Lecture Notes in Computer Science 12398

More information about this subseries at http://www.springer.com/series/7407

Zhiwen Yu · Christian Becker ·
Guoliang Xing (Eds.)

Green, Pervasive, and Cloud Computing

15th International Conference, GPC 2020
Xi'an, China, November 13–15, 2020
Proceedings

Editors
Zhiwen Yu
Northwestern Polytechnical University
Xi'an, China

Christian Becker
University of Mannheim
Mannheim, Germany

Guoliang Xing
Chinese University of Hong Kong
Shatin, Hong Kong

ISSN 0302-9743   ISSN 1611-3349 (electronic)
Lecture Notes in Computer Science
ISBN 978-3-030-64242-6   ISBN 978-3-030-64243-3 (eBook)
https://doi.org/10.1007/978-3-030-64243-3

LNCS Sublibrary: SL1 – Theoretical Computer Science and General Issues

This Springer imprint is published by the registered company Springer Nature Switzerland AG
The registered company address is: Gewerbestrasse 11, 6330 Cham, Switzerland

Preface

On behalf of the Organizing Committee, we are pleased to present the proceedings of the International Conference on Green, Pervasive and Cloud Computing (GPC 2020), held in Xi'an, China, during November 13–15, 2020. The goal of GPC is to establish a high-standard world forum for researchers and practitioners alike to share their novel ideas and experiences in the areas of green computing and communications, pervasive computing, and cloud computing. Previous editions were organized all over the world: Taichung, Taiwan (2006), Paris, France (2007), Kunming, China (2008), Geneva, Switzerland (2009), Hualien, Taiwan (2010), Oulu, Finland (2011), Hong Kong (2012), Seoul, South Korea (2013), Wuhan, China (2014), Plantation Island, Fiji (2015), Xi'an, China (2016), Cetara, Italy (2017), Hangzhou, China (2018), and Uberlândia, Brazil (2019). Due to the devastating impacts of COVID-19, GPC 2020 was postponed to November 2020.

This year, the value, breadth, and depth of the GPC conference continued to strengthen and grow in importance for both the academic and industrial communities. The strength was evidenced this year by having a number of high-quality submissions, resulting in a highly selective program. After the wide promotion of GPC 2020, we received 96 submissions in total. Each of the 96 submissions received at least three reviews. Among them 30 submissions were accepted as full papers (the acceptance rate is around 30%); and 8 submissions were accepted as short papers (posters).

GPC 2020 was a great success due to many reasons. First and foremost, the Chinese government took great efforts to cease the widespread of the coronavirus within its borders, which made it possible to host GPC 2020 in China. Secondly, we greatly appreciated the authors who submitted and presented their contributions in GPC 2020. Thirdly, the Program Committee members and reviewers dedicated their time to the advancement of knowledge. Without their hard work and guidance, the conference simply would not have happened.

We hope you enjoy the conference proceedings.

November 2020

Zhiwen Yu
Christian Becker
Guoliang Xing

Organization

Honorary Chairs

Stephen S. Yau	Arizona State University, USA
Xingshe Zhou	Northwestern Polytechnical University, China
Sumi Helal	Lancaster University, UK

General Chairs

Zhiwen Yu	Northwestern Polytechnical University, China
Christian Becker	University of Mannheim, Germany
Guoliang Xing	The Chinese University of Hong Kong, Hong Kong, China

Program Chairs

Bin Guo	Northwestern Polytechnical University, China
Raghu Ganti	IBM T. J. Watson Research Center, USA
Nic Lane	University of Oxford, UK

Program Vice Chairs

Daniele Riboni	University of Milan, Italy
Robert Ching-Hsien Hsu	Chung Hua University, Taiwan, China
Panlong Yang	University of Science and Technology of China, China

Panel Chairs

Xing Xie	Microsoft Research Asia, China
Gregor Schiele	University of Duisburg-Essen, Germany
Wendong Xiao	University of Science and Technology Beijing, China

Award Chairs

Gang Pan	Zhejiang University, China
Hui-huang Hsu	Tamkang University, Taiwan, China
Qi Han	Colorado School of Mines, USA

Poster Chairs

Xu Chen	Sun Yat-sen University, China
Wenyao Xu	State University of New York at Buffalo, USA

Workshop Chairs

Chao Chen   Chongqing University, China
Zipei Fan   The University of Tokyo, Japan
Yue-Shan Chang   National Taipei University, Taiwan, China

Special Issue Chairs

Lina Yao   University of New South Wales, Australia
Mianxiong Dong   Muroran Institute of Technology, Japan
Xiaokang Zhou   Shiga University, Japan
Zhiyong Yu   Fuzhou University, China

International Liaison Chairs

Yo-Ping Huang   National Taipei University of Technology, Taiwan,
                            China
Yuichi Nakamura   Kyoto University, Japan
Artur Lugmayr   Curtin University, Australia
Mohammad Anwar Hossain   King Saud University, Saudi Arabia
Chen-Khong Tham   National University of Singapore, Singapore
Yu Wang   University of North Carolina at Charlotte, USA

Industrial Liaison Chairs

Alvin Chin   BMW of North America, USA
Ying Liu   Cardiff University, UK
Yi (Estelle) Wang   Continental Automotive Singapore, Singapore

Local Organization Chairs

Zhu Wang   Northwestern Polytechnical University, China
Tianzhang Xing   Northwest University, China
Lei Tang   Chang'an University, China

Publicity Chairs

Zhenjiang Li   The City University of Hong Kong, Hong Kong, China
Jiangtao Wang   Coventry University, UK
Tomoko Yonezawa   Okayama University, Japan
Liang Wang   Northwestern Polytechnical University, China

Publication Chair

Yunji Liang   Northwestern Polytechnical University, China

Web Chair

Helei Cui   Northwestern Polytechnical University, China

Registration Chair

Jiaqi Liu   Northwestern Polytechnical University, China

Steering Committee

Hai Jin   Huazhong University of Science and Technology,
                                        China
Zhaohui Wu   Zhejiang University, China
Nabil Abdennadher   University of Applied Sciences, Switzerland
Christophe Cerin   Université Sorbonne Paris Nord, France
Sajal K. Das   Missouri University of Science and Technology, USA
Jean-Luc Gaudiot   University of California Irvine, USA
Kuan-Ching Li   Providence University, USA
Cho-Li Wang   The University of Hong Kong, Hong Kong, China
Chao-Tung Yang   Tunghai University, Taiwan, China
Laurence T. Yang   St. Francis Xavier University, Canada

Contents

Device-Free Sensing

Wavelet Analysis Based Noncontact Vital Signal Measurements Using mm-Wave Radar

Luyao Liu[1](✉), Wendong Xiao[1], Jiankang Wu[2], and Shenglang Xiao[3]

[1] School of Automation and Electrical Engineering, University of Science and Technology Beijing, Beijing, China
17888841360@163.com
[2] University of Chinese Academy of Sciences, Beijing, China
[3] School of Computer Science and Technology, Xidian University, Xian, China

Abstract. Instantaneous physiological signal rates related to cardiopulmonary activities are important indicators of human health assessment. Noncontact vital signals detection using microwave radar is preferable due to its zero disturbance to the subject. This paper presents a Wavelet Analysis (WA) based noncontact heartbeat and respiration signals detection algorithm using millimeter Frequency Modulated Continuous Wave (FMCW) radar. In WA, wavelet packet decomposition is applied to separate heartbeat and respiration signals from radar signal and continuous wavelet transform is used for time frequency analysis. Comparison experiments have been conducted with wearable devices on 10 subjects. Compared with the measurement result of the reference sensor, the average absolute error percentage is less than 2.0% and 3.5% for respiration and heart rate, respectively. In addition, the proposed method improves the accuracy of vital signals detection in comparison with Bandpass filter and Peak Detection (BPK).

Keywords: Heart rate · Respiration · Wavelet packet decomposition · Continuous wavelet transform · mm-Wave FMCW radar

1 Introduction

As one of the most significant physiology parameters in clinical diagnosis and disease prevention, respiration and heart rate imply a lot of valuable information can be used for diagnosis and prevention of some diseases. In fact, respiration and heart rate will show strangeness before some diseases appear especially as early as 6–24 h prior to adverse events such as Cardiac arrest [1]. There are many wearable sensors that are used to measure the vital sign rates, for example, electrocardiography (ECG), photoplethysmography (PPG), and breath belt [2–4]. Although the measurement results are more accurate, these sensors are inconvenient for some special patients suffering from empyrosis and burn [5]. Fortunately, noncontact detection using radar has attracted more attention because it has no any sensors attached to the body so that it can work in a noninvasive manner and without load for patients. The method has a good application in many aspects for example, sleep apnea monitoring, sudden infant death syndrome (SIDS) monitoring, fatigue monitoring, in-hospital monitoring, and home healthcare [6].

© Springer Nature Switzerland AG 2020
Z. Yu et al. (Eds.): GPC 2020, LNCS 12398, pp. 3–14, 2020.
https://doi.org/10.1007/978-3-030-64243-3_1

Frequency Modulated Continuous Wave (FMCW) radar has unique advantages compared with other radars. 1) As a mm-wave radar, some tiny displacements comparable to the wavelength can be detected. The high sensitivity is good at detecting the chest wall movement which is in mm order [7]. 2) FMCW radar has range resolution which can be used to distinguish the reflections from different ranges [8]. 3) FMCW radar is more robust so that it less affected by the noise [9]. 4) The FMCW wide-band radar has the potential to have a small size, be light weight, consume low amounts of power and enable real time processing [10]. In this paper, we choose a millimeter wave FMCW radar operating at 77 GHz to detect vital signals.

In the separation algorithm of vital signals, bandpass filtering (BPF) has been proposed to extract the respiration and heartbeat signals [11]. However, the method can't effectively separate the heartbeat signal from the respiratory harmonics because there are frequency overlaps. In addition to traditional simple filters, a double parameter least mean square (LMS) filter was used in [10]. Although the method can separate the vital signal more accurately, it is only been verified in simulation and has not been used for actual signal processing. In addition to the separation algorithm, there are many algorithms which was used to acquire the rate of the respiration and heartbeat. Discrete Fourier transform (DFT) is the most popular [7]. Although the DFT can obtain the rate of vital signal, it has no way to get the vital signal rate varying along time. In the paper [6], the peak detection method has been proposed to extract the rates of vital signal along time. However, this method has higher requirements for time-domain waveforms. Unless there are obvious sharp peaks as ECG signals, otherwise the result is not desirable. Afterward, in order to get the frequency variations along time, the short-time Fourier transform (STFT) has been used for radar heartbeat detection [12], but it's window cannot change along frequency and time which limits the resolution of the algorithm.

In this paper, we combine wavelet packet decomposition with continuous wavelet transform to show the feasibility and reliability of using an mm-wave FMCW radar for noncontact physiological signs detecting with acceptable low errors. The rest of this paper is organized as follows. Section 2 describes the model of FMCW radar signal. In Sect. 3, respiration and heart rate estimation algorithm based on wavelet analysis is described in details. Experimental equipment parameters and measurement results are showed in Sect. 4. In the end, the conclusion is drawn in Sect. 5.

2 FMCW Radar Signal

For FMCW radar, the transmit (TX) signal is a sinusoid whose frequency increases linearly with a positive slope of S and duration time T_d from f_{min} to f_{max} as shown in Fig. 1. (f_{min} and f_{max} is the start and end frequency respectively). This sweep in frequency is commonly referred to as a "chirp". A set of these chirps form a "Frame" which can be used as the observation window for the radar processing. Bandwidth is the frequency difference of f_{max} and f_{min} equivalently the product of slope and duration of the chirp. The received chirp is a delayed version of the transmitted chirp with a delay of τ and it can be down converted to a new signal using transmitted chirp as reference signal, the signal is named as beat signal.

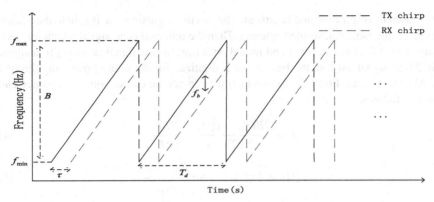

Fig. 1. Transmitted and received chirp sequences

The transmitted chirp waveform can be approximately expressed as:

$$x_T(t) = A_T e^{j(2\pi f_{min}t + \pi St^2 + \phi(t))} \quad S = \frac{B}{T_d} \quad 0 < t < T_d \tag{1}$$

with start frequency f_{min}, bandwidth B and slope S at the duration time T_d. The received radar signal is a scaled and shifted version of the transmitted signal given by:

$$x_R(t) = \alpha A_T e^{j(2\pi f_{min}(t-\tau) + \pi S(t-\tau)^2 + \emptyset(t-\tau))} \quad \tau = \frac{2R}{c} \quad \tau < t < T_d \tag{2}$$

where τ is the round trip time of the wave, c is the light speed, R denotes the distance to the radar. The transmitted and received signals are mixed to acquire the beat signal which can be approximated as:

$$y(t) = A_R e^{j(2\pi S\tau t + 2\pi f_{min}\tau + \pi S\tau^2 + \Delta\phi(t))}$$
$$= A_R e^{j(2\pi f_b t + \phi_b(t) + \Delta\phi(t))} \tag{3}$$

The residual phase noise is $\Delta\phi(t) = \phi(t) - \phi(t - 2R/c)$ which can be neglected for short range radar applications due to the range correlation effect. Additionally, the term $\pi S\tau^2$ can also be neglected in $\phi_b(t)$ as S is in 10^{12} Hz/s order while τ is in 1 ns thus the term is in the order of 10^{-6}.

3 Noncontact Vital Signals Detection Program

3.1 Theory of FMCW Radar Vital Signals Measurement

For a typical adult, the displacements of chest are about 1–12 mm and 0.01–0.5 mm caused by respiration and heartbeat respectively. In theory, the tiny chest movements can be detected by a noncontact way using a mm-wave FMCW radar. A simplified schematic diagram of a FMCW radar system is shown in Fig. 2. The human subject is at a constant distance of R_0 from the antenna, who has a periodic chest displacement

$x(t)$ caused by respiration and heartbeat. The electromagnetic wave is sent to the human subject by the radar transmitted antenna. Then the reflected echo signal which travels a distance of 2 $R(t)$ is amplified and mixed with transmitted signal resulting in a signal called beat signal. At last, the beat signal is digitized for the future processing through the ADC transform. From the formula (3) we can get the expression of frequency and phase as follows.

$$f_b = \frac{2B(R_0 + x(t))}{cT_c} \approx \frac{2BR_0}{cT_c} \tag{4}$$

$$\phi_b(t) = 2\pi f_{min}\tau = 4\pi \frac{R_0 + x(t)}{\lambda_{max}} \tag{5}$$

The change of f_b caused by $x(t)$ is very small so that it can be ignored in Eq. (4). This equation shows the connection between beat signal frequency and the constant distance, so it can be used to detect the range of a subject, R_0. According to the Eq. (5), $\phi_b(t)$ varied with $x(t)$ relative to λ_{max} so that the distance variations $x(t)$ can greatly change the phase. $x(t)$ is a periodic function denotes the chest wall displacement due to heartbeat and respiration. Hence, the vibration frequency of the respiration and heartbeat can be calculated through phase information.

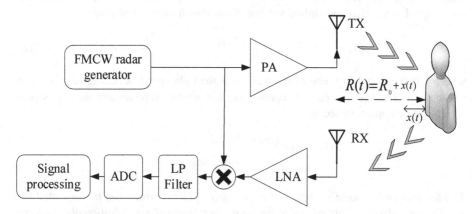

Fig. 2. Schematic diagram of FMCW radar vital signals measurement

3.2 Instantaneous Vital Signals Detection Algorithm

Respiration and Heartbeat Signals Separation
The flowchart of vital signals detection algorithm is shown in Fig. 3. The phase signal acquired is the target's chest movement mixed with other unwanted clutter. To extract the useful information, we apply the wavelet packet decomposition (WPD) to decompose the phase signal and recovery the heartbeat and respiration signals. WPD is suitable for time-frequency localization analysis of non-stationary signals. Compared with the

wavelet decomposition, the wavelet packet decomposition can divide the frequency more detailed. And this decomposition has neither redundancy nor omissions. In addition, it can adaptively select the optimal wavelet basis function according to the characteristics of the signal.

$$\emptyset_{l+1,2m}(t) = \sum h(n)\emptyset_{l,m}(t-nk) \tag{6}$$

$$\emptyset_{l+1,2m+1}(t) = \sum g(n)\emptyset_{l,m}(t-nk) \tag{7}$$

$$\emptyset_{l,m}(t) = \sum \overline{g(n)}\emptyset_{l+1,2m+1}(t-nk) + \overline{h(n)}\emptyset_{l+1,2m}(t-nk) \tag{8}$$

The equal (6) and (7) are the decomposition algorithm of high frequency and low frequency, respectively. Equation (8) provides an algorithm for reconstructing the master node of the previous layer from the branch node. l denotes the decomposition level of the wavelet packet, m shows the location of the node at l level. $h(n)$ and $g(n)$ are regarded as low pass and high pass filter, respectively.

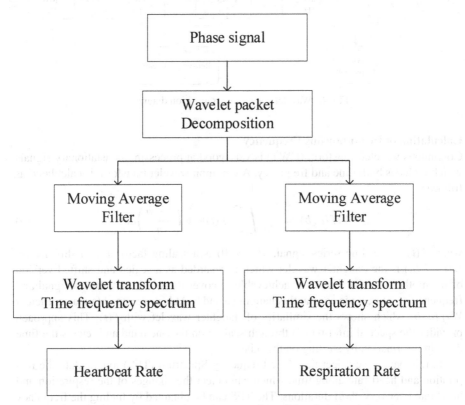

Fig. 3. Proposed signal processing procedure of the vital signal detection

In this paper, we perform 6-level wavelet packet decomposition on the obtained phase signal as the Fig. 4 shows. At the sixth level, we can get a series of wavelet coefficients including 64 nodes whose frequency increase at intervals of 0.15625 Hz. The low frequency components which include nodes from the first to the third at the sixth level are used for respiration recovery and the high frequency components which include from the seventh to the twentieth nodes are apply to recovery heartbeat signal.

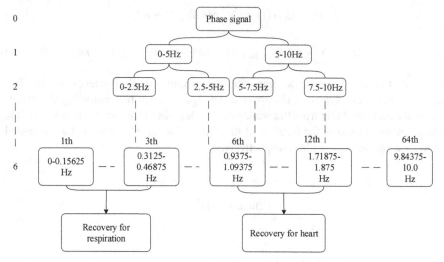

Fig. 4. Wavelet packet decomposition diagram

Calculation of Instantaneous Frequency

Continuous wavelet transform (CWT) is very good at processing nonstationary signals which includes both time and frequency. A common wavelet transform is calculated as follows:

$$WTf(a, b) = \frac{1}{\sqrt{a}} \int_{-\infty}^{+\infty} f(t)\psi * \left(\frac{t - b}{a}\right) dt \tag{9}$$

where $f(t)$ is the time series signal, $a(a > 0)$ is a scaling factor, b is a shift factor, $\psi(t - b/a)$ is the daughter wavelet which is regarded as a scaled and shifted version of the mother wavelet $\psi(t)$. It is achievable to cover the whole time-series signal and frequency of interest via constantly changing a and b. At last we can obtain a coefficient $WTf(a, b)$ which shows the similarity of daughter wavelet with $f(t)$. This approach provides the spectral information through scaling on the one hand and retains the time domain information by shifting on the other.

In this paper, we select the Time Frequency Spectrum (TFS) to calculate the respiration and heart rate along time which can detect the changes of the respiration and heart rate over very short durations. The TFS can be obtained by finding the frequency corresponding to the maximum energy at every shift. In general, the x-axis of the TFS is shifts or time and the y-axis is the frequency at that point. At last, we apply sliding window algorithm to transform the frequency into rates of vital signs along time.

4 Experiments and Results

4.1 Experimental Equipment and Parameters

We applied a single Texas Instrument (TI) mm-wave IWR1642 sensor operating at 77–81 GHz for our experiment. The system has four transmit (TX) antennas and four receive (RX) antennas by which we can get an eight elements virtual array. When collecting data, the data are transmitted through the USB interface to a PC for future signal process.

The chirp and frame configuration parameters are listed in Table 1. In our experiment, each frame contained 128 chirps and 68 points were collected per chirp. Each frame is repeated every $T_c = 50\,ms$ which means the slow time sampling rate is 20 Hz, in addition the ADC sampling rate (fast time sampling) is 3.2 MHz. The start frequency is 76.4 GHz. Each chirp cycle time is 64 μs with an idle time of 16 μs between the end of previous chirp and the start of next chirp i.e. the duration of a chirp $T_d = 48\,\mu s$. The slope of each chirp is 20 $MHz/\mu s$ equivalently, the sweeping bandwidth is 960 MHz.

Table 1. Radar configuration parameters

Parameter	f_{min}	T_d	S	B	f_{slow}	f_{fast}
Value	76.4 GHz	48 us	20 MHz/s	960 MHz	20 Hz	3.2 MHz

According to the above experimental configuration parameters, we can calculate the maximum and minimum distances and vibration frequencies that the radar can detect based on the characteristics of the FMCW radar. The result is shown in Table 2. According to the paper [10], the vibration frequency of the chest for respiration and heartbeat are approximately 0.1–0.6 Hz (6–36 times per minute) and 0.8–2 Hz (48–120 beat per minute) respectively. We can clearly see that the respiratory and heartbeat frequencies are all within the frequency range that the radar can detect from the Table 2.

Table 2. Range and vibration frequency bounds.

Parameter	Range (m)	Vibration frequency (Hz)
Max	12	10
Min	0.35	0.006

All experiments have been carried out in a common indoor laboratory environment, as shown in Fig. 5. The human subjects were asked to sit on the chair 0.5 m, 1 m and 1.5 m away from the radar respectively with the chest facing the radar. A wearable sensor CM19 was used to measure the ECG and respiration signal as reference simultaneously.

Fig. 5. Photograph of the experiment of human vital signal detection

4.2 Measurement Results

The respiration and heart rate as a reference are obtained from the reference sensor by Peak Detection. Each peak of the time domain respiration and heartbeat signal is searched. Then the vital signal rates can be calculated as:

$$R_i = \frac{1}{\Delta p} = \frac{1}{p_{i+1} - p_i} \tag{10}$$

$p_i(i = 1, 2, \ldots)$ with $p_{i+1} > p_i$ denotes a time series corresponding to discrete peak values. R_i denotes the vital signal rate between consecutive peaks.

In order to verify the performance of the FMCW radar measurement, we quoted two statistical evaluation indicators, the average absolute error (AAE) [13] and the average absolute error percentage (AAEP) [13] which are defined as respectively as follows.

$$AAE = \frac{1}{W} \sum_l^W |BPM_{est}(l) - BPM_{true}(l)| \tag{11}$$

$$AAEP = \frac{1}{W} \sum_l^W \frac{|BPM_{est}(l) - BPM_{true}(l)|}{BPM_{true}(l)} \tag{12}$$

where w represents the total number of time window within the observation time. $BPM_{true}(l)$ and $BPM_{EST}(l)$ are the truth and the estimation in the l_{th} time window, respectively.

The example of the 50 s phase signal including heartbeat, respiration and unwanted clutter is shown in Fig. 6. The larger amplitude displacements are regarded as respiration signal and vary obviously while the small fluctuations on top of the respiratory waveform denote the heartbeat signal that can't be seen clearly. It's pretty obvious that the heartbeat signal can be an order of magnitude lower than the respiration signal.

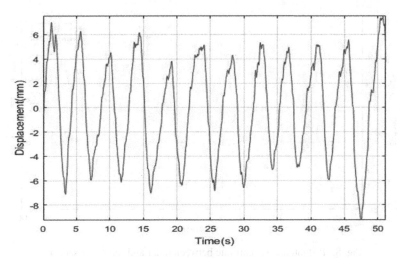

Fig. 6. Radar phase signal

Following the signal processing method previously mentioned, respiration and heart rate are acquired through continuous wavelet transform. The 120 s instantaneous breath rate (BR) and heart rate (HR) are shown in Figs. 7. and 8. For respiration, the average rate locates around 15 BPM. Compared with the reference, the traces of BR calculated from the method show high consistency and reliability. For heartbeat, the average rate locates around 68 BPM. Although there is a small deviation between the radar measurement and the reference signal, the overall trend is highly consistent so that the result of the heart rate is reliable. The high consistence of instantaneous rate measurements between radar and reference sensor demonstrates that the wavelet analysis algorithm is successful and noncontact detection using mm-wave FMCW radar is feasible and reliable.

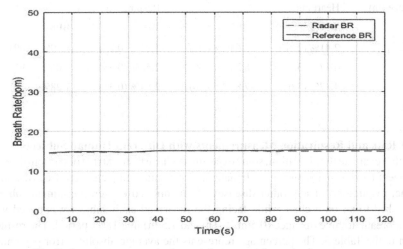

Fig. 7. Instantaneous respiration rate between radar and reference sensor

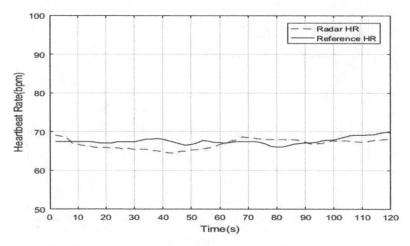

Fig. 8. Instantaneous heart rate between radar and reference sensor

Performance Evaluation of Different Algorithms

As a comparison, the bandpass filter and peak detection (BPK) is also used for processing the radar signal. Table 3 shows the AAEP and AAE of different algorithms in each distance. It is clear that the wavelet analysis (WA) is more accurate and reliable than the BPK in each distance. Especially for the detection distance is more than 1.0 m, the AAEP and AAE of BPK increase remarkably, while the wavelet analysis is still accurate. The percentage represents the average absolute error percentage (AAEP), and the content in brackets indicates average absolute error (AAE).

Table 3. WA-based and BPK-based methods from three distances

Distance (m)	Heart rate		Respiration	
	WA	BPK	WA	BPK
0.5	2.41% (2.16)	3.64% (4.07)	1.21% (0.23)	4.79% (0.69)
1.0	4.47% (3.75)	8.25% (7.00)	2.56% (0.38)	7.06% (0.97)
1.5	4.37% (3.65)	7.83% (6.56)	2.84% (0.31)	7.28% (1.30)

Heart Rate and Respiration Measurements with Different Human Subjects

To further evaluate the algorithm, some experiments have been carried out on ten different volunteers (seven males and three females). The human subjects were free of known cardiac, respiratory, or any other diseases. As mentioned earlier, the human subjects were asked to sit on a chair while facing the radar and each subject was tested with normal breath at three distance (0.5 m, 1.0 m and 1.5 m) in a 180 s period. The result is shown in the Table 3. The percentage represents the average absolute error percentage (AAEP), and the content in brackets indicates average absolute error (AAE) (Table 4).

Table 4. Measurement result of radar instantaneous vital sign rates detection from ten subjects at three difference distance

Subject	Gender	Height (cm)	Weight (kg)	Heartrate			Respiration		
				0.5 m	1.0 m	1.5 m	0.5 m	1.0 m	1.5 m
1	Male	175	63	2.41% (2.16)	4.47% (3.75)	4.37% (3.65)	1.21% (0.23)	2.56% (0.38)	2.84% (0.31)
2	Male	180	65	2.57% (1.81)	2.45% (1.75)	5.36% (3.92)	1.62% (0.26)	1.94% (0.31)	2.33% (0.31)
3	Male	173	85	3.54% (3.22)	4.80% (4.30)	4.46% (3.81)	1.76% (0.26)	2.68% (0.29)	2.52% (0.38)
4	Male	176	87	4.16% (2.47)	4.20% (2.62)	5.00% (3.02)	3.38% (0.48)	3.68% (0.39)	4.62% (0.46)
5	Male	173	70	2.48% (1.69)	6.10% (4.11)	5.90% (4.10)	1.90% (0.31)	2.4% (0.20)	3.58% (0.42)
6	Male	175	75.5	3.08% (2.22)	6.20% (4.33)	6.80% (4.88)	1.63% (0.28)	1.61% (0.22)	1.83% (0.28)
7	Male	171	60	3.91% (2.21)	8.19% (5.16)	6.81% (4.36)	1.69% (0.22)	2.72% (0.35)	3.16% (0.40)
8	Female	170	55	4.32% (2.86)	3.22% (2.10)	3.61% (2.37)	3.31% (0.49)	1.68% (0.25)	2.13% (0.32)
9	Female	165	50.5	4.09% (2.43)	4.53% (2.65)	3.94% (2.39)	1.41% (0.26)	2.39% (0.43)	2.28% (0.38)
10	Female	163	46	3.46% (3.07)	7.04% (6.43)	8.20% (7.52)	0.76% (0.08)	2.25% (0.29)	3.56% (0.38)

5 Conclusion

In this paper, we presented the wavelet analysis for vital signal analysis based on FMCW mm-wave radar. The wavelet packet decomposition can separate the respiration and heartbeat signals more clearly according to the different frequency. The continuous wavelet transform can effectively calculate the instantaneous frequency variations along time. Several experiments have been carried out with different human subjects at different distances. Experimental results show that the average absolute error percentage between radar and reference sensor is less than 2.0% and 3.5% for respiration and heart rate, respectively. What's more, the wavelet analysis improves the detection accuracy of vital signals compared with BPK. It is demonstrated that noncontact physiological signal detection based on wavelet analysis using millimeter wave FMCW radar is feasible and reliable.

References

1. Van Loon, K., et al.: Wireless non-invasive continuous respiratory monitoring with FMCW radar: a clinical validation study. J. Clin. Monitor. Comput. **30**(6), 797–805 (2016)

2. Peng, M., Wang, T., Hu, G., Hui, Z.: A wearable heart rate belt for ambulant ECG monitoring. In: 2012 IEEE 14th International Conference on e-Health Networking, Applications and Services (Healthcom) (2012)

3. Shaltis, P.A., Reisner, A., Asada, H.H.: Wearable, cuff-less PPG-based blood pressure monitor with novel height sensor. In: Conference Proceedings of the Annual International Conference of the IEEE Engineering in Medicine and Biology Society, Conference 2006. IEEE Engineering in Medicine and Biology Society, vol. 1, pp. 908–911 (2006)

4. Yang, C.M., Yang, T.L., Wu, C.C., Hung, S.H., Hsieh, H.C.: Textile-based capacitive sensor for a wireless wearable breath monitoring system. In: 2014 IEEE International Conference on Consumer Electronics (ICCE) (2014)

5. Zhao, H., Hong, H., Sun, L., Li, Y., Li, C., Zhu, X.: Noncontact physiological dynamics detection using low-power digital-IF doppler radar. IEEE Trans. Instrum. Meas. **66**(7), 1780–1788 (2017)

6. Hu, W., Zhao, Z., Wang, Y., Zhang, H., Lin, F.: Noncontact accurate measurement of cardiopulmonary activity using a compact quadrature doppler radar sensor. IEEE Trans. Biomed. Eng. **61**(3), 725–735 (2013)

7. Alizadeh, M., Shaker, G., de Almeida, J.C.M., Morita, P.P., Safavi-Naeini, S.: Remote monitoring of human vital signs using mm-wave FMCW radar. IEEE Access (2019)

8. Muñoz-Ferreras, J.-M., Wang, J., Peng, Z., Gómez-García, R., Li, C.: From doppler to FMCW radars for non-contact vital-sign monitoring

9. Wang, G., Gu, C., Inoue, T., Li, C.: A hybrid FMCW-interferometry radar for indoor precise positioning and versatile life activity monitoring. IEEE Trans. Microwave Theory Tech. **62**(11), 2812–2822 (2014)

10. He, M., Nian, Y., Gong, Y.: Novel signal processing method for vital sign monitoring using FMCW radar. Biomed. Sig. Process. Control **33**, 335–345 (2017)

11. Mostov, K., Liptsen, E., Boutchko, R.: Medical applications of shortwave FM radar: remote monitoring of cardiac and respiratory motion. Med. Phys. **37**(3), 1332–1338 (2010)

12. Wei, H., Zhang, H., Zhao, Z., Wang, Y., Wang, X.: Real-time remote vital sign detection using a portable Doppler sensor system. In: 2014 IEEE Sensors Applications Symposium (SAS) (2014)

13. Ye, C., Toyoda, K., Ohtsuki, T.: A stochastic gradient approach for robust heartbeat detection with doppler radar using time-window-variation technique. IEEE Trans. Biomed. Eng. **66**(6), 1730–1741 (2019)

Study on Feasibility of Remote Metal Detection Using Millimeter Wave Radar for Convenient and Efficient Security Check

Yixuan Lu⬤, Weixi Chen⬤, Haipeng Liu⬤, and Anfu Zhou⁽⊠⁾⬤

Beijing University of Posts and Telecommunications, Beijing, China
zhouanfu@bupt.edu.cn

Abstract. Millimeter-wave (mmWave) has advantages of sensitivity and concealment, which enables a mature application in human body security. However, all the state-of-the-art solutions are based on a huge antenna array which is too cumbersome, *i.e.*, it is difficult to move, repair, and also occupies a large amount of space. From views of the long term, it is uneconomical, high power consumption and narrow application. In this paper, we propose a new and more efficient detection system. We utilize a small radar chip with a custom-designed method to extract the spatial features of the detected objects, *e.g.*, location and energy intensity. The method establishes the image of the energy intensity changing with time and analyzes the change of reflected energy of different materials on different people to find the relationship between them. From the relationship, we can infer whether there are metal products and their positions quickly on the tested person. The proposed solution is implemented on a mmWave radar. We evaluate it thoroughly and provide more extensive experiments for its practicability.

Keywords: Millimeter wave · Body security · Metal detection

1 Introduction

With the increasingly serious anti-terrorism situation in the world, the safety inspection of dangerous goods carried by the human body has become an important part of public security [4]. To "see" whether there is a dangerous good, a popular solution is to utilize millimeter wave (mmWave, belongs to electromagnetic radiation) to image the human body, because mmWave can penetrate non-metallic covering materials such as clothing and has better resolution and anti-interference ability. Furthermore, compared with other alternative perception mediums (*e.g.*, microwave [12,21,25], X-ray [22]), mmWave detection has two advantages: *safe* (*i.e.*, mmWave penetration of millimeter wave is moderate. It is unable to leak human body's irrelevant information which may cause

© Springer Nature Switzerland AG 2020
Z. Yu et al. (Eds.): GPC 2020, LNCS 12398, pp. 15–29, 2020.
https://doi.org/10.1007/978-3-030-64243-3_2

privacy issues) and *high-efficiency* (*i.e.*, the narrower beam and the higher resolution to make the detection faster). Therefore, mmWave detection has become the most popular technology of human security inspection.

Motivated by these advantages, many researchers devote lots of efforts: Cooper team [2] developed a high-resolution imaging radar to achieve the metal detection.

However, current methods' problems fall in the two following aspects: *(i)* Unnecessary cost: All the current human security check solutions [3,16,19] are based on body imaging which is expensive and unnecessary on resource consumption. The consumption can be economized by a non-imaging method, *i.e.*, only analyzing the reflected objects' energy change to recognize different material on the human body. *(ii)* Occupying large area: All the existing solutions [1] realize security check through a huge antenna array. The smallest size of the x-ray security check machine has at least 4 to 6 m^2 large 300 kg weight. The huge equipment is too cumbersome to fit all the security situation, *e.g.*, school security, personal house security. Furthermore, the bulky facility also leads to inconvenience, *e.g.*, high power consumption and large space scale occupancy.

In this paper, we develop the primary feasibility study for the efficient metal detection system. We utilize a small mmWave radar chip with a custom-designed system for metal detection on the human body and security check. To achieve this goal, we *firstly* propose a coarse human body model consisting of multiple points extracted from reflected mmWave signals. The model depicts the human body's 3-D dynamic energy intensity distribution feature. By analyzing dynamic energy intensity features, we can find out which part of the human body has higher energy intensity which may relate to the metal item. To detect the reflection intensity of all aspects of the human body, we ask the testers to turn 360° with different sizes of metal items and use these captured data to establish the human body model. *Secondly,* we design a novel metal detection method to perceive whether the tester carries a metal on her body. The method carefully analyzes the changing trend of the reflection intensity during the tester is turning around. Specifically, the trend will change when the tester is carrying a metal. The metal will reflect more powerful mmWave signals than human skin. Therefore, if the trend pattern is different from ordinary situations, the method will regard this one as a dangerous candidate.

The proposed solution is implemented on a 76–81 GHz frequency-modulated continuous wave (FMCW) 10.4 cm × 10.4 cm mmWave radar chip. With such a small radar, we can achieve metal detection in any kind of security scenarios. To verify the reliability of the proposed system, we evaluate this method thoroughly.

We asked testers to wear different size of metal items and do different actions, *e.g.*, rotation, walking toward radar in front of the mmWave radar. The result shows that rotation is sufficient to represent the best human body character. From the rotation action's result, we can clearly identify whether the person carries metal. Furthermore, we explore the effect of human shape and location for further research.

The main contributions can be summarized as follows:

(i) We build up an efficient and reliable detection system. This well-designed system can establish a coarse human model consisting of multiple reflect signal points and embed a reliable metal detection method to perceive whether a tester carries a metal.

(ii) We implement the designed system on an FMCW mmWave radar chip and transform the collected signals into the coarse human rotating model for further determination.

(iii) We design the customized experiment and recruit volunteers for experiments. After analysis, we find that rotation is sufficient to represent the best human body character and the typical features of energy change.

2 Related Work

MmWave Metal Detection: The mmWave technology has been already developed for human identification [7,9,18,20], environment mapping [24] and item detection. The paper [2] employed the frequency-modulated continuous wave (FMCW) radar technique to achieve centimeter-scale range resolution. They use this radar to establish the image of an object to achieve metal detection. Meng *et al.* [10] developed a channel passive millimeter-wave (PMMW) imaging system for public security check with a quasi-optical scanning structure. However, these imaging systems have high resolution, but as trade-off, they need a large radar antenna and high transmitting power. In addition, the accurate human model requires more calculation which is unnecessary for metal detection. Due to these high cost of the imaging system, Kapilevich [5,6] non-imaging sensor for detecting hidden objects. They designed an FMCW sensor 94 GHz and the method with vertical scan and horizontal scan for target identification. This system reduces the complexity of calculation, but the radar module still quite big (30 cm × 40 cm × 30 cm) as for a portable detection solution.

X-rays Metal Detection: In the past 20 years, X-rays detector is the mainstream for security check. The X-ray absorption of an object depends on the absorption coefficient and the thickness of a given material. X-ray is an excellent tool to check luggage [22] without opening and manually checking each of them. However, X-ray carries the high radiation which will harm the human body. Besides, the high penetrate image will also cost lot and violate tester's privacy [11].

Other Metal Detection: Microwave is a new technology on metal detection. Some teams use Wi-Fi for detection [13–15]. Zhuge [25] uses microwave ultra-wideband (UWB) radar with a planar aperture to validate the possibility of using UWB radar to image a human body. Yurduseven [21] uses microwave imaging technique to get the indirect microwave holographic imaging of a metal gun concealed in a pouch.

3   Overview

The proposed system aims to enable the security check device to work in more types of environment especially in space limited area. Specifically, this small device with our system can be embedded into the wall or some inconspicuous facilities where is too narrow to place a big machine. Furthermore, this device can detect the human body without notification because of its small size. It gives the possibility for special human body check, *e.g.*, judge whether terrorists carry guns or identify the number of weapons held by terrorists on the battlefield.

System Scenario: The detected person is asked to stand in front of the device at a proper distance and start rotating for one circle at a slow and constant speed (shown in Fig. 1). Before the person, we place a mmWave radar in a medium height facing the human chest. When the detection process starts, mmWave signals will cover the tester's whole body and reflect the information for metal detection. The whole process only takes several seconds and without any manual assistance.

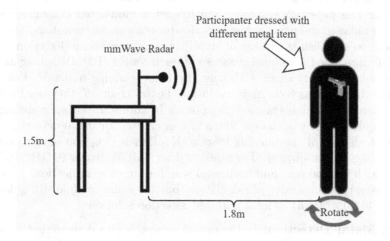

Fig. 1. Schematic diagram of the experiment

System Composition: The whole system consists of the following three modules (shown in Fig. 2).

Radar module broadcasts mmWave, receives signals and transmits the original signal to the next module. The radar firstly generates the chirp signals by a chirp signal synthesizer and broadcasts them through the transmitter antenna. Then, the reflected analog signals from the object will be recorded by the receiver and transformed into digital signals. The digital signals will be sent to the next module.

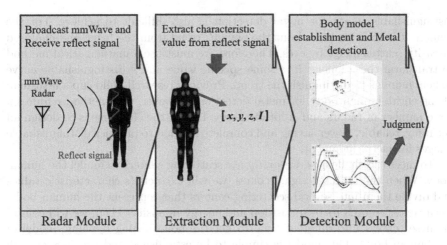

Fig. 2. System module diagram

Extraction module is to extract the characteristic value of the original reflected signal, *e.g.*, positions, the intensity of energy. The position information represents the object's 3-D location. We can use this information to build up the human model in the next module. The intensity of energy information is the reflected strength of this point. This value can be used to speculate the material of the human body. After extracting the value, the module will provide the data table of position, intensity of energy and frame number for detection module. The frame number represents a time unit (ten frames per second).

Detection module receives the characteristic value, builds up the human body model and runs the detection algorithm for judgment. The module will sum up all the intensity values in each frame to build the intensity-frame image. Secondly, it will find out the peak value, valley value and compare them with no metal image's values. Finally, *detection module* will evaluate the differences between those two image and give out the judgment whether there is a metal material on the human body.

4   Methodology

As noted before, the proposed system consists of a novel human body model and a customized detection algorithm. *Firstly*, it is difficult to distinguish and find the position of carried metal using such a small mmWave radar chip. The small scale of mmWave radar is difficult to build a fine-grained model for the human body, unlike visible light or X-ray which can show the human body's image. In addition, in previous work, it is difficult to detect the whole human body, especially the metal on its side, because previous works only enable detection in its front. Therefore, the challenge is to design a complete all-round metal detection method by using such small chips. *Secondly*, the establishment of a distinguishable image for metal detection is also difficult to achieve. For the human, it is difficult to find out the obvious trend from the fuzzy and confused intensity scatter image by eyes. Therefore, we must use a mathematical method to transform these images into some specific value and a distinguishable curve to help humans to distinguish the trend. Previous research builds up a heat map of the entire human body for metal detection. However, this method requires a large number of radars and A lot of energy. Hence, the challenge is to design an accuracy, reliable, power saving and complete method to produce distinguishable images for metal judgment.

To meet the challenges, we *firstly* use scattering centers to model the human body. When the reflected signal comes, we will extract its characteristic values and divide them into several scattering centers that represent the human body. Each center records its own position and energy intensity. Then, we will consist of these centers into different time to get the non-imaging dynamic model of the human body. This model is simple to be established and provides enough information for complete metal detection which can simplify the calculation of metal detection and is able to implement in a small chip. *Secondly*, we use a polynomial fitting method to fit the discrete points and build a curve that can estimate the general trend of intensity. We will calculate the feature values, *e.g.*, curve's peak value, valley value, gradient, entire energy and compare them with the image's features without metal. Then, we will use them for an entire evaluation and give out the judgment whether the human is carrying metal items.

4.1   Preliminaries: Radar Fundamental

In this work, we leverage a basic radar system principle that perceive the human body by analyzing the reflected electromagnetic signal. Specifically, we utilize a mmWave FMCW radar to collect the features of the reflection points on human body, *i.e.*, 3-D coordinate, angle and intensity of energy by acquiring the reflected signal information, *i.e.*, the time delay, phase or frequency shift.

Range Measurement: In the FMCW radar, the signal (called as "chirp") is increasing linearly with time. Assuming the speed of light c and the flying time τ during a chirp signal's reflection by fast-Fourier transformation (FFT), we can calculate the distance from the reflection position as $d = \frac{\tau c}{2}$.

Angle Estimation: An FMCW radar system can also estimate the arrival angle θ of the reflected signal with the horizontal plane. Angular estimation is based on the observation that a small change in the distance of an object results in a phase change in the peak of the range-FFT. This result is used to perform angular estimation, using at least two receiver antennas as shown in Fig. 3. Assuming the distance between two receivers l, the angle can be estimated as $\theta = sin^{-1}(\frac{\lambda \Delta \Phi}{2\pi l})$.

4.2   The Establishment of Human Body Model

Due to the small size limitation of the chip, we are unable to show the entire image of the human body. Therefore, we model the response signal of the human

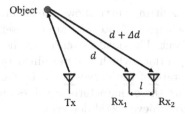

Fig. 3. Angle estimation

body as the superposition of responses from discrete, dynamic scattering centers [8]. This human model shows lots of information of the reflect object, *e.g.*, location, scattering centers' distribution, reflect intensity, approximate shape and dynamic condition. This model is the basis of further analysis.

To obtain this model, we separate the original reflected signal into different scattering centers by using CA-CFAR algorithm and extract every centers' characteristic value in each frame, *e.g.*, 3-D coordinate, energy intensity. By using Eq. 1, we put the obtained value into the equation to establish the human body model. This function combines the time, location (coordinates) and energy intensity value which shows the dynamic features of human body model. In this equation, the 3-D human model is represented by $m(x, y, z, T)$ which is changing over time T. Each scattering center is parameterized by energy intensity $I_i(T)$ and three-dimensional coordinates $x_i(T)$, $y_i(T)$, $z_i(T)$ from the scattering center, which varies as a function of time T:

$$m(x, y, z, T) = \sum_{i=1}^{N_{SC}} I_i(T)\delta(x - x_i(T))\delta(y - y_i(T))\delta(z - z_i(T)) \qquad (1)$$

where N_{SC} is the number of scattering centers and $\delta(.)$ is the Dirac delta function.

4.3   Metal Detection

After building up the entire human body model, we design a novel metal detection method to analyze the changing trend of reflected energy intensity at different time. In the process of analysis, we will find the abnormal changes at the specific time. These abnormal changes can help us find the general law of energy intensity change and summarize the special features of human carrying metal.

More concretely, we use the intensity-frame image for analysis to build up the changing trend of reflected energy intensity. Specifically, we sum up all intensity values in each frame to make the intensity-frame scatter image. Based on the scatter image, we use a polynomial fitting method to fit the discrete points and build a curve to make the plot more visual and easier to compare the difference. After trying different degrees of polynomial fitting functions, we decide to set the degree of the fitting function to 7, because in this degree, the curve and show the best performance. This fitting curve shows the general trend of intensity. In this curve, the abnormal changes of intensity are represented by the peak value, valley value and the gradient. These values represent the size of reflect area and the strength of reflecting surface which is determined by the material. Besides the descent and increase rate of the curves could be variable by many diverse situations. We will compare these characteristic values and find the relationship between these behavior to achieve metal detection.

5   Experiment

5.1   Dataset

We invite 8 participants (including 6 men and 2 women) to participate in our experiments. They are divided into four categories: tall, short, fat and thin according to their size. They are asked to rotate slowly at a constant speed for 10 turns at 1.8 m far from the mmWave wave radar (shown in Fig. 1). Each participant rotates with metal gun, metal plate, and no metal item. The metal plate has larger metal area than the metal gun. During the rotation, the radar records all human information captured of each frame into a computer for future analysis. As noted in Sect. 3, we install our mmWave chip in an empty room and put the chip in the middle of the room 1.5 m high.

5.2   Implementation Details

Hardware: We use an FMCW 10.4 cm × 10.4 cm mmWave chip to implement our design. The mmWave signal's frequency is 77 GHz to 81 GHz and its bandwidth is 4 GHz. The frame duration is 100 ms (10 frames per second). When the radar system is on the work, the radar will broadcast mmWave continuously to detect the surrounding object. It operates as follows: Firstly, the chirp signal synthesizer generates a chirp signal and transmits this signal to both the transmitter antenna and the mixer. Secondly, the chirp signal is transmitted by the transmitter antenna. The broadcasting signal is reflected to the receiver antenna by the objects. Thirdly, the reflection of the chirp by an object generates a reflected chirp captured by the receiver antenna. This reflected chirp is transmitted to the mixer. Fourthly, the mixer combines the receiver antenna and transmitter antenna signals to produce an intermediate frequency (IF) signal by subtracting the frequency and phase of the transmitted and received signals respectively. Then, the IF signal is processed by the FFT (Fast-Fourier-Transformation) to get the range-doppler image. To get the angle information, the device process the IF signal by another FFT operation and estimate the angle. Finally, we use CA-CFAR algorithm to extract the dynamic point from the original signal and transmit these data to the software for further analysis. We use 4 receiving antennas and 3 transmitting antennas to achieve the object detection. The transmitting power is 12 dB and the ADC sampling rate is 37.5 Msps.

Fig. 4. Picture to the tester with metal gun

Software: The hardware will be connected to the PC and transmit the receiving information of the position, number of frames and energy intensity of each point to the processing module. We use MATLAB R2017b 9.3 to process data. We put the energy intensity and frame number of each point collected into two matrices. The "for" loop structure is used to process each frame of data. When the program find that the frame number of two neighboring points are different, we consider that all the points of this frame are collected. Then, we sum the energy intensity of this frame and use the "scatter" function to plot the energy intensity of each frame in the graphics window. Finally, we use the "polyfit" function to produce a curve and use this curve to fit these discrete points which can indicate the energy intensity trend and compare different situations.

5.3   System Performance

Metal on the Tester's Front: The experiment in this section evaluates the scenario of human with metal in the front (see Fig. 4). 8 participants are asked to rotate with metal gun, metal plate and no metal item in the front. We plot the energy intensity points in one rotation and display the intensity-frame curve. We can combine the information of peak, gradient, and the difference between the two peaks to determine whether the person has metal.

From Fig. 5, we got the following insights: *(i)* Fig. 5(a) shows two peaks and one valley in one circle rotation of the human body. The first peak is occurred when the participants facing the radar, *i.e.*, the intensity is very high because the reflected area is large. When the participant rotates about 90°, side of tester is shown to the radar which has less area, the intensity goes to the valley. Another peak is taken place when the tester's back is facing the radar. The peak is a little bit lower than the front because the surface in the back is a smoother and less rough area than the front.

(ii) Figure 5(d) shows that wearing a metal plate has a higher peak than wearing a metal gun, and the peaks of both cases are greater than those of wearing no metal items. The reason is that the metal has stronger reflected intensity than other materials. The larger the area of metal, the higher the peak will go. Besides, two peak values in rotation are different. There is no metallic

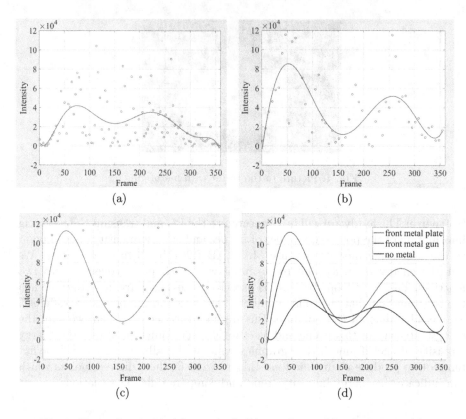

Fig. 5. Tester front with (a) no metal; (b) metal gun; (c) metal chest; (d).

item on the tester's back, so the second peak value won't go as high as the first peak.

(*iii*) Figure 5(d) shows that the gradient of the metal curve is higher than the no metal curve. The reason is when the tester wearing metal turns his side to the radar, reflected strength and reflected area both decrease quickly.

Metal on the Tester's Side: In this experiment, we place the metal on the side of the human body instead of the front. This experiment is a supplement to the previous experiment making it possible to calculate the approximate position of the hidden item and prove the correctness of the theory that we stated in the last section. 8 participants wear the same metal items on the sides and rotate. Through computer processing, we obtain the intensity-frame images (Fig. 6).

We got the following insights: (*i*) As shown in Fig. 6(a), We find 3 peaks in the image. The first and third peaks are corresponding to tester's front and back. The appearance of the second peak is because of the metal plate on the side. When the tester turns over 90°, the reflected strength of side increase rapidly to offset the decrease of reflected area. Therefore, it becomes a new peak in the image.

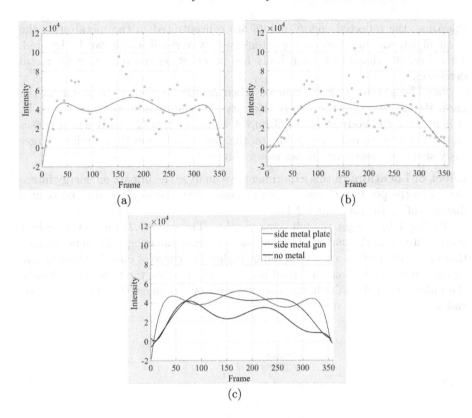

Fig. 6. Tester side with (a) metal plate; (b) metal gun; (c).

(ii) As shown in Fig. 6(b), the image of the tester side with the metal gun is similar to the previous image. They both have two peaks and one valley. However, the valley is higher than the previous situation. The difference between peak and value very small. The reason for the higher valley is the increasing reflect strength which is unable to offset the decrease of reflected area. It can only make the gradient smaller and the valley value higher.

5.4   System Practicability

Effect of Body Shape: This experiment aimed to analyze the impact on the energy intensity value with different body shapes. We divided 8 participants into 2 groups. Four participants who were 175 cm tall 70 kg in weight were considered as Group A, and 4 participants 170 cm tall 60 kg were considered as Group B. They wear a metal plate on the front and rotate at a distance of 1.8 m from Radar.

By Fig. 7(a), we got the following insights: *(i)* The first peak was when participants face the radar. The peak value of two groups is basically the same. At this time, the reflected energy points are concentrated in the metal area, the effect of human shape on energy intensity is very small which can be ignored. Therefore, the shape of human body has no effect on the judgment for metal detection.

(ii) The second peak is occurred when people are facing the radar on the back. We can find that the energy intensity of Group A is higher than Group B. It is because the body shape of Group A is larger than Group B which causes Group A has more reflection points on the person of Group B. Therefore, larger body shape has relatively higher energy intensity.

Effect of Location. In this experiment, we analyze the impact on energy intensity when the position changes. 8 participants wore metal plate and rotate at a distance of 1.2 m, 1.8 m, and 2.4 m.

By Fig. 7(b), we got the following insights: The curve 1.2 m have the highest energy intensity. The curve 2.4 m is at the bottom of the image. It can be inferred that closer the testers are to the radar, higher the curve of energy intensity will be captured. In addition, the trend is more obvious when the testers are close to the radar, but it doesn't change the character of the image (two peaks and one valley).

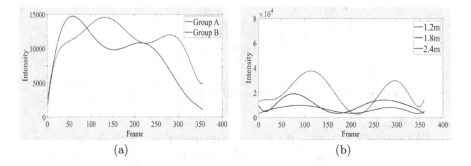

Fig. 7. Testers in different (a) body shape; (b) Location

6   Discussion and Future Work

Real-Time System: The current system can only artificially determine whether the tester is carrying metal objects, but it's unable automatically do the quantitative analysis for metal detection. Therefore, We need to develop a standard by combining wave, gradient, and other information. However, there are many challenges in developing this standard. *Firstly,* environmental impacts have a significant impact on standards. The multi-path effect may interfere the true result. Therefore, the avoidance of environmental interference is the challenge. *Secondly,* setting standards requires a large amount of data to find a stable standard. The number of our participants is far from achieving the universality of the standard. In our future work, we will recruit more testers in our experiments for collecting data and use these data for statistical analysis to find a proper threshold of automatic metal detection. In addition, after establishing standard, we will deal with the false positive and false negative problems to enhance the accuracy of the system.

Multiple Person Metal Detection: Our current situation is that there can only be one person in the test scope. Due to the large range of radar detection, we're enable to test more than one person simultaneously. Therefore, it is possible to detect multiple people by using one chip. The previous multiple people sensing and people tracking papers [17,23] gives up some ideas in multi-people data processing. In our future work, we will try the multiple persons detection which can enhance the security-check efficiency. Preliminary idea is to use cluster mining algorithm to separate each person in the detection area. Each cluster represents a person. We can calculate each cluster's frame-intensity image to detect metal item.

Specific Location on the Human Body: In our current research, our device can only detect whether there is a metal item hiding in the human body and find out the metal in an aspect of the human body. However, the accuracy of the system is unable to fit the true situation. Our algorithm is unable to determine the accurate location of the carrying metal item. More concretely, if the metal is hidden in the waist in the front and another is in the chest at the same aspect, our device only knows there was a metal item in the front of the human body, but it will not distinguish each item's accuracy location. Therefore, our future work needs to improve the accuracy of the metal detection which could point out the exact area of the human body.

Detection in Another Method: We have tried another scene besides rotating in place. We asked 8 participants to move from a distance of 3.2 m to 1.8 m. We found that energy intensity quickly increased. As shown in Fig. 8, the closer the tester is to the radar, the more energy points there are. The image of different

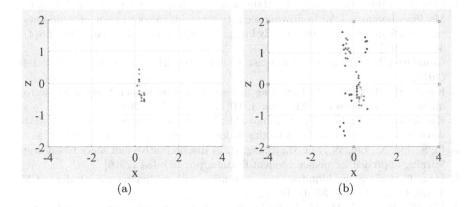

Fig. 8. Tester location to the radar (a) far to radar; (b) close to radar.

testers is slightly the same. We are unable to distinguish the difference by eyes. Therefore, it is difficult to determine whether a person is carrying metal. Our experimental scenario of rotating in place not only fix the distance to the radar but also detects the energy situation on all sides of the person. In comparison, the rotated scene is the best one for metal detection.

7 Conclusion

In this work, we design and implement a novel security check application with a small mmWave radar. The proposed solution enables security devices to work in the indoor environment especially in space-limited area. The application facilitates the detection of whether the detected person has the metal item on her body. We further explore its practicability from three aspects: metal in different parts of the body, the different distance of tester's location, and different tester's body shapes. Given the convenience of the proposed solution, we believe this metal detection system can be used in various security applications.

Acknowledgment. The research is supported by National Science and Technology Major Program of the Ministry of Science and Technology and project name is Research on 5G channel emulation and performance validation with 2018ZX03001031, NSFC (61772084, 61832010), the Fundamental Research Funds for the Central Universities (2019XD-A13).

References

1. Baştan, M., Yousefi, M.R., Breuel, T.M.: Visual words on baggage X-ray images. In: Real, P., Diaz-Pernil, D., Molina-Abril, H., Berciano, A., Kropatsch, W. (eds.) CAIP 2011. LNCS, vol. 6854, pp. 360–368. Springer, Heidelberg (2011). https://doi.org/10.1007/978-3-642-23672-3_44
2. Cooper, K., et al.: A high-resolution imaging radar at 580 GHz. IEEE Microwave Wirel. Compon. Lett. **18**(1), 64–66 (2008)
3. Gonzalez-Valdes, B., Alvarez, Y., Mantzavinos, S., Rappaport, C.M., Las-Heras, F., Martinez-Lorenzo, J.A.: Improving security screening: a comparison of multistatic radar configurations for human body imaging. IEEE Antennas Propag. Mag. **58**(4), 35–47 (2016)
4. Gunaratna, R.: Global threat forecast. Counter Terrorist Trends Anal. **10**(1), 1–6 (2018)
5. Kapilevich, B., Einat, M.: Detecting hidden objects on human body using active millimeter wave sensor. IEEE Sens. J. **10**(11), 1746–1752 (2010)
6. Kapilevich, B., Pinhasi, Y., Anisimov, M., Litvak, B., Hardon, D.: FMCW MM-wave non-imaging sensor for detecting hidden objects, pp. 101–104 (2011)
7. Li, S., Liu, X., Liu, W., Ma, H., Zhang, H.: A discriminative null space based deep learning approach for person re-identification, pp. 480–484 (2016)
8. Lien, J., et al.: Soli: ubiquitous gesture sensing with millimeter wave radar. ACM Trans. Graph. (TOG) **35**(4), 142 (2016)
9. Liu, W., Zhang, C., Ma, H., Li, S.: Learning efficient spatial-temporal gait features with deep learning for human identification. Neuroinformatics **16**, 457–471 (2018)

10. Meng, Y., Qing, A., Lin, C., Zang, J.: Passive millimeter wave imaging system for public security check. In: 2017 International Applied Computational Electromagnetics Society Symposium (ACES), pp. 1–2. IEEE (2017)
11. Murphy, M.C., Wilds, M.R.: X-rated X-ray invades privacy rights. Crim. Justice Policy Rev. **12**(4), 333–343 (2001)
12. Nanzer, J.A.: A review of microwave wireless techniques for human presence detection and classification. IEEE Trans. Microw. Theory Tech. **65**(5), 1780–1794 (2017)
13. Qian, K., Wu, C., Yang, Z., Liu, Y., Jamieson, K.: Widar: decimeter-level passive tracking via velocity monitoring with commodity Wi-Fi. In: Moharir, S., Gopalan, A. (eds.) Proceedings of the 18th ACM International Symposium on Mobile Ad Hoc Networking and Computing, Chennai, India, 10–14 July 2017. ACM (2017). https://doi.org/10.1145/3084041.3084067
14. Qian, K., Wu, C., Zhang, Y., Zhang, G., Yang, Z., Liu, Y.: Widar2.0: passive human tracking with a single Wi-Fi link, pp. 350–361 (2018)
15. Qian, K., Wu, C., Zhou, Z., Zheng, Y., Yang, Z., Liu, Y.: Inferring motion direction using commodity Wi-Fi for interactive exergames, pp. 1961–1972 (2017)
16. Sato, H., et al.: Passive millimeter-wave imaging for security and safety applications. In: Terahertz Physics, Devices, and Systems IV: Advanced Applications in Industry and Defense, vol. 7671, p. 76710V. International Society for Optics and Photonics (2010)
17. Wei, T., Zhang, X.: mTrack: high-precision passive tracking using millimeter wave radios, pp. 117–129 (2015)
18. Wei, T., Zhou, A., Zhang, X.: Facilitating robust 60 GHz network deployment by sensing ambient reflectors, pp. 213–226 (2017)
19. Wetter, O.E.: Imaging in airport security: past, present, future, and the link to forensic and clinical radiology. J. Forensic Radiol. Imaging **1**(4), 152–160 (2013)
20. Yang, Y., Guo, B., Wang, Z., Li, M., Yu, Z., Zhou, X.: BehaveSense: continuous authentication for security-sensitive mobile apps using behavioral biometrics. Ad Hoc Netw. **84**, 9–18 (2019)
21. Yurduseven, O.: Indirect microwave holographic imaging of concealed ordnance for airport security imaging systems. Prog. Electromagnet. Res. **146**, 7–13 (2014)
22. Zentai, G.: X-ray imaging for homeland security. In: 2008 IEEE International Workshop on Imaging Systems and Techniques, pp. 1–6. IEEE (2008)
23. Zhen, M., et al.: Gait recognition for co-existing multiple people using millimeter wave sensing (2020)
24. Zhou, A., Yang, S., Yang, Y., Fan, Y., Ma, H.: Autonomous environment mapping using commodity millimeter-wave network device, pp. 1126–1134 (2019)
25. Zhuge, X., Savelyev, T., Yarovoy, A., Ligthart, L., Matuzas, J., Levitas, B.: Human body imaging by microwave UWB radar. In: 2008 European Radar Conference, pp. 148–151. IEEE (2008)

Long-Range Gesture Recognition Using Millimeter Wave Radar

Yu Liu[1], Yuheng Wang[1], Haipeng Liu[1], Anfu Zhou[1(✉)],
Jianhua Liu[2], and Ning Yang[2]

[1] Beijing University of Posts and Telecommunications, Beijing, China
zhouanfu@bupt.edu.cn
[2] OPPO Co., Ltd., Beijing, China

Abstract. Millimeter wave (mmWave) based gesture recognition technology provides a good human computer interaction (HCI) experience. Prior works focus on the close-range gesture recognition, but fall short in range extension, *i.e.*, they are unable to recognize gestures more than one meter away from considerable noise motions. In this paper, we design a long-range gesture recognition model which utilizes a novel data processing method and a customized artificial Convolutional Neural Network (CNN). Firstly, we break down gestures into multiple reflection points and extract their spatial-temporal features which depict gesture details. Secondly, we design a CNN to learn changing patterns of extracted features respectively and output the recognition result. We thoroughly evaluate our proposed system by implementing on a commodity mmWave radar. Besides, we also provide more extensive assessments to demonstrate that the proposed system is practical in several real-world scenarios.

Keywords: Gesture recognition · Millimeter wave radar · Long-range scenario · Convolutional neural networks

1 Introduction

Contactless gesture recognition is a popular approach to realize natural human-computer interaction (HCI) for a better experience, so more and more external physical gesture devices [1–3] will be replaced by "in air" gestures [4,5]. To realize this HCI, researchers focus on wireless signal sensing. Compared with candidate sensing methods (*e.g.*, WiFi signal [6–9], sonic wave [10], and ultrasonic wave [11]), millimeter wave (mmWave) is sensitive to detect tiny variations, *i.e.*, centimeter-level finger movements. While visible [13] and infrared [14] light sensing are much more accurate on imaging a hand and thus gesture recognition, mmWave has unique advantages of privacy protection and energy consumption. Therefore, mmWave is the most suitable choice for contactless gesture recognition. Especially, mmWave is mainly used in 5G technology [15], so it will not only be a new radio access standard but a potential sensing tool.

© Springer Nature Switzerland AG 2020
Z. Yu et al. (Eds.): GPC 2020, LNCS 12398, pp. 30–44, 2020.
https://doi.org/10.1007/978-3-030-64243-3_3

The research on mmWave gesture recognition has obtained many achievements. At the practical application level, it can be used in the automotive industry to provide a safe and intuitive control interface for drivers. However, not all gestures of passengers sitting in the car can be accurately recognized, and the model will be low accuracy due to the interference of distance and the items in the car [16]. In addition, a short-range 60 GHz mmWave radar sensor that is sensitive to fine dynamic hand motions has been created but this model can only be used in a limited distance [17]. Therefore, prior work using mmWave radar is limited by the distance problem, which is an unavoidable challenge for us. Specifically, they can only realize gesture recognition under a short range situation, if the range is extended, the radar receives more reflective signal information, and the traditional method can not separate the interferer information and the effective information, thus distant gestures can not be recognized accurately.

In this paper, we design a long-range gesture recognition model with a customized Convolutional Neural Network (CNN). Firstly, in this model, we realize the accurate recognition of long-range gestures. Based on the basic principle of radar, we analyze the expressions of transmitting signals and reflected signals. We can accurately judge the distance, angle, velocity and other information of hands through the calculation of Fast Fourier Transformation (FFT) and Range-Doppler (R-D) algorithm. As long as the object is within the detection range of radar signal, we can realize the accurate location of the object. Secondly, our CNN is able to classify gestures correctly. In the previous CNN, all data is often processed in the same layer, which leads to some interference data to affect the result [18,19]. However, we divide our CNN into five sub-layers, each layer processes the corresponding features, with less interference, and finally combine the results for judgment. Different layers of CNN handle different features separately, so they will not interfere with each other. It ensures that the model can maintain high accuracy even if the extended distance leads to more interference.

We evaluate the proposed model thoroughly by implementing on a mmWave radar. Our experiments demonstrate that the accuracy of the model is sufficient be applied in certain real-world situations. Moreover, we conduct various extensive tests to explore the influence of different factors on the accuracy of the model. Specifically, we simulate a family living room by placing appropriate amounts of furnitures (*e.g.*, televisions, chairs) to make the real domestic facilities. Then we arrange participants to perform four gestures which are designed in advance and get the accuracy of the model judgement to evaluate the practicability of our model.

In conclusion, our contributions are as follows:

(i) We construct a long-range gesture recognition model by extracting the spatial-temporal features of hands' reflection points. Then we design a CNN to learn the points' features for recognition.

(ii) We utilize a mmWave radar sensor to implement the proposed model and thus recognize gestures automatically.

(iii) We verify that our proposed model is robust within several real-world situations (*e.g.*, family living room, multiple people, and real-time situation) and discuss the current limitations with several potential solutions.

2   Related Work

mmWave Sensing: mmWave has widely been used not only for high-speed networks [20–22], but also for human sensing [23] (*e.g.*, vehicular communications [24], drone tracking [25,26], material identification [27]). In addition, because of its large bandwidth, it can capture small changes in motion. This feature is often used in applications such as finger tracking [28]: combining efficient, dynamic path tracking algorithms and radar to track pathing; Gesture Recognition [29]: utilizing the feasibility of human gesture recognition using the spectra of radar measurement parameters for recognition. But the disadvantage of these methods is ignoring the distance between users and radar. Besides, the calculation of algorithms is too complicated and slow.

Other Long-Range Gesture Recognition Solutions: *(i)* *Visible Light:* Using visible light for communication and perception is a low-cost, green and low-carbon technology [12]. It also has the advantage of avoiding the interference of other electromagnetic waves. For example, LiGest [13], is a hand gesture recognition model based on visible light. However, LiGest suffers from the low penetration of visible light and the high cost of optical instruments. *(ii)* *Infrared Light:* Infrared light is not in direct contact with the object and has the advantage of high sensitivity and quick response. At present, there are two popular infrared sensor electronic devices: Leapmotion [14] and Kinect [30] for recognition. Both of them are able to monitor human details, *e.g.*, judging the position of the palm, identifying the palm and fingertips. However, they cannot determine all attributes for each frame. *(iii)* *WiFi signal:* WiFi signal is widely used in our daily life, including mobile device networking, wireless sensor networks [2,31] and also gesture recognition. Many models utilized WiFi signal has been applied for daily life. The latest study proposes WiMU, a WiFi based multi-users gesture recognition system [6], which provides a lower accuracy. Comparing to mmWave, the system is not sensitive enough to recognize complex gestures. *(iv)* *Sonic and Ultrasonic Wave:* The main idea is to combine the Doppler effect and the division of power levels short-time Fourier transforms on the frequency domain [32]. Moreover, some studies estimates range and receives signal strength (RSS) of reflected signal to recognize gestures [10]. However, the systems are not stable enough due to the narrow bandwidth and the external environment factors.

3   Overview

The proposed model aims at an attempt of mmWave based gesture recognition in a long-range scenario, which can be applied to many aspects in our daily life. Specifically, the model can cooperate with smart home system to provide better user experience, *e.g.*, controlling smart home appliances by "in air" gesture at a distance. For instance, a user can directly wave her hands up and down to control the light's state instead of touching the switch. Moreover, when a user is sitting on the couch and wants to draw curtains in the distance, what she only has to do is pointing at the radar and swiping her hand left or right. Therefore, our model is able to replace multiple unnecessary and troublesome movements, and acquire more comfortable and convenient experience.

Our model consists of following three modules which are shown in Fig. 1:

(i) Signal Transformation: This module captures reflected mmWave signals on gesturing hand and feeds them into the next *Information Extraction* module. In this module, we use the mmWave radar sensor to send the FMCW signal. When the signal arrives at hands, it will be reflected and received by the radar receiver. Then, the signal will be input into the next module after certain preprocessing methods.

(ii) Information Extraction: This module constructs the signal into a gesture point cloud model and provides it to the next *Neural Network* module for recognition. In the point cloud model, each of the inner point has its own five features, namely the x-y-z coordinate of the reflection point, velocity, and intensity. From the model, we can also observe the trend of gestures' change clearly.

(iii) Convolutional Neural Network: This module learns the changing pattern of the point cloud model and returns a classification result of the gesture. We input the point cloud data into this module. In advance, we creates an customized artificial CNN for handling the five features, every feature has its own layers. After the data passing CNN, the system will give the type of the gestures.

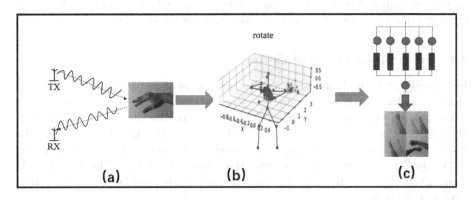

Fig. 1. The model consists of three modules: (a) Signal Transformation (b) Information Extraction (c) Neural Network

4   Methodology

As noted before, our method consists of gesture point cloud model and the customized CNN. *Firstly,* the model can depict the changing trend of gestures in space, however, there is a challenge existing when constructing the model: Long-range gestures will be interfered by some useless signals occurred by any surrounding object which reflects the mmWave signals, because the mmWave radar is omnidirectional. The problem will adversely impact the feature extraction process. Specifically, previous studies set the distance between the radar and the user very small, so there are less interfering objects in the detection range of radar and we will lose much effective information at the meanwhile. *Secondly,* leveraging on the model, we custom-design a CNN to classify gestures automatically. The design of CNN is one of the most innovative and challenging part of our solution: The CNN is responsible to process all features comprehensively and analyze the most reasonable changing trend, but we find that common convolutional neural networks cannot be used. Specifically, traditional convolutional neural network, such as VGG [24], have high network complexity and require too many parameters. Besides, it can be proved by our preliminary experiments that as the network deepens, vanishing gradient problem will appear, and lead to network degradation problems accordingly.

To meet the challenge, we propose two following methods: *Firstly,* the point cloud model we built contains valid information points and useless information points generated by the reflection of other interfering objects. Thus we adopt CA-CFAR technique to reduce the influence. With this technique, dynamic hot points with valid information can be selected after the Range-Doppler (R-D) image is calculated, so we obtain features effectively such as the distance, velocity and energy intensity of each spot. *Secondly,* we recommend a novel multi-branch CNN architecture instead of common networks used in the past. It not only solves the problems caused by traditional networks, but also gets better learning by passing each feature through a layer. We analyze features by layering to avoid cross interference between data, so as to obtain better accuracy.

4.1   Point Cloud Model of Gesture

In this module, we build a new 3D point cloud model of gestures with tendency in space, in order to remove as many interference points as possible. The proposed model adopts the radar principle that we perceive the gestures by analyzing the difference between the transmitted and the reflection signals from the hand. Please note that we omit the specific technical details, but readers can learn more in [33]. In Eq. 1, we show the set of reflection point information. The X, Y, Z, V, I respectively represent five features, and the lower corner marker i represents the ith point in the set.

$$P_i = \{X_i, Y_i, Z_i, V_i, I_i\} \tag{1}$$

After collecting the reflective point information data, we are ready to process the data. We take 30 frames (3 s) of initial point data to represent a gesture. By analyzing the trend of the point cloud, we can determine the changing pattern of gestures. Then, we prepare to deal with the initial data. Firstly, we will find the mean of five features of all reflection points of a gesture, taking the average value as a standard point as shown in Eq. 2, and then subtract the mean from each reflection point in turn to get D-value point as shown in Eq. 3.

$$P_0 = \{\bar{X}, \bar{Y}, \bar{Z}, \bar{V}, \bar{I}\} \tag{2}$$

$$\delta P_i = \{(X_i - \bar{X}), (Y_i - \bar{Y}), (Z_i - \bar{Z}), (V_i - \bar{V}), (I_i - \bar{I})\} \tag{3}$$

Then, we can get a 3D point cloud (pc) model with 5 * 30 * 65 size matrix as shown in Eq. 4.

$$PC = (\{F_1, F_2, F_3, F_3, \ldots F_j\}, j = 1, 2, 3 \ldots 30,$$
$$F_j = \{P_0, \delta P_1, \delta P_2, \ldots, \delta P_n\}, n = 1, 2, 3, \ldots 64) \tag{4}$$

As a result, we acquire the new 3D point model, which can focus points in the space near the standard point (shown in Fig. 2) and input the model to the next CNN.

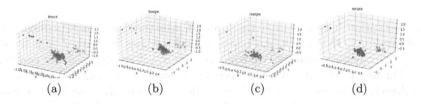

(a)   (b)   (c)   (d)

Fig. 2. The point cloud of four gestures: (a) knock; (b) left swipe; (c) right swipe (d) rotate.

4.2   The Model of Convolutional Neural Network

We built a customized multi-branch CNN to process feature information and recognize gestures as shown in Fig. 3. Since each point in the point cloud contains five features in the information, these features can calculate the valid information for each reflection point we need. Therefore, the CNN is divided into five layers in according to the features, that is, $N = \{X, Y, Z, V, I\}$. Each layer corresponds to X, Y, Z coordinates, velocity and intensity of energy. Firstly, we establish a ResNet class for each corresponding network. Through the ResNet layer, features can enter their corresponding networks. After passing through the networks, we extract the spatiotemporal information of a feature, but this cannot fully represent the gesture information. Therefore, the results after each network calculation go into the combine layer, in which these results are combined into a final result, as follows:

$$scr = N(Cat(X(x), Y(y), Z(z), V(v), I(i))) \tag{5}$$

Thus, the final result of jth gesture recognized as $j = max(src)$.

Implementation and Training: The corresponding network contains two parts: CONV1 network and CONV block. CONV1 network has a 7×7 convolution layer with 2×2 strides, and uses batch normalization followed by

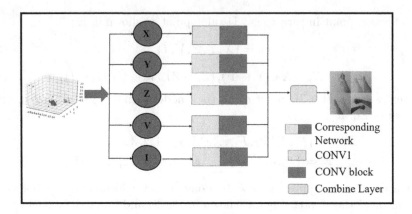

Fig. 3. The structure of Neural Network

ReLU activation functions after the layer. It uses the 3×3 max pooling with 2×2 strides. CONV block is a residual block for ResNet with 2×2 strides and 3×3 convolution layers. We connect feature values together into combine layer. The first layer is 3×3 convolution layers with 1×1 strides. We use batch normalization followed by the ReLU activation functions after the layer. We use a layer of fully connected layer with 65,280 input to obtain classification scores. The batch size is 64 and total training epochs are 200. The initial value of learning rate lr is 0.001. For each 200 epoch we set lr $=$ lr $\times$ 0.1. The optimization function of the network is Adam. We implement our network in PyTorch.

5   Experiment

5.1   Implementation Details

Gesture Design: In following experiments, participants are invited to perform four gestures in Fig. 4: knock, left swipe, right swipe and rotate. For gesture (a), knock, we ask participants to raise their right arm and tap it up and down twice in the air before returning to their original position. For gesture (b), left swipe, we ask participants to raise their right arm, sliding it across their chest to the left hand side, and then return to the original position. For gesture (c), right swipe, we ask participants to raise their right arm to the front of their left arm, sliding it across their chest to the right, and then return to their original position. For gesture (d), rotate, we ask participants to roll their hands in front of their chest, alternating up and down, for a period of time.

Data Collection: The experiment is performed as follows: Firstly, we place the mmWave radar in an empty room that will eliminate other interference. Then we arrange the participants stand 2.4 m in front of radar and make four different gestures introduced above. In each experiment, we ask 30 different participants, each of whom repeats the same gesture 50 times.

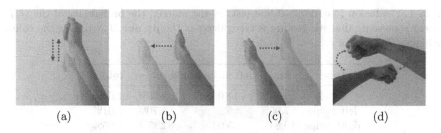

Fig. 4. Predefined gestures for interacting with applications: (a) knock; (b) left swipe; (c) right swipe; (d) rotate.

Hardware: We utilize a commodity mmWave radar that is an integrated single-chip mmWave sensor based on FMCW radar technology operating in 76 to 81 GHz bands with continuous linear frequency modulation pulses up to 4 GHz. The sampling rate of the radar is 37.5 Msps and the frame duration of it is 200 ms. This sensor provides us with rewritable functionality, for changing the internal programming module to get a multi-mode sensor.

Software: There are three software components to handle with data: Firstly, we use the Code Composer Studio (CCS) 9.1.0 to receive the point cloud data from the mmWave radar. CCS is a Integrated Device Electronics (IDE) that supports the embedded microcontroller and processor product line. Then, we need Matlab R2017b to save the point cloud data as a ".csv" file. At last, we use the Spyder 3.3.6, a simple IDE for python 3.7.3, the convolutional neural network and data processing are both implemented in Python language.

5.2 Performance Analysis

We design an experiment to test the accuracy under ideal conditions to investigate the model's performance. Specifically, we perform the standard test on 30 participants (15 men and 15 women). They are asked to make a sequence of four gestures, each repeats 50 times, at a distance of 2.4 m from the radar. After all the gesture information is collected, we process the data and get the corresponding off-line accuracy rate. By averaging the off-line accuracy of four gestures, we get a total off-line accuracy of 88.11%.

Micro Analysis: To make it easier for readers to understand the four gestures' accuracies, we built the confusion matrix shown in Table 1.

From the confusion matrix, we have several conclusions: *(i)* The rotate gesture has the highest accuracy rate nearly 99%, because its unique motion trajectory can be distinguished from other gestures, so it is not easy to be misjudged. This shows that the model has a high accuracy in judging some unique gestures. *(ii)* The accuracy rates of other three gestures are not high enough, because the transformation modes of the three are similar, especially in a long-range scenario, so they are easy to be mistaken.

Table 1. Confusion Matrix of off-line test. In the matrix, the probability of the (i, j) element represents that ith gesture is recognized as the jth one. The darker the color, the higher the accuracy

Types	knock	left swipe	right swipe	rotate
knock	85.17%	11.03%	2.76%	1.03%
left swipe	7.05%	86.24%	5.70%	1.01%
right swipe	10.84%	5.94%	82.17%	1.05%
rotate	0.72%	0.00%	0.00%	99.28%

Surpass on Classification Method: We confirm the effectiveness of our proposed network by comparing it with the ordinary method Resnet18 [34]. The result of this is 62.78% which is much more lower than our 88.11%.

5.3 Forecast Accuracy for New Users

We collect gesture data from 30 people and do a leave-one-subject-out validation (Table 2) to test the model's accuracy in identifying new users. Each of the models tested is learned from the gestures of the other 29 people. Therefore, we obtain a total of 30 models for the experiment.

Table 2. Results of leave-one-subject-out validation.

People	Acc	People	Acc	People	Acc	People	Acc	People	Acc
No. 1	83.00%	No. 7	83.50%	No. 13	91.00%	No. 19	84.50%	No. 25	94.00%
No. 2	85.43%	No. 8	88.00%	No. 14	91.50%	No. 20	76.50%	No. 26	77.00%
No. 3	92.00%	No. 9	86.00%	No. 15	94.50%	No. 21	69.50%	No. 27	67.00%
No. 4	95.50%	No. 10	93.00%	No. 16	88.00%	No. 22	94.50%	No. 28	74.17%
No. 5	95.50%	No. 11	99.00%	No. 17	81.00%	No. 23	82.00%	No. 29	77.50%
No. 6	59.00%	No. 12	83.00%	No. 18	94.00%	No. 24	85.00%	No. 30	77.50%
Average	86.09%								

In the first column, we represent 30 participants with numbers. The second column shows the test results for each model for the new user. We can see that the average accuracy of the model for new users is 86.09%, which shows that our model is feasible for gesture recognition of unfamiliar users who have not been known by our model. This is slightly less accurate than offline accuracy in Sect. 5.2, but it still maintains an acceptable accuracy.

5.4 Practical Application Analysis

To verify the performance of the model in real situations, we simulate three real-life scenarios. Comparing to experiments in Sect. 5.2, we add several chairs and a television to create the effect of the living room in the family. We will test the impact caused by these pieces of furniture on our model in following scenes.

In the first scene, we ask two participants, still standing 2.4 m from the radar, to repeat each of four gestures 30 times, collecting a total of 60 pieces of gesture data. The room is as shown in Fig. 5. In the second and third scene, we keep the number of participants and the number and types of gestures still the same. We only change the placement of tables and chairs in the room.

(a)   (b)   (c)

Fig. 5. Three scenes: (a) scene1; (b) scene2; (c) scene3.

Table 3. Results of practical experiment

Types/Accuracy	Knock	Left swipe	Right swipe	Rotate
Scene1	48.33%	38.33%	51.67%	98.00%
Secne2	35.00%	5.00%	23.33%	96.67%
Scene3	38.33%	3.33%	30.00%	98.33%

From Table 3, we can find following three insights: *(i)* Rotate's accuracy has remained roughly the same, suggesting that the uniqueness of the gesture mode gives it a high degree of accuracy. This kind of gestures is less affected by the external environment, and can be applied in real life. *(ii)* However in these three scenarios, we only collected 60 pieces of data for each gesture, so the lack of data may also has contributed to the sharp decline in accuracy. *(iii)* The accuracy of the first three gestures has decreased greatly, which is not enough to support the application of the model in real life. We believe that this model is greatly affected by external environment factors, and does not have a good performance for gestures that are not easy to distinguish. Therefore, we try to split out the noise points manually and achieve a higher accuracy of the three scenarios are respectively 84.59%, 70.00%, 59.58%.

6   Discussion

In this section, we have a case-by-case discussion on factors which might affect the model. The distance factor, the multi-people factor and the real-time situation are discussed in turn. We explore the performance and practical application of our model under the influence of different factors. These discussions allow us to evaluate and test the model more thoroughly.

6.1   Distance Influence

During the study, we find that the distance between hand and radar is an important factor that affects the accuracy of model judgment. Here, we divide the room area with bricks, each brick is a square which has the side length of 0.6 m, as shown in Fig. 6. In order to better explore the distance influence on the model, we take the number of bricks as a variable to verify whether the accuracy of the model in different blocks will be affected. First, there are 80 participants in this experiment, each of whom stands at the 5th brick and repeats each of four gestures 50 times, so we collect 400 pieces of data for each gesture. The accuracy in Sect. 5.2 is about the same as our previous experiment. Therefore, we change the distance between participants and the radar, asking them stand at the 4th brick and keep everything else the same.

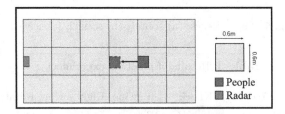

Fig. 6. The room was divided into bricks.

We use the model of the 5th brick to test whether the data collected from the 4th brick is accurate. The result is that the data collected from the 4th brick is not accurate. However, when we input the data collected by participants standing at the 4th brick into the model, and we test participants standing on the 4th brick and the 5th block respectively, and then find that the model could run normally with high accuracy (listed in Table 4).

Table 4. The results of distance influence. The origin model only has the data of 5th brick and the new model has the data of both 5th and 4th bricks.

Scenes	Knock	Left swipe	Right swipe	Rotate
5th brick (origin model)	65.00%	79.25%	87.00%	99.25%
4th brick (origin model)	3.50%	22.25%	12.00%	98.00%
5th brick (new model)	61.75%	82.50%	88.00%	99.00%
4th brick (new model)	63.25%	80.00%	83.33%	99.85%

From Table 4, we can find that the model is very sensitive to distance factor, and the gesture data from different distances will lead to different judgment results. Therefore, in practical application, we need to collect as much informa-tion as possible from different distances so that the model can accurately judge gestures at different positions.

In our future work, we manage to reduce the distance sensitivity of the model and realize accurate judgment of gestures at different positions.

6.2   Multiple People Influence

We apply the model to the multi-people environment, and design two scenarios shown as Fig. 7.

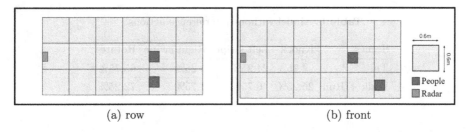

(a) row   (b) front

Fig. 7. The two scenarios: (a) two participants stand in one row (b) one participant stands in front of another

In this experiment, we recruit three participants and divide each two of them into three groups. Each group will experiment with two scenes separately. Among them, the participant who stands on the 5th brick is set as the target person we want to identify, and the other participant is the interferer. Each group asked to do each of the four gestures 30 times simultaneously, so we can get 90 pieces of data of each gesture. The experiment results of two scenarios are shown in Table 5.

Table 5. Results of multiple people

Scenes	Knock	Left swipe	Right swipe	Rotate
Multi-people (row)	37.78%	2.22%	22.22%	100.00%
Multi-people (front)	47.78%	1.00%	17.78%	98.89%

From the results, we can find that only rotate can the model judged correctly with a high accuracy. However, the accuracy of another three gestures is too low to be used. Thus, this model hasn't accomplished to recognize multiple people's concurrent gestures. When we are recording the gesture data, there is usually a lot of interference data. Therefore, we believe splitting out the gestures from noises may tackle this problem, and we have made a preliminary manual efforts which achieving a better accuracy of 69.72% (front), 78.19% (row).

6.3   Real-Time Consideration

In the real situation, the model usually encounters a lot of interferences, which leads to a decreased accuracy. Therefore, we consider several interference actions, *i.e.*, walk, run, and some tiny gestures which are similar to our model gestures. In this experiment, we ask 80 participants to do each of these two interference actions (distance and other requirements remained the same), and to repeat each action 50 times. We can get 400 pieces of data for each action.

In consequence of not considering the model of interference before this experiment, the model will mistake these interference actions into different gestures. The results are shown as Table 6:

Table 6. Model without interference actions

Scenes	Knock	Left swipe	Right swipe	Rotate
Tiny	4.75%	24.25%	5.25%	65.75%
Walk + Run	25.25%	0.75%	1.75%	72.25%

From the Table 6, some tiny gestures may be mistaken into rotate or other gestures. The action of walk or run is also an interference for our model. This will cause the accuracy of the model decreased sharply. We specifically collect 1,600 pieces of data on these two types of interference and feed them into the model. Later, when we test the gesture with the interference actions again, the results from the Table 7 show that the model is able to automatically identify and removes the interference, then identifying the correct gesture.

Table 7. Model with interference actions

Scenes	Knock	Left swipe	Right swipe	Rotate
Tiny	80.75%	75.00%	78.20%	97.75%
Walk + Run	84.25%	85.25%	80.25%	98.25%

7   Conclusion

In this paper, we introduce a long-range gesture recognition model based on mmWave sensing. We utilize a mmWave radar to collect spatial and temporal characteristics of gestures, and then input gesture data into a customized convolutional neural network for automatic gesture recognition. On this basis, we also carry out several real scenario experiments to verify the practicability of the model. With the rapid development of 5G technology, mmWave frequency band will be fully developed and utilized in the future. Therefore, we believe mmWave sensing technology will provide a wider range of services for mankind.

Acknowledgment. The research is supported by National Key R&D Program of China (2019YFB2102202), NSFC (61772084, 61832010), the Fundamental Research Funds for the Central Universities (2019XD-A13) and OPPO research foundation.

References

1. Li, G., Wu, H., Jiang, G., Xu, S., Liu, H.: Dynamic gesture recognition in the Internet of Things. IEEE Access **7**, 23713–23724 (2018). https://doi.org/10.1109/ACCESS.2018.2887223
2. Naosekpam, V., Sharma, R.K.: Machine learning in 3D space gesture recognition. Jurnal Kejuruteraan **31**, 243–248 (2019)
3. Liang, Y., Zhou, X., Yu, Z., Guo, B.: Energy-efficient motion related activity recognition on mobile devices for pervasive healthcare. MONET **19**(3), 303–317 (2014)
4. Liu, W., Zhang, C., Ma, H., Li, S.: Learning efficient spatial-temporal gait features with deep learning for human identification. Neuroinformatics **16**, 457–471 (2018). https://doi.org/10.1007/s12021-018-9362-4
5. Li, S., Liu, X., Liu, W., Ma, H., Zhang, H.: A discriminative null space based deep learning approach for person re-identification. In: CCIS 2016, pp. 480–484 (2016)
6. Venkatnarayan, R.H., Mahmood, S., Shahzad, M.: WiFi based multi-user gesture recognition. IEEE Trans. Mob. Comput. (2019). https://doi.org/10.1109/TMC.2019.2954891
7. Qian, K., Wu, C., Zhou, Z., Zheng, Y., Yang, Z., Liu, Y.: Inferring motion direction using commodity Wi-Fi for interactive exergames. In: ACM CHI, Denver, USA, 6–11 May 2017 (2017)
8. Qian, K., Wu, C., Yang, Z., Liu, Y., Jamieson, K.: Widar: decimeter-level passive tracking via velocity monitoring with commodity Wi-Fi. In: ACM MobiHoc, Chennai, India, 10–14 July 2017 (2017)
9. Qian, K., Wu, C., Zhang, Y., Zhang, G., Yang, Z., Liu, Y.: Widar2.0: passive human tracking with a single Wi-Fi link. In: ACM MobiSys, Munich, Germany, 10–15 June 2018 (2018)
10. AlSharif, M.H., Saad, M., Al-Naffouri, T.Y.: Hand gesture recognition using ultrasonic waves. Article (2017)
11. Das, A., Tashev, I., Mohammed, S.: Ultrasound based gesture recognition. In: Conference Paper, March (2017)
12. Hu, Q., Yu, Z., Wang, Z., Guo, B., Chen, C.: ViHand: gesture recognition with ambient light. In: SmartWorld/SCALCOM/UIC/ATC/CBDCom/IOP/SCI 2019, pp. 468–474 (2019)
13. Venkatnarayan, R.H., Shahzad, M.: Gesture recognition using ambient light. Proc. ACM Interact. Mob. Wearable Ubiquit. Technol. **2**(1), 28 (2018). Article ID 40
14. Lee, B., Park, K., Ghan, S., Chin, S.: Designing canonical form of finger motion grammar in leapmotion contents. In: 2016 International Conference on Mechatronics, Control and Automation Engineering (2016)
15. Sakaguchi, K., Haustein, T., et al.: Where, when, and how mmWave is used in 5G and beyond. IEICE Trans. Electron. **100**, 790–808 (2017)
16. Smith, K.A., Csech, C., Murdoch, D., Shaker, G.: Gesture recognition using mmWave sensor for human-car interface. IEEE Sens. Lett. **2**, 1–4 (2018)
17. Hazra, S., Santra, A.: Robust gesture recognition using millimetric-wave radar system. IEEE Sens. Lett. **2**, 1–4 (2018)
18. Liu, K., Liu, W., Gan, C., Tan, M., Ma, H.: T-C3D: temporal convolutional 3D network for real-time action recognition. In: AAAI, pp. 7138–7145 (2018)

19. Liu, W., Yan, C.C., Liu, J., Ma, H.: Deep learning based basketball video analysis for intelligent arena application. Multimedia Tools Appl. **76**(23), 24983–25001 (2017)
20. Song, Y., Liu, L., Ma, H., Vasilakos, A.V.: A biology-based algorithm to minimal exposure problem of wireless sensor networks. IEEE Trans. Netw. Serv. Manag. **11**(3), 417–430 (2014)
21. Zhou, A., Yang, S., Yang, Y., Fan, Y., Ma, H.: Autonomous environment mapping using commodity millimeter-wave network device. In: INFOCOM 2019, pp. 1126–1134 (2019)
22. Zhou, A., et al.: Robot navigation in radio beam space: leveraging robotic intelligence for seamless mmWave network coverage. In: MobiHoc 2019, pp. 161–170 (2019)
23. Meng, Z., et al.: Gait recognition for co-existing multiple people using millimeter wave sensing. In: AAAI (2020)
24. Molchanov, P., Gupta, S., Kim, K., Kautz, J.: Hand gesture recognition with 3D convolutional neural networks. NVIDIA, Santa Clara, California, USA (2015)
25. Dogru, S., Baptista, R., Marques, L.: Tracking drones with drones using millimeter wave radar. In: Silva, M.F., Luís Lima, J., Reis, L.P., Sanfeliu, A., Tardioli, D. (eds.) ROBOT 2019. AISC, vol. 1093, pp. 392–402. Springer, Cham (2020). https://doi.org/10.1007/978-3-030-36150-1_32
26. Wei, T., Zhang, X.: mTrack: high-precision passive tracking using millimeter wave radios. Department of Electrical and Computer Engineering (2015)
27. Dwivedi, S.: Simulation analysis on applicability of meta material and PBG based mm-Wave planar antenna for advanced cellular technologies. Open J. Antennas Propag. **5**, 23–35 (2017)
28. Rasekh, M.E., Marzi, Z., Zhu, Y., Madhow, U., Zheng, H.: Noncoherent mmWave path tracking (2017)
29. Liu, C., Li, Y., Ao, D., Tian, H.: Spectrum-based hand gesture recognition using millimeter-wave radar parameter measurements. IEEE Access **7**, 79147–79158 (2019). https://doi.org/10.1109/ACCESS.2019.2923122
30. Chuang, C.-H., Chen, Y.-N., Deng, M.-S., Fan, K.-C.: Gesture recognition based on kinect (2014)
31. Liu, L., Song, Y., Zhang, H., Ma, H., Vasilakos, A.V.: Physarum optimization: a biology-inspired algorithm for the Steiner tree problem in networks. IEEE Trans. Comput. **64**(3), 819–832 (2013)
32. Binh, N.D.: Gestures recognition from sound waves. Research Article EAI Endorsed Transactions on Context-aware Systems and Applications (2016)
33. Principle of Radar. Texas Instrument
34. He, K., Zhang, X., Ren, S., Sun, J.: Deep residual learning for image recognition. In: IEEE Conference on Computer Vision and Pattern Recognition. IEEE Computer Society (2016)

Towards Fine-Grained Indoor White Space Sensing

Fan Wu[1]([envelope]), Yunlong Xiang[1], Zhenzhe Zheng[1], Yuben Qu[1], Xiaofeng Gao[1], Linghe Kong[1], Guihai Chen[1], and Biao Liu[2]

[1] Department of Computer Science and Engineering, Shanghai Jiao Tong University, Shanghai, China
{fwu,gao-xf,gchen}@cs.sjtu.edu.cn,
{xiangyunlong,zhengzhenzhe,quyuben,linghe.kong}@sjtu.edu.cn
[2] Gaoxin Technology Group Co., Ltd., Shenzhen, China
liubiao@gosuncn.com

Abstract. Exploring white spaces in the indoor environment has been recognized as a promising way to satisfy the rapid growth of the wireless spectrum demand. Although a few indoor white space exploration systems have been proposed in the past few years, they mainly focused on exploring white spaces at a small set of candidate locations. However, what we need are the white space availabilities at arbitrary indoor locations instead of only those at the candidate locations. In this paper, we first perform an indoor TV spectra measurement to study the characteristics of indoor white spaces in a fine-grained way. Then, we propose a Fine-gRained Indoor white Space Estimation mechanism, called FRISE, which could accurately estimate the white space availabilities at arbitrary indoor locations. FRISE mainly consists of a method to determine the positions of candidate locations and an accurate spatial interpolation algorithm. Furthermore, we evaluate the performance of FRISE based on real-world measured data. The evaluation results show that FRISE outperforms the existing methods in estimating white spaces at arbitrary indoor locations.

Keywords: Dynamic Spectrum Access · White space · Gaussian process

1 Introduction

The fast growth of the mobile devices and applications has led to the increasing demand of wireless spectra for communication. Unfortunately, the amount of unlicensed wireless spectra that are free to use is very limited, while most of the licensed spectra are underutilized [17]. Facing the shortage of the wireless spectra, the concept of Dynamic Spectrum Access (DSA) was proposed to improve the wireless spectrum utilization.

In 2008, the Federal Communication Commission (FCC) issued the rule that allows unlicensed devices to access locally unoccupied TV spectra, which are usually referred to as TV white spaces [7]. Although the unlicensed use of TV white

© Springer Nature Switzerland AG 2020
Z. Yu et al. (Eds.): GPC 2020, LNCS 12398, pp. 45–60, 2020.
https://doi.org/10.1007/978-3-030-64243-3_4

spaces is allowed, FCC also requires that unlicensed devices should not interfere with any of the licensed TV transmissions. Therefore, all user devices (especially the unlicensed ones) should get the spectrum's availability information before accessing it.

In the indoor environment, there exist more white spaces than the outdoor scenarios because of the existence of the indoor obstacles (e.g., walls) [19]. The existing indoor white space exploration systems [10,19] aim at constructing an indoor white space availability map, which indicates the availabilities of the TV spectra at different indoor locations. Users could submit their indoor locations, and then receive the corresponding list of white spaces according to the current indoor white space availability map. The construction of the indoor white space availability map can be divided into two steps: *recovery at candidate locations* and *estimation at arbitrary locations*.

Step I Recovery at Candidate Locations: In order to construct the indoor white space availability map, a set of candidate locations should be selected to cover every of the rooms and corridors. Due to limitations on budget and runtime cost, existing approaches turn to carefully deploying a certain number of spectrum detectors at a part of the candidate locations, and then recover the status of TV spectra at the other candidate locations based on indoor spectrum's characteristic of spatial-spectral correlations.

Step II Estimation at Arbitrary Locations: Given the signal strengths at candidate locations, the signal strengths at arbitrary indoor locations are estimated based on some spatial interpolation method.

However, the existing works could not perform Step II in an accurate enough way. All existing works assume that the positions of candidate locations are given beforehand. Whereas our experiment results in Sect. 2 demonstrate that different positions of candidate locations would lead to different performances of estimation. Furthermore, existing works apply a kind of constant spatial interpolation to do the estimation. We have also shown that directly applying the constant interpolation approach would lead to high error rates of estimation.

Unfortunately, it is difficult to solve the above two problems. The first challenge is how to determine the positions of candidate locations. The other challenge is accurate spatial interpolation. In this paper, we propose FRISE, a Fine-gRained Indoor white Space Estimation mechanism. In response to the first challenge, FRISE uses mutual information to describe the "importance" of each of the indoor locations. Besides, we determine the positions of candidate locations in sequence, and iteratively choose the most "important" locations. In this way, the position determination could be achieved in polynomial time. For the second challenge, we build a Gaussian process model for the signal strengths at arbitrary locations, the kernel function of which could approximately describe the correlations between any pair of locations. Furthermore, the spectral and temporal correlations are also considered to improve the performance of the interpolation. The main contributions of this paper are summarized as follows:

- We perform indoor TV spectra measurement in a lab room and a corridor. The measurement results demonstrate the influence of different positions of candidate locations and the inaccuracy of the constant interpolation, which motivates this work.

– FRISE improves the accuracy of estimation at arbitrary locations by first determining the proper positions of candidate locations and then applying an accurate spatial interpolation method to do the estimation. To the best of our knowledge, FRISE is the first mechanism that studies the position determination of candidate locations.

– We evaluate the performance of FRISE with extensive real-world measured data. The evaluation results demonstrate that FRISE leads to a maximum 38.5% less white space error compared to the constant interpolation and 47.0% less white space error compared to the random determination for positions of candidate locations, respectively.

The rest of the paper is organized as follows. In Sect. 2, we present our indoor TV spectra measurement experiment. Then we propose the detailed system design of FRISE in Sect. 3. In Sect. 4, we evaluate FRISE. Related works and conclusions are given in Sect. 5 and Sect. 6, respectively.

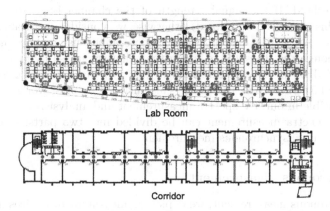

Fig. 1. Map of the lab room and corridor.

2   Indoor TV Spectra Measurement

In this section, we present our indoor TV spectra measurement. Different from the existing TV spectra measurement, which measured the TV spectra only at the candidate locations, we measure the TV spectra in a more fine-grained way. The measurement is carried out in two typical indoor environments: a lab room (abbr. $10\,m \times 45\,m$) and a long corridor (abbr. $120\,m$ long), the maps of which are shown in Fig. 1.

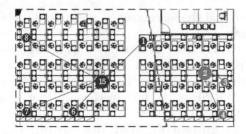

Fig. 2. Example of constant interpolation.

2.1 Equipment and Setup

Our measurement device consists of a USRP N210, a log periodic PCB antenna, and a laptop. The USRP N210 is equipped with the SBX daughter-board with 5–10 dBm noise figure. We measure 56 UHF digital TV channels between 470 MHz–566 MHz and 606 MHz–958 MHz with 8 MHz channel bandwidth.

We can get the status of a channel by comparing its signal strength with a preset threshold. If the signal strength of the channel is greater than the threshold, this channel is occupied, otherwise we consider it vacant. We use a threshold of −84.5 dBm/8 MHz, which is determined using the same way as [10,19]. Although the threshold is higher than that suggested by FCC, which is −114 dBm/8 MHz, we set the threshold in this way due the device limitation. Since the −84.5 dBm/8 MHz threshold is also utilized by prior works, we believe that it is feasible in our TV spectra measurement and analysis.

The TV spectra measurement can be divided into two parts: synchronous measurement and asynchronous measurement.

2.2 Synchronous Measurement

In the synchronous measurement, we deploy 22 measurement devices in the lab room (blue points in Fig. 1) and continuously measure the signal strengths of TV channels for a period of 2 weeks. We synchronously measure the signal strengths of 56 TV channels every 5 min in the two weeks period. The observations are as follows:

The Constant Interpolation Could Not Accurately Estimate the Status of TV Channels. The constant interpolation is commonly utilized by the existing indoor white space exploration systems to estimate the status of TV channels at arbitrary indoor locations. We analyze the performance of the constant interpolation based on the measurement results. We first give a simple example. Figure 2 shows a part of the lab room, which contains the measurement locations 1, 2, 3, 4, 6, 7, 8, and 15. We choose location 2 and 15 as the candidate locations. If we apply the constant interpolation to do the estimation at arbitrary locations, then the status of TV channels at location 3 and 4 are considered the same as location 2, while the status of TV channels at location 1, 6, 7, and 8 are considered the same as location 15. We compare the real status of the 56 TV channels with the estimated values at each time slot (5 min), and calculate the average errors of the estimation. Here we denote the *white space error* as the ratio between the number of channels whose status are incorrectly estimated and the total number of channels. We give the detailed definition of white space error in Sect. 4.1. The results are shown in Table 1. For instance, at location 1, the status of an average of 4.5 channels are incorrectly estimated, which is about 8% of the 56 channels. At location 4, about 16% of the channels (9.1) are estimated to wrong status. These high white space error make constant interpolation not accurate enough, and thus it is essential to design an accurate algorithm to do the estimation at arbitrary locations.

Table 1. Performance analysis about constant interpolation

Candidate locations	15				2	
Locations	1	6	7	8	3	4
# of errors	4.5	8.8	6.8	6.3	5.7	9.1
White space error	8%	16%	12%	11%	10%	16%

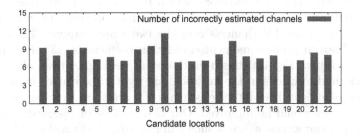

Fig. 3. Influence of positions of candidate locations.

Different Positions of Candidate Locations Lead to Different Performances of Estimation. We also observe that different positions of candidate locations would lead to different performances of the estimation at arbitrary locations. Here, we first set location 1 as the candidate location, and calculate the average number of channels whose status are incorrectly estimated over the remaining 21 locations. Then, we set location 2, 3, ..., 22 as the candidate location in sequence, and compare the performance of estimation under different candidate locations. The results are shown in Fig. 3. The y-axis refers to the average number of incorrectly estimated channels under different candidate locations. For instance, when we use location 1 as the candidate location, the status of an average of 9.18 channels are incorrectly estimated at the remaining 21 locations.

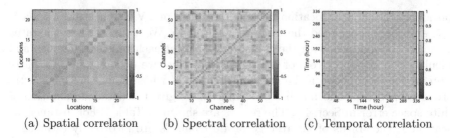

(a) Spatial correlation   (b) Spectral correlation   (c) Temporal correlation

Fig. 4. Correlations of indoor TV spectra.

It is observed that when the positions of the candidate locations are different, the number of incorrectly estimated channels are also different, which leads to different estimation performances. Hence, it is important for us to determine a proper set of positions for candidate locations in order to get a higher estimation accuracy.

There Exist Spatial-Spectral-Temporal Correlations Among TV Spectra. We then study the correlations of TV spectra between different locations, channels, and time slots, which we call spatial-spectral-temporal correlations.

We focus on the spatial correlation in a room or corridor, instead of that between different rooms or corridors, which is already studied. Based on the measured data, we get a vector for each measured location that contains the signal strengths of all TV channels over the two weeks interval. Then we calculate the Pearson product-moment correlation coefficients [13] of all pairs of locations, and draw Fig. 4(a) based on the result. In Fig. 4(a), we observe that the 22 measured locations in the lab room are tightly correlated. If the spatial correlation could be utilized into the estimation at arbitrary locations, we believe that its accuracy would be improved. Our observations on spectral correlation are similar to prior works, which is shown in Fig. 4(b). A channel may be tightly correlated with some channels while almost independent to others.

Furthermore, we also study the temporal correlation of TV spectra while existing works on indoor white space exploration mainly focus on the spatial and spectral correlations. Figure 4(c) illustrates the Pearson product-moment correlation coefficients between different time slots in the two weeks interval. We observed that the temporal correlation shows the periodical property. For some time slots, they may have relatively small Pearson product-moment correlation coefficients with their neighbors but be tightly correlated with the time slots which are one period after or before them. The temporal correlation could help us simplify the process of training FRISE, because we do not need to synchronously measure the TV spectra in the training process.

2.3   Asynchronous Measurement

Due to the limitation of budget, we do not have enough measurement devices to support a synchronous fine-grained measurement. We instead apply an asynchronous way to do the measurement.

We choose two typical indoor environments, the lab room and a long corridor, to do the measurement. We measure the TV spectra at the same lab room with the synchronous measurement, and choose 105 locations (red points in room of Fig. 1). We mount our measurement device on a cart, and measure all the TV channels at one location after another. We also record the time after every measurement. In the long corridor, we choose 27 locations (red points in the corridor of Fig. 1) and perform the measurement in the same way. Every day we perform one round of measurement. The asynchronous measurement lasts for a period of two weeks.

3   System Design

This section shows the design of FRISE. At first, we give an overview of FRISE. Then, we describe the implementation of the multitask Gaussian process based spatial interpolation. After that, we introduce the mutual information based method to determine the positions of candidate locations.

3.1   System Overview

The indoor white space exploration systems aim at constructing an indoor white space availability map, which indicates the white space availabilities of the whole indoor environment. The construction of the map could be divided into two steps: recovery at candidate locations (Step I) and estimation at arbitrary locations (Step II). Existing works mainly focus on Step I. They assume that a set of candidate locations are given in advance, and try to select a part of candidate locations to deploy spectrum detectors. Based on the measurement results of spectrum detectors, the signal strengths of TV spectra at all candidate locations could be accurately recovered.

Given the signal strengths at all candidate locations, FRISE aims at estimating those at arbitrary locations (Step II) in a more accurate way. FRISE improves the accuracy of the estimation in two ways:

- FRISE first applies a mutual information based method to determine the proper positions of candidate locations.
- FRISE further uses a multitask Gaussian process based spatial interpolation by considering the spatial-spectral-temporal correlations among TV spectra.

Since the algorithm to determine the positions of candidate locations is based on the estimation results, in the following parts, we first assume the positions of candidate locations are given and describe the multitask Gaussian process based spatial interpolation algorithm. Then we present the algorithm to determine the positions of candidate locations.

3.2   Multitask Gaussian Process Based Spatial Interpolation

Gaussian process is usually used to predict a single output (or task) based on one or more inputs. However, there exist dozens of TV channels with correlations. If we simply train a Gaussian process model independently for each channel, we would "waste" the correlations among channels. Hence, we explore a multitask Gaussian process regression model [1,20], which estimates the signal strength of some channel not only based on the same channel's information, but also based on the signal strengths of other correlated channels.

Given the set of N inputs $\boldsymbol{x}_1, \boldsymbol{x}_2, \ldots, \boldsymbol{x}_N$ with $\boldsymbol{x}_i = (p_i, q_i, t_i)^T$ where (p_i, q_i) is the coordinate of the an location, and t_i refers to the time. The corresponding signal strengths of TV channels are defined as

$$\boldsymbol{y} = (y_1^1, \ldots, y_N^1, y_1^2, \ldots, y_N^2, \ldots, y_N^M), \tag{1}$$

where y_i^ℓ is the signal strength of the ℓth TV channel at location (p_i, q_i) when the time is t_i. Here M refers to the number of TV channels.

According to the Gaussian process theory [1,15], $\boldsymbol{y}$ can be assumed to obey a multivariate Gaussian joint distribution with a mean value 0, which means that

$$\boldsymbol{y} \sim \mathcal{N}(\boldsymbol{0}, K), \tag{2}$$

where K is the covariance matrix. The covariance matrix K is defined by a kernel function $k(\boldsymbol{x}_i, \boldsymbol{x}_{i'}, \ell, \ell')$ which refers to the covariance between two observations y_i^ℓ and $y_{i'}^{\ell'}$. According to the multitask Gaussian process theory [1], $k(\boldsymbol{x}_i, \boldsymbol{x}_{i'}, \ell, \ell')$ can be rewritten as

$$k(\boldsymbol{x}_i, \boldsymbol{x}_{i'}, \ell, \ell') = K_{\ell\ell'}^c k^x(\boldsymbol{x}_i, \boldsymbol{x}_{i'}), \tag{3}$$

where K^c is an $M \times M$ positive semi-definite matrix that specifies the spectral correlation and k^x is a covariance function which describes the spatial-temporal correlations. $K_{\ell\ell'}^c$ is the element at ℓth row and ℓ'th column of K^c, which refers to the correlation between channel ℓ and ℓ'. If we let K^x be the matrix of covariances between all pairs of training inputs. The covariance matrix K in Eq. (2) can be denoted as

$$K = K^c \otimes K^x, \tag{4}$$

where $\otimes$ refers to the Kronecker product [8].

Given the signal strengths of TV channels at the candidate locations, that is $\boldsymbol{y}$, we try to estimate the signal strengths of arbitrary indoor locations. For example, if we want to know the signal strength of channel ℓ at location (p_*, q_*) when the time is t_*, where the corresponding input is $\boldsymbol{x}_* = (p_*, q_*, t_*)^T$, we have the following results

$$\begin{bmatrix} \boldsymbol{y} \\ y_*^\ell \end{bmatrix} \sim \mathcal{N}\left(\boldsymbol{0}, \begin{bmatrix} K & (K_*^\ell)^T \\ K_*^\ell & K_{**}^\ell \end{bmatrix} \right), \tag{5}$$

with

$$K_{**} = k(\boldsymbol{x}_*, \boldsymbol{x}_*, \ell, \ell) = K_{\ell\ell}^c k^x(\boldsymbol{x}_*, \boldsymbol{x}_*), \tag{6}$$

and

$$K_*^\ell = K_\ell^c \otimes K_*^x, \tag{7}$$

where K_ℓ^c is the ℓth column of K^c, and K_*^x is the vector of covariances between x_* and the input $x_1, x_2, \ldots, x_N$,

$$K_*^x = [k^x(x_*, x_1), k^x(x_*, x_2), \ldots, k^x(x_*, x_N)]^T. \tag{8}$$

The probability distribution of y_*^ℓ given the observations y is a Gaussian [9,15]:

$$y_*^\ell | y \sim \mathcal{N}(K_*^\ell K^{-1} y, K_{**}^\ell - K_*^\ell K^{-1}(K_*^\ell)^T). \tag{9}$$

We use the mean value

$$\bar{y}_*^\ell = K_*^\ell K^{-1} y \tag{10}$$

as the estimation of y_*^ℓ, and the variance

$$\text{var}(y_*^\ell) = K_{**}^\ell - K_*^\ell K^{-1}(K_*^\ell)^T \tag{11}$$

as the uncertainty of the estimation.

As shown in Eq. (3), the kernel function can be expressed as the product of two parts: $K_{\ell\ell'}^c$ and $k^x(x_i, x_{i'})$ We study their expressions one by one.

The matrix K^c is required to be positive semi-definite [1]. A common parametrization to guarantee positive-semidefiniteness of K^c is to use the Cholesky decomposition $K^c = LL^T$, where L is a lower triangular.

$$L = \begin{bmatrix} \theta_{11}^c & 0 & \cdots & 0 \\ \theta_{21}^c & \theta_{22}^c & \cdots & 0 \\ \vdots & \vdots & \ddots & \vdots \\ \theta_{M1}^c & \theta_{M2}^c & \cdots & \theta_{MM}^c \end{bmatrix}. \tag{12}$$

The spatial-temporal kernel function $k^x(x_i, x_{i'})$ can be written as the product as a spatial kernel and a temporal kernel:

$$k^x(x_i, x_{i'}) = k^s(p_i, q_i, p_{i'}, q_{i'}) k^t(t_i, t_{i'}), \tag{13}$$

where the spatial kernel $k^s(p_i, p_{i'}, q_i.q_{i'})$ indicates the spatial correlation, and the temporal kernel $k^t(t_i, t_{i'})$ describes the temporal correlation. Considering that the signal strengths may change differently at different directions, we utilize the commonly used anisotropic Gaussian kernel to describe the spatial correlation:

$$k^s(p_i, p_{i'}, q_i.q_{i'}) = \sigma_s^2 \exp\left(-\frac{(p_i - p_{i'})^2}{\theta_p}\right) \exp\left(-\frac{(q_i - q_{i'})^2}{\theta_q}\right),$$

where σ_s^2 is the maximum allowable spatial covariance.

For the temporal kernel, we present a periodical kernel to describe the temporal correlation:

$$k^t(t_i, t_{i'}) = \sigma_t^2 \exp\left(-\frac{\sin^2(\nu\pi(t_i - t_{i'}))}{\theta_t}\right), \tag{14}$$

where σ_t^2 is the maximum allowable temporal covariance, ν is the periodical frequency.

The noise of TV spectra is also an important part of the real-world measurement. Here, we consider a general Gaussian noise, where different channels have different noise variance. For example, the noise of channel ℓ is $n_\ell \sim \mathcal{N}(0, \sigma_\ell^2)$ with σ_ℓ^2 referring to the noise variance. Thus, The kernel function (3) becomes

$$k(\boldsymbol{x}_{ij}, \boldsymbol{x}_{i'j'}, \ell, \ell') = K_{\ell\ell'}^c k^s(p_i, p_{i'}, q_i.q_{i'}) k^t(t_j, t_{j'}) \atop +\sigma_\ell^2 \delta(\ell, \ell') \delta(\boldsymbol{x}_i, \boldsymbol{x}_{i'}), \tag{15}$$

where $\delta(\ell, \ell')$ and $\delta(\boldsymbol{x}_i, \boldsymbol{x}_{i'})$ refer to the Kronecker delta function.

In order to avoid the redundancy in the parameters of kernels K^c, k^s, and k^t, we further let $\sigma_s^2 = \sigma_t^2 = 1$, which means the spatial kernel and temporal kernel have unit variances. In this way, the parameters of $k(\boldsymbol{x}_{ij}, \boldsymbol{x}_{i'j'}, \ell, \ell')$ could be denoted as

$$\boldsymbol{\theta} = \{\theta_p, \theta_q, \theta_t, \nu, \theta_{11}^c, \theta_{21}^c, \theta_{22}^c, \ldots, \theta_{MM}^c, \sigma_1^2, \sigma_2^2, \ldots, \sigma_M^2\}.$$

Given a set of training data with observations $\boldsymbol{y}_o \in \mathbb{R}^d$ and the corresponding inputs X_o, the value of $\boldsymbol{\theta}$ can be determined by maximizing the marginal likelihood $p(\boldsymbol{y}_o|X_o, \boldsymbol{\theta})$. Considering the fact that $\boldsymbol{y}_o|X_o \sim \mathcal{N}(\boldsymbol{0}, K_o)$ with K_o referring to the corresponding covariance matrix, the logarithm marginal likelihood is

$$\log p(\boldsymbol{y}_o|X_o, \boldsymbol{\theta}) = -\frac{1}{2} \log|K_o| - \frac{1}{2} \boldsymbol{y}_o^T K_o^{-1} \boldsymbol{y}_o - \frac{d}{2} \log 2\pi.$$

The logarithm marginal likelihood can be maximized by running the multivariate optimization algorithm (e.g.., conjugate gradients, Nelder-Mead simplex, etc.). After the optimization, we can get the proper value of $\boldsymbol{\theta}$. Then, we can estimate the signal strengths of TV channels at different indoor locations.

3.3 Determining the Positions of Candidate Locations

We have shown that different positions of candidate locations would lead to different accuracies in estimation at arbitrary locations. In this part, we propose the algorithm to determine the proper positions of candidate locations, which has never been studied before. We first assume the number of candidate locations n is given, and then study how to determine a proper n.

We consider our space as a discrete set of locations $\mathcal{V}$. The possible candidate locations set $\mathcal{S}$ is thus a subset of $\mathcal{V}$: $\mathcal{S} \subset \mathcal{V}$. Now the problem becomes: find a subset $\mathcal{A}^* \subset \mathcal{S}$ with $|\mathcal{A}^*| = n$ that maximize the estimation accuracy. It is difficult to directly maximize the estimation accuracy, because we cannot give a certain mapping from the candidate locations to the estimation accuracy. Instead, we utilize the optimization criterion, proposed by Caselton and Zidek in 1984 [2], that search for $\mathcal{A}^*$ that most significantly reduce the estimation uncertainty in the rest of the space $\mathcal{V} \setminus \mathcal{A}^*$, which is equal to

$$\mathcal{A}^* = \operatorname{argmax}_{\mathcal{A} \subset \mathcal{S}, |\mathcal{A}|=n} H(\mathcal{Y}_{\mathcal{V} \setminus \mathcal{A}}) - H(\mathcal{Y}_{\mathcal{V} \setminus \mathcal{A}}|\mathcal{Y}_{\mathcal{A}}), \tag{16}$$

where $\mathcal{A}$ is the positions of candidate locations, $\mathcal{Y}_\mathcal{A}$ is the set of random variables of signal strengths of all channels over the training time period at the candidate locations $\mathcal{A}$. $H(\mathcal{Y}_{\mathcal{V}\backslash\mathcal{A}})$ refers to the entropy of $\mathcal{Y}_{\mathcal{V}\backslash\mathcal{A}}$. If $\boldsymbol{y}_{\mathcal{V}\backslash\mathcal{A}} \in \mathbb{R}^r$ obey Gaussian distribution, then

$$H(\mathcal{Y}_{\mathcal{V}\backslash\mathcal{A}}) = \frac{1}{2}\log((2\pi e)^r \mathrm{Cov}(\boldsymbol{y}_{\mathcal{V}\backslash\mathcal{A}})), \tag{17}$$

where $\mathrm{Cov}(\boldsymbol{y}_{\mathcal{V}\backslash\mathcal{A}})$ refers to the covariance of $\boldsymbol{y}_{\mathcal{V}\backslash\mathcal{A}}$.

Actually, the criterion $H(\mathcal{Y}_{\mathcal{V}\backslash\mathcal{A}}) - H(\mathcal{Y}_{\mathcal{V}\backslash\mathcal{A}}|\mathcal{Y}_\mathcal{A})$ is equivalent to the *mutual information* $I(\mathcal{Y}_\mathcal{A}; \mathcal{Y}_{\mathcal{V}\backslash\mathcal{A}})$ between the position set $\mathcal{A}$ and the rest of space $\mathcal{V}\backslash\mathcal{A}$. Thus, Eq. (16) is equal to finding a set $\mathcal{A}^*$ which maximize the mutual information:

$$\mathcal{A}^* = \mathrm{argmax}_{\mathcal{A}\subset\mathcal{S},|\mathcal{A}|=n}I(\mathcal{Y}_\mathcal{A}; \mathcal{Y}_{\mathcal{V}\backslash\mathcal{A}}). \tag{18}$$

The problem of mutual information maximization has been proven to be an NP-complete problem [9]. We apply a greedy approach that determines the positions of candidate locations in sequence, choosing the position for next candidate location which provides the maximum increase in mutual information. The performance analysis of the greedy approach can be found in [9]. For the ease of presentation, we let $H(\mathcal{A}) = H(\mathcal{Y}_\mathcal{A})$, $\mathrm{MI}(\mathcal{A}) = I(\mathcal{Y}_\mathcal{A}; \mathcal{Y}_{\mathcal{V}\backslash\mathcal{A}})$, and use $\mathcal{A} \cup \alpha$ to denote $\mathcal{A} \cup \{\alpha\}$. In this way, we determine the position of next candidate location by choosing a position α that maximizes:

$$\begin{aligned}
&\mathrm{MI}(\mathcal{A} \cup \alpha) - \mathrm{MI}(\mathcal{A}) \\
&= H(\mathcal{A} \cup \alpha) - H(\mathcal{A} \cup \alpha|\bar{\mathcal{A}}) - [H(\mathcal{A}) - H(\mathcal{A}|\bar{\mathcal{A}} \cup \alpha)] \\
&= H(\alpha|\mathcal{A}) - H(\alpha|\bar{\mathcal{A}}),
\end{aligned} \tag{19}$$

where $\bar{\mathcal{A}} = \mathcal{V}\backslash(\mathcal{A} \cup \alpha)$.

Since $\boldsymbol{y}_\alpha|\boldsymbol{y}_\mathcal{A}$ and $\boldsymbol{y}_\alpha|\boldsymbol{y}_{\bar{\mathcal{A}}}$ obey Gaussian distributions whose means and covariances can be calculated based on Eq. (10) and Eq. (11), we can easily get that

$$\begin{aligned}
H(\alpha|\mathcal{A}) - H(\alpha|\bar{\mathcal{A}}) &= \frac{1}{2}\log\frac{|\mathrm{Cov}(\boldsymbol{y}_\alpha|\boldsymbol{y}_\mathcal{A})|}{|\mathrm{Cov}(\boldsymbol{y}_\alpha|\boldsymbol{y}_{\bar{\mathcal{A}}})|} \\
&= \frac{1}{2}\log\frac{|K_{\alpha\alpha} - K_{\alpha\mathcal{A}}K_{\mathcal{A}\mathcal{A}}^{-1}K_{\mathcal{A}\alpha}|}{|K_{\alpha\alpha} - K_{\alpha\bar{\mathcal{A}}}K_{\bar{\mathcal{A}}\bar{\mathcal{A}}}^{-1}K_{\bar{\mathcal{A}}\alpha}|},
\end{aligned}$$

where $K_{\alpha\alpha}$ is the covariance matrix of different channels and times at position α, $K_{\alpha\mathcal{A}}$ is the covariance matrix of different channels and times between position α and positions set $\mathcal{A}$, $K_{\mathcal{A}\mathcal{A}}$ is the covariance matrix of positions set $\mathcal{A}$. $K_{\mathcal{A}\alpha}$, $K_{\alpha\bar{\mathcal{A}}}$, $K_{\bar{\mathcal{A}}\bar{\mathcal{A}}}$, and $K_{\bar{\mathcal{A}}\alpha}$ are defined in a similar way. The values of these matrices can be obtained using the kernel function k in Eq. (15).

The detailed algorithm is shown in Algorithm 1. We apply a strategy that sets the number of candidate locations as small as possible while the performance of Step II is guaranteed. In this way, the performance of Step I can be satisfactory as well.

Algorithm 1: Candidate locations determination

Input : $\mathcal{V}$: discrete set of all locations,
$\mathcal{S}$: possible positions for candidate locations,
$K_{\mathcal{V}\mathcal{V}}$: covariance matrix of $\mathcal{V}$,
T_{err} error threshold.
Output: n: number of candidate locations,
$\mathcal{A}^*$: positions of candidate locations.

1 $n \leftarrow 0; \mathcal{A} \leftarrow \emptyset$;
2 **repeat**
3   **for** $\alpha \in \mathcal{S} \backslash \mathcal{A}$ **do**
4        $\eta_\alpha \leftarrow \frac{|K_{\alpha\alpha} - K_{\alpha\mathcal{A}}K_{\mathcal{A}\mathcal{A}}^{-1}K_{\mathcal{A}\alpha}|}{|K_{\alpha\alpha} - K_{\alpha\bar{\mathcal{A}}}K_{\bar{\mathcal{A}}\bar{\mathcal{A}}}^{-1}K_{\bar{\mathcal{A}}\alpha}|}$;
5     $\alpha^* \leftarrow \arg\max_{\alpha \in \mathcal{S}\backslash\mathcal{A}} \eta_\alpha$;
6     $n \leftarrow n+1; \mathcal{A} \leftarrow \mathcal{A} \cup \alpha^*; \mathcal{C} \leftarrow \mathcal{V}/\mathcal{A}$;
7     $\mathrm{Cov}(\boldsymbol{y}_\mathcal{C}|\boldsymbol{y}_\mathcal{A}) \leftarrow K_{\mathcal{C}\mathcal{C}} - K_{\mathcal{C}\mathcal{A}}K_{\mathcal{A}\mathcal{A}}^{-1}K_{\mathcal{A}\mathcal{C}}$;
8     $\mathrm{Var}(\boldsymbol{y}_\mathcal{C}|\boldsymbol{y}_\mathcal{A}) \leftarrow diag(\mathrm{Cov}(\boldsymbol{y}_\mathcal{C}|\boldsymbol{y}_\mathcal{A}))$
9 **until** $\max \mathrm{Var}(\boldsymbol{y}_\mathcal{C}|\boldsymbol{y}_\mathcal{A}) \leq T_{err}$;
10 $\mathcal{A}^* \leftarrow \mathcal{A}$;
11 **return** $n, \mathcal{A}^*$;

---

4 Performance Evaluation

In this section, we extensively evaluate the performance of FRISE based real-world measurement data. We first give the setup of the evaluation and then present the evaluation results.

4.1 Evaluation Setup

The evaluation is based on the results of asynchronous TV spectra measurement in Sect. 2. For the asynchronous measurement, we measure the TV channels in a lab room and a long corridor, respectively, and get 14 measurement datasets, which contain the signal strengths of 56 TV channels at different locations, in a two weeks period. We use the data of the first week to train FRISE, and use the other week's data to evaluate its performance. We choose *Estimation Error* and *White Space Error* as the evaluation criteria. Their definitions are shown as follows:

- *Estimation Error (EE)*: is the relative error between the estimation and the real value.

$$\|\hat{\boldsymbol{y}} - \boldsymbol{y}\|_2 / \|\boldsymbol{y}\|_2,$$

where $\boldsymbol{y}$ is the vector containing real signal strengths of TV channels and $\hat{\boldsymbol{y}}$ is the corresponding estimated values.
- *White Space Error (WSE)*: is defined as the ratio between the number of channels whose status are mis-identified and the total number of channels.

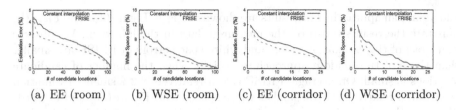

(a) EE (room)   (b) WSE (room)   (c) EE (corridor)   (d) WSE (corridor)

Fig. 5. Multitask Gaussian process interpolation vs constant interpolation.

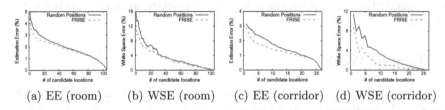

(a) EE (room)   (b) WSE (room)   (c) EE (corridor)   (d) WSE (corridor)

Fig. 6. Comparison of different approaches determining the positions of candidate locations.

4.2   Performance of Gaussian Process Based Interpolation

In Fig. 5, we compare the estimation error and white space error between multitask Gaussian process interpolation of FRISE and constant interpolation. We vary the number of the selected candidate locations from 1 to 105, and run the two interpolation algorithms based on the room data sets. The results are shown in Fig. 5(a) and Fig. 5(b). In Fig. 5(a), we observe that the estimation errors decrease as the increment of the number of candidate locations. Besides, the estimation errors of FRISE are smaller than the constant interpolation. Actually, the average estimation error is 1.90% for FRISE and 2.42% for the constant interpolation. This means that FRISE leads to an estimation error which is relatively 21.6% smaller than the constant interpolation. Figure 5(b) demonstrates the white space errors. We observe similar results to the estimation error. The average white space error is 3.26% for FRISE, which is relatively 28.3% smaller than constant interpolation, the average white space error of which is 4.55%. Figure 5(c) and Fig. 5(d) are the comparison results based on the data measured in the corridor. The results are similar to Fig. 5(a) and Fig. 5(b). On average, FRISE gets a relatively 15.6% smaller estimation error and a relatively 38.5% smaller white space error, compared to the constant interpolation.

4.3   Different Positions of Candidate Locations

We then study the performance of the mutual information based algorithm to determine the positions of the candidate locations. For the convenience of comparison, we choose the positions of the candidates among the measured indoor locations (105 in the lab room, 27 in the corridor). We compare the estimation error and the white space error between the mutual information based method and a random approach. The results are shown in Fig. 6. Figure 6(a) and Fig. 6(b) illustrate the results based on the measured data in the lab room. We observe that both of the estimation errors and white space errors of FRISE are smaller than those of the random approach, especially when the number of candidate locations is small. On average, FRISE gets a relatively 8.2% smaller estimation error and a relatively 17.0% smaller white space error. Figure 6(c) and Fig. 6(d) illustrate the estimation errors and the white space errors based on the data measured in the corridor. The average estimation error for FRISE is relatively 16.2% smaller than the random approach. For the white space error, this number is 47.0%.

5   Related Work

As a new kind of dynamic spectrum access approach, utilizing indoor white spaces to do communications gains increasing attentions. At first, researchers mainly focused on exploring and utilizing white spaces in the outdoor scenario [4,6,14,16]. Then, in 2013, Ying et al. [19] discovered the problem of indoor white space exploration and proposed the first indoor white space exploration system, WISER. Then in 2015, Liu et al. [10] presented a cost efficient indoor white space exploration mechanism, called FIWEX. In addition, there are some other works focused on indoor white space exploration recently [18,21].

Gaussian process is a Bayesian modeling technique which has been widely used in machine learning [15], deep learning [12], queuing analysis [5], sensor networks [9]. Multitask Gaussian process [20] is used to predict multiple correlated outputs, and has been applied for robot inverse dynamics [3] and time series analysis [11]. However, considering the unique characteristics of indoor white spaces, the existing works of multitask Gaussian process cannot be directly applied to the indoor white space estimation. We learn a proper kernel for indoor white spaces and then propose an accurate white space estimation mechanism.

6   Conclusion

In this paper, we have performed an indoor TV spectra measurement in a lab room and a corridor for a period of 2 weeks. The measurement results demonstrate that the constant interpolation leads to high estimation error rates and different positions of candidate locations lead to different estimation accuracies. Based on the measurement observations, we propose FRISE, which is a Fine-gRained Indoor white Space Estimation mechanism. FRISE mainly consists of a mutual information based method to determine the positions of candidate locations and a multitask Gaussian process based spatial interpolation algorithm. We evaluate the performance of FRISE based on the measurement data. The evaluation results demonstrate that FRISE leads to a maximum 38.5% less white space error compared to the constant interpolation and a maximum 47.0% less white space error compared to the estimation based on random positions of candidate locations.

Acknowledgement. This work was supported in part by National Key R&D Program of China No. 2019YFB2102200, in part by China NSF grant No. 62025204, 61972252, 61972254, 61672348, and 61672353, in part by Joint Scientific Research Foundation of the State Education Ministry No. 6141A02033702, in part by Alibaba Group through Alibaba Innovation Research Program, and in part by Tencent Rhino Bird Key Research Project. The opinions, findings, conclusions, and recommendations expressed in this paper are those of the authors and do not necessarily reflect the views of the funding agencies or the government.

References

1. Bonilla, E.V., Chai, K.M., Williams, C.: Multi-task gaussian process prediction. In: Proceedings of NIPS, pp. 153–160 (2007)
2. Caselton, W.F., Zidek, J.V.: Optimal monitoring network designs. Stat. Prob. Lett. **2**(4), 223–227 (1984)
3. Chai, K.M., Williams, C., Klanke, S., Vijayakumar, S.: Multi-task Gaussian process learning of robot inverse dynamics. In: Proceedings of NIPS, pp. 265–272 (2009)
4. Chen, Z., Zhang, Y.: Providing spectrum information service using TV white space via distributed detection system. IEEE Trans. Veh. Technol. **68**(8), 7655–7667 (2019)
5. Choe, J., Shroff, N.B.: Use of the supremum distribution of Gaussian processes in Queueing analysis with long-range dependence and self-similarity. Stochast. Models **16**(2), 209–231 (2000)
6. Deb, S., Srinivasan, V., Maheshwari, R.: Dynamic spectrum access in DTV whitespaces: design rules, architecture and algorithms. In: Proceedings of MobiCom, pp. 1–12. ACM (2009)
7. FCC: FCC adopts rules for unlicensed use of TV white spaces (2008). https://apps.fcc.gov/edocs_public/attachmatch/DOC-286566A1.pdf
8. Graham, A.: Kronecker Products and Matrix Calculus: With Applications. Wiley, New York (1982)
9. Krause, A., Singh, A., Guestrin, C.: Near-optimal sensor placements in Gaussian processes: theory, efficient algorithms and empirical studies. J. Mach. Learn. Res. **9**, 235–284 (2008)
10. Liu, D., Wu, Z., Wu, F., Zhang, Y., Chen, G.: FIWEX: compressive sensing based cost-efficient indoor white space exploration. In: Proceedings of MobiHoc, pp. 17–26. ACM (2015)
11. Nickerson, P., Baharloo, R., Davoudi, A., Bihorac, A., Rashidi, P.: Comparison of Gaussian processes methods to linear methods for imputation of sparse physiological time series. In: 2018 40th Annual International Conference of the IEEE Engineering in Medicine and Biology Society (EMBC), pp. 4106–4109. IEEE (2018)
12. Novak, R., et al.: Bayesian deep convolutional networks with many channels are Gaussian processes. In: ICLR (2019)
13. Onwuegbuzie, A.J., Daniel, L., Leech, N.L.: Pearson product-moment correlation coefficient. In: Encyclopedia of Measurement and Statistics, pp. 751–756 (2007)
14. Rahman, M.A., Asyhari, A.T., Azad, S., Hasan, M.M., Munaiseche, C.P., Krisnanda, M.: A cyber-enabled mission-critical system for post-flood response: Exploiting TV white space as network backhaul links. IEEE Access **7**, 100318–100331 (2019)
15. Rasmussen, C.E., Williams, C.K.I.: Gaussian processes for machine learning (2006). http://www.gaussianprocess.org/gpml/chapters/RW.pdf

16. Saeed, A., Harras, K.A., Zegura, E., Ammar, M.: Local and low-cost white space detection. In: Proceedings of ICDCS, pp. 503–516. IEEE (2017)
17. Taher, T.M., Bacchus, R.B., Zdunek, K.J., Roberson, D.: Long-term spectral occupancy findings in Chicago. In: Proceedings of DySPAN, pp. 100–107. IEEE (2011)
18. Xiao, H., Liu, D., Wu, F., Kong, L., Chen, G.: CORTEN: a real-time accurate indoor white space prediction mechanism. In: Proceedings of MASS, pp. 415–423. IEEE (2018)
19. Ying, X., Zhang, J., Yan, L., Zhang, G., Chen, M., Chandra, R.: Exploring indoor white spaces in metropolises. In: Proceedings of MobiCom, pp. 255–266. ACM (2013)
20. Yu, K., Tresp, V., Schwaighofer, A.: Learning Gaussian processes from multiple tasks. In: Proceedings of ICML, pp. 1012–1019. ACM (2005)
21. Zheng, X., Yi, F., Liu, D., Wu, F., Chen, G.: MISEN: a mobile indoor white space exploration method. In: Proceedings of ICC, pp. 1–6. IEEE (2019)

Evaluating mmWave Sensing Ability of Recognizing Multi-people Under Practical Scenarios

Lipeng Feng[ID], Shibo Du[ID], Zhen Meng[ID], Anfu Zhou[✉][ID],
and Huadong Ma[ID]

Beijing University of Posts and Telecommunications, Beijing, China
zhouanfu@bupt.edu.cn

Abstract. Visual tracking is a scheme to locate people's position in space. However, there are privacy concerns that raw video may cause leakage of personal information. Many people do not accept cameras deployed in their homes or workspaces.Recently, millimeter-wave (mmWave) gait recognition has been recognized as an alternative solution, which has the advantages of low power consumption and user privacy protection.However, performance analysis particularly under multi-person application scenarios in different environments remains to be explored.In this work, we collect and evaluate over the mmWave sensing point cloud dataset from mmWave FMCW radars. Our study reveals the change of point cloud as people population and their distance varies.

Keywords: Millimeter-wave perception · Co-existing multi-people recognition

1 Introduction

As the next generation of wireless communication technology, millimeter wave can greatly improve the wireless network rate to multi-Gbps. In the foreseeable future, mmWave modules will be widely installed in mobile phones, wearable, smart hardware, or more widely Internet of things devices, becoming a mainstream communication technology.

We found that in addition to ultra-high-speed wireless transmission, the characteristics of mmWave such as short wavelength, large bandwidth, and directed beam also make it possible to perceive human gait with high resolution and robustness. Moreover, compared with other methods, mmWave sensing has its unique advantages. For example, the accuracy of the acoustic gait recognition method will be greatly reduced when it is faced with interference during the surrounding noises [20]. The accuracy of gait recognition based on visible image analysis is also relatively low in the environment with low or no light. At the same time, the design of the gait recognition equipment for image identification has serious privacy leakage problem, which is not convenient for its universal

© Springer Nature Switzerland AG 2020
Z. Yu et al. (Eds.): GPC 2020, LNCS 12398, pp. 61–74, 2020.
https://doi.org/10.1007/978-3-030-64243-3_5

deployment and use [1]. More importantly, mmWave can penetrate nonmetallic materials such as plastics, so mmWave modules can be hidden inside nonmetallic devices [10].

mmWave technology can provide more intelligent and effective biometrics. For example, this report focuses on gait recognition. mmWave equipment can identify human identity information based on human gait. Similarly, mmWave gait recognition can be used for Intelligent security identification in homes and businesses. It could also be used in areas such as health testing, robotics, and new retail. mmWave gait recognition waking up does not need users to do any action, mmWave device will take the initiative to detect the user's gait and identify the user. mmWave gait recognition can be applied to property security to prevent private valuables from being stolen. Users can install mmWave devices in laptops, mobile phones, and other items, and let your devices know you through gait recognition technology. When someone steals your devices but cannot imitate your gait, the system will alarm. mmWave gait recognition can also be applied to smart homes to ensure safety for the elder. In the family, if the elder suddenly falls down or other emergencies happened, mmWave gait recognition devices can immediately identify and immediately notify the family.

At present, the mmWave gait recognition theory has been widely recognized, it has the advantages of low power consumption, environmental protection, and user privacy protection [2]. This system collects real-time gait point cloud data through mmWave equipment. After analyzing the point cloud data in the background, it introduces the neural network algorithm for training. When the model training is completed, real-time gait recognition can be carried out. However, in neural network learning of the gait point cloud data set of the identified object, the system often encounters a variety of problems, resulting in inaccurate training results. Among these problems, a large part of them is caused by the complexity of the working environment and the occlusion between the tested objects when the mmWave device collects the gait point cloud data. In order to further improve the accuracy of mmWave gait recognition, we will conduct a series of experimental analyses from the data acquisition end. The specific analysis of the experimental environment involves many factors. In order to accurately analyze the influence of each variable on the clustering effect of the point cloud, we will use the control variable method to explore the phenomena such as the minimum recognition distance of mmWave equipment and the occlusion problem.

This paper discusses the mmWave FMCW radar's high tracking accuracy human tracking recognition system performance research experiment. With the help of mmWave sensors, we can get sparse clouds and form time-dependent tracks. In the different experimental background, we test and evaluate the mmWave FMCW radar data acquisition and DB-scan clustering algorithm, and prove that our system can still maintain high recognition accuracy when there are static or dynamic occlusion and low error in short distance recognition in the two-person scene. In order to further clarify the minimum recognition distance of mmWave FMCW radar for multiple objects under test, we also designed a series of experiments to analyze the mmWave FMCW radar sensing ability based on the feedback point cloud data. In the above experiments, we verified the basic performance of mmWave FMCW radar. Combining with the clustering algorithm, we measured the ideal effective multi-person recognition distance is about 45 cm based on mmWave FMCW radar. In this paper, our innovation lies in combining the basic recognition performance of mmWave FMCW radar and the clustering algorithm to analyze the occlusion problem and the problem of too close distance in the case of multi-person recognition.

2 Related Works

2.1 Application Prospect of MmWave

In recent years, some experiments and researches have realized the tracking or recognition of human behavior characteristics through Wi-Fi signals [16–19] or video monitoring [14,15]. Compared with video monitoring, mmWave FMCW radar has many advantages, such as better anti-interference, lower energy consumption, and higher accuracy [11]. Therefore, mmWave FMCW radar has a wide application prospect in various fields [12]. With the development of mmWave technology, mmWave recognition has been applied in speed measurement, distance measurement, gesture recognition [3,4], single-person tracking identification [5], multi-person recognition and other fields [13]. In order to realize the large-scale deployment of mmWave recognition equipment, designers must rely on the theoretical basis of wireless sensor networks to solve the problem of network topology and network minimum exposure [13].

2.2 Recognition Using mmWave Signals

Previous studies used mmWave signals of different frequencies for vital signs detection [6–8]. [9] Experiments verified the feasibility of mmWave in monitoring vital signs. There's still a lot of work to be done, using mmWave to identify people's movements or study health status through the gait [1].

3 System Design and Experimental Process

3.1 Overview of Main Experiment

We deployed a mmWave FMCW radar in a closed laboratory in accordance with the basic working requirements of the mmWave equipment. After the determination of various parameters in the experimental environment, we launch the mmWave equipment and began to collect experimental data. We invited volunteers to participate in the gait point cloud data collection experiment as subjects to complete a series of movements according to the specified requirements. The mmWave device sends the antenna to transmit the wireless signal, which is modulated by the user's gait and reflected, and the reflected signal is captured by

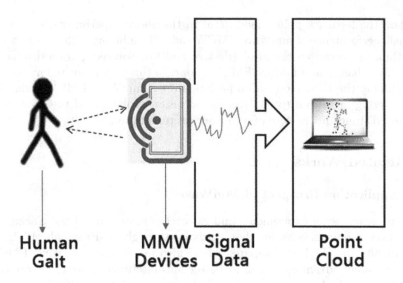

Human   **MMW** **Signal**   **Point**
Gait   **Devices** **Data**   **Cloud**

Fig. 1. Flow chart of the main experiment.

the mmWave receiving antenna. Then, the mmWave device will capture the signal for processing, and obtain the distance, angle, Doppler frequency shift, and other information (Fig. 1).

The mmWave FMCW radar can pre-process the original FMCW signal to obtain a three-dimensional point cloud. These point cloud data are preprocessed and point cloud sequences are generated. We mainly collect the spatial coordinates, velocity, and SNR of each point in the 3D point cloud. A series of clustering algorithms are used to analyze the above data and eliminate noise points. In short, this process is to clean the collected data and improve data quality (Fig. 2).

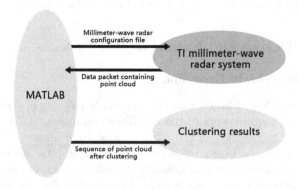

Fig. 2. Software configuration.

3.2 Hardware Configuration and Data Acquisition

The mmWave FMCW radar is set to transmit 16 chirps per frame. The start frequency of the chirp is set to 77 GHz. The bandwidth B is 4 GHz. The Chirp Cycle Time Tc is set to 131.14 µs. The Idle Time is set to 81 s. The ADC Valid Start Time is set to 7 s. The Ramp End Time is set to 57.14 s. The Frequency Slope is set to be 70 GHz/ms. With such a configuration, the mmWave FMCW radar has a range resolution of 4.4 cm and a maximum unambiguous range of 8m. In terms of velocity, it can measure a maximum radial velocity of 2.35 m/s, with a resolution of 0.3 m/s. The mmWave FMCW radar EVM has three transmitting antennas and four receiving antennas. The device can emit and receives the FMCW mmWave signal, which outputs all the points detected in each frame in the form of a point cloud. With this data, the device can parse the three-dimensional position, speed, and peak value of each reflected point.

Human gait is the behavior characteristic of human walking. The reflection signals generated by the human body during dynamic changes are caused by the superposition of reflections from multiple surface energy points. So we call these points the Surface Energy Points of the Gait (SEPs). We break down the reflective surfaces of body parts into surface energy points. To obtain the characteristics of these surface energy points, we transformed the received signal into the representation of the eigenvalues related to Range Doppler and Angle according to the following principle module, including the distance, speed, and Angle of each SEP.

The point cloud data obtained by mmWave radar equipment is unstructured, and the point cloud is relatively sparse, so humans cannot intuitively understand these data. Therefore, a set of clustering algorithms is specially designed to analyze the features of point cloud data to classify and predict the point cloud data of human gait.

4 Experiment Evaluation and Analysis

4.1 Basic Working Performance of mmWave FMCW Radar

Max distance is calculated only at the zero degrees bore sight, performance decreases as target move to the side angles. Angular resolution is defined as how far apart two objects need to be (in angle) for them to be detected as different/separate objects. Angular accuracy is how accurately the angle of the object is detected. The FOV provided by the antenna spacing is a theoretical max FOV that can be achieved. The antenna gain would typically reduce as we move away from the center and hence the max range would reduce as you move at an angle. Based on the antenna pattern, you look at the gain provided by the antenna at the desired angle and based on the Radar Cross Section. You can use the sensing estimator tool to help you estimate what the kind of min antenna gain you would need for your use case and then estimate the angle at which that is achievable from the antenna pattern (Table 1).

Table 1. Performance parameters of the mmWave FMCW radar.

Azimuth FoV(deg)	Elevation FoV(deg)	Azimuth angular resolution	Elevation angular resolution	Max distance
±60	±15	15	60	47 m

4.2   Minimum Effective Clustering Distance Between Two Persons

Through the clustering algorithm to mark and process the point cloud, we observe that when the minimum effective clustering distance between two people to be tested is reached, about 25% to 30% of the frames recognize the point cloud of two or more people who are close to each other as a person's point cloud, and too few points in a person's point cloud will also lead to noise-related recognition errors. The above two problems there is a nonlinear positive proportion between the distance between the two people and the recognition effect of the clustering algorithm, and there may be significant differences between the left and right sides in a relatively small area (Figs. 3 and 4).

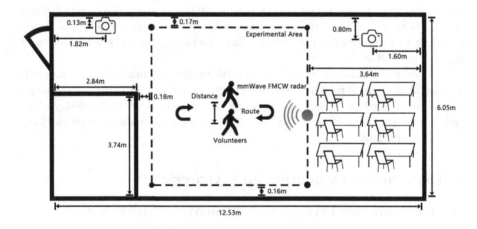

Fig. 3. Experimental environment.

We designed an experiment to explore the effect of clustering by adjusting the distance between two volunteers. A room with a length of 12.53 m and a width of 6.05 m is selected as the experimental environment. There is a rectangle about 6.00 m × 6.00 m rectangular activity area in the middle. We define this environment like an office or family place. We have installed mmWave FMCM radar, which is 1.00m away from the ground, at the middle point on the right side of the rectangular active area. Then we chose two volunteers who were close to each other. At the same time, we stipulated that the movement track of the two volunteers was fixed. They moved to the horizontal direction of mmWave FMCM radar at the same speed side by side. The longitudinal length of the motion track

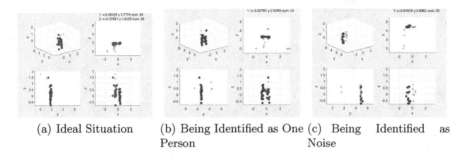

(a) Ideal Situation   (b) Being Identified as One Person   (c) Being Identified as Noise

Fig. 4. Clustering Point Cloud Imaging with Close Distance Between Two Persons. The blue or red dots in each picture are the feature points successfully identified by the clustering algorithm. The green star points are noise points determined by the clustering algorithm. We present the 3D graph, top view, side view, and front view of the point cloud after clustering in a certain frame under three conditions (Color figure online).

is fixed, that is, it is the same as the length of one side of the rectangle. We define different distance relationships and adjust the horizontal distance between two volunteers to analyze the overall impact of the distance between people on DB-scan clustering algorithm recognition and mmWave FMCM radar data collection. Among them, the distance between the two volunteers was 0 cm (hands holding hands), 15 cm, 30 cm, 45 cm, which respectively corresponded to the four types of common interpersonal relationship and distance relationship between walking, i.e. relatives or lovers, friends, colleagues or friends, strangers. Through mmWave FMCM radar data collection and DB-scan clustering algorithm operation, we get the clustering effect of distance relationship of four common interpersonal states as follows. At the same time, according to the video recorded by the installed synchronous camera device and the real-time point cloud image generated by MATLAB, it is compared.

To show the quality of point cloud more intuitively, we chose to draw a broken line statistical chart, using the distance between two volunteers from 0cm to 45 cm as the x-axis, calculating the number of point cloud per capita under each distance relationship as the y-axis, and drawing the broken line to reflect the trend of the number of point cloud per capita with the change of distance between the two people. By processing data and drawing images, we can find that when the distance between two people is 0 cm, the number of per capita point clouds is the largest at this time, and the feedback value in the current experimental operation is about 55, which means that it is difficult to distinguish the two people closer together after DB-scan clustering algorithm processing under the current distance relationship. With the increasing distance between the two people, the number of point clouds per capita shows a trend of rapid reduction and slow reduction until the distance between the two people reaches 45 cm. At this time, the number of point clouds per capita is about 27, nearly stable, which means that under the current distance relationship, the DB-scan clustering algorithm can distinguish the two adjacent people very well (Fig. 5).

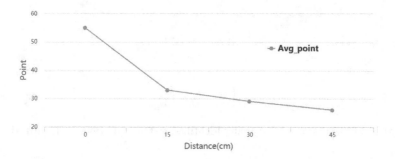

Fig. 5. The relationship between point cloud quality and two person distance.

The experimental results show that when two volunteers who are close to each other move parallel to the mmWave FMCM radar in the experimental environment near the office or home, the results of data collection and data processing show that there are three situations: successful clustering, clustering into one person, and clustering failure. When the distance between two people is 0 cm, it has the worst clustering success rate. Only 9% of the average probability successfully identifies different volunteers. Besides, 85% of the probability identifies the same person, and 6% of the probability is unrecognizable. When the distance between two people is gradually increasing, the probability of successful recognition is increasing, and there is a significant change when the distance is between 30 cm and 45 cm, reaching 70% of the better recognition probability. It can be seen that as the distance between people decreases, the quality of point cloud will become worse, and the recognition effect will become worse, so it is easy to identify two volunteers as the same person; as the distance between people increases, the quality of point cloud will improve, and the recognition effect will become better so that different people can be distinguished well. We conclude that in the appropriate experimental environment, the minimum distance between two people when they are moving is not less than 45cm when using the mmWave FMCM radar data collected by DB-scan clustering algorithm, to obtain better quality point cloud and achieve better recognition effect (Table 2).

Table 2. Clustering under four conditions.

Distance (cm)	Clustering falls into one categorie (percentage)	Point cloud is too sparse to cluster (percentage)	Successful clustering falls into two categories (percentage)
0	85%	6%	9%
15	75%	5%	20%
30	60%	6%	34%
45	16%	14%	70%

4.3   Occlusion Relationship Effect

During the experiment, we noticed that when undefined objects are occluding the objects to be tested, the clustering system may not be effective or it is difficult to effectively capture the objects to be tested. Therefore, we designed two groups of experiments to explore the influence of static occlusion and dynamic occlusion on the clustering recognition effect of the measured objects.

Static Occlusion Experiment. The static occlusion experiment is to study the influence of static occlusion on mmWave FMCM radar data collection and DBscan clustering algorithm. The experimental environment is defined as close to the office or home, and its core area is a 6.00 m × 6.00 m rectangular open environment, which we call the active area. We installed mmWave FMCM radar at a height of 0.80 m at the midpoint of one side of the active area. We choose a 1.70 m-tall, well-balanced volunteer to do a round-trip uniform movement along the horizontal direction of the activity area along the length of 2.40 m. The distance between the volunteer and mmWave FMCW radar is 3.00 m, which is in line with the good receiving distance of mmWave FMCW radar. We installed a smooth rectangular partition composed of multiple materials between volunteers and mmWave FMCM radar, which is 1.80 m away from mmWave FMCW radar. The height of the occluder was slightly lower than the experimenter's height (1.50 m), and the length of the occluder was close to the volunteer's trajectory length of 2.40 m. Then we began to experiment and collect data at the same time (Table 3, Fig. 6).

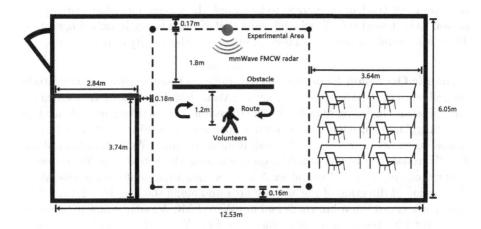

Fig. 6. Experimental environment.

Table 3. Static occlusion experiment clustering result.

Successful clustering falls into one categorie (percentage)	Point cloud is too sparse to cluster (percentage)	Clustering falls into two or more categories (percentage)
63%	5%	32%

The experimental results show that when a volunteer moves parallel to mmWave FMCM radar at a constant speed and has a static rectangular halo covering the volunteer's moving track, the results of data collection and data processing show that there are three main situations: successful clustering, clustering failure, and other phenomena. We have carried out several groups of the same experiment to take the average value and reduce the experimental error. The results show that the DB-scan algorithm can recognize the target object successfully when the processed data image shows the point cloud distribution which is close to the shape of human body, and the average probability is 63%; when the processed data image shows the discrete and sparse point cloud distribution, the DB-scan algorithm cannot recognize the target object successfully, that is, the average probability of recognition failure is 32% When the processed data image presents other abnormal point cloud distribution such as too free and too dense, we define this situation as other situations, with an average probability of 5%. Therefore, we can draw a conclusion that if mmWave FMCM radar is used to collecting data and DB-scan clustering algorithm is used to process data, when a symmetrical person moves at a constant speed in the experimental environment near the office or home, if there is a smooth and uniform static shelter covering the movement track of the person to be tested, the success rate of identifying the person to be tested is 63%, which means that if there is any in actual operation The static occlusion will have a certain impact on the quality of point cloud.

Dynamic Occlusion Experiment. Dynamic occlusion experiment is to study the influence of dynamic occlusion on mmWave FMCW radar data acquisition and DB-scan clustering algorithm. The experimental environment is defined as a rectangular open environment with a core area of $6.00\,\text{m} \times 6.00\,\text{m}$, which is similar to an office or a family. We call it an active area. We installed mmWave FMCW radar at a height of 0.80m on one side of the active area. We choose a 1.70-meter-tall, balanced volunteer A to do a round-trip uniform exercise along the horizontal direction of the activity area and along the length of 2.40 m. The distance between the volunteer A and mmWave FMCW radar is 3.00 m, which is consistent with the good receiving distance of mmWave FMCW radar. We chose a volunteer B whose figure was similar to that of volunteer A is between volunteer A and mmWave FMCW radar. The velocity and trajectory of volunteer B and volunteer A were the same, 1.80m away from mmWave FMCW radar. At the same time, volunteers A and B started to exercise at the same time. At the same time, we started to conduct experiments and data collection at the same time (Fig. 7 and Table 4).

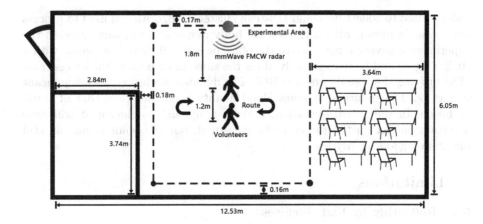

Fig. 7. Experimental environment.

Table 4. Static occlusion experiment clustering result.

Volunteers	Successful clustering falls into two categories (percentage)	Point cloud is too sparse to cluster (percentage)	Clustering falls into one categorie (percentage)
Volunteer A	70%	6%	24%
Volunteer B	75%	1%	24%

The experimental results of dynamic occlusion show that when two volunteers with similar height and body shape move uniformly in the vertical direction of launching mmWave FMCM radar in an experimental environment similar to the office, the results of data collection and data processing show that there are three situations: successful clustering, clustering into one person, and clustering failure. We have carried out several groups of the same experiment to take the average value and reduce the experimental error. We regard volunteer B as dynamic occlusion, so we mainly analyze the clustering results of volunteer A. The results show that when the processed data image shows the distribution of two groups of point clouds which are concentrated and close to the shape of human body, DB-scan algorithm successfully identifies and distinguishes the target object, and judges that the clustering is successful at this time, with an average probability of 70%; when the processed data image shows that a group of point clouds which are concentrated or close to two groups of point clouds is judged as the same group of point cloud distribution, DB-scan algorithm does not If it can identify and distinguish the target object successfully, it is judged that the clustering fails at this time, that is, the average probability of identifying a person is 24%; when the processed data image presents other abnormal point cloud distribution such as too free and too dense, we define this situation as other situations, the average probability is 6%. Therefore, we can conclude that if mmWave FMCM radar is used to collect data and DB-scan clustering algorithm is used to process data, when a person with asymmetrical body moves at a constant speed in the experimental environment close to the office or home, if there is a person with a similar figure and he moves evenly along the same motion path, the success rate of identifying the tested person is 70%. The dynamic occlusion has a significant impact on The influence of point cloud quality is smaller than that of static occlusion. In the actual operation, if there is dynamic occlusion, it will have a certain impact on the target to be measured, but the point cloud can still maintain a good quality level.

5   Limitations

5.1   Reflecting by Flat Surfaces

In the actual experiment, we find that the acquisition effect of mmWave is influenced by the reflection of some smooth planes (such as mirrors or windows) in the experimental environment. Therefore, when conducting the mmWave experiment, we should consider the interference of other smooth planes in the experimental environment to the experimental results. For example, sometimes there will be the mirror image of the target to be tested due to the reflection. This is It should not exist. In our experimental operation, there is inevitably a specular plane in the final selected experimental environment, so it is worth considering the impact of specular reflection on the quality of point cloud in the actual deployment.

5.2   Scope of Monitoring

In the actual experimental operation, due to a certain degree of site constraints, we set the maximum range of experimental environment length of each side to 8 m. In principle, the theoretical effective range of mmWave is as high as 47 m, but this ideal range is at the cost of reducing the spatial accuracy and the signal-to-noise ratio. At the same time, due to the limitation of the site and the final definition of the experimental environment as office or home, there is no test for the maximum range. At the same time, according to the hardware manual, if the object to be measured is too far away from the sensor, it is difficult to detect and distinguish from the background noise.

6   Conclusion

In this work, we collected multiple and single person data on volunteer spacing and occlusion relationships. These data are used to evaluate DB-scan clustering algorithm. Based on the original algorithm, we need to further define the distance relationship when multiple people are moving. At the same time, DB-scan clustering algorithm can achieve better recognition accuracy when reasonability occlusion. We plan to conduct in-depth research to improve the accuracy of multi-person recognition in small distance scenes.

Acknowledgements. The work is supported by National Key R&D Program of China (2019YFB2102202), NSFC (61772084, 61720106007, 61832010), the Funds for Creative Research Groups of China (61921003), the 111 Project (B18008), the Fundamental Research Funds for the Central Universities (2019XD-A13).

References

1. Beringer, R., Sixsmith, A., Campo, M., Brown, J., McCloskey, R.: The "Acceptance" of ambient assisted living: developing an alternate methodology to this limited research lens. In: Abdulrazak, B., Giroux, S., Bouchard, B., Pigot, H., Mokhtari, M. (eds.) ICOST 2011. LNCS, vol. 6719, pp. 161–167. Springer, Heidelberg (2011). https://doi.org/10.1007/978-3-642-21535-3_21

2. Chao, H., He, Y., Zhang, J., Feng, J.: Gaitset: regarding gait as a set for cross-view gait recognition. In: The Thirty-Third AAAI Conference on Artificial Intelligence, AAAI 2019, The Thirty-First Innovative Applications of Artificial Intelligence Conference, IAAI 2019, The Ninth AAAI Symposium on Educational Advances in Artificial Intelligence, EAAI 2019, Honolulu, Hawaii, USA, 27 January–1 February 2019, pp. 8126–8133 (2019)

3. Li, S., Liu, W., Ma, H.: Attentive spatial temporal summary networks for feature learning in irregular gait recognition. IEEE Trans. Multimed. **21**(9), 2361–2375 (2019)

4. Lien, J., et al.: Soli: ubiquitous gesture sensing with millimeter wave radar. ACM Trans. Graph. **35**(4), 142:1–142:19 (2016)

5. Zhao, P., et al.: mID: tracking and identifying people with millimeter wave radar. In 15th International Conference on Distributed Computing in Sensor Systems, DCOSS 2019, Santorini, Greece, 29–31 May 2019, pp. 33–40 (2019)

6. Yang, Z., Pathak, P.H., Zeng, Y., Liran, X., Mohapatra, P.: Monitoring vital signs using millimeter wave. In Proceedings of the 17th ACM International Symposium on Mobile Ad Hoc Networking and Computing, MobiHoc 2016, pp. 211–220. ACM, New York (2016)

7. Petkie, T, D., Benton, C., Bryan, E.: Millimeter-wave radar for vital signs sensing. In: Radar Sensor Technology XIII, vol. 7308, p. 73080A (2009)

8. Mikhelson, I., Lee, P.G., Bakhtiari, S., Elmer, T.W., Katsaggelos, A.K., Sahakian, A.V.: Noncontact millimeter-wave real-time detection and tracking of heart rate on an ambulatory subject. IEEE Trans. Inf. Technol. Biomed. **16**(5), 927–934 (2012)

9. Zou, H., Zhou, Y., Yang, J., Gu, W., Xie, L., Spanos, C.J.: WiFi-based human identification via convex tensor shapelet learning. In: Thirty-Second AAAI Conference on Artificial Intelligence (2018)

10. Ferris, D.D., Currie, N.C.: Microwave and millimeterwave systems for wall penetration. In: Targets and Backgrounds: Characterization and Representation IV, vol. 3375, pp. 269–280. International Society for Optics and Photonics (1998)

11. Zhou, A., Yang, S., Yang, Y., Fan, Y., Ma, H.: Autonomous environment mapping using commodity millimeter-wave network device. In: 2019 IEEE Conference on Computer Communications, INFOCOM 2019, Paris, France, 29 April-2 May 2019, pp. 1126–1134 (2019b)

12. Zhou, A., et al.: Robot navigation in radio beam space: leveraging robotic intelligence for seamless mmwave network coverage. In: Proceedings of the Twentieth ACM International Symposium on Mobile Ad Hoc Networking and Computing, Mobihoc 2019, Catania, Italy, 2–5 July 2019, pp. 161–170 (2019a)

13. Meng, Z., et al.: Gait recognition for co-existing multiple people using millimeter wave sensing. In 2020 Association for the Advancement of Artificial Intelligence Conference, New York, United States, 7–20 February 2020 (2020)
14. Liu, W., Zhang, C., Ma, H., Li, S.: Learning efficient spatial-temporal gait features with deep learning for human identification. Neuroinformatics **16**(3–4), 457–471 (2018). https://doi.org/10.1007/s12021-018-9362-4
15. Li, S., Liu, X., Liu, W., Ma, H., Zhang, H.: A discriminative null space based deep learning approach for person re-identification. CCIS **2016**, 480–484 (2016)
16. Qian, K., Wu, C., Zhou, Z., Zheng, Y., Yang, Z., Liu, Y.: Inferring motion direction using commodity Wi-Fi for interactive exergames. In: ACM CHI, Denver, USA, 6–11 May 2017 (2017)
17. Qian, K., Wu, C., Yang, Z., Liu, Y., Jamieson, K.: Widar: decimeter-level passive tracking via velocity monitoring with commodity Wi-Fi. In: ACM MobiHoc, Chennai, India, 10–14 July 2017 (2017)
18. Qian, K., Wu, C., Zhang, Y., Zhang, G., Yang, Z., Liu, Y.: Widar2.0: passive human tracking with a single Wi-Fi link. In: ACM MobiSys, Munich, Germany, 10–15 June 2018 (2018)
19. Xin, T., Guo, B., Wang, Z., Li, M., Yu, Z., Zhou, X.: FreeSense: indoor human identification with Wi-Fi signals. In: GLOBECOM 2016, pp. 1–7 (2016)
20. Xu, W., Yu, Z., Wang, Z., Guo, B., Han, Q.: AcousticID: gait-based Human Identification Using Acoustic Signal. IMWUT **3**(3), 115:1–115:25 (2019)

Machine Learning

GradSA: Gradient Sparsification and Accumulation for Communication-Efficient Distributed Deep Learning

Bo Liu[1], Wenbin Jiang[1(✉)], Shaofeng Zhao[2,3], Hai Jin[1], and Bingsheng He[4]

[1] National Engineering Research Center for Big Data Technology and System, Service Computing Technology and System Lab, Cluster and Grid Computing Lab, Huazhong University of Science and Technology, Wuhan, China
wenbinjiang@hust.edu.cn
[2] Wuhan National Laboratory for Optoelectronics, Key Laboratory of Information Storage System, Engineering Research Center of Data Storage Systems and Technology, Huazhong University of Science and Technology, Wuhan, China
[3] Library, Henan University of Economics and Law, Zhengzhou, China
[4] Department of Computer Science, School of Computing, National University of Singapore, Singapore, Singapore

Abstract. Large-scale distributed deep learning is of great importance in various applications. For distributed training, the inter-node gradient communication often becomes the performance bottleneck. Gradient sparsification has been proposed to reduce the communication overhead. However, the sparsification only arbitrarily selects a small fraction of gradients, while the efficiency of selection dimension has been overlooked. Furthermore, gradient staleness is inevitable after applying the sparsification which will ultimately lead to model divergence. In this paper, we propose a staleness-compensated sparse stochastic gradient descent algorithm, GradSA, to improve the training efficiency. Layer-level gradients are sparsified to reduce the communication overhead, which conform to the characteristics of the network structure, and historical accumulation of the approximated gradients is utilized to speed up convergence. We demonstrate the model convergence acceleration and the efficiency of our layer-level selection over existing state-of-the-art works, such as DGC, TernGrad, and 8-Bit quantization.

Keywords: Distributed deep learning · Bandwidth-constrained · Communication efficiency · Gradient sparsification

1 Introduction

Deep Learning (DL) has become one of the most promising techniques in the field of machine learning. Due to the explosive growth of data, large-scale distributed DL has attracted increasing attention in recent years. A common choice

© Springer Nature Switzerland AG 2020
Z. Yu et al. (Eds.): GPC 2020, LNCS 12398, pp. 77–91, 2020.
https://doi.org/10.1007/978-3-030-64243-3_6

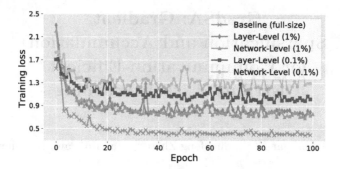

Fig. 1. Comparisons of layer-level and network-level threshold-based gradient sparsification. We record the training loss curves on ResNet-20 (Cifar-10 dataset, batchsize = 64) with different gradient sparsity rates, 1% and 0.1%.

in distributed DL, data-parallelism, has each node compute its local gradients and uniformly update model parameters by exchanging gradients with other nodes in such DL systems. However, the evolution of the interconnected network bandwidth is not as fast as computing hardware. For example, the latest NVIDIA V100 GPU features a 7TFlops peak performance and a 900 GB/s memory bandwidth with HBM2, while the fastest InfiniBand network only achieves a 200 GB/s interconnected bandwidth. Therefore, communication overhead is increasingly becoming the bottleneck on distributed GPU-based systems. When training *Deep Neural Network* (DNN) in the bandwidth-constrained environments [12] with large numbers of mobile devices or edge devices, reducing the requirement for communication bandwidth becomes much more urgent.

There have been two types of works attempting to improve communication efficiency by reducing the size of the gradients. (i) *Quantization*: these methods focus on quantizing gradients into fixed-point numbers such as a binary or ternary representation based on the law of gradient data distribution [2,13,14,19]. (ii) *Sparsification*: these methods impose sparsity onto gradients during communication, where only a small fraction of gradients is exchanged across nodes in each iteration [11,18]. However, the underlying ideas of these methods are all to reduce the scale of exchanged gradient data, which inescapably introduces extra losses, and impairs model accuracy. In general, there exists two key challenges, which are described as below.

Challenge 1: The existing literature on sparsification only concerns the whole DNN and selects sparse ones from the entire gradients, while the efficiency on selection dimension has been less investigated. Generally, gradient sparsification decreases the gradient updates into a small portion, and only uploads the "important" gradients by setting proper thresholds [11,18]. However, it is not easy to choose the optimal threshold, and comprehensively represent the distribution of gradients, which always changes across layers of the DNN architecture.

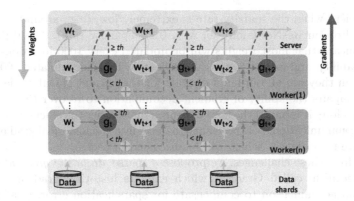

Fig. 2. Sparse training with historical gradient accumulation

To confirm this viewpoint, we take a set of experimental studies[1] and observe that: under the same low sparsity rate, choosing different sparse granularities lead to different training qualities for the same model. Two sparse granularities in Fig. 1 are respectively network-level and layer-level. Here we define the layer-level selection as deploying the same sparsity rate for each layer and selecting the same proportion of gradients from each layer. We also define the network-level selection as deploying a uniform sparsity rate, and selecting gradients from the whole population of this network. The results show that when the sparsity rate is set at 1%, the model performance of the two methods are close to each other, while the layer-level method with lower sparsity rate, 0.1%, obviously performs better than the network-level method. The accuracy degradation of network-level selection is noteworthy, and it is because that a uniform threshold solution for all layers in a DNN is not appropriate. Only selecting the maximum values in the network-level will neglect the lower-magnitude (but critically important) gradients from other layers. This improper selection will trigger a chain reaction and finally impair the training performance. Our motivation for layer-level sparsification emerges from here, which will be discussed in Sect. 4.

Challenge 2: To improve the model performance, historical gradient accumulation [13] has been adopted into the sparse distributed training. Taking the data-parallel training process with *Parameter Server* (PS) [10] communication pattern as an example (shown in Fig. 2), workers do not send all elements of the local gradient matrix to the server until the values of corresponding gradient elements reach the predefined threshold (denoted as "th" in Fig. 2), the remaining historical gradients will be accumulated to the fresh matrix of the next iteration.

To cope with the bandwidth-constrained networks, the gradient sparsity rate will be defined as low as possible by users, resulting the staleness of historical gradient accumulation. Therefore, the accumulated gradient sparsification is

---

[1] We use a famous DNN, ResNet, used in vision tasks. Except where otherwise indicated, all experiments are performed on distributed MXNet [3] with 4 workers.

still inefficient when the sparsity rate is extremely low, (e.g., around 1–5% test accuracy drop on ResNet-family [6] with 0.1% sparsity rate). The 0.1% sparsity rate means that most weights will be updated every 1000 iterations with a high probability, and unsent historical gradients will be accumulated 1000 times even though they are all outdated or stale for the current global model, which seriously impairs the ability of gradient accumulation to recover the stochastic error. Therefore, it is one of the key challenges that hinder the efficiency of sparse gradient communication. It is necessary to delve into the historical gradients and compensate for staleness, which will be discussed in Sect. 5.

To address these challenges, we propose a sparse *stochastic gradient descent* (SGD) algorithm called GradSA, which exploits historical gradient approximation and accumulation to compensate for sparsification error. GradSA also explores the selection dimension of sparsification to improve gradient quality considering the structure characteristics of DNNs. Specifically, our contributions are listed as follows.

- To eliminate the sparsification error, a historical gradient approximation and accumulation method is proposed by introducing the Taylor expansion of the stale gradient at a later time point that is temporally near to it.
- To improve the quality of sparse gradients, a layer-level selection is proposed by considering the DNN structure characteristics, and only exchanges a few gradients of statistical significance.
- We conduct experiments in comparison with state-of-the-art sparsification and quantization methods. The results show that only GradSA keeps the same validation accuracy as the baseline for all mainstream DNNs. Additionally, GradSA outperforms DGC [11] by up to 1.92× in training speed.

2   Background and Problem Setting

Data-Parallel SGD with Parameter Server. We introduce synchronous data-parallel SGD, modeling a multi-node GPU-based environment. We denote a DNN model learned from an objective function $f(w)$: $\mathbb{R}^n \to \mathbb{R}$, where w is the weight with d-dimension. We have P workers communicate using the PS architecture. Each worker maintains a local copy of w, and holds a local data shard from the entire training set $\mathcal{D} = \{x_i, y_i\}_{i=1}^{N}$, where $x_i, y_i \in \mathbb{R}$. Then, the p-th worker can calculate local gradients $\nabla f^{(p)}(w_t; x_i)$. The server is a coordinator that achieves a global weight update g_t by averaging all local gradients that send to it. Then, all of the workers pull the latest weights from the server. This process is described in Fig. 2, and defined as follows,

$$g_t = \frac{1}{P} \sum_{p=1}^{P} \nabla f^{(p)}(w_t; x_i) \tag{1}$$

$$w_{t+1} = w_t - \eta g_t \tag{2}$$

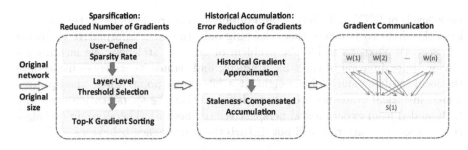

Fig. 3. Three stages of the proposed pipeline: 1) gradient sparsification, 2) historical gradient accumulation, and 3) gradient communication

where η is the learning rate. If we set the server as an independent computing node, it is obvious that the synchronization cost can be a system bottleneck in a large-scale environment.

Sparse Gradient Communication. Let $S\colon \mathbb{R}^d \to \mathbb{C}^d$ be the threshold-based sparsification function, which sorts each component of a d-dimensional vector into a descending sequence, and selects the Top-k gradients (which have k largest values) to communicate. The sparsity rate θ represents the proportion of selected ones in the entire vector. Each worker handles its local gradients before communicating in each iteration:

$$\tilde{g}_t^{(p)} = S\left(g_t^{(p)}; \theta\right) \tag{3}$$

where $g_t^{(p)}$ is the local gradients of the p-th worker at the t-th iteration, and $\tilde{g}_t^{(p)}$ is its sparse counterpart. When a server receives all the sparse gradients, it computes and updates the global model replica via:

$$w_{t+1} = w_t - \eta \cdot \tilde{g}_t = w_t - \frac{\eta}{P}\sum_{p=1}^{P}\tilde{g}_t^{(p)} \tag{4}$$

After this update period, the remaining unsent gradients will be locally stored, so they can be accumulated to the fresh local gradient of the next iteration.

3 Design Overview

The key motivations for efficiently developing sparse gradient communication on distributed training concentrate on two aspects, (i) reducing the quantity of communication set and (ii) keeping the quality of distributed training. However, only one single strategy cannot address all of the challenges. Therefore, we propose a three-stage pipeline shown in Fig. 3, in which two corresponding strategies complementary to each other, exerting their advantages on different aspects. First, to address the challenge of limited communication bandwidth, we attempt to exploit the granularity of gradient sparsification from two basic levels of DNN architecture, and obtain sparse gradients by setting a layer-level threshold to truncate them, keeping only the most informative gradients (cf. Sect. 4). Next, to tackle the problem of gradient staleness, we introduce a Taylor approximation of the stale gradient, and reduce its staleness using both the local gradient and global weight at a later time point. Then, the approximated historical gradients are accumulated so that the sparsification error can be bounded from experimental perspectives (cf. Sect. 5). Therefore, in our algorithm, a low sparsity rate will not disturb the convergence behavior.

4   Layer-Level Gradient Sparsification

In this section, we propose to use an efficient layer-level threshold solution. Compared to the original version of gradient sparsification, we introduce the layer-level Top-k selection. In each iteration, each worker handles its local gradients layer-by-layer before broadcasting, and Eq. (3) can be refined as:

$$\tilde{g}_{(l,t)}{}^{(p)} = \boldsymbol{S}\left(g_{(l,t)}{}^{(p)}; \theta\right) \tag{5}$$

A fraction $0 < \theta < 1$ is used to control the percentage of dropping. Specifically, in an arbitrary worker p, the value obtained from the Top-k sorting is the threshold, and we will select the k largest gradients based on the threshold. Here, $g_{(l,t)}{}^{(p)}$ is the local gradient partition on the l-th layer of a model, and $\tilde{g}_{(l,t)}{}^{(p)}$ is its sparse counterpart. The server computes and updates the global model replica via a layer-by-layer law which has been adopted by most DL frameworks.

Discussion: Note that there still exists a more granular selection dimension at the filter-level, selecting gradients from every filter or every filter group. However, we would not introduce this aggressive strategy considering the trade-off between the excessive costs of search space and limited performance revenue. Furthermore, immoderate sparse granularity will lead to uncertain sparsity rate and make it hardly deployed in low bandwidth environment. Taking the ResNet-20 as an example, based on our study, a filter-level trial takes up to 9× longer execution time when compared with the layer-level strategy and only achieves almost 10% sparsity rate.

5   Staleness-Compensated Historical Gradient Accumulation

Since the problem of sparsification error at low sparsity rates should be primarily solved, we propose to mitigate historical gradient staleness by two steps, (i) historical gradient approximation: instead of the wild historical gradients, we introduce a Taylor expansion on the fresh gradient to approximate them. (ii) approximated gradient accumulation: we then accumulate the approximated historical gradients with a decayed factor for the latter iteration.

5.1   Historical Gradient Approximation

To recover the stale gradients, giving them a stronger role in the object function optimization, we introduce an interesting insight into the historical gradient accumulation using a form of "look-ahead" with the gradient descent. We remove the contribution of the gradient from the previous iteration, and replace it with the contribution from the current iteration. With this insight, a straightforward and ideal method is to use the current gradients, such as $g_{t+\tau}^{(p)}$, to approximate the historical ones, $g_t^{(p)}$.

Gradient Approximation Using Taylor Expansion. The gradient $g_t^{(p)}$ can be decomposed as follow using the Taylor formula [7]:

$$g_t^{(p)} = g_{t+\tau}^{(p)} - \nabla g_{t+\tau}^{(p)}(w_{t+\tau} - w_t) + O((w_{t+\tau} - w_t)^2) \tag{6}$$

where ∇g denotes the first-order derivative of the gradient matrix with its element $\nabla g_{ij} = \frac{\partial^2 f}{\partial w_i \partial w_j}$ for $i, j \in [n]$, $O((w_{t+\tau} - w_t)^2)$ denotes the higher order remainder of the Taylor formula. Here τ is called the staleness factor. Since the residual involves the sum of an infinite number of items, which is highly nontrivial, we overlook a certain truncation terms, and only consider the simplest approximation, i.e., keeping the first-order item in the Taylor expansion:

$$(g_t^{(p)})' = g_{t+\tau}^{(p)} - \nabla g_{t+\tau}^{(p)}(w_{t+\tau} - w_t) \tag{7}$$

where $(g_t^{(p)})'$ denotes the approximation of wild gradient $g_t^{(p)}$ in Eq. (6), $\nabla g_{t+\tau}^{(p)}$ corresponds to the second-order derivative of the loss function $f(w_t; x_i)^{(p)}$, which actually is the Hessian matrix, defined as H_t.

Gradient Approximation Using Diagonal Hessian. Because exact computation of the Hessian matrix H_t is computationally expensive. We therefore adopt further diagonal approximations (i.e., $\lambda g_t^{(p)} \odot g_t^{(p)}$, where $\odot$ indicates the element-wise product, λ is a balancing factor [22]) that can be proved theoretically close to H_t and can be easily computed without introducing additional complexity (i.e., just using gradients and weights of the previous training iterations). Therefore, the approximation of wild local gradient $g_t^{(p)}$ in Eq. (7) can be written as follow:

$$(g_t^{(p)})' = g_{t+\tau}^{(p)} - \lambda g_{t+\tau}^{(p)} \odot g_{t+\tau}^{(p)} \odot (w_{t+\tau} - w_t) \tag{8}$$

Since we aim to approximate the historical gradient $\hat{g}_t^{(p)}$, which are unsent from the local worker to the server, we then execute masking operations on wild and sparse gradients $Mask(g_t^{(p)}, \tilde{g}_t^{(p)})$, and obtain $\hat{g}_t^{(p)}$, in which some elements are of the same values as $g_t^{(p)}$, and some elements are zero. Therefore, the wild gradient in Eq. (8) can be easily replaced with the historical gradient $\hat{g}_t^{(p)}$. Then, the approximation of historical gradient can be denoted as follow:

$$(\hat{g}_t^{(p)})' = \hat{g}_{t+\tau}^{(p)} - \lambda \hat{g}_{t+\tau}^{(p)} \odot \hat{g}_{t+\tau}^{(p)} \odot (w_{t+\tau} - w_t) \tag{9}$$

Please note that, compared to the original gradient exchange, our approximation has no extra communication cost and no extra computational requirement on the parameter server. The additional computations for Eq. (9) only introduce a lightweight overhead to the local workers.

The core idea behind this approximation is inspired by [22], which focuses on asynchronous SGD optimization, studies the Taylor formula of the latest gradient $g_{t+\tau}$, and successfully replaces the delayed gradient that is updated by the straggler worker. Compared to it, we inversely leverage the Taylor formula to achieve a closer approximation of the historical gradient g_t, and recover its staleness using the local gradient and global weight from the later time point. We expect the result from Eq. (6) to be exceptionally accurate in the "look-ahead" direction. Note that a small τ would be needed, which means that w_t and $w_{t+\tau}$ are close to each other. According to the upper bound of the Taylor series [7], we can see that an approximate gradient with a smaller τ will be more accurate than that with a larger one.

5.2   Historical Gradient Accumulation

After first attempting to reduce the staleness of the historical gradient, we propose to accumulate the approximated historical gradients and conclude the final sparsification error. Compared to the original gradient sparsification, we increase the steps for historical gradient accumulation, modify the object of the sparsification phase, and replace the wild gradient with the approximated accumulated gradients. Specifically, we use $h_t^{(p)}$ to denote the accumulated historical gradients of the p-th worker at t-th iteration, which accumulates all the previous unsent historical gradients:

$$h_t^{(p)} = \sum_{i=1}^{t-1} (\hat{g}_i^{(p)})' \tag{10}$$

The sparse local gradients are now computed by applying the threshold-based sparsification function in Eq. (3) to the compensated gradients:

$$\tilde{g}_t^{(p)} = S\left(g_t^{(p)} + \alpha h_t^{(p)}; \theta\right) \tag{11}$$

where α is the historical accumulation decayed coefficient ($\alpha \geq 0$). We then define the sparisification error $\varepsilon_t^{(p)}$ as the difference between the compensated local gradients $g_t^{(p)} + \alpha h_t^{(p)}$ and its sparisification results $\tilde{g}_t^{(p)}$. We follow the assumptions in [22] and conclude that the upper bound of $\varepsilon_t^{(p)}$ holds in any iteration t and will not diverge during the optimization.

6   Evaluation

6.1   Experiment Setup

In this section, we evaluate the performance of our proposed GradSA with extensive experiments. Representative DNN models are chosen, including AlexNet [9],

Inception [16], and ResNet [6], that are widely applied in classification tasks. Two famous datasets, Cifar-10 [8] and ImageNet [4], are used. The experiments are conducted on a GPU cluster of 16 nodes interconnected with both InfiniBand and Ethernet. Each node has two Tesla P100 GPUs. We develop GradSA based on MXNet, which is forked from the latest version of Apache.

The comparison contains two parts. First, to demonstrate the training efficiency of GradSA, we use the original full-size training without any gradient sparsification or optimization as the baseline. These experiments aim to measure the model accuracy fluctuations and training convergence behaviors before and after gradient optimization. Specifically, we compare it with other state-of-the-art strategies, including 8-Bit gradient quantization [2] (8-Bit for short), TernGrad [19], and DGC [11][2]. Their latest versions are obtained from GitHub. Second, to present the potentials of GradSA on supporting mobile or edge devices, we evaluate the scalability under bandwidth-constrained environment. We start by simulating the current mobile communication systems, including the recent evolution [12] (from 3 G to 5 G), as shown in Table 1.

Table 1. Characteristic summary of existing cellular standards

Generation	Regulation	Download bandwidth	Upload bandwidth	Network latency
3 G	UMTS	128–364 Kb/s	60–128 Kb/s	800 ms–2 s
3.5 G	HSPA	56 Mb/s	22 Mb/s	100–600 ms
4 G	LTE	100–300 Mb/s	50 Mb/s	100 ms
4G+	LTE-A	1 Gb/s	500 Mb/s	10–50 ms
5G	NR	5–10 Gb/s	1–5 Gb/s	<1 ms

[1] We roughly list the regulations of existing wireless cellular standards [12] and summarize the statistical data gathered from them.

During the training process, we follow the empirical hyper-parameters (learning rate, momentum, etc.) provided by the cited articles for the mentioned DNN models, and adopt the Nesterov momentum SGD optimizers [15]. Note that other hyper-parameters (including λ, α, and τ) can be exploited by performing simplified grid search, for simplicity, we constantly choose $\alpha = 0.9$, $\lambda = 0.05$, and $\tau = 10$, which help to achieve a proper test performance.

6.2   Overall Training Performance Comparison

We study the overall performance of our GradSA, the baseline with full-size gradients, 8-Bit, TernGrad, and DGC. We undertake training processes on some famous models, and record the corresponding model accuracy, compression ratio, and convergence behavior.

---

[2] Since DGC [11] is not yet open-source, we basically implement its core optimizations, i.e., momentum correction, warm-up start, gradient clipping et al. in MXNet.

Accuracy Comparison. Table 2 shows the detailed Top-1 test accuracy of these models with 4 workers after 200 epochs. The gradient sparsity is 0.1% for both DGC and GradSA (meaning that only 0.1% of the gradients are non-zero). Compared to the baseline, which has dense gradient exchange during the training process, GradSA has fully maintained the test accuracies of almost all models, which confirms that the accuracy drop ascribed to gradient staleness could be eliminated by our approximation and compensation. In contrast, 8-Bit and TernGrad only achieve moderate training performance since they both lack effective actions against gradient staleness. Note that even though GradSA and DGC all attempt to accumulate historical gradients to compensate for staleness, we perform better than DGC due to layer-level selection and proper gradient approximation. The results indicate that the Taylor-based approximation can introduce fresh gradients from the local worker, and utilize updates from other workers to boost the outdated ones.

Table 2. Training performance comparison

Training data	Model	Test accuracy (Top-1; %)					
		Baseline	8-Bit	TernGrad	DGC (refer.)	DGC	GradSA
Cifar10	Inception-v2	89.33	86.91	87.90	–	89.04	**90.40**
	ResNet-50	92.23	90.16	90.58	–	92.10	**93.12**
	ResNet-56	93.03	90.91	91.23	–	91.96	**93.84**
	ResNet-110	93.75	89.75	92.69	93.87	93.54	**94.09**
ImageNet	ResNet-50	76.36	74.04	75.29	76.15	75.90	**77.20**
	AlexNet	57.15	55.96	56.28	**58.20**	56.19	58.05

[1] We list the test Top-1 accuracy of different models with a total batch size = 128 for the ResNet-family, and a total batch size = 64 for Inception-v2 and AlexNet. The compression ratio varies slightly during every iteration, so we take averaged values after 20 iterations.

Compression Ratio Comparison. We also compare the corresponding compression ratio of these methods. When the gradient sparsity is set at 0.1% for the distributed training process, the communication costs will decrease significantly. Therefore, the gradient size reductions that DGC and GradSA offer are all high to 200× (refer that the compression ratio on the baseline is denoted as 1× for every model). In contrast, other gradient quantization methods based on bit-format data structure only achieve very restricted compression rates, such as Terngrad and 8-Bit only get 8× and 2×, respectively.

Convergence Behavior Comparison. Figure 4 depicts the convergence behaviors of three algorithms on different numbers of workers (16 workers and 32 workers, respectively). They are all terminated at the 160th epoch, and use the same group of hyper-parameters. The results show that GradSA works well and converges similar to the baseline of full-size SGD. Compared to them, the learning curve of DGC is worse than theirs due to gradient staleness. Note that when the number of workers increase to 32, the training loss on GradSA is slightly higher than that on the baseline because some hyper-parameters used for the full-size SGD are not suitable for sparse SGD, such as the learning rate and weight decay. Fortunately, since the test accuracy for GradSA can maintain the same standards as the baseline in Fig. 5(b), the side-effect is almost negligible.

Another potential advantage of our GradSA is that it is likely to speed up model convergence, and reduce the entire training time when running the same epochs. Figure 5 demonstrates the comparison of Top-1 test accuracy and wallclock time. To achieve a similar accuracy on ResNet-56 with 32 workers, the training time consumed by the baseline is 6× longer than that consumed by GradSA, and the time consumed by DGC is 1.74× longer than ours. After decreasing gradient size to an extremely tiny size, the multi-worker communication bottleneck can be fully solved, and model convergence can be accelerated significantly.

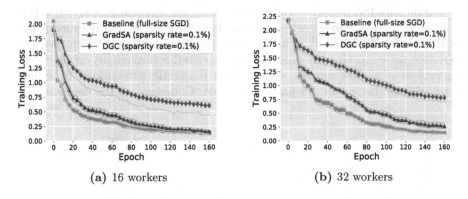

(a) 16 workers   (b) 32 workers

Fig. 4. Learning curves of ResNet-56 on Cifar-10

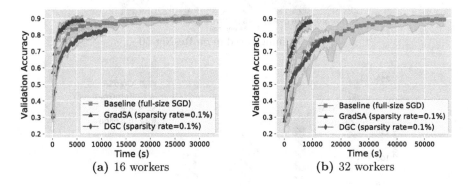

(a) 16 workers   (b) 32 workers

Fig. 5. Test accuracy v.s. wallclock time on ResNet-56

6.3 Scalability Evaluation

To evaluate the scalability of GradSA, we adjust the performance model [21], combining an analytical communication model for PS architecture with lightweight profiling on a single training worker. Our results show that GradSA can significantly reduce communication costs and achieve the best speedup under mobile network bandwidth environments, as shown in Fig. 6.

First, with recent mobile connections (from 3 G to 5 G), GradSA generally performs better than other methods, including TernGrad and 8-Bit. When the bandwidth decreases to 128 Kb/s, GradSA is still able to make the distributed training work well. GradSA outperforms TernGrad up to $4.5\times$ on the training process of AlexNet, and up to $1.46\times$ on that of ResNet-50. The oversize communication set of TernGrad and 8-Bit is a primary factor for communication inefficiency in the limited bandwidth environment, although they have no extra overhead on gradient sparsification compared to GradSA and DGC. This is largely attributed to the compact communication set in GradSA, as the extremely high gradient sparsity makes this set much smaller than other methods.

Second, GradSA performs slightly worse with the increasing bandwidth. It is because that the communication bottleneck alleviates after the network bandwidth rises to 500 Mb/s. It is noted that, compared to DGC (which uses the Allreduce pattern), GradSA only achieves the similar throughput on the training process of almost models. Our method is slightly sub-optimal in scaling to 64 workers due to the PS pattern we used. Compared to the decentralized

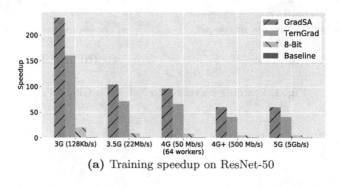

(a) Training speedup on ResNet-50

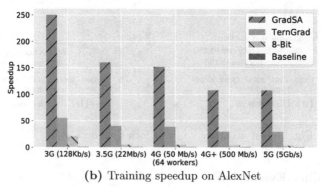

(b) Training speedup on AlexNet

Fig. 6. Training speedup on low bandwidth environments

Allreduce, centralized PS introduces explosive communication workloads linear to the number of workers, which is the reason why GradSA performs mildly when the workers increase to hundreds. Therefore, we consider to adopt the Allreduce topology in the future to achieve sub-linear communication cost growth.

7 Related Work

There have been various efforts aiming to improve the communication efficiency of distributed DL. As orthogonal lines of work, gradient quantization and sparsification have been used to obtain low-precision or low-size gradients to reduce communication costs. However, in many scenarios, methods that lead to accuracy degradation are not advisable from the perspective of systematic optimization. Our discussion will focus on a certain range of accuracy-preserving solutions.

Gradient Quantization. As a branch of research that focuses on quantizing the communication data to low-precision values, 1-Bit SGD [13], later 8-Bit gradient quantization [2] and TernGrad [19] all work well by converting the gradient into a 1-bit or other bit-format matrix. However, these quantized methods perform differently with centralized Parameter Server or decentralized Allreduce topologies. Because the quantized bit-format data structure cannot do a reduction with average and summation on the fly, they can hardly use optimized Allreduce operations to reduce communication traffic. Furthermore, another limitation of quantization is its compatibility, e.g., some studies [1] find that machine translation is less tolerant of quantization. Therefore, we prefer to choose a sparsification-based method in consideration of its flexibility for different communication topologies.

Gradient Sparsification. This type of method restricts gradient updates to a small subset of parameters, and only transmits the "important" gradients by setting thresholds. The first attempt of gradient sparsification [14] prunes gradient values below a static threshold. Subsequent works propose to use a relatively tiny portion (e.g., top 1%) [1,11] and adaptive threshold [5] for gradients based on their absolute values. However, the optimal threshold is easily chosen, considering this issue, we propose to seek a proper selection strategy to cover both the gradient data distribution and model accuracy conservation.

Sparsification Error Elimination. Since we aim to deploy DL on large scale mobile or edge networks with very low bandwidth, the gradient sparsity rate will be adjusted as low as possible. It is therefore of great necessity to guarantee the convergence of sparse SGD, particularly in distributed environments where the updates are inconsistent and stale. Several prior works [13,17,20] carry the sparsification error to the next gradient, accumulating error to avoid drift. The idea originates from Sigma-Delta Modulation [13], and has proven to be successful in many cases. As one of the state-of-the-art works, DGC [11] extends this idea by correcting momentum as well. Some works suggest conditioning gradient values by changing the DNN architecture, adding various normalization layers [1], whereas others [11] propose local gradient clipping and warm-up training.

8   Conclusion

In this paper, we present GradSA, a layer-level gradient sparsification strategy for communication efficiency on distributed DL systems. GradSA focuses on how to extremely decrease the size of exchanged gradients during the training with no obvious side-effect on the DNN accuracy. Empirical evaluations show that our approximated gradient accumulation leads to faster convergence and less training loss than baseline methods with vanilla accumulation. We further show that GradSA can achieve excellent speedup even with low bandwidth environment. In the future, we will attempt to efficiently encode and decode the communication set on GradSA, and achieve an extremely high compressed ratio, allowing designers to explore distributed DL in the mobile networks.

Acknowledgment. This work is supported by National Natural Science Foundation of China under grants No. 61832006 and No. 61672250.

References

1. Aji, A.F., Heafield, K.: Sparse communication for distributed gradient descent. In: Proceedings of the 2017 Conference on Empirical Methods in Natural Language Processing, EMNLP 2017, pp. 440–445. Association for Computational Linguistics, Copenhagen, Denmark (2017)
2. Banner, R., Hubara, I., Hoffer, E., Soudry, D.: Scalable methods for 8-bit training of neural networks. In: Proceedings of the 32nd International Conference on Neural Information Processing Systems, NIPS 2018, pp. 5151–5159. Curran Associates Inc., Montreal, Canada (2018)
3. Chen, T., et al.: Mxnet: a flexible and efficient machine learning library for heterogeneous distributed systems. In: Proceedings of Workshop on Machine Learning Systems at the 28th Annual Conference on Neural Information Processing Systems, LearningSys 2015, pp. 1–6. Montreal, Canada (2015)
4. Deng, J., Dong, W., Socher, R., Li, L., Li, F.: ImageNet: a large-scale hierarchical image database. In: Proceedings of the 22nd IEEE Conference on Computer Vision and Pattern Recognition, CVPR 2009, pp. 248–255. IEEE, Miami, USA (2009)
5. Dryden, N., Jacobs, S.A., Moon, T., Van Essen, B.: Communication quantization for data-parallel training of deep neural networks. In: Proceedings of the Workshop on Machine Learning in High Performance Computing Environments, MLHPC 2016, pp. 1–8. IEEE, Salt Lake City, USA (2016)
6. He, K., Zhang, X., Ren, S., Sun, J.: Deep residual learning for image recognition. In: Proceedings of the 29th IEEE Conference on Computer Vision and Pattern Recognition, CVPR 2016, pp. 770–778. IEEE, Las Vegas, USA (2016)
7. Jeffreys, H., Jeffreys, B.: Methods of Mathematical Physics. Cambridge University Press, Cambridge (1999)
8. Krizhevsky, A., Hinton, G.E.: Learning multiple layers of features from tiny images. Technical report, University of Toronto (2009)
9. Krizhevsky, A., Sutskever, I., Hinton, G.E.: ImageNet classification with deep convolutional neural networks. In: Proceedings of the 25th Annual Conference on Neural Information Processing Systems, NIPS 2012, pp. 1097–1105. Curran Associates Inc, Lake Tahone, USA (2012)

10. Li, M., et al.: Scaling distributed machine learning with the parameter server. In: Proceedings of the 11th USENIX Symposium on Operating Systems Design and Implementation, OSDI 2014, pp. 583–598. USENIX, Broomfield, USA (2014)

11. Lin, Y., Han, S., Mao, H., Wang, Y., Dally, B.: Deep gradient compression: reducing the communication bandwidth for distributed training. In: Proceedings of the 6th International Conference on Learning Representations, ICLR 2018. Curran Associates Inc, Vancouver, Canada (2018)

12. Ma, Z., Zhang, Z., Ding, Z., Fan, P., Li, H.: Key techniques for 5G wireless communications: network architecture, physical layer, and MAC layer perspectives. Sci. China Inf. Sci. **58**(4), 41301:1–041301:20 (2015)

13. Seide, F., Fu, H., Droppo, J., Li, G., Yu, D.: 1-Bit stochastic gradient descent and its application to data-parallel distributed training of speech DNNs. In: Proceedings of the 16th Annual Conference of the International Speech Communication Association, INTERSPEECH 2014, Singapore, pp. 1058–1062 (2014)

14. Strom, N.: Scalable distributed DNN training using commodity GPU cloud computing. In: Proceedings of the 16th Annual Conference of the International Speech Communication Association, INTERSPEECH 2015, Dresden, Germany, pp. 1488–1492 (2015)

15. Sutskever, I., Martens, J., Dahl, G., Hinton, G.: On the importance of initialization and momentum in deep learning. In: Proceedings of the 30th International Conference on Machine Learning, ICML 2013, pp. 1139–1147. PMLR, Atlanta, USA (2013)

16. Szegedy, C., et al.: Going deeper with convolutions. In: Proceedings of the 28th IEEE Conference on Computer Vision and Pattern Recognition, CVPR 2015, pp. 1–9. IEEE, Boston, USA (2015)

17. Tang, H., Yu, C., Lian, X., Zhang, T., Liu, J.: DoubleSqueeze: parallel stochastic gradient descent with double-pass error-compensated compression. In: Proceedings of the 36th International Conference on Machine Learning, ICML 2019, pp. 6155–6165. PMLR, Long Beach, USA (2019)

18. Wangni, J., Wang, J., Liu, J., Zhang, T.: Gradient sparsification for communication-efficient distributed optimization. In: Proceedings of the 32th Annual Conference on Neural Information Processing Systems, NIPS 2018, pp. 1299–1309. Curran Associates Inc, Montreal, Canada (2018)

19. Wen, W., et al.: Terngrad: ternary gradients to reduce communication in distributed deep learning. In: Proceedings of the 31st Annual Conference on Neural Information Processing Systems, NIPS 2017, pp. 1509–1519. Curran Associates Inc, Long Beach, USA (2017)

20. Wu, J., Huang, W., Huang, J., Zhang, T.: Error compensated quantized SGD and its applications to large-scale distributed optimization. In: Proceedings of the 35th International Conference on Machine Learning, ICML 2018, pp. 5325–5333. PMLR, Stockholmsmässan, Sweden (2018)

21. Yan, F., Ruwase, O., He, Y., Chilimbi, T.: Performance modeling and scalability optimization of distributed deep learning systems. In: Proceedings of the 21st ACM SIGKDD International Conference on Knowledge Discovery and Data Mining, KDD 2015, pp. 1355–1364. ACM, Sydney, Australia (2015)

22. Zheng, S., et al.: Asynchronous stochastic gradient descent with delay compensation. In: Proceedings of the 34th International Conference on Machine Learning, ICML 2017, pp. 4120–4129. PMLR, Sydney, Australia (2017)

An Improved Artificial Bee Colony Algorithm with Multiple Search Strategy

Jun Ma[1] and Yunlong Zhao[1,2(✉)]

[1] Nanjing University of Aeronautics and Astronautics, Nanjing, Jiangsu, China
3030712828@qq.com, zhaoyunlong@nuaa.edu.cn
[2] Collaborative Innovation Center of Novel Software Technology and Industrialization,
Nanjing, Jiangsu, China

Abstract. Artificial Bee Colony (ABC) has been applied to solve constrained optimization problems such as green wireless communications, path planning and so on. To solve the problem that ABC algorithm is easy to fall into local optimum, this paper proposes an Improved Artificial Bee Colony (IABC) algorithm with multiple search strategy. An opposition-based learning technique is integrated in initialization phase. Then, in order to speed up convergence rate, each employed bee searches for neighbor with adding global information. Furthermore, multiple search strategy is used to balance the exploitation and exploration during the onlooker bee phase. Inspired by Modification Rate (MR), the solution generation method of new bees whose trail have exceed *limit* is modified to increase disturbance in scout bee phase. Six benchmark functions are used to test the efficiency and stability of the algorithm, and the simulation results show IABC algorithm performs better than ABC algorithm in high dimensional space.

Keywords: Artificial Bee Colony (ABC) · Modification Rate (MR) · Multiple search strategy · Constrained optimization problem

1 Introduction

Inspired by the foraging behavior and the waggle dance behavior of honey bee swarm, a novel swarm intelligence algorithm called Artificial Bee Colony (ABC) which imitated the foraging behavior of bee swarms, was proposed by Karaboga in 2005 [1]. Owing to its excellent optimization performance and easy-to-use merit, more and more researchers have a great interest in enhancing the performance of ABC, some improved versions of ABC have been proposed for further enhancing the performance of standard ABC. Zhu and Kwong [2] proposed a global best guided ABC (GABC) by introducing a novel search equation, which can efficiently take use of the information of global best individual to improve the exploitation ability of standard ABC. Luo et al. [3] proposed a modified artificial bee colony algorithm by introducing a new search equation, in which the best solution of the previous iteration is employed to guide the search of new candidate solutions in the onlooker bee phase. Inspired by the gravity model, an attractive force model is proposed for choosing a better neighbor of a current individual to improve

© Springer Nature Switzerland AG 2020
Z. Yu et al. (Eds.): GPC 2020, LNCS 12398, pp. 92–100, 2020.
https://doi.org/10.1007/978-3-030-64243-3_7

the exploitation ability of ABC [4]. Alatas [5] proposed a chaotic artificial bee colony algorithm, in which a chaotic number generator was used to produce a chaotic number sequence for initializing a population instead of a random number sequence. In addition, a chaotic search technique was also employed.

As a kind of swarm intelligence algorithm, ABC algorithm has been applied to a variety of optimization problems. ABC algorithm and its enhanced versions have been successfully used to find high quality solutions of the job-shop scheduling problem with no-wait constraint (JSPNW) with the objective of minimizing makespan among all the jobs [6], image processing [7], predict the structure of proteins through their primary structure [8], vehicle routing problem [9], and so on [10, 11].

The rest of the paper is organized as follows. Section 2 describes the original artificial bee colony algorithm. In Sect. 3, an improved artificial bee colony algorithm is proposed. In Sect. 4, a comprehensive experimental study is carried out and some discussions are provided. Finally, some conclusions are drawn in Sect. 5.

2 Original Artificial Bee Colony Algorithm

ABC algorithm contains three groups of bees. They are employed bees, onlooker bees and scout bees. The number of employed bees and onlookers are equal, both of which account for half of the colony. The position of a food source represents a candidate solution of the optimization problem, and its nectar amount denotes the corresponding fitness value. There is only one employed bee in one food source and the main tasks of employed bees are to discover and record food sources, then transfer information to onlookers. The onlookers choose food sources according to the information transferred by the employed bees. If a food source is exhausted, the employed bee becomes a scout, and begins to find a new food source. The main steps can be described as follows:

(1) Initialize the bee colony $X = \{x_i | i = 1, 2, \cdots, SN\}$, where SN denotes the population size, x_i is the ith bee by formula (1), where φ is a random real number in [0, 1], min and max stand for lower and upper bounds of possible solutions.

$$x_i = min + (max - min) \times \varphi \tag{1}$$

(2) According to the fitness function, calculate the fitness f_i of each employed bee x_i, record the maximum nectar amount as well as the corresponding food source.
(3) Each employed bee produces a new solution v_i in the neighborhood of the solution in its memory by formula (2), where k is an integer near to $i, k \neq i$, and $\emptyset$ is a random real number in $[-1, 1]$.

$$v_i = x_i + (x_i - x_k) \times \emptyset \tag{2}$$

(4) Use the greedy criterion to update x_i. Compare the fitness of v_i. If v_i is superior to x_i. x_i is replaced with v_i; otherwise retain x_i.
(5) According to the fitness f_i of x_i, get probability value p_i via formula (3) and (4).

$$p_i = \frac{fit_i}{\sum_{i=1}^{n} fit_i} \tag{3}$$

$$fit_i = \begin{cases} \frac{1}{1+f_i} & f_i > 0 \\ 1 + abs|f_i| & f_i < 0 \end{cases} \tag{4}$$

(6) Depending on the probability p_i, onlookers choose food sources, search the neighborhood to generate candidate solutions, and calculate their fitness.

(7) Use the greedy criteria to update the food sources.

(8) Memorize the best food source and nectar amount achieved.

(9) Check whether there are some abandoned solutions or not. If true, replace them with some new randomly generated solutions by formula (1).

(10) Repeat steps (3)–(9), until the maximum number of iterations is reached or stop conditions are satisfied.

3 The Proposed ABC Algorithm

3.1 Initialization Phase

An opposition-based learning technique is integrated in initialization phase, which is described by formula (5).

$$x_i' = min + (max - x_i) \tag{5}$$

3.2 Employed Bees Phase

Aiming to making use of the global best information to speed up the convergence rate and avoiding falling into local optimum, each employed bee begins to search a new food source v_i by formula (6), where x_{best} is the best solution of the current group.

$$v_i = x_i + \emptyset \cdot (x_i - x_k) + \varphi \cdot (x_{best} - x_i) \tag{6}$$

Then, in order to add the group diversity, handle the boundary constraints by formula (7).

$$v_i = \begin{cases} min + (max - min) \cdot \varphi & v_i < min \\ max - (max - min) \cdot \varphi & v_i > max \end{cases} \tag{7}$$

3.3 Onlooker Bees Phase

Unlike the random search of standard ABC, another guiding scheme with better exploration ability is presented in the onlooker bee phase. The presented new guiding can be described by formula (8).

$$v_i = x_k + \emptyset \cdot (x_i - x_k) \tag{8}$$

In order to further balance the exploitation of ABC algorithm, in the onlooker bees phase, a random search is carried out and it is described by formula (1).

Next, opposition-based learning technique which is used to further balance the exploitation and exploration, it is also introduced in the onlooker bee phase.

Subsequently, the perturbation frequency for changing many more parameters is increased. Namely, a parameter called Modification Rate (MR) is used to control the perturbation frequency of parameters of solutions. It is also employed in the onlooker bee phase of IABC.

3.4 Scout Bee Phase

In the scout bees phase of standard ABC algorithm, there is only one scout at most and ABC algorithm is easy to fall into local optimum. Yan et al. proposed a modified artificial bee colony algorithm ABC-1, which focus on improving the search ability by adding the number of scouts and increasing disturbance. More detailed information can be found in literature [12] and Algorithm 1.

Algorithm 1: The IABC algorithm

---

1. Initialize a population of SN individuals randomly
2. Calculate the fitness value for each individual
3. Calculate the opposite individual for each individual
4. Calculate the fitness value for each opposite individual
5. for $i = 1$ to SN do
6. Determine the best individual by comparing the fitness values of individual and its corresponding opposite individual
7. Get the best individual in initialization phase
8. Set up the related parameters, i.e, $limit\ \delta, \xi, \beta, , maxCycle$
9. Set $trail_i = 0\ (i = 1,2, \cdots SN)$
10. While $iter < maxCycle$ do
11.   for $i = 1$ to SN do
12.   Set $v = x_i$
13.   Randomly generate an integer k and $k \neq i$
14.   Randomly produce a integer j within the interval [1,D]
15.   Generate a new solution v according to Eq.(6)
16.   Handle the boundary constraints according to Eq.(7)
17.   if $f(v) \leq f(x_i)$ then
18.   Replace x_i with v and set $trail_i = 0$
19.   else
20.   Set $trail_i = trail_i + 1$
21.   end if
22.   end for
23.   Calculate the probability value p_i for each onlooker bee using Eq.(5)
24.   Set $t = 0$ and $i = 1$
25.   while $t < SN$ do

26.	if $rand < p_i$ then
27.	Set $t = t + 1$ and $v = x_i$
28.	Randomly generate an integer k and $k \neq i$
29.	Randomly produce a integer $jrand$ within the interval [1,D]
30.	for $j = 1$ to D do
31.	if $rand < \beta || j == jrand$ then
32.	// β represents the modification rate which controls the perturbation frequency of parameter
33.	// rand is used to randomly generate a number between [0,1]
34.	Set $tempr = rand$ then
35.	if $tempr < \delta$ then
36.	Generate a new solution v according to Eq.(8)
37.	else if $tempr < \xi$ then
38.	Generate a new solution v according to Eq.(5)
39.	else
40.	Generate a new solution v according to Eq.(1)
41.	end if
42.	Handle boundary constraints according to Eq.(7)
43.	end if
44.	end for
45.	if $f(v) \leq f(x_i)$ then
46.	Replace x_i with v and set $trail_i = 0$
47.	else
48.	Set $trail_i = trail_i + 1$
49.	end if
50.	end if
51.	Set $i = i + 1$
52.	if $i == (SN + 1)$ then $i = 1$
53.	end while
54.	sort the $trail$ values for all individuals
55.	if $trail_{max} > limit$ then
56.	The onlooker bee of $trail_{max}$ becomes a scout
57.	if $trail_{second} > limit$ then
58.	if $trail_{third} \leq limit$ then
59.	The onlooker bee of $trail_{third}$ becomes a scout
60.	end if
61.	else
62.	The onlooker bee of $trail_{third}$ becomes a scout using
63.	end if
64.	end if
65.	Record the best solution obtained so far
66.	end while

4 Validation and Comparison

4.1 Benchmark Functions

To test the efficiency and stability of the updated ABC algorithm with multiple search strategy, we use six benchmark functions as following.

4.1.1 Sphere Function

Sphere function is a unimodal function, its optimum value is 0, and it can be defined by the following formula (9).

$$f_1(x) = \sum_{i=1}^{n} x_i^2$$
$$x_i \in [-100, 100] \tag{9}$$

4.1.2 Rosenbrock Function

Rosenbrock function is a non-convex function, its optimum value is 0, and it can be defined by the following formula (10).

$$f_2(x) = \sum_{i=1}^{n-1} \left[100(x_{i+1} - x_i^2)^2 + (x_i - 1)^2 \right]$$
$$x_i \in [-30, 30] \tag{10}$$

4.1.3 Rastrigin Function

Rastrigin function is a multimodal function, its optimum value is 0, and it can be defined by the following formula (11).

$$f_3(x) = \sum_{i=1}^{n} \left[x_i^2 - 10\cos(2\pi x_i) + 10 \right]$$
$$x_i \in [-5.12, 5.12] \tag{11}$$

4.1.4 Schwefel Function

Schwefel function is a multimodal function, its optimum value is −418.9829* D (D is number of space dimensions), and it can be defined by the following formula (12).

$$f_4(x) = \sum_{i=1}^{n} \left[-x_i \sin\left(\sqrt{|x_i|}\right) \right]$$
$$x_i \in [-500, 500] \tag{12}$$

4.1.5 Griewank Function

Griewank function is a multimodal function, its optimum value is 0, and it can be defined by the following formula (13).

$$f_5(x) = \frac{1}{4000} \sum_{i=1}^{n} x_i^2 - \prod_{i=1}^{n} \cos\left(\frac{x_i}{\sqrt{i}}\right) + 1$$
$$x_i \in [-600, 600] \tag{13}$$

4.1.6 Ackley Function

Ackley function is a multimodal function, its optimum value is 0, and it can be defined by the following formula (14).

$$f_6(x) = -20\exp\left(-0.2\sqrt{\frac{1}{n}\sum_{i=1}^{n} x_i^2}\right) - \exp\left(\frac{1}{n}\sum_{i=1}^{n}\cos(2\pi x_i)\right) + 20 + e$$
$$x_i \in [-32, 32] \tag{14}$$

4.2 Simulation and Results

In order to verify the performance of the IABC algorithm, in the simulation experiment, the colony size SN is 100, the maximum cycle number $maxCycle$ to terminate the algorithm is 1000, the parameter $limit$ is 50, $\delta = 0.95, \xi = 0.98, \beta = 0.15$, and each function is optimized over 30 independent runs by each algorithm. In order to investigate the effect of some modifications of IABC relative to ABC, performance comparisons among ABC, ABC-1 and IABC are carried out.

Best, worst, median, mean and standard deviation values achieved by ABC, ABC-1 and IABC algorithm in fifty-dimensional space and one hundred-dimensional space are shown respectively in Tables 1 and 2.

Table 1. Statistical results obtained by ABC, ABC-1 and IABC in fifty-dimensional space

Function	Algorithm	Best	Worst	Mean	Std
Sphere	ABC	1.21552e−07	2.31302e−05	3.07143e−06	3.96225e−06
	ABC-1	1.3168e−07	9.39729e−06	3.32478e−06	2.62048e−06
	IABC	1.40248e−11	2.68594e−10	7.16391e−11	4.09737e−11
Rosenbrock	ABC	2.69337	89.4186	22.9693	18.0327
	ABC-1	6.0758	73.9508	19.2997	13.4373
	IABC	0.549459	9.66236	2.86964	2.30198
Rastrigin	ABC	1.99872	9.24262	5.12676	1.84813
	ABC-1	1.05814	8.1476	4.80683	1.6449
	IABC	3.1885e−07	1.02828	0.130018	0.380818
Griewank	ABC	1.55882e−06	0.00250772	0.000228926	0.000535726
	ABC-1	3.27922e−06	0.0274681	0.00170288	0.00516979
	IABC	3.63853e−11	3.85518e−08	2.45367e−09	7.26252e−09
Ackley	ABC	0.00281789	0.0172737	0.00809974	0.00378532
	ABC-1	0.00273788	0.018134	0.00838802	0.0040022
	IABC	6.59349e−06	1.89239e−05	1.21356e−05	3.55273e−06
Schwefel	ABC	−20108.6	−19141	−19527.3	225.035
	ABC-1	−20074.5	−19035.2	−19521.2	239.661
	IABC	−20949.1	−20828.3	−20935	36.5325

It should be noted that our proposed IABC algorithm, ABC-1 ABC algorithm are cod-ed in MATLAB R2016a, The computer is Surface Laptop and the operating system is Window 10.

In Table 1, IABC algorithm performs better than ABC algorithm in fifty-dimensional space, it is superior to ABC algorithm in accuracy of solution, especially in multimodal functions and IABC algorithm performs better in stability of algorithms. On one hand,

Table 2. Statistical results obtained by ABC, ABC-1 and IABC in one hundred-dimensional space

Function	Algorithm	Best	Worst	Mean	Std
Sphere	ABC	0.00132199	0.849787	0.0735031	0.141387
	ABC-1	0.00198244	0.371583	0.0704753	0.104974
	IABC	7.84228e−05	0.00195292	0.000387935	0.000343736
Rosenbrock	ABC	93.9681	3132.62	661.24	610.48
	ABC-1	193.856	2708.3	587.432	511.377
	IABC	20.6585	309.018	126.794	61.6084
Rastrigin	ABC	34.0965	81.092	61.5411	9.65884
	ABC-1	41.3384	81.6396	63.674	9.77043
	IABC	15.9474	30.1348	23.5027	3.0932
Griewank	ABC	0.00300182	0.95744	0.150137	0.18333
	ABC-1	0.0112061	0.499583	0.136605	0.126568
	IABC	0.00059177	0.0624408	0.00620051	0.00887176
Ackley	ABC	2.0477	3.70931	2.70772	0.324902
	ABC-1	1.70362	3.18068	2.67663	0.253588
	IABC	5.7921e−06	2.36493e−05	1.25336e−05	3.50394e−06
Schwefel	ABC	−36941.5	−34777.5	−35593.5	477.051
	ABC-1	−36264.5	−34623.5	−35451.4	377.185
	IABC	−40976.6	−39183.9	−40046.3	289.404

we make full use of the global information to speed up the convergence rate. On the other hand, the ABC algorithm is improved by the new method called multiple search strategy, it mainly solve the problem that ABC algorithm is easy to fall into local optimum by adding group diversity, which increases disturbance in some way. The above analysis and explanations can be used for Table 2.

5 Conclusion

This paper proposes an improved Artificial Bee Colony (IABC) algorithm with multiple search strategy. In addition to using global information to speed up convergence rate, we also improve the performance by adding the number of scouts and introducing a perturbation factor, the proposed algorithm has strong search ability. Several simulations show the effective performance of the proposed IABC algorithm when compared with the standard ABC algorithm in high dimensional space. Finally, it can be efficiently employed to solve some optimization problems.

Acknowledgements. This research was supported by Defense Industrial Technology Development Program under Grant No. JCKY2016605B006, Six talent peaks project in Jiangsu Province under Grant No. XYDXXJS-031.

References

1. Karaboga, D.: An idea based on honey bee swarm for numerical optimization (2005)
2. Zhu, G., Kwong, S.: Gbest-guided artificial bee colony algorithm for numerical function optimization. Appl. Math. Comput. **217**(7), 3166–3173 (2010)
3. Luo, J., Wang, Q., Xiao, X.: A modified artificial bee colony algorithm based on converg E-onlookers approach for global optimization. Appl. Math. Comput. **219**(20), 10253–10262 (2013)
4. Xiang, W.L., Meng, X.L., et al.: An improved artificial bee colony algorithm based on the gravity model. Inf. Sci. **429**, 49–71 (2018)
5. Alatas, B.: Chaotic bee colony algorithms for global numerical optimization. Expert Syst. Appl. **37**(8), 5682–5687 (2010)
6. Sundar, S., Suganthan, P.N., Jin, C.T., et al.: A hybrid artificial bee colony algorithm for the job-shop scheduling problem with no-wait constraint. Soft. Comput. **21**(5), 1193–1202 (2015)
7. Ma, M., Liang, J., Guo, M., et al.: SAR image segmentation based on artificial bee colony algorithm. Appl. Soft Comput. **11**(8), 5205–5214 (2011)
8. Li, M., Duan, H., Shi, D.: Hybrid artificial bee colony and particle swarm optimization approach to protein secondary structure prediction. In: Intelligent Control & Automation. IEEE (2012)
9. Szeto, W.Y., Wu, Y., Ho, S.C.: An artificial bee colony algorithm for the capacitated vehicle routing problem. Eur. J. Oper. Res. **215**(1), 126–135 (2011)
10. Karthikeyan, S., Christopher, T.: A hybrid clustering approach using artificial bee colony (ABC) and particle swarm optimization. Int. J. Comput. Appl. (2014)
11. Karaboga, D., Akay, B.: A modified artificial bee colony (ABC) algorithm for constrained optimization problems. Appl. Soft Comput. **11**(3), 3021–3031 (2011)
12. Wang, Y., You, J.: An improved artificial bee colony (ABC) algorithm with advanced search ability. In: 2018 8th International Conference on Electronics Information and Emergency Communication (ICEIEC) (2018)

An Efficient Data Prefetch Strategy for Deep Learning Based on Non-volatile Memory

Wenbin Jiang(✉), Pai Liu, Hai Jin, and Jing Peng

National Engineering Research Center for Big Data Technology and System, Services Computing Technology and System Lab, Cluster and Grid Computing Lab, School of Computer Science and Technology, Huazhong University of Science and Technology, Wuhan 430074, China
{wenbinjiang,liunxpaisley,hjin,crystalpeng}@hust.edu.cn

Abstract. *Deep learning* (DL) systems usually utilize asynchronous prefetch to improve data reading performance. However, the efficiency of the data transfer path from hard disk to DRAM is still limited by disk performance. The emerging *non-volatile memory* (NVRAM) provides a novel solution for this problem, while few existing researches have considered it. We propose a novel efficient data prefetch strategy for DL based on a heterogeneous memory system combining NVRAM with DRAM. Benefitting from the large capacity and fast reading speed of NVRAM, the strategy uses an asynchronous reading method named *sliding NVRAM cache* (SNC) to improve the performance of the data transfer paths. A sliding window is applied to map the data from disk to NVRAM and continuously update the data, while non-ideal writing performance of NVRAM can be remitted to a large extent in this strategy. Experiments show that SNC can improve the time performance of diverse deep neural networks training by more than 30%.

Keywords: Deep learning · Data prefetch · NVRAM.

1 Introduction

Deep Learning (DL) is an important tool in data processing and analysis, and has been making great progress in many fields [6], such as image classification and video recognition, over the past decade. DL is often compute-intensive and data-hungry, accompanied with larger and larger *deep neural network* (DNN) models and datasets. Diversified types of DL acceleration hardware devices, such as NVIDIA GPUs and DaDianNao, can run so fast that input data often cannot be available in time. Recently, some novel improvements in CPUs, such as Intel *Advanced Vector Extensions* (AVX) [8], cluster of CPUs [15], and Intel Xeon Phi, worsen this kind of conflict further, especially for some applications with heavy input data, such as huge image datasets and video datasets.

© Springer Nature Switzerland AG 2020
Z. Yu et al. (Eds.): GPC 2020, LNCS 12398, pp. 101–114, 2020.
https://doi.org/10.1007/978-3-030-64243-3_8

Oftentimes, the bottleneck lies between hard disk and main memory (or called DRAM) in a single machine.

Although different DL systems [1,10] are different from each other in many respects, they fetch input data from hard disk almost in the same way in a single machine, that is, reading data asynchronously to keep pace with training. As shown in Fig. 1, there are usually two threads that work in parallel. The main thread waits for training data batches and submits them to the training processor. The prefetch thread fetches the data batches from hard disk. Asynchronous reading can overlap the time of reading data with the time of computation to some extent. The ideal situation is that the time of computation is longer than the time of reading data, which can make the training process go fluently without any data waiting.

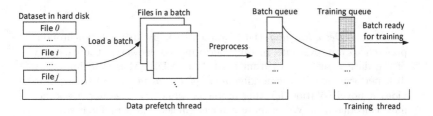

Fig. 1. The flow of asynchronous data prefetch for DL

As known to all, the scales of datasets for DL range from several MB to hundreds of GB. For a small dataset, it can be cached in DRAM if the DL system uses a large prefetch queue. Data-hungry problem can be ignored. However, for a big dataset such as ImageNet [3], it is impossible to cache it all in DRAM just once. Therefore, the system needs to read data batches from the hard disk constantly. A data batch contains dozens of samples such as pictures and segments of videos, which means that multiple disk I/O requests are sent to fetch data. The physical feature of traditional hard disk storage causes significant latency while processing multiple requests. It eventually results in longer data reading time and the entire training process slowing down. Data-hungry problem becomes serious.

The emerging of the byte-addressable *non-volatile random access memory* (NVRAM) *devices*, such as *Intel Optane DC Persistent Memory* (PMEM) [9] provides a new way to break through the data-hungry problem. NVRAM has very fast reading speed that is close to DRAM, while much higher capacity compared to it. However, although it has been verified to be very useful for many simple applications, few works have been done to approve its effectiveness in DL systems even in some emulators, because of the special reading behaviours and complexity of most DL systems.

In DL training process, traditionally, the data in a dataset are prefetched into memory sequentially from the beginning to the end of the dataset in an epoch, namely if a copy of data has been used, the opportunity that it will be accessed again is low. It means that the temporal locality of the data is low. Therefore, when we take NVRAM as a cache between hard disk and DRAM for the data movement, if the dataset is much larger than the capacity of NVRAM, the temporal locality of the data loaded into the NVRAM device becomes very poor. In other words, the probability being re-accessed of the data loaded into an NVRAM device is very low, since they will be replaced with a high probability before being re-accessed. Therefore, it is necessary to find a new way to re-organize and prefetch dataset when using NVRAM for DL systems.

As aforementioned, we focus on the situation that the time of data prefetch is longer than that of DL computation, namely the *ratio of data prefetch time to computation time* (RDC) is larger than one. NVRAM is applied to maintain the continuity of the DL computation as high as possible.

To overcome aforementioned challenges and break through the bottleneck of data reading in DL systems and exploit the potential of NVRAM, we propose a multi-thread data prefetch strategy for DL applications based on a heterogeneous memory system. The strategy uses an asynchronous reading method named *sliding NVRAM cache* (SNC) to improve the performance of the data transfer paths. A sliding window is applied to map the data from disk to NVRAM and continuously update the data, while non-ideal writing performance of NVRAM can be remitted to a large extent.

The main contributions of our work can be summarized as the following.

- NVRAM, as a novel type of memory, is introduced into DL systems to improve the system performance. To the best of our knowledge, it is the first time to introduce NVRAM to DL systems.
- Based on NVRAM, an asynchronous reading method named SNC is proposed to break through the bottleneck of data reading in DL systems, which explores the special temporal and spatial localities of the data to be prefetched. A novel sliding window algorithm is proposed for data prefetch for DL with NVRAM.
- Diversified evaluations are performed to show the advantages of our proposed strategy. Especially, a real NVRAM device is used for these evaluations, which makes the experimental results more convictive.

2   Related Work

2.1   Optimizations for Data Bottleneck in DL Systems

For DL systems, at early stage, data hungry problems were mainly noticed in distributed environments. The main reason that leads to the data hungry problems is the network bandwidth limitation between different nodes. Quite a few researches have been done for them.

You et al. [15] train some big DNNs in a cluster with 1024 CPUs. The work struggles to improve the efficiency of the communication among CPUs so as to improve the efficiency of the data fetching by utilizing larger batch sizes to prefetch data. Sreedhar et al. [14] try to load the whole dataset into the distributed memory of the system.

In fact, recently, more and more attentions have been paid to the data hungry problems in a single machine. The storage and data migration technologies that provide data for DL system obviously fall behind the fast development of computation technologies, especially the development of GPU, which then results in more and more prominent data bottleneck problems in various DL systems.

Moreover, some new improvements in CPUs aggravate this contradiction further. Intel proposes an enhanced version of Caffe named Intel-Caffe to exploit more potential of CPU by AVX [8]. Hadjis et al. [7] tap more potential of the CPU computation by rewriting some kernels of the BLAS (*Basic Linear Algebra Subprograms*) library, and combine CPU and GPU together to train networks. Due to more computation powers released from CPUs, the input data bottleneck is highlighted further. Even worse, the data prefetch and the computation are serialized in Intel-Caffe, namely cannot be run asynchronously, which worsen the performance of the DL training.

A direct approach to alleviate this problem is to replace traditional hard disks with some new storage devices that have higher access speeds. SSD being used in many practical DL systems is a good example. It also has been used for many other applications. However, SSD is still a kind of hard disk and its speed is far slower than DRAM. The effectiveness brought by it is still unsatisfactory.

Another way to improve the data reading efficiency in DL is to format dataset into some integrated files or other forms. LMDB [13] is such a kind of file supported by Caffe, which integrates all data into a single file to improve the data reading speed. LMDB is not a flexible format. It only supports the data in form of *image + single integer label*. When the dataset is updated, the LMDB file needs to be regenerated again. TFRecord is a similar way designed for TensorFlow by Google. However, besides lack of flexibility, the TFRecord file may include additional data which is to reconstruct the original data. So the TFRecord file may take much more disk space than raw data, while many datasets are already very large. To further improve the data access efficiency in an integrated file, Pumma et al. [13] present LMDBIO by optimizing LMDB. However, the work pays main attention to the situation of multiple Caffe processes running on a single server concurrently and the dataset stored in a shared file system. For the common situation that a single Caffe process runs on a single server, and the local disk holds the whole dataset, the optimization is less effective.

2.2   Development of NVRAM

Fortunately, the emerging of NVRAM provides a new opportunity to crack the data bottleneck problems in DL application. NVRAM can be used in two models: storage-based model and memory-based model [9]. For storage-based model, there are quite a few researches done and some NVRAM physical hardware devices are available. Facebook uses Bandana [5] to reduce memory footprint in the recommender system. It aggregates user model vectors that have similar behaviors in one physical 4KB (Kilobyte) block of NVRAM to accelerate the access of user model vectors.

However, for memory-based model, currently there are few physical hardware devices available. Most researches are done on some emulation platforms such as HME [4] and NVMain [12]. However, generally, these emulators usually only can support some simple and light-weight applications. For DL applications, the overheads and the complexities usually are very high, which results in that few DL research works have been done on these emulators.

In this paper, we deploy our research on some real physical NVRAM devices, benefitting from the recent emerging of the physical device of PMEM, which provides a good environment for our research. In fact, some researches have been done to evaluate the effectiveness of PMEM for some relative simple HPC applications [9,11]. Izraelevitz et al. [9] and Peng et al. [11] both evaluate the bandwidth and latency of PMEM. The former also evaluates the throughput of some database applications; The latter studies the impact of PMEM for a parallel file system. Applications mentioned above are I/O-intensive. However, for many complex applications, such as DL, few evaluations have been done. Our work attempts to exploit some effective strategy for DL applications by applying PMEM.

3 NVRAM-Based Cache Sliding Strategy for Data Prefetch

In this paper, we propose a novel data prefetch strategy for DL frameworks by leveraging byte-addressable NVRAM that works as an extension and assistant of DRAM, namely, the main memory is composed of NVRAM and DRAM, as shown in Fig. 2. Here, the byte-addressable NVRAM can be regarded as a cache between DRAM and hard disk to some extent. However, it is not a traditional cache, especially when it works for DL systems. Some special scheduling algorithms must be designed to meet special requirements of DL data prefetching. At the same time, the side-effect of the slowness of NVRAM writing (compared to NVRAM reading) should be noticed and treated carefully to improve the overall performance of NVRAM for DL systems.

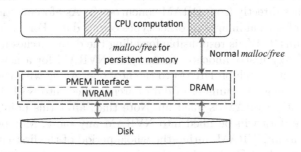

Fig. 2. The storage framework of DL system leveraging NVRAM

As mentioned before, we pay main attention to the situation that the data prefetch time is longer than the DNN computation time (Otherwise, the former can be hidden in the latter, then there is no data bottleneck problem needed to be addressed). We propose a NVRAM-based sliding cache strategy to alleviate the problem existing in this situation. Briefly, there are three stages in this strategy, which are NVRAM data initialization, NVRAM data sliding, and NVRAM data refilling. Three workers (parallel threads) are introduced into this strategy: a worker for NVRAM filling (W_f), a worker for prefetching (W_p), and a worker for the computation module (W_{cm}). Details about them are explained and discussed as follows.

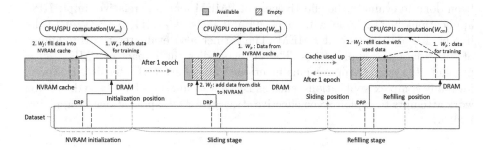

Fig. 3. Different stages of the SNC process

3.1   NVRAM Data Initialization

At the beginning of a DL training, NVRAM device shown in Fig. 3 is usually empty. In other words, there is no data in the NVRAM device available for computation. We should fill it at first by fetching data from hard disk. Inspired by the caching method of the traditional cache between CPU and DRAM, we design a similar method to initialize NVRAM, namely, fill it with some data that have been accessed in order that they can be re-accessed faster.

The left part of Fig. 3 illustrates the brief process of the initialization. The three workers are running in parallel. When the first epoch of the DL training is going, W_p fetches the data batches from the hard disk to DRAM and W_{cm} gets data batches directly from DRAM concurrently. As aforementioned, a data batch consists of several images or other types of raw data. For each data batch, once W_{cm} obtains it, W_f is responsible for filling the data batches into NVRAM simultaneously. W_f firstly allocates memory on NVRAM for a new data batch and copies the data batch on DRAM to the new one. Along with the first epoch of the training going, the number of data batches filled into NVRAM increases continuously until NVRAM is filled up. Note that, after this point at the first epoch, no more data will be filled into NVRAM any more. Moreover, W_p will not fetch data from NVRAM during the whole period of the first epoch. This is because in an epoch of DL training, the data are accessed sequentially, and no data will be accessed twice or more.

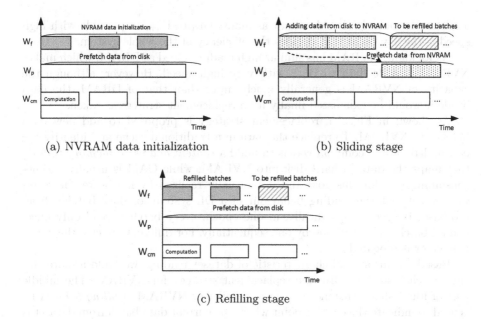

Fig. 4. Timeline analysis of main thread, prefetch thread, and backup thread in SNC. The backup thread is for data updating in the sliding stage and for data refilling when the cache is used up.

Therefore, after the first epoch, only the head part of the dataset will be cached into NVRAM. However, since the capacity of NVRAM is usually much larger than DRAM and can provide similar reading speed like DRAM, the cached data in NVRAM will benefit the performance of the DL training process much in the following epochs. To improve the performance of the initialization process, two concurrent threads are created to be in charge of the DRAM data fetching and NVRAM data filling, respectively. As shown in Fig. 4(a), W_f is responsible for the NVRAM caching, and W_p is for the DRAM data prefetching. Of course, there is a main thread (W_{cm}) that is in charge of the DL computing process.

The above initialization process lasts for one epoch. As Fig. 4(a) illustrates, compared to the DRAM data prefetching, the initialization process usually takes less time, and it can be hidden in the former. Of course, the initialization process can not save time for the first epoch, but it introduces almost no extra overhead. It just fills up NVRAM in parallel (assume that the volume of the dataset is bigger than the volume of NVRAM).

3.2 NVRAM Data Sliding

As aforementioned, after the first epoch, NVRAM is filled up and can provide data to W_{cm} instead of the hard disk in the following epochs to some extent (The basic data reading behavior of a DL system is that it reads through the dataset in units of data batches sequentially in each epoch). Then, how to design a scheme to make NVRAM submit as many data to W_{cm} as possible with high speed is the key point that decides the efficiency of the whole system.

As we know, NVRAM has similar high reading speed as DRAM, which makes NVRAM provide data to W_{cm} with very high speed. However, although the capacity of NVRAM is generally much larger than that of DRAM, the data inside it would be exhausted finally if no replacement strategy is taken.

As shown in Fig. 3, a replacement strategy is proposed to add new data batches to NVRAM. To replace the data in a traditional cache and identify the new added data, a common way is to build a *content addressed memory* (CAM) that maps the data in hard disk into NVRAM, while CAM is usually a time-consuming way for this goal and it is usually realized by hardware. However, we obverse that the reading behaviour of a DL system for data batches from a dataset is special. Specifically, in one epoch, every batch is read only once, and all batches are read one by one sequentially. For different epochs, the above behaviour is repeated.

Based on this special characteristic of dataset reading, we build a more efficient mechanism to realize the replacement strategy for NVRAM. The middle part of Fig. 3 shows this mechanism in detail. For NVRAM, a *filling point* (FP) is used to indicate the current point where the current data batch from dataset is being filled; a *reading point* (RP) denotes the point where the W_p is reading the data from NVRAM to W_{cm}. Along with the training going on, both points slide forward recurrently. In other words, as soon as they slide to the end of NVRAM, they go back to the beginning point. In the meanwhile, for reading the dataset, a *dataset reading point* (DRP) is used to indicate the position where the current file to be read is. DRP also slides from the beginning of the dataset to the end when a DL training epoch is going.

In order to improve the efficiency of this sliding stage, besides the main thread (W_{cm}) for the DL computing process, two other separate threads, which are W_f and W_p, are used for adding data from hard disk to NVRAM, and for prefetching data from NVRAM to the W_{cm}, respectively. Note that, the tasks of W_f and W_p have changed relative to the initialization stage. Figure 4(b) shows the process in detail. All three threads are executed concurrently to improve the performance of the process in this stage.

Note that, even though, some new data batches will be added into NVRAM along with the DL training going on, the available data in NVRAM will be exhausted after some time, because the speed of reading data from hard disk is usually much slower than the speed at which the data in NVRAM are consumed by W_{cm}. When W_p detects that no data is available in NVRAM, it is the time to switch to another stage in the next iteration. The switching will not make the training stop. In this new stage, W_p should read data from hard disk again to DRAM for W_{cm}. At the same time, NVRAM should be refilled. We will discuss this in the next section in detail.

According to the design of the NVRAM data sliding approach, it is clear that, when the RDC is certain, the longer the time of the NVRAM data sliding stage lasts, the higher efficiency our proposed SNC can achieve. We use *CacheSize* to represent the maximum quantity of data batches that NVRAM can hold. Therefore, *CacheSize* is the key factor of the length of sliding stage.

3.3 NVRAM Refilling for Next Sliding Stage

As aforementioned, when the data batches loaded to NVRAM are used up, the data sliding stage must stop, and a data refilling stage should be launched to refill NVRAM. At this time, W_{cm} gets data from hard disk through DRAM. The main idea of this process is also shown in the right part of Fig. 3.

We can see that this stage is similar to the data initialization stage in the first epoch, and the training computation in this stage is also intermittent as shown in Fig. 4(c).

The refilling stage mainly differs from the NVRAM initialization stage in that, the data to be refilled is read from hard disk starting at the position where the last data sliding stage stops (as *sliding position* (SP) in Fig. 3). After NVRAM is filled up, it will not be filled again until the next epoch comes and the dataset is scanned to the position where SP points to. Then a new NVRAM data sliding stage will be launched to let W_p fetch data from NVRAM again. Another difference is that, there is no need to allocate memory on NVRAM, because the data batches on NVRAM allocated in the initialization stage can be used again. So the refilling stage takes the same time as that of the initialization stage. Both of them can be regarded as the same stage. Figure 5 shows that the refilling stage and the data sliding stage are launched alternately among epochs to exploit the potential of NVRAM caching capacity.

Fig. 5. Alternation of refilling (or initialization) stage and sliding stage

To highlight the advantage of our proposed SNC, we also design and realize a *fixed NVRAM cache* (FNC) that just fixes some cached data in NVRAM for comparison. FNC has exactly the same initialization stage as SNC has in the first epoch. A prefetch thread is also applied to read data from the hard disk. In next coming epochs, the data in the NVRAM cache keep unchanged, which means that there is no sliding stage for data update. The training data is firstly fetched from NVRAM then from hard disk in each following epoch. FNC is easily implemented, however, has a disadvantage in time performance.

In the next section, we will evaluate the performance of both SNC and FNC.

4 Evaluation

4.1 Experiment Environment

As aforementioned, PMEM, as a kind of hardware solution of NVRAM, is now available. We build a PMEM based test environment for this evaluation. Table 1 shows some parameters and configuration in detail. Considering this PMEM based test platform cannot support GPU yet due to its physical restriction from the server manufacturer, we apply Intel-Caffe for this evaluation, which can also provide considerable training speed, benefitting from the new Intel high performance instruction set of AVX.

We apply SNC and FNC to Intel-Caffe respectively. Intel-Caffe integrates the data prefetch module as a layer of the network model. This layer contains an asynchronous thread for data prefetch (W_p) while the entire network model is trained in main thread (W_{cm}). We add another thread for filling NVRAM (W_f). By aid of the memkind library [2] that allows applications to allocate memory on PMEM, Intel-Caffe is able to access PMEM efficiently. The network model is still stored and updated in DRAM as original.

AlexNet and ResNet-18 are trained on ImageNet here. The training parameters are shown in Table 2. The *batch number* denotes the quantity of batches that the entire ImageNet dataset contains under a specific batch size.

Table 1. Experimental environment for PMEM

Server	Linux Kernel	CPUs	DRAM	PMEM	Disk read Speed
Sugon I620-G30	4.13.0	2 * Intel Xeon Gold 6230	128 GB	256 GB	195.23 MB/sec

Table 2. Training parameters for AlexNet and ResNet-18 on PMEM

Network	Train Mode	Batch Size	Batch Number	Max Iteration	Dataset
AlexNet	CPU	64	20019	250000	ImageNet
ResNet-18	CPU	32	40037	325000	ImageNet

4.2 Performance Evaluation

In this part, we evaluate the performance of SNC. Intel-Caffe is set to use 20 CPU cores to train the network models. The maximum size of *CacheSize* is related to the capacity of the NVRAM device and the batch size of the data read. In this evaluation, the capacity of the NVRAM device is fixed. Because the batch size of AlexNet is twice that of ResNet-18, the *CacheSize* of AlexNet is half that of ResNet-18. When we set *CacheSize* to 2000 or 5000 for AlexNet, the *CacheSizes* for ResNet-18 are 4000 or 10000, respectively.

The top-1 test accuracy results are shown in Fig. 6. It is clear that, SNC and FNC can help Intel-Caffe realize better training speeds, while keeping the model accuracies without loss.

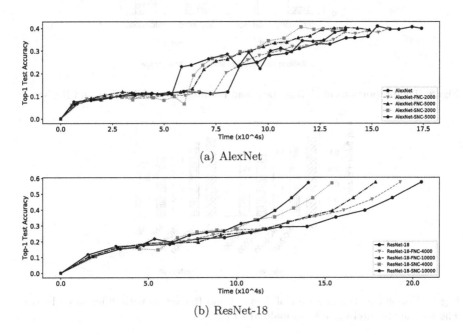

(a) AlexNet

(b) ResNet-18

Fig. 6. Top-1 test accuracy trends of some networks on ImageNet

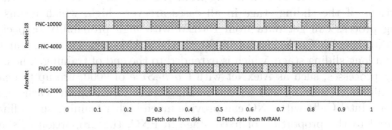

Fig. 7. The proportion of fetching data from NVRAM in FNC

Figure 7 shows the proportion of fetching data from NVRAM in FNC. Because the data cached in NVRAM is fixed, the batches always can be fetched from NVRAM at the beginning of each epoch. This results in stable and regular proportions as shown in this figure.

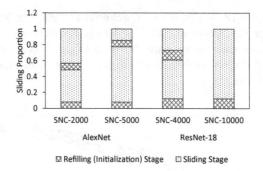

Fig. 8. The proportions of sliding stage and refilling stage of AlexNet and ResNet-18

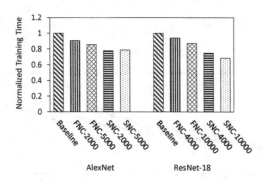

Fig. 9. Normalized training time of AlexNet and ResNet-18 with different cache sizes. The baseline of Intel-Caffe is normalized to 1.

Figure 8 depicts the proportion of the sliding stage when training AlexNet and ResNet-18 with SNC. Benefitting from the large capacity of PMEM, the proportions of the sliding stage in all cases are very high, which means the training process can get data from PMEM with high probability. Especially, for ResNet-18 with *CacheSize* of 10000, the NVRAM cache is large enough to provide a long sliding stage, which is extended to the end of training. The other training processes, such as AlexNet with *CacheSize* of 2000, use up the cache in the middle of training and need a refilling stage to fill up the cache again. Therefore, Intel-Caffe with SNC can provide much higher training speed finally. Compared to the proportion of fixed stage in FNC, the proportion of sliding stage in SNC can be much longer, which can be more efficiency.

Figure 9 shows the final time efficiency of training AlexNet and ResNet-18 with different cache sizes on PMEM. We see that, FNC can reduce the training time of AlexNet by 14.5% with *CacheSize* of 5000. SNC can reduce this time by 21.1%. SNC is not sensitive to the cache size in the training of AlexNet. Whether the *CacheSize* is 2000 or 5000, the time of training is almost identical. For ResNet-18, SNC is far more efficient than FNC. FNC reduces the training time of ResNet-18 by 12.8%, while SNC can reduce it by 24.9% and 31.3%.

5   Conclutions and Future Work

In this paper, we present a NVRAM-based cache strategy (SNC) with a sliding window to break the data I/O bottleneck in DL systems, by leveraging the high reading speed and large capacity of NVRAM. SNC takes the special character-istics of data reading in DL systems into account, and achieves an efficient data prefetch strategy for DL training. Meanwhile SNC can reduce the side effect of relatively slow writing speed of NVRAM by asynchronous data initialization and replacement. We implement SNC on Intel-Caffe. Experimental results show that SNC can improve the time performance of deep neural networks training by more than 30%. In the future, we will conduct more tests about the performance of SNC on the machine equipped with GPUs. Furthermore, we will make some research on fine-grained data prefetch method by focusing on dataset partition to explore NVRAM for DL systems further.

Acknowledgement. This work is supported by National Natural Science Foundation of China under grants No. 61832006 and No. 61672250.

References

1. Abadi, M., et al.: TensorFlow: a system for large-scale machine learning. In: Pro-ceedings of the 12th USENIX Conference on Operating Systems Design and Imple-mentation (OSDI 2016), pp. 265–283. USENIX, Berkeley (2016)
2. Cantalupo, C., Venkatesan, V., Hammond, J., Czurlyo, K., Hammond, S.D.: Memkind: an extensible heap memory manager for heterogeneous memory plat-forms and mixed memory policies. Technical report, Sandia National Lab (SNL-NM), Albuquerque, NM, United States (2015)
3. Deng, J., Dong, W., Socher, R., Li, L., Li, K., Li, F.: ImageNet: a large-scale hierarchical image database. In: Proceedings of the IEEE Conference on Computer Vision and Pattern Recognition (CVPR 2009), pp. 248–255. IEEE, Piscataway (2009)
4. Duan, Z., Liu, H., Liao, X., Jin, H.: HME: a lightweight emulator for hybrid mem-ory. In: Proceedings of Design, Automation & Test in Europe Conference & Exhi-bition (DATE 2018), pp. 1375–1380. IEEE, Piscataway (2018)
5. Eisenman, A., et al.: Bandana: using non-volatile memory for storing deep learning models. arXiv preprint arXiv:1811.05922 (2018)
6. Geng, Q., Zhou, Z., Cao, X.: Survey of recent progress in semantic image segmen-tation with CNNs. SCIENCE CHINA Inf. Sci. **61**(5), 1–18 (2018). 051101
7. Hadjis, S., Abuzaid, F., Zhang, C., Ré, C.: Caffe con Troll: shallow ideas to speed up deep learning. In: Proceedings of the Fourth Workshop on Data Analytics in the Cloud (DanaC 2015), pp. 2:1–4. ACM, New York (2015)
8. Intel Corporation: Intel distribution of Caffe (2019). https://github.com/intel/caffe
9. Izraelevitz, J., et al.: Basic performance measurements of the Intel Optane DC persistent memory module. arXiv preprint arXiv:1903.05714 (2019)
10. Jia, Y., et al.: Caffe: convolutional architecture for fast feature embedding. In: Proceedings of the 22nd ACM International Conference on Multimedia (MM 2014), pp. 675–678. ACM, New York (2014)

11. Peng, I.B., Gokhale, M.B., Green, E.W.: System evaluation of the Intel Optane byte-addressable NVM. In: Proceedings of the International Symposium on Memory Systems (MEMSYS 2019), pp. 304–315. ACM, New York (2019)
12. Poremba, M., Zhang, T., Xie, Y.: NVMain 2.0: a user-friendly memory simulator to model (non-)volatile memory systems. IEEE Comput. Archit. Lett. **14**(2), 140–143 (2015)
13. Pumma, S., Min, S., Feng, W.C., Balaji, P.: Parallel I/O optimizations for scalable deep learning. In: Proceedings of the IEEE 23rd International Conference on Parallel and Distributed Systems (ICPADS 2017), pp. 720–729. IEEE, Los Alamitos (2017)
14. Sreedhar, D., Saxena, V., Sabharwal, Y., Verma, A., Kumar, S.: Efficient training of convolutional neural nets on large distributed systems. In: Proceedings of the International Conference on Cluster Computing (CLUSTER 2018), pp. 392–401. IEEE, Los Alamitos (2018)
15. You, Y., Zhang, Z., Hsieh, C., Demmel, J., Keutzer, K.: ImageNet training in minutes. In: Proceedings of the 47th International Conference on Parallel Processing (ICPP 2018), pp. 1:1–10. ACM, New York (2018)

A Drift Detection Method Based on Diversity Measure and McDiarmid's Inequality in Data Streams

Yuan Xia[1] and Yunlong Zhao[1,2(✉)]

[1] Nanjing University of Aeronautics and Astronautics, Nanjing, Jiangsu, China
zhaoyunlong@nuaa.edu.cn
[2] Collaborative Innovation Center of Novel Software Technology and Industrialization,
Nanjing, Jiangsu, China

Abstract. Mining data stream is an important research topic due to the development of network. The distribution of data in a dynamic environment changes over time, which is a challenging problem called concept drift. Concept drift need to be detected and handled as soon as possible because it can make previous models inaccurate. In this work, we propose a method, called Diversity Measure and McDiarmid Drift Detection Method (dmm-DDM), which combines diversity measure and inequality to detect drift detection. The dmm-DDM approach proceeds by sliding a window over diversity measure result, and associate window value with weights. The algorithm compares the weighted average inside the sliding window with the maximum weighted average. A huge difference between the two weighted averages, calculated by McDiarmin's inequality, proves a concept drift. The experiment results show that the proposed method with less detection delay, less false position and less false negative than most of the compared methods.

Keywords: Concept drift · Data streaming mining · Diversity measure · McDiarmid's inequality

1 Introduction

In the past, data mining algorithms have always been studied in static data sets. However, with the development of the Internet, researchers begin algorithm research on dynamic data streams. This is a challenging task because of data distribution may changes in evolving environment which is called concept drift [1]. Generally, the occurrence of concept drift will cause the performance of the classification model to decrease. To this end, fast adaptation to concept drift is essential to ensure the effectiveness of the algorithm [2]. Typically, classification models are updated or retrained when a drift has been detected. The drift detector needs to detect drift quickly and keep low false negative and false positive to ensure that the update or retrain of the classification algorithm is effective.

Concept drift is an important issue to be considered in data stream mining. In a real environment, the data distribution is constantly changing, and the model needs to be continuously updated to adapt to the new environment.

© Springer Nature Switzerland AG 2020
Z. Yu et al. (Eds.): GPC 2020, LNCS 12398, pp. 115–122, 2020.
https://doi.org/10.1007/978-3-030-64243-3_9

Existing concept drift detection methods can be divided into two types: active methods and passive methods. Active method first monitors the stability of the data distribution by using a clear concept drift detection mechanism, and then triggers a drift adaptation mechanism to adapt the new environment. However, the passive method does not need to detect the occurrence of concept drift, and continuously adjusts the model to adapt the new environment. Gama et al. [2] classified active concept drifts into three groups: (1) sequential analysis-based methods: these methods evaluate the predictions sequentially when they are available, and they send a drift alarm when a predefined threshold is reached. The Cumulative Sum (CUSUM) [4], Page-Hinkley test (PH test) [5] and Diversity Measure as a new Drift Detection Method (DMDDM) [6] are examples of this group. (2) statistical-based methods: these methods analyze statistical parameters, such as the mean and standard deviation associated with the prediction results, to detect concept. The Drift Detection Method (DDM) [7], Early Drift Detection Method (EDDM) [8] and Reactive Drift Detection Method (RDDM) [9] are examples of this group. (3) windows-based methods: these methods usually use a fixed reference window to summarize past information, and a sliding window to summarize recent information. A significant difference between the distribution of these two windows means that a drift has occurred. These methods use statistical tests or mathematical inequalities. The Adaptive Windowing (ADWIN) [10], the SeqDrift detectors [11], the Drift Detection Methods based on Hoeffding's Bound ($HDDM_{A\text{-}test}$ and $HDDM_{W\text{-}test}$) [12] are examples of this group.

In this paper, we introduce the Diversity Measure and McDiarmid Drift Detection Method (dmm-DDM) which calculates the diversity of classifier responses based on continuously incoming data to rapidly and efficiently detect concept drift. dmm-DDM does not monitor error predictions, but instead monitors the diversity of a pair of classifiers. Then dmm-DDM uses sliding window and McDiarmid's inequality [3] to calculate and compare the diversity measure results. The experiment results show that the dmm-DDM algorithm produces less detection delay, less false positive and less false negative than other methods.

2   The Diversity Measure and McDiarmid Drift Detection Method

In a data stream environment where concept drift exists, most supervised concept drift detection methods analyze the accuracy of the model and its corresponding standard deviation, and then use window functions or cumulative values to predict whether drift occurs. However, the performance of the above methods is seriously affected by the noise point and the performance of the classifier, we try to replace the accuracy of a single classifier with a diversity measure of multiple classifiers.

In this section, we introduce the diversity measure and McDiarmid drift detection method (dmm-DDM) which is windows-based method. This method adds the diversity measure results to the sliding window, then assigns higher weights to the nearest results. Finally, the weighting scheme is used in the sliding window to detect drift faster.

2.1   Diversity Measure

Diversity is an important feature of ensemble classifiers in static data. Measuring diversity is used to analyze the effectiveness of the ensemble classifier method. Therefore, many researchers consider diversity to prune a number of component classifiers [13]. [14] researches the effect of using diversity on online ensemble learning. In this paper, we replace the classification accuracy with the diversity of component classifiers to detect concept drift. Diversity measure is used to measure the diversity of individual classifiers in ensemble.

We define diversity measure based on the prediction results of the same training data by two different classifiers h_i and h_j. In our paper, if $h_i = h_j$, the diversity measure result is 1, Otherwise the result is 0.

2.2 Drift Detection Method

The dmm-DDM slides a window of size n over the diversity measure result. It inserts diversity measure result into the window. Each element in the sliding window is associated with a weight w_i. In order to pay more attention to the later data, we need to ensure that $w_i < w_{i+1}$. we define $w_i = 1 + (i - 1) * d$, where $d \geq 0$ is a constant representing the difference between the two weights. The size of the sliding window is n. When a new data arrives, if the sliding window is not full, the calculated diversity measure result can be directly filled into the sliding window. If the content in the sliding window is full, we remove the diversity measure result that originally entered the sliding window, and then fill the newly obtained diversity measure result at the end of the sliding window. Finally, we calculate the weighted average μ_t in the sliding window at the current moment and the maximum weighted average μ_{max} observed so far. μ_{max} is calculated as follow:

$$if\ \mu_t > \mu_{max} \Rightarrow \mu_{max} = \mu_t \tag{1}$$

Where $\mu_t = \sum_{i=1}^{n} w_i \cdot D_i$. As the data in the data stream is processed one by one, the algorithm will continuously update μ_t and μ_{max}. A significant difference between μ_t and μ_{max} means the emergence of a concept drift.

On the basis of the PAC learning model [15], if the data distribution remains stable, the error rate of the model will decrease as the number of training sample increases. The predictions of a pair of component classifiers (h_i and h_j) are becoming more and more consistent. Thus, the value of μ_{max} should increase or keep constant. In other words, when the predictions of component classifiers (h_i and h_j) start to be inconsistent in an unusual way, the probability of concept drift increases and μ_t decrease over time. A significant difference between μ_t and μ_{max} indicates a drift:

$$if\ \mu_{max} - \mu_t \geq \varepsilon \Rightarrow Drift = true \tag{2}$$

The significant difference ε is determined by the McDiarmid's inequality [3]. Once the concept drift is found, we will reset μ_{max} and classifiers.

2.3 McDiarmid's Inequality

The McDiarMid's inequality is defined as follows: let $X_1, X_2, \ldots, X_n$ be n independent random variables. If a function $f : \chi^n \to \mathbb{R}$ can find a constant c_i for all i and satisfied the following for the following formula:

$$\left| f(X_1, X_2, \ldots, X_i, \ldots, X_n) - f(X_1, X_2, \ldots, X_i', \ldots, X_n) \right| \leq c_i \tag{3}$$

The above formula shows that for the function $f : \chi^n \to \mathbb{R}$, if any X is replaced, the change of the function value will not exceed the constant c_i. Therefore, for any $\varepsilon > 0$.

Algorithm 1: Diversity Measure and McDiarmid Drift Detection Method (dmm-DDM)

Require: S: data stream (labelled)
    (n, δ) = (windowSize, confidence level delta)
    win = []//win represent a sliding window
    $\mu_{max} = 0$

$\varepsilon = \boxtimes \sqrt{\dfrac{\sum_{i=1}^{n}(\frac{w_i}{\sum_{i=1}^{n}w_i})^2}{2}} \ln\frac{1}{\delta}$

Result: drift $\in$ {TRUE, FALSE}
for each example $X^t \in$ S **do**
    u = h_u prediction using X^t
    v = h_v prediction using X^t
    if (u == v) **then**
        D = 1
    else
        D = 0
    if (win.size == n) **then**
        win.pop()
    win.push(D)
    if (win.size < n) **then**
        return FALSE
    else
        $\mu_t = \sum_{i=1}^{n}(D_i \cdot w_i)/\sum_{i=1}^{n} w_i$
        if $(\mu_{max} < \mu_t)$ **then**
            $\mu_{max} = \mu_t$
        $\Delta\mu = \mu_{max} - \mu_t$
        if $(\Delta\mu > \varepsilon)$ **then**
            return TRUE
        else
            return FALSE
    Incrementally train h_v and h_u with X^t

Mcdiarmid's inequality gives a probability bound:

$$\Pr\{f - E[f] > \varepsilon\} \leq \exp\left(-\frac{2\varepsilon^2}{\sum_{i=1}^{n} c_i^2}\right) \tag{4}$$

Therefore, given a confidence level δ, the threshold is calculated by:

$$\varepsilon = \sqrt{\frac{\sum_{i=1}^{n} c_i^2}{2} \ln\frac{1}{\delta}} \tag{5}$$

Where c_i is given by:

$$c_i = \frac{w_i}{\sum_{i=1}^{n} w_i} \tag{6}$$

The number n represents the size of the sliding window, and w_i is the weight of the sliding window. When the difference between μ_t and μ_{max} is greater than the threshold ε, a drift signal is issued. The dmm-DDM algorithm pseudocode is presented in Algorithm 1.

2.4 Parameters Analysis

The parameter δ is inversely proportional to ε, which means that as δ decreases, the value of ε increases and the boundary becomes conservative. Decreasing δ may lead to a reduction in false positives and an increase in false negative. The parameter d controls the proportion of weight assigned to the sliding window element. Larger d values result in faster concept drift detection because higher weights are assigned to the latest elements; however, the false positive may increase.

3   Experiment Evaluation

We compare the proposed dmm-DDM with other methods, namely DDM, EDDM, DMDDM, PH test and ADWIN. Next we will discuss experiment datasets, settings, analysis and results.

Synthetic Data Streams. We generated three synthetic data streams, SINE1, MIXED, LED. These data streams were generated by the data stream generators in MOA (Massive Online Analysis). MOA [18] is a very popular framework for data stream analysis. It includes tools for evaluation and a collection of machine learning algorithms. There are abrupt drifts in SINE1 and MIXED, and gradual drifts in LED. Each of the above data streams contains 100,000 instances. Each data stream also contains 10% noise in order to evaluate the robustness of the drift detectors. The advantage of using synthetic data stream is that we know where the concept drift points in the data stream. We set the transition length between two concepts. In the abrupt concept drift, we set the transition length to 50. In the gradual concept drift, we set the transition length to 500. In our experiment, the drifts occur at every 20000 instances in SINE1 and MIXED for abrupt drift, and at every 25,000 instances in LED for gradual drift.

Real-World Data Streams. We extended the experiments to the real-world data stream, Electricity [16], Forest covertype [17] and Poker hand.

In dmm-DDM and DMDDM, we used Hoeffding tree (HT) and Perceptron (PER) as incremental classifiers. These two classifiers have good effects as heterogeneous classifiers in this paper. In DDM, EDDM, PH test and ADWIN, we used HT as the incremental classifier. And in the above methods all use HT to detect the accuracy.

Our work proposes a drift detector. We use delay detection, true positive, false positive, false negative and accuracy to evaluate the performance of drift detectors in synthetic data streams. In real-world data streams, we use alarm and accuracy to evaluate the performance of drift detectors.

The symbol Δ represents an acceptable drift delay. Δ has been set to 1000 on SINE1 and MIXED, and 2000 on LED. In our experiments, we set the following parameters:

$n = 100, d = 0.01, \delta = 10^{-10}$. Experiments were performed on an Intel Core i7 @ 2.6 GHz with 16 GB of RAM running macOS Catalina.

Table 1 shows the experimental results on synthetic data streams. In SINE1, the result shows that all detectors have correctly detected all drift points, and there are no false negatives. But only dmm-DDM method and ADWIN method have no false positives. And for delay detection and classifier accuracy, the dmm-DDM algorithm has the lowest delay and the highest classifier accuracy. In MIXED, dmm-DDM, DDM, ADWIN and PH detect all drift points. For false positive. Only DDM and ADWIN do not have false positives. dmm-DDM has the lowest delay and the highest classifier accuracy. In LED, dmm-DDM, DDM and ADWIN detect all drift points. ADWIN also have the highest false positives. dmm-DDM has the lowest delay, and dmm-DDM and DDM have the highest classifier accuracy. The results show that compared with other algorithms, the dmm-DDM algorithm can detect the drift in the shortest time and make the classifier have the highest accuracy.

Table 1. Results of experiments on synthetic datasets (10% noise)

	Classifier	Detectors	Delay (sample)	TP	FP	FN	Accuracy
SINE1	HT&PER	dmm-DDM	79	4	0	0	87.09%
		DMDDM	543.75	4	3	0	85.54%
	HT	DDM	141	4	6	0	86.48%
		EDDM	570.75	4	42	0	84.57%
		ADWIN	209	4	0	0	86.72%
		PH test	755.25	4	2	0	85.07%
MIXED	HT&PER	dmm-DDM	70	4	1	0	83.26%
		DMDDM	666	3	1	1	81.44%
	HT	DDM	169.75	4	0	0	83.05%
		EDDM	925	1	8	3	80.50%
		ADWIN	297	4	0	0	82.72%
		PH test	815.5	4	1	0	81.35%
LED	HT&PER	dmm-DDM	256.33	3	0	0	89.63%
		DMDDM	533.5	2	1	1	89.18%
	HT	DDM	430.67	3	0	0	89.54%
		EDDM	751	1	1	2	80.50%
		ADWIN	631.3	3	422	0	69.94%
		PH test	1571.5	2	1	1	88.43%

In real-world datasets, we cannot use the delay detection, true positive, false positive and false negative to detect drift points, because we do not know whether drifts occur in these datasets or where they occur. Therefore, we evaluate the performance of the drift detectors by the number of drifts detected and the accuracy of the classification.

Table 2 shows the experimental results on Electricity, Forest Covertype and Poker-Hand. In Electricity, DDM and EDDM have the highest accuracy, but they also have the highest number of alarms. In Forest Covertype and Poker-Hand, EDDM has the highest accuracy and a highest number of alarms. Our proposed method dmm-DDM has a higher accuracy and a lower number of alarms. Result shows that drift detection methods with more alarms often lead to higher classification accuracy. The dmm-DDM has higher accuracy in the case of a lower number of alarms, indicating that the algorithm has a good effect on the real-world data streams.

Table 2. Results of experiments on real-world datasets

Classifier	Detectors	Electricity		Forest covertype		Poker-hand	
		Alarms	Accuracy	Alarms	Accuracy	Alarms	Accuracy
HT&PER	dmm-DDM	41	83.15%	654	83.00%	1074	73.85%
	DMDDM	5	81.16%	16	82.07%	111	64.88%
HT	DDM	194	84.82%	1686	82.02%	1804	72.22%
	EDDM	183	84.77%	2217	84.91%	4615	76.49%
	ADWIN	46	82.45%	735	82.17%	819	71.39%
	PH test	57	81.93%	173	82.98%	1441	70.52%

4 Conclusion

In this paper, we introduce a new concept drift detector called dmm-DDM. This method uses the diversity of a pair of classifiers as a result and combines it with sliding windows and McDiarmid's inequality to detect drift. We use three synthetic datasets and three real-world datasets to evaluate the algorithm. The results indicate that on the synthetic datasets, the proposed method dmm-DDM can detect drift with lowest delay and has highest accuracy. dmm-DDM also has satisfactory results on TP, FP and FN. On the real-world datasets, our method has higher accuracy and a lower number of alarms than other methods.

Acknowledgements. This research was supported by Defense Industrial Technology Development Program under Grant No. JCKY2016605B006, Six talent peaks project in Jiangsu Province under Grant No. XYDXXJS-031.

References

1. Lu, J., Liu, A., Dong, F., et al.: Learning under concept drift: a review. IEEE Trans. Knowl. Data Eng. (2018)

2. Gama, J., Žliobaitė, I., Bifet, A., et al.: A survey on concept drift adaptation. ACM Comput. Surv. (CSUR) **46**(4), 44 (2014)
3. McDiarmid, C.: On the method of bounded differences. Surv. Comb. **141**(1), 148–188 (1989)
4. Basseville, M., Nikiforov, I.V.: Detection of Abrupt Changes: Theory and Application. Prentice Hall, Englewood Cliffs (1993)
5. Gama, J., Sebastião, R., Rodrigues, P.P.: On evaluating stream learning algorithms. Mach. Learn. **90**(3), 317–346 (2013)
6. Mahdi, O.A., Pardede, E., Ali, N., et al.: Diversity measure as a new drift detection method in data streaming. Knowl.-Based Syst. 105227 (2019)
7. Gama, J., Medas, P., Castillo, G., Rodrigues, P.: Learning with drift detection. In: Bazzan, A.L.C., Labidi, S. (eds.) SBIA 2004. LNCS (LNAI), vol. 3171, pp. 286–295. Springer, Heidelberg (2004). https://doi.org/10.1007/978-3-540-28645-5_29
8. Baena-García, M., del Campo-Ávila, J., Fidalgo, R., et al.: Early drift detection method. In: Fourth International Workshop on Knowledge Discovery from Data Streams, vol. 6, pp. 77–86 (2006)
9. Barros, R.S.M., Cabral, D.R.L., Gonçalves Jr., P.M., et al.: RDDM: reactive drift detection method. Expert Syst. Appl. **90**, 344–355 (2017)
10. Bifet, A., Gavalda, R.: Learning from time-changing data with adaptive windowing. In: Proceedings of the 2007 SIAM International Conference on Data Mining. Society for Industrial and Applied Mathematics, pp. 443–448 (2007)
11. Pears, R., Sakthithasan, S., Koh, Y.S.: Detecting concept change in dynamic data streams. Mach. Learn. **97**(3), 259–293 (2014)
12. Frías-Blanco, I., del Campo-Ávila, J., Ramos-Jimenez, G., et al.: Online and non-parametric drift detection methods based on Hoeffding's bounds. IEEE Trans. Knowl. Data Eng. **27**(3), 810–823 (2014)
13. Banfield, R.E., Hall, L.O., Bowyer, K.W., Kegelmeyer, W.P.: A new ensemble diversity measure applied to thinning ensembles. In: Windeatt, T., Roli, F. (eds.) MCS 2003. LNCS, vol. 2709, pp. 306–316. Springer, Heidelberg (2003). https://doi.org/10.1007/3-540-44938-8_31
14. Minku, L.L., White, A.P., Yao, X.: The impact of diversity on online ensemble learning in the presence of concept drift. IEEE Trans. Knowl. Data Eng. **22**(5), 730–742 (2009)
15. Mitchell, T.M.: Machine Learning, vol. 45, no. 37, pp. 870–877. McGraw Hill, Burr Ridge (1997)
16. Zliobaite, I.: How good is the electricity benchmark for evaluating concept drift adaptation. arXiv preprint arXiv:1301.3524 (2013)
17. Blackard, J.A., Dean, D.J.: Comparative accuracies of artificial neural networks and discriminant analysis in predicting forest cover types from cartographic variables. Comput. Electron. Agric. **24**(3), 131–151 (1999)
18. Bifet, A., Holmes, G., Kirkby, R., et al.: MOA: massive online analysis. J. Mach. Learn. Res. **11**(2), 1601–1604 (2010)

An Improved Sparse Representation Classifier Based on Data Augmentation for Time Series Classification

Juhong Lu[1,2], Fangwan Huang[1,2(✉)], and Zhiyong Yu[1,2,3]

[1] College of Mathematics and Computer Science, Fuzhou University, Fuzhou, China
hfw@fzu.edu.cn
[2] Fujian Provincial Key Laboratory of Network Computing and Intelligent Information Processing, Fuzhou University, Fuzhou, China
[3] Key Laboratory of Spatial Data Mining & Information Sharing, Ministry of Education, Fuzhou, China

Abstract. Sparse Representation-based Classification (SRC), which has achieved good performance in face recognition and other image classification, has been successfully extended to time series classification in recent years. As a generalization of the nearest subspace classifier, the performance of SRC depends on a rich set of training samples for each class, which can span as many variations of each class as possible under testing conditions. However, due to the difficulty of sample collection, many important applications can only provide a few or even a single sample for each class, which inevitably affects the performance of SRC. To address the problem of insufficient training samples, ESRC (Extended SRC) was proposed to put some samples that reflect the variations within the class into the dictionary, to obtain better generalization ability than SRC for under-sampled face recognition. In this paper, a new approach IESRC (Improved extend sparse representation based classification) is developed by splitting the dictionary into an original dictionary and auxiliary dictionary. The proposed model was first evaluated in 30 baseline data sets in the University of California, Riverside time series classification archive and then applied to classify the effects of aerobic exercise intervention in 24 young hypertensive patients based on the time series of the cardiopulmonary exercise test. Experimental results show that the proposed model can achieve better performance than SRC and ESRC in time series classification.

Keywords: Time series classification · Data augmentation · Sparse representation

1 Introduction

Time series classification has received growing research attention over recent years. There is both anecdotal and empirical evidence suggesting that dynamic time warping (DTW) combined with classifiers such as k nearest neighbor (KNN) has achieved good results in time series classification. Additionally, feature-based methods, such as the Bag-of-Words (BoW) [1], finding out whether a feature in the time series matches the existing

© Springer Nature Switzerland AG 2020
Z. Yu et al. (Eds.): GPC 2020, LNCS 12398, pp. 123–130, 2020.
https://doi.org/10.1007/978-3-030-64243-3_10

bag-of-words, represent a sequence with words, etc., fills the time series classification research gap. Inspired by face recognition in computer vision, sparse representation-based classification (SRC), by representing the test sample in an overcomplete dictionary (or directly training samples) and exploiting the discriminative nature of sparse representation to perform classification [2], has been successfully extended to time series classification. Recently, with the advent of the deep learning boom, many researchers have applied neural networks to time series classification such as convolutional neural networks (CNN), multi-channel CNN (MC-CNN) [3], multi-scale CNN (MCNN) [4], LSTM_FCN [5], etc. So many methods have been proposed, which enough to explain the importance of time series classification, and Bagnall et al. [6] summarized and evaluated some of the state-of-art time series classification methods.

Despite this emphasis on time series classification model which requires large amounts of labeled training samples to make work effective, surprisingly little is known about time series augmentation, which strengthens model generalization ability in the case that training sets are insufficient. The way to data augmentation has two main ideas, synthesizing and modification. Forestier et al. [7] proposed a method for generating a set of synthetic time series by averaging combined with varying weights evolves new time series from a dataset. It has focused research attention on a limited set of generating, the applicability of synthetic samples has received little consideration. Kegel et al. [8] proposed a feature-based generation method that evolves cross-domain time-series datasets and presented a similarity measure to assess the applicability of synthetic samples generated by other methods. The other idea to data augmentation, for instance, Le Guennec et al. [9] proposed to stretch or shrink randomly selected slices of a time series by speeding it up or down referred to as window warping (WW). For face recognition and image processing, the second idea is more widely used, such as flip, rotation, scale, crop, translation, etc. Additionally, to overcome the problem that training samples are insufficient, Deng et al. [10] proposed to extend SRC (ESRC), by appending an intra-class dictionary that reflects the variations within the class to the training samples.

In this paper, we proposed to improve extend SRC (IESRC) to address the problem of insufficient samples in time series classification. We first present experiments using 30 datasets whose training samples are less than 100 on the UCR archive [11] to assess our approach. The experiments show that the proposed model is very competitive with other traditional classification methods in case of insufficient training samples. In the second part, the proposed model applied to classify the effects of aerobic exercise intervention in 24 young hypertensive patients based on the time series of the cardiopulmonary exercise test. We show that the proposed model can achieve better performance than SRC and ESRC in time series classification. Therefore, this study fills an existing time series data augmentation research gap by proposing an improved model, and thus, it has the potential to contribute to providing a new idea for time series augmentation.

2 SRC and ESRC

Sparse representation, as a research hotspot in recent years, is actually a decomposition process of the original signal. This process relies on an overcomplete dictionary, which is prepared in advance, and the linear representation of a testing sample y can be written as

$$y = Ax + z \tag{1}$$

The training set is denoted as $A = [A_1, A_2, \ldots, A_i] \in \mathbf{R}^{M \times N}$ which is usually an over complete dictionary (or original training set when training samples are insufficient), where $A_i \in \mathbf{R}^M$ ($i = 1, 2, \ldots, N$) denotes the ith training sample, and x is the coefficient vector whose entries are zeros except those associated with class, z is a noise term. The purpose of SRC is to seek the sparest solution to $y = Ax$, where $x = [x_1, x_2, \ldots, x_N]^T$ and x_i denotes the representation coefficient corresponding to the ith training sample, by solving the following optimization problem

$$\hat{x}_1 = argmin\|x\|_1 \quad s.t. \quad \|Ax - y\| \leq \varepsilon \tag{2}$$

In Extend SRC(ESRC) proposed by Deng et al. [10], the test samples can be represented by the dictionary A and the intra-class variant dictionary shared by all samples, the model (1) can be modified to account for large variation between the training and test samples by writing

$$y = Ax + D_1\beta + z \tag{3}$$

where the intra-class variant dictionary D_I can be constructed by two methods as following.

$$D_I^{(1)} = [D_1 - c_1 e_1, D_2 - c_2 e_2, \ldots, D_l - c_l e_l] \in \mathbf{R}^{d \times n} \tag{4}$$

where $e_i = [1, 1, \ldots, 1] \in \mathbf{R}^{1 \times n_i}$, c_i is the class centroid of class i.

$$D_I^{(2)} = [P_1, P_2, \ldots, P_l] \in \mathbf{R}^{d \times \sum_i [n_i(n_i-1)/2]} \tag{5}$$

where $P_i \in \mathbf{R}^{d \times [n_i(n_i-1)/2]}$ is the pairwise difference time series between the samples of class i.

Then, x and β are the sparse representation coefficients respectively associated with A and D_I, the ESRC aims to resolve the following problem

$$\begin{bmatrix} \hat{x}_1 \\ \hat{\beta}_1 \end{bmatrix} = argmin\|\begin{bmatrix} x \\ \beta \end{bmatrix}\|_1, \quad s.t.\|[A, D_I]\begin{bmatrix} x \\ \beta \end{bmatrix} - y\|_2 \leq \varepsilon \tag{6}$$

where ε is the error tolerance.

3 Improved Extend SRC

In face recognition, the intra-class variant basis which is the atoms of dictionary D_I in model (3) can be shared by other faces, which means all face have similar features. These features can be regarded as the basic faces of all kinds of samples. For instance, a facial image with disguise and sidelight can be approximated by a natural (training) image of this person plus a variant basis image of another person [10]. Time series as one of the simplest data, it should be noted that there are differences among the intra-class variation bases from different class samples. The intra-class variation which reflect the differences of similar samples cannot be shared by all time-series data set. An auxiliary dictionary constructed by Eqs. (4) or (5) should be apart from dictionary A, which means the status of two dictionaries are different, and the atoms of an auxiliary dictionary are divide by class.

Thus, instead that a test sample is represented by two dictionaries together, it should be presented by two dictionaries respectively. The residual is computed by the two sparse representation vectors associated with class i. Although it does not extend the training sample directly, it increases the tolerance of the difference between training samples and test samples from one class in the case of deficiency, which also improves the generalization ability of the model. Improve extend sparse representation classification (IESRC) enhanced the data of time series from another perspective compared with the ERSC, which should be more suitable for time series.

Algorithm: Improve Extend Sparse Representation Classification

1: **Input:** a matrix of training set $A = [A_1, A_2, \ldots, A_k] \in \mathbf{R}^{d \times n}$ for k class, a matrix of intra-class auxiliary dictionary $D_I \in \mathbf{R}^{d \times p}$ constructed by (4) or (5), a test sample $y \in \mathbf{R}^d$, and two optional error tolerance $\varepsilon_1 > 0$ and $\varepsilon_2 > 0$.

2: Normalize the columns of A and D_I to have unit l^2-norm.

3: Solve the L1-minimization problem

$$\hat{x}_1 = argmin\|x\|_1 \quad s.t. \quad \|Ax - y\| \le \varepsilon_1 \tag{7}$$

$$\hat{\beta}_1 = argmin\|\beta\|_1 \quad s.t. \quad \|D_I\beta - y\| \le \varepsilon_2 \tag{8}$$

4: Compute the residuals

$$r_i(y) = \left\|y - A\delta_i(\hat{x}_1)\right\|_2 + \left\|y - D_I\theta_i(\hat{\beta}_1))\right\|_2 \tag{9}$$

for $i = 1, 2, \ldots, k$, where $\delta_i(\hat{x}_1) \in \mathbf{R}$ is the sparse representation vector only associated with class i in dictionary A, and $\theta_i\left(\hat{\beta}_1\right) \in \mathbf{R}$ is the sparse representation vector associated with class i in auxiliary dictionary D_I.

5: **Output:**

$$Label(y) = argmin_i r_i(y) \tag{10}$$

4   Experimental Results

In this section, we will verify the effectiveness of our proposed model IESRC though conducting two experiments on the UCR archive [11] which includes 30 baseline time-series datasets whose training sets is less than 100, to compare with other methods, and classifying 24 young hypertensive patients based on the time series of the cardiopulmonary exercise test. In the first part, we have implemented SRC [3] and ESRC [10] both based on the L1 norm minimization [12] in time series classification, for comparison. All the dataset has been split into training and testing by default. The optimal error tolerance ε in Eqs. (2), (6), (7) and (8) is set to 5~1 and 1~1e-6. The best result of classification is chosen to be within one of these error ranges. In the second part, the proposed model compared with SRC and ESRC, and all based on the OMP [13]. The preprocessing in our experiment is the linear interpolation on the data set whose samples have unequal dimensions and l2-normalization on both training and test split. All the experiments are run on a platform with 2.5 GHz CPU and 8.0 GB RAM using Matlab R2017a software.

4.1 Experiments on UCR Archive

We select 1NN-ED and 1NN-DTW, which have achieved good results in time series classification, as a simple standard baseline in comparison. In Table 1, the classifying error rate for 30 sub data set in which training samples are insufficient in UCR archive [11] is provided.

Table 1 shows that IESRC generally perform better than ESRC and SRC over the 30 data sets. The arithmetic average rank of error rate on ESRC (I) whose D_I dictionary constructed by Eq. (4) is 0.1769 and ESRC (II) whose D_I dictionary constructed by Eq. (5) is 0.1877, which is higher than IESRC (I) and IESCR (II) is 0.1780 and 0.1748 respectively. The number of WIN on SRC and ESRC (II) which has the smallest error rate when compared with other methods in a certain data set is 8, which is highest among other classification methods. Experiment results show that IESRC is very competitive. In contrast, 1NN-ED and 1NN-DTW will not perform as well as IESRC, ESRC, and SRC in the case of insufficient training samples.

4.2 Experiments on Predicting the Effect of Aerobic Exercise Intervention on 24 Young Patients with Hypertension

The experiment selects the data of 24 adolescent hypertension patients during the exercise phase in a single CPET before treatment, the sampling time series of 9 indicators, including heart rate (HR), stroke volume (SV), cardiac output (Qt), oxygen pulse (VO2/HR), oxygen consumption per kilogram (VO2/kg), tidal volume (VT), ventilation per minute (VE), respiratory exchange rate (R), and carbon dioxide ventilation equivalent (VE/VCO2).

The prediction of the hypotensive effect of aerobic exercise in patients can be regarded as a classification problem, and classify those patients with good hypotensive effects after treatment into one class and general effects fall into another class. Due to each indicator has only 24 time-series, corresponding to 24 patients. When predicting the hypertensive effect of aerobic exercise intervention for each patient, the other 23 patients are used as training samples, and themselves as a test sample.

4.2.1 Evaluating Indicator

The confusion matrix is considered as the evaluating method. The value of F1-Score ranges from 0 to 1, with 1 representing the best model output and 0 representing the worst model output.

Table 1. Testing error for 30 ucr time series dataset.

Error rate	SRC	ESRC (II)	ESRC (I)	IESRC (II)	IESRC (I)	ED	DTW
ArrowHead	**0.166**	0.171	0.171	0.189	0.189	0.200	0.297
BirdChicken	**0.150**	0.200	**0.150**	**0.150**	**0.150**	0.450	0.250
Car	0.117	0.117	0.117	**0.100**	0.117	0.267	0.267
CinCECGTorso	**0.021**	0.176	0.049	0.026	0.025	0.103	0.349
DiatomSizeReduction	**0.023**	0.029	**0.023**	**0.023**	**0.023**	0.065	0.033
ECGFiveDays	**0.029**	0.036	**0.029**	0.041	0.036	0.203	0.232
FaceFour	0.171	**0.136**	0.148	0.182	0.171	0.216	0.171
GunPoint	0.060	0.060	0.060	0.060	**0.053**	0.087	0.093
Herring	0.391	**0.359**	0.391	0.375	0.375	0.484	0.469
ItalyPowerDemand	0.040	0.034	**0.027**	0.042	0.040	0.045	0.050
Lightning2	0.262	0.279	0.262	0.246	0.262	0.246	**0.131**
Lightning7	0.329	0.384	0.343	0.384	0.370	0.425	**0.274**
Mallat	0.081	0.081	0.081	0.077	0.081	0.086	**0.066**
Meat	**0.017**	**0.017**	**0.017**	**0.017**	**0.017**	0.067	0.067
MoteStrain	0.118	0.125	0.129	0.119	**0.116**	0.121	0.165
OliveOil	**0.033**	**0.033**	**0.033**	**0.033**	**0.033**	0.133	0.167
ShapeletSim	0.472	**0.456**	0.467	0.472	0.461	0.461	0.350
SonyAIBORobotSurface1	0.243	**0.233**	0.236	0.243	0.243	0.305	0.275
SonyAIBORobotSurface2	0.125	**0.122**	0.124	0.128	0.123	0.141	0.169
Symbols	0.087	0.129	0.118	0.110	0.108	0.101	**0.050**
ToeSegmentation1	0.338	0.439	0.417	0.368	0.355	0.320	**0.228**
ToeSegmentation2	0.231	**0.154**	0.300	0.246	0.223	0.192	0.162
TwoLeadECG	0.074	0.070	0.080	0.063	**0.062**	0.253	0.096
Wine	0.167	0.167	0.167	0.167	0.167	0.389	0.426
BME	0.200	0.133	**0.093**	0.140	0.133	0.167	0.100
DodgerLoopDay	0.488	0.475	0.475	0.488	0.488	**0.450**	0.500
DodgerLoopWeekend	0.036	0.044	0.051	0.044	0.044	**0.015**	0.051
FreezerSmallTrain	0.313	0.314	0.313	0.316	0.316	0.324	**0.241**
Rock	**0.140**	0.180	0.160	**0.140**	0.160	0.160	0.400
UMD	0.347	0.479	0.278	0.354	0.306	0.236	**0.007**
WIN	**8**	**8**	7	6	7	2	7
Arithmetic average rank	0.1755	0.1877	0.1769	0.1780	**0.1748**	0.2237	0.2045

Figure 1 shows that the F1-score of IESRC (I) and IESRC (II) are higher than ESRC and SRC in the VO2/HR, HR, SV, VE/VCO2, and VT indicator. ESRC (I) and ESRC (II) has no obvious improvement, moreover, the F1-score had decreased in VE and HR compared to SRC. More intuitively, these methods are arithmetically averaged at the F1-score of the nine indicators, as shown in the AVG in Fig. 1. One can see that the effects of classifying aerobic exercise intervention in 24 young hypertensive patients by IESRC is better, compare with ESRC and SRC.

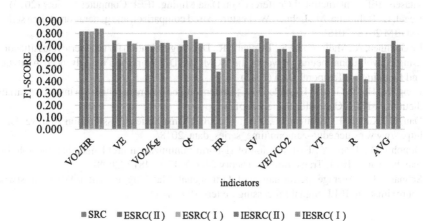

Fig. 1. The f1-score of predicting the effect of aerobic exercise intervention on 24 young patients with hypertension.

5   Conclusion

Time series classification has received growing research attention over recent years. However, the research to date has tended to focus on classification rather than data augmentation. In this paper, we propose IESRC to solve the problem of insufficient training set in time series classification. Our experimental results show that IESRC has some effects for insufficient training set problem in time series classification, which also inspired us to improve the generalization ability in the data set lacking training samples by improving the existing classification model.

References

1. Lin, J., Keogh, E., Wei, L., et al.: Experiencing sax: a novel symbolic representation of time series. Data Min. Knowl. Disc. **15**(2), 107–144 (2007)
2. Wright, J., Yang, A.Y., Ganesh, A., Sastry, S.S., et al.: Robust face recognition via sparse representation. IEEE PAMI **31**(2), 210–227 (2009)
3. Zheng, Y., Liu, Q., Chen, E., Ge, Y., Zhao, J.L.: Exploiting multi-channels deep convolutional neural networks for multivariate time series classification. Front. Comput. Sci. **10**(1), 96–112 (2016). https://doi.org/10.1007/s11704-015-4478-2

4. Cui, Z., Chen, W., Chen, Y.: Multi-scale convolutional neural networks for time series classification. arXiv preprint arXiv:1603.06995 (2016)
5. Karim, F., Majumdar, S., Darabi, H., et al.: LSTM fully convolutional networks for time series classification. IEEE Access **99**(1), 1662–1669 (2017)
6. Bagnall, A., Lines, J., Bostrom, A., et al.: The great time series classification bake off: a review and experimental evaluation of recent algorithmic advances. Data Min. Knowl. Disc. **31**(3), 606–660 (2016)
7. Forestier, G., Petitjean, F., Dau, H.A., et al.: Generating synthetic time series to augment sparse satasets. IEEE International Conference on Data Mining, IEEE Computer Society (2017)
8. Kegel, L., Hahmann, M., Lehner, W.: Feature-based comparison and generation of time series. SSDBM 2018 (2018)
9. Le Guennec, A., Malinowski, S., Tavenard, R.: Data augmentation for time series classification using convolutional neural networks. In: ECML/PKDD Workshop on Advanced Analytics and Learning on Temporal Data (2016)
10. Deng, W., Hu, J., Guo, J.: Extended SRC: Undersampled face recognition via intraclass variant dictionary. IEEE Computer Society (2012)
11. Dau, H., Keogh, E., Kamgar, K., et al.: The UCR Time Series Classification Archive. URL https://www.cs.ucr.edu/~eamonn/time_series_data_2018/
12. Donoho, D., Tsaig, Y.: Fast solution of l1-norm minimization problems when the solution may be sparse. IEEE Trans. Inform. Theory **54**(11), 4789–4812 (2008)
13. Schnass, K.: Average performance of Orthogonal Matching Pursuit (OMP) for sparse approximation. IEEE Signal Processing Letters, (99), 1–1

Concept Stability Based Isolated Maximal Cliques Detection in Dynamic Social Networks

Jie Gao[1], Fei Hao[1,2(✉)], Erhe Yang[1], Yixuan Yang[1], and Geyong Min[2]

[1] School of Computer Science, Shaanxi Normal University, Xi'an, China
{jaygao,fhao,erhyang,yxyang}@snnu.edu.cn
[2] Department of Computer Science, University of Exeter, Exeter, UK

Abstract. As the network security gradually deviates from the virtual environment to the real environment, the security problems caused by abnormal users in social networks are becoming increasingly prominent. These abnormal users usually form a group which can be regarded as an isolated network. This paper aims to detect the isolated maximal cliques from a dynamic social network for identifying the abnormal users in order to cut off the source of fake information in time. By virtue of concept stability, an isolated maximal clique detection approach is proposed. Experimental results shown that the proposed algorithm has a high F-measure value for detecting the isolated maximal cliques in social network.

Keywords: Isolated maximal clique · Concept stability · Formal Concept Analysis

1 Introduction

5G technology not only will comprehensively promote the development of the Internet of Things, big data and artificial intelligence, but also will further enhance the degree of integration between the network and the entity. Thus, network security will gradually deviate from the virtual environment and move to the real environment. For instance, the security problems caused by abnormal users in social networks are becoming increasingly prominent. By establishing a large number of fake users and stealing normal users, criminals push fake advertisements or phishing websites on social networks, and organize "water army" to post malicious comments. Incidents of normal users being deceived in social networks often occur, causing that normal users have a crisis of trust in social networks. In fact, abnormal users usually have some hidden common characteristics. For example, the IP addresses of some abnormal users are the same. Therefore, identifying and detecting abnormal users to ensure user safety in social networks is a key issue by data mining and other techniques.

Actually, these abnormal users usually have the following characteristics: 1) abnormal users usually rarely establish contact with normal users; 2) there are

Z. Yu et al. (Eds.): GPC 2020, LNCS 12398, pp. 131–144, 2020.
https://doi.org/10.1007/978-3-030-64243-3_11

usually some hidden connections among abnormal users. Abstractly, these abnormal users usually form a group which can be regarded as an isolated network. It implies that the abnormal user data represents the outlier data that are inconsistent with other existing data models in social network analysis. Outlier mining is an important research field of data mining. Outliers contain some potentially valuable information: isolated clique helps both in getting faster algorithms than for the enumeration of maximal general cliques and in filtering out cliques with special semantics [5]. This paper aims to extract as much potential information as possible with focus on the dynamic isolated cliques detection.

Social networks usually consist of nodes, such as social members or organizations, and edges indicating the relationships between these social members. Generally, a social network is mathematically formalized as a graph $G = (V, E)$ where V denotes the set of objects and E denotes the set of relationships between objects. There are two types of social networks: static social network and dynamic social network. In the real world, most social networks are dynamically evolving, that is, the nodes in the network often change, and the relationships among nodes also often change. For instance, a newcomer joins an existing community, or someone in a community may be affected by a specific event and migrate to another community. As the ownership of the nodes changes constantly, so does the structure of the network.

Clique is a common existing topological structure in the network. It is composed of nodes and their common attributes and reveals the characteristics of social networks and the commonality of groups. Clique detection not only plays an important role in many applications, such as recommendation system [13] and public opinion monitoring, but also provides an effective coarse knowledge granularity for understanding social network structure [3]. However, finding a maximum clique is not only NP-hard but also hard to approximate within a factor of $n^{(1-\epsilon)}$ [8]. There are numerous computational approaches for maximal clique finding and enumeration. Ito, Iwama and Osumi [7] studied the linear-time enumeration of isolated cliques. Roughly speaking, isolation means that the connection of the maximal clique to the rest of the graph is limited, that is, there are few edges with one endpoint in the clique and one endpoint outside the clique [14].

Formal Concept Analysis (FCA) as a categorization method aims at grouping objects described by common attributes [9]. In this framework, a category is more precisely defined as a maximal set of objects sharing a maximal set of attributes. As far as we know, there is no previous work on isolated maximal clique detection using FCA. With the help of FCA's powerful analysis ability, our recent research [4] has proved that a particular concept, called the equiconcept in a concept lattice represents the maximal cliques of social graph. This paper can be considered a continuation of previous work. Specifically, this paper takes into account the dynamic environment and focuses on the detection and changes of isolated maximal cliques under dynamic social networks by using concept stability. Concept stability is an effective measure of FCA for selecting interesting concepts and noise reduction [11]. And it reflects the dependency of the intent on the particular object of the extent [16].

Different from the existing algorithms on maximal clique detection, we adopt the concept stability measure for mining isolated maximal cliques from a dynamic social network. The major contributions of this paper are summarized as follows:

- Our research scenario is a dynamic social network, which is closer to the actual situation. Then, by using the concept stability, the bridge between FCA and network topology, isolated maximal cliques can be easily detected in dynamic situations.
- A concept stability based isolated maximal cliques detection approach is proposed. First, we propose and prove the concept stability based isolated maximal cliques detection theorem. Besides, some interesting properties of concept stability are presented as well. Then, based on the proposed theorem, an algorithm of detecting isolated maximal clique with concept stability is devised.
- We conduct the experiments on two classical networking datasets for validating the effectiveness of the proposed algorithm. Experimental results have shown the proposed algorithm has a high F-measure value for detecting the isolated maximal cliques in social network.

The remainder of this paper is structured as follow. Section 2 sketches the preliminaries about clique, FCA and concept stability. Then, the problem definition of isolated maximal clique detection is presented in Sect. 3. Section 4 describes concept stability based isolated maximal clique detection approach from a dynamic social network. Experimental results are reported in Sect. 5. Finally, Sect. 6 concludes this paper.

2   Preliminaries

In this section, we briefly outline the key notions used in the rest of this paper, including three aspects: clique, FCA and concept stability.

2.1   Clique

Definition 1. *[3] (Clique): Given an undirected graph $G = (V, E)$, a clique $Q \subseteq G$ is a subset of the vertices such that every two distinct vertices are adjacent.*

Definition 2. *[4] (Maximal Clique): Given an undirected graph $G = (V, E)$, a clique $Q \subseteq G$ is maximal if it cant be extended by including one more adjacent vertex.*

Definition 3. *[6] (Isolated Maximal Clique): Let $G = (V, E)$ be an undirected graph. A maximal clique $Q \subseteq G$ is isolated if for any two vertices $v_i \in V$, $v_j \notin V$, there doesn't exist an edge $(v_i, v_j) \in E$. That is, there is no edge that connects an object in the maximal clique to any object outside it.*

2.2   FCA

Formal Concept Analysis (FCA) is a mathematical theory oriented at data analysis and visualization. It provides tools for understanding the data by representing it as a hierarchy of concepts or, more exactly, a concept lattice.

Definition 4. *[3] (Formal Context): A formal context is formed as a triple $K = (U, A, I)$, where U is a set of objects, A represents a set of attributes, and I is the binary relation between U and A (i.e.., $I \subseteq O \otimes A$). Suppose $o \in U$ and $a \in A$, each $(o, a) \in I$ denotes that object o has the attribute a, otherwise $(o, a) \notin I$.*

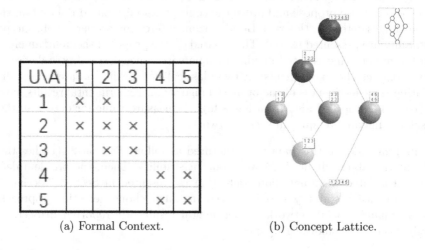

U\A	1	2	3	4	5
1	×	×			
2	×	×	×		
3		×	×		
4				×	×
5				×	×

(a) Formal Context.   (b) Concept Lattice.

Fig. 1. Example of formal context and its corresponding concept lattice.

Example 1. Figure 1(a) shows a formal context. The set of objects U and the set of attributes A are $\{1, 2, 3, 4, 5\}$, and in which "×" denotes that there exists the binary relation between U and A. For example, the object "1" has the attributes "1" and "2".

Definition 5. *[3] For a formal context $K = (U, A, I)$, the operators $\uparrow$ and $\downarrow$ on $X \subseteq U$ and $Y \subseteq A$ are respectively defined as*

$$X^{\uparrow} = \{a \in A | \forall x \in X, (x, a) \in I\} \tag{1}$$

$$Y^{\downarrow} = \{x \in U | \forall a \in Y, (x, a) \in I\} \tag{2}$$

$\forall x \in U$, let $\{x\}^{\uparrow} = x^{\uparrow}$, and $\forall a \in A$, let $\{a\}^{\downarrow} \in a^{\downarrow}$.

Definition 6. *[3] (Concept): For a formal context $K = (U, A, I)$, if (X, Y) satisfies $X^{\uparrow} = Y$ and $Y^{\downarrow} = X$, (X, Y) is called a concept, X is the extent of the concept, Y is the intent of the concept.*

Definition 7. *[3] (Equiconcept): For a formal context $K = (U, A, I)$, if (X, Y) satisfies $X^\uparrow = Y$, $Y^\downarrow = X$ and $X = Y$, (X, Y) is called an equiconcept, where X is called extent, and Y is called intent.*

Definition 8. *(Timed Equiconcept): A equiconcept $< (X, Y), t >$ is timed with t means that the concept (X, Y) is an equiconcept at time t. In the remainder, we use abbreviation form $< X, t >$ for timed equiconcept.*

Definition 9. *[3] Let $C(K)$ denote the set of all formal concepts of the formal context $K = (U, A, I)$. If $(X_1, B_1), (X_2, B_2) \in C(K)$, then let*

$$(X_1, B_1) \le (X_2, B_2) \Leftrightarrow X_1 \subseteq X_2 (\Leftrightarrow B_1 \supseteq B_2) \tag{3}$$

then "$\le$" is a partial relation of $C(K)$.

Definition 10. *[3] (Concept Lattice): A concept lattice $L = (C(K), \le)$ can be obtained by all formal concepts $C(K)$ of a context K with the partial order $\le$. Its graphical representation is a Hasse diagram.*

Example 2. Figure 1(b) illustrates the concept lattice for the context of Fig. 1(a). Each blue node represents a concept. The upper labels and lower labels of the nodes represent intents and extents of the concepts, respectively. Thus, we can obtain equiconcepts $(\{1, 2\}, \{1, 2\})$, $(\{3, 4\}, \{3, 4\})$ and $(\{4, 5\}, \{4, 5\})$.

2.3   Concept Stability

Definition 11. *(Stability): Given a formal context $K = (U, A, I)$ and a concept $c = (X, Y)$ of K. The intensional stability essentially depicts a proportion of the subsets of X whose closure is equal to Y. It is defined as follows [1, 10]:*

$$\sigma(c) = \frac{|\{x \in \varphi(X) \,|\, x^\uparrow = Y\}|}{2^{|X|}} \tag{4}$$

Actually, intensional stability measures the dependency between the intent Y and the object of the extend X. The stability index [15] can be computed by locating the closed set $X's$ associated minimal generator. In this paper, we calculate concept stability by invoking the DFSP algorithm [15] that is the first algorithm handles efficiently and straightforwardly concept stability computation.

3   Problem Statement

In this paper, we will mainly investigate how to detect the isolated maximal clique in a dynamic social network by using the theory of FCA and concept stability. A formal description of this problem is given below.

Given a dynamic social network $G = \{G_1, G_2, G_3 \ldots G_t\}$, where $G_t = (V_t, E_t)$ represents the network structure at time t. The G_t at each moment can be regarded as a static network in which the vertices set V_t includes the individuals in the social network, and the edge set $E_t = \{(v, w)|v, w \in V_t)\}$ represents the relationship between individuals. The isolated maximal clique detection problem is to detect all isolated maximal clique at every moment by using unique properties of concept stability.

In order to illustrate the problem addressed in this paper, a simple example of isolated maximal clique identification is given in Fig. 2.

Example 3. Figure 2 is a topology graph of a dynamic network $G = \{G_a, G_b\}$ at different time slots. The shadow part ($\{8, 9, 10\}$) represents the isolated maximal clique at time a. When the time goes from a to b, the node 11 is added. Obviously, maximal isolated cliques ($\{8, 9, 10\}$) are changing to ($\{8, 9, 10, 11\}$) over time.

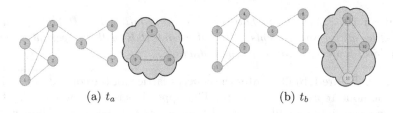

(a) t_a (b) t_b

Fig. 2. Simple example of isolated maximal clique detection.

4   Concept Stability Based Isolated Maximal Clique Detection

This section provides a new isolated maximal clique detection approach based on concept stability. To clarify our approach, we will detail our study through the following issues: 1) construct formal contexts for a dynamic social network; 2) explore the relation between concept stability and network topology; 3) propose an algorithm for detecting isolated maximal clique.

4.1   Formal Context Construction from Dynamic Social Network

We divide the dynamic social network $G = \{G_1, G_2, G_3 \ldots G_t\}$ into t (t is the number of time nodes) static network G_t according to the time nodes. A static social network G_t can be formalized as a classical mathematical relationship visualized as an undirected graph. We utilize the modified adjacency matrix as a formal context of G_t. Then, by invoking incremental concept lattice generation algorithm, we get all concepts and construct the concept lattice of static network G_t.

The modified adjacency matrix is defined as follows:

Definition 12. *[3] (Modified Adjacency Matrix): Let G be a graph with n vertices that are assumed to be ordered from v_1 to v_n. The $n \times n$ matrix A' is called a modified adjacency matrix, in which*

$$A' = \begin{cases} a_{ij} = 1 & \text{if there exists an edge from } v_i \text{ to } v_j \text{ and } i \neq j \\ a_{ij} = 1 & \text{if } i = j \\ a_{ij} = 0 & \text{otherwise} \end{cases} \tag{5}$$

Example 4. Continue Example 3, the constructed formal context K_a is presented in Table 1. And then we build the corresponding concept lattices L_a as shown in Fig. 3.

Table 1. Formal context K_a of G_a.

G_a	1	2	3	4	5	6	7	8	9	10
1	×	×	×	×						
2	×	×	×	×						
3	×	×	×	×						
4	×	×	×	×	×					
5			×	×	×	×				
6				×	×	×				
7				×	×	×				
8							×	×	×	
9							×	×	×	
10							×	×	×	

4.2 Isolated Maximal Clique Detection

This section introduces several interesting properties about concept stability and provides the isolated maximal clique detection algorithm as shown in *Algorithm* 1. In addition, the complexity of algorithm is analyzed and an illustrative example is presented to show that how does the algorithm run.

Proposition 1. *[6] Given a social graph $G = (V, E)$ and its corresponding concept lattice $L(K)$, if a maximal clique C is isolated, there is an equiconcept (A, B) corresponding to C and its stability equals to $\frac{2^{|A|}-1}{2^{|A|}}$.*

Proposition 2. *Given a social graph $G = (V, E)$ and its corresponding concept lattice $L(K)$, the equiconcept (A, B) corresponding to an isolated maximal clique locates between the top and bottom of the concept lattice.*

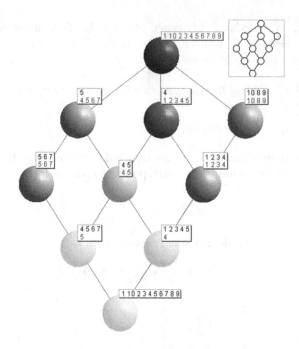

Fig. 3. Concept lattice L_a of K_a.

Proof. Suppose a concept (X, Y) is a son concept of the concept (A, B), then by Definition 9, $X \subseteq A$ and $B \subseteq Y$. Thus $\exists x \in X \Rightarrow x \in A$. Due to $|x^\uparrow| \geq |Y|$, and B is a subset of Y, thus $|x^\uparrow| > |B|$. That means x is associated with items not included in B. Moreover, corresponding node x is associated with nodes outside the isolated clique. This goes against Definition 3 of isolated maximal clique. Therefore, (A, B) cannot have son concept. Similarly, it can be proved that it is impossible (A, B) have father concept. Thus, the equiconcept (A, B) corresponding to an isolated maximal clique locates between the top and bottom of the concept lattice. □

Proposition 3. *Given a concept (A, B), if the $|A| = 1$, then the stability value of the concept (A, B) is equal to 0.5.*

Proof. According to Definition 11, the intensional stability depicts a proportion of the subsets of A whose closure is equal to B. Since $|A| = 1$, thus $\varphi(A) = \{A, \emptyset\}$. That is, all subsets of A have only the empty set and itself. Due to $A^\uparrow = B$ and $\emptyset^\uparrow = \emptyset$, only one subset A satisfies the stability condition in Definition 11. So, the stability of (A, B) is equal to 1/2. □

Proposition 4. *Given a social graph $G = (V, E)$ and its corresponding concept lattice $L(K)$, the intensional stability of the son concept of the equiconcept is equal to the extensional stability of the grandfather concept.*

Proof. Suppose the concept (X, Y) is the son concept of a equiconcept, due to the symmetry of the concept lattice of social networks, the concept (Y, X) must be a grandfather concept of the equiconcept. That means, the extent of son concept is the intent of grandfather concept. Thus, the intensional stability of (X, Y) is equal to the extensional stability of (Y, X).   □

Based on the above property of concept stability, the pseudo code for isolated maximal cliques detection algorithm is given in Algorithm 1. The algorithm goes through two parts. The first part aims to obtain all timed equiconcepts as a basis for mining interesting clique. At the second part, the main purpose of the algorithm is to select interesting concepts that captures isolated cliques using concept stability theory.

Algorithm 1. Concept Stability based Isolated Maximal Cliques Detection Algorithm

---

Require:
    $G = \{G_1, G_2, G_3 \ldots G_t\}$ //t represents *time*
Ensure:
    Set of isolated maximal clique $\hat{I}$ of G
1: Initialize $\hat{I} = \emptyset$, $\hat{E} = \emptyset$
2: **begin**
3: Construct formal contexts for G_t by Definition 3
4: $L_t \leftarrow$ Build concept lattices of G_t
5: **for** each concept $(A, B) \in L_t$ **do**
6:    **if** (A, B) is an equiconcept **then**
7:      $\hat{E} \leftarrow \hat{E} \cup < (A, B), t >$
8:      $\sigma (A, B) \leftarrow$ calculate the stability index σ of (A,B)
9:      **If** $\sigma (A, B) == \frac{2^{|A|} - 1}{2^{|A|}}$ **then**
10:        $\hat{I} \leftarrow \hat{I} \cup < (A, B), t >$
11:      **end if**
12:   **end if**
13: **end for**
14: **return** $\hat{I}$
15: **end**

A dynamic network G is the inputs of the algorithm. Our algorithm starts by initializing $\hat{I}$ (set of isolated maximal cliques and time nodes) and $\hat{E}$ (set of timed equiconcepts) to $\emptyset$ (Line 1). Then, we build formal context for G_t. Next, the concept lattice is constructed by our ongoing research which is an algorithm for quickly generating concept lattice based on dynamic network (Line 4). After that, we extract the equiconcepts that captures all maximal cliques from lattices L_t and time dimension into $\hat{E}$ (Lines 5–7). By invoking DFSP to calculate the stability value σ of timed equiconcept (Line 8), it is determined that if its stable value satisfies the Proposition 1 (Line 9), its corresponding clique is isolated maximal clique at that moment. DFSP [15] is the first algorithm to deal with the concepts stability calculation efficiently and directly. Lines 10–14 insert the detected isolated maximal clique into $\hat{I}$ and return $\hat{I}$.

Complexity Analysis: The first part of algorithm has $O(t_1)$ time complexity which is the time needed to generate concept lattice. Let $|\hat{E}|$ denote the number of timed equiconcepts. Thus. the second part of algorithm has $O(|\hat{E}| *t_2)$ time complexity, where t_2 is the time needed to calculate stability index by using DFSP.

Illustrative Example: Let us consider the dynamic network $G = \{G_a, G_b\}$ given by Fig. 2. First, we build formal context for G_a (Table.1) and G_b. Next, the concept lattices L_a (Fig. 3) and L_b are constructed. After that, we extract timed equiconcepts which represent maximal clique in social graph from concept lattice. So, we get $<\{1, 2, 3, 4\}, ab>, <\{4, 5\}, ab>, <\{5, 6, 7\}, ab>, <\{8, 9, 10\}, a>,$ $<\{8, 9, 10, 11\}, b>$ and then store into $|\hat{E}|$. Finally, by calling the DFSP to calculate the stability value, there are two equiconcepts conform to the Eq. (4). The stability index of $<\{8, 9, 10\}, a>, <\{8, 9, 10, 11\}, b>$ respectively equal to $7/8, 15/16$. Hence, clique $\{8, 9, 10\}$ is an isolated maximal clique at time a; clique $\{8, 9, 10, 11\}$ is an isolated maximal clique at time b.

5   Experiments

In this section, we conduct the experiments on two networking datasets to evaluate the proposed approach. The goal of the experiments is to examine whether using concept stability is feasible and efficient for detecting isolated maximal clique. All algorithms are implemented in JAVA language and are run on an Inter(R) Core (TM) i7-8565U @ 1.80 GHz 1.99 GHz, 20 GB RAM computer.

5.1   Data Set and Configurations

In this paper, two datasets of social network are adopted. Data I [12] is a classical dataset on the social network of frequent associations between 62 dolphins in a community living off Doubtful sound, New Zealand. Data II [2] is a network that represents the schedule of games between college football teams in a single season. Figure 4 shows the visualization of both dolphin living network and football network.

Due to the structural specificity of isolated maximal clique, this structure does not exist in most real social networks, but this structure is also the basis for mining isolated communities, so we randomly add data to the existing dataset for synthetic dynamic networks.

5.2   Experimental Results

This section mainly evaluates the proposed approach with two important metrics: *precision/recall* ratio of isolated maximal clique detection. For a given parameter k and time t, a set of isolated maximal cliques are obtained, the corresponding *precision* and *recall* ratio are defined as follows:

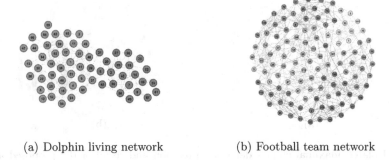

(a) Dolphin living network   (b) Football team network

Fig. 4. The visualization of Dolphin living network and Football team network.

- *Precision* is the ratio of the number of isolated maximal k-cliques in the detection results to the total number of isolated maximal k-cliques obtained by that detection.
- *Recall* is the ratio of the number of isolated maximal k-cliques in the detection results to the total number of existing isolated maximal k-cliques.
- *F1-score* is used to evaluate how well an algorithm can find the isolated maximal k-cliques from a social graph by fitting the Precision and Recall, denoted as $F1 = \frac{2*Precision*Recall}{Precision+Recall}$.

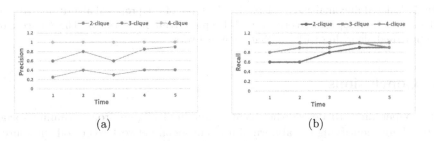

Fig. 5. Isolated maximal cliques detection precision and recall of the proposed algorithm in Dolphin living network. (a) The precision of the proposed algorithm with various k at different time. (b) The recall of the proposed algorithm with various k at different time.

As shown in Fig. 5 and Fig. 6, the precision and recall of the proposed detection algorithm are measured at different times with different k. Obviously, as the k increases, the detection precision and recall ratio of the isolated maximum k-cliques also increase. In particular, when we try to find the isolated maximum 4-cliques, the precision and recall are reach 100%. In addition, we also evaluated the proposed algorithm with various k values based on the $F1$ score, which is used to evaluate the efficient of each algorithm to find the isolated maximal clique from the social network. Figure 7 reports that the proposed algorithm can effectively find the largest isolated group, especially the group with larger k.

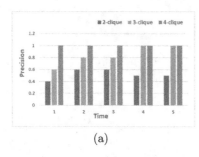
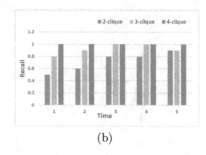

(a)   (b)

Fig. 6. Isolated maximal cliques detection precision and recall of the proposed algorithm in Football team network. (a)The precision of the proposed algorithm with various k at different time. (b) The recall of the proposed algorithm with various k at different time.

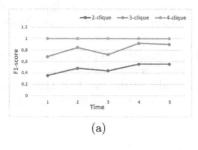
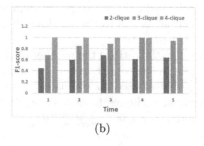

(a)   (b)

Fig. 7. Isolated maximal cliques detection $F1$ score of the proposed algorithm. (a) The $F1$ score of the proposed algorithm with Dolphin living network. (b) The $F1$ score of the proposed algorithm with Football team network.

6   Conclusions

This paper aims to detect the isolated maximal cliques from dynamic social network for identifying the abnormal users in social network to cut off the source of fake information in time, and reduce the occurrence of security incidents. We have proposed the concept stability based isolated maximal clique detection algorithm. Firstly, we used a modified adjacency matrix to construct the formal context and generated the concept lattice of a dynamic social network. Then, some unique properties of concept stability have been presented and proved. Based on the properties, a detection algorithm of isolated maximal clique has been further proposed. The proposed algorithm has been evaluated by using two classical datasets. Experimental results have shown the proposed algorithm has a high $F1$ score for detecting the isolated maximal cliques from dynamic social networks.

Acknowledgment. This work was funded in part by the National Natural Science Foundation of China (Grant No. 61702317), the Natural Science Basic Research Plan in Shaanxi Province of China (Grant No. 2019JM-379), and the Fund Program for the

Scientific Activities of Selected Returned Overseas Professionals in Shaanxi Province (Grant No. 2017024). This is also a part of a project that has received funding from the European Union's Horizon 2020 research and innovation programme under the Marie Sklodowska-Curie grant agreement No. 840922. This work reflects only the authors' view and the EU Commission is not responsible for any use that may be made of the information it contains.

References

1. Babin, M.A., Kuznetsov, S.O.: Approximating concept stability. In: Domenach, F., Ignatov, D.I., Poelmans, J. (eds.) ICFCA 2012. LNCS (LNAI), vol. 7278, pp. 7–15. Springer, Heidelberg (2012). https://doi.org/10.1007/978-3-642-29892-9_7
2. Girvan, M., Newman, M.E.: Community structure in social and biological networks. Proc. Natl. Acad. Sci. **99**(12), 7821–7826 (2002)
3. Hao, F., Min, G., Pei, Z., Park, D.S., Yang, L.T.: k-clique community detection in social networks based on formal concept analysis. IEEE Syst. J. **11**(1), 250–259 (2017)
4. Hao, F., Pei, Z., Yang, L.T.: Diversified top-k maximal clique detection in social internet of things. Future Gener. Comput. Syst. **107**, 408–417 (2020)
5. Hüffner, F., Komusiewicz, C., Moser, H., Niedermeier, R.: Enumerating isolated cliques in synthetic and financial networks. In: Yang, B., Du, D.-Z., Wang, C.A. (eds.) COCOA 2008. LNCS, vol. 5165, pp. 405–416. Springer, Heidelberg (2008). https://doi.org/10.1007/978-3-540-85097-7_38
6. Ibrahim, M.H., Missaoui, R., Messaoudi, A.: Detecting communities in social networks using concept interestingness. In: Proceedings of the 28th Annual International Conference on Computer Science and Software Engineering, pp. 81–90. IBM Corp. (2018)
7. Ito, H., Iwama, K., Osumi, T.: Linear-time enumeration of isolated cliques. In: Brodal, G.S., Leonardi, S. (eds.) ESA 2005. LNCS, vol. 3669, pp. 119–130. Springer, Heidelberg (2005). https://doi.org/10.1007/11561071_13
8. Johan, H.: Clique is hard to approximate within n1-epsilon. In: Proceedings of the 37th Annual Symposium on Foundations of Computer Science, pp. 627–636 (1996)
9. Klimushkin, M., Obiedkov, S., Roth, C.: Approaches to the selection of relevant concepts in the case of noisy data. In: Kwuida, L., Sertkaya, B. (eds.) ICFCA 2010. LNCS (LNAI), vol. 5986, pp. 255–266. Springer, Heidelberg (2010). https://doi.org/10.1007/978-3-642-11928-6_18
10. Kuznetsov, S.O.: On stability of a formal concept. Ann. Math. Artif. Intell. **49**(1–4), 101–115 (2007)
11. Kuznetsov, S.O., Makhalova, T.P.: Concept interestingness measures: a comparative study. In: CLA, vol. 1466, pp. 59–72 (2015)
12. Lusseau, D., Schneider, K., Boisseau, O.J., Haase, P., Slooten, E., Dawson, S.M.: The bottlenose dolphin community of doubtful sound features a large proportion of long-lasting associations. Behav. Ecol. Sociobiol. **54**(4), 396–405 (2003)
13. Matin, A.I., Jahan, S., Huq, M.R.: Community recommendation in social network using strong friends and quasi-clique approach. In: 8th International Conference on Electrical and Computer Engineering, pp. 453–456. IEEE (2014)
14. Molter, H., Niedermeier, R., Renken, M.: Enumerating isolated cliques in temporal networks. In: Cherifi, H., Gaito, S., Mendes, J.F., Moro, E., Rocha, L.M. (eds.) COMPLEX NETWORKS 2019. SCI, vol. 882, pp. 519–531. Springer, Cham (2020). https://doi.org/10.1007/978-3-030-36683-4_42

15. Mouakher, A., Yahia, S.B.: On the efficient stability computation for the selection of interesting formal concepts. Inf. Sci. **472**, 15–34 (2019)
16. Roth, C., Obiedkov, S., Kourie, D.: Towards concise representation for taxonomies of epistemic communities. In: Yahia, S.B., Nguifo, E.M., Belohlavek, R. (eds.) CLA 2006. LNCS (LNAI), vol. 4923, pp. 240–255. Springer, Heidelberg (2008). https://doi.org/10.1007/978-3-540-78921-5_17

Echo State Network Based on L_0 Norm Regularization for Chaotic Time Series Prediction

Li Li[1,2], Fangwan Huang[1,2(✉)], and Zhiyong Yu[1,2,3]

[1] College of Mathematics and Computer Science, Fuzhou University, Fuzhou, China
hfw@fzu.edu.cn
[2] Fujian Provincial Key Laboratory of Network Computing and Intelligent Information Processing, Fuzhou University, Fuzhou, China
[3] Key Laboratory of Spatial Data Mining & Information Sharing, Ministry of Education, Fuzhou, China

Abstract. The echo state network introduces a large and sparse reservoir to replace the hidden layer of the traditional recurrent neural network, which can solve the gradient-based problem of most recurrent neural networks in the training process. However, there may be an ill-posed problem when the least square method is used to calculate the output weight. In this paper, we proposed an echo state network based on L_0 norm regularization. The main idea is to limit the number of output connections to compute the output effectively by removing unimportant ones. The simulation results of the chaotic time series prediction show the effectiveness of the proposed model.

Keywords: Echo state networks · L_0 norm regularization · Orthogonal matching pursuit · Chaotic time series prediction

1 Introduction

Chaos is a universal phenomenon of irregular motion characteristics of the nonlinear dynamic system [1]. Recently, it has become an important research field to predict the nonlinear time series extracted from chaotic systems. The prediction of chaotic time series is to predict the future state of the system by analogy or extension of the development process and trend reflected by the sequence [2]. To obtain the time correlation in the sequence for better predicting, the nonlinear system prediction must have some intelligence information processing ability. Recurrent neural network (RNN), which can effectively keep the input information through finding the correlation between data points with a large time span through the self-connection of its hidden layer, has been widely used in chaotic time series prediction. However, the Back Propagation Through Time (BPTT) algorithm adopted in RNN training phase brings problems like vanishing gradient or exploding gradient, causing the network performance degrades [3]. The echo state network (ESN) proposed by Jaeger [4] is a new RNN architecture using a large and sparse reservoir to replace the hidden layer of the traditional RNN. It only needs to train

© Springer Nature Switzerland AG 2020
Z. Yu et al. (Eds.): GPC 2020, LNCS 12398, pp. 145–152, 2020.
https://doi.org/10.1007/978-3-030-64243-3_12

the output weights of the network that can greatly reduce the computational complexity and avoids the gradient problems by the BPTT algorithm. In addition, ESN has been proved that it performs well at nonlinear mapping [5, 6].

ESN has been widely used since proposed, especially in time series prediction [7, 8]. The reservoir is the core of ESN, which contains a large number of randomly and sparsely connected neurons. Because of its large size, it often needs to pay a high computational cost in the process of solving the problem, which reduces the performance of the network. Besides, the least-square method used to compute the output weights in ESN may cause an ill-posed problem [9], affecting the generalization of ESN. To solve these problems, the feature selection ability of the regularization method can be used to decrease the complexity of the model and makes it easy to explain. Regularization modifies the training criteria for linear regression by adding different kinds of norms to the loss function to impose constraint [10]. Han proposed an improved ESN based on L_1 norm regularization to improve the numerical stability of the model solution and controls the complexity of the network [11]. Xu used $L_{1/2}$ regularization to get a sparse solution in order to solve the ill-posed problem and improve the generalized performance [12]. But for regular factor value, it usually needs to be adjusted to a very small value to make the model perform better, which is time-consuming and not conducive to model fitting.

In this paper, we propose an improved model introducing L_0 norm regularization to ESN. L_0 norm regularization is an intuitive sparse method, similar to the Dropout [13], and it is popular in sparse coding (SC) recently. By adding an L_0 norm to the loss function, it keeps the important connection from the reservoir to the output layer and sets the unimportant values to 0. Then the output weights can be solved effectively and accurately due to the limitation of the number of effective output connections. To solve the NP-hard problem [14] brought by the L_0 norm regularization, we take an example by the SC to use the greedy algorithm to solve the non-convex function. The greedy algorithm used in this paper is the famous Orthogonal Matching Pursuit [15].

2   Preliminaries

ESN is a simple but powerful novel RNN architecture that introduces the concept of "reservoir computing". It consists of input layer, reservoir, and output layer. The core reservoir always contains a large number of neurons, which are randomly generated and sparsely connected. The architecture of ESN is shown in Fig. 1.

In Fig. 1, the $W_i \in R^{N \times I}$, $W \in R^{N \times N}$ and $W_f \in R^{O \times N}$ (the solid arrows) represent the weight matrixes of Input-Reservoir, Reservoir-Reservoir, and Output-Reservoir, respectively. Both of them are randomly generated during network initial phase and remain unchanged. And the $W_o \in R^{(I+N) \times O}$ (the dotted arrows) represents the weights matrix of readout, the only one that needs to be trained in ESN.

At time t, equations of the reservoir state update and the network output are shown below:

$$u(t) = \varphi\left(W_i x(t) + W u(t-1) + W_f y(t-1) + \xi\right) \tag{1}$$

$$y(t) = \psi\left(W_o(x(t); u(t))\right) \tag{2}$$

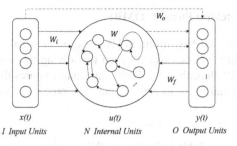

Fig. 1. An ESN architecture with feedback connections.

where the $x(t) \in R^I$, $u(t) \in R^N$ and $y(t) \in R^O$ represent the input, reservoir state, and output vectors, respectively. φ and ψ are the active functions of reservoir and output, which in general are chosen as a tanh function and a linear function, respectively. And ξ is a small noise term.

To train W_o better, a pair of input-output sequences $(x(1), y(1)), \dots, (x(s), y(s))$ of length s is used in this paper. In the initial phase, after the W_i, W and W_f are randomly generated, put the sequence $x(1), \dots, x(s)$ as input to the network for training. The initial states of the reservoir need to be discarded and then recorded from time h as $u(h), \dots, u(s)$. The corresponding input and reservoir state vectors are combined to form a matrix M, and the sequence $y(h), \dots, y(s)$ as the corresponding target output vectors is formed into matrix Z. The equation can be defined as followed:

$$Z = MW_o \tag{3}$$

Then the output weights can be computed by using the least square method as follow:

$$\widehat{W_o} = arg\ min_{W_o}\ \|Z - MW_o\|_2^2 \tag{4}$$

The original ESN computes the solution of (6) is as followed:

$$\widehat{W_o} = M^\dagger Z = \left(M^T M\right)^{-1} M^T Z \tag{5}$$

However, there may be an ill-posed problem when using the above method. A solution to this problem is to use regularization, which has the general form:

$$\widehat{W_o} = arg\ min_{W_o}\ \|Z - MW_o\|_2^2 + \lambda \|W_o\|_\alpha^\alpha \tag{6}$$

where λ is a regular value of particular norm that balances the two objective terms, and $\|W_o\|_\alpha^\alpha$ is taken as the α norm regularization of W_o.

3   ESN Based on L_0 Norm Regularization

In this paper, we are applying the L_0 norm regularization to ESN. But there exists the main difficulty that the L_0 norm belongs to an NP-hard problem, causing the target function of ESN to be non-convex. Recently, in the field of compressed sensing (CS), different L_0 norms are used to build mathematical models to obtain a sparse solution. In solving the non-convex function, CS draws on the experience of SC which always uses the greedy algorithm to make the L_0 norm works well.

3.1 Orthogonal Matching Pursuit (OMP)

Pati et al. proposed the OMP algorithm in [16]. It is an improved method of Matching Pursuit (MP) algorithm [17] that usually used for solving the non-convex function in SC. Different with MP algorithm, the OMP algorithm requires the residual after each iteration to be orthogonal to the effective atom. The process of the OMP algorithm is shown in Table 1.

Table 1. Process of OMP algorithm.

Steps	Details
0	Initialize the signal $\omega = R_0\omega$, $k = 0$, dictionary $D_0 = \emptyset$, constant error $\delta > 0$
1	Compute the inner product $\{\langle R^k\omega, p_i\rangle \mid p_i \in D\backslash D_k\}$
2	Find the effective atom $p_{jk} \in D\backslash D_k$ satisfying
	$\left\lvert\langle R^k\omega, p_{jk}\rangle\right\rvert \geq \beta \sup_r \left\lvert\langle R^k\omega, p_r\rangle\right\rvert$, where $0 < \beta \leq 1$, $D_k = D_k \cup \{p_{jk}\}$
3	Compute $p_k^* = arg\ \min_p \lVert\omega - D_kp\rVert_2$.
4	Compute the new residual $R^k\omega = \omega - D_kp_k^*$
5	If $R^k\omega < \delta$, stop; else $k = k + 1$, continue with steps 1-5

3.2 OMP-ESN Algorithm

In this paper, the OMP algorithm works by using the reservoir state matrix as a dictionary, selecting the effective "atom" from the matrix by keeping the import connections from the reservoir to the output layer and setting the unimportant ones to 0 to impose a constraint. The process of the OMP-ESN algorithm is shown in Table 2.

From Table 2, assume that the input-output sequence is put into running the ESN. And at time h after the ESN runs, the reservoir states $u(h), \ldots, u(s)$ computed as (1) are recorded to the matrix M with the corresponding input. The target outputs $y(h), \ldots, y(s)$ are put into matrix Z. Then we use the OMP algorithm to select the effective "atom" according to the Table 1 from the matrix M. And the output weights W_o computed, with a sparse number of non-zero features, which is an approximate solution of the following NP-hard problem:

$$\min_{\omega \in W_o} \lVert Z - MW_o\rVert_2^2\ s.t\ \lVert W_o\rVert_0 \leq k \tag{7}$$

Where $\lVert \cdot \rVert_0$ indicates the number of non-zero items in W_o and k represents the maximum number of output connections allowed.

For fast convergence, the OMP algorithm computes the covariance matrix M^TM in first. Then for each target output, it computes M^TZ and performs the decomposition with a Cholesky-based algorithm.

Table 2. Process of OMP-ESN algorithm.

Steps	Details
0	Initial the ESN with randomly generated weights matrix of W_i, W, and W_f, and set the initial reservoir state $u(0) = 0$
1	Drive the reservoir by the input-output sequence, and compute the reservoir states as (1). Then collect the states from time h
2	Form the needed matrix M and Z
3	Based on the OMP algorithm, select the optimal non-zero feature in U according to the parameter k
4	Compute the output weights W_o as (2)
5	Test the trained ESN

4   Simulations

In this section, we apply the proposed OMP-ESN model to three typical chaotic time series datasets and evaluate its performance compared with two frequently-used models: ESN with L_1 norm regression (L1-ESN) and ESN with L_2 norm regression (L2-ESN). The normalized root mean square error (NRMSE) is selected as the evaluation criterion for the prediction accuracy, defined as:

$$\text{NRMSE} = \sqrt{\frac{\langle \|y[i] - y^*[i]\|^2 \rangle}{\langle \|y[i] - <y^*[i]> \|^2 \rangle}} \tag{8}$$

Where $y[i]$ is the true output, $y^*[i]$ is the target output, and $\langle \cdot \rangle$ is the mean.

4.1   Datasets Description

These datasets are the majority of tasks performed by known ESN researches. Below we provide a brief description of them.

Mackey-Glass (MG) Time-Series. The input signal is generated from the MG time-delay differential system, the equation is defined as followed:

$$y(t+1) = y(t) + \delta\left(0.2\frac{y\left(t - \frac{\tau}{\delta}\right)}{1 + y\left(t - \frac{\tau}{\delta}\right)^{10}} - 0.1y(t)\right) \tag{9}$$

In this paper, we generated MG time series for 6,000 data points with $\delta = 0.1$, $\tau = 17$, and initial $y(0) = 0.1$ as the system usually sets.

Lorenz System. This system is defined by the following three differential equations:

$$\frac{dx}{dt} = p(y - x), \frac{dy}{dt} = x(q - z) - y, \frac{dz}{dt} = xy - rz \tag{10}$$

In this paper, we set the initial input $x(0) = 12$, $y(0) = 2$, $z(0) = 9$, and the system parameter $p = 10$, $q = 28$ and $r = 8/3$ to keep the chaotic system.

Moore-Spiegel. This dynamical systems, which manifests interesting synchronization properties, is defined by the following three differential equations:

$$\frac{dx}{dt} = y, \frac{dy}{dt} = z, \frac{dz}{dt} = -z - \left(t - r + rx^2\right)y - tx \tag{11}$$

In this paper, we set r = 100 to keep the chaotic system.

The last two systems both generate 10,000 data points in our simulations.

4.2 Experimental Setup

In this paper, we use the first 70% of the time series as the training set, the next 15% of time series are used as the validation set to find the optimal parameters of ESN models, and the last 15% of the time series are used for evaluating the final model performance as a test set. Simulations are implemented in Python, by adapting the code from [18]. In this code, all of parameters adjusted by the genetic algorithm (GA).

After a lot of experiments, we conclude that 6 parameters of ESN models, and the parameters of the regression method used to solve the output, need to be adjusted. The bounds for these parameters are shown in Table 3 (The last three columns are the parameters of the three regression methods, respectively).

Table 3. Parameters search range with resolution n.

	N	ρ	ξ	$W_{IS}/W_{OS}/W_{FS}$	$\lambda_{L2\text{-}ESN}$	$\lambda_{L1\text{-}ESN}$	k(OMP)
min	250	0.5	0.0	0.1	0.001	0.00001	50
max	500	1.4	0.1	0.9	1.0	0.001	250
n	5	0.09	0.01	0.08	0.1	0.1	5

In Table 3, N is the reservoir size, ρ is the reservoir spectral radius and ξ is a small noise in the reservoir. And W_{IS}, W_{OS} and W_{FS} is the scaling of input, output and feedback vectors, respectively.

4.3 Results Discussion

The optimal configuration of each ESN model after turning is shown in Table 4. We found that the reservoir spectral radius is usually $\rho > 1$. According to the definition of ESN, the spectral radius to maintain the "echo" property should be $\rho < 1$. In fact, the most recent researches advocate using a spectral radius in the range [1.1, 1.2] can make the reservoir perform [18].

After using the optimal configuration to set the corresponding network model, we ran 30 times and get the mean and standard deviation of NRMSE to evaluate the performance of each model. In addition, the mean training time of running a model is also considered. The final results are shown in Table 5.

Table 4. The optimal configuration of ESN, L1-ESN, and OMP-ESN.

Datasets	Model	λ	k	N	ρ	ξ	W_{IS}	W_{OS}	W_{FS}
MG	L2-ESN	0.037	/	486	1.348	0.0	0.776	0.363	0.694
	L1-ESN	1.0E-5	/	447	1.4	0.036	0.787	0.516	0.237
	OMP-ESN	/	224	428	1.304	0.001	0.853	0.497	0.369
Lorenz	L2-ESN	0.031	/	478	0.5	0.001	0.614	0.797	0.705
	L1-ESN	1.0E-5	/	443	0.767	0.0	0.820	0.471	0.788
	OMP-ESN	/	141	364	0.872	0.0	0.822	0.636	0.108
MS	L2-ESN	0.574	/	453	1.160	0.0	0.666	0.454	0.639
	L1-ESN	1.0E-5	/	318	1.096	0.001	0.895	0.818	0.398
	OMP-ESN	/	239	457	1.118	0.0	0.9	0.174	0.365

Table 5. Comparison results of the L2-ESN, L1-ESN, and OMP-ESN.

Datasets	Model	Error	Time(s)
MG	L2-ESN	1.663E-2 ± 7.213E-2	1.49
	L1-ESN	2.945E-2 ± 3.310E-3	5.81
	OMP-ESN	**4.902E-4 ± 9.615E-5**	**1.42**
Lorenz	L2-ESN	7.270E-4 ± 2.753E-5	3.79
	L1-ESN	5.903E-2 ± 2.213E-1	8.47
	OMP-ESN	**5.022E-4 ± 5.976E-4**	**2.57**
MS	L2-ESN	5.546E-2 ± 1.502E-1	**2.66**
	L1-ESN	1.387 ± 4.558	8.54
	OMP-ESN	**2.464E-2 ± 6.981E-3**	2.89

From the Table 5, it can be seen that the OMP-ESN model we proposed in this paper is outperformed in performance than the L2-ESN and L1-ESN model in three tasks. And the efficiency of OMP-ESN is the best except for the MS tasks. Although it is not as good as L2-ESN in the MS tasks, the accuracy is much better than it, and the time difference is not very big.

5 Conclusion

In this paper, combining with the OMP algorithm, we focus on an L_0 norm regularization which is an NP-hard problem actually for chaotic time series prediction. The simulation results in three chaotic time series show that the OMP-ESN model we proposed is viable, and it can perform well than the commonly used L2-ESN and L1-ESN model in the most tasks.

In the future, we will further improve the OMP-ESN model so that it can be applied to different real scenario tasks with good performance, and find more L_0 norm regularization methods that can be applied to ESN.

References

1. Haykin, S., Principe, J.: Making sense of a complex world [chaotic events modeling]. IEEE Signal Process. Magaz. **15**(3), 66–81 (1998)
2. Yu, Z.: Chaos and symbol analysis and practice of time series (in Chinese). National University of Defense Technology Press, Changsha (2007)
3. Namikawa, J., Tani, J.: Building recurrent neural networks to implement multiple attractor dynamics using the gradient descent method. Advances in Artificial Neural Systems (2009)
4. Jaeger, H.: The "Echo State" approach to analyzing and training recurrent neural networks. Bonn, Germany: German National Research Center for Information Technology GMD Technical Report **148**(34), 13 (2001)
5. Qiao, J.F., Bo, Y.C., Han, G.: Application of ESN-based multi indices dual heuristic dynamic programming on wastewater treatment process. Acta Automatica Sinica **39**(7), 1146–1151 (2013)
6. Ongenae, F., Van, L.S., Verstraeten, D., Verplancke, T., Benoit, D., De, T.F., Dhaene, T., Schrauwen, B., Decruyenaere, J.: Time series classification for the prediction of dialysis in critically ill patients using echo state networks. Eng. Appl. Artif. Intell. **26**(3), 984–996 (2013)
7. Sheng, C., Zhao, J., Liu, Y., et al.: Prediction for noisy nonlinear time series by echo state network based on dual estimation. Neurocomputing **82**, 186–195 (2012)
8. Peng, Y., Wang, J.M., Peng, X.: Researches on time series prediction with echo state networks. Acta Electronica Sinica **38**(b02), 148–154 (2010)
9. Chatzis, S.P., Demiris, Y.: Echo state Gaussian process. IEEE Trans. Neural Netw. **22**(9), 1435–1445 (2011)
10. Haykin, S.: Neural Networks: a compressive foundation. Tsinghua University Press, Beijing (2001)
11. Han, M., Ren, W.J., Xu, M.L.: An Improved Echo State Network via L1-norm Regularization. J. Autom. **000**(011), 2428–2435 (2014)
12. Xu, M., Han, M., Kanae, S.: $L_{1/2}$ norm regularized echo state network for chaotic time series prediction. In: Hirose, A., Ozawa, S., Doya, K., Ikeda, K., Lee, Minho, Liu, D. (eds.) ICONIP 2016. LNCS, vol. 9949, pp. 12–19. Springer, Cham (2016). https://doi.org/10.1007/978-3-319-46675-0_2
13. Iosifidis, A., Tefas, A.: DropELM: Fast Neural Network Regularization with Dropout and DropConnect. Neurocomputing **162**, 57–66 (2015)
14. Dicker, L., Huang, B.S., Lin, X.L.: Variable selection and estimation with the seamless-L_0 penalty. Statistica Sinica **23**(2), 929–962 (2013)
15. Goodfellow, I., Haykin, Y., Courville, A.: Deep learning. MIT press, US (2016)
16. Pati, Y.C., Rezaiifar, R., Krishnaprasad, P.S.: Orthogonal matching pursuit: recursive function approximation with applications to wavelet decomposition. In: Proceedings of 27th Asilomar Conference on Signals, Systems and Computers, IEEE, pp. 40–44 (1993)
17. Manat, S., Zhang, Z.: Matching pursuit in a time-frequency dictionary. IEEE Trans. Signal Process. **12**, 3397–3451 (1993)
18. Bianchi, F.M., Maiorino, E., Kampffmeyer, M.C., et al.: An overview and comparative analysis of recurrent neural networks for short term load forecasting. arXiv preprint arXiv:1705.04378 (2017)

Recommendation Systems

MI-KGNN: Exploring Multi-dimension Interactions for Recommendation Based on Knowledge Graph Neural Networks

Zilong Wang⬛, Zhu Wang(✉)⬛, Zhiwen Yu, Bin Guo, and Xingshe Zhou

Northwestern Polytechnical University, Xi'an 710129, China
wangzhu@nwpu.edu.cn

Abstract. To achieve more accurate recommendations, a consensus of the research community is that not only explicit information (i.e., historical user-item interactions) but also implicit information (i.e., side information) should be utilized. Generally, both explicit and implicit information can be categorized according to the following assumptions: 1) Users with same behaviors are similar; 2) Items related to the same user are similar; 3) Items with same attributes are similar; and 4) Users with same interests are similar. However, none of existing studies has fully explored such information. To this end, we put forward Multi-dimension Interactions based Knowledge Graph Neural Networks (MI-KGNN), i.e., a GNN-based recommendation model that characterizes the similarity between users and items through embedding propagation in the knowledge graph. Specifically, apart from the traditional user-item and item-user interactions, we define another two types of interactions by introducing three different bipartite graphs. On one hand, we explore the interaction between items and the neighborhood during the information aggregation process. On the other hand, we explore the interaction between users and the neighborhood during embedding propagation. These interactions allow information to propagate in the direction indicated by the above four assumptions. In such a way, MI-KGNN effectively extracts both semantic information and structural information in the knowledge graph. Experimental results show that MI-KGNN significantly outperforms state-of-the-art methods in top-K recommendations.

Keywords: Recommender system · Knowledge graph · Graph neural networks · Embedding propagation · Multi-dimension interactions

1 Introduction

With the development of information technology and the Internet, people have gradually entered the era of information overload from the era of lack of information. In this era, both information consumers and information producers have

---

This work is partially supported by the National Natural Science Foundation of China (No. 61725205, 617772428), and the Fundamental Research Funds for the Central Universities (No. 3102019AX10).

Z. Yu et al. (Eds.): GPC 2020, LNCS 12398, pp. 155–170, 2020.
https://doi.org/10.1007/978-3-030-64243-3_13

encountered great challenges: as an information consumer, how to find the information of interest from a large amount of information is very difficult; as an information producer, how to make the produced information stand out and be concerned by the users is also a challenging issue. The recommender system is regarded as an effective way to address such challenges, and has attracted more and more attention.

During the last decade, lots of efforts have been devoted to the studies on optimizing collaborative filtering, which is a classic technique for the recommender system [17]. Collaborative filtering techniques predict possible future user behaviors by exploring historical interactions (i.e., explicit information) between users and items. Although collaborative filtering is successful in many applications, it is not effective when historical interactions are sparse [4,5]. In order to solve this problem, researchers choose to characterize users and items by utilizing both historical interaction information and side information (i.e., implicit information) [8,12,14,29]. For example, more and more studies [2,11,13,22,24–26] use knowledge graphs (KG) as side information because KG contains rich semantic information, which contributes to the diversity and explainability of the recommendation result. The early KG-aware recommender systems can be divided into two categories: embedding-based approaches [10,11,15,24,26] and path-based approaches [3,7,18,19,27,30], both of which have certain shortcomings. For instance, embedding-based approaches are not suitable for end-to-end training and the results are unexplainable, and path-based approaches rely too much on the choice of meta-paths that require manual guidance for extraction.

Recently, the Graph Neural Network (GNN) based approach [21–23] has attracted more and more attention, which enables end-to-end representation learning of the nodes (i.e., users and items). It addresses the drawbacks of previous approaches to some extent by exploring the semantic and structural information in KG. Currently, GNN-based approaches mainly extend the GNN architecture to KG-aware recommender systems. For example, Knowledge Graph Attention Network (KGAT) [23] uses the attention mechanism to adjust the collaborative knowledge graph which consists of the user-item bipartite graph and the knowledge graph. In order to capture user preferences, KGAT pays attention to the long-range connectivity in the graph. However, user preferences are diluted during multiple propagations. KGCN [22] adds high-dimensional representations of users to the information transfer process and uses KG to learn the preferences of different users. KGCN-LS [21] is proposed to address the overfitting problem of the KGCN model. It mitigates the overfitting problem with label smoothing regularization and achieves better performance than KGCN.

While KGCN and KGCN-LS can capture user preferences more accurately, they still have not fully utilized all the possible information for node embedding. Thereby, we propose to explore possible information in a more systematic way. Specifically, we categorize possible information according to the following assumptions: 1) Users with same behaviors are similar; 2) Items related to the same user are similar; 3) Items with same attributes are similar; and 4) Users with same interests are similar. Collaborative filtering methods mainly utilize the first two assumptions to update the recommendation model without KG, and existing GNN-based methods have weakened at least one of these assumptions.

In this paper, we propose Multi-dimension Interactions based Knowledge Graph Neural Networks (MI-KGNN) to fully explore possible information indicated by the above four assumptions. Apart from the traditional user-item and item-user interactions, MI-KGNN further utilizes the interaction between items and the neighborhood during information aggregation, as well as the interaction between users and the neighborhood during embedding propagation. In such a way, the MI-KGNN model meets all the four assumptions by appropriately adjusting the loss function. Obviously, the key difference between MI-KGNN and KGCN-LS lies in the way information is exchanged during embedding propagation, which is very important in the GNN model.

We evaluate MI-KGNN based on three datasets: MovieLens-20M (movie), Dianping-Food (restaurant), and Last.FM (music). Experiment results show that in top-K recommendations, the recall rate of MI-KGNN significantly outperforms the state-of-the-art method KGCN-LS by 7.1%, 3.2% and 1.5%, respectively.

The contribution of this work can be summarized as follows:

- To characterize users and items from different aspects, we propose a new GNN-based recommendation model MI-KGNN by exploring multi-dimension interactions in a more systematic way based on a set of assumptions.
- We give mathematical analysis and calculation of MI-KGNN and prove that the model does meet the theoretical assumptions and is able to fully characterize hidden user preferences in an end-to-end manner.
- We conduct extensive experiments based on three different datasets. Results show that MI-KGNN significantly outperforms state-of-the-art methods in top-K recommendations.

2   Related Work

Most existing recommender systems adopt algorithms such as collaborative filtering to mine historical interactions between users and items for recommendations. Although CF-based systems perform well in dense datasets, they become less effective while the interaction is sparse. To solve the data sparsity issue and the cold-start problem, researchers usually introduce side information to enhance the recommender system.

The knowledge graph provides an effective way for the extraction of side information as it consists of rich semantic and structural information. In general, KG-aware recommender systems can be divided into three categories: embedding-based, path-based and GNN-based. Embedding-based approaches leverage the structural information in KG to learn the implicit representations of users and items. For example, collaborative knowledge base embedding (CKE) [28] extracts the item's textual representation and visual representation and integrates semantic information in KG. While embedding-based systems perform well on tasks such as KG completion, they can't be used for end-to-end training and are poorly explainable. The performance of path-based systems, e.g., personalized entity recommendation (PER) [27], depends on the choice of the meta-path which requires manual design.

To address the shortcomings of embedding-based and path-based approaches, GNN-based approaches have been proposed. One line of GNN-based studies focuses on mining rules in KG. Ma et al. [11] propose a joint optimization framework that extracts rules from KG and use these rules to assist with recommendations. However, the extracted rules are less versatile and cannot capture user preferences. The other line of researches focuses on extracting user preferences. Wang et al. propose Neural Graph Collaborative Filtering (NGCF) [24] and KGAT [23] to capture user preferences hidden in long-range connectivities. The performance of KGAT is slightly better than NGCF as it introduces the attention mechanism in the model. However, the embedding propagation process of both NGCF and KGAT reduces the characteristics of different users. The KGCN model [22] leverage interactions with the user's hidden state during embedding propagation to avoid the above issue. KGCN-LS [21] mitigates the overfitting problem of KGCN by introducing label smoothing regularization. Compared with other models, KGCN-LS can accurately learn user preferences and achieve better recommendation performance, yet it has not fully leveraged interactions between items and the neighborhood during the embedding propagation process. In this work, we propose to address this issue by exploring multi-dimension interactions in a more systematic way according to a set of assumptions.

3   MI-KGNN

In this section, we first give a formal definition of the KG-aware recommendation problem. Then we present four basic assumptions and analyze the shortcomings of existing solutions. Finally, we elaborate the proposed model and give mathematical verification.

3.1   Problem Definition

Classical recommendation approaches analyze the user-item interaction matrix $A \in \mathbb{R}^{m \times n}$ to determine suitable items for the user. When user u and item v have historical interactions, $a_{uv} = 1$, otherwise $a_{uv} = 0$. The KG-aware recommender system adds a knowledge graph $\mathcal{G}$ that is composed of entities and relationships. Generally, a knowledge graph $\mathcal{G}$ contains a set of triples (h, r, t), where h is the head entity, t is the tail entity, and r is the relationship between the head entity and the tail entity. For example, the triple (*The Avengers 4, film.film.director, Russo brothers*) means that the film "*The Avengers 4*" is directed by *Russo brothers*. Each triple contains a fact which is conducive to the representation of users and items. Our task is to use the above data to learn the characteristics of users and items to predict the possibility of new interactions in matrix A. Specifically, we need to build a model that learns the user representation $\mathbf{u} \in \mathbb{R}^d$ and the item representation $\mathbf{v} \in \mathbb{R}^d$, and then learn a prediction function $\hat{y} = F(\mathbf{u}, \mathbf{v}|W, A, \mathbf{G})$ which outputs the possibility of a new interaction between user $\mathbf{u} \in \mathbb{R}^d$ and item $\mathbf{v} \in \mathbb{R}^d$. W is the model parameters of function of F.

3.2   Problem Analysis

To improve the recommendation performance, we propose to learn more accurate node representations by exploring not only explicit information (i.e., historical user-item interactions) but also implicit information (i.e., side information in knowledge graph). The classical collaborative filtering algorithm in recommender system is based on two basic assumptions: 1) users with same behaviors are similar (A1); 2) items related to the same user are similar (A2). These assumptions allow information to be propagated in the user-item bipartite graph, as shown in the top right of Fig. 1.

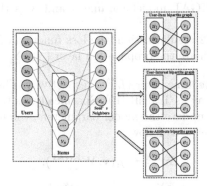

Fig. 1. Illustration of multi-dimension interactions.

In the KG-aware recommender system, each item in the user-item bipartite graph corresponds to an entity in the KG. We define entities in the KG that have corresponding items in the user-item bipartite graph as seeds. The seeds and their neighbors can form another bipartite graph, and neighbors of a seed can be regarded as its attributes, as shown in the bottom right of Fig. 1. Thereby, based on the idea of collaborative filtering, a straightforward assumption is that items with same attributes are similar (A3).

Furthermore, neighbors of a seed may also contribute to the representation of the user who interacted with the corresponding item. They represent the user's possible preferences that might have resulted in certain historical interactions. Users and neighbors of the seeds form the 3rd bipartite graph, as shown in the middle right of Fig. 1. Similarly, another straightforward assumption is that users with same interests are similar (A4). Inspired by the collaborative filtering approach, we propose to develop a GNN-based KG-aware recommendation model by utilizing all the above four assumptions for node representation.

While some existing KG-aware recommendation models are also designed based on these assumptions, their updating direction ignores or weakens at least one of the assumptions. In the rest of this section, we will analyze two representative models KGAT and KGCN.

KGAT fuses the user-item bipartite graph and KG into a collaborative knowledge graph in which users do not interact directly with the neighbors of seeds. KGAT mainly consists of three layers: the embedding layer, the propagation layer and the prediction layer. The loss function of KGAT is defined as follows:

$$L^{\mathrm{KGAT}} = L^{\mathrm{EM}} + \sum_{(u,v^+,v^-)\in O} -\ln \sigma \left(y(u,v^+) - y(u,v^-) \right) + \lambda ||\mathbf{W}^{\mathrm{KGAT}}||_2^2, \quad (1)$$

where L^{EM} is the loss function of the embedding layer, $\sigma\left(\cdot\right)$ is the sigmoid function, $O = \{(u,v^+,v^-)|(u,v^+) \in \mathbf{R}^+, (u,v^-) \in \mathbf{R}^-\}$ denotes the training set, in which $(u,i) \in \mathbf{R}^+$ while $A_{ui} = 1$ and $(u,i) \in \mathbf{R}^-$ while $A_{ui} = 0$. $\mathbf{W}^{\mathrm{KGAT}}$ is parameters of the KGAT model parameter, and λ is the L2 regularization parameter.

Regardless of the L2 regularization, the loss function of KGAT mainly consists of two parts, which are the propagation layer ($\sum_{(u,v^+,v^-)\in O} -\ln \sigma(y(u,v^+) - y(u,v^-)))$ and the embedding layer (L^{EM}) respectively. The embedding layer is designed in the same way as TransR [10]. Specifically, as KGAT uses the gradient descent method to update the model parameters, the updating direction in a single embedding layer is as follows:

$$\Delta \mathbf{u}^{\mathrm{EM}} = g_1(\mathbf{v}, \mathbf{W}^{\mathrm{KGAT}}), \quad (2)$$

$$\Delta \mathbf{v}^{\mathrm{EM}} = g_2(\mathbf{v}_{\mathrm{N}}, \mathbf{u}, \mathbf{W}^{\mathrm{KGAT}}), \quad (3)$$

where $\mathbf{u}$ and $\mathbf{v}$ represent the embedding of user u and item v. $\mathbf{v}_{\mathrm{N}}$ is the embedding of v's neighbors, $\Delta \mathbf{u}$ and $\Delta \mathbf{v}$ are the increments of $\mathbf{u}$ and $\mathbf{v}$, and g ($\mathbf{v}$ only represents a function related to $\mathbf{v}$).

Furthermore, $y\left(\cdot\right)$ in Eq. (1) is the prediction function, which is defined as the inner product as follows:

$$y(u,v) = \mathbf{u} \cdot \mathbf{v}. \quad (4)$$

Thereby, the updating direction in a single propagation layer is as follows:

$$\Delta \mathbf{u}^{\mathrm{ppg}} = g_3(\mathbf{v}), \quad (5)$$

$$\Delta \mathbf{v}^{\mathrm{ppg}} = g_4(\mathbf{u}). \quad (6)$$

Based on Eq. (2) (6), the updating direction of user embedding and item embedding in KGAT can be represented as follows:

$$\Delta \mathbf{u}^{\mathrm{total}} = g_1(\mathbf{v}, \mathbf{W}^{\mathrm{KGAT}}) + g_3(\mathbf{v}), \quad (7)$$

$$\Delta \mathbf{v}^{\mathrm{total}} = g_2(\mathbf{v}_{\mathrm{N}}, \mathbf{u}, \mathbf{W}^{\mathrm{KGAT}}) + g_4(\mathbf{u}). \quad (8)$$

Based on Eq. (7), by repeating the embedding layer for multiple times, information of the two-hop neighbors will be propagated to the central node, i.e., the user's preference information is transmitted to the user node during embedding propagation. In particular, the experimental results of KGAT demonstrate that the best performance is obtained when the embedding layer is repeated for 4 times. However, since the user's preference information needs to pass through the seed node first, the information will be weakened when the model parameters are updated. Thereby, we can conclude that in KGAT the updating direction of the user's embedded value is not close enough to one's actual interest.

The second representative model is KGCN, which considers user embedding during message propagation, i.e., allows users to interact directly with the seed's neighbors. For different users, the embedding of the same item is different. The embedding formula of the seed node in a single KGCN layer is as follows:

$$
\mathbf{v}^u = \sigma \left(\mathbf{W}(\mathbf{v} + \sum_{v_N \in \mathbf{N}_v(i)} \frac{\exp(\mathbf{u} \cdot \mathbf{r}_{v,v_N})}{\sum_{v_N \in \mathbf{N}_v(i)} \exp(\mathbf{u} \cdot \mathbf{r}_{v,v_N})} \cdot \mathbf{v}_N) + \mathbf{b} \right),
\tag{9}
$$

where $\mathbf{v}^u$ is the embedding of item v from the perspective of user u. v_N represents the neighbor of item v, $\mathbf{N}_v(i)$ represents the set of v's neighbors, and $\mathbf{v}_N$ is a member of $\mathbf{N}_v(i)$. $\mathbf{r}_{v,v_N}$ is the relation between item v and its neighbors v_N. $\mathbf{W}$ and $\mathbf{b}$ are the trainable parameters, $\sigma(\cdot)$ is the activation function. The prediction function is the inner product of the embedding of u and the embedding of v, defined as:

$$
\hat{y}_{uv} = \mathbf{u} \cdot \mathbf{v}^u,
\tag{10}
$$

During the model training process, KGCN also uses the gradient descent method to update the model parameters. The loss function of KGCN is as follows:

$$
L^{\mathrm{KGCN}} = \sum_{u \in U} \left(\sum_{v:a_{uv}=1} L_c(a_{uv}, \hat{y}_{uv}) - \sum_{i=1}^{T^u} E_{v_i \sim P(v_i)} L_c(a_{uv_i}, \hat{y}_{uv_i}) \right)
$$
$$
+ \lambda \|\mathbf{W}^{\mathrm{KGCN}}\|_2^2,
\tag{11}
$$

where L_c is cross-entropy loss, P is a negative sampling distribution, and T^u is the number of negative samples for user u. In KGCN, P follows a uniform distribution and $T^u = |\{v : a_{uv} = 1\}|$. The last term is the L2-regularizer. According to Eq. (9), (10) and (11), we can derive the updating direction of user embedding and item embedding as follows:

$$
\Delta \mathbf{u} = f_1(\mathbf{v}^u) + f_2(\mathbf{r}, \mathbf{v}_N, \mathbf{W}),
\tag{12}
$$

$$
\Delta \mathbf{v} = f_3(\mathbf{u}, \mathbf{W}).
\tag{13}
$$

According to Eq. (12) and (13), we can see v's neighbors will not directly impact the updating direction of v's embedded value, although multi-layer KGCN will propagate the influence of v's neighbors and $\mathbf{v}_N$ will eventually affect $\mathbf{v}^u$. In other words, $\mathbf{v}_N$ has a weak effect on v during the model's updating phase. Thereby, we conclude that the updating direction of the item's embedded value is not close enough to its neighbors in the KGCN model.

3.3 Implementation of MI-KGNN

In the previous section, we proved that existing models did not fully meet the four assumptions. In this section, we will present the detailed design of the proposed MI-KGNN model, which explores all the possible information indicated these assumptions.

As presented in Sect. 3.1, a collaborative knowledge graph can be viewed as three bipartite graphs. However, it is not the best choice to perform node embedding on three bipartite graphs at the same time. We choose to perform node embedding only in KG, and increase the interaction between users and seed neighbors as well as the interaction between seeds and their neighbors during embedding propagation in KG. Accordingly, we design the MI-KGNN layer, which is used to aggregate useful information in KG to enhance the recommendation performance, as shown in Fig. 2.

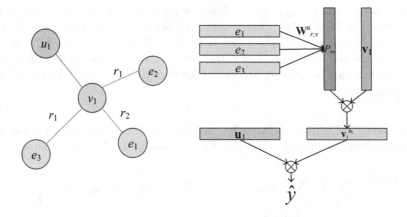

Fig. 2. Overview of a single MI-KGNN layer

First, similar to KGCN, we allow users to interact directly with neighbors of the seed in MI-KGNN, so that the model meets assumption A4. As a result, the user's preference can be characterized based on the seed's neighbors. After normalization, the weight of the interaction is as follows:

$$\mathbf{W}_{r,v}^u = \frac{\exp(\mathbf{u} \cdot \mathbf{r}_{v,v_N})}{\sum\limits_{v_N \in \mathbf{N}_v(i)} \exp(\mathbf{u} \cdot \mathbf{r}_{v,v_N})}, \tag{14}$$

where $\mathbf{N}_v(i)$ represents the set of item v's neighbors, which can be called as v's receptive field. The preference of user u for item v is the weighted combination of the information of the entities in v's receptive field by weighting:

$$p_{uv} = \sum\limits_{v_N \in \mathbf{N}_v(i)} \mathbf{W}_{r,v}^u \cdot \mathbf{v}_N. \tag{15}$$

Next, we need to aggregate the user preferences p_{uv} and the item embedding $\mathbf{v}$ in KG. The aggregator agt: $\mathbb{R}^d \times \mathbb{R}^d \to \mathbb{R}^d$ in MI-KGNN is defined as follows:

$$agt(\mathbf{v}, p_{uv}) = \sigma\left(\mathbf{W}_1\left(\mathbf{v} + p_{uv}\right) + \mathbf{W}_2 Q(\mathbf{v}, p_{uv}) + \mathbf{b}\right), \tag{16}$$

where $\mathbf{W}_1$, $\mathbf{W}_2$ and $\mathbf{b}$ are the trainable parameters, $Q(\mathbf{v}, p_{uv}) : \mathbb{R}^d \times \mathbb{R}^d \to \mathbb{R}^d$ is the element-wise product function. The difference between the proposed aggregator and the one used in KGCN is that we take into account interactions between the item and its neighbors during the aggregation process, which make the model addresses assumption A3. Once the scope of the receptive field is no longer limited to one-hop neighbors, the aggregation process can be repeated for multiple times to obtain information of nodes that are far away. Specifically, during the first aggregation process, a seed node will aggregate all the information of selected one-hop neighbors. Meanwhile, one-hop neighbors of the seed node will also aggregates the information of the two-hop neighbors. Then, during the second aggregation process, the information of selected two-hop neighbors will be integrated into the embedding of the seed node. Obviously, if we need to explore the information of the h-hop neighbors of the seed node, the aggregation process should be repeated for h times, which can be defined as follows:

$$\mathbf{v}^u = \mathbf{v}^h = agt(\mathbf{v}^{h-1}, p_{uv}^{h-1}), \tag{17}$$

$$p_{uv}^{h-1} = \sum_{v_N \in \mathbf{N}_v(i)} \mathbf{W}_{r,v}^u \cdot \mathbf{v}_N^{h-1}, \tag{18}$$

where $\mathbf{v}^h$ is the item embedding $\mathbf{v}$ after the hth aggregation process, which aggregates the neighbor information and its own information in the h-1th aggregation process. Particularly, if the maximum depth of information propagation is h, the activation function is $ReLU$ for the first h-1 times of aggregation, and tan for the hth aggregation process. In this case, $\mathbf{v}^h$ can be regarded as $\mathbf{v}^u$, i.e., the embedding of item v from the perspective of user u.

Finally, the prediction function used in the MI-KGNN model is inner product as described in Eq. (10). The loss function of MI-KGNN is defined as follows, which has one more constraint (i.e., another parameter matrix) compared with the loss function of KGCN.

$$L = \sum_{u \in U} \left(\sum_{v:a_{uv}=1} L_c(a_{uv}, \hat{y}_{uv}) - \sum_{i=1}^{T^u} E_{v_i \sim P(v_i)} L_c(a_{uv_i}, \hat{y}_{uv_i}) \right) \\ + \lambda \|\mathbf{W}_1 + \mathbf{W}_2\|_2^2. \tag{19}$$

According to Eq. (17), (18) and (19), we can derive the updating direction of user embedding and item embedding in MI-KGNN as follows:

$$\Delta\mathbf{u} = h_1(\mathbf{v}^u) + h_2(\mathbf{r}, \mathbf{v}_N, \mathbf{W}_1, \mathbf{W}_2), \tag{20}$$

$$\Delta\mathbf{v} = h_3(\mathbf{u}, \mathbf{W}_1) + h_4(\mathbf{v}_N, \mathbf{u}, \mathbf{W}_1, \mathbf{W}_2). \tag{21}$$

Accordingly, we can see that by considering only a single MI-KGNN layer, the updating direction of the model's parameters is already in line with all the four assumptions. Compared with KGCN, the proposed MI-KGNN model increases the interaction between items and their neighbors during the aggregation process, so that the updating direction of item embedding is in line with all the four assumptions.

MI-KGNN has the same problem of overfitting as KGCN. We use the label smoothing regularization in KGCN-LS to alleviate this problem. While the computational complexity of MI-KGNN is similar to KGCN-LS, the running time of MI-KGNN is slightly longer than KGCN-LS, as we consider more interactions during the aggregation process.

4   Experiments

4.1   Dataset Description

To evaluate the effectiveness of MI-KGNN, we utilize the following three datasets, which are same as KGCN-LS:

Table 1. Statistics and hyper-parameter settings for the datasets (H: depth of the receptive field, d: dimension of embeddings, n: neighbor sampling size, λ: L2 regularizer weight, α: learning rate, β: label smoothness regularizer weight).

	Movie	Music	Restaurant
#users	138,159	1,872	2,298,698
#items	16,954	3,846	1,362
#interactions	13,501,622	42,346	23,416,418
#entities	102,569	9,366	28,115
#relations	32	60	7
#triples	499,474	15,518	160,519
h	1	1	2
d	32	16	8
n	16	8	4
λ	1×10^{-7}	9.1×10^{-5}	9.8×10^{-8}
α	2×10^{-2}	5×10^{-4}	2×10^{-2}
batch size	65,535	128	65,535
β	1	0.1	0.5

- **MovieLens-20M**: a stable benchmark dataset, which consists of approximately 20 million ratings and 465,000 tag applications applied to 27,000 movies by 138,000 users.

- **Last.FM**: a music listening dataset, which contains artist listening records of 1892 users from Last.FM online music platform. The music recommendation dataset is smaller than the other two datasets.
- **Dianping-Food**: a restaurant recommendation dataset provided by Dianping.com, which consists of 10 million interactions between nearly 2.3 million users and 1.3 thousand restaurants.

Since differences in knowledge graphs will largely affect the results, we use the same knowledge graphs as the KGCN-LS experiment. Similarly, data preprocessing is also similar to KGCN-LS. More detailed dataset related information is presented in Table 1.

4.2 Baselines

The baseline we selected in the experiment is as follows:

- **SVD** [9]: a CF-based model which measures node similarity through interaction. NCF [6] is also a well-known CF-based method. The performance of NCF is slightly lower than SVD on our dataset, and the two are very similar, so we present the better one here.
- **LibFM** [16]: a feature-based model trained with the user ID and the item ID as features.
- **LibFM + TransE** [1]: Unlike LibFM, the used feature is the representation after learning by the TransE method.
- **PER** [27]: a path-based method, which extracts qualified meta-paths as connectivity between a user and an item.
- **CKE** [28]: an embedding-based method that combines various item embeddings from different sources including TransR on KG.
- **RippleNet** [20]: a state-of-the-art algorithm that spread user preferences on KG to learn the potential interests of users.
- **KGCN** [22]: a GNN-based method which transforms a heterogeneous KG into a user-personalized weighted graph.
- **KGCN-LS** [21]: a GNN-based method which optimizes the over-fitting problem of KGCN.

Table 2. The results of Recall@K in top-K recommendation.

Model	Movie				Music				Restaurant			
	R@2	R@10	R@50	R@100	R@2	R@10	R@50	R@100	R@2	R@10	R@50	R@100
MI-KGNN	**0.05**	**0.16**	**0.358**	**0.483**	**0.045**	**0.125**	**0.286**	**0.374**	**0.047**	0.168	**0.366**	0.485
KGCN-LS	0.043	0.157	0.334	0.468	**0.045**	0.119	0.275	0.36	**0.047**	**0.17**	0.34	**0.487**
KGCN-avg	0.04	0.152	0.325	0.448	0.032	0.112	0.265	0.364	0.039	0.157	0.324	0.475
RippleNet	0.045	0.13	0.278	0.447	0.032	0.101	0.242	0.336	0.04	0.155	0.328	0.44
CKE	0.034	0.107	0.244	0.322	0.023	0.07	0.18	0.296	0.034	0.138	0.305	0.437
PER	0.022	0.077	0.16	0.243	0.014	0.052	0.116	0.176	0.023	0.102	0.256	0.354
LibFM+TransE	0.041	0.125	0.28	0.396	0.032	0.102	0.259	0.326	0.044	0.161	0.343	0.455
LibFM	0.039	0.121	0.271	0.388	0.03	0.103	0.263	0.33	0.043	0.156	0.332	0.448
SVD	0.036	0.124	0.277	0.401	0.029	0.098	0.24	0.332	0.039	0.152	0.329	0.451

Table 3. The results of AUC in CTR prediction.

	Movie	Music	Restaurant
MI-KGNN	**0.979**	**0.804**	0.847
KGCN-LS	**0.979**	0.803	**0.85**
KGCN-avg	0.975	0.774	0.844
RippleNet	0.96	0.77	0.833
CKE	0.924	0.744	0.802
PER	0.832	0.633	0.746
LibFM+TransE	0.966	0.777	0.839
LibFM	0.959	0.778	0.837
SVD	0.963	0.769	0.838

Specifically, as the KGAT model uses different datasets and different knowledge graphs, we did not take it as a baseline in this work.

4.3   Experimental Settings

We divide the dataset into a training set, a validation set, and a test set with a ratio of 3:1:1, and repeat the experiment for 5 times to obtain the average performance. Like the KGCN-LS experiment, we perform click-through rate (CTR) prediction and top-K recommendation, and use AUC and recall to evaluate the performance. The experiment is conducted with Python 3.6, TensorFlow 1.12.0, and NumPy 1.14.3. The hyper-parameter settings are shown in Table 1.

Table 4. R@10 of MI-KGNN w.r.t. neighbor sampling size n.

n	2	4	8	16	32
Movie	0.140	0.139	0.152	**0.16**	0.157
Music	0.102	0.113	**0.125**	0.124	0.124
Restaurant	0.160	**0.168**	0.163	0.157	0.148

Table 5. R@10 of MI-KGNN w.r.t. depth of support set h.

h	1	2	3	4
Movie	**0.16**	0.113	0.081	0.032
Music	**0.125**	0.112	0.103	0.066
Restaurant	0.147	**0.168**	0.102	0.035

4.4   Results and Discussion

The results of CTR prediction and top-K recommendation are presented in Table 2 and Table 3, respectively. Specifically, according to our experiments, some of the results of KGCN-LS in Table 3 is slightly different from those reported in [21], but the overall performance of KGCN-LS does not change much.

As shown in Table 2, MI-KGNN performs as well as KGCN-LS in the CTR prediction experiment. The next better models are KGCN, RippleNet and LibFM+TransE, as all of them use the information in KG to assist the recommendation. In the CTR prediction experiment, the worst performing model is PER. This does not mean that PER is useless, as the performance of PER depends on the choice of the meta path which is difficult to design in KG.

In the top-K recommendation experiment, MI-KGNN significantly outperforms KGCN-LS. Specifically, compared with KGCN-LS, the average recall rate of MI-KGNN has increased by 7.1%, 3.2% and 1.5% in the film, music and restaurant datasets, respectively. Obviously, by exploring more interactions, MI-KGNN has better performance than KGCN-LS. Specifically, we can see that MI-KGNN's performance improvement on the movie dataset is higher than the other two datasets. The reason might be that the number of entities in the movie dataset is the largest, and MI-KGNN optimizes the representation of these entities. In the KGCN-LS experiment, the model performed best on the restaurant dataset when the information of the two-hop neighbors was considered. The addition of two-hop neighbor information causes the information of one-hop neighbor to interact with the central node more during the propagation process, which is similar to MI-KGNN. Therefore, in the restaurant dataset, MI-KGNN's performance improvement is not obvious. Nevertheless, we can conclude that the representation of users and items learned by the MI-KGNN model can better reflect user preferences and item attributes.

Furthermore, as shown in Table 3, models with better performance in CTR prediction do not necessarily perform well in top-K recommendation. For example, the LibFM+TransE model with better performance in CTR prediction is not as good as RippleNet in top-K prediction. The reason might be that RippleNet can capture user preferences much better, and the recommended item is more comprehensive than LibFM+TransE.

In the experiment, we made some adjustments to the hyperparameters, which are used to determine the number of neighbors and the number of propagation layers. Detailed results can be found in Table 4 and 5. Accordingly, we find that while more neighbors can provide more information, there might be some noise in the information, which will interfere with the final recommendation. Thereby, we need to choose the right number of neighbors.

Meanwhile, since MI-KGNN mimics the embedding propagation mechanism in GCN, MI-KGNN also encounters an over-smooth problem after stacking multiple layers, as shown in Table 5. For example, the recall rate of MI-KGNN on the movie dataset decreases from 0.16 to 0.032 while h increases from 1 to 4.

5   Conclusions and Future Work

In this work, we propose the MI-KGNN model for KG-aware recommendation. Inspired by the idea of collaborative filtering, we identify 4 basic assumptions and design a GNN-based model to address them by systematically exploring possible information indicated by these assumptions. Compared with existing models, MI-KGNN increases the interaction between central nodes and neighbor nodes when aggregating information, which makes node embedding in KG more precise. Experiments on three widely used datasets show that MI-KGNN outperforms state-of-the-art baselines.

There are some shortcomings in this work, which will be our future work. First, we look forward to finding a better way to solve the over-fitting problem of the proposed model. While more interactions are explored in MI-KGNN, we did not introduce new regularization other than the L2-regularizer. Even though we adopted the label smoothing regularization proposed in KGCN-LS, the over-fitting problem is only relieved rather than solved. Second, in the current model we did not choose neighbors based on their influences on the central node. Thereby, we plan to improve the choosing strategy of neighbors in future.

References

1. Bordes, A., Usunier, N., Garcia-Duran, A., Weston, J., Yakhnenko, O.: Translating embeddings for modeling multi-relational data. In: Advances in Neural Information Processing Systems, pp. 2787–2795 (2013)
2. Cao, Y., Wang, X., He, X., Hu, Z., Chua, T.S.: Unifying knowledge graph learning and recommendation: towards a better understanding of user preferences. In: The World Wide Web Conference, pp. 151–161. ACM (2019)
3. Catherine, R., Cohen, W.: Personalized recommendations using knowledge graphs: a probabilistic logic programming approach. In: Proceedings of the 10th ACM Conference on Recommender Systems, pp. 325–332. ACM (2016)
4. Cheng, H.T., et al.: Wide & deep learning for recommender systems. In: Proceedings of the 1st Workshop on Deep Learning for Recommender Systems, pp. 7–10. ACM (2016)
5. Cheng, Z., Ding, Y., Zhu, L., Kankanhalli, M.: Aspect-aware latent factor model: rating prediction with ratings and reviews. In: Proceedings of the 2018 World Wide Web Conference, pp. 639–648. International World Wide Web Conferences Steering Committee (2018)
6. He, X., Liao, L., Zhang, H., Nie, L., Hu, X., Chua, T.S.: Neural collaborative filtering. In: Proceedings of the 26th International Conference on World Wide Web, pp. 173–182. International World Wide Web Conferences Steering Committee (2017)
7. Hu, B., Shi, C., Zhao, W.X., Yu, P.S.: Leveraging meta-path based context for top-n recommendation with a neural co-attention model. In: Proceedings of the 24th ACM SIGKDD International Conference on Knowledge Discovery & Data Mining, pp. 1531–1540. ACM (2018)
8. Hu, L., Jian, S., Cao, L., Chen, Q.: Interpretable recommendation via attraction modeling: learning multilevel attractiveness over multimodal movie contents. In: IJCAI, pp. 3400–3406 (2018)

9. Koren, Y.: Factorization meets the neighborhood: a multifaceted collaborative filtering model. In: Proceedings of the 14th ACM SIGKDD International Conference on Knowledge Discovery and Data Mining, pp. 426–434. ACM (2008)

10. Lin, Y., Liu, Z., Sun, M., Liu, Y., Zhu, X.: Learning entity and relation embeddings for knowledge graph completion. In: Twenty-Ninth AAAI Conference on Artificial Intelligence (2015)

11. Ma, W., et al.: Jointly learning explainable rules for recommendation with knowledge graph. In: The World Wide Web Conference, pp. 1210–1221. ACM (2019)

12. McInerney, J., et al.: Explore, exploit, and explain: personalizing explainable recommendations with bandits. In: Proceedings of the 12th ACM Conference on Recommender Systems, pp. 31–39. ACM (2018)

13. Monti, F., Bronstein, M., Bresson, X.: Geometric matrix completion with recurrent multi-graph neural networks. In: Advances in Neural Information Processing Systems, pp. 3697–3707 (2017)

14. Nandanwar, S., Moroney, A., Murty, M.N.: Fusing diversity in recommendations in heterogeneous information networks. In: Proceedings of the Eleventh ACM International Conference on Web Search and Data Mining, pp. 414–422. ACM (2018)

15. Palumbo, E., Rizzo, G., Troncy, R.: Entity2rec: learning user-item relatedness from knowledge graphs for top-n item recommendation. In: Proceedings of the Eleventh ACM Conference on Recommender Systems, pp. 32–36. ACM (2017)

16. Rendle, S.: Factorization machines with LIBFM. ACM Trans. Intell. Syst. Technol. (TIST) **3**(3), 57 (2012)

17. Sarwar, B.M., Karypis, G., Konstan, J.A., Riedl, J., et al.: Item-based collaborative filtering recommendation algorithms. In: WWW, vol. 1, pp. 285–295 (2001)

18. Shi, C., Zhang, Z., Luo, P., Yu, P.S., Yue, Y., Wu, B.: Semantic path based personalized recommendation on weighted heterogeneous information networks. In: Proceedings of the 24th ACM International on Conference on Information and Knowledge Management, pp. 453–462. ACM (2015)

19. Sun, Y., Han, J., Yan, X., Yu, P.S., Wu, T.: Pathsim: meta path-based top-k similarity search in heterogeneous information networks. Proc. VLDB Endow. **4**(11), 992–1003 (2011)

20. Wang, H., et al.: Ripplenet: propagating user preferences on the knowledge graph for recommender systems. In: Proceedings of the 27th ACM International Conference on Information and Knowledge Management, pp. 417–426. ACM (2018)

21. Wang, H., et al.: Knowledge graph convolutional networks for recommender systems with label smoothness regularization. arXiv preprint arXiv:1905.04413 (2019)

22. Wang, H., Zhao, M., Xie, X., Li, W., Guo, M.: Knowledge graph convolutional networks for recommender systems. In: The World Wide Web Conference, pp. 3307–3313. ACM (2019)

23. Wang, X., He, X., Cao, Y., Liu, M., Chua, T.S.: KGAT: knowledge graph attention network for recommendation. arXiv preprint arXiv:1905.07854 (2019)

24. Wang, X., He, X., Wang, M., Feng, F., Chua, T.S.: Neural graph collaborative filtering. arXiv preprint arXiv:1905.08108 (2019)

25. Wu, Y., Liu, H., Yang, Y.: Graph convolutional matrix completion for bipartite edge prediction. In: KDIR, pp. 49–58 (2018)

26. Ying, R., He, R., Chen, K., Eksombatchai, P., Hamilton, W.L., Leskovec, J.: Graph convolutional neural networks for web-scale recommender systems. In: Proceedings of the 24th ACM SIGKDD International Conference on Knowledge Discovery & Data Mining, pp. 974–983. ACM (2018)

27. Yu, X., et al.: Personalized entity recommendation: a heterogeneous information network approach. In: Proceedings of the 7th ACM International Conference on Web Search and Data Mining, pp. 283–292. ACM (2014)

28. Zhang, F., Yuan, N.J., Lian, D., Xie, X., Ma, W.Y.: Collaborative knowledge base embedding for recommender systems. In: Proceedings of the 22nd ACM SIGKDD International Conference on Knowledge Discovery and Data Mining, pp. 353–362. ACM (2016)

29. Zhang, Y., Yin, H., Huang, Z., Du, X., Yang, G., Lian, D.: Discrete deep learning for fast content-aware recommendation. In: Proceedings of the Eleventh ACM International Conference on Web Search and Data Mining, pp. 717–726. ACM (2018)

30. Zhao, H., Yao, Q., Li, J., Song, Y., Lee, D.L.: Meta-graph based recommendation fusion over heterogeneous information networks. In: Proceedings of the 23rd ACM SIGKDD International Conference on Knowledge Discovery and Data Mining, pp. 635–644. ACM (2017)

MGCN4REC: Multi-graph Convolutional Network for Next Basket Recommendation with Instant Interest

Yan Zhang, Bin Guo[✉], Qianru Wang, Yueqi Sun, and Zhiwen Yu

Northwestern Polytechnical University, Xi'an 710129, China
guob@nwpu.edu.cn

Abstract. Sequential patterns involved in users' historical behaviors have received extensive attention in recommendation system, which is important to represent item-level preferences. The existing works often combine the long- and short-term patterns to capture user's preferences. But the short-term preferences modeled by the recent behavior patterns cannot clearly indicate the users' instant interest. In this paper, we propose a sequential recommendation model MGCN4REC based on multi-graph to learn the representation of users and items and then model preferences and instant interests simultaneously. Firstly, this paper utilizes multi-graph convolutional network (MGCN) to learn users and items embeddings from multi-graph. Secondly, to aggregate preferences and instant interests, we use the attention mechanism to find the degrees of dependencies on these two features. Finally, this paper conducts experiments on real data sets of Amazon to evaluate the performance of MGCN4REC model, and the results show that our model outperforms the current state-of-the-art sequential recommendation methods over 15% on the metrics.

Keywords: Sequential recommendation · Multi-graph convolution network · Instant interest · Attention mechanism

1 Introduction

Recommendation systems strive to recommend items that users are willing to purchase or interact with in modern e-commerce applications, however, the large number of user interactions (such as browsing, clicking, collecting, shopping carts, purchasing) in e-commerce makes it a great challenge to identify the users' consumption patterns and interest preferences.

Existing recommendation systems model the user-item interactions mainly in two ways. The first one is traditional recommendation systems that focus on mining static associations from user-item interactions, which are represented by collaborative filtering models [3–5]. The second one is sequential recommendation systems [6, 7] that try to capture the patterns hide in the successive user's interaction behaviors, and the user's long-term preferences and short-term preferences can be dynamically represented.

© Springer Nature Switzerland AG 2020
Z. Yu et al. (Eds.): GPC 2020, LNCS 12398, pp. 171–185, 2020.
https://doi.org/10.1007/978-3-030-64243-3_14

Specifically, the user's long-term preferences reflect in the historical behaviors and the short-term preferences are determined by recent purchases items.

Although the existing sequential recommendation models have achieved promising results, two shortcomings are remained. Firstly, these methods directly use the item sequence to represent the relationship between items. However, they fail to take into account that different users pay attention to different aspects. Secondly, most of the existing models neglect users' instant interests. Specifically, instant interests refer to an instant and specific purchase demand and are more helpful than the short-term preferences. For example, we can learn from the Q&A function in Amazon's earphone information page, as shown in Fig. 1, user's search contents ("airplane use", "workouts") reflects the attention to different aspects when having the same instant purchase needs ("earphone"), which can't be captured in their historical behaviors and more accurate than short-term preferences.

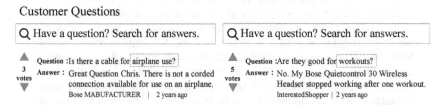

Fig. 1. Q&A in an item page of Amazon. User1 and user2 have different instant requirements when buying an earphone.

To address the above challenges, we propose a sequential recommendation model MGCN4REC. Firstly, inspired by the works in user and item representation learning [8–11], we model the users' historical interaction sequence as a multi-graph (user relationship graph, item relationship graph, and user item bipartite graph), and learn a more feasible representation of each user and item through graph convolution network. Secondly, we use a recurrent neural network to model users' preferences from historical interaction sequence and instant interests from users' question-and-answer data. Finally, we use attention mechanism to aggregate users' preferences and instant interests and make the recommendation.

In summary, the main contributions of this paper are as follows:

- This paper proposes a sequential recommendation model (MGCN4REC) based on preferences and instant interests. We leverage instant interests to better represent short-term preferences and uses the attention mechanism to aggregate preferences and instant interests.
- This paper firstly models the user-item interaction sequence as a multi-graph structure, and leverages a graph convolution network to learn the embedding representation of users and items in the same feature space.
- To evaluate our model, experiments are conducted on Amazon's real dataset and the results show that MGCN4REC outperforms than the state-of-art baselines over 15%.

2   Related Work

Among many Internet-based services [12] such as e-commerce, the recommendation system plays a vital role, and it has also attracted widespread attention in industry and academia. The related work in this paper mainly includes two aspects of representation learning and sequential recommendation system.

2.1   Representation Learning

For user and item representation learning, the recommendation system evolves according to the embedding between different entities in addition to three models: user-based recommendation based on user similarity, item-based recommendation based on user similarity of item interactions, and user extraction Interact with the characteristics of items and recommend model-based items with these characteristics. All three models inevitably need to embedding users and items to obtain the user-user, item-item, and user-item similarity. The user-based usage scenario is that the number of users is much larger than the number of items and few items appear, mainly focusing on the calculation of user-user similarity. On the contrary, the item-based usage scenario is that the number of items is much larger than the number of users and few new users appear, focusing on calculating items-items similarity. Model-based mainly focuses on calculating the correlation between users and items.

Barkan et al. [9] consider the user's historical interaction sequence as a natural sentence and they propose the item2vec, which maximizes the probability of the appearance of other items in the window under each central item to learn the vector representation of each item. Perozzi et al. [10] converts the historical interaction sequence of the user into a graph and they propose deepwalk, which utilize deep first search (DFS) on each node to obtain multiple item sequences and learn the vector representation of each item through item2vec. Different from DeepWalk, Grover et al. propose an item sequence sampling method by jointly utilizing broad first search (BFS) and deep first search (DFS), called Node2Vec, which allocates sampling probabilities according to the distance between items and the source item. After getting the sequence, they use Item2Vec to learn the representation of each item.

Most of the existing works focus on learning the similarity between items or learning the low-dimensional embedding of users and items separately. One challenge exists when directly combining the embedding of the user and his item sequence since they are in different vector space, making it impossible to directly use their inner product to get a recommendation list. Wu et al. [13] propose SR-GNN which constructs the user's interaction sequence of each session into a directed graph, and then utilizes a gated neural network to learn the representation of each node and users' current session. Grbovic et al. [14] propose list embedding which personalizes recommendations by leveraging Word2vec to model users and items into a sequence. However, due to the specificity of Airbnb data, the method is not robust to our work.

Therefore, this work intends to learn the embedding representation of each node from the user relationship graph, item relationship graph, and user-item interaction bipartite graph through graph convolutional neural network, so as to obtain the similarity between users and items.

2.2 Sequential Recommendation System

In recent years, researchers have begun to focus on various sequential recommendation scenarios, such as the next-basket recommendation [15, 16], session-based recommendation [17–19], and next item recommendation [7, 20].

The existing works of sequential recommender systems are mainly based on sequential pattern mining. Due to the huge success of deep neural networks in the past few years, sequential data modeling methods have made great progress in several applications such as NLP, social media, and recommender systems. For example, Wang *et al.* [16] make the next-time recommendation by hierarchical interactions, which captures the sequential patterns and the user's overall preferences through historical interaction sequences. Hidasi *et al.* [17] utilize recurrent neural networks (RNNs) to model the entire session and then build a session-based recommender system, which have significantly better performance than item-based methods. Tang *et al.* [19] utilize the horizontal convolution kernel and vertical convolution kernel in the convolutional neural network (CNN) to capture the user's long-term interest and short-term interest and make recommendations respectively. Li *et al.* [20] utilize the w-item2vec method to learn the vector of items, and then expresses the user's long-term and short-term preferences and makes recommendations. Although these models consider the user's sequence information, there are still shortcomings in terms of representing user long-term preferences and short-term preferences. In contrast, the method proposed in this paper combines the user's preferences with the instant interests to make recommendations. The preferences and instant interests are obtained from the user's historical interaction sequence with the item and the user's current question text.

In summary, the main work of this paper is to make a unified representation of users and items, and calculate their correlations. Based on this vector, model users' preferences and instant interests to perform sequential recommendations.

3 MGCN4REC Framework

3.1 Preliminaries

Let $U = \{u_1, u_2, \ldots, u_n\}$ denotes the set of users, $I = \{i_1, i_2, \ldots, i_m\}$ denotes the set of items, where n and m denote the number of users and items respectively. In addition, $E = \{e_1, e_2, \ldots, e_{(m+n)}\}$ denotes the embedding vector of all users and items, where e_u is the embedding vector of a user ($e_u \in R^d$, $u \in U$), and e_i is the embedding of the item i_i ($e_i \in R^d$, $i \in I$). For each user $u \in U$, we assume that his/her enquiry time is t_q. Its historical baskets before the question time t_q are represented as:

$$B^u_{<t_q} = \{ \left[e^u, b^u_{t_1} \right], \left[e^u, b^u_{t_2} \right], \ldots, \left[e^u, b^u_{t_{q-1}} \right] \Big| b_{t_j} \subset I \}$$

For each basket, there are usually more than one item in it ($|b_{t_j}| \rangle 1$), Therefore, we utilize the mean pooling operation to present the embedding of the shopping basket at each timestep:

$$b_{t_j} = \frac{1}{|b_{t_j}|} \sum_{k=1}^{|b_{t_j}|} e_{i_k}, \ e_{i_k} \in E$$

where $|b_{t_j}|$ represents the number of items in the shopping basket at the timestep t_j, and e_{i_k} represents the embedding representation of the item i_k in the user's shopping basket. Similarly, the basket after t_q is donated as $b^u_{t_{q+1}}$.

To recommend items with preferences and instant interests, we formalize the problem as the following objective function:

$$L = \sum_u L_u(f(B^u_{<t_q}, s^u), b^u_{t_{q+1}}) \tag{1}$$

Formula (1) is used to indicate the difference between the recommended item and the actual purchased item at the next time t_{q+1}: where $f(\cdot)$ represents a function that predicts the probability of being recommended for other items from an aggregated preferences of traditional preferences and instant interests; $L_u(\cdot)$ represents the loss between the recommended items and the actual purchased items in this method. However, users may not immediately purchase the items they are interested in after asking questions: from the conclusion of Caser [19], it can be known that there is a skipping behavior in the user's interaction (the previous several sequence behaviors do not directly affect the purchase behavior at t + 1, but affect the behavior at t + 2 or even t + 3). Based on this, the aggregated preferences of traditional preferences and instant interests may affect the purchasing behavior at multiple moments after t_{q+1}. Therefore, we redefine the objective function as formula (2), where $B^u_{t>t_q} = U_{t>t_q}b^u_t$ represents a group of items to be purchased after time t_q.

$$L = \sum_u L_u(f(B^u_{<t_q}, s^u), B^{u}_{>t_{q+1}}) \tag{2}$$

In this section, we formally define next-basket recommendation problem, and present the MGCN4REC system in detail, as shown in Fig. 2. MGCN4REC is mainly composed of three modules: multi-graph-based joint embedding of users and items, preferences and instant interests modeling, attention-based preferences aggregating. Firstly MGCN4REC converts the user's historical interaction sequence into a graph, including a user relationship graph taking users as the nodes and the number of items that two nodes interact as the edge weights, an item relationship graph taking items as the nodes and the number of users that two nodes are purchased as the edge weights, the user-item bipartite graph taking users and items as the nodes and the interaction between user and item as edges. Secondly, the graph convolutional network(GCN) is used to learn the representation of each node from three types of graphs, which can obtain the similarity between the users and items. Afterwards, the preferences of users are obtained through a Bi-RNN, and the users' instant interests are analyzed from the user's question text at the current moment. Finally, the user's preferences and instant interests are aggregated based on the attention mechanism for accurate recommendations.

3.2 Multi-graph-Based User-Item Representation

At the first stage of GCN-Rec, the purpose of multi-graph-based user item vector representation learning is to generate a unified representation for each user and project by learning the similarity between them from a large number of user historical interactions.

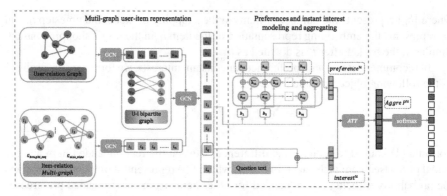

Fig. 2. Architecture of the MGCN4REC system.

In pervious works, sequential recommendations have always used one-hot coding or added an additional embedding layer to the deep learning architecture for items representation [17, 22]. However, for item sets on large e-commerce platforms, on the one hand, the one-hot coding network may cost expensive time, and it is often not well optimized due to the high sparsity [23]. On the other hand, the additional embedding layer will cause a certain loss of neural networks [17]. The item2vec mines similarities between items from user's historical interaction sequences, but it ignores the user interaction intensity for different items, which cannot effectively represent the item features with less interaction and user features. However, the graph neural networks (GNN) can learn from different types of graphs to the rich structural information and the relationships between different nodes, so MGCN4REC uses graph convolutional networks to abstract the representations of users and items.

Different types of heterogeneous graphs can present the characteristics of different dimensions of nodes. For example, we can learn the similarity between items from the shopping relationship graph, which represents those items may be purchased together. Furthermore, we could learn the competition among items from the attention item graph, meaning which item is selected from multiple items. Therefore, this paper uses the multi-graph to represent the relationship between items.

For the representation of items, we first get the sequence of the user's interaction history, $s_u = \left\{ i_1^u, i_2^u, i_3^u, \ldots, i_n^u \right\}$ (u denotes the index of the user), and the purchase relationship graph between items is represented from the historical interaction sequence, $G_{bought\_seq} = \left\{ I, e_{bought\_seq} \right\}$ (I denotes the item set and e_{bought_seq} denotes the edge set, $e_{seq} = \left\{ \left(i_1^1, i_2^1 \right), \left(i_2^1, i_3^1 \right), \ldots \left(i_{(n-1)}^{|U|}, i_n^{|U|} \right) \right\}$, $\left(i_{(n-1)}^{|U|}, i_n^{|U|} \right)$ denotes that $i_{(n-1)}^{|U|}$ has the link with $i_n^{|U|}$). Second, we create a graph of the relationships between simultaneous purchases $G_{also-bought} = \left\{ I, e_{also-bought} \right\}$, where $e_{also-bought}$ indicates that there is an edge between other purchased items at the same time and this item. Third, we create a graph between purchased items and simultaneous browsing items $G_{also-view} = \left\{ I, e_{also-view} \right\}$, where $e_{also-view}$ indicates an edge between the other items browsed and the purchased item. Then calculate the adjacency matrix $A^{|I|*|I|}$ and degree matrix $D^{|I|*|I|}$ of each graph, using the graph convolutional neural network for each graph.

Specifically, the graph convolutional network aggregates the feature information of its neighbor nodes to update its own features for each node in the graph, and then nonlinearly transform the feature information to gain robust feature representations. The feature update function is as follows:

$$h_{v_i}^{l+1} = \sigma \left(\sum_j \frac{1}{c_{ij}} h_{v_j}^l W^l \right) \tag{3}$$

where j indicates the neighboring nodes of v_i, and c_{ij} is a normalization constant for the edge (v_i, v_j), originating from the symmetrically normalized adjacency matrix $D^{-\frac{1}{2}}AD^{-\frac{1}{2}}$ in MGCN4REC.

Convert the update function to compute the nodes in the entire graph, so every neural network layer can then be described as a non-linear function:

$$H^{l+1} = f(H^l, A) \tag{4}$$

with $H^0 = X$ and $H^L = Z$. L is the number of layers, and X is the input features of nodes. In this paper, we use all aspects extracted from all reviews of each item to represent its initial features, and utilize each user's sentiment scores on all aspects to represent the user's initial feature. The specific propagation rule in convolutional layers $f(\cdot)$ can be written as:

$$f(H^l, A) = \sigma(\widehat{D}^{-\frac{1}{2}} \widehat{A} \widehat{D}^{-\frac{1}{2}} H^l W^l) \tag{5}$$

where W^l is a weight matrix for the neural network layer $layer_l$ and $\sigma(\cdot)$ is a non-linear activation function such as ReLU. $\widehat{A} = A + E$, where E is the identity matrix and $\widehat{D}$ is the diagonal degree matrix of $\widehat{A}$, i.e. $\widehat{D} = D + E$.

Since multi-graph can learn the features of nodes from different perspectives, the convolutional neural network is used to the graph G_{bought_seq} of the relationship between items purchased sequences, the graph $G_{also-bought}$ of the relationships between simultaneous purchases and the graph $G_{also-view}$ between purchased items and simultaneous browsing items to obtain the representation of each item:

$$Z_{item} = \left[Z_{seq}, Z_{also-bought}, Z_{also-view} \right]$$

For the representation of the user, repeat formulas (3)–(5), and will get the embedding for each user representing Z_{user}.

Take Z_{user} and Z_{item} as X, use the graph convolutional network for the bipartite graph of users and items interaction, and repeat formula (3)-(5) to obtain the embedding representation of all users and items:

$$Z = \left\{ z_{u_1}, z_{u_2}, \ldots, z_{u_m}, z_{i_1}, z_{i_2}, \ldots, z_{i_n} \right\}$$

3.3 User Preferences and Interests Modeling

The user's decision-making process is mainly affected by two factors: preferences and instant interests. In fact, the user's interaction process is a series of implicit feedback over time. Therefore, unlike traditional recommendation systems that explore user-item interaction from a static way, this paper uses serialized modeling to process the next basket recommendation problem. Specifically, the system designs two models of preferences and instant interests learning to distinguish the user's preferences from the instant interests, and then makes personalized recommendations by combining the user's preferences and instant interests.

Preferences Modeling

As the preferences of the user runs through the entire sequence of the user, they depend not only on the previous purchase sequence but also on the future purchase sequence. Inspired by the bidirectional RNN [24], this paper applies CLSTM to a bidirectional architecture Bi-CLSTM, making full use of the interaction sequence of the forward and backward directions to express the preferences of the user. Therefore, the system developed a deep neural network based on GRU [25] to model the stable preferences of users. After initialization, the hidden state h_j of each interaction is updated from the previous hidden state h_{j-1} at the jth time of the interaction:

$$i_j = \delta(W_{vi}b_j + W_{hi}h_{j-1} + W_{ci}c_{j-1} + \widehat{b_i}),$$
$$f_j = \delta(W_{vf}b_j + W_{hf}h_{j-1} + W_{cf}c_{j-1} + \widehat{b_f}),$$
$$c_j = f_jc_{j-1} + i_j \tanh(W_{vc}b_j + W_{hc}h_{j-1} + \widehat{b_c}),$$
$$o_j = \delta(W_{vo}b_j + W_{ho}h_{j-1} + W_{co}c_j + \widehat{b_o}),$$
$$h_j = o_j \tanh(c_j) \tag{6}$$

where i_j, f_j, and o_j correspond to the input gate, forget gate, and output gate of the GRU, b_j is the vector representation of the basket at the current time, c_j is the value of the GRU memory unit, $\widehat{b}$ is the bias term, and h_j is the hidden status of timestep t_j.

At each time t_q, calculate the hidden state $\overrightarrow{h_{t_q}}$ of the forward RNN based on the previous hidden state $\overrightarrow{h_{t_q-1}}$ and the corresponding basket representation b_{t_q} of the current time; calculate the hidden state $\overleftarrow{h_{t_q}}$ of the forward RNN based on the back hidden state $\overleftarrow{h_{t_q+1}}$ and the corresponding basket representation b_{t_q}; therefore, the hidden state h_{t_q} of the bidirectional RNN at each moment t_q can be expressed by the hidden state of the forward RNN and the hidden state of the backward RNN:

$$h_{t_q} = concatenate(\overrightarrow{h_{t_q}}, \overleftarrow{h_{t_q}}) \tag{7}$$

Represent the preferences of user u through the average pooling layer as

$$preference^u = average(h_1, h_2, \ldots, h_{t_q}) \tag{8}$$

Instant Interests Modeling

As shown in the user question data of Fig. 1, the user's question can clearly reflect the user's instant interests and the characteristics most interested in the item in the recent period.

Instant interests are represented by the embedding vector of the item being questioned at the time t_q and the vector of the question text:

$$interest^u = [e_{t_q} | Score_{a_1}, Score_{a_2}, \ldots, Score_{a_m}], \quad e_{t_q} \in E \tag{9}$$

where $Score_{a_i}$ is the emotional score of the $aspect_i$ in the user's question text. After obtaining the preferences and instant interests of user u at the question time t_q, by combining the stable preferences and dynamic instant interests, the aggregated preferences $P^u_{t_q}$ of user u at the question time t_q can be obtained, and then through the fully connected layer to make personalized recommendations.

3.4 Attention-Based Preferences Aggregating

If simply using the user aggregation preferences $P^u_{t_q}$ obtained in Sect. 3.3 for recommendation, it means that the degree of dependence on each user's preferences and instant interests is same. But in fact, the impact of preferences and instant interests on the final decision-making behavior of users is essentially different. Among them, instant interests determine the items that users want to buy, and preferences determine the details of item. And may be different for different users depend on preferences and instant interests, user A may be more in line with historical habits when shopping, while user B may prefer novel items. Therefore, the system introduces an attention mechanism [2] to aggregate the user's preferences and instant interests. The aggregated preferences after the introduction of the attention mechanism is expressed as follows:

$$Aggre \, P^u_{t_q} = \beta [preference^u, interest^u]^T \tag{10}$$

$$\beta^u_i = \frac{exp(Aggre \, p^u_i)}{\sum_{j=1}^{||preference|+|interest||} exp(Aggre \, p^u_j)} \tag{11}$$

Finally, the system uses a fully connected layer to find the relationship between the aggregation preferences $P^u_{t_q}$ and the target term, as shown in formula (12). And $\hat{y}^u$ represents the probability of user u interacting with the item after asking a question:

$$\hat{y}^u = sigmoid \, (W \, (Aggre \, p^u)^T + b) \tag{12}$$

3.5 Model Training

The Loss function of this system includes two parts: the first is the difference between the recommendation made by aggregated preferences and the actual purchase of items as shown in formula (2); the other part introduces an auxiliary loss function that is he error between the predicted preferences and the real preferences at each $t + 1$ moment in preferences modeling. The user's preferences modeling is introduced in the Sect. 3.3.1. The GRU layer can obtain the set of items that may be purchased at time t + 1. The system reduces the error between the predicted set and the real set at each time, so that the recommendation can obtain better accuracy. The set of items that may be purchased at t + 1 can be expressed as:

$$\hat{b}^u_{t+1} = f_R(b^u_t, h_t) \tag{13}$$

where $f_R(\cdot)$ is a function based on the RNN structure, $h_t \in R^d$ is the hidden state at time t, and it is a dynamic representation of user preferences. In this article, $f_R(\cdot)$ selects GRU. At the same time, we introduce the error between the predicted value and the true value at each time:

$$L_R = \sum_{t=1}^{t_q-1} L_t(\hat{b}^u_t, b^u_t) \tag{14}$$

where $L_R(\cdot)$ is a loss function that measures the error between predicted preferences and true preferences. A cross-entropy loss function is used in this system, as shown in formula (15):

$$L = \sum_u (\gamma L_u(\hat{y}^u, B^u_{t>t_q}) + (1 - \gamma)L_R) \tag{15}$$

where $\gamma \in (0, 1)$ is a parameter that balances the relative importance of the two-part loss function. Due to the large number of items, if all negative samples are used to reduce the Loss function, the time complexity and space complexity of training will be too high. Therefore, in this paper, the system uses the negative sampling technique to train the $L_U(\cdot)$ function.

4 Experiment

4.1 Dataset

We collect amazon reviews and q&a records in [26]. Users are used to comment on items they buy and subsequent users can take comments as an advice. We first obtain the comment records to obtain the initial characteristics of the user and the item, and then leverage the user's history to construct the commodity graph and the user graph. To extract features from item review data, we first used Stanford CoreNLP (A kind of NLP's analysis tool) to extract feature words and emotional scores (on a scale of 1 to 5), and then we use TF-IDF technique to select the feature with the highest frequency as the feature of the current item.

We conduct experiments with two sub-datasets of the amazon dataset, Electronics and Baby, in [26]. Since our model is mainly aimed at recommending to users after asking questions, we filter out users who have never asked a question. The statistics of the two datasets are shown in Table 1.

Table 1. Statistics of dataset

	Number of User	Number of items	Number of users with purchase after question	Number of users who purchase question-related
Electronics	196,114	65,124	19,445	4,881
Baby	17,217	4,982	1,321	213

4.2 Baselines

As the method in this paper firstly includes the representation learning of users as well as items and the sequential recommendation module, we compare our model with two user-item representation models and two sequential recommendation models:

- Item2vec [9], which represents item vector based on Word2Vec and we use it to replace the GCN module in this article as the baseline;
- node2vec [11], which represents item vector based on GNN. Based on depth-first search and breadth-first search, the model constructs sequences by exploring nodes that are similar to the structure and essence of the target node, so as to obtain the representation of each node and we use it instead of the GCN module as the baseline in this paper;
- DREAM [18], which is a sequential recommendation model based on CNN while instant interest is not considered. We take the historical interaction as the input of LSTM for personalized recommendation;
- Caser [19] ,which is a sequential recommendation model based on CNN and embeddings of both item and user are considered. In order to adapt to the problems in this paper, user embedding represents users' stable long-term preferences. Caser's vertical convolution kernel and horizontal convolution kernel are used to extract users' short-term preferences, which is different from the immediate interest of this paper;
- BINN [20], which is a sequential recommendation model based on RNN and contains the item2vec module to learn the item representation. Bidirectional RNN is used to model the user's long-term preferences, and the recent session is used to model the user's short-term preferences, which is different from the instant interest of this paper.

4.3 Evaluation Metric

To evaluate the performance of the MGCN4REC model in this article, we use Recall @K and HT@K, which are widely used in recommendation systems. Given the top-K recommendation results R_K^u of the user u, the calculation formula is shown in (16):

$$Recall@K = \frac{1}{|U|} \sum_u \frac{|R_K^u \cap B_{t>t_q}^u|}{|B_{t>t_q}^u|},$$

$$HR@K = \frac{I(R_K^u \cap B_{t>t_q}^u \neq 0)}{|U|} \tag{16}$$

where $\left| B^u_{t>t_q} \right|$ is the number of purchases after user asks, and|U| is the number of users.

4.4 Experimental Results

Performance Comparison

The results of the MGCN4REC model and comparative algorithms are as shown in Table 2, in which the first column represents the two data sets, the second column shows performances on different evaluation metrics: each index of the optimal data is in bold and suboptimal results are shown underlined. The last column represents the improvement of MGCN4REC model compared with the suboptimal results.

Table 2. Performance comparisons of MGCN4REC with baseline methods on two datasets (Bold scores are the best in each row, while underlined scores are the second best).

Datasets	Metric	Item2vec	Node2vec	DREAM	Caser	BINN	MGCN4REC	Improve
Baby	Recall@5	0.0041	0.0426	0.0043	0.0225	0.0038	**0.051**	+19.7%
	Recall@10	0.0481	0.0571	0.0337	0.0388	0.0452	**0.0672**	+17.7%
	Recall@20	0.168	0.197	0.126	0.156	0.155	**0.226**	14.6%
	HR@5	0.0721	0.078	0.0313	0.0562	0.0681	**0.091**	+16.7%
	HR@10	0.136	0.1459	0.08375	0.11	0.125	**0.162**	+11.1%
	HR@20	0.205	0.224	0.156	0.192	0.212	**0.253**	+12.9%
Electronics	Recall@5	0.0162	0.0186	0.0115	0.01	0.0158	**0.0223**	+19.8%
	Recall@10	0.0263	0.0271	0.0215	0.025	0.0254	**0.0301**	+11.1%
	Recall@20	0.1682	0.186	0.11	0.135	0.1574	**0.201**	+8.1%
	HR@5	0.0595	0.0659	0.0408	0.0408	0.0569	**0.076**	+15.3%
	HR@10	0.109	0.109	0.0766	0.0733	0.112	**0.134**	+19.6
	HR@20	0.1954	0.2031	0.112	0.1506	0.1685	**0.2325**	+14.5%

According to the experiment results, the performances of the 3 baselines (Item2vec, node2vec, BINN) with the item representation are almost higher than that of the remained two baselines, which proves that it is very important to study the representation of the user and the item in recommendation system. In addition to the MGCN4REC algorithm proposed in this paper, Item2vec with aggregated preferences has achieved almost the best performance in all metrics. This is because item2vec algorithm learns item representation and models users' long- and short-term preferences. At the same time, it proves that the user-item representation learning based on multi-graph are effective. Compared with the recommendation system with long- and short-term preferences aggregation, DREAM has the lowest performance, because it only considers users' long-term preferences.

In the Baby dataset, our MGCN4REC model achieves an average improvement of more than 10% in the performance comparing with the other baselines in all metrics. On the Electronics dataset, MGCN4REC outperforms than the baselines on all metrics:

each metric is improved by an average of 15% over the comparison algorithm that works best with the same parameters.

Impact of Multi-graph

We also study the effect of multi-graph user-item representation on the performance of the recommendation system. Table 3 shows the comparison results of MGCN4Rec with and without multi-graph on HR@10.

Table 3. MGCN4Rec with and without multi-graph on HR@10

Datasets	Metrics	Only G_{bought_seq}	Only G_{also_bought}	Only G_{also_view}	Multi-graph
Baby	HR@10	0.138	0.143	0.139	0.162
Electronics	HR@10	0.116	0.118	0.117	0.134

According to the Table 3, our model MGCN4Rec with multi-graph outperforms than without multi-graph model over 10% on HR@10. Therefore, the user-item representation based on mulit-graph can better learn the similarity between users and items, then improving recommendation performance.

Impact of Preferences Dimensionality d

We also study the effect of user preferences dimension d on the performance of the recommendation system. Figure 3 shows HR@10 for MGCN4REC and other baselines with the preferences dimensionality d varying from 16 to 256 while keeping other optimal hyper-parameters unchanged. We make some observations from this figure.

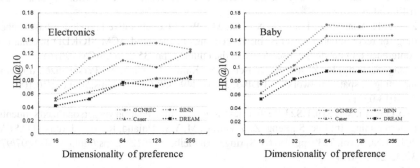

Fig. 3. Effect of the preferences dimensionality d on HR@10 for neural sequential models.

The performance of each model tends to converge as the dimensions increase, and larger dimensions do not necessarily lead to better model performance. Moreover, the model presented in this paper is superior to the baseline in almost all dimensions.

5 Conclucion

This paper proposes a sequential recommendation model based on multi-graph to learn the representation of users and items, and then to model the preferences and instant interest simultaneously. For the part of user-item representation learning, this paper utilize graph convolutional neural network (GCN) to learn the similarity between user-item representation from different graphs. For preferences, this paper utilize recurrent neural network (RNN) to learn users' stable preferences from the shopping basket of historical interaction sequence. For instant interests, this paper utilize the user's question text to model the user's instant interests. In order to aggregate preferences and instant interests, attention mechanism is introduced to calculate users' attention distribution, so as to obtain users' dependence on these two preferences. By comparing with two state-of-art methods of representation learning and three sequential recommendation systems, the results show that our MGCN4REC model can more effectively represent users and items, thus making more effectively recommendation.

References

1. Karatzoglou, A., Baltrunas, L., Shi, Y.: Learning to rank for recommender systems. In: Proceedings of the 7th ACM Conference on Recommender Systems, pp. 493–494. ACM (2013)
2. Koren, Y., Bell, R., Volinsky, C.: Matrix factorization techniques for recommender systems. Computer **8**, 30–37 (2009)
3. Koren, Y.: Collaborative filtering with temporal dynamics. In: Proceedings of the 15th ACM SIGKDD international conference on Knowledge discovery and data mining, pp. 447–456. ACM (2009)
4. Liu, Q., Zeng, X., Zhu, H., Chen, E., Xiong, H., Xie, X., et al.: Mining indecisiveness in customer behaviors. In: 2015 IEEE International Conference on Data Mining, pp. 281–290. IEEE (2015)
5. Zhang, F., Yuan, N.J., Lian, D., Xie, X., Ma, W.Y.: Collaborative knowledge base embedding for recommender systems. In: Proceedings of the 22nd ACM SIGKDD international conference on knowledge discovery and data mining, pp. 353–362. ACM (2016)
6. Shang, S., Ding, R., Zheng, K., Jensen, C.S., Kalnis, P., Zhou, X.: Personalized trajectory matching in spatial networks. VLDB J. **23**(3), 449–468 (2013). https://doi.org/10.1007/s00 778-013-0331-0
7. Yap, G.E., Li, X.L., Yu, P.S.: Effective next-items recommendation via personalized sequential pattern mining. In: Lee, S., Peng, Z., Zhou, X., M, Y.S., Unland, R., Yoo, J. (eds.) DASFAA 2012. LNCS, vol. 7239, pp. 48–64. Springer, Heidelberg (2012). https://doi.org/10.1007/978-3-642-29035-0_4
8. Mikolov, T., Sutskever, I., Chen, K., Corrado, G.S., Dean, J.: Distributed representations of words and phrases and their compositionality. In: Advances in Neural Information Processing Systems, pp. 3111–3119 (2013)
9. Barkan, O., Koenigstein, N.: Item2vec: neural item embedding for collaborative filtering. In: 2016 IEEE 26th International Workshop on Machine Learning for Signal Processing (MLSP), pp. 1–6. IEEE (2016)
10. Perozzi, B., Al-Rfou, R., Skiena, S.: Deepwalk: Online learning of social representations. In: Proceedings of the 20th ACM SIGKDD international conference on Knowledge discovery and data mining, pp. 701–710. ACM (2014)

11. Grover, A., Leskovec, J.: node2vec: Scalable feature learning for networks. In: Proceedings of the 22nd ACM SIGKDD International Conference on Knowledge Discovery and Data Mining, pp. 855–864. ACM (2016)

12. Ricci, F., Rokach, L., Shapira, B.: Introduction to recommender systems handbook. In: Ricci, F., Rokach, L., Shapira, B., Kantor, P.B. (eds.) Recommender Systems Handbook, pp. 1–35. Springer, Boston, MA (2011). https://doi.org/10.1007/978-0-387-85820-3_1

13. Wu, S., Tang, Y., Zhu, Y., Wang, L., Xie, X., Tan, T.: Session-based recommendation with graph neural networks. In: Proceedings of the AAAI Conference on Artificial Intelligence, vol. 33, pp. 346–353 (2019)

14. Grbovic, M., Cheng, H.: Real-time personalization using embeddings for search ranking at airbnb. In: Proceedings of the 24th ACM SIGKDD International Con-ference on Knowledge Discovery & Data Mining, pp. 311–320. ACM (2018)

15. Rendle, S., Freudenthaler, C., Schmidt-Thieme, L.: Factorizing personalized markov chains for next-basket recommendation. In: Proceedings of the 19th in-ternational conference on World wide web, pp. 811–820. ACM (2010)

16. Wang, P., Guo, J., Lan, Y., Xu, J., Wan, S., Cheng, X.: Learning hierarchical representation model for nextbasket recommendation. In: Proceedings of the 38th International ACM SIGIR conference on Research and Development in Information Retrieval, pp. 403–412. ACM (2015)

17. Hidasi, B., Karatzoglou, A., Baltrunas, L., Tikk, D.: Session-based recommenda-tions with recurrent neural networks (2015). arXiv preprint arXiv:1511.06939

18. Yu, F., Liu, Q., Wu, S., Wang, L., Tan, T.: A dynamic recurrent model for next basket recom-mendation. In: Proceedings of the 39th International ACM SIGIR Conference on Research and Development in Information Retrieval, pp. 729–732. ACM (2016)

19. Tang, J., Wang, K.: Personalized top-n sequential recommendation via convolutional sequence embedding. In: Proceedings of the Eleventh ACM International Conference on Web Search and Data Mining, pp. 565–573. ACM (2018)

20. Li, Z., Zhao, H., Liu, Q., Huang, Z., Mei, T., Chen, E.: Learning from history and present: Next-item recommendation via discriminatively exploiting user behaviors. In: Proceedings of the 24th ACM SIGKDD International Conference on Knowledge Discovery & Data Mining, pp. 1734–1743. ACM (2018)

21. Donkers, T., Loepp, B., Ziegler, J.: Sequential user-based recurrent neural network recom-mendations. In: Proceedings of the Eleventh ACM Conference on Recommender Systems, pp. 152–160. ACM (2017)

22. Quadrana, M., Karatzoglou, A., Hidasi, B., Cremonesi, P.: Personalizing session-based rec-ommendations with hierarchical recurrent neural networks. In: Proceedings of the Eleventh ACM Conference on Recommender Systems, pp. 130–137. ACM (2017)

23. Bengio, Y., Courville, A., Vincent, P.: Representation learning: a review and new perspectives. IEEE Trans. Pattern Anal. Mach. Intell. **35**(8), 1798–1828 (2013)

24. Schuster, M., Paliwal, K.K.: Bidirectional recurrent neural networks. IEEE Trans. Sig. Process. **45**(11), 2673–2681 (1997)

25. Hochreiter, S., Schmidhuber, J.: Long short-term memory. Neural Comput. **9**(8), 1735–1780 (1997)

26. He, R., McAuley, J.: Ups and downs: Modeling the visual evolution of fashion trends with one-class collaborative filtering. In: Proceedings of the 25th International Conference On World Wide Web, pp. 507–517. International World Wide Web Conferences Steering Committee (2016)

Urban Computing

Using Deep Active Learning to Save Sensing Cost When Estimating Overall Air Quality

Dehao Lei[1,2], Zhiyong Yu[1,2,3(✉)], Peiguan Li[1,2], Lei Han[1,2], and Fangwan Huang[1,2]

[1] College of Mathematics and Computer Science, Fuzhou University, Fuzhou, China
yuzhiyong@fzu.edu.cn
[2] Fujian Provincial Key Laboratory of Network Computing and Intelligent Information Processing, Fuzhou University, Fuzhou, China
[3] Key Laboratory of Spatial Data Mining and Information Sharing, Ministry of Education, Fuzhou, China

Abstract. Air quality is widely concerned by the governments and people. To save cost, air quality monitoring stations are deployed at only a few locations, and the stations are actuated at partial time. Therefore, it is necessary to study how to actively collect a subset of air quality data to maximize the estimation accuracy of air quality at other locations and time. In order to solve this challenge, we propose the active variational adversarial model (AVAM) that selects the most valuable unlabeled samples through two iterative phases of active learning. In the first phase of our model, a candidate set with unlabeled samples is selected through traditional active learning. In the second phase, variational auto-encoder (VAE) is used to obtain the compressed representation of the candidate set and the training set with labeled samples, then a discriminator based on three-layer neural network is trained from the compressed representation. Finally the discriminator can output the most valuable unlabeled samples from the candidate set. The experimental results show that the AVAM proposed in this paper is superior to active learning models with the first or second phase only.

Keywords: Active learning · Air quality estimation · Variational adversarial

1 Introduction

Monitoring air quality is helpful for the health of people. Since air quality stations are very expensive to establish and maintain, with the goal to save cost, air quality monitoring stations are deployed at only a few locations, and the stations are actuated at partial time. As a result, we can only monitor partial air quality data. To acquire the overall air quality data of the whole area during a whole time period, air quality estimation can be adopted. Air quality estimation aims to estimate air quality at other locations and time based on the air quality data already monitored.

Most existing work focus on the accuracy of estimation only, without paying attention to the collecting cost of data used for estimation. In fact, according to the viewpoint of active learning [1], different known data can get different accuracy of the estimated

© Springer Nature Switzerland AG 2020
Z. Yu et al. (Eds.): GPC 2020, LNCS 12398, pp. 189–204, 2020.
https://doi.org/10.1007/978-3-030-64243-3_15

results. Therefore, it is necessary to study an active spatio-temporal data sampling strategy so that only a small number of samples need be collected to obtain the desired estimation accuracy. In other words, active sampling is performed on a fixed number of known samples and estimation algorithms, which leads to higher estimation accuracy.

A small number of existing work addressed on this challenge. However, they adopt a shallow estimation algorithm which may not be able to capture the complex interaction between the influencing factors. In view of the success of deep learning in many fields, we try to study the effect of deep learning model on air quality estimation, and more importantly, the active sampling strategy corresponding to deep learning. We call such a framework deep active learning. It samples a batch of the most informative sample through active learning strategy, then these sample are manually labeled and added to the training set, finally a deep neural network model is trained. In this paper, we propose a deep active learning model called active variational adversarial model (AVAM), which is an improvement of Variational Adversarial Active Learning (VAAL) [20]. VAAL selects from the full samples, while AVAM selects from the filtered samples, which adds a selection mechanism to make the selected sample more informative. And AVAM can save sensing cost when estimating overall air quality.

The main contributions of this paper are listed as follows:

- Propose the active variational adversarial model (AVAM) that combines deep learning and active learning. AVAM has two selection phases to output the most valuable unlabeled samples to be labeled next. AVAM contains a deep learning model suitable for air quality estimation which has better performance than baseline methods.
- Evaluate AVAM on an air quality dataset with 44 stations in southern China from August 2014 to April 2015.

2   Related Work

Data Estimation. Rana [2] and Zhu [3] respectively proposed the compressed sensing method to collect and estimate noise and traffic condition data under the condition of less sampling. In other words, spatio-temporal data completion is achieved through the data reconstruction technology of compressed sensing and the spatio-temporal correlation (such as sparsity) of the data itself. Similarly, Yang [4] proposed a technology based on sparse representation which can reveal the spatial and temporal correlation of traffic flow and then find out which sections of traffic flow will affect the traffic flow of the section to be speculated. Zheng et al. [5] proposed cross domain data fusion, using a small amount of air quality monitoring stations measured value and a large number of multi-sources heterogeneous information (weather, traffic, road structure, POI), equivalent to adding dimensions to the data characteristics of no air quality monitoring station area and then speculated their air qualities through machine learning techniques. Some of the methods used in air quality prediction can also provide references for air quality class estimation. For example, some statistical models such as linear regression, regression tree [6] and neural network [7] have been applied to the real-time prediction air quality. Song [8] and Zhu [9] used time series method and BP neural network method to establish models of air quality prediction and then predicted and analyzed the concentrations of SO_2,

NO_2 and particulate matter. Lin [10] and Meng [11] proposed an AQI prediction model and an AQI classification prediction method based on random forest. Su [12] and Yang [13] applied the grey theory model to predict the changing trend of AQI and predicted the concentration of pollution factors in the next 10 years. Chang [14] selected kriging interpolation and combined the idea of active learning to provide a kriging model of air quality estimation for any given location based on the lack of air quality data.

Active Learning. Iglesias [15] proposed a sample selection method based on committee voting (query by committee, QBC). This method trained two or more classifiers to form a committee based on the labeled sample set. Each committee member in the committee voted on the unlabeled samples and then the samples with the most inconsistent voting results were selected as candidate samples. Wang [16] proposed the study of uncertainty based active learning algorithm, including the Least Confidence, Margin Sampling, and Entropy Sampling, which were all calculated based on the probability in the prediction to find the most informative unlabeled samples.

Deep Active Learning. Gal [17, 18] proposed dropout using in the neural network prediction phase (i.e., the test samples pass the network randomly) lead to unbiased MonteCarlo estimated the mean and variance and then measured the uncertainty of unlabeled data through variance, and put forward Bayesian active learning by disagreement (BALD) which maximized the mutual information between predictions and model posterior. Yoo [19] proposed the active learning method by introducing a loss prediction module to estimate the loss value of unlabeled data. Sinha [20] used VAE and adversarial network to learn the query strategy of unlabeled data and labeled data distribution in potential space. Tran [21] proposed the Bayesian generative active deep learning model which used the traditional pool-based active learning method to select samples and then trained the generative adversarial model to generate samples.

3 Problem Description

Air Quality Index (AQI) describes the extent to which the air is clean or polluted, and the impact on health. The air quality report issued by the environmental monitoring department every day includes the concentration values of various pollutants. However, these abstract data have no specific meaning for most people and it is no way to judge the current air quality level from them. Therefore, the environmental protection agency calculates the AQI through several major pollution criteria. People can clearly judge whether the air quality is healthy through the number. The major pollutants participating in the AQI assessment are $PM_{2.5}$, PM_{10}, NO_2, O_3, SO_2, CO. Specifically, the air monitoring station will monitor and record the air quality data which obtain $PM_{2.5}$, PM_{10}, NO_2, O_3, SO_2 pollutant concentration information and then obtain the AQI through calculation. The calculation formula is presented as follows:

$$I = \frac{I_h - I_L}{C_h - C_l}(C - C_l) + I_l \tag{1}$$

where I is the AQI, C is pollutant concentration, C_l, C_h are the limit values of the pollutant concentration, I_l, I_h are the corresponding limit values of AQI.

In this article, we use standards published by the U. S. environmental protection agency to divide the air quality index into six levels. Each level has a corresponding AQI's range, state, and class. We regard each AQI level as the class to be estimated and the higher class value represents the worse air quality, as shown in Table 1.

Table 1. Description of air quality and air pollution index

AQI	Air Quality Index Level (State)	Class
0–50	Level I (Good)	0
51–100	Level II (Moderate)	1
101–150	Level III (Mild pollution)	2
151–200	Level IV (Moderate pollution)	3
201–300	Level V (Severe pollution)	4
301–500	Level VI (Serious pollution)	5

We use the AQI class to describe air quality. Our objective is to identify the relationship between AQI, time, spatial position and meteorological features, and establish an effective model. When given a specified time, a specified spatial position and meteorological data, the air quality class can be estimated by our model.

Given air quality data $\{AQI_S^t\}_{t=1}^T$, meteorological data $\{M_S^t\}_{t=1}^T$, where S is the set of air quality monitoring stations $\{S_1, S_2, \ldots, S_n\}$ and T is the timestamp set of the known AQI, we aim to actively collect a subset of unknown air quality data to estimate the AQI for each monitoring station $\{AQI_S^k\}_{k=1}^K$ at time k where K is the timestamp set of the unlabeled AQI.

4   Data Preprocessing

4.1   Data Description and Missing Data Processing

In this experiment, we use air quality data sets and meteorological data sets [22]. The data set contains air quality data and meteorological data from 437 air monitoring stations in 43 cities from May 2014 to April 2015. Each air quality data contains information on pollutant concentration at a specific time and each meteorological data contains information on meteorological characteristics at a specific time.

Our aim is to estimate the air quality class at a given time and location with maximum accuracy through actively collecting a small number of samples. This requires the data set to be complete, in other words, it requires hourly air quality data and meteorological data at each station from May 2014 to April 2015. However, there are a lot of missing data in the existing data set. So we need to fill in the missing values of the data.

There are three spline interpolation methods to solve the problem for the data missing value completion: linear interpolation, Quadratic-Spline interpolation, and Cubic-Spline interpolation.

Air quality data of each station should be normally recorded hourly. So the complete air quality data for a single station has 8,760 records a year. We selected the station 9017 with most data records which has 8,556 air quality data and then extracted the AQI data. Next, we used the above three methods to experiment with AQI data and then selected the best method to complete the missing data. In the experiment, 500, 1000, 1500, 2000 and 2500 records were randomly missing from the AQI data of station 9017. We used MAPE:

$$MAPE = \sum_{t=1}^{n} |\frac{observed_t - predicted_t}{observed_t}| \times \frac{100}{n} \tag{2}$$

as the evaluation standard and recorded the time spent in each experiment, details are shown in Table 2.

Table 2. Performance comparison of different interpolation methods

	MAPE			TIME		
	Linear	Quadratic	Cubic	Linear	Quadratic	Cubic
500	7.36	7.64	7.87	0.085 s	0.086 s	0.078 s
1000	7.84	8.23	8.47	0.126 s	0.102 s	0.107 s
1500	8.10	8.26	8.48	0.119 s	0.122 s	0.124 s
2000	8.30	8.56	8.78	0.141 s	0.142 s	0.144 s
2500	8.65	8.96	9.18	0.161 s	0.167 s	0.170 s

As shown in Table 2, the time of various methods is basically the same and MAPE value of linear interpolation shows the best result in each missing case. Therefore, linear interpolation is used to complete missing values of air quality data and meteorological data. There are too much missing data in most monitoring stations. So we screened more than 6000 existing data and finally selected 44 stations in southern China from August 2014 to April 2015.

4.2 Data Feature Processing

The final data record is shown in Table 3. The data features of this paper include time feature, space feature and meteorological feature. Time features include year, month, day, hour all of which are class feature. Spatial features include longitude and latitude which have specific meanings and belong to numerical features. Meteorological features include weather, temperature, humidity, pressure, wind speed and wind direction, among which weather and wind direction are class feature. Different number of weather and wind direction characteristics represents different weather and wind direction, details as shown in Table 4 and Table 5.

In the process of data processing, we used embedding [23] and z-score (zero-mena normalization) to reduce the spatial dimension of the discrete variable, and then elimi-nated dimensional relationships between variables to make data comparable. For class

Table 3. About final complete data record

Station_id	Year	Month	Day	Hour		Latitude	Longitude	Weather
4002	14	8	1	0		22.53424	113.98487	1
Temperature	Pressure	Humidity	wind_speed	wind_direction	aqi	Class		
31	998.3	76	0.8	3	38	0		

Table 4. About different weather labels corresponding to different meanings

0	1	2	3	4	5	6	7	8
Sunny	Cloudy	Overcast	Rainy	Sprinkle	Moderate rain	Heaver rain	Rain storm	Thunder storm
9	10	11	12	13	14	15	16	
Freezing rain	Snowy	Light snow	Moderate snow	Heavy snow	Foggy	Sand storm	Dusty	

Table 5. About different wind direction labels corresponding to different meanings

0	1	2	3	4	9	13	14	23	24
No	East	West	South	North	Unstable	South east	North east	South west	North west

features, embedding makes it possible to express the variable meaningfully after the transformation. For numerical features, we used z-score which can uniformly convert different data of magnitude into the same order, and uniformly used the calculated z-score value to ensure the comparability between data.

We detailed the embedding settings for class features (see Table 6). Dimension represents the dimension after one-hot encoding. We reduced the dimensions of the class features to two or three dimensions and made them more meaningful. More importantly, it is beneficial to the training of neural networks.

5 Proposed Method

In this section, the active variational adversarial model proposed in this paper and related knowledge are introduced in detail.

5.1 Acquisition Function for the First Phase of Active Learning

The acquisition function is the most important part of active learning. In active learning, we used the acquisition function to actively select most representative unlabeled data. Then we formulated the acquisition function, given a estimation model θ, unlabeled

Table 6. Embedding setting. Dimension is treated by feature one-hot encoding.

Data	Feature	Dimension	Embedding
Time	Year	15	2
	Month	12	2
	Day	31	3
	Hour	24	3
Meteorological	Weather	16	2
	Wind direction	24	3

data set D_U, and input $x \in D_U$. The most informative sample X^* was selected from the unlabeled data set D_U by:

$$x^* = \arg \max_{x \in D_U} a(x, \theta) \tag{3}$$

where $a(x, \theta)$ is the acquisition function. Next, we proposed several commonly acquisition functions as follows:

(1) The samples with the maximum information entropy are the ones where the current classifier is least able to determine its classification. Therefore, select unlabeled points based on predictive entropy (Entropy):

$$a(x, \theta) = -\sum_{m} p(y = m|x, \theta) \log p(y = m|x, \theta) \tag{4}$$

where y is the class label, m is a real number.

(2) Look for the prediction sample with the least confidence in the classifier, the one with the lowest probability of predicting the most likely category. So select the sample with the least confidence (LC):

$$a(x, \theta) = 1 - \max_{y} p(y|x, \theta) \tag{5}$$

(3) Look for the prediction sample with the most dilemma of the classifier. In other words, select the sample which the probabilities of the two most likely categories predicted are very close (Margin):

$$a(x, \theta) = -(\max_{m \in L} p(y = m|x, \theta) - \max_{m \in L \setminus m+} p(y = m|x, \theta)) \tag{6}$$

where L contains all categories, m+ is the m that maximizes the first half of the equation, and when you maximize the second half, you should delete this m.

We referred to reference [18] and used their approximate distribution method to approximate three methods above and generate the corresponding three methods Entropy_dropout, LC_dropout, Margin_dropout.

(4) Entropy_dropout:

$$a(x, \theta_d) = -\sum_m p(y = m|x, \theta_d) \log p(y = m|x, \theta_d) \tag{7}$$

where θ_d is a estimation model, which uses dropout during the test phase.

(5) LC_dropout:

$$a(x, \theta_d) = 1 - \max_y p(y|x, \theta_d) \, a(x, \theta_d) = 1 - \max_y p(y|x, \theta_d) \tag{8}$$

(6) Margin_dropout:

$$a(x, \theta_d) = -(\max_{m \in L} p(y = m|x, \theta_d) - \max_{m \in L \setminus m+} p(y = m|x, \theta_d)) \tag{9}$$

(7) Random sample (RS): sample the data in the D_U by using a random function.

5.2 The Second Phase of Active Learning

The second stage of active learning in this paper is Variational Adversarial Active Learning. The VAAL [20] draws lessons from generative adversarial networks to learn the active sampling strategy. The VAAL model comprises a variational autoencoder (that learns the potential space of unlabeled data and labeled data) and a discriminator (that discriminates between unlabeled and labeled data). The purpose of VAAL is that in the minimax game between VAE and adversarial network, deceive the adversarial network to predict all data as labeled data through train VAE, and train the adversarial network to discriminate the distribution of different typed data in the potential space so as to distinguish labeled data from unlabeled data.

5.3 Active Variational Adversarial Model

The main technical contribution of this paper is to combine acquisition function for the first phase and the second phase of active learning for selecting the more valuable candidate set. As a result, the discriminator can better discriminate the labeled data from the unlabeled data and find the most uncertain data in the unlabeled data (see Fig. 1).

In our model, X_1^* and X_2^* were screened out by selecting two different acquisition functions from the unlabeled dataset, and merged into candidate set. Then we used a variational autoencoder for labeled dataset and partial unlabeled dataset representation learning, in which the encoder used gaussian priori to learn the low-dimensional space as the underlying distribution and reconstructed the input data of the decoder. In order

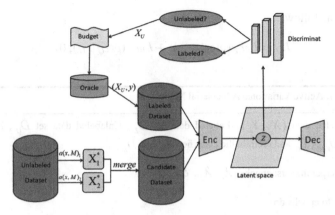

Fig. 1. Network architecture of our proposed model

to discover the missing features of labeled data in transductive representation learning, we can benefit from using unlabeled data and performed transductive representation learning. The objective function of the VAE in transductive representation learning is presented as follows:

$$L_{VAE}^{trd} = \mathbb{E}_{z \sim p(z_L | x_L)}[-\log q(x_L | z_L)] + KL(p(z_L | x_L) \| q(z))$$
$$+ \mathbb{E}_{z \sim p(z_U | x_U)}[-\log q(x_U | z_U)] + KL(p(z_U | x_U) \| q(z)) \qquad (10)$$

where $q(x|z)$ is the probability distribution of the generative model and $p(z|x)$ is the distribution of the hidden variable z calculated from x. $q(z)$ is the distribution of the space of hidden variables and prior distribution. In the experiment, we used the reparameterization trick to calculate the gradient [24].

The transductive representation that VAE learned is the representation of the underlying characteristics of labeled and unlabeled data. In AVAM, we assigned a value to the potential space of the data, that is, labeled it 1 if the data is labeled, and labeled it 0, otherwise. Then we created a discriminator network and formed an adversarial network with VAE to learn the adversarial representation of the data in the potential space. In the process of minimax game between VAE and discriminator network, train VAE to fool the discriminator that predicts all inputs as labeled data and train discriminator network to distinguish the distribution of different typed data in the potential space so that labeled data were distinguished from unlabeled data. On the other hand, the discriminator attempts to efficiently estimate the probability of unlabeled data. We defined the objective function under the adversarial role of the VAE as follows:

$$L_{VAE}^{adv} = L_{BCE}(q(x_L | z_L), 1) + L_{BCE}(q(x_U | z_U), 1) \qquad (11)$$

where L_{BCE} is simply a binary cross-entropy cost function. The final loss function of VAE as follows:

$$L_{VAE} = \lambda_1 L_{VAE}^{trd} + \lambda_2 L_{VAE}^{adv} \qquad (12)$$

where λ_1 and λ_2 are hyperparameters corresponding to L_{VAE}^{trd} and L_{VAE}^{adv} on learning a valid variational Adversarial representation. The final loss function of the discriminator is presented as follows:

$$L_D = L_{BCE}(p(z_L|x_L), 1) + L_{BCE}(p(z_U|x_U), 0) \tag{13}$$

Algorithm 1. Active Variational Adversarial Model

Input: Labeled data (X_L, Y_L), Labeled data set D_L, Unlabeled data set D_U, Initialized models for θ_{VAE}, θ_D and pretrain the classifier θ with D_L.

Input: Hyperparameters: epochs, λ_1, λ_2, α_1, α_2.

    for e = 1 to epochs **do**

        Pick the most informative X_1^* and X_2^* from D_U with $a(x,\theta)$ in (5) and (6)

        $X_U \leftarrow X_1^* \cup X_2^*$

        Sample $(x_L, y_L) \sim (X_L, Y_L)$

        Sample $x_U \sim X_U$

        Compute L_{VAE}^{trd} by using Equation (10)

        Compute L_{VAE}^{adv} by using Equation (11)

        $L_{VAE} \leftarrow \lambda_1 L_{VAE}^{trd} + \lambda_2 L_{VAE}^{adv}$

        $\theta_{VAE} \leftarrow \theta_{VAE} - \alpha_1 \nabla L_{VAE}$

        Compute L_D by using Equation (13)

        $\theta_D \leftarrow \theta_D - \alpha_2 \nabla L_D$

    end for

    return Trained θ_{VAE}, θ_D

    Our full algorithm is shown in Algorithm 1. Through Algorithm 1, we can obtain the parameters θ_{VAE}, θ_D. For the sampling strategy in AVAM, we used the probability associated with the prediction of the discriminator network as the score to select b samples with the lowest score and sent them to Oracle for marking. The sampling strategy in AVAM is shown in Algorithm 2.

Algorithm 2. Sampling Strategy in AVAM

Input: $b, X_L, X_U,$

Output: $X_L, X_U;$

    Select samples(X^*) with $\min_b \{\theta_D(z_U)\}$

    $Y^* \leftarrow ORACLE(X^*)$

    $(X_L, Y_L) \leftarrow (X_L, Y_L) \cup (X^*, Y^*)$

    $X_U \leftarrow X_U - X^*$

    Return X_L, X_U

---

6 Experiments

We divide the experiment into two parts. The first part is learning of AQI level, which proves the effectiveness of the DNN model we designed. Therefore, we apply the DNN to the AVAM. The second part is active learning of AQI level, which verifies the feasibility of the AVAM.

6.1 Learning of AQI Level

In this section, we aim to design a deep neural network for AQI category estimation. And the validity of the proposed deep neural network is verified by comparing it with the traditional machine learning algorithm for classification problems.

Dataset. We used the data after data preprocessing of Chapter 4.

Data Partitioning. The data set was randomly scrambled and divided into training set, validation set, and test set according to the proportion of 70%, 10%, and 20%.

Implementation Details. We used a simple neural network with three hidden layers of sizes 256, 128, 128. Learning rate starts at 10^{-3}, its decay is set to 0.6 and its change is related to the loss of the validation set. Training dropout rate is set to 0.1. L_2 regularization is set to 10^{-3} in the output layer.

Machine Learning Algorithm (Baseline). We compared the designed DNN with the following five traditional machine learning algorithms.

- **k-NearestNeighbor:** KNN is classified by measuring the distance between different features. In other words, if most of the k nearest samples of a sample in the feature space belong to a certain category, then the sample is also classified into this category. In the experiment, we set the main parameter K to three.

- **Logistic Regression:** The goal of logistic regression is to find a decision boundary that is sufficiently distinguishable to separate the two classes well. In the experiment, we set the main parameter penalty to L2 regularization.
- **Decision Tree:** The basic idea is to select one feature when split one node at a time so that the resulting dataset is as pure as possible.
- **Random Forest:** Random forest is bagging of the decision tree, and its core idea is a double-random process of random put back sample sampling (row sampling) and random no put back feature sampling (column sampling). Parameter n_estimators is set to 27, which represents the number of trees in the forest
- **Gradient Boosting:** Gradient boosting is a machine learning technique for regression and classification problems that generates predictive models in the form of a set of weak predictive models.

Evaluation Metrics. We used prediction accuracy to evaluate our algorithms.

Table 7. Comparison between DNN and machine learning algorithm

Method	DNN	Logistic regression	Decision tree	Random forest	Gradient boosting
Accuracy	79. 88%	60.78%	76. 82%	79. 39%	69. 08%

The results are shown in Table 7. For DNN, we did 5 experiments and took the average result as the final result. Experimental results show that the DNN we designed has the best performance compared to the machine learning algorithm and is an effective deep learning model for AQI category estimation.

6.2 Active Learning of AQI Level

In this section, we used the method AVAM presented in this paper to compare with the baseline and verify the feasibility of our approach.

Dataset. We used the data after data preprocessing of Chapter 4.

Data Partitioning. The data set was randomly scrambled and divided into training set, sample set, validation set and test set according to the proportion of 5%, 65%, 10%, and 20%. The validation set and the test set are consistent with the data partitioning in Sect. 5.1.

Implementation Details. The architecture used in the task module for category estimation of AQI is the designed network in Sect. 6.1, where VAE has five layers with size 32, 16, 8, 16, 32, respectively. The discriminator is a 3-layer neural network. Adam [25] is used as the optimizer for VAE and discriminator module with an equal learning rate of 2×10^{-4}. In the first phase of active learning, we used two methods to sample 7% data respectively and combined them into the candidate set. Finally, we sampled 5% of the whole data from the candidate set in each batch.

Comparison Targets (Baseline). We compared our method with random sampling (RS), LC-based sampling, Margin-sampling, and Entropy-based sampling and VAAL. Details of the methods are shown in Sect. 5.1 and Sect. 5.2. We referred to reference [18] and used their approximate distribution method to approximate methods LC, Margin, Entropy, and generate the corresponding three methods LC_dropout, Margin_dropout, Entropy_dropout.

Evaluation Metrics. We used prediction accuracy to evaluate our algorithms.

The result is shown in Fig. 2. Each point is an average of 3 trial with different initial labeled samples and has a corresponding error bar. Experimental results show that both LC-based and Margin-based methods are better than the other three methods. In the last active learning cycle, the LC, the Margin and the entropy methods show 79.75%, 79.79%, and 79.77% respectively, while the VAAL and RS show 78.9% and 78.92% respectively. Our method shows the highest performance for all active learning cycles. In the last cycle, our method achieves an accuracy of 79.82%.

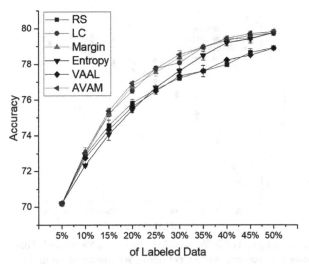

Fig. 2. The initial training set is 5%. We sampled 9 times and 5% unlabeled data each time (up to 50% of labeled data and averaged over 3 repetitions). We compared our method containing methods LC and Margin with five acquisition functions (RS, LC, Margin, Entropy, VAAL).

Since the approximate distribution method in reference [18] has better experimental effect, we considered adding this method to the traditional active learning method. Figure 3 shows the comparison of three traditional active methods Margin, LC, and Entropy with the corresponding three methods Margin_dropout, LC_dropout, and Entropy_dropout after the approximate treatment of reference [18]. The results show that the approximation method is better than the original method. Therefore, we conducted another set of comparative experiments. We compared our method AVAM_dropout, which contains methods LC_dropout and Margin_dropout, with four acquisition functions. The result is shown in Fig. 4. In the last active learning cycle, the LC_dropout, the

Margin_dropout, and the entropy_dropout show 79.73%, 79.68%, and 79.64% respectively, while the RS shows 78.92% respectively. In the last cycle, our method achieves an accuracy of 79.85%. In general, our method shows higher performance.

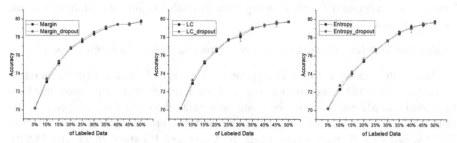

Fig. 3. The traditional active learning methods (Margin, LC, Entropy) are compared with the methods of Bayesian (Margin_dropout, LC_dropout, Entropy_dropout).

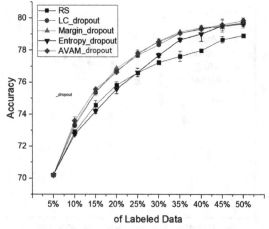

Fig. 4. The initial training set is 5%. We sampled 9 times and 5% unlabeled data each time (up to 50% of labeled data and averaged over 3 repetitions). We compared our method AVAM_dropout, which contains methods LC_dropout and Margin_dropout, with four acquisition functions (RS, LC_dropout, Margin_dropout, Entropy_dropout).

7 Conclusion

This paper studies how to actively collect a subset of unknown air quality data to estimate air quality categories at other time and locations. To address this problem, we propose an active variational adversarial model (AVAM) that selects the most valuable unlabeled samples. The experimental results show that the proposed model is more effective than the traditional active learning method. This paper does not consider the influence of traffic conditions, personnel flow, road network and points of interest on air quality categories. In the future, we will not only consider these factors but also study other methods to further improve the estimation accuracy.

Acknowledgement. This work is supported by the National Natural Science Foundation of China under grant No. 61772136.

References

1. Settles, B.: Active Learning Literature Survey. Computer Sciences Technical Report 1648, University of Wisconsin–Madison (2009)
2. Rana, R.K., Chou, C.T., Kanhere, S.S., Bulusu, N., Hu, W.: Ear-phone: an end-to-end participatory urban noise mapping system. In: 9th International Conference on Information Processing in Sensor Network (IPSN), pp. 105–116 (2010)
3. Zhu, Y., Li, Z., Zhu, H., Li, M., Zhang, Q.: A compressive sensing approach to urban traffic estimation with probe vehicles. IEEE Trans. Mob. Comput. **12**, 2289–2302 (2013)
4. Yang, S., Shi, S., Hu, X., M, Wang: Spatiotemporal context awareness for urban traffic modeling and prediction: sparse representation based variable selection. PLoS ONE **10**(10), e0141223 (2015)
5. Zheng, Y., Liu, F., Hsieh, H.P.: U-air: when urban air quality inference meets big data. In: 19th ACM SIGKDD International Conference on Knowledge Discovery and Data Mining(KDD), pp. 1436–1444 (2013)
6. Burrows, W.R., Benjamin, M., Beauchamp, S., Lord, S., McCollor, E.R., Thomson, B.: CART decision-tree statistical analysis and prediction of summer season maximum surface ozone for the vancouver, montreal, and atlantic regions of canada. J. Appl. Meteorol. **34**(8), 1848–1862 (2010)
7. Subcommittee S T C A Q. Air Quality Forecasting: A Review of Federal Programs and Research Needs. Environmental Policy Collection (2001)
8. Song, Y.C., Zhen, S.: Application of BP neural network and time series model in air quality prediction of Baotou city. J. Arid Land Res. Environ. **27**(7), 65–70 (2013)
9. Zhu, C.L., Jiang, Z.F., Wang, Q.: A prediction model of ambient air quality based on B-P neural network. Comput. Eng. Appl. **22**, 223–227 (2007)
10. Lin, K., Shao, F.: Study on air quality prediction based on random forest and neural network. J. Qingdao Univ. (Eng. Technol. Ed.) **33**(02), 32–36 (2018)
11. Qian, M.: Classification and prediction of air quality based on random forest perspective. J. Chongqing Technol. Bus. Univ. (Nat. Sci. Ed.) **35**(03), 30–34 (2018)
12. Su, J., Wu, H.P.: Predicting the change trend of ambient air quality by using grey theory model - taking the prediction of ambient air quality in Jingjiang city as an example. Pollut. Control Technol. 23(04): 10–12 + 22 (2010)
13. Yang, J.W., Sun, B.L.: The prediction of air pollutant concentration in Pingdingshan city based on grey Markov model. Math. Pract. Theor. **44**(02), 64–70 (2014)
14. Chang, H., Yu, Z., Yu, Z.: Air quality estimation based on active learning and Kriging interpolation. Big Data **4**(06), 57–67 (2018)
15. Iglesias, J.E., Konukoglu, E., Montillo, A., Tu, Z., Criminisi, A.: Combining generative and discriminative models for semantic segmentation of CT scans via active learning. Inf Process Med Imaging **22**, 25–36 (2011)
16. Wang, D., Shang, Y.: A new active labeling method for deep learning. In: 2014 International Joint Conference on Neural Networks (IJCNN). IEEE (2014)
17. Gal, Y.: Uncertainty in deep learning. University of Cambridge (2016)

18. Gal, Y., Islam, R., Ghahramani, Z.: Deep Bayesian Active Learning with Image Data (2017)
19. Yoo, D., Kweon, I.S.: Learning loss for active learning. In: Proceedings of the IEEE Conference on Computer Vision and Pattern Recognition (2019)
20. Sinha, S, Ebrahimi, S., Darrell, T.: Variational Adversarial Active Learning (2019). arXiv preprint arXiv:1904.00370
21. Tran, T., Do, T.T., Reid, I., et al.: Bayesian Generative Active Deep Learning (2019). arXiv preprint arXiv:190411643
22. Zheng, Yu., et al.: Forecasting fine-grained air quality based on big data. In: Proceedings of the 21th ACM SIGKDD International Conference on Knowledge Discovery and Data Mining. ACM (2015)
23. Wang, D., Cao, W., Li, J., Ye, J.: DeepSD: supply-demand prediction for online car-hailing services using deep neural networks. In: 2017 IEEE 33rd International Conference on Data Engineering (ICDE). IEEE (2017)
24. Kingma, D.P., Welling, M.: Auto-encoding variational bayes (2013). arXiv preprint arXiv: 13126114
25. Kingma, D.P., Ba, J.: Adam: a method for stochastic optimization. In: International Conference on Learning Representations (2015)

Interpretable Multivariate Time Series Classification Based on Prototype Learning

Dengjuan Ma, Zhu Wang[✉], Jia Xie, Bin Guo, and Zhiwen Yu

Northwestern Polytechnical University, Xi'an, China
wangzhu@nwpu.edu.cn

Abstract. Recently, the classification of multivariate time series has attracted much attention in the field of machine learning and data mining, due to its wide application values in biomedicine, finance, industry and so on. During the last decade, deep learning has achieved great success in many tasks. However, while many studies have applied deep learning to time series classification, few works can provide good interpretability. In this paper, we propose a deep sequence model with built-in interpretability by fusing deep learning with prototype learning, aiming to achieve interpretable classification of multivariate time series. In particular, an input sequence is classified by being compared with a set of prototypes, which are also sequences learned by the developed model, i.e., exemplary cases in the problem domain. We use the matched subset of the MIMIC-III Waveform Database to evaluate the proposed model and compare it with several baseline models. Experimental results show that our model can not only achieve the best performance but also provide good interpretability.

Keywords: Multivariate time series · Interpretable classification · Deep learning · Prototype

1 Introduction

The multivariate time series classification problem, aiming to identify the label for multivariate data streams, has been widely studied in the field of data mining. In the era of Internet of Things, a huge amount of time series are being produced day by day, such as electronic health records (EHR) in health care, stock records in financial domain, weather records in meteorology. How to effectively use these time series to guide production and life is a challenging problem.

The existing methods for multivariate time series classification include bag of patterns [1], shapelets [2] and deep learning methods [3, 4]. Both bag-of-patterns and shapelets need to parse the time series, which aims to convert the time series into a wide range of subsequences or pattern sets as feature candidates. Usually, the process of feature extraction is time-consuming and highly complex. Deep learning-based methods can automatically learn the feature representation from time series and have achieved great success in many classification tasks. However, the deep learning model

© Springer Nature Switzerland AG 2020
Z. Yu et al. (Eds.): GPC 2020, LNCS 12398, pp. 205–216, 2020.
https://doi.org/10.1007/978-3-030-64243-3_16

is regarded as a "black box" that lacks transparency, which limits its application in many key decision-making scenarios.

Many studies have been conducted to overcome the shortcoming of deep learning. The first approach is the hidden analysis method [5], which explains the deep neural network by visualizing, anti-mapping, and marking the features learned by hidden neurons. The second approach is the simulated model [6], which uses model compression methods by constructing a simple model and imitating the decision function of the original deep model to achieve model transparency. The third one is the sensitivity analysis method [7], which makes each attribute change within the possible range, investigates and predicts the impact of these attribute changes on the model's output. The last one is the attention mechanism [8], which mimics the human visual attention mechanism and focuses on the specific parts that are critical to the output. However, in the reasoning process of capturing the original model, the post-hoc explanations may be incomplete or inaccurate.

Other than these above approaches, we choose to adopt the idea of prototype learning to build a deep learning model with built-in interpretability. Prototype learning is a form of case-based reasoning [9], which obtains the learning result by comparing the input with several prototypes in the problem domain. It mimics the problem-solving process of human beings and can be better interpreted. For example, doctors diagnose new patients based on previous diagnosis experience. In the past two years, there have been several attempts to apply prototype learning to deep neural networks to build models with built-in interpretability. Oscar et al. [10] applied prototype learning to build interpretable image classifiers. Yao et al. [11] and Alan et al. [12] applied prototype learning to model one-dimensional time series. However, little work has been done on applying prototype learning to multivariate time series modeling.

To facilitate interpretable modelling of multivariate time series, we propose a multivariate time series classification model by fusing deep neural networks and prototype learning (MTSPL). The model obtains classification results by comparing the input sequences with the prototype sequences, and thus achieves built-in interpretability. Furthermore, we introduce a prototype diversity penalty mechanism that explicitly accounts for prototype clustering and encourages the model to learn more diverse prototypes. To summarize, the main contributions of this paper are as follows:

- To the best of our knowledge, this is the first attempt to adopt prototype learning for multivariate time series classification. We fuse deep neural networks with prototype learning and develop a multivariate time series classification model with built-in interpretability.
- Experiments on real-world data sets show that MTSPL outperforms state-of-the-art baseline methods and achieves satisfactory classification results. Specifically, we visualize the learned prototypes to showcase the interpretability of the obtained results.

The rest of this paper is organized as follows. Section 2 introduces the related work, followed by the detailed description of the proposed MTSPL model in Sect. 3. Section 4 verifies the model through experiments, and Sect. 5 concludes the paper.

2 Related Work

In this section, we mainly introduce recent works on multivariate time series classification and interpretable deep learning.

2.1 Multivariate Time Series Classification

To classify multivariate time series, a classical approach is to design specific similarity/distance measures and then build classification models accordingly. For example, Lines et al. [13] proposed a similarity measure that quantifies the distance between two series after compensation for localized distortions. The similarity/distance measure is employed with Elastic ensemble (EE) which is a combination of 11 nearest neighbor classifiers. Wistuba et al. [14] used a method called UFS to select representative patterns from multivariate time series. Ghalwash et al. [15] searched for shapelets by sliding windows, and then used the found shapelets to construct a classification model. Keogh et al. [16] used shapelets to build a decision tree with information gain as the metric, and adopted the Euclidean distance between shapelets and time series as the basis for classification. Although bag-of-patterns and shapelets can provide interpretability, the process of feature extraction is time-consuming and highly complex.

In recent years, deep learning has been used for multivariate time series classification, and has achieved great performance. Zheng et al. [17] first proposed a multi-channel deep convolutional neural network (MCDCNN), which applied independent convolution on each channel of multivariate time series and used a second convolution on the cascaded convolution channels. Zhao et al. [18] proposed a time convolutional neural network for classification of multivariate time series, applying the same convolution on all channels. Zhang et al. [19] proposed a multi-scale convolutional encoder and decoder architecture for abnormal diagnosis of multivariate time series. The convolutional encoder was used to extract time series features, based on the feature map that encodes the correlation between time series and time information, the time series is reconstructed using a convolutional encoder, and errors are used to detect and diagnose anomalies. Liu et al. [20] proposed a tensor scheme for multivariate time series classification and a new deep learning structure-Multivariate Convolutional Neural Network (MVCNN), which considers multivariate and lag-feature characteristics. These methods can automatically learn the feature representation from time series and has achieved satisfactory performance in many classification tasks. However, deep learning is regarded as a "black box" that lacks transparency, none of the above work had considered the interpretability of deep learning.

2.2 Interpretability

Many interpretable methods have been proposed to overcome the opacity of deep learning. Guo et al. [21] explored the internal structure of LSTMs to make interpretable predictions of multivariate time series. Irene et al. [22] first proposed the use of DNN with Layerwise Relevance Propagation (LRP) for EEG analysis. Through LRP, a single experiment DNN decision was transformed into a heat map, indicating that which data point is related to the decision result. Strobelt et al. [23] visualized changes in the internal state of RNN to understand the role of hidden units. Goodfellow et al. [24] used global average pooling to generate Class Activation Maps (CAM) to provide explanations for deep CNN. Qin et al. [25] proposed a two-stage attention mechanism to determine which input sequence and which input value are most relevant to the decision outcome. Tian et al. [26] explained the RNN decision by adding time decay factor and attention mechanism to identify important time nodes and diagnostic codes. These methods explained deep learning by extracting and highlighting the most relevant parts of the training process. However, in the process of capturing the reasoning of original model, the post-hoc explanations may be incomplete or inaccurate.

To address this issue, some studies have focused on building models with built-in interpretability. Some traditional techniques, such as typical linear models and decision trees, are considered inherently interpretable models. However, they can't model complex relationships of time series, thus the performance is usually unsatisfactory. To build models that are interpretable and highly accurate, Oscar et al. [10] applied prototype learning to modeling image data to build interpretable image classifiers. Yao et al. [11] and Alan et al. [12] applied prototype learning to modeling one-dimensional time series data. These models are case-based reasoning, which explain the output of the model by comparing the similarity between inputs and typical cases, rather than highlighting the most relevant part of the input. By combining the advantages of deep learning with the interpretability of case-based reasoning, prototype learning is able to construct a deep neural network with high accuracy and interpretation.

3 Method

In this section, we first introduce the overall architecture of the proposed model in Sect. 3.1, and then introduce components of the model in Sects. 3.2 to 3.4.

3.1 Model Architecture Overview

Multivariate input data is represented as $\chi = \{X_1, X_2, \ldots, X_N\}, X_n \in \mathbb{R}^{N \times l}$, where N is the number of multivariate dimensions, l is the length of the time series. Every X_n has a corresponding label y_n. Given a multivariate time series $\chi = \{X_1, X_2, \ldots, X_N\}$, the task is to train a classifier to predict the corresponding labels $\mathcal{Y} = \{y_1, y_2, \ldots, y_N\}$.

Figure 1 shows the overall framework of the proposed model. The basic architecture of the model is similar to the one proposed by Li et al. [10]. The framework consists of three parts: data encoding, prototype learning, and fully connection layer.

It has been proven that convolutional neural network (CNN) can achieve great performance on classification tasks, so we propose to use convolutional neural network to encode the multivariate time series. However, while convolutional neural network has unique advantages on image processing due to its special structure of local weight sharing, which reduces the complexity of the network, time series data is very different from image data. Specifically, image data is generally a 3-dimensional tensor, so we first need to convert multivariate time series to a 3-dimensional tensor. After data conversion, a low-dimensional time series embedding is learned in the data encoding component. With low-dimensional embeddings, the next step is to learn the prototype of each class.

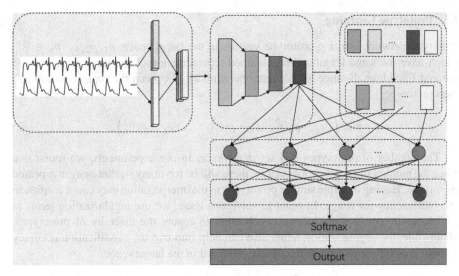

Fig. 1. Overall framework of the proposed model.

Here, the class prototype is the feature representation (embedding) of each class, which contains the same embedding size as the time series. The intuition is learning a class prototype for each class, which has a smaller distance from data samples in the same class, but a larger distance from data samples in different classes.

3.2 Data Encoding

Data Preprocessing. Obviously, the format of image data and time series data is different. Each RGB image includes three channels, and each channel consists of a two-dimensional array. In other words, the image can be represented as a 3-D tensor. In addition, time series have a time attribute. In order to convert a multivariate time series into a 3-D tensor, we first take a sliding window of specific size (e.g., 750 points) so that we can process the data and do batch classification. Then we convert each time series into a 3-D tensor, and then stitch them together. The depth of the stitched tensor is the number of time series variables.

Encoding. The encoding of time series is to learn a low-dimensional embedding for each time series through the neural network based on function c. In order to extract the characteristics of multivariate time series, we use the multi-layer convolution neural network. Specifically, four convolutional layers are applied on each transformed data. We set the default number of filters for the four convolutional layers as 32 and set the number of kernels as 3, remove the fully connected layer of CNN, and obtain a potential representation $h(X_n)$. The embedding process can be expressed as:

$$e_i = c(X_i) \in \mathbb{R}^p, \tag{1}$$

where i is the ith multivariate time series, and p is the dimension of embedding.

3.3 Prototype Learning

Prototype network learns n prototype vectors in the latent space, $p_1, p_2, \ldots p_n \in \mathbb{R}^p$, which have the same length as the obtained representation of the input data. We use squared Euclidean distance to calculate the similarity between the representation and each prototype.

$$s = \left(||e_i - p_1||_2^2, ||e_i - p_2||_2^2, \ldots, ||e_i - p_1||_n^2 \right), \tag{2}$$

The number of prototypes n is set in advance. In our experiments, we found that when the number of prototypes n is large, there will be too many similar or even repeated prototypes. Having multiple similar prototypes in the interpretation may cause confusion and inefficiency for usage. In order to solve this issue, we use regularization terms to punish prototypes that are close to each other to ensure the diversity of prototypes. Meanwhile, the regularization terms also can help improve the classification accuracy and the prototype coverage of the data represented in the latent space:

$$R(P) = \sum_{i=1}^{n} max_{i>j} \left(threshold, ||p_i - p_j||_2^2 \right), \tag{3}$$

where *threshold* is used to classify whether two prototypes are close or not. We set *threshold* $= 1.0$ in our experiment.

3.4 Fully Connection

In the prototype network, the embedded input is compared with each prototype in the latent space to obtain a similarity vector s. Then, the final classification result is obtained using a fully connected layer:

$$f = Ws, \tag{4}$$

where $W \in \mathbb{R}^{o \times n}$, o is the number of classes.

In order to distinguish the category of multivariate time series, we use the Softmax layer to calculate the output probability:

$$y_i = \frac{exp(f_i)}{\sum_j exp(f_j)}. \tag{5}$$

In this work, we improve the classification accuracy by minimizing the cross-entropy loss:

$$\mathcal{L} = \sum_{i=1}^{N} y^{(i)} log \, \hat{y}^{(i)} + \left(1 - y^{(i)} \right) log \left(1 - \hat{y}^{(i)} \right). \tag{6}$$

Moreover, in order to improve interpretability, Li et al. [10] proposed two interpretability regularization terms. The minimization of R_1 requires each prototype to be as close as possible to at least one training sample in the latent space. The minimization of R_2 requires training samples in latent space are close to at least one prototype vector, which means that R_1 will promote the generation of meaningful prototype vectors in the latent space, and R_2 will cluster the training samples around the prototypes in the latent space.

$$R_1(P, \mathcal{X}) = \sum_{i=1}^{N} \min||c(X_i) - p_i||_2^2, \qquad (7)$$

$$R_2(P, \mathcal{X}) = \sum_{i=1}^{N} \min||p_i - c(X_i)||_2^2, \qquad (8)$$

where P is the set of prototypes.

Thus, the loss function is updated to:

$$Loss = \mathcal{L} + \lambda_1 R_1(P, \mathcal{X}) + \lambda_2 R_2(P, \mathcal{X}) + \lambda R(P). \qquad (9)$$

4   Experiment

In this section, we present the performance evaluation results of the proposed MTSPL model, which is implemented based on Tensorflow. Firstly, we introduce the data sets, metrics and benchmarks used in the experiment. Then, we validate MTSPL's performance on Myocardial infarction (MI) detection, followed by analysis of the result's interpretability.

4.1   Experimental Settings

Datasets. The MIMIC-III dataset is a large open database published by the MIT Computational Physiology Laboratory [27], which contains data from 53,423 de-private patients in the intensive care unit of Beth Tsrael Deaconess Medical Center from 2001 to 2012. There are three parts: MIMIC-III Clinical Database, MIMIC-III Waveform Database and MIMIC-III Waveform Database Matched Subset. The dataset we used in this paper is MIMIC-III Waveform Database Matched Subset, which contains all MIMIC-III waveform database records associated with the MIMIC-III clinical database records.

We selected the data of patients who are admitted for the first time and are over 18 years old. Patients' ICU types are divided into CCU and non CCU, and we focus on CCU patients. In total, there are 1,354 patients with MI in the MIMIC-III database, and the MIMIC-III Waveform Database matched subset contains 331 patients with MI. We set the ratio of training set and test set as 7:3.

As the device maybe unstable at beginning, we gave up the first hour's data of each patient, and then we take a sliding window of specific size (e.g., 750 points) to partition the time series into segments of 750 points. Example data of patients with MI and non-MI are shown in Fig. 2 (a) and Fig. 2 (b):

Since the two variables differ greatly in value, the parameters and accuracy of the model may be affected, so we first need to normalize the multivariate time series and map the data to the range of 0 to 1. The normalized results are shown in Fig. 3.

Metrics. To evaluate the proposed model, we adopted classification accuracy and Area Under Curve (AUC) as the evaluation metrics.

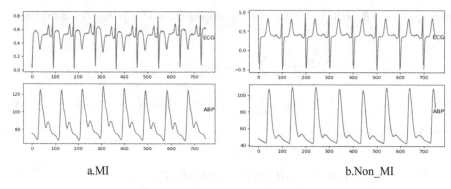

a.MI   b.Non_MI

Fig. 2. Patients with MI and non-MI.

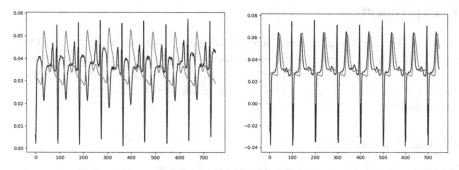

Fig. 3. Normalized time series.

Baselines. We compared MTSPL with two different benchmark models. The details of the benchmarks are provided as follows:

- RNN (Doctor-AI) [28]: RNN + Softmax. It concatenates multi-hot vector with a difference of time stamp as the input feature, and a Softmax layer is added after bi-LSTM.
- CNN: CNN + Softmax. It uses four convolutional layers and 1 dimensional filter, followed by a Softmax layer.

4.2 Result

We set $\lambda_1 = 0.05$, $\lambda_2 = 0.05$, $\lambda = 0.01$, learning rate $= 0.001$, and use the multi-layer convolution neural network to train the model MTSPL.

The number of prototypes has an impact on the model's performance, as shown in Fig. 4. When the number of prototypes is small, the generated prototypes are not enough to summarize all types of samples, resulting in a decrease in training accuracy. When the number of prototypes is large, there will be some similar or even repeated prototypes, resulting in low model training efficiency.

As shown in Fig. 4, when $n = 10$ the model can achieve the best performance. We further optimize the prototypes based on prototype diversity, and finally get 7 prototypes.

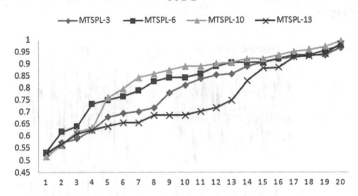

Fig. 4. The influence of different number of prototypes.

Table 1 lists the classification accuracy and AUC of each model, showing that our model is superior to all other baselines.

Table 1. Classification accuracy of each model on MIMIC-III.

Model	AUC	ACC
Bi-LSTM	0.9714	0.9835
CNN	0.9901	0.9922
MTSPL	**0.9933**	**0.9975**

Specifically, according to Table 1, we can see that MTSPL has a higher accuracy. The reason should be that the proposed model can effectively capture potentially important information and learn the evolutionary pattern of the data. The reason why CNN achieves better performance than Bi-LSTM may be that we convert multivariate time series into 3-D vectors, which is equivalent to inputting data as pictures. CNN can extract features from such data more accurately, and thus outperforms the Bi-LSTM model.

4.3 Interpretation

Since the prototype is generated during training, a prototype-based model is with built-in interpretability. In our case, the learned prototypes correspond to evolutionary patterns of the data, which can be used for disease classification. To verify the effectiveness of prototype learning, we visualized some representative prototypes generated in the training process, as shown in the left part of Fig. 5. From the generated prototypes, we found that prototype learning can help learn the main differences between MI and non-MI. For example, the prototype can learn the ST segment elevation of ECG signal, which is very important for MI diagnosis. Based on the generated prototypes, one can obtain the final classification result by compare them with the input, as shown in the right part of Fig. 5.

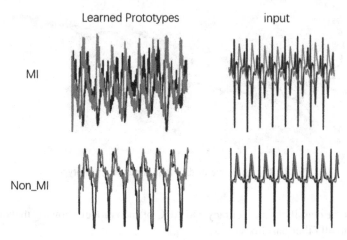

Fig. 5. Learned prototypes.

5   Conclusion

In this work, we proposed an interpretable multivariate time series modeling approach called MTSPL, which combines prototype learning and deep learning to achieve interpretability and high classification accuracy. The model promotes diversity of obtained prototypes by penalizing prototypes that are too close in the latent space. At the same time, the classification accuracy and prototype coverage of the data represented in the latent space are improved. We observed that there is a trade-off between the interpretability of the prototype and the accuracy of the model. When the number of prototypes is small, most of the learned prototypes will be representative ones, but the classification accuracy will decrease. When the number of prototypes is large, some of the generated prototypes may not be representative, although better classification performance can be obtained. Experiments on MIMIC-III Waveform Database matched subset showed that MTSPL is not only as accurate as other advanced deep learning models, but also produces more interpretable results and provides efficient support for clinicians to make decisions.

Acknowledgments. This work is partially supported by the National Natural Science Foundation of China (No. 61725205, 617772428), and the Fundamental Research Funds for the Central Universities (No. 3102019AX10).

References

1. Senin, P., Malinchik, S.: SAX-VSM: interpretable time series classification using sax and vector space model. In: ICDM 2013, pp. 1175–1180 (2013)

2. Grabocka, J., Schilling, N., Wistuba, M., Schmidt-Thieme, L.: Learning time-series shapelets. In: KDD 2014, pp. 392–401 (2014)
3. Cui, Z., Chen, W., Chen, Y.: Multi-scale convolutional neural networks for time series classification. arXiv preprint arXiv:1603.06995 (2016)
4. Zheng, Y., Liu, Q., Chen, E., Ge, Y., Zhao, J.L.: Time series classification using multi-channels deep convolutional neural networks. In: Li, F., Li, G., Hwang, S., Yao, B., Zhang, Z. (eds.) WAIM 2014. LNCS, vol. 8485, pp. 298–310. Springer, Cham (2014). https://doi.org/10.1007/978-3-319-08010-9_33
5. Assaf, R., Schumann, A.: Explainable deep neural networks for multivariate time series predictions. In: IJCAI 2019, pp. 6488–6490 (2019)
6. Wu, M., Hughes, M.C., Parbhoo, S., Zazzi, M., Roth, V., Doshi-Velez, F.: Beyond sparsity: tree regularization of deep models for interpretability. In: AAAI 2018, pp. 1670–1678 (2018)
7. Montavon, G., Samek, W., Müller, K.-R.: Methods for interpreting and understanding deep neural networks. Digit. Signal Process. **73**, 1–15 (2018)
8. Vaswani, A., et al.: Attention is All you Need. In: NIPS 2017, pp. 5998–6008 (2017)
9. Kolodner, J.L.: An introduction to case-based reasoning. Artif. Intell. Rev., **6**(1), 3–34 (1992)
10. Li, O., Liu, H., Chen, C., Rudin, C.: Deep learning for case-based reasoning through prototypes: a neural network that explains its predictions. In: AAAI 2018, pp. 3530–3537 (2018)
11. Ming, Y., Xu, P., Qu, H., Ren, L.: Interpretable and steerable sequence learning via prototypes. In: KDD 2019, pp. 903–913 (2019)
12. Gee, A.H., García-Olano, D., Ghosh, J., Paydarfar, D.: Explaining deep classification of time-series data with learned prototypes. In: KHD@IJCAI, pp. 15–22 (2019)
13. Lines, J., Bagnall, A.: Time series classification with ensembles of elastic distance measures. Data Min. Knowl. Disc. **29**(3), 565–592 (2014). https://doi.org/10.1007/s10618-014-0361-2
14. Wistuba, M., Grabocka, J., Schmidt-Thieme, L.: Ultra-fast shapelets for time series classification. arXiv preprint arXiv:1503.05018(2015)
15. Ghalwash, M.F., Obradovic, Z.: Early classification of multivariate temporal observations by extraction of interpretable shapelets. BMC Bioinform. **13**, 195 (2012)
16. Ye, L., Keogh, E.J.: Time series shapelets: a new primitive for data mining. In: KDD 2009, pp. 947–956 (2009)
17. Zheng, Y., Liu, Q., Chen, E., Ge, Y., Zhao, J.L.: Exploiting multi-channels deep convolutional neural networks for multivariate time series classification. Front. Comput. Sci., **10**(1), 96–112 (2016). https://doi.org/10.1007/s11704-015-4478-2
18. Zhao, B., Huanzhang, L., Chen, S.: Convolutional neural networks for time series classification. J. Syst. Eng. Electron. **28**(1), 162–169 (2017)
19. Zhang, C., et al.: A deep neural network for unsupervised anomaly detection and diagnosis in multivariate time series data. In: AAAI 2019, pp. 1409–1416 (2019)
20. Liu, C.-L., Hsaio, W.-H., Yao-Chung, T.: Time series classification with multivariate convolutional neural network. IEEE Trans. Ind. Electron. **66**(6), 4788–4797 (2019)
21. Guo, T., Lin, T., Antulov-Fantulin, N.: Exploring interpretable LSTM neural networks over multi-variable data. In: ICML 2019, pp. 2494–2504 (2019)
22. Sturm, I., Bach, S., Samek, W., Müller, K.-R.: Interpretable Deep Neural Networks for Single-Trial EEG Classification. CoRR abs/1604.08201 (2016)
23. Strobelt, H., Gehrmann, S., Pfister, H., Rush, A.M.: LSTMVis: a tool for visual analysis of hidden state dynamics in recurrent neural networks. IEEE Trans. Vis. Comput. Graph., **24**(1), 667–676 (2018)
24. Goodfellow, S., Goodwin, A., Eytan, D., Greer, R., Mazwi, M., Laussen, P.: Towards understanding ECG rhythm classification using convolutional neural networks and attention mappings. In: MLHC 2018, pp. 83–101 (2018)

25. Qin, Y., Song, D., Chen, H., Cheng, W., Jiang, G., Cottrell, G.W.: A dual-stage attention-based recurrent neural network for time series prediction. In: IJCAI 2017, pp. 2627–2633 (2017)
26. Bai, T., Zhang, S., Egleston, B.L.: Interpretable representation learning for healthcare via capturing disease progression through time. In: KDD 2018, pp. 43–51 (2018)
27. Johnson, A.E.W., et al.: MIMIC-III, a freely accessible critical care database. Sci. Data (2016). https://doi.org/10.1038/sdata.2016.35
28. Choi, E., Bahadori, M.T., Schuetz, A., Stewart, W.F., Sun, J.: Doctor AI: predicting clinical events via recurrent neural networks. In: MLHC 2016, pp. 301–318 (2016)

A Driver-Centric Vehicle Reposition Framework via Multi-agent Reinforcement Learning

Chenxi Liu, Mingyu Deng, Chao Chen[✉], and Chaocan Xiang

College of Computer Science, Chongqing University, Chongqing 400044, China
cschaochen@cqu.edu.cn

Abstract. The e-hailing platforms have transformed the way people travel, live, and socialize. The efficiency of the platform is substantially influenced by the distribution differences between demands and supplies in the city. Therefore, an appropriate reposition vehicle strategy can significantly balance this distribution difference, which will promote platform benefits, customer goodwill and greatly alleviate traffic congestions. Due to the complicated relationship between vehicles and the temporal correlation of reposition actions, it is a challenging task to reposition vehicles in the city. Existing studies mostly focus on individual drivers that can hardly capture the relationship between drivers and long-term variations of demands and supplies in the city. In this paper, we introduce the reinforcement learning with geographic information and propose a geographic-based multi-agent deep deterministic policy gradient algorithm (gbMADDPG). The algorithm is driver-centric which takes the passenger searching time as an optimization goal to reduce the idle time of vehicles. We will demonstrate the effectiveness of our proposed algorithm framework through simulation experiments based on real data.

Keywords: Vehicle reposition · Multi-agent reinforcement learning · Deep reinforcement learning

1 Introduction

With the popularity of mobile devices and cellular mobile networks, the way people's daily travel has been transformed dramatically [2,3]. Unlike the traditional unknown waiting time to be served, people can choose the way of "E-Hailing" to find a vehicle whenever they need to travel. The e-hailing platforms, such as Didi Chuxing[1] and Uber[2], provide the services that match passengers with vacant vehicles, which can reduce passenger's waiting time, improve vehicle utilization efficiency (e.g. reduce the empty time of the vehicle) and alleviate city's traffic pressure.

However, a major challenge for e-hailing platforms is to balance the distribution of demands and supplies. Although online e-hailing platforms have expanded

---

[1] Didi Chuxing. [n. d.]. ([n. d.]). https://www.didiglobal.com/.

[2] Uber. [n. d.]. ([n. d.]). https://www.uber.com/.

© Springer Nature Switzerland AG 2020
Z. Yu et al. (Eds.): GPC 2020, LNCS 12398, pp. 217–230, 2020.
https://doi.org/10.1007/978-3-030-64243-3_17

the range of ride-hailing, its efficiency is affected by the distribution between demands and supplies. If we can add a balancing mechanism to guide vehicles to calibrate demand and supply in each region, it will greatly improve the service quality of the e-hailing platforms and benefit all aspects of the e-hailing system (e.g. improving platforms matching rate, increasing the driver's income and passengers satisfaction). Thus, how to reposition vehicles is an important issue that needs to be solved in the e-hailing platforms.

It is not a new issue in the relevant research fields. There are many data mining methods [4–6,25] which based on the historical travel data to mine the relationship between the passenger's potential travel patterns and geography information or other information that can be used to recommend the region to the drivers. Traditional methods focus on analyzing the static data, while they exist two major issues. One is that the reposition actions will change the relationships of demands and supplies in the region, but this change will not be reflected because of the historical static data are constant. The other is that reposition action not only influences the current time but also the future. These issues reflect the limitation of traditional data mining methods. They lack consideration of the dynamic environment, which depends on the reposition actions that had been taken before.

We can view the reposition problem as a Markov Decision Process (MDP), and by making sequential decisions, we can get different results. Therefore, our problem transforms into how to find the best sequential decision. Reinforcement learning (RL) [19] is well suited to solving MDP problems. The agent adjusts its policy by interacting with the dynamic environment to obtain a reward and maximize them so that it can form a strategy that matches each station with the best action. Some researchers have utilized RL to study the vehicle reposition problem [23]. However, traditional RL is hard to model from the urban-level, it will generate a huge action space and state space, and it is almost impossible to learn a repositioning strategy with such a huge action and state space.

In recent years, the deep neural network has made great success in multiple fields, especially in deep reinforcement learning (DRL) [14]. Instead of using tables to collect value, it used a neural network to approximate the real function that matches the state and action to solve the complicated problems more efficiently. Hence, we get a new strategy to solve the reposition vehicle problem–the DRL. Yet, there are still some challenges when using DRL to solve this problem:

– **The Proper Reward Setting.** The RL is reward-driven [10], which is trained based on rewards from environment feedback [1]. So, the RL's optimization objective is determined by the reward from the environment in some sense. The previous studies had taken accumulated driver income (ADI) or the order response rate (ORR) [7] as the reward to guide the vehicles to satisfy the demands. Obviously, these settings consider more about the benefits of the platforms but take less consideration for the vehicles (e.g. the search time of the vehicles when hunting for a passenger). In real cases, we should consider more about the vehicles, not only for the efficiency of vehicles but also for urban transportation [26].

- **Urban-level Reposition.** Although we can use DRL to solve high-dimensional problems, it is still difficult to train an optimization policy in constant time. There could be thousands of vehicles in urban, if we use the DRL to solve the urban-level reposition problem directly, it will incur high computational costs [15]. One approach is that we can use a multi-agent reinforcement learning (MARL) method. To be specific, we can treat each vehicle as an agent, thus decomposing high-dimensional problems into many low- dimensional problems. But this approach will bring a new issue about how to coordinate so many agents to maximize our rewards. We need a new model.
- **Geographic Information.** As our problem is based on the city, geographic information is important information. It can help us understand the urban structure and the relationship between regions. Thus, if we merge geographic information with DRL, we will solve our problem more rationally.

To address the above challenges, we propose a geographic-based multi-agent RL algorithm. Our major contributions are as follows:

- We constructed a reasonable urban model based on the MARL framework for the purpose of solving the problem more efficiently.
- We define a reward that considers both the search time of the vehicle and the ORR, guiding the vehicle to learn the policy that reduces the search time while guaranteeing the whole order response rate.
- We propose a geographic-based multi-agent reinforcement learning algorithm and a geographic-based multi-agent deep deterministic policy gradient (gbMADDPG). The algorithm can efficiently train large scale agents at each time, and achieve an optimization result.
- Last but not least, we use the real taxi data sets from Manhattan to simulate real-world traffic and apply our proposed algorithm to the simulator to demonstrate the effectiveness of the framework.

The rest of the paper is structured as follows. We introduce the related work in Sect. 2. Then we will narrate the preliminaries and the urban model in Sect. 3. The algorithm is described in Sect. 4 and the related experiments are presented in Sect. 5. Finally, we conclude this work in Sect. 6.

2 Related Works

Vehicle Reposition. As an important part of urban transportation service, taxi and ride-sharing services have provided great travel convenience for the passenger. Many studies have focused on maximizing the efficiency of the vehicles to reduce the cruised distance when hunting a passenger. In [8], the authors proposed an advanced data mining algorithm to extract the taxi-patterns for efficient passenger-finding. In [25], a taxi recommender system was proposed based on the pick-up behaviors of high-profit drivers and the mobility patterns of passengers. These methods usually make recommendations at the individual level. Actually, they will change the demands and supplies in turn [22], which cannot guarantee long-term optimization. In reference [21], the authors modeled the problem as a Markov Decision Process (MDP), which provides a good reference for the work of this paper.

Reinforcement Learning. To solve the MDP problem, reinforcement learning [19] is an effective way. Traditional reinforcement learning is based on tabular, namely tabular-Q Learning. Its limitations are obvious, as the state increases, it needs to expand the form, and it cannot deal with unknown states. The deep reinforcement learning [14] is developed with a deep neural network as a function approximator. There are many DRL algorithms, such as DQN [14], A3C [13], which have demonstrated their effectiveness in dealing with MDP problems through successful applications in games [17]. However, the real-world MDP problem is more complicated than that in games. There may be a lot of agents, not just one, that will make the environment change more dramatically, which is fatal to the training of the RL algorithm for the high computational cost.

Multi-agent Reinforcement Learning. MARL is a novel method to solve the MDP problem with multiple agents. Researchers have proposed many algorithms, such as MFMARL [24], MADDPG [11]. The essential idea of these algorithms is that if the agents can exchange information with each other, they will make the environment stationary in a sense [11]. Inspired by the domain of Natural Language Processing (NLP), the authors introduced the attention mechanism into the MADDPG algorithm [12], but did not extend to large-scale agents. Recently, some researchers [7,10] have applied MARL methods to real-world problems. For instance, in [10], researchers proposed a fleet management approach and demonstrated the powerful capabilities in processing complicated large-scale multi-agent problems in high-dimensional space. Similar to fleet management problems, the vehicle reposition problem can also be solved by the MARL method.

3   Problem Statement

Our problem is how to reposition vehicles in the city. In fact, the vehicles in a region have the same state, which means we can treat them as homogeneous vehicles. By this means, we make the vehicles in the same region have the same reposition actions, which significantly reduces the complexity of the problem and makes it possible to obtain the optimization results. The goal of the vehicle reposition is to reduce the average search time (AST) of the vehicle when searching for a passenger and also to guarantee the order response rate (ORR). We represent our problem with a spatial illustration in Fig. 1. In this scenario, we use square-grid to split the map and divide the time into 30 min intervals. At each interval, we generate orders according to the real taxi data that we collected and match the order with the nearest vehicle. The vehicles are guided to the region determined by the reposition action, which can be the current region or the adjacent regions. Our goal in the problem is to formulate a repositioning strategy for each region in the city so that we can minimize the idle time of

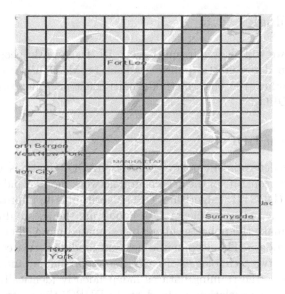

Fig. 1. The square-grid division of the city

vehicles. To solve this problem, we introduce reinforcement learning. Formally, we define the problem as a Markov Game G, which is represented by a tuple $G = (N, S, A, R, P, \gamma)$, where N, S, A, R, P, γ are the number of agents, set of states, joint action space, reward function, transition possibility, and a future reward discount factor respectively. The specific definitions are as follows:

Agent N: As we split the map with square-grid, we take each grid as a region and also an agent. The vehicles in the same region are homogeneous which means they will have the same reposition policy. When they are repositioned to another region, their policy will change to that region's reposition policy.

State $s_t^i \in S$: Each region has a state s_t^i at time t. It is defined as the number of available vehicles and orders in each region. The global state s_t is made up of each region's state s_t^i with the current time (one-hot encoding).

Action $a_t^i \in A$: The action of each agent a_t^i represents the current target region of repositioning. It only can be the neighbor regions, i.e. up, right, down and left, or the current region itself. So there have $|a_t^i| = 5$. The vehicles in the region will find a random position in the target reposition region and navigate to that position. If there are available orders when navigating, they will serve the order.

Reward $r_t^i \in R$: The reward is also associated with each region. The region attempts to maximize the accumulate reward with the discount γ: $\sum_{k=0}^{\infty} \gamma^k r_{t+k}^i$. r_t^i refers to the reward that the agent received at time, which reflects the overall service quality of the current region at time t. The reward is inversely proportional to the average search time in the region. With such a setup, we encourage vehicles to go to the region with less competition, which can reduce the time spent in hunting a passenger. But this may have other adverse effects, we will see in Sect. 5.

4 Methodologies

In this section, we will show our multi-agent RL framework: geographic-based multi-agent deep deterministic policy gradient (gbMADDPG) algorithm. We first briefly introduce the basic method, multi-agent deep deterministic policy gradient (MADDPG).

4.1 Multi-agent DDPG

Multi-agent deep deterministic policy gradient (MADDPG) [11] is extended from DDPG [9]. DDPG consisits of the deep neural network module and deterministic policy gradients (DPG) [18] algorithm. DPG algorithm is an improved algorithm from the stochastic policy gradients [20]. It outputs the action directly, such a mechanism can make the policy gradient be estimated more efficiently and also need less training data. The deep neural network module is related to DQN [14] algorithm, it uses two technologies of DQN, the replay buffer, and dual network structure. It makes the training data as independently identically distribution (IID) and break the correlation of the data. In DDPG, the performance object is:

$$\mathcal{J}_\beta(\theta) = \int_S p^\beta(s) Q^u\left(s, u_\theta(s)\right) ds \tag{1}$$

when we extend DDPG algorithm to a multi-agent environment, if we know the actions taken by all agents, it can make the environment stationary [11], which is the primary motivation behind MADDPG. The performance object of each agent changed to:

$$\mathcal{J}_{\beta_i}(\theta_i) = \int_S p^\beta(s) Q^u\left(s, u_{\theta_1}(s), \ldots, u_{\theta_N}(s)\right) ds \tag{2}$$

where $p^\beta(s)$ is the probability distribution of the states with the joint policy β which taken by the agents, and u_{θ_i} refers to the ith agent's evaluate policy, θ_i is the parameter of the network. Actually, this is an off-policy [19] training progress that allows agents to explore more fully.

4.2 Geographic-Based MADDPG

As the vehicle only influences other vehicles in a certain range, their actions' influences are related to the distance. Therefor, when they are too far apart, their actions are unimportant to each other. In this work, we use this distance information to propose a geographic-based MADDPG (gbMADDPG) algorithm.

We give the overall architecture of the algorithm framework in Fig. 2. It is a centralized training and decentralized execution [5] architecture that can use additional information in training, which is required for the gbMADDPG algorithm. Furthermore, we use a distributed reward setting which enables agents to evaluate their own policies and adjust them more quickly. There are two important modules in the algorithm.

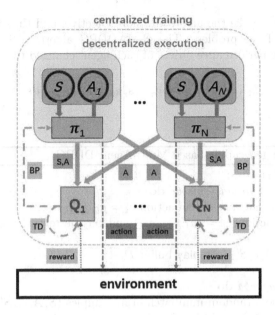

Fig. 2. The overall algorithm framework

Distance Convolution. We use the convolution to aggregate the distance information. Like other convolution operation, we define the kernel ω first:

$$\omega = \begin{bmatrix} \frac{1}{d_4} & \frac{1}{d_3} & \frac{1}{d_2} & \frac{1}{d_3} & \frac{1}{d_4} \\ \frac{1}{d_3} & \frac{1}{d_2} & \frac{1}{d_1} & \frac{1}{d_2} & \frac{1}{d_3} \\ \frac{1}{d_2} & \frac{1}{d_1} & 1 & \frac{1}{d_1} & \frac{1}{d_2} \\ \frac{1}{d_3} & \frac{1}{d_2} & \frac{1}{d_1} & \frac{1}{d_2} & \frac{1}{d_3} \\ \frac{1}{d_4} & \frac{1}{d_3} & \frac{1}{d_2} & \frac{1}{d_3} & \frac{1}{d_4} \end{bmatrix} \tag{3}$$

where d_i refers to the distance between the region and operation region: $d_i = \frac{1}{d_{mh}}$, d_{mh} is the Manhattan Distance and the adjacent regions' distance is 1. Hence, the convolution operation is given by Eq. (4):

$$A_t^i = A_t \cdot \omega \tag{4}$$

where A_t is the joint actions of all agents at time t. After convolution operation, the joint actions change to A_t^i for agent i.

Agent Approximation. Even though the distance convolution has embedded the distance information, each action is still individual. For the current region, it doesn't care about each nearby region's specific reposition action. It is more interested in the overall reposition action of the neighborhood. We reduce the action from convolution operation and calculate an overall action:

$$a_{\text{reduce}_t}^i = \text{reduce}\left(\{a_t^i | a_t^i \in A_t^i\}\right) \tag{5}$$

These mechanisms make the algorithm more effective, and they further reduce the complexity of the problem. The gbMADDPG algorithm is elaborated in Algorithm 1. The performance object of each agent changed to:

$$\mathcal{J}_{\beta_i}(\theta_i) = \int_S p^\beta(s) Q^u(s, u_{\theta_i}(s), a_{\text{reduce}}) \, ds \tag{6}$$

Algorithm 1: geographic-based Multi-Agent DDPG

Initial global state S;

for *episode = 1 to max-episode* **do**

    For each agent i, select an action $a_i = \mu_{\theta_i}(S)$;

    Executes actions $A = (a_1, \ldots, a_N)$ and get the reward r and new state S';

    Store (S, A, r, S') in replay buffer D;

    $S \leftarrow S'$;

    foreach *agent i* **do**

        Sample a random minibatch of M samples (S, A, r_i, S') from D;

        Execute a convolution for agent i, get the joint action $A_i = A \cdot \omega$;

        Reduce the joint action A_i and get

        $a_{reduce\,i} = reduce(\{a_i | a_i \in A_i\})$;

        Set $y_i = r_i + \gamma Q_i^{\mu_{\theta_i'}}(S', a_i, a_{reduce\,i})$;

        Update critic network by minimize the loss:

$$\mathcal{L}(\theta_i) = \frac{1}{M} \sum \left(y_i - Q_i^{\mu_{\theta_i}}(S, a_i, a_{reduce\,i}) \right)^2$$

        Update actor using the sampled policy gradient:

$$\nabla_{\theta_i} J \approx \frac{1}{M} \sum \nabla_{\theta_i} \mu_i(S) \nabla_{a_i} Q_i^{\mu_{\theta_i}}(S, a_i, a_{reduce\,i})$$

    Soft update target network for each agent i:

$$\theta_i' \leftarrow \tau\theta_i + (1 - \tau)\theta_i'$$

---

5   Experiments

In this section, we conduct experiments to verify the effectiveness of the algorithm that we proposed. We will first introduce our simulator briefly. Then, we will show the performance of our proposed gbMADDPG algorithm from the perspective of drivers, platforms, and passengers. Finally, we will conduct an ablation study to analyze the effectiveness of the convolution module.

5.1 Simulator

Reinforcement learning is a method that interacts with the environment and learns from the environment. Thus, we adopt the simulator[3] and extend it to a reinforcement learning environment according to our problem demands.

The Datasets Description. We use the Manhattan datasets of New York TLC Trip Record YELLOW Data which is provided by the NYC Taxi and Limousine Commission (TLC)[4] includes the orders such that both pick-up and drop-off are within the Manhattan area. The order information contains pick-up and drop-off dates, pick-up and drop-off locations, trip distances, itemized fares, rate types, payment types, and driver-reported passenger counts. As each day the passengers have similar travel patterns, drivers also begin their work in the same place, for evolution convenience, we only take records in one day to simulate the traffic in the Manhattan, it has more than two hundred thousand served orders.

The Simulator Design. In order to simulate the real-world transportation travel, we use the orders to represent passengers, and the locations of pick-up and drop-off in the orders are corresponding to the origin and destination positions of the passengers respectively. Then we divide the time into segments at 30-min intervals. At the beginning of each time slot t, the region will generate a reposition action a to indicate the vehicle in the region according to the current state s. At the end of the time slot, each region will return a reward r that is calculated by the average search time of the vehicles in the region. For the passenger, it will become available at the pick-up time and have a 10 min lifetime, it will match with the nearest idle vehicle unless the nearest vehicle can't reach the pick-up position before the end of the lifetime. For the vehicle, when it is hunting a passenger, it is idle and can be matched with a passenger nearby. Once matched, it becomes busy and the simulator will generate the shortest route for passengers to reach their destination. When it arrives, it becomes idle again and can continue to match with passengers.

5.2 Performance Evaluation

To evaluate the performance of the proposed algorithm, we use the RANDOM method and MADDPG as the benchmark for comparison. Each experiment we have run three times with 800 training episodes and 100 evaluation episodes, and calculate its average value.

- RANDOM: The agent will generate reposition action randomly without considering any information.
- MADDPG: The MADDPG algorithm is introduced in Sect. 4.1. We use an MLP model [16] as the neural network and there are two hidden layers in the MLP model.

---

[3] Comset. https://github.com/Chessnl/COMSET-GISCUP.
[4] Nyc taxi and limousine commission. https://www1.nyc.gov/site/tlc/about/data-and-research.page.

Table 1. Performance comparison of methods at different fleet sizes.

Method	5000		6000		7000	
	AST	ORR	AST	ORR	AST	ORR
RANDOM	312.45	85.25%	421.92	91.05%	542.91	94.87%
MADDPG	309.78	85.18%	384.87	90.63%	529.50	94.24%
gbMADDPG	242.71	83.19%	347.78	89.69%	520.13	94.26%

– gbMADDPG: The gbMADDPG algorithm is introduced in Sect. 4.2. We use the MLP model which is the same as MADDPG used.

The results of these methods are summarized in Table 1. We can see that the gbMADDPG algorithm achieves the best performance at any fleet size in reducing AST. As gbMADDPG algorithm imports the prior knowledge of geographic information, it can let the network focus on effective action, so that the training efficiency is improved. The performance of the MADDPG algorithm is similar to the random method at fleet size of 5000, possibly because the original MADDPG algorithm is difficult to optimize the policies of agents. Even though we have simplified the problem to dozens of agents, there are still too many inputs in critic network of MADDPG, it needs much more training episodes to find the relation between the q value and the actions. We also can observe from Table 1 that the ORR is reduced in gbMADDPG and MADDPG compared to the random method. Such observation may because the MADDPG algorithms encourage vehicles to search a passenger in a less competition region which will reduce the AST overall. But usually, the regions with more orders are intensely competition, so that the ORR is reduced as there are fewer vehicles in regions with more orders.

5.3   Consideration of ORR

The ORR is an important indicator of the e-hailing platforms, which reflects the effectiveness of the vehicle reposition. In this subsection, we will consider the ORR. In Sect. 5.2, we compared the gbMADDPG algorithm's average search time with the random algorithm, it has reduced the time significantly also reduced the ORR. So we introduce the ORR into the reward:

$$r_t^i = r_{\text{origin}_t}^i \times (1/2)^{|c_t^i - c_{\text{origin}}|} \tag{7}$$

where c_t^i is the current ORR in region i at time t, c_{origin} is the average ORR in the random method. We named this variant algorithm as gbMADDPG_v1. We run the gbMADDPG_v1 with the same neural network structure in MADDPG with 5000 vehicles in the simulator and calculate the average value with the 100 evaluation episodes. The final result is shown in Fig. 3. We find that the gbMADDPG truly reduces the ORR, which is fatal to the e-hailing platform, and the improved algorithm gbMADDPG_v1 guarantees the ORR, even has a little increase. As we have stated in Sect. 1, RL is reward-driven. By modifying the reward mechanism, our algorithm can reduce the average search time while maintaining the ORR, which will benefit both the platform and drivers.

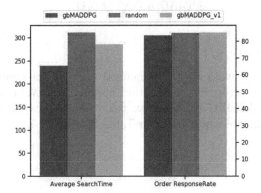

Fig. 3. The effectiveness of different reward design. The left Y-axis denotes the average search time and the right Y-axis denotes the ORR in one day.

5.4 Passenger Satisfaction

To investigate passenger satisfaction, we take reciprocal of passengers' average waiting time as the evaluation indicator. Less waiting time will increase passenger satisfaction. Take the same experiment settings as in Sect. 5.3, we get the passenger satisfaction percentage histogram Fig. 4. We can see from Fig. 4 that the gbMADDPG_v1 achieves the highest passenger satisfaction which makes a 2.84% increase compared to the gbMADDPG. Such increase is due to the gbMADDPG_v1 algorithm considering the ORR to make the passengers' demands served more quickly as the distribution of demands and supplies is more reasonable. From the above experiments, we can conclude that the gbMADDPG_v1 algorithm can benefit the drivers, e-hailing platforms and passengers.

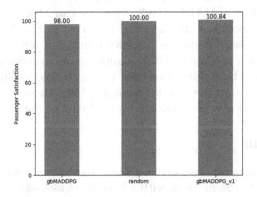

Fig. 4. The passenger satisfaction of different algorithms.

Table 2. The effectiveness of the convolution module.

Method	AST
gbMADDPG	242.71
gbMADDPG_v2	295.11

5.5   Ablation Study

In this subsection, we will evaluate the effectiveness of the convolution module in gbMADDPG. We drop the convolution module in gbMADDPG, and name this variation gbMADDPG_v2. Then we take the same experiment settings in Sect. 5.3, the results are summarized in Table 2 and Fig. 5.

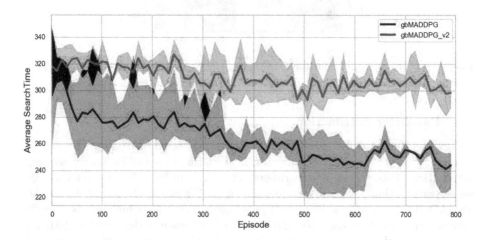

Fig. 5. Training comparison of gbMADDPG and gbMADDPG_v2 without the convolution module.

As seen in Table 2, with the convolution module, gbMADDPG achieves better performance than gbMADDPG_v2. Also, we can observe the effectiveness of the convolution module from the training curves in Fig. 5. The light areas' upper bound and lower bound are the max value and min value of the methods. The convolution module not only significantly improves the performance but also accelerates the training progress. Hence the geographic information is important information to the vehicle reposition, the convolution module utilizes this information so that it becomes an essential part of the algorithm.

6   Conclusions

In this paper, we introduce reinforcement learning into urban-level vehicle reposition and formulate the problem with a feasible model setting. Given this setting, we proposed the geographic-based multi-agent DDPG algorithm that uses convolution operation to aggregate nearby agents' action information with a centralized training and decentralized execution architecture. Furthermore, we have extended our proposed algorithm framework in the simulator using real taxi data to simulate the urban traffic, and demonstrate the effectiveness of our framework from drivers, e-hailing platforms and passengers perspectives.

References

1. Arulkumaran, K., Deisenroth, M.P., Brundage, M., Bharath, A.A.: A brief survey of deep reinforcement learning. arXiv preprint arXiv:1708.05866 (2017)
2. Chen, C., Ding, Y., Wang, Z., Zhao, J., Guo, B., Zhang, D.: Vtracer: when online vehicle trajectory compression meets mobile edge computing. IEEE Syst. J. **14**(2), 1635–1646 (2019)
3. Chen, C., Ding, Y., Xie, X., Zhang, S., Wang, Z., Feng, L.: Trajcompressor: an online map-matching-based trajectory compression framework leveraging vehicle heading direction and change. IEEE Trans. Intell. Transp. Syst. **21**(5), 2012–2028 (2019)
4. Chen, C., et al.: Crowddeliver: planning city-wide package delivery paths leveraging the crowd of taxis. IEEE Trans. Intell. Transp. Syst. **18**(6), 1478–1496 (2016)
5. Foerster, J., Assael, I.A., De Freitas, N., Whiteson, S.: Learning to communicate with deep multi-agent reinforcement learning. In: Advances in Neural Information Processing Systems, pp. 2137–2145 (2016)
6. Guo, S., et al.: ROD-revenue: seeking strategies analysis and revenue prediction in ride-on-demand service using multi-source urban data. IEEE Trans. Mob. Comput. **19**, 2202–2220 (2019)
7. Jin, J., et al.: Coride: joint order dispatching and fleet management for multi-scale ride-hailing platforms. In: Proceedings of the 28th ACM International Conference on Information and Knowledge Management, pp. 1983–1992 (2019)
8. Li, B., et al.: Hunting or waiting? Discovering passenger-finding strategies from a large-scale real-world taxi dataset. In: 2011 IEEE International Conference on Pervasive Computing and Communications Workshops (PERCOM Workshops), pp. 63–68. IEEE (2011)
9. Lillicrap, T.P., et al.: Continuous control with deep reinforcement learning. arXiv preprint arXiv:1509.02971 (2015)
10. Lin, K., Zhao, R., Xu, Z., Zhou, J.: Efficient large-scale fleet management via multi-agent deep reinforcement learning. In: Proceedings of the 24th ACM SIGKDD International Conference on Knowledge Discovery & Data Mining, pp. 1774–1783 (2018)
11. Lowe, R., Wu, Y., Tamar, A., Harb, J., Abbeel, O.P., Mordatch, I.: Multi-agent actor-critic for mixed cooperative-competitive environments. In: Advances in Neural Information Processing Systems, pp. 6379–6390 (2017)
12. Mao, H., Zhang, Z., Xiao, Z., Gong, Z.: Modelling the dynamic joint policy of teammates with attention multi-agent DDPG. In: Proceedings of the 18th International Conference on Autonomous Agents and MultiAgent Systems, pp. 1108–1116. International Foundation for Autonomous Agents and Multiagent Systems (2019)
13. Mnih, V., et al.: Asynchronous methods for deep reinforcement learning. In: International Conference on Machine Learning, pp. 1928–1937 (2016)
14. Mnih, V., et al.: Human-level control through deep reinforcement learning. Nature **518**(7540), 529–533 (2015)

15. Pham, T.H., De Magistris, G., Tachibana, R.: Optlayer-practical constrained optimization for deep reinforcement learning in the real world. In: 2018 IEEE International Conference on Robotics and Automation (ICRA), pp. 66–6243. IEEE (2018)
16. Pinkus, A.: Approximation theory of the MLP model in neural networks. Acta Numerica **8**, 143–195 (1999)
17. Silver, D., et al.: Mastering the game of go with deep neural networks and tree search. Nature **529**(7587), 484 (2016)
18. Silver, D., Lever, G., Heess, N., Degris, T., Wierstra, D., Riedmiller, M.: Deterministic policy gradient algorithms (2014)
19. Sutton, R.S., Barto, A.G.: Reinforcement Learning: An Introduction. MIT Press, Cambridge (2018)
20. Sutton, R.S., McAllester, D.A., Singh, S.P., Mansour, Y.: Policy gradient methods for reinforcement learning with function approximation. In: Advances in Neural Information Processing Systems, pp. 1057–1063 (2000)
21. Tang, H., Kerber, M., Huang, Q., Guibas, L.: Locating lucrative passengers for taxicab drivers. In: Proceedings of the 21st ACM SIGSPATIAL International Conference on Advances in Geographic Information Systems, pp. 504–507 (2013)
22. Wang, S., Li, L., Ma, W., Chen, X.: Trajectory analysis for on-demand services: a survey focusing on spatial-temporal demand and supply patterns. Transp. Res. Part C: Emerg. Technol. **108**, 74–99 (2019)
23. Wen, J., Zhao, J., Jaillet, P.: Rebalancing shared mobility-on-demand systems: a reinforcement learning approach. In: 2017 IEEE 20th International Conference on Intelligent Transportation Systems (ITSC), pp. 220–225. IEEE (2017)
24. Yang, Y., Luo, R., Li, M., Zhou, M., Zhang, W., Wang, J.: Mean field multi-agent reinforcement learning. arXiv preprint arXiv:1802.05438 (2018)
25. Yuan, N.J., Zheng, Y., Zhang, L., Xie, X.: T-finder: a recommender system for finding passengers and vacant taxis. IEEE Trans. Knowl. Data Eng. **25**(10), 90–2403 (2012)
26. Zhang, R., Ghanem, R.: Demand, supply, and performance of street-hail taxi. IEEE Trans. Intell. Transp. Syst. **21**, 4123–4132 (2019)

Demand-Responsive Windows Scheduling in Tertiary Hospital Leveraging Spatiotemporal Neural Networks

Zhiyuan Wang[1], Ruiying Guo[1], Linghong Hong[2], Cheng Wang[1], and Longbiao Chen[1(✉)]

[1] Fujian Key Laboratory of Sensing and Computing for Smart City,
School of Informatics, Xiamen University, Xiamen, China
`longbiaochen@xmu.edu.cn`
[2] Xiang'an Hospital of Xiamen University, Xiamen, China

Abstract. Long waiting queues have been a stressful problem in many tertiary public hospitals, which significantly impact the accessibility and quality of health care. One of the key challenges to solve this problem is to provide enough registration windows to serve hospital visit demand under the limited medical and human resources. Traditional window shift scheduling methods are usually based on experiences and biased historical data, which may not accurately reflect the actual hospital visit demand. In this work, we propose a demand-responsive window scheduling framework by accurately modeling and forecasting the fine-grained hospital visit demand from real-world human mobility data. Specifically, in the first phase, we extract hospital visit demand from taxi drop-off events around hospitals, and build a graph model to capture their spatiotemporal patterns. In the second phase, we propose a spatiotemporal graph neural network (ST-GNN) to accurately forecast the hospital visit demand, which simultaneously captures the spatial correlation by graph convolutional networks (GCN) and the temporal dependency by gated recurrent units (GRU). Finally, we exploit a queuing theory model to achieve demand-responsive windows scheduling. Evaluation results using real-world data from Xiamen City show that our framework accurately forecasts hospital visit demand, and effectively schedules hospital registration windows, which consistently outperforms the baselines.

Keywords: Hospital management · Graph neural network · Human mobility data · Deep learning

1 Introduction

The problem of long waiting queues in tertiary hospitals is troubling patients, which may affect the medical experience of patients and delay the treatment of emergency and critical patients [1]. For example, the average queuing time in Detroit VA Medical Center is as long as 42.3 min [2]. Due to the limitation of

© Springer Nature Switzerland AG 2020
Z. Yu et al. (Eds.): GPC 2020, LNCS 12398, pp. 231–243, 2020.
https://doi.org/10.1007/978-3-030-64243-3_18

medical and human resources, the hospitals' administrations can not schedule enough service windows to satisfy the demand, causing it necessary to exploit effective registration windows scheduling strategies to reduce queuing time.

The registration windows scheduling requires the forecast of the amount of the hospital visit demand in the next period of time to schedule the shift in advance, e.g., 6 h. The conventional methods are to forecast hospital visit demand based on experiences [3] and the data in the hospital visit registration system [4]. However, experience-based methods are not able to respond to real-time demand. While the methods based on the historical registration system data can not reflect the actual queuing situation since the registration system can not reflect the over-demand part due to the limited capacity [5]. Therefore, existing methods can not model and forecast the hospital visit demand veritably, hindering the demand-responsive registration windows scheduling (Fig. 1).

(a) Serious queuing problem in hospital   (b) The windows closed due to scheduling

Fig. 1. Real situation of the queuing window in the hospital

Fortunately, with the advance of mobile and ubiquitous computing, we can now harness various kinds of human mobility data [6], such as taxi trajectories, bus riderships, and bike-sharing usages. Based on these human mobility data, we are able to sense the dynamics of real-world hospital visit demand and schedule registration windows scheduling, which compensates the existing methods' drawbacks. However, it is challenging due to the following issues:

- **How to effectively model the spatiotemporal hospital visit demand pattern using mobility data?** Hospitals in urban space satisfy a geographical distribution, and the hospitals have various sizes in space. In addition, the hospital visit is scattered around the hospital with strong temporal dynamics. Traditional grid-based approaches [7] do not take the spatial distribution into consideration. Therefore, we need to model the spatial distribution of hospitals to capture the correlation between them.
- **How to accurately predict hospital visit demand for windows scheduling?** Hospital visit demand varies significantly, depending on the impacts of temporal contexts, human mobility, etc. Moreover, the hospitals

may demonstrate potential correlations due to the dynamics in spatial distribution. Capturing the temporal dependency and spatial correlation among hospital visit demand patterns is not trivial using state-of-the-art time series models, such as ARIMA [8] and LSTM [9]. Therefore, we need to foster more effective methods for accurate hospital visit demand forecasting.

In this paper, we propose a demand-responsive window scheduling framework with accurately modeling and forecasting the fine-grained hospital visit demand from real-world human mobility data in two phases: hospital visit demand graph modeling and registration windows scheduling. In the first phase, we extract hospital visit demand from taxi drop-off events around hospitals, and build a graph model to capture the spatiotemporal patterns. In the second phase, we propose a spatiotemporal graph neural network (ST-GNN) to accurately forecast the hospital visit demand, and exploit an effective demand-responsive window scheduling mechanism based on the demand forecast using queuing theory. In summary, our contributions include:

- We propose a two phases framework to exploit an effective hospital windows scheduling strategy with accurate hospital visit demand forecast. In the first phase, we extract the taxi drop-off points of tertiary hospitals and model the hospital visit demand spatiotemporal graph. In the second phase, we propose a spatiotemporal graph neural network (ST-GNN) model, which models the spatial correlation by graph convolution neural networks (GCN) and temporal dependency by gated recurrent units (GRU). Then base on the queuing theory, we derive an effective demand-responsive registration windows scheduling strategy.
- We evaluate the proposed framework using real-world taxi drop-off data collected from the Xiamen taxi system in two separate months and hospital boundary data of Xiamen City. Results show that the proposed framework accurately forecasts hospital visit demand with only an average 5% error on RMSE, which consistently outperforms other baseline methods. Our model finds effective windows scheduling strategies, and the model performs well in two case studies of real-world situations.

2   Preliminary and Framework Overview

2.1   Preliminaries

Definition 1. *Hospital Visit Demand: we define hospital visit demand d_i as reflected in dynamic human data such as taxi arrivals.*

Definition 2. *Time Span: we divide the duration of observation data into equal time spans Δt, each time span lasts for a period of time, e.g., one hour.*

Definition 3. *Hospital Status: the status of tertiary hospital i at time quantum t is defined as $V_i(t)$, where $V_i(t)$ is the number of the hospital visit demand in tertiary hospital i at time quantum t, respectively.*

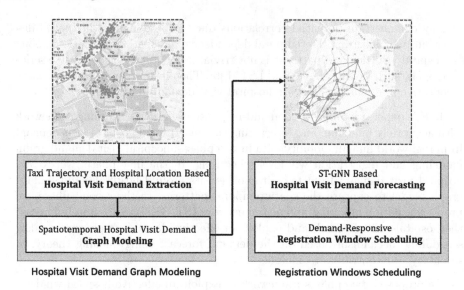

Fig. 2. Framework overview.

2.2 Framework Overview

As shown in Fig. 2, we propose a two-phase framework. In the hospital visit demand graph modeling phase, we determine the arrival area of the taxi according to the tertiary hospital boundary polygon and map the taxi drop-off point to represent the number of hospital visit demand in the time series. Then we take the hospital visit demand as node value, the road network distance as edge weight to build the graph model in the urban space. In this way, the spatiotemporal graph can measure both the spatial and temporal dynamics in urban space in any period. In the demand-responsive windows scheduling phase, we build a spatiotemporal graph neural network (ST-GNN) to forecast each tertiary hospital visit demand in time series, simultaneously capturing the spatial correlation by graph convolutional networks (GCN) and the temporal dependency by gated recurrent units (GRU). Then, according to the forecast results, we dynamically schedule the windows based on the queuing theory.

3 Hospital Visit Demand Graph Modeling

In the hospital visit demand graph modeling phase, we take the whole urban space as a layer space, then model hospitals into the graph in this space to represent the spatial distribution of hospitals. The intrinsic spatial pattern of hospital visit demand is not trivial. For example, a general hospital with relatively abundant medical resources has a rush of the visits even at midnight for emergency, while some specialized hospitals are more chosen by patients during the daytime. Therefore, we propose a spatiotemporal graph model to overcome this challenge. We elaborate on the details as follows.

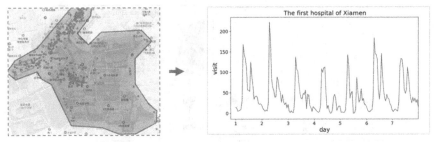

(a) Taxi drop-off and hospital boundary   (b) One week of hospital visit demand

Fig. 3. The case of extracting the hospital visit demand by mapping taxi drop-off data.

3.1 Taxi Trajectory and Hospital Location Based Hospital Visit Demand Extraction

To represent the number of hospital visit demand of each tertiary hospital, we introduce the real-world human mobility data to sense the dynamics of demand, specifically, we use the taxi arrival data in this work. We delimit the local scope through the tertiary hospital boundary polygon dataset, and map the taxi drop-off point on the time series to the corresponding hospital. Figure 3 is an example of extracting the hospital visit demand by mapping taxi drop-off data.

3.2 Spatiotemporal Hospital Visit Demand Graph Modeling

To model the spatial correlation between tertiary hospitals, we represent the urban tertiary hospitals' system as a weighted undirected spatiotemporal graph $G(V, E)$, where V denotes the graph nodes that represent the tertiary hospitals in the urban, and E denotes the set of edges between all the pairs of tertiary hospitals. Based on this graph structure, we model the spatiotemporal dynamics of hospital visit demand using nodes value and edges weight as follows:

Node Values (X): we define the value of node $v \in V$ as $X_v^{(t)}$, which is calculated as the hospital visit demand of hospital v during $[t, t + \Delta t]$. Consequently, we denote the node values of graph G as a matrix $X \in R^{N_t \times N_s}$, where N_t is the number of time spans, and $N_s = |V|$ is the number of tertiary hospitals.

Edge Weights (W): we define the weight of edge $e_{i,j} = \{v_i, v_j\} \in E$ as $W(v_i, v_j)$, which is calculated based on the geographical correlation between tertiary hospital v_i and hospital v_j. In our work, we model the edge weights as the road network distance between hospitals.

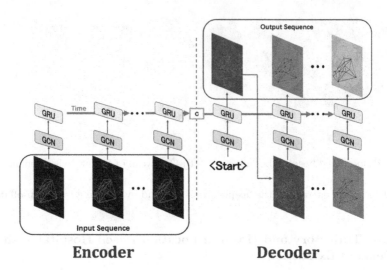

Fig. 4. Model architecture for the spatiotemporal graph neural network (ST-GNN).

4   Registration Windows Scheduling

In the demand-responsive windows scheduling phase, we propose a spatiotemporal graph neural network (ST-GNN) model, which models the spatial correlation by graph convolution neural networks (GCN) and temporal dependency by gated recurrent units (GRU). Then base on the queuing theory, we derive the demand-responsive registration windows scheduling strategy.

4.1   ST-GNN Based Hospital Visit Demand Forecasting

It is difficult to capture the dynamics of urban space of hospital visit demand patterns using traditional time series analysis methods (e.g., Auto-Regressive Integrated Moving Average [8], Feedforward Neural Networks [10] and Long Short-term Memory Neural Networks [9]). To overcome these challenges, we introduce the spatiotemporal graph neural network (ST-GNN) to model the spatial correlation and temporal dependency of the urban medical system for an accurate forecast. Figure 4 shows the framework of the model.

GCN-Based Spatial Correlation Modeling
In spatial correlation modeling, current works usually employ a grid to divide the urban space, mapping the data into Euclidean domains, and then use convolutional neural networks (CNN) [11] to model the spatial correlation in urban space. However, in our problem, the distribution of tertiary hospitals is irregular and scattered. Therefore, we introduce a graph structure based on the distribution of hospitals to model the spatial pattern and exploit graph convolutional networks (GCN) [12] to capture the potential correlation of graph structure data.

It is challenging to construct a convolution operator in vertexes. To overcome this challenge, Bruna et al. [13] proposed spectral networks and locally connected networks on graphs based on graph spectrum theory. Graph spectrum is the set of graph eigenvalues of the adjacency matrix of the graph. With spectral graph convolution, we can easily define the convolution operator on a graph in the Fourier domain. The spectral graph convolution is defined as

$$X * \mathcal{G} y = U \left((U^T x) \odot (U^T y) \right) \tag{1}$$

where U is the eigenvectors of the graph Laplacian matrix, x is the value of node X, y is the value of node Y, and $\odot$ is the element-wise Hadamard product. To applicate graph neural networks model efficiently, we use graph convolutional neural network architecture designed by Kipf et al. [14].

RNN-Based Temporal Dependency Introducing
The pattern of hospital visit demand is affected by closeness (such as sudden illness caused by accident), period (such as the daily and weekly routine of visits), and trend (such as influenza affects for a period of time), which requires the model to response the long short-term dependency. To capture the temporal dynamics of each hospital in urban space, we introduce the gated recurrent unit (GRU) [15]. In the time series forecast, the gated recurrent unit is commonly used to capture patterns over long short-term with relatively little expense. We replace the matrix multiplications in GRU with the graph convolution defined in Eq. 1, which lead to our graph gate recurrent unit as

$$
\begin{aligned}
r^{(t)} &= \sigma \left(\Theta_{r*\mathcal{G}} \left[X^{(t)}, H^{(t-1)} \right] + b_r \right) \\
u^{(t)} &= \sigma \left(\Theta_{u*\mathcal{G}} \left[X^{(t)}, H^{(t-1)} \right] + b_u \right) \\
C^{(t)} &= \tanh \left(\Theta_{C*\mathcal{G}} \left[X^{(t)}, \left(r^{(t)} \odot H^{(t-1)} \right) \right] + b_c \right) \\
H^{(t)} &= u^{(t)} \odot H^{(t-1)} + \left(1 - u^{(t)} \right) \odot C^{(t)}
\end{aligned}
\tag{2}
$$

where $X(t)$, $H(t)$ denote the input and output of at time t, $r(t)$, $u(t)$ are reset gate and update gate at time t, respectively. $*\mathcal{G}$ denotes the convolution defined in Eq. 1 and Θ_r, Θ_u, Θ_C are parameters for the corresponding filters.

Encoder-Decoder-Based End-to-End Forecast
The encoder-decoder framework [16] is an end-to-end learning framework, and is widely used in natural language processing [17]. In this work, we build a spatiotemporal encoder-decoder model with the combination of GCN and GRU. At training step, we feed the historical time series into the encoder and initialize the decoder with a context vector. The decoder generates predictions given previous ground truth observations.

4.2   Demand-Responsive Registration Windows Scheduling

In this section, with the results of future hospital visit demand forecasted, we schedule the hospital registration windows rationally based on the queuing theory. We formulate the windows scheduling problem as a queuing theory problem

[18] with multiple windows and the hospital visit demand is reflected by the forecast data.

Proposition 1. *We suppose the opening number of hospital registration windows is N, the processing registration speed of a single-window is u, and the arrival speed of patients which is reflected by the data is v. In this case, the average arrival rate λ of patients in each window can be represented as $\lambda = \frac{v}{N}$. Assuming that the hospital acceptance capacity is unlimited, i.e., the hospital reception capacity does not affect the speed of registration.*

Normally, after our searching, the average processing registration speed of a single-window should be set as 53 s per patient.

According to queuing theory, the intensity of the service can be defined as

$$\rho = \frac{\lambda}{\mu} \tag{3}$$

the average length of queues is

$$L_q = \frac{\rho^2}{1 - \rho} = \frac{\rho\lambda}{\mu - \lambda} \tag{4}$$

In this way, the average time of waiting can be represented as

$$W = \frac{L_q}{\lambda} = \frac{\rho}{u - \lambda} = \frac{v}{u^2 N - uv} \tag{5}$$

Assuming that the queuing time of patients should be limited within reasonable time, thus, the number of windows should be adjusted to keep the W within a reasonable range.

5   Evaluation

5.1   Dataset Description

We use the Xiamen taxi trajectory data set in September 2016 and September 2017. It includes taxi passenger status, longitude, latitude, recorded time points, and other pieces of information. After processing the data, we obtained the taxi alighting point. Then combining with the boundary data of Xiamen tertiary hospital, we mapped the alighting points of 20 tertiary hospitals in Xiamen City, to obtain the hospital visit demand arrived with taxis of each hospital in each hour.

To evaluate our forecast result, we split the datasets as training data, validation data, and test data by choosing the last 20% as test data, the first 70% hours as training data and the rest of the hours as validation data. Hospital visit demand counting period is empirically set as one hour.

5.2 Evaluation on Visit Forecast

Evaluation Metrics

We use two metrics commonly used in time series forecast, (1) Root Mean Squared Error (RMSE), and (2) Mean Absolute Error (MAE) to measure the forecast error, which are defined as follows:

$$RMSE = \sqrt{\frac{1}{n} \sum_{i=1}^{n} (y_i - \hat{y}_i)^2} \tag{6}$$

$$MAE = \frac{1}{n} \sum_{i=1}^{n} |y_i - \hat{y}_i| \tag{7}$$

Baselines

We compare our method with two sets of baselines: machine learning algorithms and deep learning algorithms. We choose state-of-the-art time series models: ARIMA, SVR, FNN, and LSTM as baseline methods.

- *ARIMA:* Auto-regressive integrated moving average (ARIMA) [19] is widely used in time series analysis. This method models the hospital visit demand as time series' value and does not consider changes in related random variables.
- *SVR:* Support vector regression (SVR) [20] is a regression method of Support Vector Machine. SVR uses the same principles as the SVM to minimize error, individualizing the hyperplane which maximizes the margin between classes.
- *FNN:* Feedforward neural networks (FNN) [10] is the basic architecture of deep learning method. We design the neural networks with two hidden layers, and use Adam optimization algorithm to iterate network weights.
- *LSTM:* Long short-term memory (LSTM) Neural Networks [9] have feedback connections, i.e. memory cells and forget gates, which capture the time dependency of visits pattern while overcoming gradient vanishing and gradient exploding problem. This baseline employs recurrent neural networks with LSTM hidden units to forecast hospital visit demand.

We put the hospital visit demand per hour in the past six hours into models, and it forecasts the hospital visit demand in the next six hours. The forecast results are measured with evaluation metrics.

Results

Table 1 shows that the spatiotemporal graph neural network (ST-GNN) performs the best among other baselines. In comparison, ST-GNN shows at least 10% and 25% improvements on RMSE and MAE relative error reduction respectively. To conclude, ST-GNN's ability to model spatial correlation and temporal dependency contributes to the accurate prediction of spatiotemporal sequence.

Table 1. Forecast Evaluation in 2016 & 2017

Methods	September 2016		September 2017	
	RMSE	MAE	RMSE	MAE
ARIMA	7.45	5.57	9.41	7.39
SVR	5.83	3.94	7.31	4.58
FNN	6.26	4.38	7.17	5.17
LSTM	4.92	3.38	6.15	4.41
ST-GNN	**4.45**	**2.53**	**5.54**	**2.93**

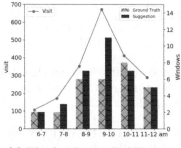

(a) The first hospital of Xiamen

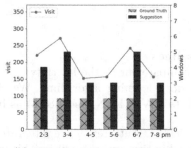

(b) Xiamen university hospital

Fig. 5. Hospital visit demand and windows opening of the two hospitals

5.3 Case Studies on Windows Scheduling

We choose two typical Tertiary hospitals to applicate our model, i.e., the first hospital of Xiamen and Xiamen university hospital. The former is the biggest hospital in Xiamen City, and the latter is set mainly for students in Xiamen university with only two registering windows.

Weekday Scheduling
The first hospital of Xiamen has highly specialized equipment and expertise, which is generally chosen by citizens in the daytime. We forecast the hospital visit demand from 6 am to 12 am on November 14, 2019, with the proposed model, and give suggestions for windows scheduling.

It is a typical case that the hospital allocates the windows relatively reasonable, but for the 9 to 10 rush hour, the restriction of opening windows resulted in an average queue time of 12 min. While as shown in Fig. 5(a), our model gives a more effective scheduling plan.

Physical Constraint Condition
Xiamen university hospital faces severe windows constraints. There are only two registration windows in Xiamen university hospital, so it has a relatively

large physical constraint on the flexibility of windows scheduling. As shown in Fig. 5(b), the hospital visit demand is generally higher than the maximum capacity of the windows, and the problem of long waiting queues in this hospital is serious.

6   Relative Work

We describe the related work from two perspectives, i.e., spatiotemporal sequence forecast and graph neural networks.

6.1   Spatiotemporal Sequence Forecast

Spatiotemporal sequence forecast is mainly to model spatial correlation and temporal dependency. Nowadays, machine-learning-based methods perform well in spatiotemporal sequence forecast problems, which have special designs for capturing the spatiotemporal features [21]. It can be divided into classical methods and deep learning methods. Classical feature-based methods are state-space models and gaussian process, such as Spatiotemporal indicator [22], STARIMA [23] and GP [24]. For deep learning methods, Srivastava et al. [25] proposed to use multi-layer FC-LSTM networks to forecast spatiotemporal sequence, but it does not consider spatial correlation well. Shi et al. [26] proposed the Convolutional LSTM (ConvLSTM) to capture spatial correlation with FC-LSTM's architecture, which added the consideration of spatial correlation. Zhang et al. [27] proposed a grid-based method to divide the city and proposed Deep Spatio-Temporal Residual Networks (ST-ResNet) to represent the long-term patterns.

6.2   Graph Neural Networks

Recently, the graph neural networks perform well in non-Euclidean domains, which employ graph structure to model the spatiotemporal characteristic. Specifically, the Graph Convolutional Network (GCN) is the pioneering work in graph neural networks and the graph convolutional neural network architecture designed by Kipf et al. [14] is extensively used. Sometimes it combines GCN with RNN to model both spatial correlation and temporal dependency. Yu et al. [28] proposed Spatio-Temporal Graph Convolutional Networks (STGCN) for traffic forecast, introducing graph convolution and gated temporal convolution through a designed block. And Li et al. [29] proposed Diffusion Convolutional Recurrent Neural Network (DCRNN) for long-term forecast.

7   Conclusion and Future Work

In this paper, we investigated the problem of hospital visit demand forecast in urban space for effective registering windows scheduling. We proposed a spatiotemporal data-driven framework, which overcomes the challenges by leveraging advanced graph neural networks to achieve accurately forecast. Specifically, in the first phase, we formulated the forecast problem into the hospital visit demand spatiotemporal graph. In the second phase, we proposed a spatiotemporal graph neural network (ST-GNN) model, it models the spatial correlation by graph convolution neural networks (GCN) and temporal dependency by gated recurrent units (GRU) to forecast hospital visit demand accurately. Then we scheduled the effective windows scheduling based on the queuing theory.

In the future, there are still several challenging issues to be investigated. Firstly, the data bias in representing hospital visit demand by taxi drop-off data can not be ignored. It requires the multi-data fusion to represent real hospital visit demand accurately. Secondly, for long-term demand predictions (e.g., one day ahead), we plan to incorporate the attention mechanism in the ST-GNN model to enable accurate and consistent multi-step predictions. Thirdly, we plan to incorporate external data sources, i.e. social events, weather situations, and traffic conditions, to model the real dynamics in urban space.

Acknowledgement. We would like to thank the reviewers for their constructive suggestions. This research is supported by NSF of China No. 61802325, NSF of Fujian Province No. 2018J01105, and the China Fundamental Research Funds for the Central Universities No. 20720170040.

References

1. Mustafa, N., Salim, T.A., Watson, A.: The impact of waiting time on hospital service perception and satisfaction: the moderating role of gender. Int. J. Bus. Manag. Sci. **8**(1) (2018)
2. Qian, Yu., Yang, K.: Hospital registration waiting time reduction through process redesign. Int. J. Six Sigma Compet. Advant. **4**(3), 240–253 (2008)
3. Marcilio, I., Hajat, S., Gouveia, N.: Forecasting daily emergency department visits using calendar variables and ambient temperature readings. Acad. Emerg. Med. **20**(8), 769–777 (2013)
4. Luo, L., Luo, L., Zhang, X., He, X.: Hospital daily outpatient visits forecasting using a combinatorial model based on ARIMA and SES models. BMC Health Serv. Res. **17**(1), 469 (2017)
5. Taylor, N.B.: The contram dynamic traffic assignment model. Netw. Spatial Econ. **3**(3), 297–322 (2003)
6. Vazquez-Prokopec, G.M., et al.: Using GPS technology to quantify human mobility, dynamic contacts and infectious disease dynamics in a resource-poor urban environment. PLoS ONE **8**(4), e58802 (2013)
7. Verdie, Y., Lafarge, F., Alliez, P.: LOD generation for urban scenes. ACM Trans. Graph. **34**(ARTICLE), 30 (2015)
8. Yuan, C., Liu, S., Fang, Z.: Comparison of china's primary energy consumption forecasting by using ARIMA (the autoregressive integrated moving average) model and GM (1, 1) model. Energy **100**, 384–390 (2016)
9. Hochreiter, S., Schmidhuber, J.: Long short-term memory. Neural Comput. **9**(8), 1735–1780 (1997)
10. Huang, G.-B., Zhu, Q.-Y., Siew, C.-K., et al.: Extreme learning machine: a new learning scheme of feedforward neural networks. Neural Netw. **2**, 985–990 (2004)

11. Krizhevsky, A., Sutskever, I., Hinton, G.E.: Imagenet classification with deep convolutional neural networks. In: Advances in Neural Information Processing Systems, pp. 1097–1105 (2012)
12. Schlichtkrull, M., Kipf, T.N., Bloem, P., van den Berg, R., Titov, I., Welling, M.: Modeling relational data with graph convolutional networks. In: Gangemi, A., et al. (eds.) ESWC 2018. LNCS, vol. 10843, pp. 593–607. Springer, Cham (2018). https://doi.org/10.1007/978-3-319-93417-4_38
13. Bruna, J., Zaremba, W., Szlam, A., LeCun, Y.: Spectral networks and locally connected networks on graphs. arXiv preprint arXiv:1312.6203 (2013)
14. Kipf, T.N., Welling, M.: Semi-supervised classification with graph convolutional networks. arXiv preprint arXiv:1609.02907 (2016)
15. Chung, J., Gulcehre, C., Cho, K., Bengio, Y.: Empirical evaluation of gated recurrent neural networks on sequence modeling. arXiv preprint arXiv:1412.3555 (2014)
16. Cho, K., et al.: Learning phrase representations using RNN encoder-decoder for statistical machine translation. arXiv preprint arXiv:1406.1078 (2014)
17. Zhou, J., Xu, W.: End-to-end learning of semantic role labeling using recurrent neural networks. In: Proceedings of the 53rd Annual Meeting of the Association for Computational Linguistics and the 7th International Joint Conference on Natural Language Processing (vol. 1: Long Papers), pp. 1127–1137 (2015)
18. Kleinrock, L.: Queueing Systems. Volume I: Theory (1975)
19. Box, G.E.P., Pierce, D.A.: Distribution of residual autocorrelations in autoregressive-integrated moving average time series models. J. Am. Stat. Assoc. 65(332), 1509–1526 (1970)
20. Drucker, H., Burges, C.J., Kaufman, L., Smola, A.J., Vapnik, V.: Support vector regression machines. In: Advances in Neural Information Processing Systems, pp. 155–161 (1997)
21. Shi, X., Yeung, D.-Y.: Machine Learning for Spatiotemporal Sequence Forecasting: A Survey. arXiv preprint arXiv:1808.06865 (2018)
22. Ohashi, O., Torgo, L.: Wind speed forecasting using spatio-temporal indicators. In: ECAI, pp. 975–980. Citeseer (2012)
23. Cliff, A.D., Ord, J.K.: Model building and the analysis of spatial pattern in human geography. J. Roy. Stat. Soc.: Ser. B (Methodol.) 37(3), 297–328 (1975)
24. Senanayake, R., O'Callaghan, S., Ramos, F.: Predicting spatio-temporal propagation of seasonal influenza using variational Gaussian process regression. In: Thirtieth AAAI Conference on Artificial Intelligence (2016)
25. Srivastava, N., Mansimov, E., Salakhudinov, R.: Unsupervised learning of video representations using LSTMs. In: International Conference on Machine Learning, pp. 843–852 (2015)
26. Xingjian, S.H.I., Chen, Z., Wang, H., Yeung, D.Y., Wong, W.K., Woo, W.C.: Convolutional LSTM network: a machine learning approach for precipitation nowcasting. In: Advances in Neural Information Processing Systems, pp. 802–810 (2015)
27. Zhang, J., Zheng, Y., Qi, D.: Deep spatio-temporal residual networks for citywide crowd flows prediction. In: Thirty-First AAAI Conference on Artificial Intelligence (2017)
28. Yu, B., Yin, H., Zhu, Z.: Spatio-temporal graph convolutional networks: a deep learning framework for traffic forecasting. arXiv preprint arXiv:1709.04875 (2017)
29. Li, Y., Yu, R., Shahabi, C., Liu, Y.: Diffusion convolutional recurrent neural network: data-driven traffic forecasting. arXiv preprint arXiv:1707.01926 (2017)

Prediction Technology for Parking Occupancy Based on Multi-dimensional Spatial-Temporal Causality and ANN Algorithm

Jian He[1] and Jiahao Bai[2(✉)] (iD)

[1] Beijing Advanced Innovation Center for Future Internet Technology, Beijing 100124, China
[2] Faculty of Information Technology, Beijing University of Technology, Beijing 100124, China
jiahaoformail@163.com

Abstract. The Granger causality model is extended by supplementing spatial, weather, and other factors. Therefore, a multi-dimensional spatial-temporal causality model for the prediction of the parking occupancy is proposed, and the prediction algorithm for parking occupancy based on multi-dimensional spatial-temporal causality and ANN is carefully designed. The CityPulse dataset provided by the European Union FP7 project is introduced to train the network, and verify our algorithm. The experimental results show that our new technology for prediction of parking occupancy can effectively improve the accuracy of the prediction, compared with other algorithms only rely on time or spatial factors.

Keywords: Parking occupancy · Spatial-temporal causality · Neural network

1 Introduction

Since the end of the last century, the Intelligent Transportation System (ITS) has been rapidly promoted and developed in different countries around the world. Because it has taken advantages of information processing and computer technologies to significantly improve the efficiency of transportation services, and ease traffic congestion [1]. With the development of wireless communication technology and the improvement of automobile configuration, ITS has become more and more widely used in transportation service. Drivers could easily obtain helpful transportation information through ITS [2–4]. For example, the parking guidance information (PGI) subsystem, being an important part of the ITS, can provide the drivers with the required parking information and enable them to find the most suitable parking lot [5]. Available PGIs usually inform drivers about the real-time parking occupancy through pre-deployed sensors, so that drivers can easily find a suitable parking lot [6]. Since the parking information changes dynamically during the driver's journey to a parking lot, and the parking occupancy may be greatly changed during driving to the parking lot. After arriving at the parking lot, it may spend the driver more time and fuel consumption to search for parking availability [7]. The study from Shin et al. shows that the cruising cars searching for a parking space is determined to account for 30% of the total traffic in a city, and increases the traffic flow peak [8].

© Springer Nature Switzerland AG 2020
Z. Yu et al. (Eds.): GPC 2020, LNCS 12398, pp. 244–256, 2020.
https://doi.org/10.1007/978-3-030-64243-3_19

Furthermore, cars will spend unnecessary time and extraneous energy during searching for a parking space, and produce more carbon dioxide. For example, In Schwabing, Germany, the annual total economic loss is about 20 million euros, caused by searching for free parking space.

Lots of experiments show that it is possible to predict the parking occupancy for a period of future time, combined with the previous parking occupancy and other traffic information (such as the traffic flow around the parking lot). And it will help drivers to efficiently find a suitable parking lot, and avoid the negative influence caused by the vehicle flow in the parking lot [9, 10]. Therefore, we draw on the idea of causality from C.W.J. Granger. That is, if the past values of a time series X provide statistically significant information about future values of Y (usually through a series of t-tests and F-tests on lagged values of X), then time series X is said to Granger-cause Y. Meanwhile, we extend the concept of temporal causality by supplementing spatial relevance, and apply it to analyze the spatial-temporal causality of parking occupancy. Since there are lots of other different factors that can simultaneously effect the parking occupancy, and it is difficult to determine how each of the factors effects on the parking occupancy, and the degree of it effect. According to such challenges described above, artificial neural network (ANN) technology is introduced to accurately predict the parking occupancy. Meanwhile, open data about smart city (namely CityPulse) provided by the European Union FP7 project are used to train the relationship among different spatial-temporal causality of the parking occupancy [12], and verify our algorithm.

The rest of the paper is organized as follows. In Sect. 2, the related researches on the prediction of parking occupancy are introduced and analyzed. In Sect. 3, how spatial and temporal factors effect on the prediction of parking occupancy is firstly analyzed, and a prediction algorithm for parking occupancy based on multi-dimensional spatial-temporal causality and ANN is proposed. In Sect. 4, the CityPulse public data are used to verify our algorithm, and the test result is analyzed. The conclusion and our future works are presented in Sect. 4.

2 Related Work

Using the available data about vehicles and parking lot to establish analytical models, and then predict future parking occupancy has drawn worldwide attention since 1990 s [13]. According to the available reference document, the factors effect on parking occupancy include the time (daily rush hours, weekly, etc.), weather (whether it rains or not), events and others. The method of predicting parking occupancy can be divided into two categories based on real-time on-line data or off-line. Namely, real-time on-line prediction and off-line prediction.

2.1 Real-Time On-Line Prediction

This method uses publicly available data for prediction, and it has a notable feature that does not depend upon real-time data from users. Time series modeling is very popular technology in this method. For example, Wu et al. [17] proposed a prediction algorithm for parking probability based on correlations among different time lags. Ziat et al. [18]

applied representation learning methods to the heterogeneous time series, so as to jointly predict traffic information and parking occupancy. Vlahogianni et al. [19] proposed a prediction system for parking time series based on neural network, and applied survival analysis to predict the probability of the future available parking space. These methods can well predict the time-dependent parking behavior, but they are less concerned on space-dependent features. Therefore, some researchers have studied on the prediction of parking occupancy based on the spatial factors along with time series. For instance, Richter et al. [20] proposed and compared five different clustering strategies based on spatial-temporal historical parking data. Rajabiou et al. [21] proposed an autoregressive model for parking availability based on temporal and spatial correlation. The above methods established a complete space-time model using historical data, and took into account the temporal and spatial correlation for parking information, but they did not consider other factors that are very helpful for the prediction result, such as the weather, and event etc. In addition, there are some researchers who did not consider the feature of time series, but only consider the weather, traffic congestion or other factors so as to predict the parking occupancy. Pflügler et al. [22] proposed a prediction model based on multi-dimensional publicly available data, and assessed the contribution of various factors so as to improve the prediction results. The results showed that time, weekends, weather had a significant influence on parking prediction, while events, holidays, and other factors had a weaker influence.

Considering the challenges of existing off-line prediction technology of parking occupancy, this paper proposes a parking analysis model based on multi-dimensional spatial-temporal causality. It can simultaneously pay attention to the weather and other influencing factors while considering about temporal and spatial relationships. At the same time, it combines spatial-temporal causality with ANN to predict the parking occupancy.

3   Prediction Methodology

After analyzing the spatial-temporal correlation of parking occupancy, a multi-dimensional spatial-temporal causality model is proposed, and a prediction algorithm of parking occupancy based on multi-dimensional spatial-temporal causality and ANN is designed.

3.1   Multidimensional Spatial-Temporal Causality Model

The available parking data in a week from 18th to 24th on August 2014 for a parking lot at Aarhus, Denmark, is plotted in Fig. 1, in which reveals the change regulation of parking availability along with the time from Monday to Sunday. It can be seen that the trends of parking availability during the weekdays are similar. In particular, time points of the morning peak and the evening flat peak curves are quite similar for each day curve. Although the peak value of the parking availability up and down fluctuates over the weekend, the form and change regulation of the curves are basically similar, it indicates that the trend of parking availability is cyclically changing in days with significant similarities.

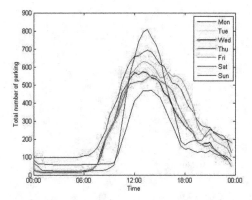

Fig. 1. The plotting of the parking availability in a week

Pflügler found that the location and traffic factors are important causes of parking occupancy [22]. From a qualitative analysis point of view, when a road is close to a parking lot and its distance is relatively short, the vehicle traveling on the road is more likely to enter the parking lot, and its location correlation is relatively strong. As the distance between the parking lot and the road increases, the destination of the vehicle is difficult to determine, thus its correlation is weakened. Therefore, we can consider the parking lot as the center point, and sum the influence of each road on the parking availability from inside to outside under a specific radius according to the traffic flow information of each road. We can divide the parking lots into different regions with spatial feature according to the summation on the influence of each road around the parking lot. It provides us with a kind of spatial factors to predict the parking occupancy, so as to improve the accuracy of prediction. Figure 2 shows an example of the division according to the spatial factor which is calculated by the distances between the parking lot and the road, and the number of the road around each parking lot. In Fig. 2, there are three parking lots. Each red dot stands for a parking lot, which is located in Aarhus City. The data comes from the CityPulse data set.

Being a statistical concept of causality based on the time series, Granger causality is widely used in analyzing the causality of economic variables. Since time series modeling is also an effective method for the prediction of parking occupancy as well. We extend the Granger causality by supplementing the spatial factor described above so as to simultaneously pay attention to temporal and spatial correlation on the prediction of parking occupancy. In order to quantitatively describe the spatial factors, we make a statistical analysis of the CityPulse public data. The statistical result shows that the number of roads around the parking lot is closely related with the parking occupancy. Therefore, each parking lot is considered as the center of a specified radius circle, and the spatial factor of the parking lot is calculated by the summation of the roads in the circle. Figure 3 shows an example of the selected roads in a circle with1 km radius around a parking lot in Aarhus. In the Fig. 3, the red mark is the parking lot, the black circle is the divided area boundary, and the blue mark is the selected road.

Let $Z(n)$ to be the spatial information within the circle with radius φ centered on the parking lot n (indicated by the subscript $n + \varphi$ below), then $Z(n)$ equals to

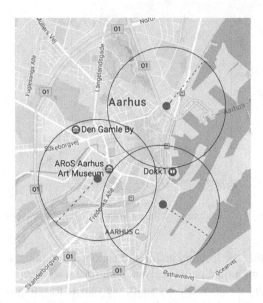

Fig. 2. Road division around each parking lot

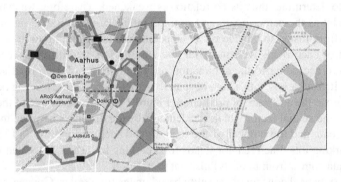

Fig. 3. The selected roads in a circle with 1 km radius around a parking lot

$\{x_{n+\varphi}^1, x_{n+\varphi}^2, \ldots, x_{n+\varphi}^P\}$, which contains P number of roads information in divided area that could affect the parking occupancy at parking lot n. Extended the Granger causality model which includes the spatial-temporal causality model is shown in Eq. 1, where $\{y_{m-t}\}_{t=1}^T$ is the time series variable of the prediction result y, $\{x_{m-t,n+\varphi}^P\}_{t=1,p=1}^{T,P}$ is the spatial-temporal variable of the Granger reason x, T is the maximum time lag in the past observation period, weights w_{j_1} and w_{j_2} represent the influence on the past parking occupancy and roads around the parking lot.

$$y_{m,n} = \sum_{t=1}^{T} w_{j_1} \cdot y_{m-t} + \sum_{p=1}^{P} \sum_{t=1}^{T} w_{j_2} \cdot x_{m-t,n+\varphi}^p \tag{1}$$

In addition to spatial-temporal factors, there are multi-dimensional correlations and dependencies influencing on parking occupancy. Pflügler pointed out that the weather has a significant influence on parking availability [22]. Figure 4 shows the statistically analyzed results of CityPule data. It can be seen that the prediction error is significantly reduced after adding weather factors. Hence, the weather is the Granger causality of the parking occupancy.

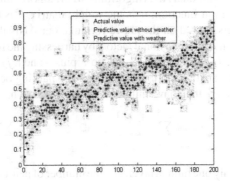

Fig. 4. The influence of weather factors

Let $\{z_{m-t}^q\}_{t=1,q=1}^{T,Q}$ be the time series variable of the influencing factor z, time series $\{y_{m-t}\}_{t=1}^{T}$ performs the following regressions:

$$y_{m,n} \approx \sum_{t=1}^{T} w_{j1} \cdot y_{m-t} + \sum_{q=1}^{Q} \sum_{t=1}^{T} w_{j3} \cdot z_{m-t}^q \qquad (2)$$

where $z^q(q = 1,...,Q)$ are the Q dimensional related factors such as temperature, humidity, etc. w_{j3} is the degree about the influence of the relevant factors.

3.2 Parking Occupancy Prediction

There are many factors that can affect parking occupancy in the spatial-temporal causality model. Perhaps there are some correlations among different influencing factors. At the same time, an individual influencing factor may also have complex deep features. It is difficult to analyze the complex relationship between different influencing factors using traditional autoregressive methods, which may lead to inaccurate prediction of parking occupancy rate. Therefore, we introduce ANN to learn the correlations among different factors so as to accurately predict the parking occupancy. The reason why we introduce ANN is described as follows.

1) ANN can be used to deal with multi-dimensional, and highly correlated data, even though it is unclear that multidimensional features are related to each other.
2) ANN performs better on the analysis of the regular and complex features compared with other general machine learning method.
3) ANN can continuously improve the model through training, with the advantages of easy modification, flexibility, and strong growth.

Considering the above advantages, the ANN is selected as the prediction algorithm of parking occupancy based on multi-dimensional spatial-temporal causality.

$$y = \sigma(w_1 \cdots \sigma(w_2\sigma(w_1 \cdot x + \theta_1)+\theta_2)\cdots+\theta_l)+\theta \tag{3}$$

Equation 3 outlines the traditional ANN algorithm, where x is a column vector containing n inputs, σ is the activation function, w is the weight matrix, θ is the bias, and l is the number of hidden layers. Based on the above formula, our ANN that fuses the spatial-temporal features with multi-dimensional factors by harnessing the following regressions defined as Eq. 4, where j_1 equals to t, j_2 equals to T plus p and t, j_3 equals to $2T$ plus P, q and t, y and x^p are the spatial and temporal factors of parking occupancy, z^q is the Q dimensional related factors than have influence on the prediction.

$$y_{m,n} \approx \sum_{k=1}^{K} w_k \sigma_k \left(\sum_{t=1}^{T} w_{ij_1} \cdot y_{m-t} + \sum_{p=1}^{P} \sum_{t=1}^{T} w_{ij_2} \cdot x_{m-t,n+\varphi}^p + \sum_{q=1}^{Q} \sum_{t=1}^{T} w_{ij_3} \cdot z_{m-t}^q + \theta_k \right) + \theta \tag{4}$$

In this model, there is only one hidden layer, and the number of neurons in the hidden layer is K. The number of input neurons in the neural network corresponds to the dimensions of the multi-dimensional data, and is determined by the dimensions of y, x, and z as described above.

4   Analysis of Experimental Results

The CityPulse data published in the EU FP7 project (available at http://iot.ee.surrey.ac.uk:8080/index.html) are used to train the ANN, and verify the prediction algorithm of parking occupancy based on multi-dimensional spatial-temporal causality and ANN.

4.1   Data Selection and Normalization

The research materials related to the website about CityPulse are studied and analyzed before using the data [23–25]. We select the valid data related with the parking lot from August 1st to October 20th in 2014, including 2452 parking data, and the related weather and traffic data around the parking lot. All of the data are preprocessed with the same sampling time. According to the difference on value units and ranges of the data, all of the data are normalized according to Eq. 5, and the normalized data could be renormalized according to Eq. 6, where X is the original data, X^* is the normalized data, X_{max} and X_{min} are the maximum and minimum values of the original data respectively.

$$X^* = (X - X_{min})/(X_{max} - X_{min}) \tag{5}$$

$$X = X^*(X_{max} - X_{min}) + X_{min} \tag{6}$$

In order to effectively apply the spatial-temporal features, the valid time-related data are divided into 3 lag data, the interval is 30 min for each lag data. For example, when predicting the parking occupancy after half an hour, the current data, the previous 30 min data, and the previous one-hour data could be used as the data for realizing the correlation.

Similarly, the previous 30 min data, the previous one-hour data, and the previous one and half hours data are used to predict the current parking occupancy. The data used in this paper in the range that is centered on the parking lot has six related roads within a radius of one kilometer. Besides, the related weather and environmental data (such as temperature and humidity) are also used as well.

4.2 Neural Network Construction

There are totally 53 input neurons to be the input of neural network, including days of the week, time, weather information (such as: air pressure, dew point, humidity, temperature, wind direction, wind speed), traffic information with time lag about the six roads, and previously parking occupancy rate. The number of output neurons is 1, and the output is the prediction value of parking occupancy rate. There are two hidden layers for the neural network, and the number of neurons for the hidden layer is 7, 5 respectively. The design of the hidden layer is based on the experience and the analysis of experimental results. Back propagation (BP) neural network is used because of its extensive effect, simple structure, and convenience in the mathematical analysis [26]. The activation function of the hidden layer and the output layer is the logarithmic sigmoid transfer function and the training function is the gradient descent adaptive learning rate training function.

During generating training and verification data set for the neural network, we divide the parking occupancy rate into 10 sections by 0.1 intervals, the proportion of data in each interval is calculated, and the data is randomly selected according to the proportion between training data and original data. Among them, 200 pieces of data are selected as verification set, and the rest are used as training set. Some training samples are shown in Table 1.

4.3 Analysis of Experimental Results

Matlab R2012b is adopted to implement the algorithm, and the preprocessed data are used for verification. We predict the parking occupancy after 30 min using the actual historical values based on the CityPulse open data, and then compare the prediction results with the actual parking occupancy. In the experiment, the capacity of the parking lot is 56. Since the parking information was updated per 30 min, the prediction lag should also be a multiple of 30 min. If the sampling frequency of the data is higher, and more detailed information is provided, the model can predict the future parking occupancy with smaller time granularity.

In order to objectively evaluate the prediction effect, the mean absolute error (MAE) is introduced to measure the prediction effect. The MAE is calculated according to Eq. 7, where X^* is the predicted value, X is the actual value, and N is the total number of samples.

$$MAE = \frac{1}{N} \sum_{i=1}^{N} |X^* - X| \tag{7}$$

In order to measure the performance of our prediction technology after supplementing spatial-temporal causality and multi-dimensional influencing factors, several

Table 1. Training samples used for the experiment

Sample	Week of day	Time	Air pressure	Air pressure (with time lag)			Other weather info	Road1	Road1 (with time lag)			Other road info	Parking occupancy (with time lag)			Parking occupancy
				30 min	1 h	1 h 30 min			30 min	1 h	1 h 30 min		30 min	1 h	1 h 30 min	
S(1)	0.3333	0.6876	0.2632	0.2895	0.2632	0.2632	...	0.3530	0.4706	0.5294	0.2353	...	0.0893	0.2679	0.1071	0.0536
S(2)	0.8333	0.4375	0.3684	0.3684	0.3421	0.3684		0.4118	0.1765	0.1765	0.2353		0.2857	0.4643	0.2321	0.1964
S(3)	0.5	0.3333	0.2632	0.2632	0.2632	0.2632		0.2353	0.1765	0.6471	0.1176		0.625	0.4821	0.5	0.2321
S(4)	0.6667	0.3333	0.3947	0.3684	0.3947	0.3684		0.1765	0.1765	0.2941	0.3530		0.6071	0.4107	0.5714	0.3214
S(5)	0.6667	0.6875	0.5263	0.5526	0.5526	0.5526		0.2941	0.2941	0.3530	0.1176		0.3571	0.3929	0.6429	0.4821
S(6)	0.6667	0.7708	0.5263	0.5263	0.5263	0.5263		0.2353	0.0588	0.2353	0.1765		0.5536	0.5536	0.4821	0.5179
S(7)	1	0.4167	0.4474	0.4474	0.4737	0.4474		0.2941	0.4118	0.4706	0.4118		0.625	0.6786	0.6964	0.625
S(8)	0	0.3959	0.5526	0.5526	0.5526	0.5526		0.3529	0.2941	0.1765	0.1176		0.7321	0.8214	0.625	0.7143
S(9)	0.1667	0.875	0.9474	0.9211	0.9211	0.9211		0.0588	0.1176	0.4706	0.2941		0.7321	0.8214	0.75	0.8036
S(10)	0.5	0.7917	0.8684	0.8684	0.8947	0.8947		0.1176	0.2941	0.5294	0.2941		0.3571	0.3393	0.875	0.9107

different algorithms are used to predict the same data set. For example, Kalman filtering algorithm has been used to predict the traffic status [27, 28]. Hence, the Kalman filtering algorithm is also used to predict the parking occupancy as well, and its predicting result is compared with others. In addition, the following prediction algorithms are compared: neural network prediction algorithm based on spatial factors (road information) and weather; linear regression prediction algorithm based on time series; neural network prediction algorithm based on time series; neural network prediction algorithm based on spatial-temporal factors and weather without time lag; neural network prediction algorithm based on spatial-temporal causality (including weather factors with time lag). Prediction results include parking occupancy after 30 min, and after 1 h respectively. The experimental results are renormalized and shown in Table 2. The results show that the prediction errors of parking spaces by linear regression method based on time series after 30 min and after 1 h are 3.753 and 5.034 respectively, while the errors of neural network prediction based on time series are 3.021, 3.866 respectively. Compared with linear regression, neural network prediction error is smaller and prediction accuracy is higher. In terms of time series prediction and the Kalman filtering prediction, they err 3.059 and 3.739 respectively, which is better than neural network. However, when other dimensional factors (such as weather, road, etc.) are gradually introduced, the neural network also reduces the prediction errors as well, and its prediction becomes better and better. Additionally, it can be seen from Table 2 that time correlation is a very important factor for neural network, compared with the predict results 5.486 (30 min), and 6.372 (1 h) which only includes roads factors and weather factors, the predicted error with time series is reduced to 3.021 (30 min), 3.866 (1 h). Meanwhile, the prediction accuracy is significantly improved when the temporal factor is supplemented. When concerning about temporal correlation, supplementing road and weather factors can greatly improve the accuracy of the prediction, while the error sharply drops to 2.562 for 30 min, and 3.475 for an hour respectively. With multi-dimensional spatial-temporal causality, the accuracy of the prediction is further improved, and the error is reduced to a minimum of 2.488 for 30 min, and 3.418 for an hour respectively, which is less than the error of linear regression and Kalman filtering. It proves that our algorithm based on multi-dimensional spatial-temporal causality and ANN can efficiently improve the predicting accuracy of parking occupancy.

Table 2. Comparison on the results of different prediction method

Prediction methodology	MAE	
	30 min	1 h
Road, Weather (Neural network)	5.486	6.372
Time series (Linear regression)	3.753	5.034
Time series (Kalman filter)	3.059	3.739
Time series (Neural network)	3.021	3.866
Time series, Road, Weather (Neural network)	2.562	3.475
Multi-dimensional Spatial temporal casual factors (Neural network)	2.488	3.418

The prediction results of multi-dimensional input are shown in Fig. 5. It indicates that some points are deviant from the regression trend. There are some possible reasons, such as road accidents, emergencies, or special event in the surrounding area, and so on.

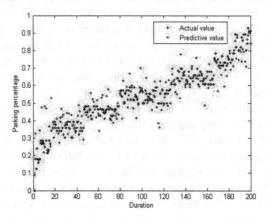

Fig. 5. Prediction result of multi-dimensional input

5   Conclusion

Accurate prediction of parking occupancy is an important part of the ITS study. In this paper we propose a multi-dimensional spatial-temporal causality model of parking occupancy, and established a prediction algorithm of parking occupancy based on ANN. It can estimate the parking occupancy at the time of the driver arriving at the parking lot according to the estimated time of arrival.

The model proposed in this paper mainly consider the multidimensional spatial and temporal causality related to the parking data, and used public data sets to verify the validity of the model. The experimental results show that the parking occupancy mainly depends on the spatial-temporal correlation factors, spatial-temporal causality can effectively improve prediction accuracy. In addition, other influencing factors (such as seasonal factors in the parking) can also contribute to the prediction accuracy, and we would like to try to use other algorithms to improve the prediction accuracy such as RNN in the future.

Acknowledgement. This work is supported by the National Nature Science Foundation of China (no. 61602016), and Beijing Science and Technology Project (no. D171100004017003). The authors would like to acknowledge Dr. Ruihai Dong in School of Computer Science, University College Dublin for improving the language in the article.

References

1. Figueiredo, L., Jesus, I., Machado, J.A.T.: Towards the development of intelligent transportation systems. Intell. Transp. Syst., 1206–1211 (2001)

2. Nugent, C.D., Hong, X., Hallberg, J.: Assessing the impact of individual sensor reliability within smart living environments. In: IEEE International Conference on Automation Science and Engineering, pp. 685–690 (2008)
3. Rahim, A., et al.: Vehicular social networks: a survey. Pervasive Mobile Comput. **43**, 96–113 (2017)
4. Ning, Z., Xia, F., Ullah, N., Kong, X., Hu, X.: Vehicular social networks: enabling smart mobility. IEEE Commun. Mag. **55**(5), 16–55 (2017)
5. Teng, H., Qi, Y., Martinelli, D.R.: Parking difficulty and parking information system technologies and costs. J. Adv. Transp. **42**(2), 151–178 (2008)
6. Yang, Z., Liu, H., Wang, X.: The research on the key technologies for improving efficiency of parking guidance system. Intell. Transp. Syst., **2**, 1177–1182 (2003)
7. Liu, S., Guan, H., Yan, H.: Unoccupied parking space prediction of chaotic time series. In: Tenth International Conference of Chinese Transportation Professionals, pp. 2122–2131 (2010)
8. Shin, J.H., Jun, H.B.: A study on smart parking guidance algorithm. Transp. Res. Part C Emerg. Technol. **44**(4), 299–317 (2014)
9. Blythe, P.T.: Forecasting available parking space with 1argest Lyapunov exponents method. J. Central South Univ. **21**(4), 1624 (2014)
10. Tamrazian, A., Qian, Z., Rajagopa, R.: Where is my parking spot? Transp. Res. Record J. Transp. Res. Board **2489**, 77–85 (2015)
11. Granger, C.W.J.: Investigating causal relations by econometric models and cross-spectral methods. Econometrica **37**(3), 424–438 (1969)
12. Zhang, G., Patuwo, B.E., Hu, M.Y.: Forecasting with artificial neural networks: the state of the art. Int. J. Forecast. **14**(1), 35–62 (1998)
13. Arnott, R., Rowse, J.: Modeling parking. J. Urban Econ. **45**(1), 97–124 (1999)
14. Caicedo, F., Blazquez, C., Miranda, P.: Prediction of parking space availability in real time. Expert Syst. Appl. **39**(8), 7281–7290 (2012)
15. Rajabioun, T., Foster, B., Ioannou, P.: Intelligent parking assist. Control Autom., 1156–1161 (2013)
16. Nandugudi, A., Ki, T., Nuessle, C.: PocketParker: pocketsourcing parking lot availability, pp. 963–973 (2014)
17. Wu, H.K., Sahoo, J., Liu, C.Y.: Agile urban parking recommendation service for intelligent vehicular guiding system. Intell. Transp. Syst. Mag. IEEE **6**(1), 35–49 (2014)
18. Ziat, A., Leroy, B., Baskiotis, N.: Joint prediction of road-traffic and parking occupancy over a city with representation learning. In: International Conference on Intelligent Transportation Systems, pp. 725–730 (2016)
19. Vlahogianni, E.I., Kepaptsoglou, K., Tsetsos, V.: A real-time parking prediction system for smart cities. J. Intell. Transp. Syst. **20**(2), 192–204 (2016)
20. Richter, F., Martino, S.D., Mattfeld, D.C.: Temporal and spatial clustering for a parking prediction service. In: International Conference on TOOLS with Artificial Intelligence, pp. 278–282 (2014)
21. Rajabioun, T., Ioannou, P.A.: On-Street and off-street parking availability prediction using multivariate spatiotemporal models. IEEE Trans. Intell. Transp. Syst. **16**(5), 2913–2924 (2015)
22. Pflügler, C., Köhn, T., Schreieck, M.: Predicting the availability of parking spaces with publicly available data. In: Informatik, pp. 361–374 (2016)
23. Ali, M.I., Gao, F., Mileo, A.: CityBench: a configurable benchmark to evaluate rsp engines using smart city datasets. In: International Semantic Web Conference, pp.374–389 (2015)
24. Bischof, S., Karapantelakis, A., Sheth, A.: Semantic modelling of smart city data. Position Paper in W3C Workshop on the Web of Things: enablers and services for an open Web of Devices, 1–5 (2014)

25. Kolozali, S., Bermudez-Edo, M., Puschmann, D.: A knowledge-based approach for real-time IoT data stream annotation and processing. Internet Things, 215–222. IEEE (2015)
26. Hanafizadeh, P., Ravasan, A.Z., Khaki, H.R.: An expert system for perfume selection using artificial neural network. Expert Syst. Appl. **37**(12), 8879–8887 (2010)
27. Okutani, I., Stephanedes, Y.J.: Dynamic prediction of traffic volume through Kalman filtering theory. Transp. Res. Part B **18**(1), 1–11 (1984)
28. Ji, H., Xu, A.: The applied research of Kalman in the dynamic travel time prediction. In: International Conference on Geoinformatics, pp. 1–5. IEEE (2010)

An Improved Leaky-ESN for Electricity Load Forecasting

Qiaoying Lin[1,2], Fangwan Huang[1,2(✉)], Zhiyong Yu[1,2,3], and Li Li[1,2]

[1] College of Mathematics and Computer Science, Fuzhou University, Fuzhou, China
hfw@fzu.edu.cn
[2] Fujian Provincial Key Laboratory of Network Computing and Intelligent Information Processing, Fuzhou University, Fuzhou, China
[3] Key Laboratory of Spatial Data Mining and Information Sharing, Ministry of Education, Fuzhou, China

Abstract. In the recent decade, recurrent neural networks become a hot research field, with the powerful capability to capture temporal information from time series. To avoid the vanishing/exploding gradient problem caused by the gradient descent algorithm involved in most recurrent networks, echo state network (ESN) was proposed to contain a large but sparse reservoir instead of traditional hidden layers. However, the performance of ESN is very sensitive to the parameters of the reservoir. In this paper, we focus on the improvements of ESN in the background of electricity load forecasting. With the goal of effectively and efficiently computation in the context of pervasive and cloud computing, two versions of adaptive echo state network (AESN) are designed to adopt a modular control strategy to automatically adjust some parameters of the reservoir. Applying AESN on two synthetic datasets and two real world electricity datasets, experimental results demonstrate that AESN is viable.

Keywords: Echo state network · Time series prediction · Leaky integrator · Modular control strategy

1 Introduction

With the rapid development of data storage technologies and the emergence of Internet-enabled devices, we have stepped into the data explosion era. Data grows exponentially so that we could explore much information, such as from the electricity grid, hospital system, or public transportation network, to make our lives more convenient. Therefore, researches about effectively and efficiently computing in the context of pervasive and cloud computing have received a lot of attention now.

In this paper, we would focus on the electricity load forecasting filed. The main characteristic of electricity load is its periodicity, which might change hourly, daily, weekly, or monthly, etc. [1]. Although it is a kind of continuous time series, it is still highly sensitive to some exclusive variations, such as temperature, humidity, and holiday. Also, it could be indirectly affected by economic development, population growth, or

© Springer Nature Switzerland AG 2020
Z. Yu et al. (Eds.): GPC 2020, LNCS 12398, pp. 257–269, 2020.
https://doi.org/10.1007/978-3-030-64243-3_20

global warming [2]. Some of those direct and indirect variations could be estimated while some could not.

To solve the problems above, statistical methods, machine learning algorithms and neural networks are widely applied and proposed for higher model accuracy. A novel recurrent neural network (RNN) paradigm, called echo state network (ESN), was proposed by Jaeger and Haas in 2001 [3] to avoid the vanishing/exploding gradient problem caused by the gradient descent algorithm, which lowers the training complexity of neural networks at the same time. In the architecture of ESN, hidden layers of the traditional RNNs are replaced by a large but sparse reservoir. In addition, ESN only needs to obtain the output weight matrix, while the input weight matrix and the reservoir weight matrix are randomly generated and remain unchanged during the training process. In the last decade, applications or modifications of the ESN model are mainly focused on approaches to deepen the reservoir, to compute the output weight matrix, or ensemble approaches with other models, which in a way increase the model accuracy but also make it more complex. Meanwhile, the selection of model parameters, such as the number of neurons in the reservoir, spectral radius and sparsity of the reservoir, still remains a problem.

This paper presents the following contributions:

- Due to the cost of parameter optimization without exact rules, a modular control strategy based on leaky-ESN is proposed to automatically adjust the leaking rate and the sparsity of the reservoir.
- The proposed models were applied on two synthetic datasets for time series prediction and two real-world datasets for electricity load forecasting. Performances are proved to be better than the traditional ESN and leaky-ESN on all datasets. When applying on the two synthetic datasets, two improved versions of ESN proposed in the reference [4] are introduced for comparison, where our proposed models still have better performance.

The rest of this paper is organized as followed. In Sect. 2, we present some recent researches in the field of electricity load forecasting. Theories of ESN architecture are presented in Sect. 3. In Sect. 4 and Sect. 5 we present our proposed novel model and experimental results, respectively. Conclusion and future works are presented in Sect. 6.

2   Related Work

According to forecast duration, the electricity load forecasting can be classified into short-term, middle-term, long-term forecasting, which is hourly or daily, weekly, and monthly or even yearly, respectively [5]. So far, researches in this field could be generally concluded as the following three categories:

- Statistical mathematical approaches [6], such as Autoregressive (AR), Auto Regressive Moving Average (ARMA), Autoregressive Integrated Moving Average (ARIMA) [7], Generalized Auto Regressive Conditional Heteroskedasticity model (GARCH) [8], and Grey Forecast models [9, 10], etc.
- Machine learning approaches [11], such as Support Vector Machine (SVR) [12, 13], the hybrid method of Regression Trees and Neural Networks [14], etc.

- Deep learning approaches, such as Recurrent Neural Networks (RNN) [15–17], Long Short-term Memory (LSTM) [18], Echo State Networks (ESN) [19–21], Deep Belief Network [22], etc.

Different approaches have their own advantages. Compared with the other two kinds of approaches, deep learning is powerful for autonomous learning and obtaining useful and valuable information from a large amount of training data. The core of deep learning is the hidden layers, where the weight of each neuron in the hidden layers is obtained during the training process. Considering the temporal characteristics of electricity load, researches on different RNNs, containing memory units, have drawn great attention. And the introduction of ESN helps to avoid the vanishing/exploding gradient problem caused by the gradient descent algorithm and slow convergence. Meanwhile, it also can lower the training complexity [23–25].

However, ESN still has its drawbacks. Taking them into account, recent researches and improvements of ESN can be generally concluded as followed:

- Because there are many parameters required during the construction of the ESN architecture, in most cases, a variety of intelligent optimization algorithms such as Genetic Algorithms (GA) are used to optimize the parameters [26].
- Linear regression methods always look for the output weights that are suitable for the training set, which could easily lead to overfitting. To solve this problem, it is necessary to add some intervention to the ESN model to appropriately reduce its training accuracy. Common improvements include increasing white noise [27] on neurons during training or using ridge regression instead of linear regression [28].
- Adjust and optimize the structure of the reservoir. A typical attempt is to deepen the reservoir or replace internal neurons with different neurons, such as merged integral neurons [29].

3 Preliminary

ESN is a novel recurrent neural network, which is suitable for sequential processing tasks, such as text or time-series. Its training process is simple but having high accuracy compared to other neural networks. Instead of setting hidden layers, ESN introduces a large but sparse reservoir, which helps to overcome the existing problems of slow convergence speed and avoid the vanishing/exploding gradient problem caused by the gradient descent algorithm in the most neural network models.

The architecture of ESN is illustrated in Fig. 1., which consists of an input layer with I neurons, a reservoir with N neurons and an output layer with O neurons.

Assume that at time step t, $x[t] \in R^I$ denotes the external input, $h[t] \in R^N$ denotes the echo state, and $y[t] \in R^O$ denotes the output vector. W_i^r, W_r^r, W_r^o, W_o^r, and W_i^o, denote the weight matrix from the input layer to the reservoir, with size $N \times I$, the weight matrix of internal connections within the reservoir, with size $N \times N$, the weight matrix from the reservoir to the output layer, with size $O \times N$, the weight matrix from the output layer to the reservoir, with size $N \times O$, and the weight matrix from the input layer to the output layer, with size $O \times I$, respectively.

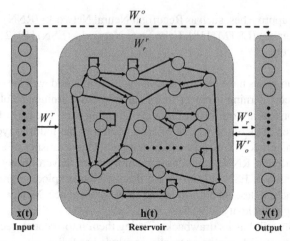

Fig. 1. ESN architecture, where the solid arrow represents the randomly initialized weight matrix, while the dotted arrow represents the weight matrix to be trained.

The process of training the ESN model consists of two steps: the collection of echo states and the computation of outputs.

During the training process, equations of the traditional ESN are given as followed:

$$h[t] = f\left(W_i^r \times x[t] + W_r^r \times h[t-1] + W_o^r \times y[t-1] + \xi\right) \tag{1}$$

$$y[t] = W_i^o \times x[t] + W_r^o \times h[t] \tag{2}$$

The Eq. (1) indicates the process of collecting echo states, where W_i^r, W_r^r and W_o^r are randomly initialized. The Eq. (2) indicates the process of computing outputs, where W_r^o and W_i^o are obtained after performing regression methods.

The equations of leaky-ESN to collect echo states [30, 31], where the reservoir consists of leaky-integrator neurons, are given as followed:

$$h'[t] = f\left(W_i^r \times x[t] + W_r^r \times h[t-1] + W_o^r \times y[t-1] + \xi\right) \tag{3}$$

$$h[t] = \alpha \times h[t-1] + (1-\alpha) \times h'[t] \tag{4}$$

The reservoir plays a vital role in ESN. It contains a large number of neurons, which are not fully connected. At time step t, the echo state $h[t]$ is a kind of high-dimensional nonlinear expansion formed after the external input $x[t]$ passing through the reservoir, which also preserves some transient memory information [23].

Compared to other neural networks, such as feed forward network and recurrent neural network, ESN model is relatively easier to be constructed, but during the training process, some key parameters in the network are required to be empirically selected and adjusted: N which denotes the number of neurons in the reservoir, λ and S which denotes the spectral radius and the sparsity of W_r^r, respectively, and α which denotes the leaking rate when computing the echo states.

First of all, the most critical parameter in leaky-ESN is the number of neurons N in the reservoir. The larger N is, the more complex leaky-ESN network structure is. This parameter is similar to the construction of some traditional neural networks when setting the number of hidden layers and the number of neurons of each hidden layer. Theoretically, if there are more neurons in the reservoir, it is easier to obtain the nonlinear combination of external inputs, but it might also cause the over-fitting of output vectors.

Secondly, it is about the configuration of λ and S of the weight matrix W_r^r. The value of λ affects the length of time for leaky-ESN to remember useful information, while the sparsity S ensures the sparse connection of neurons in the reservoir, which has its value in an exact range, $[0, 1]$.

Thirdly, the value of the leaking rate α decides how much information of the last echo state and the current echo state should be taken into consideration, which also has its value in an exact range, $[0, 1]$.

4 AESN for Electricity Load Forecasting

From the perspective of the parameter setting, the leaking rate of ESN model cannot be changed once set, which limits the flexibility of the model. In order to improve the adaptability of the leaky-ESN, inspired by CW-RNN [32], we divide the reservoir into equal-sized modules and define the working period for each module. By judging whether the current time step can be divisible by the working period of a module, the information of the module can be updated or maintained, so as to automatically adjust the leaking rate. We abbreviate the above model as AESN-I. On this basis, we hope to further automatically adjust the sparse connection of the reservoir. Different from the traditional ESN, we initialize the reservoir in a fully-connected state, and then use the adaptive leaking rate obtained by AESN-I to control the dropout of neurons, thus achieving a similar effect with the sparse connection adopted by the traditional ESN. We call this model AESN-II for short. Details of AESN-I and AESN-II are presented as followed.

4.1 The Modular Control Strategy

In this subsection, the modular control strategy is defined and described for the automatic adjustment of later proposed AESN models. Assuming that the reservoir with N neurons is divided into k modules of equal size, the number of neurons in each module is $m = \frac{N}{k}$. Firstly, the working period for each module is defined as the Eq. (5):

$$T_i = 2^{i-1}, i = 1, 2, 3, \ldots, k \tag{5}$$

According to the working period of each module, the updated sub-vector of the module at time step t are obtained by the following Eq. (6):

$$u_i[t] = \begin{cases} (1, 1, 1, \ldots, 1)^T, & if t mod T_i = 0 \\ (0, 0, 0, \ldots, 0)^T, & if t mod T_i \neq 0 \end{cases}, i = 1, 2, 3, \ldots, k \tag{6}$$

Finally, by concatenating the sub-vectors of each module together, we obtain the updated vector of the entire reservoir at time step t. To sum up briefly, neurons in the reservoir are updated in modules, and the update frequency of modules is closely related to the working period of modules. This means that the number of neurons involved in the update process can change flexibly at different time steps, thus achieving adaptive adjustment of the leaking rate.

4.2 AESN-I with Initial Sparsely-Connected Reservoir

In the traditional form of leaky-ESN, the leaking rate is a fixed constant running over the whole dataset each time. In AESN-I, the modular control strategy is utilized, where the form of constant is replaced by the form of vector as a leaking rate. During the training process, the Eq. (4) is modified as the Eq. (7)–(8):

$$u'[t] = 1 - u[t] \tag{7}$$

$$h[t] = u'[t] \odot h[t-1] + u[t] \odot h'[t] \tag{8}$$

In the Eq. (8), entries with the same positions in $u'[t]$ and $u[t]$ are inversed, with the value of either 0 or 1. Figure 2 illustrates the entries in $u'[t]$ and $u[t]$ at time step $t = 10$, where $h[t]$ is the concatenation of the first two sub-vectors of $h'[t]$ and the last two sub-vectors of $h[t-1]$.

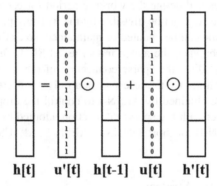

$$\begin{array}{ccccc} \mathbf{h[t]} & \mathbf{u'[t]} & \mathbf{h[t\text{-}1]} & \mathbf{u[t]} & \mathbf{h'[t]} \end{array}$$

Fig. 2. Process of computing the echo state at time step $t = 10$ where entries of $u'[t]$ and $u[t]$ are indicated.

4.3 AESN-II with Initial Fully-Connected Reservoir

Based on the AESN-I architecture, we further designed AESN-II with the capability to automatically adjust the sparse connections within the reservoir, where the reservoir is initially fully-connected. On the basis of the modification of AESN-I, the Eq. (3) is modified as the following Eq. (9) to obtain $h'[t]$:

$$h'[t] = f\left(W_i^r \times x[t] + W_r^r \times (u[t] \odot h[t-1]) + W_o^r \times y[t-1] + \xi\right) \tag{9}$$

In this model, $u[t]$, as an adaptive leaking rate in the AESN-I, is utilized to control the dropout of neurons. Therefore, the initial fully-connected reservoir performs similarly as a sparse reservoir adopted by the traditional form of ESN or leaky-ESN.

5   Experiments and Results

5.1   Dataset Description

In this section, our proposed approaches are applied to two synthetic datasets and two real-world electricity load datasets.

Mackey-Glass (MG) Time-Series: The MG time-delay differential equation can be described as followed:

$$\frac{dx}{dt} = \alpha \frac{x_{\tau_{MG}}}{1 + x_{\tau_{MG}}^n} - \beta x \tag{10}$$

where α, β, τ_{MG}, n are real numbers and $x_{\tau_{MG}}$ represents the value of x at time step $t - \tau_{MG}$. In this paper, it is generated as $\alpha = 0.2$, $\beta = 0.1$, $\tau_{MG} = 17$, $n = 10$.

Multiple Superimposed Oscillator (MSO): MSO is the superimposition of different sine waves with incommensurable frequencies, which requires decoupled internal states to be represented simultaneously. Since neurons in the reservoir are coupled, it is challenging for ESN to deal with MSO [33]. Many researches apply the ESN model on MSO [34–36], with the definition as followed:

$$y(t) = \sin(0.2t) + \sin(0.311t) + \sin(0.42t) + \sin(0.51t) + \sin(0.63t) + \sin(0.74t) \tag{11}$$

North-American (NA) Electricity Utility: This real-world dataset consists of time series of hourly electricity consumption and temperature data, in a period from January 1st, 1991 to October 12th, 1992. It is provided by [1].

Australian Energy Market Operator (AEMO) Data: This real-world dataset consists of time series of electricity demand and price every 30 min, in the year of 2016. It is provided by [37].

5.2   Experimental Settings

To avoid the overfitting and help to guide the parameter optimization, training set, validation set, and test set were involved in our experiments. For the first two synthetic datasets, we divided each into 3 sub-datasets, where 70% for training, 15% for validation and the rest 15% for testing. Daily electricity load predictions were applied on NA and AEMO real-world electricity datasets, where the last two months were used as the validation set and the test set, respectively. When applying NA dataset, temperature was used as an exogenous variable, while electricity price was used as an exogenous variable when applying AEMO dataset.

A Python implementation of the traditional form of ESN, provided by [4], was modified to construct the traditional ESN, leaky-ESN, AESN-I and AESN-II. During the computation, ridge regression was applied to train the readout. Normalized root mean squared error (NRMSE) was used as the evaluation criterion for results comparison. The equation is presented as followed:

$$\hat{y} = \frac{1}{n}\sum\nolimits_{i=1}^{n} y_i' \tag{12}$$

$$NRMSE(y, y') = \sqrt{\frac{\frac{1}{n}\sum_{i=1}^{n}(y_i - y_i')^2}{\frac{1}{n}\sum_{i=1}^{n}(y_i - \hat{y})^2}} \tag{13}$$

where y denotes the predicted value and y' denotes the ground truth.

With the goal of fair comparison among traditional ESN, leaky-ESN, AESN-I and AESN-II, the following configurations in Table 1 were kept to be in the same range or value for parameter selection and adjustment.

Table 1. Configuration table for the fair experimental comparison

Parameter	Range/Value
Number of neurons in the reservoir N	100–500
Spectral radius of the reservoir R	0.5–1.4
Number of initially discarded outputs D	100
Input scaling IS	0.1–0.9
Output scaling OS	0.1–0.9
Feedback scaling FS	0.0–0.6
Regularization parameter (Ridge Regression) λ	0.001–1.0
Noise ξ	0.0–0.1

In addition, the leaking rate α was optimized in the range of $[0, 1]$ during the construction of leaky-ESN. When constructing AESN-I and AESN-II, the number of modules M was optimized in the range of $[2, 8]$. Except for AESN-II, which contains a fully-connected reservoir, the other 3 models require the optimization of the sparsity of the reservoir ρ within the range of $[0.25, 0.5]$.

After the process of parameter optimization, each test set was run on the constructed model for 32 times to get the mean and standard deviation of NRMSEs.

5.3   Results Discussion

Synthetic Dataset
In the reference [4], Principal Component Analysis (PCA) and kernel Principal Component Analysis (kPCA) are introduced for dimensionality reduction during the training process of ESN. Since MG and MSO time series utilized in the experiments are the same both in this paper and in the reference [4], these 2 improved versions of ESN are

also involved in the comparison of the results. Besides, only ridge regression for readout training is considered for fair comparison.

The configuration table of experimental results is depicted in the Table 2. In the Table 3, experimental results applying on these two synthetic datasets are compared among ESN, leaky-ESN, ESN + PCA, ESN + kPCA, AESN-I and AESN-II. It can be concluded that the two versions of AESN perform not only better than the traditional ESN and leaky-ESN, but also have higher prediction accuracy compared to some recent improved versions of ESN, ESN + PCA and ESN + kPCA. MG is a kind of simple signal compared to MSO, consequently, it is intuitive that all models achieve low prediction error and AESN-I is outperformed among them. Although MSO is challenging for traditional ESN architecture to deal with, which can be proved from the prediction results, the leaky-ESN helps to lower the prediction error. Both AESN-I and AESN-II, containing leaky-integrator neurons in the reservoir, present better performance and AESN-II has the lowest prediction error.

Table 2. Configuration table of experimental results: α – leaking rate, M – number of modules, N – number of neurons in the reservoir, R – spectral radius of the reservoir, ρ – sparsity of the reservoir, ξ – noise when updating ESN states, IS – input scaling, OS – output scaling, FS – feedback scaling, λ – regularization parameter of ridge regression.

		α	M	N	R	ρ	ξ	IS	OS	FS	λ
MG	ESN	–	–	378	1.22	0.25	0.0	0.550	0.212	0.250	0.625
	Leaky-ESN	0.345	–	492	1.40	0.419	0.0	0.869	0.341	0.538	0.635
	AESN-I	–	2	369	1.19	0.272	0.0	0.644	0.775	0.061	0.001
	AESN-II	–	2	366	1.33	1	0.0	0.442	0.616	0.080	0.001
MSO	ESN	–	–	298	1.15	0.25	0.01	0.345	0.147	0.045	0.438
	Leaky-ESN	0.128	–	499	1.03	0.331	0.01	0.1	0.180	0.119	0.471
	AESN-I	–	4	481	0.96	0.342	0.0	0.1	0.156	0.097	0.496
	AESN-II	–	4	417	1.15	1	0.0	0.1	0.287	0.123	0.237

Real-World Electricity Dataset

In this section, NA and AEMO electricity datasets were applied for 24-h electricity load forecasting. The configuration table of experimental results and the comparison of the results among ESN, leaky-ESN, AESN-I and AESN-II are depicted in the Table 4 and the Table 5, respectively. Since electricity load data are highly sensitive to some exclusive variations, which are more complex than synthetic datasets, the prediction accuracy would be lower compared to experiments applying on synthetic datasets. However, it still can be concluded that the two versions of AESN are both viable.

Considering both NA and AEMO electricity datasets, the prediction accuracy of ESN is slightly lower or higher than the prediction accuracy of leaky-ESN. Hence, AESN-I and AESN-II, which involve leaky-integrator neurons in the reservoir by automatically adjusting the leaking rate, would only slightly improve the prediction accuracy.

Table 3. Results comparison among ESN, leaky-ESN, ESN + PCA, ESN + kPCA, AESN-I and AESN-II.

		NRMSE
MG	ESN	$3.064\text{E}^{-2} +- 1.648\text{E}^{-4}$
	Leaky-ESN	$4.185\text{E}^{-3} +- 1.460\text{E}^{-2}$
	ESN + PCA	$6.483\text{E}^{-3} +- 9.126\text{E}^{-3}$
	ESN + kPCA	$4.283\text{E}^{-3} +- 1.893\text{E}^{-4}$
	AESN-I	**$8.456\text{E}^{-4} +- 1.945\text{E}^{-3}$**
	AESN-II	$1.457\text{E}^{-3} +- 1.285\text{E}^{-3}$
MSO	ESN	$9.427\text{E}^{-1} +- 1.675\text{E}^{-2}$
	Leaky-ESN	$1.546\text{E}^{-1} +- 3.165\text{E}^{-2}$
	ESN + PCA	$7.642\text{E}^{-1} +- 1.189\text{E}^{-1}$
	ESN + kPCA	$5.959\text{E}^{-1} +- 3.233\text{E}^{-2}$
	AESN-I	$7.590\text{E}^{-2} +- 8.142\text{E}^{-3}$
	AESN-II	**$5.427\text{E}^{-2} +- 1.592\text{E}^{-2}$**

Table 4. Configuration table of experimental results: α – leaking rate, M – number of modules, N – number of neurons in the reservoir, R – spectral radius of the reservoir, ρ – sparsity of the reservoir, ξ – noise when updating ESN states, IS – input scaling, OS – output scaling, FS – feedback scaling, λ – regularization parameter of ridge regression.

		α	M	N	R	ρ	ξ	IS	OS	FS	λ
NA	ESN	–	–	258	0.77	0.436	0.06	0.183	0.730	0.258	0.672
	Leaky-ESN	0.936	–	232	0.68	0.480	0.08	0.192	0.708	0.016	1.0
	AESN-I	–	8	131	0.58	0.379	0.02	0.181	0.390	0.0	0.549
	AESN-II	–	6	355	0.86	1	0.0	0.132	0.608	0.0	1.0
AEMO	ESN	–	–	318	0.87	0.313	0.02	0.353	0.885	0.328	0.261
	Leaky-ESN	0.402	–	332	0.83	0.323	0.02	0.311	0.825	0.234	0.353
	AESN-I	–	2	393	0.75	0.436	0.01	0.147	0.828	0.388	0.460
	AESN-II	–	6	285	1.30	1	0.03	0.537	0.172	0.0	0.761

In these two datasets, it is intuitive that AESN-I, with the initial sparsely-connected reservoir, is not so satisfied compared to AESN-II, with the initial fully-connected reservoir and lowest prediction error. In AEMO electricity dataset, prediction accuracies of AESN-I and AESN-II are almost the same.

Table 5. Results comparison among the traditional ESN, leaky-ESN, AESN-I and AESN-II.

		NRMSE
NA	ESN	$4.136E^{-1} +- 1.447E^{-2}$
	Leaky-ESN	$3.944E^{-1} +- 9.871E^{-3}$
	AESN-I	$3.892E^{-1} +- 1.214E^{-2}$
	AESN-II	$\mathbf{3.574E^{-1} +- 9.956E^{-3}}$
AEMO	ESN	$6.006E^{-1} +- 2.356E^{-2}$
	Leaky-ESN	$6.120E^{-1} +- 3.838E^{-2}$
	AESN-I	$5.898E^{-1} +- 2.092E^{-2}$
	AESN-II	$\mathbf{5.854E^{-1} +- 2.426E^{-2}}$

6   Conclusions and Future Work

In this paper, we focus on the electricity load forecasting, in the context of pervasive and cloud computing. Applying on the two synthetic datasets, MG and MSO, and two real-world datasets, NA and AEMO electricity load datasets, we compare our two proposed models, AESN-I and AESN-II, with the traditional ESN, leaky-ESN and two improved versions of ESN, ESN + PCA and ESN + kPCA. It is proved that the modular control strategy is viable on the ESN architecture. The idea of automatically adjusting sparsity and leaking rate reduces prediction errors, on the basis of ensuring the sparse connections within the reservoir.

For future works, we will extend experimental results of our proposed models for further analysis, such as applying on different real-world datasets, and comparing them with statistical mathematical methods or machine learning algorithms. Moreover, we are also interested in investigating other control strategies to reduce the cost during the process of parameter optimization, with the goal of effectively and efficiently computation.

Acknowledgments. This work is supported by the National Natural Science Foundation of China under Grant No. 61772136, 61672159, the Technology Innovation Platform Project of Fujian Province under Grant No. 2014H2005, the Research Project for Young and Middle-aged Teachers of Fujian Province under Grant No. JT180045, the Fujian Collaborative Innovation Center for Big Data Application in Governments, the Fujian Engineering Research Center of Big Data Analysis and Processing.

References

1. Amjady, N., Keynia, F.: Short-term load forecasting of power systems by combination of wavelet transform and neuro-evolutionary algorithm. Energy **34**(1), 46–57 (2009)
2. Ertugrul, Ö.F.: Forecasting electricity load by a novel recurrent extreme learning machines approach. Int. J. Electrical Power Energy Syst. **78**, 429–435 (2016)

3. Jaeger, H.: The "echo state" approach to analysing and training recurrent neural networks-with an erratum note. German National Res. Center for Inf. Technol. GMD Tech. Report **148**(34), 13 (2001)
4. Løkse, S., Bianchi, F.M., Jenssen, R.: Training echo state networks with regularization through dimensionality reduction. Cogn. Comput. **9**(3), 364–378 (2017)
5. Alfares, H.K., Nazeeruddin, M.: Electric load forecasting: literature survey and classification of methods. Int. J. Syst. Sci. **33**(1), 23–34 (2002)
6. Islam, B.U.: Comparison of conventional and modern load forecasting techniques based on artificial intelligence and expert systems. Int. J. Comput. Sci. Issues (IJCSI) **8**(5), 504 (2011)
7. BVBCET, H., SSIT, T.: Short Term Load Forecasting Using Time Series Analysis: A Case Study for Karnataka, India (2012)
8. Anand, N.C, Scoglio, C., Natarajan, B.: GARCH—Non-linear time series model for traffic modeling and prediction. In: Network Operations and Management Symposium. pp. 694–697, IEEE (2008)
9. Bahrami, S., Hooshmand, R.A., Parastegari, M.: Short term electric load forecasting by wavelet transform and grey model improved by PSO (particle swarm optimization) algorithm. Energy **72**, 434–442 (2014)
10. Dudek, G.: Artificial immune system with local feature selection for short-term load forecasting. IEEE Trans. Evol. Comput. **21**(1), 116–130 (2016)
11. Mateo, F., Carrasco, J.J., Millán-Giraldo, M., et al.: Machine learning techniques for short-term electric power demand prediction. In: European Symposium on Artificial Neural Networks (2013)
12. Hu, Z., Bao, Y., Xiong, T.: Comprehensive learning particle swarm optimization based memetic algorithm for model selection in short-term load forecasting using support vector regression. Appl. Soft Comput. **25**, 15–25 (2014)
13. Hu, Z., Bao, Y., Xiong, T., et al.: Hybrid filter–wrapper feature selection for short-term load forecasting. Eng. Appl. Artif. Intell. **40**, 17–27 (2015)
14. Cheepati, K.R., Prasad, T.N.: Performance comparison of short term load forecasting techniques. Int. J. Grid Distrib. Comput **9**(4), 287–302 (2016)
15. Vermaak, J., Botha, E.C.: Recurrent neural networks for short-term load forecasting. IEEE Trans. Power Syst. **13**(1), 126–132 (1998)
16. Khan, G.M., Zafari, F., Mahmud, S.A.: Very short term load forecasting using Cartesian genetic programming evolved recurrent neural networks (CGPRNN). In: 12th International Conference on Machine Learning and Applications. vol. 2, pp. 152–155, IEEE (2013)
17. Zhang, B., Wu, J.L., Chang, P.C.: A multiple time series-based recurrent neural network for short-term load forecasting. Soft. Comput. **22**(12), 4099–4112 (2017). https://doi.org/10.1007/s00500-017-2624-5
18. Hochreiter, S., Schmidhuber, J.: Long short-term memory. Neural Comput. **9**(8), 1735–1780 (1997)
19. Kobialka, H.U., Kayani, U.: Echo state networks with sparse output connections. In: Diamantaras, K., Duch, W., Iliadis, L.S. (eds.) ICANN 2010. LNCS, vol. 6352, pp. 356–361. Springer, Heidelberg (2010). https://doi.org/10.1007/978-3-642-15819-3_47
20. Deihimi, A., Showkati, H.: Application of echo state networks in short-term electric load forecasting. Energy **39**(1), 327–340 (2012)
21. Han, M., Xu, M.: Laplacian echo state network for multivariate time series prediction. IEEE Trans. Neural Netw. Learn. Syst. **29**(1), 238–244 (2017)
22. Dedinec, A., Filiposka, S., Dedinec, A., et al.: Deep belief network based electricity load forecasting: An analysis of Macedonian case. Energy **115**, 1688–1700 (2016)
23. Butcher, J.B.: Reservoir Computing with high non-linear separation and long-term memory for time-series data analysis. Keele University (2012)

24. Lukoševičius, M.: A practical guide to applying echo state networks. In: Montavon, G., Orr, G.B., Müller, K.R. (eds.) Neural Networks: Tricks of the Trade. LNCS, vol. 7700, pp. 659–686. Springer, Heidelberg (2012). https://doi.org/10.1007/978-3-642-35289-8_36

25. Yildiz, I.B., Jaeger, H., Kiebel, S.J.: Re-visiting the echo state property. Neural Netw. **35**, 1–9 (2012)

26. Jiang, F., Berry, H., Schoenauer, M.: Supervised and evolutionary learning of echo state networks. In: Rudolph, G., Jansen, T., Beume, N., Lucas, S., Poloni, C. (eds.) PPSN 2008. LNCS, vol. 5199, pp. 215–224. Springer, Heidelberg (2008). https://doi.org/10.1007/978-3-540-87700-4_22

27. Jaeger, H.: Short term memory in echo state networks. GMD-Report 152. GMD-German National Research Institute for Computer Science (2002)

28. Shi, Z., Han, M.: Ridge regression learning in ESN for chaotic time series prediction. Control Decis. **22**(3), 258 (2007)

29. Lukoševicius, M, Popovici D, Jaeger H, et al.: Time warping invariant echo state networks. International University Bremen, Technical Report (2006)

30. Lun, S.X., Yao, X.S., Qi, H.Y., et al.: A novel model of leaky integrator echo state network for time-series prediction. Neurocomputing **159**, 58–66 (2015)

31. Lun, S., Yao, X., Hu, H.: A new echo state network with variable memory length. Inf. Sci. **370**, 103–119 (2016)

32. Koutnik, J., Greff, K., Gomez, F., et al.: A Clockwork RNN. Computer ence. pp. 1863–1871 (2014)

33. Holzmann, G., Hauser, H.: Echo state networks with filter neurons and a delay&sum readout. Neural Netw. **23**(2), 244–256 (2010)

34. Jaeger, H., Lukoševičius, M., Popovici, D., et al.: Optimization and applications of echo state networks with leaky-integrator neurons. Neural networks **20**(3), 335–352 (2007)

35. Jaeger, H., Haas, H.: Harnessing nonlinearity: predicting chaotic systems and saving energy in wireless communication. Science **304**(5667), 78–80 (2004)

36. Ceperic, V., Baric, A.: Reducing complexity of echo state networks with sparse linear regression algorithms. In: 2014 UKSim-AMSS 16th International Conference on Computer Modelling and Simulation. pp. 26–31, IEEE (2014)

37. Australian Energy Market Operator. https://aemo.com.au/energy-systems/electricity/national-electricity-market-nem/data-nem/data-dashboard-nemAccessed 31 March 2020

Human Computer Interaction

MateBot: The Design of a Human-Like, Context-Sensitive Virtual Bot for Harmonious Human-Computer Interaction

Ziqi Wang[1], Bin Guo[1(✉)], Hao Wang[1], Helei Cui[1], Yang He[2], and Zhiwen Yu[1]

[1] Northwestern Polytechnical University, Xi'an 710129, China
guob@nwpu.edu.cn
[2] CEIEC Tower A, Guohai Plaza, No 17, Fuxing Road, Haidian District,
Beijing 100036, China

Abstract. The virtual bot is one of the hot topics in artificial intelligence, where most of the current studies focus on chatbots. Nevertheless, the context-sensitive virtual bot, especially with rich human-like interactions (e.g., appearance change, context-aware narration/recommendation) regarding the ambient changes (e.g., location, focused scene) through various built-in sensors, would have broader application. Towards this direction, we propose MateBot, a human-like, context-sensitive virtual bot, which supports harmonious human-computer interaction on smartphones. The design of MateBot consists of three parts. First, a context sensing network is used to recognize the input background information and face information, and modify the appearance of the virtual bot through the conversion of the encoding network. Second, a human-like bot appearance generation network can generate a virtual bot image with a human-like appearance through the GAN network and modify the appearance of the virtual bot with context-sensitive information. Third, a personalized conversation network is devised to communicate with human users. Furthermore, we apply MateBot to the intelligent travel scenario to justify its practicality, and the experiment results show that the bot can better increase the user's sense of substitution and improve the communication efficiency between human users and virtual bots.

Keywords: Virtual bot · Context-sensitive · MateBot

1 Introduction

In the past decade, virtual bots have become one of the important directions in the evolution of artificial intelligence (AI). At present, the specific research on virtual bots [21, 27] is mainly focused on chatbots. The early dialogue systems, such as Eliza Weizenbaum [22], Parry Colby [2], and Alice Wallace [21], are all dedicated to learning human dialogue through text. Despite the huge

© Springer Nature Switzerland AG 2020
Z. Yu et al. (Eds.): GPC 2020, LNCS 12398, pp. 273–287, 2020.
https://doi.org/10.1007/978-3-030-64243-3_21

breakthroughs, these chatbots still have some scope limitations. At present, fully open domain chatbots are still a target that needs to be worked hard to develop. Meanwhile, along with the progress in deep learning technology, the social chatbot have multi-domain goals, such as free dialogue, task dialogue, e.g. However, the current research on virtual bots is mainly focused on communicating with human users, that is, continuously promoting the authenticity and fluency of text generation to improve the shaping level of virtual bots. We believe that the research on virtual bots should simultaneously breakthrough in different aspects, including a human-like virtual image and the sensitivity to the situation. There is no doubt that a virtual bot with a human-like appearance and intelligence is more comfortable for common users. So we want to create a virtual bot that not just looks exactly like a human in all aspects, but is context-sensitive, that is, the virtual bot can make corresponding changes in appearance and expression according to different situations and user changes.

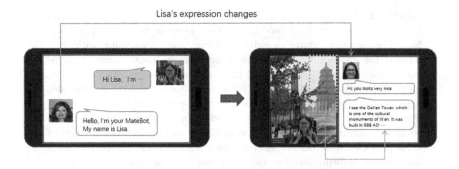

Fig. 1. The usage of MateBot: a snapshot

In this paper, as is shown in Fig. 1, the virtual bot we designed is a context-sensitive bot. Context-sensitive refers to the fact that the virtual bot should have the ability to change its image or behavior according to changes in the external environment. The context-sensitive in this paper consists of two parts: face-sensitive and background-sensitive. Specifically, face-sensitive is mainly for extracting physiological features to improve the appearance features of the virtual bot. When the virtual bot has similar appearance features to the user, it can provide users with a better sense of substitution and companionship. While background-sensitive is worthwhile, virtual bots can change their behavior patterns by sensing the external background, which is reflected in appearance, specifically changing the expression. For example, when the virtual bot senses that the environment is a well-known attraction, it will show a happy expression. A context-sensitive, high-fidelity virtual bot designed in this paper can recognize different situations through cameras, so that a virtual bot with high-fidelity appearance can change images and behaviors. In order to prove the practicality of this design, we tested and applied Mate Bot through the scene of Xi'an tourism(Xi'an, a worldwide famous tourist destination). When you use MateBot in tourism, it can provide different introductions and explanations by identifying different attractions. For example, in Xi'an, when terracotta warriors and horses are recognized, virtual robots will show a serious expression and introduce you to the context of "the first batch of Chinese World Heritage terracotta warriors and horses, located in ..." can also be used in life application. For example, when you go to the beach, the character image of the virtual robot will automatically change to add elements such as sunglasses.

The contributions of our work are listed as follows:

(1) We design a context-sensitive and human-like network to generate a virtual bot called MateBot.
(2) MateBot can adjust its appearance and communication methods according to different context.
(3) In order to verify the practicability of MateBot, we tested our design on a travel scene and achieved good experimental results

2   Related Work

Virtual Chatbot. The current research on virtual bots is mainly focused on the research of chatbots. The earliest chatbot Eliza Weizenbaum [22], proposed in 1966, was used to imitate a psychologist in clinical treatment, which also made it possible for people and computers to have a natural language conversation to a certain extent. Eliza decomposes the input through keyword matching rules, and then generates a response based on the reorganization rules corresponding to the decomposition rules. Nowadays, along with the rapid development of machine learning and deep learning technology, chatbots have undergone greater development. The typical representative products are Microsoft XiaoIce [27], Amazon Echo, Apple Siri, etc.

In the design of traditional chatbots, the designer only pays attention to the chat scene itself. Therefore, chatbots can only imitate human dialogue behaviors and do not respond to the environment. Therefore, an end-to-end architecture is often used, so it will lead to a very simple system structure, such as RNN-based systems proposed by Li [10], Vinyals [18], Shang et al. [20]. Subsequently, neural network-based models enables chat robots to be trained on large-scale corpora, greatly expanding the topics of chat.

Face Generation and Appearance Change. Generative Adversarial Networks (GAN) [8] shows powerful effects in various tasks that require computer image processing, such as image generation [1,5,6,16,26], super-resolution imaging [9], and facial image synthesis [7,11,19]. A typical GAN has two networks, one is a generator and the other is a discriminator. It is iInspired by the two-player zero-sum game, t. The two networks compete to achieve the best generation effect.

An optimized version of the GAN network is a conditional GAN, which is an adversarial generation model under certain conditions. The classified information is provided by image generators and discriminators, and samples with certain constraints are generated. At present, there are many applications, such as generating images from text descriptions.

Dialog Generation. In recent years, researchers have done a lot of research on the personalized dialogue system. Li et al. [10] first incorporate implicit persona in dialogue generation using user embeddings, which encodes each user into a dense vector. Qian et al. [15] define several profile key-value pairs, including name, gender, age, location, etc., and explicitly express a profile value in the response. Faced with the lack of personalized dialogue data sets, Zhang et al. [24] contribute a persona-chat dataset, and further propose two generative models, persona-Seq2Seq and Generative Profile Memory Network, to incorporate persona information into responses. Yavuz et al. [10] explored the use of copy mechanism in persona-based dialogue models. The above works are all based on the RNN model, while the Transformer model proposed by Google has greatly improved the structure of the sequence modeling model and become a new favorite in many NLP tasks. Based on the Transformer model, BERT [23], GPT2 [17] and other pre-training language models have achieved state-of-the-art results in a variety of NLP tasks. Zhang et al. [25] present a large, tunable neural conversational response generation model based on GPT2, which can generate more relevant, contentful and context-consistent responses than strong baseline systems. However, the existing models still have problems such as difficult to control the subject of generating text, and difficult to contain specific emotions. In this paper, we use a transformer codec-based generator to perform text generation through joint training of two data sets.

3   The MateBot Architecture

As shown in Fig. 2, our model architecture is divided into three parts: stage1: context-sensitive network (Sect. 4.1), stage2: appearance translation network (Sect. 4.2), and stage3: dialogue network (Sect. 4.3). Among them, the context-sensitive network is used for identifying context information, segmenting images and encoding different parts respectively. The appearance translation network performs different transformations on the appearance of MateBot according to the context-sensitive encoding information. Dialogue Network is responsible for the human-machine communication part of MateBot.

So, specifically, our task is to use the picture information entered by the camera, splitting the face information and context information, use the context information to generate a high-quality external appearance of a virtual bot with corresponding characteristics, and context information makes the appearance of the virtual bot more consistent with the external environment. Each generated result is expected to be fully integrated with the image information read from the camera, reflecting similar appearance and expressions. As a result, these generated images can be used as the basis for the behavior of the virtual bot and human communication. Furthermore, the comparison of context and face information in the image is difficult to extract because it contains many

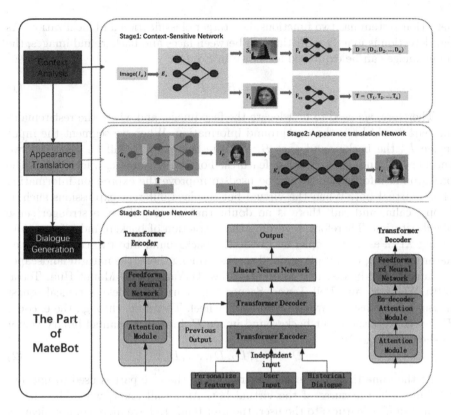

Fig. 2. MateBot generation networks (MGNet)

distracting factors, and high-quality virtual bot appearance generation requires many accessories to change. To this end, we propose a three-stage framework named MateBot.

4   MateBot: Detailed Design

4.1   Context-Sensitive Network

Our context-sensitive network contains a lightweight network variant based on Dense net [3]. We use generator E_s to split input image information into background and face parts, and two encoders, represent the information lost from the background part and the face part using vectors. In detail, the purpose of this network architecture is to decompose the input image I_a into a background part B_i and a face part P_i through E_s, and generate two different latent codes through F_s and F_{cs} to express features in vector space.

Given an input image I_a, we perform the segmentation of the background part B_i and the face part P_i by an object detection system. The entire object detection system has two functions, i.e., target classification and localization. As our detection is mainly to distinguish between faces and background images, the input image can be expressed as shown in Eq. (1):

$$I_a = B_i + P_i \tag{1}$$

Therefore, we need to first locate the face image, and where the rest remaining part would be is the background information. When we segment the input image I_a, the background part B_i and the face part P_i will be sent into two encoders F_s and F_{cs} to obtain features. For the features extracted from the background information, it can be used to improve the expression information of the virtual bot. When the virtual bot displays different expressions such as happy, calm, and sad, there is no doubt that users will feel a stronger sense of substitution. Therefore, regarding the extraction of background information, taking Xi'an as an example, we divide the background into two categories, i.e., natural landscapes and playground scenes. Among them, the natural landscapes are further subdivided into four categories: DaYan Tower, Mount Hua, Terracotta Warriors, and Bell Tower. Scenes take four categories as typical: ghost house, roller coaster, carousel, and ferric wheel. Therefore, through the encoder F_s, we convert the input background image B_i into an 8-channel binary vector as shown in Eq. (2):

$$D = (D_1, D_2, D_3, \ldots, D_n) \tag{2}$$

At the same time, the feature extraction of the face part is used to improve the human-like features of the virtual bot. As we all know, when the virtual bot has similar features to the user, the user tends to have more communication with the bot. Therefore, it is a feasible way to extract the basic physiological characteristics of the user based on the face image information and thus improve the appearance of the virtual bot. Therefore, it is a feasible way to extract the basic physiological characteristics of the user based on the face image information and thus improve the appearance of the virtual bot. Therefore, we divide the basic physiological characteristics of the face into 8 categories: gender, hair/or not, black hair/blonde hair, wearing glasses/or not, straight hair/curly hair, young/old, bearded/or not, obese/or not. We believe that these eight types of features can clearly show a person's basic appearance features. Therefore, through the generator F_{cs}, the face image information can be expressed using an eight-channel binary vector shown in Eq. (3):

$$T = (T_1, T_2, T_3, \ldots, T_n) \tag{3}$$

4.2   Appearance Translation Network

Appearance translation network contains a decoder-based generator G_s and an encoder-decoder based generator K_s. The purpose of the first generator G_s is to generate a face image I_p with certain physiological characteristics through the input of the latent code T_i for the appearance of the virtual bot. The role of the second generator K_s is to combine the image I_p and the latent code D_i to generate a face image with a specific expression.

At present, many face image generators do not consider fixed features and style requirements. For example, to specifically generate a woman with blond hair and red lips features, for the needs of the virtual bot, we need to use the generation of features that adjust the face image model. Therefore, in generator G_s, we use AdaIN [4] after each convolutional layer to add and adjust features in Eq. (4):

$$I_p = AdaIN(X_i, t) \tag{4}$$

G_s belongs to the output information of each convolutional layer, and t is the feature information transformed from the latent code T_i. Through the method of AdaIN, the feature t possessed by T_i can be migrated to the newly generated face image I_p layer by layer, and the final generation result can be expressed as shown in Eq. (5):

$$I_p = t_{s,i} \frac{X_i - \mu(X_i)}{\sigma(X_i)} + t_{b,i} \tag{5}$$

Because P_i is the extracted portrait features, and I_p is the appearance of the generated virtual bot with the same physiological characteristics as P, therefore, I_p and P_i should have a certain similarity. For this principle, in Eq. (6), we use KL divergence to optimize our network:

$$D_{kl}(p||q) = \int p(z) \frac{p(z)}{q(z)} dz \tag{6}$$

According to the definition of KL divergence, because we pursue the similarity in physiological characteristics between P_i and I_p, in Eq. (7), we will reduce KL divergence as the optimization goal:

$$L_{kl} = \min[D_{kl}(P_i||I_p)] \tag{7}$$

Even though G_s can generate a virtual bot appearance I_p with certain physiological characteristics, the generated appearance still lacks the necessary expressions, especially different expressions according to different situations. Therefore, we designed a generator K_s, which can generate face images I_s with different expressions based on the existing image I_p and latent code D_i. The essence of generator K_s is an image-to-image translator. This article focuses on the domain of expression translation: $K_s(I_p, d) \rightarrow I_s$, Which $d \in D_i$, representing target emoticons. In order to improve the quality of the image I_s and make it more natural and realistic, we have added an adversarial loss to the generator K_s as shown in Eq. (8):

$$L_{al} = E_{I_p}[\log(I(x))] + E_{I_p}[\log(1 - I(K_s(I_p, d)))] \tag{8}$$

L_{al} represents the adversarial loss of the generator K_s, where K_s generates an image $K_s(I_p, d)$ conditioned on both the face image I_p and the target expression label d, and the $I(x)$ is a probability distribution over the input image I_p.

By minimizing the adversarial loss, we can ensure the fidelity of the image, but in the process of generator K_s reconstructing the image, it is difficult to ensure that the information of the input image I_p is completely restored to the output image I_s. We added reconstruction loss to optimize the generator as shown in Eq. (9):

$$L_{rl} = E_{l_p,d,d'}[|||I_p - K_s(K_s(I_p,d),d')||_1]$$ (9)

We choose the L1 norm as our reconstruction loss. Therefore, total losses consist of adversarial losses and reconstruction losses in Eq. (10):

$$L_F = L_{al} + \mu L_{rl}$$ (10)

μ where corresponding parameter of loss $L_r l$. In this paper, we use $\mu = 10$ in all experiments.

4.3 Dialogue Network

The dialogue network is based on the model that consist of a 12-layer Transformer encoder and decoder. The input of the entire model is divided into three parts, which are the current user input dialogue content, the dialogue content that has occurred in the dialogue, and the personalized feature information given to the bot. The three parts of the input content are first converted into vectors of the same dimension through word embedding. In order to consider the position information of different words in the sequence during the encoding process, the following formula is used to perform position encoding as shown in Eq. (11) and Eq. (12):

$$PE(pos, 2i) = \sin(\frac{pos}{10000^{\frac{2i}{d_{model}}}})$$ (11)

$$PE(pos, 2i + 1) = \cos(\frac{pos}{2i})$$ (12)

Where *pos* presents the position of the word and i represents the dimension of the word. The position encoding vector is then added to the word embedding vector of the corresponding word as an input vector representation. In the encoding phase, the input vector will first get the vector representation of the context of each word through the self-attention module, the formula is as follows. The Q, K, and V vectors are obtained by multiplying the word embedding vector of each word of the input sequence by three weight matrices as shown in Eq. (13):

$$Attention(Q, K, V) = softmat(\frac{QK^T}{\sqrt{d_k}})V$$ (13)

Then input the output vector representation through the feed-forward neural network, that is, the fully connected layer, at the encoding stage. In addition to the self-attention module and feedforward neural network module in the decoding phase, there is an additional codec attention module that performs attention calculation with the output vector of the encoding phase to obtain the current user input, historical conversation content, and personalized feature information. The degree of influence of the decoding time jointly determines the content generated at the current decoding time.

5   Evaluation

In this section, we show the evaluation results of our MateBot prototype.The experimental evaluation is mainly divided into two parts. In the first parts, we introduced the experimental dataset we used in detail. In the second part, we show the different results of the three generated networks. We test the accuracy of MateBot's context recognition, the ability to generate virtual appearances and expressions, and the ability to personalize communication.

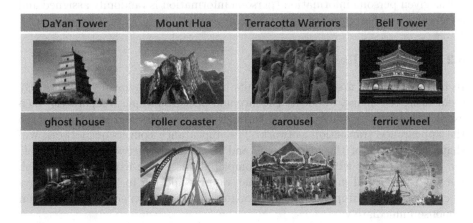

Fig. 3. Xi'an attractions data set (XaD)

5.1   Dataset

Regarding the dataset, the background recognition part uses our collected Xi'an attractions data set (XaD), the face recognition and generation part uses the public data set CelebA [13] and CK+ [14], and the dialogue part uses the Dailydialog [12] and persona-Chat [24] dataset.

XaD. Xi'an attractions data set (XaD) contains 4000 attractions image. As is shown in Fig. 3, these images are divided into 8 categories: DaYan Tower, Mount Hua, Terracotta Warriors, Bell Tower, ghost house, roller coaster, carousel, ferric wheel. We crop the image to 128 × 128, and then randomly choose 200 images as the test set, and remaining as the training set.

CelebA. We use all 202599 face images in the Celeb Faces Attributes (CelebA) dataset. These images are labeled with 40 binary attributes. We first crop the image from 178×218 to 178×178, then resize them to 128×128. We randomly choose 1000 pictures as the test set, and remaining as the training set.

CK+. This database is extended based on the Cohn-Kanadel (CK) dataset. It contains a total of 981 images with an image size of 40×40. It is divided into 7 categories according to different expressions: anger, contempt, disgust, fear, happy, sadness, surprise.

Dailydialog. This dataset contains a daily conversation dataset crawled from a spoken English website. We use all the data in this dataset for network training in the daily conversation part.

Persona-Chat. This dataset comes from real conversations between crowd-sourced people. These crowdsourced people are randomly paired and asked to act as given persona information (persona information is randomly assigned and created by another group of crowdsourced people).

5.2 Evaluation Results

In this section, we first show the results of MateBot Generating Network. By segmenting the image, we locate the face and background parts separately, then extract the corresponding features through two encoders and input them into the appearance translation network. The appearance conversion network will shape the details of the virtual bot, and the dialogue network is responsible for communicating with users. We completed the entire experiment through the Android virtual machine. Note that we also add 0.5 to 2 s random delays to enhance the anthropomorphism, though the dialogue generation module can response immediately.

Context-Sensitive Results. Figure 4 shows the separation of two images from our context-sensitive network. We observe that compared to other algorithms, we can extract more information from the image, which is mainly related to the way we use instance subdivision. By extracting background information and facial information separately, we can simultaneously control different appearance and emotional changes of the virtual robot in the appearance conversion network. In the image segmentation step, we used Mask RNN [21] for training, and the accuracy rate can reach 97.5%. Although our data set is small, it can still achieve good results, and the model also has a certain generality. It can be used in other virtual robot instances and respond accordingly. Here, we only use the pictures of Xi'an Tourism as our example dataset for testing our network and showing the results. But the model in this paper can be applied to other scenarios if the training dataset is changed to other attractions.

Appearance Translation Results. We first train the second part of our model on the CelebA dataset and CK+ dataset. Considering the diversity of physiological features and the stability of the model, we train the model multiple times to ensure the quality of the reconstructed picture. Our method can change people's appearance characteristics, such as hair color, age, and so on, in multiple fields. Compared with other virtual bot modeling methods, our model enables the virtual bot to have a human-like appearance and improve its appearance characteristics according to different users.

Fig. 4. Split input image into background image and face image

Table 1. The attributes of appearance characteristics

Characteristics	Attributes	Characteristics	Attributes
Gender	Male, Female	Age	Young, Old
Hair	Bald	Hair color	Black, Blond
Hair curl	Curly, Straight	Glasses	Eyeglasses
Makeup	Pale skin, Lipstick	Obese	Chubby, Double Chin

Furthermore, compared with other methods, as shown in Table 1, we consider different combinations of attributes to make them work together on appearance features. For example, plump cheek and double chin attributes point to the appearance feature of obesity. Therefore, it can be seen from Fig. 6 that we are more natural and delicate in changing the appearance of the virtual bot, and it is in line with the law of human change.

Figure 6 shows the results of our joint training on the Celeb A and CK datasets. Our virtual bot has three expressions: happy, calm, and resistant. Compared with other models, our model can make the virtual bot make different expressions according to different scenes. This change makes the virtual bot more real and humanoid. Figures 5 and 6 show the training results of our network.

When different user appearance features are identified, our virtual bot also completes the corresponding appearance feature changes. When the information read from the camera is background image information, our virtual bot has a certain expression change. As can be seen from Fig. 6, when the image is a well-known scenic spot such as the DaYan Tower, our virtual bot has produced Happy mood, and when the image is a sight such as a haunted house, our virtual bot shows a sense of resistance.

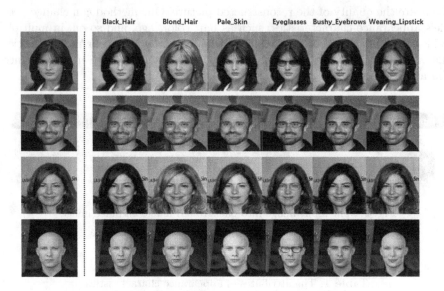

Fig. 5. We show the conversion results in this figure of some typical attributes in Table 1, such as: Black Hair, Blond Hair, Pale Skin, Eyeglasses, Bushy Eyebrows, Wearing Lipstick

Fig. 6. Three expressions of the appearance conversion network: resistant, calm, happy

Table 2. Perplexity of each model

Model	Perplexity
RNN Seq2Seq	35.63
RNN Seq2Seq+Attention	29.8
HRED	26.81
Transformer (Ours)	22.45

Fig. 7. Virtual bot dialogue diagram

Dialogue Results. We first trained our model on the Dailydialog dataset. In order to ensure the training quality and model stability, we jointly trained the Persona-Chat dataset. The Perplexity index can be used to measure how well a probability prediction model predicts a sample. The lower the degree of confusion, the better the performance of the model. The definition of confusion is given in the following formula. Y_i represents the i_{th} word in a sentence sequence Y:

$$PPL = \exp\{-\frac{1}{N}\sum_{i=1}^{n}\log p(Y_i)\} \tag{14}$$

As is shown in Table 2, compared with the existing models, our model has less confusion and better dialogue effect.

Figure 7 shows the results of our joint training on the Dailydialog and Persona-Chat dataset. It can be seen from the figure that during the dialogue between the virtual bot and the user, the semantics are clear, the dialogue is smooth, and the personify.

6 Conclusion

In this paper, we propose MateBot, a context-sensitive virtual bot shaping network. Through this network, our virtual bot can change its appearance and emotional characteristics for different scenarios and human users. In order to increase the authenticity of the virtual bot, we adopt joint training between different data sets and different attributes. In addition, we still guarantee the generalization ability of the network. It is expected that our work can be applied to more virtual bots. As for future work, we will add more expressions and appearance features to MateBot, optimize the delay time, and add more attribute information to personalized virtual bots.

Acknowledgment. This work was supported in part by the National Key R&D Program of China (2019QY0600), in part by the National Natural Science Foundation of China (No. 61772428, 61725205, 61902320, 61972319), in part by the Natural Science Basic Research Plan in Shaanxi Province of China (No. 2020JQ-215), and in part by the Fundamental Research Funds for the Central Universities (No. 3102019QD1001).

References

1. Arjovsky, M., Chintala, S., Bottou, L.: Wasserstein generative adversarial networks. In: International Conference on Machine Learning, pp. 214–223 (2017)
2. Colby, K.M.: Artificial paranoia: a computer simulation of paranoid processes, vol. 49. Elsevier (2013)
3. Hu, Y.T., Huang, J.B., Schwing, A.: MaskRNN: instance level video object segmentation. In: Advances in Neural Information Processing Systems, pp. 325–334 (2017)
4. Huang, X., Belongie, S.: Arbitrary style transfer in real-time with adaptive instance normalization. In: Proceedings of the IEEE International Conference on Computer Vision, pp. 1501–1510 (2017)
5. Huang, X., Li, Y., Poursaeed, O., Hopcroft, J., Belongie, S.: Stacked generative adversarial networks. In: Proceedings of the IEEE Conference on Computer Vision and Pattern Recognition, pp. 5077–5086 (2017)
6. Karras, T., Laine, S., Aila, T.: A style-based generator architecture for generative adversarial networks. In: Proceedings of the IEEE Conference on Computer Vision and Pattern Recognition, pp. 4401–4410 (2019)
7. Kim, T., Kim, B., Cha, M., Kim, J.: Unsupervised visual attribute transfer with reconfigurable generative adversarial networks. arXiv preprint arXiv:1707.09798 (2017)
8. Krizhevsky, A., Sutskever, I., Hinton, G.: Advances in Neural Information Processing Systems (NIPS) (2012)
9. Ledig, C., et al.: Photo-realistic single image super-resolution using a generative adversarial network. In: Proceedings of the IEEE Conference on Computer Vision and Pattern Recognition, pp. 4681–4690 (2017)
10. Li, J., Galley, M., Brockett, C., Spithourakis, G.P., Gao, J., Dolan, B.: A persona-based neural conversation model. arXiv preprint arXiv:1603.06155 (2016)
11. Li, M., Zuo, W., Zhang, D.: Deep identity-aware transfer of facial attributes. arXiv preprint arXiv:1610.05586 (2016)
12. Li, Y., Su, H., Shen, X., Li, W., Cao, Z., Niu, S.: Dailydialog: a manually labelled multi-turn dialogue dataset. arXiv preprint arXiv:1710.03957 (2017)
13. Liu, Z., Luo, P., Wang, X., Tang, X.: Deep learning face attributes in the wild. In: Proceedings of the IEEE International Conference on Computer Vision, pp. 3730–3738 (2015)
14. Lucey, P., Cohn, J.F., Kanade, T., Saragih, J., Ambadar, Z., Matthews, I.: The extended Cohn-Kanade dataset (CK+): A complete dataset for action unit and emotion-specified expression. In: 2010 IEEE Computer Society Conference on Computer Vision and Pattern Recognition-Workshops, pp. 94–101. IEEE (2010)
15. Qian, Q., Huang, M., Zhao, H., Xu, J., Zhu, X.: Assigning personality/identity to a chatting machine for coherent conversation generation. arXiv preprint arXiv:1706.02861 (2017)

16. Radford, A., Metz, L., Chintala, S.: Unsupervised representation learning with deep convolutional generative adversarial networks. arXiv preprint arXiv:1511.06434 (2015)
17. Radford, A., Wu, J., Child, R., Luan, D., Amodei, D., Sutskever, I.: Language models are unsupervised multitask learners. OpenAI Blog 1(8), 9 (2019)
18. Shang, L., Lu, Z., Li, H.: Neural responding machine for short-text conversation. arXiv preprint arXiv:1503.02364 (2015)
19. Shen, W., Liu, R.: Learning residual images for face attribute manipulation. In: Proceedings of the IEEE Conference on Computer Vision and Pattern Recognition, pp. 4030–4038 (2017)
20. Sordoni, A., et al.: A neural network approach to context-sensitive generation of conversational responses. arXiv preprint arXiv:1506.06714 (2015)
21. Wallace, R.S.: The anatomy of ALICE. In: Epstein, R., Roberts, G., Beber, G. (eds.) Parsing the Turing Test, pp. 181–210. Springer, Dordrecht (2009). https://doi.org/10.1007/978-1-4020-6710-5_13
22. Weizenbaum, J., et al.: Eliza–a computer program for the study of natural language communication between man and machine. Commun. ACM 9(1), 36–45 (1966)
23. Yavuz, S., Rastogi, A., Chao, G.L., Hakkani-Tur, D.: Deepcopy: grounded response generation with hierarchical pointer networks. arXiv preprint arXiv:1908.10731 (2019)
24. Zhang, S., Dinan, E., Urbanek, J., Szlam, A., Kiela, D., Weston, J.: Personalizing dialogue agents: i have a dog, do you have pets too? arXiv preprint arXiv:1801.07243 (2018)
25. Zhang, Y., et al.: Dialogpt: large-scale generative pre-training for conversational response generation. arXiv preprint arXiv:1911.00536 (2019)
26. Zhao, J., Mathieu, M., LeCun, Y.: Energy-based generative adversarial network. arXiv preprint arXiv:1609.03126 (2016)
27. Zhou, L., Gao, J., Li, D., Shum, H.Y.: The design and implementation of xiaoice, an empathetic social chatbot. arXiv preprint arXiv:1812.08989 (2018)

User Behavior Analysis Toward Adaptive Guidance for Machine Operation Tasks

Analysis of Behavior Differences Through Skill-Improving Experiments

Long-fei Chen[✉], Yuichi Nakamura, and Kazuaki Kondo

Graduate School of Engineering, Academic Center for Computing and Media Studies, Kyoto University, Kyoto, Japan
yuichi@media.kyoto-u.ac.jp, {chenlf,kondo}@ccm.media.kyoto-u.ac.jp

Abstract. An adaptive guidance system that supports equipment operators requires a comprehensive model of task and user behavior that considers different skill and knowledge levels as well as diverse situations. In this study, we investigated the relationships between user behaviors and skill levels under operational conditions. We captured sixty samples of two sewing tasks performed by five operators using a head-mounted RGB-d camera and a static gaze tracker. We examined the operators' gaze and head movements, and hand interactions to essential regions (hotspots) to determine behavioral differences among continuous skill improving experiences. The experimental results indicate that some features, such as task execution time and user head movements, are good indexes for skill level and provide valuable information that can be applied to obtain an effective task model. Operators with varying knowledge and operating habits demonstrate different operational features, which can contribute to the design of user-specific guidance.

Keywords: Human behavior analysis · Skill improving · Adaptive guidance · Egocentric vision · RGB-d · Machine operation · Gaze · Hotspots

1 Introduction

In the domain of assembling or operational applications, smart assistant systems have been well adopted and evaluated [1–5]. Implementing such systems can optimize task processes, improve outcomes, save physical energy, reduce mental workload, and provide economic benefits [6,7].

One of the most important points of such assistant systems is the preparation of appropriate guidance content that meet the requirements of a variety of users in rapidly changing task situations [7]:

> *"The trade of between the positive and negative aspects of overlaid AR content is likely related to the experience-level of the individuals. Future AR applications should tailor AR content to address the needs of each individual."*

© Springer Nature Switzerland AG 2020
Z. Yu et al. (Eds.): GPC 2020, LNCS 12398, pp. 288–302, 2020.
https://doi.org/10.1007/978-3-030-64243-3_22

Understanding the behavior of users with a variety of skill levels is one of the key components to this problem. For example, an expert user may accomplish a task efficiently with minimal operations while novice users or users with intermediate skills may search for items, hesitate or make mistakes with unfamiliar task procedures, or take additional time to check the outcomes [18]. Accordingly, an effective system must (i) include a variety of guidance content and (ii) be designed such that it is suitable for a sufficient variety of possible users. In other words, we need to provide guidance content and instructions considering a sufficient variety of possible users. Analyzing and modeling various user behaviors can provide useful information about the difficulty of each operation step and how a guidance system can help users with various skill levels perform a specific task.

We consider that the above processes comprise three components: (a) modeling task procedures, (b) analyzing and modeling various user behaviors, and (c) designing adaptive user instructions based on user skill levels and operational difficulties. For (a), we previously proposed a method [8] that creates the structure of a task model using hand-machine interaction regions (i.e., hotspots) as important operational segments. Concerning (b), we previously proposed a method [9] that integrates expert and beginners' operational behaviors to acquire an extensive task model. This method partially provides a solution for dealing with behavior diversity. However, this integration requires prior knowledge of user skill levels, i.e., which operational behavior samples were provided by experts and which were provided by beginners.

In this study, we deal with this remaining problem through the analysis of the relationships among user behaviors, skill levels, and operational difficulties. Note that the actual design of adaptive user instructions based on user behaviors (c) is left for future work. Basically, relationships among body, head, eye, hand, and task-relevant objects in typical operational tasks have shown complicated temporal and spatial patterns and large variations [10], which include essential user behavior information. To deal with this problem, we systematically gathered the behaviors of five participants who gradually learned operational tasks, and analyzed various features changing by user skill levels and operational difficulties. The framework of our approach is illustrated in Fig. 1. Our experiments successfully showed close relationships between operational behaviors, operational difficulties, and operator skill levels.

2   Related Work

Skill Learning. Skill learning is more than simply following the rules to accomplish the task. A traditional Japanese expression describes the learning process as "Shu-Ha-Ri" [11], which can be translated as "obey, break, and create". Obeying the rules and facts is suitable for early stages of learning. A similar theory has been presented in the literature [12]. In that study, skills acquisition is defined in five stages: novice, advanced beginner, competence, proficiency, and expertise. The novice learning process has been described as "being contingent on concept

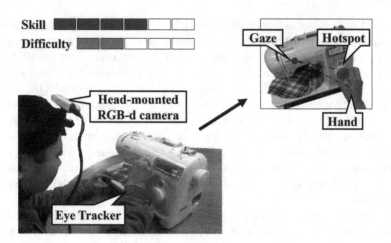

Fig. 1. A participant using a sewing machine. We analyze the operational behaviors using the operator's head movements, gaze, hands movements, and touches. Here, the goal is to find clues that indicate the skill level of the operator and the difficulty of the task.

formation and the impact of fear, mistakes, and the need for validation" [13]. These aspects provide vital clues to analyze behavior change and skill improvements of novice learners. Considering the purpose of the guidance, it is ideal to provide appropriate information to all users, but the highest priority is to support users from novices to intermediate levels. Therefore, we aim to concentrate on the process of gradually improving skills from first-time users.

Skill Comparison Studies. Concering skill levels and learning states, several studies have investigated the relationship between user behaviors and skill levels in a variety of applications. In surgery and sports, the quality of actions, such as accurate pose and economy and fluidity of body movement, can indicate high skill levels. Al-Naser et al. [14] quantified the quality of daily human actions by capturing body poses using wearable IMUs, and gauged the performance of any participant using expert action data. Uemura et al. [15] noticed a significant difference in the hand motion between expert and novice surgeons, i.e., expert surgeon hand motions are more stable. These studies have shown behavior differences between expert and novice surgeons in some feature domains, such as performance time, speed of using instruments, number of errors or procedure repetitions during an operation, and eye-hand coordination [15]. Some studies have adopted deep features to assess human skills in videos. Doughty et al. [16] proposed a supervised deep ranking model to determine skills in a pairwise manner for non-specific task using CNNs. Li et al. [17] adopted a RNN-based spatial attention model to assess hand manipulation skills. Rather than simply comparing skills between operational experiences, we aim to explicitly analyze the continuous skill learning process and investigate user behavior differences with semantic explanations.

Behavior Analysis Methods. For machine operation experiences, reliable and automatic measurements based on multiple features are required to investigate the intricate temporal and spatial patterns, as well as large variations in each operational procedure and the difficulty of individual procedures. Previous studies have investigated the relationship between gaze, head, body, and operational characteristics. Land and Hayhoe [18] tracked eye movements in tea- and sandwich-making tasks. Pelz et al. [19] monitored eye, hand, and head coordination in a block-copying task. One noteworthy observation is that, in a task that involves sequential movements, the gaze often shifts to the next object in the sequence prior to completion of the current activity.

Here, we aim to automatically detect user behaviors in machine operation tasks. A sewing task is a quick operational process that does not involve significant wait time between operations. We use a combination of features to describe user behaviors in prior to and during operation.

For a more comprehensive understanding of behavior differences, we systematically gathered and analyzed user behavior records of a continuous learning process of operators who were initially novices. Through this analysis, we aimed to delineate features to characterize skill levels and investigate differences between users, which we refer to as inter-person variability. We also expect to provide reliable semantic explanations of features that are closely related to skill levels and describe how such features relate to the actual guiding process.

3 Key Idea

A future goal is to develop a comprehensive machine operation model that can be adopted to guide a variety of users with different skill levels. This study focuses on modeling changes of behavior caused by different skill levels and inter-person variability by systematically analyzing data obtained from machine operation experiments.

We investigated an environment in which an operator can interact with a machine on or around a table primarily using their hands. The operational behaviors include gaze, head motions, and hand motions associated with physical contact (touches) with the machine.

We investigated users with different skill levels, such as novice, expert, as well as intermediate level users who have some experience. Differences other than skill levels may affect behaviors, e.g., some users may focus on completing a task quickly, some may exam the task process or results carefully, and others may devise behaviors they find convenient.

In this study, our key idea is to gather and analyze data related to the learning process of multiple novice operators, i.e., someone who has no previous experience using the machine. We investigate how user behaviors change during continuous skill improvement. We are also interested in identifying indications of skills improvement. We also examine inter-person variability. In addition to the above analyses of multiple users, we asked users to rate the difficulty of each operation in each experience, and investigated how the subjective perception of the difficulty of the task procedures vary among users and how such perceptions change through learning.

The experimental environment was as follows. We selected a sewing machine as a good representative of machines commonly used in daily life. The sewing machine is placed on a table. The operators are seated in front of the table. All required materials are within reach. Interactions with the sewing machine include various actions in a variety of patterns, such as push, slide, rotate, seize, and cut. Such actions are not easy for first-time users. Thus, such users require guidance or usage learning.

To capture the operational behaviors of users during a task, we use a head-mounted RGB-d camera to take advantage of egocentric vision (first-person vision). A fixed gaze tracker is set at the machine surface to capture operator gaze points. Features, such as head and hand motions, and hand–machine interactions, are extracted from the data captured by the RGB-d camera and the gaze tracker.

We examine quantitative and qualitative relationships among features, how features change as learning progresses, and inter-person variability. We expect that features that are primarily correlated to skill levels and operational diffi-culties will be delineated as the amount of data captured is sufficient to reveal inter- and intra-person differences.

4   Operational Behavior Detection

From the egocentric vision and gaze tracking data, we extract basic features, such as hand motions, and higher order features, such as the relationship between basic features.

4.1   Visual Features

A 2D global map of the sewing machine surface is prepared beforehand. Every egocentric view is aligned on the global map and global locations of detected visual features are obtained.

Hand and Hotspots. To detect a hand, we first segment the foreground from RGB-d images by considering the common operation distance. Then, a skin-color model is constructed for each user at the initial period of operation. Hand locations are detected in every frame by filtering with this skin-color model and depth. As crucial interaction areas on the machine surface, hotspots are detected automatically by clustering the touches in spatio-temporal locations between the hand and machine. After hotspots have been extracted, we mapped them to the global map using SIFT features and homography transformation. Detailed descriptions of the above processes can be found in the literature [21].

Gaze. A commercial gaze tracker was installed on the base of the machine (Fig. 1). The gaze tracker continuously captures the user's gaze during the task process. We match the view field of the gaze tracker to the global map and align gazing targets on the map.

4.2   Behavioral Features

In object-related actions, eyes are often involved in identifying objects for future use and planning operations to be performed on such objects [18]. Based on this observation, we define a basic operational unit (OU) as the sequential of "pure-gazing (saccade/fixation)", "hand-approaching", and "operating".

The pure-gazing period is the period between the end of the previous physical hand–machine contact and the moment the hand is within sight range. The hand-approaching period is the period between the end of a pure-gazing period and the time at which the hand operation begins. The operating period is the period in which physical touches occur. Each record of an operational experience can be divided into a sequence of such OUs. Detailed behaviors of each period may vary, for example, in some OUs, pure gaze period is skipped, or two or more staffs are gazed at sequentially. Our modeling of operational units deals with those variations as that the duration is zero, and the duration is the sum of gazing periods for two or more staffs, respectively.

We obtain the following behavioral features using the above visual sensing and the above definition of basic units.

Temporal Duration. For each OU, the absolute duration of each period is measured as a behavioral feature.

Distance, Velocity, Frequency, and Variance. We consider the distances among the hand, gaze target, and the hotspot are also essential features to characterize behaviors. In the global 2D map, distances are calculated during each OU. In addition, we use distance changing speed, its variance, and the frequency of distance change speed. They are defined as:

$$V = \mathcal{D}(d^*),$$
$$\delta^2 = E[(d^* - \bar{d})^2] \tag{1}$$
$$f = \mathcal{C}[d]/T.$$

Here, $\mathcal{D}$ is the differential and E is the expectation. d^* is the distance between two regions and $\bar{d}$ is its mean. $\mathcal{C}$ is the number of sign changes of the distance in a period. The frequency is derived by dividing number of sign changes by the period duration T.

Head Movement. Head motion is represented in angular velocity in each direction, where x is the horizontal direction and y is the vertical direction, which is estimated using the global motion vector of the egocentric RGB-d camera [20] as follows:

$$V_{head_x} = \arctan(V_{global_x}/s_{img} * s_{sensor}/f), \tag{2}$$

where s_{img} and s_{sensor} are the size of image in pixels and the size of the camera CMOS sensor in mm, respectively and f is the focal length in mm. V_{head_x} and V_{global_x} represent the components for x direction.

We also calculate the correlation between gaze and head motion to investigate their synergy.

4.3   Correlation to Skill Level and Difficulty

The correlation between each of the above features and user skill level, and the correlation between each feature and the difficulty of an operation step are important clues for modeling a task and user behaviors.

However, estimating the skill level of a user at a certain trial in an experiment is difficult. For this purpose, we assume that the skill level of each operator improves monotonically through the experience accumulating process. Thus, we rank the skill level as ordinal data aligned by task trial, e.g., the skill of a user in trial 1 is considerably no better than the skill in trial 3.

Operational difficulty is obtained by subjective rating of task procedures using a six-point scale. The difficulty score may change in different trials. For example, in trial 1, a user could find rotating a dial very difficult; however, the same procedure may feel easier in subsequent trials. The change in perceived difficulty may be related to skill level improvement.

Thus, the correlation between feature values and skill levels is considered for each trial whereas the correlation to difficulty is considered for each step of the operation.

5   Experimental Results

5.1   Experimental Conditions

Sewing Tasks Recording. We recruited five participants and recorded six operational trials for each of two sewing tasks for each participant, i.e., a total of 60 trials. Note that none of the participants had experience using a sewing machine. Task 1 is "sew a specific symbol" that consists of 11 standard operation steps (procedures) in the official manual, and task 2 is "cut the thread and restore the machine to initial state" that includes 5 standards steps. Each participant performed the two tasks alternately and repeatedly. Each participant wore a head-mounted RGB-d camera (Intel RealSense D415 [22], 30 fps), and egocentric vision from the camera was recorded. Gaze points were recorded using a fixed commercial gaze tracker (Tobii Eye Tracker 4C [23], 90 Hz). Prior to measuring, we first calibrated the gaze tracker for each operator using calibration points on a computer screen. Then, we applied the obtained alignment of the gaze tracker to the machine surface. By this procedure, we can register the user's gaze to the machine surface.

Parameters. Each participant was asked to rate the difficulty of each operation steps from 0 to 5 (easiest to most difficult) after each trial. To filter out noise caused by detection errors, we ignored touches to hotspots for less than the threshold duration (<0.3 s).

5.2   Behavior Changes Through Skill Improvements

For each operation step, we first detected the operating period based on touches to a hotspot. Then, we detected the pre-operating periods using gaze and hand clues as mentioned above in Sect. 4. To simplify the notation in the following sections, the pure-gazing, hand-approaching, and operating periods in the OU are denoted G, A, and O, respectively.

We extracted the aforementioned features from all trial records. Then, we compared the difference between them in the continuous skill improving experience records.

- **Overall**

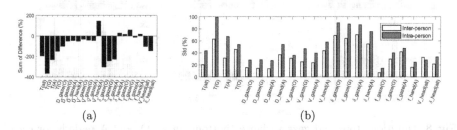

(a)   (b)

Fig. 2. (a) Overall trends of features among trials (sum of differences) and (b) inter- and intra-person standard deviations of features (averaged for two tasks).

Figure 2 (a) shows the overall trends of features by accumulating differences among trials. The sum of differences among trials of a feature for in participant is calculated as follows:

$$\mathbb{D} = \sum_{i=2}^{n}(f_i - f_{i-1})/\frac{1}{n}\sum_{j=1}^{n}f_j. \tag{3}$$

Here, f is the feature value, and i and j are the index of trial. Then, the differences are averaged for all participants. From the first to the final trial, the value difference of individual features ranged from 13% to 366%. Some features show an obvious uptrend as experience increases (i.e., *hand speed* in approaching hotspots), whereas some features show an obvious downtrend (e.g., *duration*, *gaze variance*, and *head movement*). Other features do not show a clear trend among trials.

The inter- and intra-person variations of different features are shown in Fig. 2 (b). The inter- and intra-person variations are based on standard deviation.

$$\delta_{intra} = Std(\mathbf{f}_u) \text{ and } \delta_{inter} = Std(\{\bar{\mathbf{f}}_u\}) \tag{4}$$

Here, $\mathbf{f}_u$ is the set of feature values of a user from all trials and $\bar{\mathbf{f}}_u$ is the mean value. The standard deviation of individual features ranges from 6.8% to 70% for inter-person variations and from 14% to 99% for intra-person variations, respectively. Note that *duration* and *gaze variance* show large variability both within and between participants.

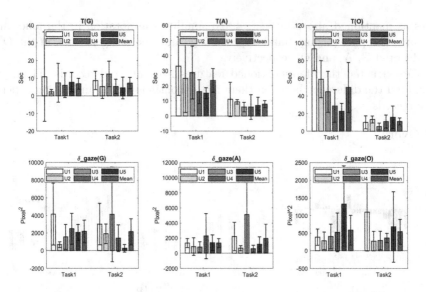

Fig. 3. Duration (top) and gaze variance (bottom) in G, O, and A periods for each participant (averaged for all trials).

- **Inter-person differences**

After considering overall trends, we looked at detailed behavior differences among participants. As can be seen in Fig. 2 (b), two groups of features show the greatest inter-person variability, (i) *duration* (especially in G) and (ii) *gaze variance* (all periods). Detailed feature values of each user for *duration* and *gaze variance* are shown in Fig. 3. As can be seen, participant 1 had the longest G and the longest O time. This indicates that the participant tended to search or hesitate more before taking action and performed slowly during task execution. When providing guidance for this type of user, explicit instructions may be appropriate. Participant 3 searches a lot in the pre-operation periods; however, they concentrate when performing a specific operation. In contrast, participant 5 made decisions quickly prior to beginning the operation and checked the progress or outcomes more during the operation. When providing guidance for this type of user, timing is important, i.e., guidance should be offered at suitable period(s) of the process, e.g., whether prior to begin or during the operation.

- **Trends with skill improvement (Intra-person)**

In our investigation of behavior changes with skill improvement, we primarily focused on features that showed significant trends over all participants, that is, (i) *duration*, (ii) *gaze*, and (iii) *head movement*, as shown in Fig. 2 (a). Figure 4 shows the detailed changes of multiple features from early to late trials (1–6).

(i) Duration. The overall execution time almost decreased monotonically for the two tasks (Fig. 4 (a)). For task 1, overall execution time of all participants

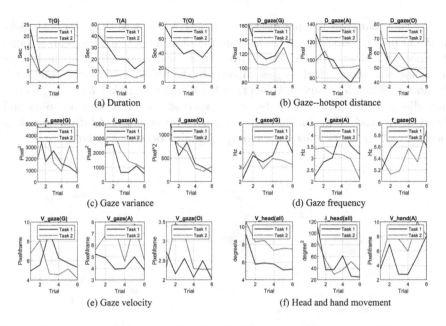

Fig. 4. Detailed trends of features in trials (1–6) of different periods in OUs (averaged over five participants) of two tasks.

decreased from an average of approximately 120 s to 50 s, and for task 2 overall execution time decreased from approximately 50 s to 30 s. The duration commonly dropped within the first two trials, particularly in the G period.

The results show that for initial experiences, low-skilled users required more time to complete the task. The process involves a significant amount of pure-gazing (search or hover) and longer hand-approaching times prior to each operation step. Once the user got familiar with the task after a few trials, the time reduction was small.

Note that operating time demonstrates a slight upward trend in some of the later trials. Presumably, this is caused by the participants' intention to further improve of their performance. For example, one participant stated that he tried to stitch the symbol better by adjusting the cloth more carefully than in previous trials.

(ii) Gaze Movement. The average distance of gaze–hotspot (Fig. 4 (b)) and the overall gaze variance (Fig. 4 (c)) decreased in both tasks as user experience increased. At the initial trials, the gaze showed large distance and variance in all G, A, and O periods, which indicated frequent searches or checks during the tasks. This may occur because novices require more searches to retain relevant information prior to the operation and more result checks during the operation. As skill improved, users located their gaze closer to the interacting area from the beginning of OU, and the gaze movement range is much narrower. However, movement velocity did not decrease significantly (Fig. 4 (e)).

We note that gaze–hotspot distance demonstrates a bowl shape for both tasks in the G period, which indicates that users did a lot of searching search (large distance with large variance) at the early trials before operation. In the middle trials, users tend to shift their gaze directly to the future operation region (small distance with small variance). When they became more familiar with the process, they did not need to concentrate on the specific spot to locate hotspots and direct their hands. This indicates user memory formulation of future operation locations. Then, users relied on memory to guide operations in later trials.

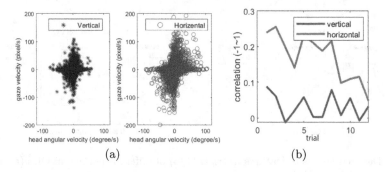

Fig. 5. (a) Correlation between gaze and head. Movement is shown in horizontal and vertical directions respectively. (b) Change of correlation scores between gaze and head with skill improvement (averaged for all participants).

(iii) Head Movement. The average head velocity and variance both decrease monotonically from early to later trials for all users, as shown in Fig. 4 (f). This shows that the stability, i.e., less motion, of the user's head could indicate a high skill level.

The overall correlation of gaze and head movement is shown in Fig. 5 (a). Note that gaze and head movements are almost uncorrelated in the vertical direction, and are weakly correlated in the horizontal direction compared to the kitchen operation scenes in a previous study [20].

We then confirmed head–gaze movement correlation trends during skill improvement, as shown in Fig. 5 (b). From the average score on the horizontal axis, the correlation between gaze-head movement decreases as the skill level increases. This is presumably because a skilled user well knows the location of a target and tends to use eye movement. The mental and physical cost of eye movement is much less than moving the head; thus, we tend not to move the head unless it is essential.

We can conclude that, in our experimental environment, head movement is a more reliable indicator of user skill level compared to gaze movement.

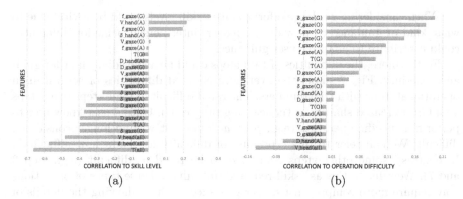

Fig. 6. (a) Correlation of features to skills, (b) Correlation of features to operation difficulties.

- **Reliable clues to skill levels and operational difficulties**

Correlations among behavioral features, skill improvements, and subjective difficulty provide useful information for task modeling and guidance design, i.e., features with strong correlation can be good indexes for user skill levels and operational difficulty.

The correlation coefficient of features to the ordinal scale of skill level was calculated using Spearman's rank correlation [24], and the correlation coefficient of features to operational difficulty scores was derived using the Pearson correlation [25].

The correlation coefficients of all features to the subjective skill levels are shown in Fig. 6 (a). The top three features with strong correlation to skills are (i) *duration*, (ii) *head variance* and *velocity*, and (iii) *gaze–hotspot distance* and *variance*. We can consider the design of user skill assessment approaches based on these features.

Figure 6 (b) depicts the correlation coefficients of the features and the user-rated difficulty scores over all the operation steps of both tasks. The result show that (i) the *gaze variance* and *velocity* of the G period, and (ii) the *gaze velocity* and *frequency* in the O period are strongly correlated to operational difficulty. This implies that the more difficult an operation step is, the more frequently the operator will search other regions prior to initiating operation. In addition, faster gaze movement during the operation will occur, which is probably due to result checking. The above analysis provides clues for designing a metric to indicate operational difficulties for user guidance.

6 Discussion

When considering creation of user guidance content, e.g., to generate an extensive task model from a variety of user records, we can consider top skill-correlated features could be efficient indexes to select high-skilled records to generate the baseline of the task model.

When considering guidance offerings, user skill levels could be a vital clue to what kind of guidance to provide. Moreover, inter-person behavior differences could contribute to adaptive user guidance.

Furthermore, the difficulties of task steps could be a subsidiary hint for guidance offerings. Fig. 7 shows the average user-rated difficulties of several main operational steps with trial numbers. The rated difficult of some steps (e.g., steps 4 and 6) decreased sharply as the learning progressed. Once a user knew how to perform a specific operation (e.g., *push a button*), it was no longer considered difficult. We call refer to this type kind of difficulty as "know-how difficulty". In contrast, some other steps continued to be rated as difficult (e.g., step 3 and 7). We refer to this as "skill-required difficulty". These types of operations may require more comprehensive user guidance, such as showing the details of a method or an alternative easier way.

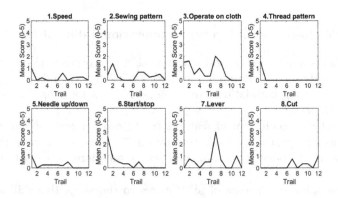

Fig. 7. Average user ratings of operational difficulties for several steps with over increasing experiences (averaged by all participant for 12 trial of the two sewing tasks).

7 Conclusion

In this paper, we introduced an approach for detecting the characteristics of skill and behaviors in machine operation. Sixty instances of two sewing machine operation tasks performed by five participants with continuous skill improvements were recorded. We measured the operational behaviors with features extracted from user's gaze, head movements, hand movements, and hotspots in both temporal and spatial domains, and confirmed if such features are good indexes of operator skill levels and operational difficulties. The experimental result shows good potential for those features, particularly for task duration, head movement, and gaze properties. In future, we need to design metrics based on these features to consider inter-person differences and to design content for adaptive guidance systems.

References

1. Bleser, G., et al.: Cognitive learning, monitoring and assistance of industrial workflows using egocentric sensor networks. PLoS ONE **10**(6), e0127769 (2015)
2. Damen, D., Haines, O., Leelasawassuk, T., Calway, A., Mayol-Cuevas, W.: Multiuser egocentric online system for unsupervised assistance on object usage. In: Agapito, L., Bronstein, M.M., Rother, C. (eds.) ECCV 2014. LNCS, vol. 8927, pp. 481–492. Springer, Cham (2015). https://doi.org/10.1007/978-3-319-16199-0_34
3. Damen, D., et al.: You-do, i-learn: discovering task relevant objects and their modes of interaction from multi-user egocentric video. In: BMVC, vol. 2 (2014)
4. Friedrich, W., Jahn, D., Schmidt, L.: ARVIKA-augmented reality for development, production and service. In: ISMAR, vol. 2002 (2002)
5. Tang, A., et al.: Comparative effectiveness of augmented reality in object assembly. In: Proceedings of the SIGCHI Conference on Human Factors in Computing Systems. ACM (2003)
6. Ong, S.K., Yuan, M.L., Nee, A.Y.C.: Augmented reality applications in manufacturing: a survey. Int. J. Prod. Res. **46**(10), 2707–2742 (2008)
7. Henderson, S., Feiner, S.: Exploring the benefits of augmented reality documentation for maintenance and repair. IEEE Trans. Visual Comput. Graphics **17**(10), 1355–1368 (2010)
8. Chen, L., et al.: Hotspot modeling of hand-machine interaction experiences from a head-mounted RGB-d camera. IEICE Trans. Inf. Syst. **102**(2), 319–330 (2019)
9. Chen, L., et al.: Hotspots integrating of expert and beginner experiences of machine operations through egocentric vision. In: 2019 16th International Conference on Machine Vision Applications (MVA). IEEE (2019)
10. Land, M.F.: Vision, eye movements, and natural behavior. Vis. Neurosci. **26**(1), 51–62 (2009)
11. Fujiwara, R.: Ideology of shuhari (1993)
12. Dreyfus, S.E.: The five-stage model of adult skill acquisition. Bull. Sci. Technol. Soc. **24**(3), 177–181 (2004)
13. Daley, B.J.: Novice to expert: an exploration of how professionals learn. Adult Educ. Q. **49**(4), 133–147 (1999)
14. Al-Naser, M., et al.: Quantifying quality of actions using wearable sensor. In: Lemaire, V., Malinowski, S., Bagnall, A., Bondu, A., Guyet, T., Tavenard, R. (eds.) AALTD 2019. LNCS (LNAI), vol. 11986, pp. 199–212. Springer, Cham (2020). https://doi.org/10.1007/978-3-030-39098-3_15
15. Uemura, M., et al.: Analysis of hand motion differentiates expert and novice surgeons. J. Surg. Res. **188**(1), 8–13 (2014)
16. Doughty, H., Damen, D., Mayol-Cuevas, W.: Who's better? Who's best? Pairwise deep ranking for skill determination. In: Proceedings of the IEEE Conference on Computer Vision and Pattern Recognition (2018)
17. Li, Z., et al.: Manipulation-skill assessment from videos with spatial attention network. arXiv preprint arXiv:1901.02579 (2019)
18. Land, M.F., Hayhoe, M.: In what ways do eye movements contribute to everyday activities? Vis. Res. **41**(25–26), 3559–3565 (2001)
19. Pelz, J., Hayhoe, M., Loeber, R.: The coordination of eye, head, and hand movements in a natural task. Exp. Brain Res. **139**(3), 266–277 (2001)
20. Li, Y., Fathi, A., Rehg, J.M.: Learning to predict gaze in egocentric video. In: Proceedings of the IEEE International Conference on Computer Vision (2013)

21. Chen, L., et al.: Hotspots detection for machine operation in egocentric vision. In: 2017 Fifteenth IAPR International Conference on Machine Vision Applications (MVA). IEEE (2017)
22. Intel RealSense Depth Camera D415
23. Tobii Eye Tracker 4C
24. Spearman, C.: The proof and measurement of association between two things (1961)
25. Pearson, K.: VII. Note on regression and inheritance in the case of two parents. Proc. Royal Soc. London **58**(347–352), 240–242 (1895)

Behavior Fingerprints Based Smartphone User Authentication: A Review

Imane Lamiche, Bin Guo$^{(\boxtimes)}$, Yafang Yang, and Zhiwen Yu

Northwestern Polytechnical University, 127 YouYi XiLu Xi'an, Shaanxi 710072, China
stic0303@gmail.com, guob@nwpu.edu.cn

Abstract. Nowadays, humans have become too dependent on their smartphone devices for a broad range of tasks: shopping, bank interactions, socialization ...etc. Wide-speared dependence on smartphone devices raises numerous security and privacy risks. To deal with these evolving threats, various authentication methods based on user behavioral biometrics have been proposed in recent research. Behavioral biometrics are used to identify the smartphone user continuously without seeking his/her cooperation which makes the task more convenient. In this paper, we review the current behavioral biometrics authentication methods on smartphones. We present an analytical study of several proposed mechanisms and discuss the strengths and limitations of available approaches. A comparative evaluation of the various state of the art obtained results is discussed. Finally, a list of open problems, challenges, and future directions are carried out for future studies on this research area.

Keywords: Biometrics · Behavioral biometrics · Smartphone authentication

1 Introduction

Since today's mobile devices have the ability to collect a massive amount of user data, smartphone security becomes of a paramount importance. Any unauthorized access to these sensitive data may lead to a privacy violation. To enhance the smartphone security, several authentication methods have been proposed in the last decade including traditional authentication methods such as passwords, personal identification number (PIN) and physiological biometrics-based authentication solutions such as face (Fathy et al. 2015) and fingerprints (Jo et al. 2016). However, these methods still suffer from several drawbacks such as the necessity of additional hardware and susceptibility to external factors. Behavioral biometrics such as gait (Gadaleta and Rossi 2018) and keystroke dynamics (Antal and Szabo 2015) represent a robust alternative for the pre-existing authentication mechanisms. Recent smartphone devices come with numerous embedded sensors that continuously and passively monitor user behavior to identify the smartphone owner. Therefore, it provides a high performance and security level for smartphone users.

In this paper, we mainly survey the state of the art behavioral biometric methods for smartphone authentication due to its promising reported state of art results. We discuss

© Springer Nature Switzerland AG 2020
Z. Yu et al. (Eds.): GPC 2020, LNCS 12398, pp. 303–317, 2020.
https://doi.org/10.1007/978-3-030-64243-3_23

the existing mechanisms with respect to the type of traits and sensors used for behavioral data acquisition, the proposed learning methodologies, and evaluate results with regard to usability and security aspects. We specifically provide a detailed review of behavioral traits in unimodal and multimodal biometric authentication systems, analyze the strengths and weaknesses of each approach and finally outline the most challenging problems in this research area. Several survey papers have been published on behavioral biometric authentication systems, however, some reviews focus only on particular behavioral traits (Teh et al. 2016; Wan et al. 2018), whereas others (Alzubaidi and Kalita 2016; Meng et al. 2015) survey both physiological and behavioral biometrics methods. Unlike the existing works, we delve deeper to review the existing works explicitly on behavioral biometrics for smartphone authentication. Specifically, the main contributions of our work can be summarized as:

- We intensely review the existing studies of behavioral biometrics authentication systems on smartphones by categorizing them into two groups: unimodal authentication methods and multimodal authentication methods.
- We analyze the methodologies used in each category and investigate the applicability of the proposed methods with regard to the usability and security aspects.
- We find out the challenges and open problems in this research area and provide future research directions for future studies in this field.

The remainder of this review is organized as follows. Section 1 reviews various state of art authentication methods. Section 2 discusses and compares the advantages and limits of the aforementioned mechanisms. Section 3 reports the open problems and challenges faced in this research area. Finally, we conclude this work in Sect. 4.

2 Behavioral Biometrics Authentication Solutions on Smartphones

Behavioral biometrics are based on user behavioral traits such as gait and touch interactions. In this section, behavioral biometrics based smartphone authentication methods were divided into two categories: Uni-modal authentication methods and Multi-modal authentication methods. Figure 1 shows the taxonomy of the existing related works adopted in this review.

2.1 Uni-Modal Behavioral Authentication Systems

Unimodal authentication system refers to a single biometric trait based authentication system such as gait, keystroke dynamics, and handwaving.

Gait Based Authentication
Gait behavioral biometric aims to identify the smartphone user based on the way he/she walks. Embedded sensors like accelerometer and gyroscope provide three-axis data (x, y, and z) where features can be extracted from this data to build gait behavioral modal of the smartphone user. Several studies have been published on gait based smartphone authentication methods. Table 1 compares several studies on gait based smartphone authentication approaches.

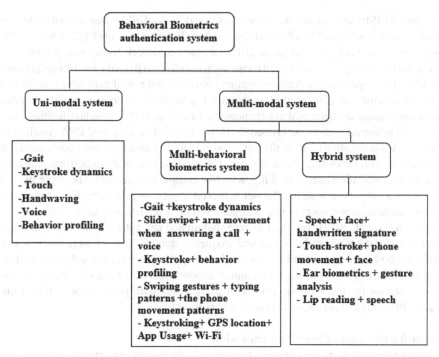

Fig. 1. Taxonomy of the existing studies reviewed in this paper.

Table 1. Examples of Gait based smartphone authentication methods

Studies	Dataset#of users	Classifier/distance metric	Sensor(s)	Results
(Zhong et al. 2015)	51	GDI Nearest Neighbor	Accelerometer	EER 7.22%
(Muaaz and Mayrhofer 2016)	35	Adapted Gaussian Mixture Models	Accelerometer	EER 3.031%
(Muaaz and Mayrhofer 2017)	35	DTW	Accelerometer	EER 13%
(H. Li et al. 2019)	2 datasets: -30 -11 (realistic scenarios)	CNN for feature extraction Bayes, SVM, RT, MLP	Accelerometer	Acc 93.63%
(Kala et al. 2019)	30	SVM, RF	Accelerometer	Acc 0.9973

In (Sprager and Juric 2015), the authors proposed a novel efficient gait authentication approach by analyzing accelerometer signals using higher-order statistics. The proposed method was able to operate on multi-channel and multi-sensor data by combining feature-level and sensor-level fusion. The proposed approach was evaluated on two datasets OU-ISIR dataset and the dataset collected by McGill University with 744 and 20 subjects respectively. The obtained results have shown an average EER of 6% to 12% respectively. In (Gadaleta and Rossi 2018), a user framework IDNet was proposed to recognize the smartphone user based on the signals collected from the built-in accelerometer and gyroscope sensors. Authors applied convolutional neural networks as universal feature extractor and combined classification results from subsequent walking cycles into a multi-stage decision making framework. Less than 0.15% misclassification rates have been achieved in their experiments. (H. Li et al. 2019), proposed IWA (Intelligent Walking Authentication), an intelligent, convenient, and identity-based authentication method designed for mobile phone devices. The proposed method can perform real-time identity authentication during walking, with low computational costs. The experimental results on a 30 person walking dataset achieved a success rate of 93.63% whereas a 91.00% authentication success rate was achieved on a realistic-scenarios dataset of 11 people. (Kala et al. 2019) presented a simple automated gait authentication system using accelerometer data, where both time and frequency domain features were extracted. A different combinations of window sizes and overlap models were trained and tested on a public dataset of 30 individuals, containing accelerometer data recorded by the smartphone's sensor for the walking activity of participants with phone kept in their right pocket. Promising experimental results were reported.

Keystroke Dynamics Based Authentication
Keystroke dynamics are widely used to continuously identify smartphone users based on their typing patterns. With the variety of touchscreen smartphones, typing behavior has changed to be easier to extract from smartphone virtual keyboards with discriminative features for user identity recognition. Table 2 shows several studies on keystroke dynamics based smartphone authentication methods.

Table 2. Examples of keystroke dynamics based smartphone authentication methods

Studies	Dataset#of users	Features	Classifier/distance metric	Results
(Clarke and Furnell, 2007)	30	4 digit PIN 6 alphabets	Neural Network	EER 8.5% EER 15.2%
(Giuffrida et al. 2014)	20	8-9 characters	kNN,Manhatta weighted, Manhattan scaled weighted	EER 8%
(Antal et al. 2015)	42	10 characters	NB,RF,KNN,C4.5, SVM,MLP	Acc 93.04% EER 12.9%
(Alsultan et al. 2016)	–	free-text	DT,SVM	EER 0.169%

(Giuffrida et al. 2014) proposed sensor-enhanced keystroke dynamics to characterize the typing behavior of users via unique sensor features. By using standard machine learning techniques to perform user authentication, the proposed approach achieved an EER of 0.08%. (Darabseh and Namin 2015) investigated the performance of keystroke features on a subset of most frequently used English words using four features key duration, flight time latency, digraph time latency, and word total time duration. Experiments were conducted to measure the performance of each feature individually then the results from the different combinations of these features. Results using 28 users data showed that digraph time offers the best performance result among all four keystroke features, followed by flight time with the FAR values slightly above 3% and 6% respectively and reduces EER of the authentication process by 2.4%. (Alsultan et al. 2016) introduced a user authentication approach based on free-text keystroke dynamics in Arabic language text. The proposed approach involves the use of the keyboard's key-layout. The method extracts timing features from specific key-pairs in the typed text. SVMs and Decision Trees (DT) were used to classify individuals based on the proposed timing features. The Experimental results reported low false accept rates and false reject rates 0.512 and 0.169% using DT and SVM respectively.

Touch Dynamics Based Authentication

Touch dynamic biometrics aim to measure and assess users' touch rhythm on smartphone devices. Data is obtained when a user interacts with the touchscreen, without requiring any specific task to be done. Table 3. shows several studies on touch dynamics based smartphone authentication methods. (Yang et al. 2019) proposed *BehaveSense*, an accurate and efficient continuous authentication method for security-sensitive mobile apps using touch-based behavioral biometrics. Four different types of touch operations were explored where the One-Class SVM (*OCSVM*) classifier was used to train the model. A series of experiments were conducted to validate the effectiveness of the proposed method. An approximately 95.85% of accuracy was achieved. (Ooi and Teoh 2019) considered that the series of touch strokes continuously performed by the user can be perceived as a temporal behavior characteristic of the person. The authors proposed the use of a temporal regression forest to unearth this hidden but vital temporal information. By incorporating this temporal information in the authentication process, the proposed model was able to achieve average equal error rates of ~ 4.0% and ~ 2.5% respectively, on two datasets. (Alghamdi and Elrefaei 2018) proposed a dynamic authentication of smartphone users based on their gestures on touchscreen. Four types of gestures were acquired tapping, scrolling, dragging and zooming for user authentication. Different classifiers including medians vector proximity (MVP), k-nearest neighbor (k-NN) and random forest (RF) were applied to classify features. The experimental results showed that the MVP classifier achieved the best results when using single gestures and the k-NN reported the best results when two gestures are combined. The k-NN classifier reaches an equal error rate of 0% using only three gestures.

Voice Based Authentication

Voice behavior is used to identify smartphone users based on their way and pattern of speaking. Each human has different voice signatures. Table 4. presents several studies on voice based smartphone authentication methods.

Table 3. Examples of touch dynamics based smartphone authentication methods

Studies	Dataset#of users	Classifier/distance metric	Results
(Serwadda et al. 2013)	190	10 classifiers	EER 10.5-42.0
(Antal et al. 2015)	71	k-NN, Random forests and SVM algorithms were used.	Acc 65% to 100%
(Alghamdi and Elrefaei, 2018)	20	medians vector proximity (MVP), k-NN, RF	EER 0%
(Yang et al. 2019)	31	One-Class SVM (OCSVM	Acc 95.85%

Table 4. Examples of voice based smartphone authentication methods

Studies	Dataset#of users	Classifier/distance metric	Results
(Kunz et al. 2011)	14	HMMs	EER 15%
(J. H. Liu et al. 2016)	181 speakers	–	EER 1.17%.
(Larcher et al. 2014)	RSR2015 dataset	Joint linear discriminant analysis and probabilistic linear discriminant analysis	EER of 0.10%.
(Wang et al. 2019)	18	two-class SVM classifier	Acc 93.5% EER 5.4%

(Larcher et al. 2014) presented novel approaches of extracting and using features from deep learning models for text-dependent speaker verification. Four types of deep models were investigated: deep Restricted Boltzmann Machines, speech-discriminant Deep Neural Network (DNN), speaker-discriminant DNN, and multi-task joint-learned DNN. Joint linear discriminant analysis and probabilistic linear discriminant analysis were used as classifiers for identity vector based deep features. Experiments on the RSR2015 data corpus showed that deep feature based methods can obtain significant performance improvements compared to the traditional baselines achieving an EER of 0.10%. (J. H. Liu et al. 2016) developed an effective voiceprint based IAS (termed as DREiSV-IAS for Mandarin smartphone users. Authors built up a Mandarin corpus MTDSR2015, which considered as the first public and free Mandarin database recorded by smartphones for text-dependent speaker recognition research. The experiments validated the effectiveness of their proposed DR-EiSV-IAS which achieves the best EER value of 1.17%. (Wang et al. 2019) designed a robust software-only anti-spoofing system on smartphones called VoicePop. Experiments using two-class SVM classifier on a dataset from 18 participants collected by three types of smartphones, showed that VoicePop can achieve over 93.5% detection accuracy at around 5.4% equal error rate.

Behavior Profiling Based Authentication
Behavior profiling refers to verifying the identity of the smartphone user based on the applications and services they use. Table 5. compares some studies on Behavior profiling based smartphone authentication methods.

Table 5. Examples of behavior profiling based smartphone authentication methods

Studies	Dataset#of users	Classifier/distance metric	Results
(F. Li et al. 2011)	MIT Reality dataset	–	EER 2.2%
(F. Li et al. 2014)	76	RBFN,FF-MLP, rule-based approach	EER 9.8%
(Datta&Manousakis, 2016)	34	two-class SVM	Acc > 85%,
(Tiwari et al. 2019)	30	–	Acc 85%

(Bassu et al. 2013) proposed an authentication approach to profile users' behavior based on mobile usage context (app usage, location, time, bandwidth usage and human device interaction) where Naive Bayes model was used for authentication. (F. Li et al. 2014) studied the feasibility of behavior profiling technique based historical application usage to continuously verify mobile users. An EER of 9.8% was achieved. Furthermore, a novel behavior profiling framework was proposed in a modular way that would not reject user's access only after a number of consecutive abnormal application usages. Experiments on the MIT Reality dataset achieved a FRR and FAR values of 11.45% and 4.17%, respectively. (Datta and Manousakis 2016) presented a smartphone user authentication method based on usage statistics. Two public datasets were used to evaluate the proposed approach. An accuracy rate of over 85% was achieved when using two-classs SVM. (Tiwari et al. 2019) offered a different perspective of login, where users need only to remember their recent activities on smartphones. Machine learning techniques were used to learn the user's behavior and create a continuously improving user profile. An accuracy value of 85% was achieved on a dataset of 30 real-world users.

Handwaving Based Authentication
Hand-waving biometric refers to the waving pattern of a smartphone user while holding his/her device. Humans wave in a different manner, leading to a behavior that can be used to identify the smartphone owner in a unique way. Table 6. presents several studies on handwaving based smartphone authentication methods.

(Lee et al. 2016) proposed a user authentication method based on users' biometric information. The proposed approach acquires the acceleration data and rotation angle values when a user shakes his/her device. Experiments on 30 participants using six classification algorithms achieved an average value of accuracies over the six classification algorithms of 97.87%. (Zhu et al. 2017) proposed ShakeIn, a handshake user authentication scheme for secure unlocking smartphones. the authors demonstrated that their

Table 6. Examples of handwaving based smartphone authentication methods

Studies	Dataset#of users	Classifier/distance metric	Results
(Gesture et al. 2015)	8	One-class Support Vector Machine	TP 92.83% FP 3.67%.
(Lee et al.2016)	30	J48, Logistic Simple, Logistic, MLP, SMO,RF	Acc 97.87%.
(Zhu et al. 2017)	20	SVM	EER 1.2%
(Yan et al. 2018)	150	DTW-LSTM	TPR:96.87% FPR 0.1%

method can effectively capture the unique and reliable biometrical features of users while shaking their devices. Real experiments on 20 volunteers dataset were conducted. Results showed that ShakeIn can achieve an average equal error rate of 1.2% with only a small number of shakes even in the presence of shoulder-surfing attacks. (Yan et al. 2018) proposed an efficient authentication method based on handshaking. The authors suggested starting the training with few training samples then expanding dynamically by adding samples when users successfully are authenticated. A DTW-LSTM Online Stacking (DLOS) classifier was adopted to verify the effectiveness of the proposed method on a dataset from 150 participants through a built-in accelerometer and gyrometer sensors. Results showed that DLOS can achieve True Positive Rate (TPR) of 90.12% starting with few training samples and TPR of 96.87% after several authentications with False Positive Rate (FPR) of 0.1%.

Signature Based Authentication

The signature biometric is the behavioral patterns generated when an individual composes a signature. Various features including the variations in timing, the pressure applied to the pen and speed can be extracted to distinguish users. Table 7. resumes some studies on signature based smartphone authentication methods.

(Krish et al. 2013) evaluated the performance of the dynamic signature verification mechanism on a database consisting of 25 users acquired with Samsung Galaxy Note.

The verification algorithm used combines two approaches: feature-based (using Mahalanobis distance) and function-based (using DTW). Experimental results showed an EER value of 0.525%. (Sae-Bae and Memon 2014) studied online signature verification on touch interface-based mobile devices. The authors proposed a simple and effective method for signature verification using the feature vector derived from attributes of several histograms of the online signature. Two datasets were used for evaluation MCYT-100 and SUSIG data sets. Moreover, a finger drawn signatures dataset on touch devices was collected from an uncontrolled environment to approve the effectiveness of the proposed algorithm in mobile settings. (Espinosa et al. 2016) developed a free-form handwriting gesture user authentication for smartphones by means of seven static and eleven dynamic handwriting features. The experiment was conducted with the participation of 30 individuals. Neural Network classifier was used for user authentication

Table 7. Examples of signature based smartphone authentication methods

Studies	Dataset#of users	Classifier/distance metric	Results
(Blanco-Gonzalo et al. 2014)	43	DTW	EER 0.19%
(Sae-Bae and Memon, 2014)	Two datasets 100 person 94 person	DTW, HMMs	EER 0.35%
(Espinosa et al. 2016)	30	Neural Network classifier	Acc 96.67%.
(Fischer and Plamondon, 2017)	SUSIGVisua SUSIGBlind MCYT-100 SG-NOTE	DTW, sigmalog normal analysis	EER 1%

achieving a recognition rate of 96.67%. (Fischer & Plamondon 2017) presented a user-centered system for signature verification by performing such a kinematic analysis to verify the identity of the user. Several benchmark datasets were used to demonstrate the effectiveness of the combined approaches DTW and sigmalog normal analysis, with an EER value around 1% for RF(Random forgeries) and an EER value between 2% and 4% for SF(skilled forgeries).

2.2 Multimodal Behavioral Authentication Systems

Multimodal behavioral biometrics refer to the fusion of information from different modalities for user authentication. The information fusion process can be done at different levels including feature level, score level, and decision level fusion. Table 8. presents different existing multimodal behavioral authentication methods.

Multi-Behavioral Biometrics

A Multi-behavioral biometrics authentication system combines different behavioral traits such as keystroke dynamics and behavioral profiling for smartphone user authentication. (Kumar et al. 2016) studied the fusion of three biometric authentication modalities, swiping gestures, typing patterns and the phone movement patterns acquired during typing or swiping. Different features including features from windows of continuous swipes, thirty features from windows of continuously typed letters, and nine features from corresponding phone movement patterns while swiping/typing were used to build the authentication system. The performance of the proposed approach evaluated on 28 users' dataset has achieved an authentication accuracy of 93.33% using the feature-level fusion method. (Lamiche et al. 2019) proposed a new multimodal authentication method to strengthen the smartphone authentication system. The proposed system acquires gait patterns and keystroke dynamics simultaneously and continuously without user intervention. A real multimodal dataset was collected under realistic scenarios including 20 subjects. The experimental results achieved an accuracy value of 99.11% when using a multilayer classifier. (Anusas-Amornkul 2019) presented a biometric authentication

Table 8. Different existing multimodal behavioral authentication methods

Studies	Modalities	Dataset#of users	Fusion level	Classifier/distance metric	Performance
Multi-behavioral biometrics system					
(Saevanee et al. 2014)	linguistic analysis, keystroke dynamics and behavioral profiling.	30	Score fusion	K-NN, the Radial Basis function (RBF), FF-MLP	EER 3.3%
(Sitova et al. 2016)	Hand Movement, Orientation, and Grasp	100	Score fusion	Scaled Manhattan, Scaled Euclidean, SVM	EER 7.16%
(Kumar et al. 2016)	Swiping gestures, typing patterns and the phone movement patterns	28	Feature fusion Score fusion	k-NN(k = ll),RF	Acc 93.33%
(Lamiche et al. 2019)	Gait + keystroke	20	Feature fusion	SVM, RF,RT NB,MLP	Acc 99.11% FAR 0.684%, FRR 7% EER 1%
(X. Liu et al. 2018)	Multi-source user machine usage	10	Decision fusion	SVM one class.	EER 5.5%.
Hybrid biometrics system					
(Morris et al. 2006)	Speech, face and handwritten signature	60	Score fusion	Gaussian mixture models	EER 1%
(McCool et al. 2012)	Face and speaker	150	Score fusion	–	EER 11.9%
(KumarMohanta & Mohapatra, 2014)	Ear and speech	50	Score level	Euclidean distanceBhattacharya distance	Acc 93.5%
(Abate et al. 2017)	Ear biometrics and gesture analysis	100	score-level weighted decision level	DWT, Euclidean distance.	EER 0.1004
(Akhtar et al. 2018)	Touchstroke, phone-movement and face patterns	95	feature level	MLP,RF	EER 0.01%

based on smartphone sensors and keystroke dynamics to strengthen password authentication on smartphone devices. Multiple classification techniques including Naïve Bayes, k Nearest Neighbors (kNN) and Random Forest were used in their work. Experiments showed that Random Forest can achieve high performance when all smartphone sensors data are combined with keystroke dynamics with accuracy and EER values of 97.90% and 5.1% respectively.

Hybrid Biometrics

Hybrid biometrics authentication system refers to a multi-modal system that involves various forms of biometrics such as face patterns, keystroke, gait …etc. (Abate et al. 2017) proposed a novel multi-modal method to authenticate smartphone users based on ear biometrics and gesture analysis. The experiments conducted on a specifically built multi-modal database including 100 subjects confirmed the effectiveness of the proposed method on mobile environments. (Akhtar et al. 2018) presented an implicit multimodal biometric system for smartphones, using touchstroke, phone-movement and face patterns. A mobile multimodal dataset was collected from 95 subjects. Two classifiers were used to measure the performance of the proposed system under different scenarios: sitting, standing and walking. (Zhang et al. 2018) proposed a multi-biometric fusion authentication system based on Lip reading and speech biometrics for smartphones. Features were extracted separately from both modalities, then a feature fusion method was applied to combine both biometric features. Authors adopted MFCC to extract speech features, GMM to train specific user's speech model, and LBP to extract lip features.

3 Discussion

As discussed above, several studies have been proposed within the field of behavioral biometrics based smartphone authentication. It is well known that behavioral biometrics offer passive and continuous authentication solutions. Unimodal behavioral biometrics systems can provide an acceptable performance however there are numerous challenges related to the application of this type of biometrics. Biometric sensors are highly susceptible to outside factors leading to poor data acquisition, such as noise in voice biometric based authentication systems. Furthermore, the emotional or physical state of the user is changeable over time and can be under various environmental conditions. Moreover, unimodal biometrics are vulnerable to malicious attacks such as spoof and robot attacks. Multimodal biometric systems are mostly more reliable than unimodal systems since it combines various biometrics, therefore a high-security level can be achieved. Furthermore, the fusion of multiple modalities overcomes numerous challenges of the unimodal systems including non-universality of some characteristics, intra-class distinctions, Noisy signals, and high error rates. With the popularity of the novel innovative smartphone devices, all the overmentioned biometrics systems become applicable on mobile devices. However, numerous limits have to be considered while the choice and implementation of authentication modalities such as computational costs, hardware limitations, speed, the time necessary for the authentication process and energy consumption. A balance between security and usability of behavioral biometrics-based authentication systems should be seriously considered.

4 Open Issues and Challenges

We carried out a literature review on behavioral biometrics based smartphone authentication systems. Based on our survey, we find out many challenges and open problems to be explored by researchers in the future.

Variation of User's Behavior: The behavioral characteristics of the smartphone user may change by means of the user state. For example, in keystroke dynamics, based authentication user's typing features may vary during walking or under different levels of fatigue which increases the false rates. More adaptive solutions to user's behavioral habits change should be considered in the future behavioral biometrics based authentication systems.

Balancing Security, Performance, and Usability: How to balance the security, performance, and usability is one of the main goals to be addressed in behavioral biometrics based authentication systems. Most state of the art studies focus on achieving a high performance even it comes at the expense of usability and security. However, the high performance alone cannot measure the success of an authentication system. Balancing security, performance, and usability is a critical research topic to be considered.

Resource Consumption: Smartphones   are   resource-constrained   computational devices, therefore, future authentication solutions should be more concerned about the consumption of the computing resources of the smartphones including energy, memory, CPU usage, and battery consumption.

Controlled Environments: Most of the studies were conducted in a controlled environment under laboratory conditions which do not necessarily reflect real-life scenarios. Smartphone users may use their devices under different environmental conditions or positions. To enhance authentication, it is an important topic to explore how to conduct a study under realistic conditions.

Small Databases: The majority of reviewed approaches were evaluated on small datasets. More involved users may lead to distinct results, therefore, It is needed to conduct experiments on a larger dataset to enhance the evaluation of the behavioral biometrics authentication systems.

Vulnerability of Biometrics: Behavioral biometrics authentication systems are generally vulnerable to several potential attacks such as Shoulder-surfing attack. The user's behavior can be easily observed and imitated. Therefore, to provide a proper method toward protecting user privacy is a challenging research topic worth to be considered.

5 Conclusion

The immerging usage of smartphone devices increases the amount of sensitive information stored in such devices. Therefore, smartphone authentications mechanisms become the main concern of researchers. In this paper, we reviewed various human behavior fingerprints based smartphone authentication methods. We analyzed and discussed numerous existing solutions by categorizing them into two groups based on either unimodal or multimodal behavioral biometrics. By comparing the existing works we find out that multimodal behavioral biometrics present high-level security solutions on smartphone devices. Finally, we came out with several open issues and future directions that should be considered in future research studies.

Acknowledgement. This work was partially supported by the National Key R&D Program of China (2019YFB1703901) and the National Natural Science Foundation of China (No. 61772428, 61725205, 61902320, 61972319).

References

Abate, A.F., Nappi, M., Ricciardi, S.: Smartphone enabled person authentication based on ear biometrics and arm gesture. In: 2016 IEEE International Conference on Systems, Man, and Cybernetics, SMC 2016 - Conference Proceedings (2017)

Akhtar, Z., Buriro, A., Crispo, B., Falk, T.H.: Multimodal smartphone user authentication using touchstroke, phone-movement and face patterns. In: 2017 IEEE Global Conference on Signal and Information Processing, GlobalSIP 2017 – Proceedings (2018)

Alghamdi, S.J., Elrefaei, L.A.: Dynamic authentication of smartphone users based on touchscreen gestures. Arab. J. Sci. Eng. **43**(2), 789–810 (2017). https://doi.org/10.1007/s13369-017-2758-x

Alsultan, A., Warwick, K., Wei, H.: Free-text keystroke dynamics authentication for Arabic language. IET Biometrics **5**(3), 164–169 (2016)

Alzubaidi, A., Kalita, J.: Authentication of smartphone users using behavioral biometrics. IEEE Commun. Surv. Tutorials **18**(3), 1998–2026 (2016)

Antal, M., Bokor, Z., Szabó, L.Z.: Information revealed from scrolling interactions on mobile devices. Pattern Recogn. Lett. **56**, 7–13 (2015a)

Antal, M., Szabo, L.Z.: An evaluation of one-class and two-class classification algorithms for keystroke dynamics authentication on mobile devices. In: Proceedings - 2015 20th International Conference on Control Systems and Computer Science, CSCS 2015 (2015)

Antal, M., Szabó, L.Z., László, I.: Keystroke dynamics on android platform. Procedia Technol. **19**, 820–826 (2015b)

Anusas-Amornkul, T.: Strengthening password authentication using keystroke dynamics and smartphone sensors. In: ACM International Conference Proceeding Series (2019)

Bassu, D., Cochinwala, M., Jain, A.: A new mobile biometric based upon usage context. In: 2013 IEEE International Conference on Technologies for Homeland Security, HST 2013 (2013)

Blanco-Gonzalo, R., Miguel-Hurtado, O., Liu-Jimenez, J.: Performance evaluation of handwritten signature recognition in mobile environments. IET Biometrics **3**(3), 139–146 (2014)

Clarke, N.L., Furnell, S.M.: Authenticating mobile phone users using keystroke analysis. Int. J. Inf. Secur. **6**(1), 1–14 (2007)

Darabseh, A., Namin, A.S.: Keystroke active authentications based on most frequently used words. In: IWSPA 2015 - Proceedings of the 2015 ACM International Workshop on Security and Privacy Analytics, Co-Located with CODASPY 2015 (2015)

Datta, T., Manousakis, K.: Using SVM for user profiling for autonomous smartphone authentication. In: 2015 IEEE MIT Undergraduate Research Technology Conference, URTC 2015 (2016)

Espinosa, F.A.T., Guerrero, G.G.E., Vea, L.A.: Modeling free-form handwriting gesture user authentication for android smartphones. In: Proceedings - International Conference on Mobile Software Engineering and Systems, MOBILESoft 2016 (2016)

Fathy, M.E., Patel, V.M., Chellappa, R.: Face-based active authentication on mobile devices. In: ICASSP, IEEE International Conference on Acoustics, Speech and Signal Processing – Proceedings (2015)

Fischer, A., Plamondon, R.: Signature verification based on the kinematic theory of rapid human movements. IEEE Trans. Hum.-Mach. Syst. (2017)

Gadaleta, M., Rossi, M.: IDNet: smartphone-based gait recognition with convolutional neural networks. Pattern Recogn. **74**, 25–37 (2018)

Gesture, M., Hong, F., Wei, M., You, S., Feng, Y., Guo, Z.: Waving authentication: your smartphone authenticate you on. In: Conference on Human Factors in Computing Systems – Proceedings (2015)

Giuffrida, C., Majdanik, K., Conti, M., Bos, H.: I sensed it was you: authenticating mobile users with sensor-enhanced keystroke dynamics. In: Dietrich, S. (ed.) DIMVA 2014. LNCS, vol. 8550, pp. 92–111. Springer, Cham (2014). https://doi.org/10.1007/978-3-319-08509-8_6

Jo, Y.H., Jeon, S.Y., Im, J.H., Lee, M.K.: Security analysis and improvement of fingerprint authentication for smartphones. Mob. Inf. Syst. (2016)

Kala, N., Bhatia, T., Aggarwal, N.: Person identification and characterization from gait using smartphone. In: 2019 11th International Conference on Communication Systems and Networks, COMSNETS 2019 (2019)

Krish, R.P., Fierrez, J., Galbally, J., Martinez-Diaz, M.: Dynamic signature verification on smart phones. In: Corchado, J.M., et al. (eds.) PAAMS 2013. CCIS, vol. 365, pp. 213–222. Springer, Heidelberg (2013). https://doi.org/10.1007/978-3-642-38061-7_21

Kumar, R., Phoha, V.V., Serwadda, A.: Continuous authentication of smartphone users by fusing typing, swiping, and phone movement patterns. In: 2016 IEEE 8th International Conference on Biometrics Theory, Applications and Systems, BTAS 2016 (2016)

KumarMohanta, T., Mohapatra, S.: Development of multimodal biometric framework for smartphone authentication system. Int. J. Comput. Appl. (2014)

Kunz, M., Kasper, K., Reininger, H., Möbius, M., Ohms, J.: Continuous speaker verification in realtime. Lecture Notes in Informatics (LNI), Proceedings - Series of the Gesellschaft Fur Informatik (GI) (2011)

Lamiche, I., Bin, G., Jing, Y., Yu, Z., Hadid, A.: A continuous smartphone authentication method based on gait patterns and keystroke dynamics. J. Ambient Intell. Humanized Comput. **10**(11), 4417–4430 (2019)

Larcher, A., Lee, K.A., Ma, B., Li, H.: Text-dependent speaker verification: classifiers, databases and RSR2015. Speech Commun. **60**, 56–77 (2014)

Lee, T.K., Kim, T.G., Im, E.G.: User authentication method using shaking actions in mobile devices. In: Proceedings of the 2016 Research in Adaptive and Convergent Systems, RACS 2016 (2016)

Li, F., Clarke, N., Papadaki, M., Dowland, P.: Behaviour profiling for transparent authentication for mobile devices. In: 10th European Conference on Information Warfare and Security 2011, ECIW 2011 (2011)

Li, F., Clarke, N., Papadaki, M., Dowland, P.: Active authentication for mobile devices utilising behaviour profiling. Int. J. Inf. Secur. **13**(3), 229–244 (2013). https://doi.org/10.1007/s10207-013-0209-6

Li, H., Yu, J., Cao, Q.: Intelligent walk authentication: implicit authentication when you walk with smartphone. In: Proceedings - 2018 IEEE International Conference on Bioinformatics and Biomedicine, BIBM 2018 (2019)

Liu, J.H., Zou, Y.X., Huang, Y.C.: An effective voiceprint based identity authentication system for Mandarin smartphone users. In: Proceedings - International Conference on Pattern Recognition (2016)

Liu, X., Shen, C., Chen, Y.: Multi-source interactive behavior analysis for continuous user authentication on smartphones. In: Zhou, J., et al. (eds.) CCBR 2018. LNCS, vol. 10996, pp. 669–677. Springer, Cham (2018a). https://doi.org/10.1007/978-3-319-97909-0_71

McCool, C., et al.: Bi-modal person recognition on a mobile phone: using mobile phone data. In: Proceedings of the 2012 IEEE International Conference on Multimedia and Expo Workshops, ICMEW 2012 (2012)

Meng, W., Wong, D.S., Furnell, S., Zhou, J.: Surveying the development of biometric user authentication on mobile phones. IEEE Commun. Surv. Tutorials (2015)

Morris, A.C., et al.: Multimodal person authentication on a smartphone under realistic conditions. In: Mobile Multimedia/Image Processing for Military and Security Applications (2006)

Muaaz, M., Mayrhofer, R.: Accelerometer based gait recognition using adapted Gaussian mixture models. In: ACM International Conference Proceeding Series (2016)

Muaaz, M., Mayrhofer, R.: Smartphone-based gait recognition: from authentication to imitation. IEEE Trans. Mob. Comput. **16**(11), 3209–3221 (2017)

Ooi, S.Y., Teoh, A.B.J.: Touch-stroke dynamics authentication using temporal regression forest. IEEE Signal Process. Lett. **26**(7), 1001 (2019)

Sae-Bae, N., Memon, N.: Online signature verification on mobile devices. IEEE Trans. Inf. Forensics Secur. **26**(7), 1001–1005 (2014)

Liu, X., Shen, C., Chen, Y.: Multi-source interactive behavior analysis for continuous user authentication on smartphones. In: Zhou, J., et al. (eds.) CCBR 2018. LNCS, vol. 10996, pp. 669–677. Springer, Cham (2018b). https://doi.org/10.1007/978-3-319-97909-0_71

Serwadda, A., Phoha, V.V., Wang, Z.: Which verifiers work?: a benchmark evaluation of touch-based authentication algorithms. In: IEEE 6th International Conference on Biometrics: Theory, Applications and Systems, BTAS 2013 (2013)

Sitova, Z., et al.: HMOG: new behavioral biometric features for continuous authentication of smartphone users. IEEE Trans. Inf. Forensics Secur. (2016)

Sprager, S., Juric, M.B.: An efficient HOS-based gait authentication of accelerometer data. IEEE Trans. Inf. Forensics Secur. **10**(7), 1486–1498 (2015)

Teh, P.S., Zhang, N., Teoh, A.B.J., Chen, K.: A survey on touch dynamics authentication in mobile devices. Comput. Secur. **59**, 210–235 (2016)

Tiwari, P.K., Velayutham, T., Singh, G., Mitra, B.: Behaviour based authentication: a new login strategy for smartphones. In: 2019 2nd International Conference on Advanced Computational and Communication Paradigms, ICACCP 2019 (2019)

Wan, C., Wang, L., Phoha, V.V.: A survey on gait recognition. ACM Comput. Surv. **51**(5), 1–35 (2018)

Wang, Q., et al.: VoicePop: a pop noise based anti-spoofing system for voice authentication on smartphones. In: Proceedings - IEEE INFOCOM (2019)

Yan, J., Qi, Y., Rao, Q., Qi, S.: Towards a user-friendly and secure hand shaking authentication for smartphones. In: Proceedings - 17th IEEE International Conference on Trust, Security and Privacy in Computing and Communications and 12th IEEE International Conference on Big Data Science and Engineering, Trustcom/BigDataSE 2018 (2018)

Yang, Y., Guo, B., Wang, Z., Li, M., Yu, Z., Zhou, X.: BehaveSense: continuous authentication for security-sensitive mobile apps using behavioral biometrics. Ad Hoc Netw. **84**, 9–18 (2019)

Zhang, X., Zhang, J., He, T., Chen, Y., Shen, Y., Xu, X.: A speech and lip authentication system based on android smart phone. In: ACM International Conference Proceeding Series (2018)

Zhong, Y., Deng, Y., Meltzner, G.: Pace independent mobile gait biometrics. In: 2015 IEEE 7th International Conference on Biometrics Theory, Applications and Systems, BTAS 2015 (2015)

Zhu, H., Hu, J., Chang, S., Lu, L.: ShakeIn: secure user authentication of smartphones with single-handed shakes. IEEE Trans. Mob. Comput. **16**(10), 2901–2912 (2017)

A System to Find the Change of One's Vision Implicitly

Xiaolin Fang[1,2]($\boxtimes$), Weiwei Wu[1], Ran Bi[3], Wei Bian[4], and Zenghui Zhang[4]

[1] School of Computer Science and Engineering, Southeast University, Nanjing, China
{xiaolin,weiweiwu}@seu.edu.cn
[2] Key Laboratory of Embedded System and Service Computing (Tongji University),
Ministry of Education, Shanghai, China
[3] School of Computer Science and Technology, Dalian University of Technology,
Dalian, China
biran@dlut.edu.cn
[4] Tianjin Jinhang Institute of Computing Technologies, Tianjin, China
bianwei8427@163.com, ht8357@sina.com

Abstract. Myopia has become one of the most serious health problems in the world as it grows rapidly in the young people. Efficient vision monitoring methods are required to determine myopia in its early stages so as to take it for further treatment. Current technologies for vision examination are usually either expensive or time costly. This paper proposes a nearsightedness monitoring system, which exploits the widely used smartphones to detect the deterioration of nearsightedness by monitoring and analyzing the distance between the eyes and the smartphone screen. The detection process is implicit since the system is implemented on the daily used phones and people do not have to be interrupted frequently. The proposed system consists of two key components: activity recognition component and the eye detecting component. The activity recognition component is used to determine whether a person is watching the phone. Once a person is watching the phone, the eye detecting component can be triggered to click a photograph of the person using the front camera of the phone and localize the two eyes on the picture taken. The distance between eyes and the screen is estimated by the ratio of the two-eye distance in the picture and the width of the picture. This paper uses the 3-axis acceleration sensor and the front camera which are equipped on most of the smartphones for activity recognition and eye detection respectively. A prototype for has been developed in order to evaluate the effectiveness of the system under various environmental conditions. From more than half year monitoring period which consisted of about 20 volunteers, we were able to accurately detect the degradation of nearsightedness in two volunteers.

1 Introduction

The number of people affected by myopic has grown rapidly in the last three decades. According to a survey in 2015, over 25% of all adult Americans or 70 million people have myopic problem, and almost 300 million people in India suffer from myopia [1]. China, as the largest populated country in the world, has almost half or 600 million myopic people [2]. Additionally, almost 90% of the students in Chinese universities are nearsighted.

Eyeglasses is the primary option to treat the visual symptoms of those with myopia [3–5]. However, glasses may have the potential to make myopia worse, as they increase the necessity to focus by the eyes [6]. Efficient mechanism is required for people with myopia to check whether their nearsightedness is becoming worse, so as to remind them of their eye health, change eyeglasses or visit a doctor for further treatments.

Current technologies for accurate vision examination is typically performed by a specialized doctor, the ophthalmologist, or by an optometrist or orthopedist [7–9]. Usually, an autorefractor or retinoscope are used to give an initial objective assessment of the refractive status of each individual eye, then a phoropter is used to subjectively refine the patient's eyeglass prescription. Adults and children are usually advised to have eye examinations regularly, as the eye sight varies swiftly. However, the vision examination process is a time-consuming work and hence the myopia patients are probably unwilling to undergo the vision examination as per the doctor advise. Most of the myopia patients find that their nearsightedness is becoming worse only when they have problems to see things clearly. By this time, the nearsightedness would have already become worse, and the treatment becomes much more difficult.

The eye chart examination is an inaccurate way to test ones' vision. People can test their vision every day using an eye chart. However, most people leave the eye charts unused over a period of time. When they find some problem of their vision, it would have already been too late. Additionally, this examination can neither record the vision degradation process not it can remind the myopia patients to perform an accurate vision examination.

This paper presents a system to monitor the status of nearsightedness. It will automatically detect whether a person is watching a phone, and estimate the distance between their eyes and the screen. Through a long time monitoring, the system will be able to predict if one's nearsightedness is getting worse.

This paper employs a 3-axis acceleration sensor and the front camera which are equipped on the smartphones currently to perform the detection process. The 3-axis acceleration sensor is used to determine whether a user is watching a phone. It achieves activity recognition by analyzing the 3-axis acceleration pattern in different environmental conditions. It then takes the picture of the user's head and send it to the cloud center. The cloud center detects the two eyes through face detection algorithm and sends back the positions of them. The eye-screen distance is then estimated by calculating the ratio of the two-eye distance and the picture width. The activity recognition is implemented before the eye-screen distance estimation so as to the reduce the number of pictures sent to cloud center, thus reducing the transmission cost. The system provides an oscillograph of the historical data from which the users can view the changing process of their nearsightedness at any time. It will store the pictures on the cloud center and record eye-screen distance in case data is lost by the user. Once the user's nearsightedness is becoming worse, an alarm is triggered thus warning the people from long time affects of myopia.

The contributions of this paper are as follows.

- To the best of our knowledge, this is the first work to study the nearsightedness monitoring problem with the exploration of widely used smart phone.
- A system is provided to analyze the status of one's nearsightedness without the interruption of the users.
- The system provides an user friendly interface. People can also view the changing process of one's nearsightedness.
- When one's nearsightedness is getting worse, the system will remind people to visit a doctor for further treatment and also be able to remind people not to read very closely for long intervals of time.
- Experiments are conducted under various environmental conditions on thirteen volunteers to evaluate the effectiveness of our system.

The rest of this paper is organized as follows. Section 2 reviews the related works. Section 3 presents the overview of our system. The activity recognition is performed in Sect. 4 and the eye-screen distance estimation is described in Sect. 5. The performance evaluation results are presented in Sect. 6 and Sect. 7 discuss other factors needed to be considered in the system. Section 2 introduces the related work and Sect. 8 concludes the paper.

2 Motivation and Challenges

2.1 Motivation

Myopia is one of the serious concerns around the globe that is often neglected by the people. It has also become common among youngsters and can only be found after a long term of near reading. By the time people find symptoms of myopia, like seeing things unclear, it would have already been too late for efficient treatment of the condition. Therefore, it is important for some efficient method to detect whether the myopia in its early stages.

An ophthalmologist can accurately tell the status of a person's eyes. However, it is costly and time consuming and hence people ignore regular visits to their ophthalmologist. Most people think it as a trouble and are unwilling to see a doctor. Usually, when a person's degree of myopia becomes more serious, they need to get closer to objects so as to see them clearer. Inspired by this observation, we try to detect whether a person is seeing things closer. Smartphones in today's world are equipped with many sensors, camera and has become an indispensable equipment in daily life. Thus, they can be used to detect if a person is watching his phone closer. Therefore, we have designed a system to detect the status of myopia using smartphones.

2.2   Challenges and Approach

The goal of our system is to detect the change in the eye-screen distances along a long period of time. Therefore, the quality of the eye-screen distance measurement is very critical. The eye-screen distance measurement is affected by the following problems: when and how to estimate the eye-screen distance and how to eliminate the fluctuation in the eye-screen distances over a period of time.

Because people use smartphone frequently, eye-screen distance varies rapidly. For example, a person might turn his head around or move his hand suddenly while watching his phone. Therefore, when to estimate the eye-screen distance is crucial. The time to sample the eye-screen distance is dependent on whether a person is watching his phone in a normal and stable mode. To address this challenge, we have divided our proposed method into two components. The first component, activity recognition component, will address the challenge of when to capture the data.

Additionally, the smartphones are rarely equipped with telemeters and hence accurate detection of the eye-screen distance is hard. But most of the smartphones are commonly equipped with sensors like accelerator, gyroscope, and camera. Hence, it is a challenge to estimate the eye-screen distance with such sensors. In order to estimate distance, we have incorporated a second component in the proposed method, called Eye Localization. This component uses the ratio of the distance between two-eyes that is captured on the picture taken with the width of the picture to estimate the eye-screen distance. It is difficult to accurately measure the eye-screen distance. However, in the process of monitoring of the nearsightedness, we do not require the accurate distance between eye and screen. Instead, our goal is to observe the changes in the eye-screen distance. Therefore, we use a relative distance rather than an absolute distance to illustrate the status of a person's nearsightedness.

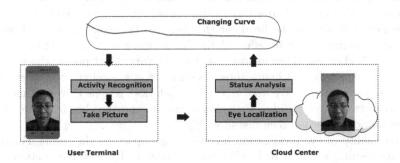

Fig. 1. System architecture

As mentioned earlier, the eye-screen distance varies in a short time. But, it also varies over days. However, this fluctuation of the eye-screen distance does not mean that the nearsightedness has changed, but it is rather a normal phenomenon. Therefore, eliminating such fluctuation of the eye-screen distance is another challenge. To address this challenge, we use three steps in order to eliminate the fluctuation in the eye-screen distances. Initially, an outlier detection method is employed to filter the outliers which are otherwise called as noise data. Then, a representation method is used to select one eye-screen distance to average the distances calculated in a particular day. Finally, the least squares method is adopted to find the tendency of degradation of a person's nearsightedness.

3   System Overview

An overview of our system is shown in Fig. 1. As shown in the picture, the system initializes activity recognition component as soon as the user turns on their cell phone. At the right time, it will take the picture of the user and send to the cloud center. The cloud center runs face recognition software which detects the face and localizes the two eyes. The original picture and the position of the two eyes are stored in the cloud center. An analysis process is performed periodically. People can see the changing curve of the status of their eyes, and it can also alert people to take a treatment when a deterioration of their nearsightedness occurs. Because the system is implemented implicitly at the background, therefore, it will not interrupt people' daily use of the phones.

The activity recognition component is used to capture the stable state of the activities of watching the smartphone screen. A temporary or sudden movement of the head or body will have a strong impact on monitoring the result. Therefore, the activity recognition is very important. In the entire monitoring processes, a high quality of activity recognition can greatly reduce the transmission data amount and improve the monitoring accuracy.

The key component of our system is the accurate localization of the two eyes in a given picture. The eye-screen distance is estimated by the ratio of the distance between the two eyes in the picture and the width of the picture. Other metrics can also be used to estimate the eye-screen distance, such as the size of the face, the size of the head, or the distance between two ears. However, these measurement may be effected by the person's hair in a picture. When the hairstyle changes, these measurement might vary. Most people change their hairstyles frequently and hence these metrics are not good choices to estimate the eye-screen distance. We need a metric which does not vary over a time. The distance between two eyes has such characteristic, and thus has been chosen for the estimation the eye-screen distance (Fig. 2).

The quality of eye localization has a strong impact on the result. For more accurate results, we need to localize the iris center. The distance between the two iris centers of a person can indicate the absolute distance between two eyes. However, the distance between the two iris centers of a person changes slightly when the eyeball moves. For example, when a person looks far away, the distance between his iris centers is larger. Contrarily, if a person looks at his nose tip, then his eyes converge, and thus the distance between his iris centers is closer. In this paper, the slight distance variation caused by looking far away or looking at one's nose tip. This is because our system alway takes picture when a person

(a) Hold phone far away   (b)   Hold phone near

Fig. 2. Moving range of one's hand

is looking at the phone which is held by the hand, the length of one's hand is limited, thus, the moving range of one's hand is limited, so the two-eye distance variation is limited.

4   Activity Recognition

The goal of our activity recognition is to improve the performance of eye-screen distance estimation and reduce the data transmission cost. Therefore, we need to initially detect if the user is watching his phone. We use the 3-axis acceleration sensors to detect the watching activity.

Through analysis of the characteristics of the 3-axis acceleration data, it is easy to find that all the curves for 3-axis acceleration data in x-axis, y-axis and z-axis vary in very small ranges. For example, the values of x-axis varies within the range of $[-0.5, 0]$, and the values of y-axis and z-axis have the same characteristic. In a special case where a person places his phone on the table, the varying ranges of the 3-axis acceleration data are smaller than that in watching activities, the variance is also little. But other activities show great difference from the watch activity, where the variance is greatly larger.

Hence, the degree of the varying range is a strong feature to classify whether one is watching his phone. We use the features similar as that in [10]. The used features include average acceleration for each axis, standard deviation for each axis, and average of the square roots of the sum of the squared values of each axis $\sqrt{x^2 + y^2 + z^2}$. Finally, we used a decision tree method to detect the watching activity. The activity recognition accuracy can achieve above 85%.

Note that, the activity recognition component may have errors, and it may take the wrong picture, which may not include a person's head. In this case, it does not matter, because the face recognition and eye-screen distance estimation process will avoid and filter these errors. For other errors, the outlier detection method in the eye-screen distance estimation can filter some of the errors.

In order to reduce the energy consumption, we do not detect the watching activity all the time. It is only detected at the first few minutes when the screen is unlocked by the user. And once it captures the required number of pictures for a day, then the system stops implementing the activity recognition and the eye-screen distance estimation components.

5 Eye-Screen Distance Estimation

5.1 Eye Localization

Our system needs to compute the distance between two eyes of a person on a picture taken so as to estimate the eye-screen distance. Therefore, the first problem that needs to be addressed is to localize the two eyes on a picture. This paper uses Face++ system for localizing two eyes on a given picture [11]. Face++ is a cloud service platform. It provides service that developers can quickly integrate facial recognition feature into their products. It focuses on the development of the world's best face detection, identification, analysis and reconstruction techniques. Figure 3 shows an example of the eye localization in Face++ system. Experiments suggested that the localization accuracy is quite high for our system.

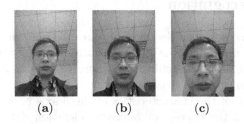

(a)   (b)   (c)

Fig. 3. Eye localization

5.2 Eye-Screen Distance

As shown in Fig. 3, when the face of person is far from the screen, then the two eyes are closer to each other in the captured picture (Fig. 3(a)). In contrast, when the face of person is closer to the screen, then the two-eye distance is far from each other Fig. 3(c). Therefore, based on this observation, we can use the distance between two eyes in the picture to estimate the eye-screen distance.

The eye-screen distance estimation is illustrated in Fig. 4. In Fig. 4, s is the position of camera and 2α is the angle of the camera's view. When the face of the person is sd_1 away from the camera, then the width of the camera's field view is AB, where e_1 and e_2 are the positions of the two eyes. When the face of the person is sd_2 away from the camera, then the width of the camera's field view is CD, where e_1' and e_2' are the positions of the two eyes.

$$\frac{AB}{2 \cdot sd_1} = \frac{CD}{2 \cdot sd_2} = \tan \alpha \tag{1}$$

The eye-screen distance is estimated by the ratio of the distance between two eyes and the picture width. For the above mentioned scenario,

$$ratio_1 = \frac{e_1 e_2}{AB} \tag{2}$$

$$ratio_2 = \frac{e_1' e_2'}{CD} \tag{3}$$

Also it should be noted that $e_1 e_2 = e_1' e_2'$. Therefore, from Eq. (1), (2) and (3),

$$\frac{ratio_1}{ratio_2} = \frac{sd_2}{sd_1} \tag{4}$$

Equation 4 shows that the estimated distance has an inverse relation to the real eye-screen distance based on the previously mentioned fact that the eyes are closer if the person's face is far away and eyes are distant if the face is near by.

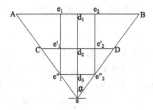

Fig. 4. Eye-screen distance estimation

Let the distance between the centers of the two eyeballs be e, and the distance between the face and the screen be d, then the distance between the two eyes can be represented as $ratio = \frac{e}{2d \tan \alpha}$. Assume that the actual distance between the centers of the two eyeballs be e and the angle of the camera's view $2 \cdot \alpha$, then we can get the absolute eye-screen distance d by Eq. (5).

$$d = \frac{e}{2 \cdot ratio \cdot \tan \alpha} \tag{5}$$

This paper uses the ratio of the distance between the two eyes and the picture width to estimate the eye-screen distance rather than measuring the accurate eye-screen distance. Hence it is a relative distance and the user can use this distance to find the status of a person's eyes. If the ratio is larger, then the real eye-screen distance is smaller, and vice-versa. Therefore, if the ratio is becoming more and more bigger, it indicates the system that the nearsightedness may be becoming worse.

5.3 Find Outliers

Figure 5 is an example of the raw data of the distances between the two eyes collected from a user. The x-axis represents the days and the y-axis represents the distance between two eyes. It is to be noted that in our paper, this distance is relative. The points in a day are ploted vertically in Fig. 5, some points in day may be far away from others, and these points are considered to be outliers. We need to a mechanism to filter such outliers.

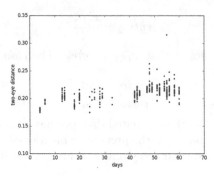

Fig. 5. Raw data

In this paper, we have used the LOF (Local Outlier Factor) method [12] to filter such outliers. Let, $d(p,q)$ be the distance between p and q, the $k\text{–}dis(p)$ of a point p be the distance between p and its kth nearest neighbor, the $N_k(p)$ as all the neighbors whose distances to p are less than $k\text{–}dis(p)$. and $reach\text{–}dist_k(p,o) = max\{k\text{–}dis(o), d(p,o)\}$

$$lrd_k(p) = \frac{|N_k(p)|}{\sum\limits_{o \in N_k(p)} reach\text{–}dist_k(p,o)} \tag{6}$$

Intuitively, the local reachability density of an object p is the inverse of the average reachability distance based on the kth nearest neighbors of p. The local outlier factor of an object p is defined as follows:

$$LOF_k(p) = \frac{\sum\limits_{o \in N_k(p)} \frac{lrd_k(o)}{lrd_k(p)}}{|N_k(p)|} \tag{7}$$

The local outlier factor of object p represents the degree to which we call p as an outlier. We can observe that the lower p's local reachability density is, and the higher the local reachability densities of p's k-nearest neighbors are, and then the higher is the LOF value of p.

LOF values will be affected by the choice of k value. By experimentation, we found that $k = 6$ can derive an acceptable effect. As shown in Fig. 6(**a**), k is set to 3, and some of the outliers have been filtered out, but not all. As shown in Fig. 6(**b**), when k is set to 6, most of the obvious outliers are filtered out from the data. Note that, the outlier is defined in one day, that is, we filter those points which are apparently different from other points for each day.

5.4 Median as Representation

Although the LOF method can filter many outliers in the raw data, there still exists some uncertainty in the filtered result. The LOF will filter those points which are obviously different from other points. However, for a given day, some

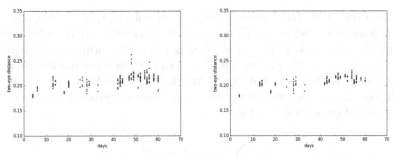

(a) Filter outliers with LOF by setting (b) Filter outliers with LOF by setting
$k = 3$ $k = 6$

Fig. 6. Different LOF settings

points that are not marked by LOF may still be different from others. We need
to eliminate the impact of such situations. Therefore, we have considered two
additional solutions, one is averaging the distance in each day, and the other is
to find the median distance in each day. By experimentation, we have confirmed
that using the median distance as the representation for each day is a better
solution. An example is shown in Fig. 7(a).

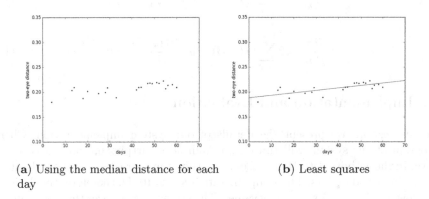

(a) Using the median distance for each   (b) Least squares
day

Fig. 7. Median and least squares

5.5 Least Squares

The method of least squares is a standard approach in regression analysis to
the approximate the solution of an over determined system for fitting a given
data set as shown in Fig. 7(b). Least squares iteratively minimizes the sum of
the squares of the errors between a model function and the given data set. The
objective of this approach is to adjust the parameters of a model function to best

fit the data set. A simple data set consists of n points $(x_i, y_i), i = 0, ..., n - 1$, where x_i is an independent variable and y_i is a dependent variable whose values are found by observation. The model function has the form $f(x, \beta)$, where β consists of the adjustable parameters. The goal is to find the parameter values in β for the model function that "best" fits the data. The least squares method finds the optimum parameters when the sum of squared errors is minimum. The sum of squared errors is defined as

$$S = \sum_{i=0}^{n-1} (f(x, \beta) - y_i)^2 \tag{8}$$

Objective of our method is to detect the worsening of a person's nearsightedness, we use a straight line in two dimensions to demonstrate the tendency of the nearsightedness. A straight line model function can be given by

$$f(x, \beta) = \beta_1 x + \beta_0 \tag{9}$$

The least squares will calculate the optimum β_1 and β_0 for a given dataset.

The minimum S is found by setting the gradient to zero. Since the model consists of 2 parameters, there are 2 gradient equations:

$$\frac{\partial S}{\partial \beta_0} = 2 \sum_{i=0}^{n-1} (f(x, \beta) - y_i) \frac{\partial f(x, \beta)}{\partial \beta_0} = 0 \tag{10}$$

$$\frac{\partial S}{\partial \beta_1} = 2 \sum_{i=0}^{n-1} (f(x, \beta) - y_i) \frac{\partial f(x, \beta)}{\partial \beta_1} = 0 \tag{11}$$

6   Implementation and Evaluation

In this section, we present the details of our system implementation. Client program of our system will run on an Android smartphone, and is written in Java. In the activity detection process, we study the characteristic of acceleration data of a period of 4.5 s. The sampling rate is set to 10 Hz, therefore, the decision window consists of 45 x, y, z-axis values. The system always uses the front camera to take pictures when it detects the user is watching his phone. We use 640×480 frames and compress each frame into a JPEG image (quality level $= 50$) to reduce the transmission cost.

6.1   Dataset

We have studied 20 volunteers (with or without myopia) in Southeast University who uses Android smartphones as a part of data collection process. About 10 pictures of every volunteer will be captured every day. Actually more than 10 pictures would be Because of many reasons such as, no Internet access, data collection for some volunteer's on those days was not possible. We have ignored such cases based on the fact that the nearsightedness is unlikely to change in a few days. The collected data includes the pictures taken by the volunteers every day and the eye locations in the picture recognized by the Face++ system. We have collected about 10000 pictures from 20 people for half year. Data of some volunteers may missed for some days, for reasons like when they lost or broke their smartphone, however, it does not matter since the changing trend can also be found for a long time, and some the missed data would not influence the detection result.

6.2   Detection Result

It is quite difficult to find the changing trend from the raw data. However, after the application of out-lier filtering, the median representation, the least squares process and simple threshold setting, it is clear to find whether one's vision is become worse or not. Figure 8 shows how the vision of 20 volunteers is changing. It can be found that there are three people whose vision is becoming worse. Among the three detected people, two are true positive, and one is false positive. The left 17 people are all not found to have vision changing after the eye test after half year.

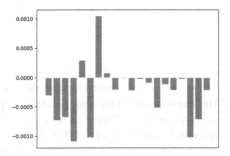

Fig. 8. Changing rate of one's vision

Among the collected data, the plots do not reveal appropriate information. However, after the application of out-lier filtering, the median representation and the least squares process, we were able to accurately detect two people whose farsightedness is getting worse. The eye-screen distance changing curves of these two people are shown in Fig. 9(b) and Fig. 9(a). The y-axis of these figure represents the ratio of the distance between the two eyes in the picture and the width of the picture. From Fig. 9(b), the changing tendency cannot be observed by a naked eye. But the Least Squares method of our system detect the tendency as shown in Fig. 9(b). The missed data in this figure is because of some reason the system fails and the error is found after a long time. But it still reveals the vision's changing process. Once all the people undergoes their vision examinations, our system predicted those two people whose eye-screen distances become closer. Myopia of both of these two people changes by −0.25 Diopters. For the people in Fig. 9(b), both two eyes decrease by −0.25 Diopters. And for the people in Fig. 9(a), only one eye decreases by −0.25 Diopters. In our system, if the people are classified by checking whether the least square line increases or not, then one false positive case is found and there is no true negative case.

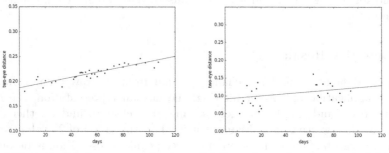

(a) First people whose nearsightedness is becoming worse

(b) Second people whose nearsightedness is becoming worse

Fig. 9. Experiment illustration

7   Discussion

We were able to accurately detect the exact two people whose nearsightedness is becoming worse for the experiment. This was possible as the eye localization accuracy in our system is quite high. Based on our test, 0.5 cm difference in actual eye-screen distance can be easily detected. If the system can take the right picture, then it can certainly detect whether one's vision is changing. Therefore, taking the right pictures is very important in our system. Our activity recognition module is a lightweight component which can filter many cases such as sudden movement in the hand or head, walking, and so on. But it can not take the right picture every time as the person using this system may watch his phone at different distances. Hence, it is essential to capture images while the person is watching his phone at the distance within a threshold.

Our system cannot accurately measure the distance between one's eyes and the phone while he is using the phone. It estimates the eye-screen distance by the ratio of the distance between the two eyes in the picture and the width of the picture. A more accurate approach can be used to measure the eye-screen distance instead of estimation.

It does not include a module for identifying different persons using the same phone. It assumes that a single person will be using the phone all the time. This identification can be achieved by other components such as fingerprint recognition, face recognition, behavior recognition and so on. Eye-screen distance pattern can also be mined to identify the owner of a phone and a stranger. This branches a new research topic. In our future work, a hybrid of eye-screen distance pattern mining and face recognition, fingerprint recognition or other technologies will be used to achieve the identification of different people.

It also assumes that people do not change their smartphones frequently. Different types of smartphones may be equipped with different types of cameras. If they do change, the new smartphone might be equipped with a camera whose focal length is different than the previous. Hence the picture size varies and so does the calculation of eye-screen distance of our system. Our system does not include the normalization of pictures taken by different types of cameras.

8 Conclusions

This paper proposes a nearsightedness monitoring system which utilizes the widely used smartphones to detect the deterioration of nearsightedness by monitoring and analyzing the distance between the eyes and the smartphone screen. The system is implemented implicitly and will not interrupt the users frequently. After the activity monitoring module, a picture will be taken to localize the two eyes. The distance between eyes and the screen is estimated by the ratio of the distance between the two eyes in the picture and the width of the picture. An outlier filter is incorporated to filter out most of the noise, accompanied with the Least Square method to detect the changing tendency of eye-screen distance. From a half-year monitoring of about 20 volunteers, although it is impossible to find the changing trend of one's vision from the raw data, but after a series of data filtering and processing, we were able to accurately detect the two volunteers whose nearsightedness is becoming worse.

Acknowledgments. This work was supported in part by National Key Research & Development Program of China under Grant 2017YFB1003000, 2018YFB2100300, National Natural Science Foundation of China under grant No. 61972083, 61632008, 61972088, 61972086, 61702097, 61602084, 61672154, 61602111, Key Laboratory of Computer Network and Information Integration of Ministry of Education of China under Grant No. 93K-9, Jiangsu Provincial Key Laboratory of Network and Information Security under Grant No. BM2003201 and Collaborative Innovation Center of Novel Software Technology and Industrialization, Jiangsu Provincial Scientific and Technological Achievements Transfer Fund under Grant No. BA2016052.

References

1. Smith, M.J., Walline, J.J.: Controlling myopia progression in children and adolescents. Adolesc. Health Med. Ther. **6**, 133–140 (2015)
2. Lin, B., Liao, X., Department of Ophthalmology: Study on the influencing factors and prevention measures of juvenile myopia in China. China Health Stand. Manag. **8**(20), 1–2 (2017)
3. Jung, J.J., Lim, E., Baek, S., Kim, Y., Gong, S., Kim, U.: Attempts to reduce the progression of myopia and spectacle prescriptions during childhood: a survey of eye specialists. Korean J. Ophthalmol. **25**(6), 417–420 (2011)

4. Smith III, E.L.: A case for peripheral optical treatment strategies for myopia. Optom. Vis. Sci. **88**(9), 1029–1044 (2011)
5. Cheng, S., Cai, Z., Li, J., Fang, X.: Drawing dominant dataset from big sensory data in wireless sensor networks. In: Computer Communications, pp. 531–539 (2015)
6. Jamal, N., Cooper, J., Schulman, E.: Current status on the development and treatment of myopia. Optom. Vis. Sci. **83**(5), 179–199 (2012)
7. Monger, L.J., Wilkins, A.J., Allen, P.M.: Identifying visual stress during a routine eye examination. J. Optom. **8**(2), 140–145 (2015)
8. Stainer, M.J., Anderson, A.J., Denniss, J.: Examination strategies of experienced and novice clinicians viewing the retina. Ophthalmic Physiol. Opt. **35**(4), 424–432 (2015)
9. Kahn, J.H., Robinett, D.A.: The physical examination of the eye. Emerg. Med. Clin. North Am. **26**, 1–16 (2008)
10. Kwapisz, J.R., Weiss, G.M., Moore, S.A.: Activity recognition using cell phone accelerometers. SIGKDD Explor. Newsl. **12**(2), 74–82 (2011)
11. Megvii Inc.: Face++ research toolkit. www.faceplusplus.com, December 2013
12. Breunig, M.M., Kriegel, H.-P., Ng, R.T., Sander, J.: LOF: identifying density-based local outliers. In: Proceedings of the 2000 ACM SIGMOD International Conference on Management of Data, SIGMOD 2000, pp. 93–104. ACM, New York (2000)

Internet of Things and Edge Computing

Energy-Aware Marginal Multi-attribute Federated Query in IoT Networks

Xiaocui Li and Zhangbing Zhou[✉]

China University of Geosciences (Beijing), Beijing, China
lixiaocui.cugb@gmail.com, zhangbing.zhou@gmail.com

Abstract. The popularity of smart things constructs sensing networks for the *Internet of Things* (*IoT*), and promotes intelligent decision-makings in industrial *IoT* applications, where multi-attribute query processing is an essential ingredient. Considering the huge number of smart things and large-scale of the network, traditional query processing mechanisms may not be applicable, since they mostly depend on a centralized index tree structure. To address this issue, this paper proposes an energy-aware *M*arginal multi-attribute *F*ederated *Q*uery mechanism (*MFQ*) in edge computing, where an energy-aware marginal query graph is established to facilitate multi-attribute query for marginal smart things contained in marginal edge networks. The experimental results show that *MFQ* performs better compared with the rivals in reducing network traffic and energy consumption for industrial *IoT* applications.

Keywords: Multi-attribute federated query · Energy-aware marginal query graph · Edge computing · IoT networks

1 Introduction

With the prevalence of smart things being ubiquitously deployed, tremendous data with multi-attributes are dynamically generated in the *Internet of Things* (*IoT*) networks. This development promotes spatial keyword queries with multi-attribute, which takes into account the spatial location, text description, and attributes of smart things [1,2]. Considering huge amounts of smart things involved in the query processing, smart things are typically scarce in their computational, communication, and energy resources [3]. In this setting, we argue that it is an indispensable ingredient for decreasing energy consumption of networks by aggregating sensory data of certain smart things requires to reduce the amount of data packets to be transmitted in *IoT* networks. Generally, sensory data of smart things should be in-network gathered, and processed in a localized fashion when possible, while only results should be aggregated and routed to the centre for further exploration. Due to this concern, edge computing [4,5], as the complement of cloud computing, has been proposed in recent years, which enables spatial multi-attribute queries to be handled in a distributed and localized manner. Considering the functional diversity of smart things and

© Springer Nature Switzerland AG 2020
Z. Yu et al. (Eds.): GPC 2020, LNCS 12398, pp. 335–346, 2020.
https://doi.org/10.1007/978-3-030-64243-3_25

the complexity of potential events to be studied, developing a collaborative and interactive mechanism is essential to support the marginal multi-attribute federated query in edge computing.

Recently, many query expansion methods have been proposed to improve the results of spatial keyword attribute queries [6,7]. In [8], authors study continuous range queries over multi-attribute trajectories for data acquisition of mobile objects in edge computing, thereby supporting the query for moving object trajectories. In [9], authors propose a spatial keyword query method that can support semantic approximate query, which makes it possible for users to obtain semantically relevant objects. In addition, some researchers focus on improve the efficiency of queries [10,11]. For graph queries, in most real scenarios, only critical vertices on the shortest path are desirable and it is unnecessary to query all vertices. In [12], authors propose a top-k Critical Vertices query (kCV) on the shortest path, where the performance of kCV is verified on centralized and distributed platforms. In [13], authors consider that different sub-retrieval queries (e.g., image retrieves text and text retrieves image) have unique characteristics. Thus, authors propose a task-dependent and query-dependent subspace learning approach for cross-modal retrieval. Generally, these techniques have been developed to enable querying smart things. However, considering the fact that the network greenness requires reducing network traffic and energy consumption [14], sensory data of smart things should be processed in a localized and distributed manner as much as possible. Therefore, an energy-aware marginal multi-attribute federated query is a promising challenge in edge networks.

To address this issue, we propose an energy-aware Marginal multi-attribute Federated Query mechanism (MFQ) in edge computing, where an energy-aware marginal query graph is established to facilitate multi-attribute query for marginal smart things contained in marginal edge networks. In this paper, major contributions are summarized as follows:

- We propose a novel MFQ mechanism for addressing the multi-attribute query problem in IoT networks, which can be modeled and formulated as an optimization problem.
- Extensive experiments have been conducted to evaluate the efficiency of MFQ. The experimental results show that MFQ performs better compared with the rivals in reducing network traffic and energy consumption.

The remainder of this paper is organized as follows. Section 2 introduces energy model, which are used in this paper. Section 3 presents marginal multi-Attribute federated query mechanism in marginal edge networks. Section 4 shows the implementation and evaluates the approach developed in this paper. Section 5 reviews and discusses related techniques. Section 6 concludes this paper.

2   Energy Model

The first-order radio model [15] is applied in this paper. Parameters of this energy model are presented in Table 1. The energy consumption for transmitting

Table 1. Parameters are used in the energy model.

Name	Description
b	The number of bits in one packet
d	The transmission distance
α	The transmission attenuation index
E_{lct}	A constant of energy consumption for the transmit and receiver electronics
ϵ_{mpl}	A constant of energy consumption for the transmit amplifier
$E_{Tx}(b, d)$	Energy consumption for transmitting a b bit packet with a distance d
$E_{Rx}(b)$	Energy consumption for receiving a b bit packet
$E_{ij}(b)$	Energy consumption for transmitting a b bit packet from a smart thing SmT_i to another smart thing SmT_j

a b bit data packet with a distance d are denoted as $E_{Tx}(b, d)$, and the energy consumption for receiving a b bit data packet are denoted as $E_{Rx}(b)$, which can be calculated as follows:

$$E_{Tx}(b, d) = E_{lct} \times b + \epsilon_{mpl} \times b \times d^{\alpha} \tag{1}$$

$$E_{Rx}(b) = E_{lct} \times b \tag{2}$$

Note that E_{lct} is the constant of energy consumption for transmission and receiver electronics, and ϵ_{mpl} is the constant of transmission amplifier. α depends on the surrounding environment. Generally, when smart things are barrier-free for forwarding data packets, α is set to 2. Otherwise, α is set to a value between 3 to 5. $E_{ij}(b)$ indicates the energy consumption for transmitting a packet of b bits from one thing to another, which is calculated as follows:

$$E_{ij}(b) = E_{Tx}(b, d) + E_{Rx}(b) \tag{3}$$

3   Marginal Multi-attribute Federated Query

Definition 1 Marginal Multi-attribute Federated Query. A marginal multi-attribute federated query is defined as a tuple $fq = (Rn, Kd, Ctn)$, where:

- $Rn = (x, y, wt, ht)$ is a rectangle region of fq, where x and y are the top-left coordinate, and wt and ht are the width and height of fq, respectively.
- $Kd = \{kd_1, kd_2, \ldots, kd_n\}$ represents a set of queried attributes that are interested by fq.
- Ctn is a set of constraints defined by fq.

Generally, $fq.Rn$ is a two-dimensional network space, where smart things are deployed. In addition, $q.Rn$ may be covered by an edge network, or by multiple contiguous edge networks, and fq is processed through the collaboration of multiple edge nodes.

3.1 Cost Calculation of Queried Packets Transmitting for Marginal Edge Nodes

Given coordinates of SmT_i (x_i, y_i) and SmT_j (x_j, y_j), we define by:

$$dT = \sqrt{(x_i - x_j)^2 + (y_i - y_j)^2} \div r \qquad (4)$$

where r represents communication radius of SmT_i or SmT_j, and dT represents the spatial scope of transmitted data. Accordingly, we define that ψ is a baseline parameter to specify the spatial scope of smart things which require to transmit queried packets. For example, if dT is not more than specified ψ, which means that SmT_i is within the scope of interactive data.

Algorithm 1 Cost Calculation of Queried Packets Transmitting

Require:
- ψ : a parameter of boundary distance percentage
- nmb : the number of edge nodes
- RS : collections of queried results of all edge networks

Ensure:
- mtx_{wgt} : a weighted adjacency matrix

1: **for** $i = 0; i < nmb; i++$ **do**
2:   **for** $j = 0; j < nmb; j++$ **do**
3:     **if** $i \neq j$ **and** gd_i **and** gd_j are marginal **then**
4:       $gdRS \leftarrow \emptyset$
5:       **while** each $RS_j \subset RS \neq NULL$ **do**
6:         $Temp \leftarrow$ get certain kind of attribute set from RS_j
7:         $O \leftarrow \emptyset$
8:         **while** $Temp \neq NULL$ **do**
9:           **if** $dT \leq \psi$ **then**
10:            $O \leftarrow O \cup \{o\}$
11:          **end if**
12:         **end while**
13:         $gdRS \leftarrow gdRS \cup O$
14:       **end while**
15:       $mtx_{gd}[i][j] \leftarrow gdRS$
16:       $b \leftarrow$ Obtain transmission data of $gdRS$
17:       $d \leftarrow$ Euclidean distance of gd_i and gd_j
18:       $mtx_{wgt}[i][j] \leftarrow E_{ij}(b)$
19:     **end if**
20:   **end for**
21: **end for**

Cost calculation of queried packets transmitting for marginal edge nodes is presented in Algorithm 1. Firstly, queried results of each edge network are obtained (lines 6–7). Then, queried packets for marginal edge nodes are obtained by ψ and dT (lines 9–11). Furthermore, $E_{ij}(b)$ of gd_i and gd_j is calculated by Eq. 3 (lines 16–17), where d of gd_i and gd_j is defined as a 2-d Euclidean distance. Finally, the result of transmitting cost for marginal edge nodes is stored in $mtx_{wgt}[i][j]$ (line 18).

3.2   Marginal Multi-attribute Federated Query Model

The transmitting of queried packets can be modeled as an optimization problem. An energy-aware marginal query graph is established to facilitate multi-attribute query, where the energy consumption is considered as the decision factor:

$$F = \Sigma_{i=1}^{n} \Sigma_{j=1}^{n} w_{ij} \times k_{ij} \tag{5}$$

where:

$$k_{ij} = \begin{cases} 1, & (w_{ji} \neq 0 \text{ and } w_{ij} \leq w_{ji}) \\ 0, & (\text{otherwise}); \end{cases} \tag{6}$$

where w_{ij} ($w_{ij} \neq 0$) represents the energy consumption of transmitting queried packets from gd_i to gd_j, and k_{ij} is determined by the comparison of the energy values between gd_i and gd_j. By F, we can achieve a minimum of energy consumption for data communication within a reasonably acceptable range.

4   Implementation and Evaluation

The prototype assessment has been taken in a Java program, and experiments have been conducted on a desktop with an Intel i5-6500 CPU at 3.20 GHz, 16-GB of memory and 64-bit Windows 10 system.

4.1   Baseline Methods

MFQ is benchmarked with two baseline methods of energy consumption for packet routing for queries, namely *Query-Greedy* (*Q-G*) and *Query-Random* (*Q-R*):

- *Q-G*: Each edge node routes packets to a certain edge node which has the most residual energy, and is within the communication range.
- *Q-R*: Each node routes packets to a random edge node as long as that edge node has enough residual energy and is within the communication range.

In this paper, we evaluate three approaches, namely *MFQ*, *Q-R* and *Q-G*, using the metrics of energy consumption of transmitted queried packets, the lower the better. In addition, we vary one parameter and keep others fixed to observe the impact of each parameter on methods in the evaluation metric. To reduce the randomness caused by the environmental configuration, experiments with a certain parameter setting is conducted twenty times, and an average value is presented as the experimental results.

Table 2. Parameters settings of experiments.

Parameters name	Value
Network query region	300 m × 300 m
Number of smart things (smt)	80 to 140
Skewness degree of IoT networks (sd)	0.1 to 0.6
Number of queried attributes (qt)	2 to 8
Percentage of boundary distance (ψ)	0.1 to 0.8
Energy consumption for transmitting and receiver electronics (E_{lct})	100 nJ/bit
Energy consumption for transmitting amplifier (ϵ_{mpl})	0.1 nJ/(bit × m^2)
Number of bits in one packet (b)	2
Attenuation transmission index (α)	2

4.2 Experiment Settings

Synthetic Datasets: In order to evaluate *MFQ*, synthetic datasets are generated by simulating a network deployed in a relatively skewness distribution. Specific parameters in experiments are presented in Table 2. Without loss of generality, a query is assumed to be relevant with 2 to 8 kinds of attributes, since queries are typically not very complex for the majority of domain applications. Besides, when kinds of attributes that queries interest are large in number, queries should hardly be clearly explained and easily understood. The number of smart things ranges from 80 to 140 with an increment of 20, and a smart thing is randomly assigned with a sensing attribute. Due to the fact that smart things may be distributed unevenly in the network, a skewness degree (denoted sd) is adopted to quantify this character and ranges from 0.1 to 0.6. Generally, sd is calculated as $(dn - sn) \div N$, where (i) dn and sn refer to the number of smart things deployed in dense and sparse sub-regions, respectively, and (ii) N is the sum of dn and sn [16].

Experimenting Parameters: In this experiments, we vary three setting parameters that may have an impact on *MFQ*:

- **Number of Smart Things (smt):** Energy consumption for numbers of smart things are deployed in *IoT* networks.
- **Varying of Skewness Degrees (sd):** Energy consumption for various skewness degrees when smart things are distributed in *IoT* networks.
- **Varying of Boundary distance** (ψ): Energy consumption for various percentages of boundary distance.
- **Kinds of Queried Attributes (qt):** Energy consumption for kinds of queried attributes specified by *fq*.

4.3 Evaluation Results

Impact of Smart Things for Energy Consumption. Figure 1 depicts the comparison of the energy consumption for *MFQ*, *Q-G*, and *Q-R* with the number

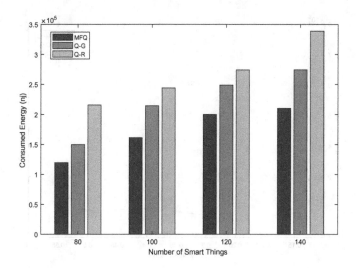

Fig. 1. Energy consumption of *MFQ*, *Q-G*, and *Q-R* with the number of smart things.

of smart things ranging from 80 to 140. Besides, the skewness degree is set to 0.6, percentage of boundary distance is set to 0.8, the number of attributes is set to 4 in a query specification. Figure 1 shows that our proposed method *MFQ* has the minimum energy consumption compared with the other methods. In fact, *Q-G*, and *Q-R* route all sensory data of smart things whose attributes is associated with specified query specifications to the centre. However, *MFQ* in our work gathers sensory data of smart things in edge networks, processes these data in a localized fashion, and only routes the result of certain edge networks to the centre. This result indicates that *MFQ* can perform better than *Q-G*, and *Q-R* in decreasing energy consumption when the network is relatively large in the number of smart things. In addition, with the increase of the number of smart things, energy consumption for *MFQ*, *Q-G*, and *Q-R* is increases accordingly. This is reasonable that when smart things are relatively larger in number, the amount of sensory data generated by smart things are processed in networks may be larger. Thus, more energy should be consumed.

Impact of Skewness Degrees for Energy Consumption. Figure 2 shows the comparison of the energy consumption for *MFQ*, *Q-G*, and *Q-R*, when the skewness degree is set from 0.1 to 0.6. The number of smart things is set to 140, and other parameters are set to the same values as those in Fig. 1. Figure 2 shows that *Q-G*, and *Q-R* methods consume much more energy than our *MFQ*. Besides, when the skewness degree is larger, energy consumption of *MFQ* is relatively smaller. Most of gathering and routing packets of sensory data should be carried out in dense sub-regions when the skewness is large, which indicates that transmission distance of most packets may be shorter. However, when smart things in networks are deployed with relatively small skewness degree, which

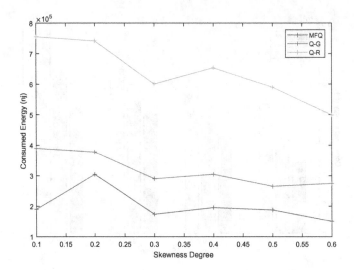

Fig. 2. Energy consumption of *MFQ*, *Q-G*, and *Q-R* with various skewness degrees.

means that smart things are distributed relatively evenly, thereby the average transmission distance of sensory data packets may be longer. In general, when smart things are distributed in a skewed fashion, Fig. 2 shows *MFQ* is more efficient in terms of network energy consumption.

Impact of Boundary Distance for Energy Consumption. Figure 3 shows the comparison of energy consumption for *MFQ*, *Q-G*, and *Q-R*, with skewness degree ranging from 0.1 to 0.8. Other parameters are the same setting as those in Fig. 1. Figure 3 depicts energy consumption of *MFQ* is lower than the competitive methods. In addition, Fig. 3 also indicates that the increase of energy consumption of *Q-G*, and *Q-R* is almost linear with the increase of the percentage of boundary distance. Since in our experiments, energy is mainly consumed in collecting and aggregating sensory data packets along a marginal query graph developed in this paper. Specially, the construction of that is mainly affected by the percentage of boundary distance. However, both *Q-G*, and *Q-R* methods adopt the strategy that edge nodes route packets to (i) a certain edge node which have the most residual energy, and (ii) a random edge node as long as that edge node has enough residual energy. Thus, *Q-G*, and *Q-R* are not bound by the percentage of boundary distance, and energy consumption of those is stable.

Impact of Queried Attributes for Energy Consumption. Figure 4 shows the comparison of the energy consumption for *MFQ*, *Q-G*, and *Q-R*, as the number of attributes rangs from 2 to 8. The skewness degree is set to 0.6, and other parameters are set to the same values as those in Fig. 1. It is intuitive that the energy consumption of our proposed *MFQ* is less than that of *Q-G*, and *Q-R*. Figure 4 also shows that the energy consumption is gradually decreased with respect to the increasing of the number of queried attributes. This result

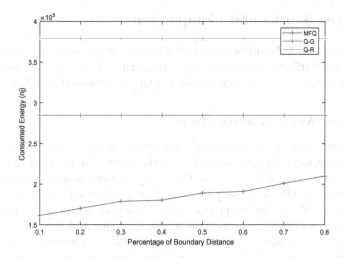

Fig. 3. Energy consumption of *MFQ*, *Q-G*, and *Q-R* with various percentages of boundary distance.

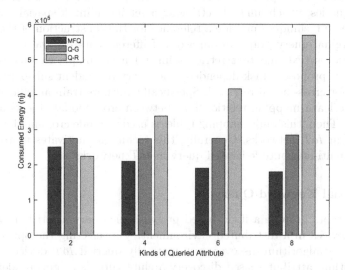

Fig. 4. Energy consumption of *MFQ*, *Q-G*, and *Q-R* with kinds of queried attributes.

is reasonable since the majority of query processing tasks is conducted locally in edge networks, only processing results of edge networks are routed to the centre. Figure 4 depicts *MFQ* should decrease the network traffic and energy consumption significantly, when the number of queried attributes is more.

5   Related Works and Comparison

In recent years, several studies strive to design the energy-aware processing methods for multi-attribute queries in edge computing. Here we elaborate on the relevant techniques and give comparisons with our proposed *MFQ* method.

5.1   Energy-Aware Routing Query

Routing-based queries are increasingly important in the recent two decades. In most real scenarios, only critical vertices on the shortest path are desirable and it is unnecessary to query all vertices. Therefore, authors propose a top-k critical vertices query on the shortest path [12]. The performance of that is verified on centralized and distributed platforms for large-scale real-world networks, and experimental results show this method is high efficiency and accuracy. To further improve the query efficiency, authors develop a query framework [17], where a series of optimization techniques are designed. Extensive experiments on large datasets have verified the performance of the developed query framework. In [18], authors further optimize query results and propose top-k collective spatial keyword queries, which aims at retrieving a set including k spatial objects. In general, these techniques provide a reference for the construction of the energy-aware marginal query graph in our work. Different sub-retrieval queries (e.g., image retrieves text and text retrieves image) have unique characteristics, in [13], authors propose a task-dependent and query-dependent subspace learning approach for cross-modal retrieval. Specifically, authors train an efficient linear classifier to learn mapping relationships between cross-modal objects and their categories. Then, this built mapping table, is used to guide cross-modal retrieval of objects in *IoT* networks. Generally, this technique motivates us to develop marginal multi-attribute federated query in *IoT* networks.

5.2   Spatial Keyword Query

In [19], authors propose a flood-based probabilistic query algorithm for querying *IoT* devices in a distributed environment. Via selecting the optimal path, this proposed algorithm discovers automatically queried *IoT* devices. Besides, this algorithm, attribute-based discovery architecture, is protocol-independent, so that it can be deployed and implemented on top of on any network layer protocol. This attribute-based discovery architecture provides guidance for querying smart things with multi-attribute in marginal edge networks in our work. Most of existing spatial keyword query techniques only focus on queries of location proximity and strict text matching. These make semantically related objects can not be provided to users and even may lead to empty answer problem. Furthermore, the current index structures (e.g., IR-tree) may be inappropriate for handling numeric attributes which are usually contained in the descriptive information related to spatial objects. In [9], authors propose a spatial keyword query method and construct a hybrid index tree for supporting text semantic matching queries. Specially, authors leverage a conditional generative adversarial network technology to generate a series of queried keywords associated with semantics of the user's original query. Generally, this technique supports both strict and approximate text semantic matching queries of spatial keywords, which can better satisfy user's preferences. Meanwhile, this technique also provides a technical reference for our multi-attribute query in our work. The greenness of edge computing requires reducing network traffic and energy consumption at the network edge. Therefore, sensory data of smart things should be processed in a localized and distributed manner as much as possible. In [20], authors devise an attribute-based multi-keyword search scheme in resource-constrained IoT networks. This technique can drastically decrease both computational and storage costs.

To summarize, the above mentioned related techniques have been developed to enable querying smart things, which have inspired us for developing our technique. However, they may not be efficient when the network is large in scale, in terms of the communication cost and energy consumption. In this paper, we mainly considers smart things deployed in skewness distribution IoT networks to process the marginal multi-attribute query.

6   Conclusion

This paper proposes an energy-aware Marginal multi-attribute Federated Query mechanism (MFQ) in edge computing, where an energy-aware marginal query graph is established to facilitate multi-attribute query for marginal smart things contained in marginal edge networks. Extensive experiments have been conducted to evaluate the efficiency of MFQ proposed in this paper. The experimental results show that MFQ performs better compared with the rivals in reducing network traffic and energy consumption for industrial IoT applications.

Acknowledgments. This work was supported by the National Natural Science Foundation of China (Grant no. 61772479 and 61662021).

References

1. Cheng, S., Cai, Z., Li, J., Hong, G.: Extracting kernel dataset from big sensory data in wireless sensor networks. IEEE Trans. Knowl. Data Eng. **29**(4), 813–827 (2017)
2. Fan, K., Pan, Q., Wang, J., Liu, T., Yang, Y.: Cross-domain based data sharing scheme in cooperative edge computing. In: 2018 IEEE International Conference on Edge Computing (EDGE), pp. 87–92 (2018)
3. Tang, J., Zhou, Z.: Searching the internet of things using coding enabled index technology. In: Li, S. (ed.) GPC 2018. LNCS, vol. 11204, pp. 79–91. Springer, Cham (2019). https://doi.org/10.1007/978-3-030-15093-8_6
4. Du, M., Kun, W., Yuanfang, C., Xiaoyan, W., Yanfei, S.: Big data privacy preserving in multi-access edge computing for heterogeneous internet of things. IEEE Commun. Mag. **56**(8), 62–67 (2018)
5. Donno, M.D., Tange, K., Dragoni, N.: Foundations and evolution of modern computing paradigms: cloud, IoT, edge, and fog. IEEE Access, **7**, 150 936–150 948 (2019)

6. Gao, Z., Zheng, J.: Queries based on data attribute spatial index in wireless sensor networks. In: 2018 International Conference on Intelligent Transportation, Big Data and Smart City (ICITBS), pp. 183–186 (2018)

7. Li, Y., Zhu, R., Mao, S., Anjum, A.: Fog computing-based approximate spatial keyword queries with numeric attributes in IoV. IEEE Internet of Things J. **7**, 4304–4316 (2020)

8. Xu, J., Lu, H., Guting, R.H.: Range queries on multi-attribute trajectories. IEEE Trans. Knowl. Data Eng. **30**(6), 1206–1211 (2017)

9. Meng, X., Li, P., Zhang, X.: A personalized and approximated spatial keyword query approach. IEEE Access **8**, 44 889–44 902 (2020)

10. Kim, M., Lee, H.T., Ling, S., Wang, H.: On the efficiency of the-based private queries. IEEE Trans. Dependable Secure Comput. **15**(2), 357–363 (2018)

11. Yuan, X., Yuan, X., Zhang, Y., Li, B., Wang, C.: Enabling encrypted Boolean queries in geographically distributed databases. IEEE Trans. Parallel Distrib. Syst. **31**(3), 634–646 (2020)

12. Ma, J., Yao, B., Gao, X., Shen, Y., Guo, M.: Top-k critical vertices query on shortest path. IEEE Trans. Knowl. Data Eng. **30**(10), 1999–2012 (2018)

13. Wang, L., Zhu, L., Yu, E., Sun, J., Zhang, H.: Task-dependent and query-dependent subspace learning for cross-modal retrieval. IEEE Access **6**, 27 091–27 102 (2018)

14. Sampaio, H.V., de Jesus, A.L.C., do Nascimento Boing, R., Westphall, C.B.: Autonomic IoT battery management with fog computing. In: Miani, R., Camargos, L., Zarpelão, B., Rosas, E., Pasquini, R. (eds.) GPC 2019. LNCS, vol. 11484, pp. 89–103. Springer, Cham (2019). https://doi.org/10.1007/978-3-030-19223-5_7

15. Heinzelman, W.R., Chandrakasan, A., Balakrishnan, H.: Energy-efficient communication protocol for wireless microsensor networks. IEEE Comput. Soc. **18**, 8020 (2000)

16. Zhou, Z., Zhao, D., Hancke, G., Shu, L., Sun, Y.: Cache-aware query optimization in multiapplication sharing wireless sensor networks. IEEE Trans. Syst. Man Cybern. Syst. **PP**(99), 1–17 (2016)

17. Li, J., Zhong, Y., Zhu, S.: Diversified routing queries in dynamic road networks. IEEE Access **7**, 25 452–25 458 (2019)

18. Sun, D., Zhou, X., Yang, Z., Yifu, Z., Gao, Y.: Top-k collective spatial keyword queries. IEEE Access **7**, 2169–3536 (2019)

19. Sharma, S.: Attribute based discovery architecture for devices in internet of things (IoT). In: 2019 IEEE 5th International Conference for Convergence in Technology (I2CT), pp. 1–4 (2019)

20. Practical attribute-based multi-keyword search scheme in mobile crowdsourcing: IEEE Internet of Things J. **5**(4), 3008–3018 (2018)

A Novel UAV Charging Scheme for Minimizing Coverage Breach in Rechargeable Sensor Networks

Kulaea T. Pauu[1], Han Xu[2(✉)], and Bang Wang[1]

[1] School of Electronic Information and Communications,
Huazhong University of Science and Technology, Wuhan 430074, China
{xuh,wangbang}@hust.edu.cn
[2] School of Journalism and Information Communication,
Huazhong University of Science and Technology, Wuhan 430074, China
2603933919@qq.com

Abstract. In wireless rechargeable sensor networks, one of the most important issues is how and when to recharge the sensor nodes. Existing studies show that not all of the sensors can be properly recharged in time due to the limitation of solar or wind-based charging technologies. As a result, some sensors will be interrupted and cannot function well due to exhaustion of their energy. A recent promising technology is the use of wireless energy transfer technology together with UAV-based wireless charger, which has the opportunity of powering sensors with manageable yet perpetual energy. In this paper, considering not only the remaining energy of the sensors but also the coverage rate of the scenario, we propose a complete coverage and energy knowledge partial charging scheme (Co-EPaCS) to find and plan a charging schedule for the UAV charger in order to minimize the total network coverage breach. Simulation results show that the proposed scheme significantly outperform other methods in terms of coverage rate, energy consumption of all nodes and network lifetime.

Keywords: Wireless rechargeable sensor networks · Wireless energy transfer · Uav-based wireless charger · Coverage

1 Introduction

Wireless sensor networks (WSNs) have been widely deployed to support diverse applications, such as environment monitoring, military surveillance [2,11,23]. Traditional sensor networks usually assume to deploy numerous small nodes each powered by an on-board battery with limited capacity. With such configurations, how to maximize network lifetime yet guaranteeing application requirements, like coverage quality and data transmission rate, has become a critical issue in sensor networks, as well as sensor activity scheduling and energy efficient routing [4,12,20].

© Springer Nature Switzerland AG 2020
Z. Yu et al. (Eds.): GPC 2020, LNCS 12398, pp. 347–361, 2020.
https://doi.org/10.1007/978-3-030-64243-3_26

Recently, some have proposed to use rechargeable nodes each equipped with a chargeable battery to sustain a very long, or even perpetual operational time for sensor networks [3]. Many energy replenishment techniques can be used to charge a node by harvesting energy from environmental sources, like sun, wind, etc. [10, 14]. However, the cost of equipping each node with such an energy harvesting unit, e.g., a solar panel or windmill, may be too prohibitive. Also energy harvesting may be too dependent on unpredictable environmental conditions, which may degrade single node battery performance. In addition, in order to avoid disasters like collapsed bridges in different countries [19] and bush fires in Australia [18], wireless sensor nodes should be deployed on the bridge to monitor the health of the bridge and to detect early fire in forest. These nodes may have little or no access to the ambient source, which may cause constant interruption of power supply.

Another approach for charging rechargeable nodes is to use the wireless power transfer (WPT) technology [24], where a charger with sufficient energy to get close enough to each individual node and transfer power wirelessly. The wireless power transfer method makes the charging process easy since no complicated mechanical mechanism is required to operate the sensor node. In the literature, many have studied how to use a wheeled mobile charger to charge nodes. Although the mobile charger is assumed to have large energy capacity, its movement also consumes energy. Hence, a key research issue is how to plan a charging route to efficiently charge as many as possible the mostly needed nodes in each single charging tour.

Several charging schemes have been proposed to design efficient charging tours [6, 9, 13, 17, 21, 22]. For example, He et al. [6] proposed a greedy charging scheme, named Nearest-Job Next with preemption (NJNP), which always selects the nearest requesting node to be charged by the mobile charger first. Analytical results on the number of charging requests served and the charging latency of each sensor node are provided. However, their solution cannot be guaranteed that all of the to-be charged sensors could be charged prior to their energy depletion time. Wang et al. [17] considered a practical model where mobile chargers have limited capacity and their movements consume energy. Their aim is to maximize the recharge profit, the recharged energy less the traveling cost. In addition, the authors also considered the sensor's alive time to avoid node failure before the mobile charger can recharge it. Two algorithms are proposed suitable to the context of the problem. Considering both the traveling time of the mobile charger and the charging time for a node, Ren et al. [13] designed a novel charging scheme. The authors assumed that when charging a node, the node should be fully recharged to its battery capacity. Efficient sensor charging algorithms are proposed so as to charge as many nodes as possible in a given time span. Shih and Yang [22] combined the charging issue with the network coverage quality. Besides using the residual energy for node selection, they also took into account network coverage to prioritize those coverage-critical nodes for the next charging tour. In these schemes, they assume that when charging a node, the node should be fully recharged to its battery capacity. Wu et al. [21] argued that it may not be necessary to fully charge a node each time. Instead, they proposed a partial charging scheme to minimize the depletion of each node by charging a single node with an amount of energy to its some energy level.

Since Unmanned Aerial Vehicle (UAV) can move with required speed to cover sensors distributed in a large-scale area that is even inaccessible to human, some have proposed to use UAV instead of wheeled mobile charger to charge nodes [1,9]. The UAV-based wireless power transfer is able to maintain the wireless sensor network as a long-term monitoring system by regularly charge these sensor nodes. UAV charger has better performance and competence due to its fast-moving speed to charge sensor nodes, but similar to the wheeled mobile charger, the key issue of designing a UAV charging tour is to select which nodes to be charged and how to charge them. Johnson et al. [9] studied the use of a UAV as a WPT charger and proposed a single node should be charged to its full battery capacity in each flight. The UAV also needs to recharge its own energy. Previous works redirect the UAV back to the base station which is connected to the power grid [1]. However, such infrastructure could be unavailable in ad-hoc applications such as pollution, forest, bridge monitoring. To this end, a solar energy harvesting base station is required so it can charge the UAV when its energy is depleted. As a result, the network will no longer rely on electricity from the power grid.

In our work, we also study the UAV charging problem. Compared with the previous studies, we consider a scenario where in a remote harsh environment. A base station that uses a large solar panel to harvest energy for charging the UAV which is then responsible for charging sensor nodes is builded. This is motivated from the fact that many sensor networks are deployed in desolated areas without accessing power grids. Although theoretically a rechargeable sensor node will never die as long as it can be recharged in time, it would temporarily loss its functionality if it has depleted its energy while not yet been recharged. As such, network operational quality such as area coverage could be much degraded due to those temporary powered-off nodes.

Some past research only considered the residual energy of the sensor nodes as the only clue to recharge sensors. However, it is obvious that only considering the residual energy of sensors is not enough to avoid the occurrences of coverage holes in the network. In this paper, considering both the residual energy and coverage degree of sensors, we design a complete coverage and energy knowledge partial charging scheme (Co-EPaCS) to find and plan a charging schedule for the UAV so as to minimize network coverage breach. In our work, the network coverage breach is avoided by deploying more nodes equipped with rechargeable batteries. The coverage breach is temporary and it can be self-recovered after the nodes are recharged. We assume that all nodes can work continuously, then a discrete time model is adopt in which the continuous timeline is divided into consecutive slots each with equal length. For each slot, all sensors are in active state and at the beginning of each slot we choose active sensors with remaining energy less than a given threshold to become a candidate. A charging tour plan is then given according to the candidate's priority.

The rest of the paper is organized as follows. Section 2 outlines the problem description to help understand the approach of this paper. Section 3 introduces the proposed charging scheme. Section 4 evaluates the performance of the proposed algorithms and shows the simulation results and Sect. 5 concludes the paper.

2   Problem Description

2.1   Network Model and Assumptions

We consider a sensor network consists of rechargeable nodes that are all randomly deployed in a 2D rectangular field. The set of rechargeable sensors are assumed to be static and homogenous and is denoted by $V_s = \{s_i\}, i = 1, 2, 3, ...n$. Here s_i means a sensor node. Moreover, we consider that each sensor s_i is equipped with Global Positioning System (GPS) and each sensor can communicate with other sensors if the distance between these two sensors is less than a sensor's communication range R_c. A binary coverage model is assumed where the region covered by a sensor node is a disk with radius R_s. Here R_s is the sensing radius of s_i. In other words, each grid point can be considered as covered by s_i with a probability 1 if it is within the sensing radius of s_i and with a probability 0 (uncovered) when it is beyond s_i's sensing range [7,16].

Under such assumptions, the location and energy level of each sensor s_i can be known before the UAV starts its charging task from the base station v_{bs}. Figure 1 illustrates a sample of this work's network model.

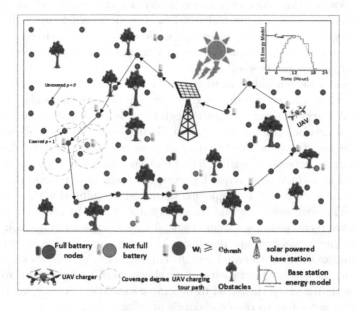

Fig. 1. Network model of the work.

In Fig. 1, we can see that the sensors are randomly deployed in a rectangular field located in a remote area, a single UAV charger UAV_c is employed to perform the charging task to the sensor nodes. The UAV's power source is from a solar powered base station located in the field. The arrow depicts the charging path of the UAV, which starts from the base station v_{bs} and must return back to v_{bs}. The sensors' energy level are differentiated in three colors. The green color represents full battery, the yellow color represents not full battery and the red color represents a sensor node's battery is less than or equal to a pre-defined energy threshold. It means these nodes need to be charged immediately before they exhaust their energy. When performing a charging tour task, the UAV will start flying from v_{bs} and must return back to v_{bs} after finishing its charging tour task to recharge itself or rest for the next charging tour. Each sensor node s_i is powered by a rechargeable battery of limited energy, and it consumes energy when performing sensing, data processing, data transmissions and receptions. The UAV_c flies at a constant speed v within the deployment field and replenishes the energy supply to a sensor s_i with a fixed charging rate r. The UAV_c energy consumption while flying is e_f, while hovering is e_h and while transferring energy to a sensor s_i is e_t during a charging tour. The total energy consumption of the UAV_c for traveling and charging should not exceed its battery capacity E_{UAV}, as shown in (1), where $t_{charging}$ is the charging time.

$$(t \times e_f) + (t \times e_h) + ((r \times e_t) \times t_{charging}) < E_{UAV} \qquad (1)$$

We adopt an approximate one-day energy charging model for the base station [8], which uses a quadratic curve to model the solar energy harvested in the daytime, while in the night, the harvested energy is zero.

2.2 Partial Recharging Model

Let B_i denote the total battery capacity of a sensor s_i and E_i denotes the amount of energy of a sensor s_i before charging, to partially charge s_i, we use a unit charging strategy. We use $\triangle_i$ to denote an amount of energy needed to be replenished to s_i at each charging tour. Thus, the amount of energy needed to charge to a sensor s_i to its full capacity is $\triangle_i = B_i - E_i$. In our work, we assume that the energy charge to s_i at each time is a value in $\{\frac{\triangle_i}{2}, \frac{\triangle_i}{3}..., \frac{\triangle_i}{k}\}$ where k is an integer. The minimum amount of energy charged per charging tour is $\triangle_{min} = \min\{\triangle_i\}$. We also assume that the UAV can charge each sensor node with a fixed number of charging times no more than K per tour, where K is the number of possible charging to a sensor s_i per tour and it is a given non-negative constant integer. Since the UAV has limited energy capacity, it is hard to cover too much sensor nodes in a single flight tour. As a result, a sensor can only be charged once in a charging tour. Therefore, we set $K = 1$. Moreover, we adopt a discrete time model where the total time of each tour T, is divided into consecutive slots $\tau_q, q = 1, 2, ...$ each with equal length.

2.3 Problem Definition

To define the problem clearly, we us an undirected metric graph $\mathcal{G} = (\mathcal{V}, \mathcal{E})$ to represent the rechargeable sensor network. Here vertex set $\mathcal{V} = \{s_i, v_{\mathrm{bs}}\}$. Elements in $\mathcal{V}$ are connected through edges in $\mathcal{E}$, which are possible UAV flight paths. The UAV is able to travel along edges and stop at some nodes to charge them. Given a set of to-be-charged sensors V_c, we let $TOUR \triangleq P((v_{\mathrm{bs}}, 0) \rightarrow (s_1, e_1) \rightarrow (s_2, e_2) \rightarrow \dots \rightarrow (s_j, e_j) \dots \rightarrow (v_{\mathrm{bs}}, 0))$ be the charging tour for the UAV charger UAV_c. Here $s_j \in V_c$, e_j is the amount of energy charged to sensor s_j. The total energy consumed by UAV_c cannot exceed its energy capacity E_{UAV}, in addition, the total amount of energy being charged to a node s_i by UAV_c per tour should not be greater than its energy demand $B_i - E_i$. Let $Z_j = 1$ if a target TAG_j in the region can be covered by at least one sensor, $Z_j = 0$ otherwise, the total time coverage breach occurs during a slot τ_q can be defined as $\sum_j t_j(1 - Z_j)$. Here t_j is the duration TAG_j can not be covered by at least one sensor.

The problem is to find a charging tour $TOUR$ for UAV_c to charge the nodes in V_c from the network $\mathcal{G}$ so that the network coverage breach is minimized. Since the value of the total coverage breach is related to the total time, we can use breach rate instead as the coverage performance criteria. The problem can be formulated as follows.

$$\mathcal{G} \Rightarrow \{V_c, TOUR\} \Big|_{\arg\min \sum_q \frac{\sum_j t_j(1 - Z_j)}{\tau_q}} \tag{2}$$

3 Complete Coverage and Energy Knowledge Partial Charging Scheme (Co-EPaCS)

In this section, we will explain how the complete coverage and energy knowledge partial charging scheme (Co-EPaCS) works. There are two steps in our scheme, the first one is to find a subset of sensors to charge and to decide when to start a charging tour, the second one is to plan a charging tour for the UAV and recharging of sensors.

3.1 Finding a Subset of Sensors to Charge and Deciding When to Start a Charging Tour

The first stage of Co-EPaCS is to find a subset of sensors V_c to charge and to decide when to launch a charging tour for the UAV. In our work, once V_c is found, the base station v_{bs} will not receive any charging requests from other sensors in V_s before the UAV finishes its current charging task. Choosing an appropriate time to begin the charging tour depicts a design challenge that can significantly affects the solution performance in terms of energy consumption, thus we designed a pre-defined energy threshold, denoted by e_{thresh} that triggers the launching time of a charging tour. The pseudo-codes for the first step of Co-EPaCS are given in Algorithm 1. In line 1, the weights, denoted by w_i which combines both remaining energy E_i and coverage sets CS_i for each sensor s_i, aiming to avoid or delay existence of a coverage hole, is calculated. The design of the weights w_i is shown in (3). T_i^{CS} denotes the total number of cover sets for a sensor s_i. It means when a sensor s_i is about to exhaust its energy, its sensing range can be covered by T_i^{CS} sets of sensors. Apparently, the larger T_i^{CS} is, the less possibility coverage breach occurs.

Algorithm 1 Finding a subset of sensors to charge and deciding when to start a charging tour

---

Require:

    Sensor nodes V_s, cover sets CS_i, sensor residual energy E_i, sensor battery capacity B_i, charging rate r, sensor energy consumption rate θ.

Ensure:

    Subset of sensors to charge V_c and energy threshold e_{thresh}

1: $w_i \leftarrow \left\lfloor \frac{(B_i - E_i) + (r \times e_t)}{B_i} \right\rfloor \times \frac{1}{T_i^{CS} + 1}$

2: $l_w \leftarrow w_i$

3: $l_u \leftarrow \emptyset$

4: **for** $i \leftarrow 1$ to length $(l_w) - 1$ **do**

5:    $e_{\text{thresh}} \leftarrow \left\lfloor \frac{(B_i - \theta) + (r \times e_t)}{B_i} \right\rfloor \times \frac{1}{\lfloor AVG_C \rfloor}$

6:    **if** $l_w \geq e_{\text{thresh}}$ **then**

7:        $l_u \leftarrow s_i + i^{\text{th}}$ node in l_w

8:        UAV start to charge all the sensor nodes in l_u

9:    **else**

10:      $l_u \leftarrow \emptyset$

11:      UAV start to charge all the sensor nodes in l_w

12:    **end if**

13: **end for**

14: **return** V_c

15: **return** e_{thresh}

$$w_i = \left\lfloor \frac{(B_i - E_i) + (r \times e_t)}{B_i} \right\rfloor \times \frac{1}{T_i^{CS} + 1} \tag{3}$$

In line 2, the calculated weights w_i in (3) are sorted in a list denoted by l_w accordingly. An empty list of urgent nodes denoted by l_u is shown in line 3. Here, the urgent nodes are defined as the nodes that exceeds the energy threshold e_{thresh} and its energy battery will exhaust very soon. In line 5, the energy threshold e_{thresh} is calculated according to (4) which is derived from (3). Here θ is the energy consumption of a sensor s_i.

$$e_{\text{thresh}} = \left\lfloor \frac{(B_i - \theta) + (r \times e_t)}{B_i} \right\rfloor \times \frac{1}{\lfloor AVG_C \rfloor} \tag{4}$$

We use $\lfloor AVG_C \rfloor$ as the average number of cover sets for all the sensors. When a senor s_i's total number of cover sets T_i^{CS} is smaller than $\lfloor AVG_C \rfloor$, this sensor is likely to be considered have a coverage hole. As shown in line 6 to 13, if a sensor s_i's weight w_i in the weights list l_w is greater than the pre-defined energy threshold e_{thresh}, s_i will be added to the urgent nodes list l_u, the UAV will begin its charging tour and start to charge all the sensors V_c in l_u immediately, else it will start to charge all the sensors V_s in l_w.

3.2   Planning UAV Charging Tour and Charging the Sensors

The second step of Co-EPaCS is planning a charging tour for the UAV and charging the sensors, as shown in Algorithm 2. Here we use a *for loop* to compute which sensors should be charged, how much energy UAV_c needs to fly to the sensors, recharge them and fly back to the base station v_{bs} without exceeding its battery capacity E_{UAV}. Assuming a subset of sensors V_c in the urgent list l_u is computed according to Algorithm 1, if UAV_c's current energy level $\triangle E_{UAV}$ is greater than a pre-defined minimum energy level $\triangle E_{UAV\,min}$, UAV_c will first calculate how much energy it will consume to fly to the sensors in V_c to recharge them and then fly back to the base station v_{bs} before starting the charging tour. For each sensor s_i in V_c, the distance between UAV_c and s_i is computed, denoted as $dist_i$. For the most urgent sensor s_d that needs charging, if $dist_d$ is less than the distance UAV_c's remaining energy can take, which denoted as $dist_{\triangle E_{UAV}}$, UAV_c will immediately fly to s_d and perform the charging task. If $dist_d \geq dist_{\triangle E_{UAV}}$, we need to find another sensor from V_c where UAV_c's remaining energy can reach, then UAV_c will fly to this sensor to recharge it. Note that once UAV_c flies to a new destination sensor, its coordinate will be updated. However, if there is no sensor where UAV_c's remaining energy can reach, UAV_c will fly back to v_{bs} to recharge itself. As shown in line 25 to 34, if the current weight w_i of a sensor to be charged in the urgent list l_u is greater than the pre-defined energy threshold e_{thresh}, that sensor will exhaust its energy soon and needs to be charged immediately. The amount of energy e_j to be charged to those sensors is $\lfloor \frac{B_i - E_i}{2} \rfloor$. The UAV will start its tour from sensor s_i with the highest weights w_i in the urgent nodes list l_u then flies to the sensor s_i with the second highest weight, and so forth else if the urgent list l_u is empty, the UAV_c charges the sensors in the weights list l_w in the same order else it flies back to the base station. Although this path planning is not the most energy-efficient, it ensures that the sensor who will exhaust its energy soon will be charged first to avoid coverage hole and prolongs the lifetime of the sensor network.

4   Performance Evaluation

4.1   Parameter Settings

We consider a sensor network consisting of 240 sensor nodes randomly deployed within a $1,000\,\mathrm{m} \times 1,000\,\mathrm{m}^2$ area. The sensing range R_s of a node is $121\,\mathrm{m}$. The UAV and the base station are both co-located in the center of the field. The base station's solar energy maximum charging rate C_{max} is set to $0.1 - 0.6$. The energy capacity of the UAV is $E_{UAV} = 300\,\mathrm{kJ}$. The battery (NiMH battery $1.2\,\mathrm{V}/2.5\,\mathrm{Ah}$) capacity of each sensor $s_i \in V_s$ is $B_i = 10.8\,\mathrm{kJ}$ [15]. The residual energy of each sensors are generated in the range of 20%–60% of $10.8\,\mathrm{kJ}$. The UAV_c travels at a constant speed of $v = 7.33\,\mathrm{m/s}$. The energy consumption rate for flying is

$e_f = 121.9\,\mathrm{W}$, for hovering is $e_h = 92.28\,\mathrm{W}$ and for energy transferring is $e_t = 20\,\mathrm{W}$. The charging rate r is 0.2. The energy consumption rate θ of each sensor s_i is $1.625\,\mathrm{mW}$. A node is Urgent when its energy level reaches threshold $e_{\mathrm{thresh}} = 0.1$. The energy charging efficient rate of the UAV to a sensor is $4\,\mathrm{J/s}$.

Algorithm 2 Planning UAV Charging Tour and Charging of Sensors

---

Require:
UAV charger UAV_c, base station v_{bs}, UAV total battery capacity E_{UAV}, UAV current energy $\triangle E_{\mathrm{UAV}}$, distance the UAV can take $dist_{\mathrm{GoBack}}$, destination distance $dist_d$, UAV velocity v, UAV Traveling Time t.

Ensure:
A charging tour $TOUR$ for the UAV_c so that in every charging tour an amount of energy e_j is charged to the sensors and the traveling length of the UAV_c is not greater than its total battery capacity E_{UAV}.

1: $V_c \leftarrow l_u$
2: **for** $i \leftarrow 1$ to length $|V_c|$ **do**
3:     $dist_{\mathrm{GoBack}} \leftarrow \sqrt{(v_{\mathrm{bs}}(Y) - UAV_c(Y))^2 + (v_{\mathrm{bs}}(X) - UAV_c(X))^2}$
4:     $\triangle E_{\mathrm{UAV}} \leftarrow E_{\mathrm{UAV}} - (dist_{\mathrm{GoBack}}/v \times e_f) + (t \times e_h) + (r \times e_t)$
5:     $dist_d \leftarrow \sqrt{(s_d(Y) - UAV_c(Y))^2 + (s_d(X) - UAV_c(X))^2}$
6:     **if** $\triangle E_{\mathrm{UAV}} > \triangle E_{\mathrm{UAVmin}}$ **then**
7:         **if** $dist_d < dist_{\mathrm{UAV}}$ **then**
8:             choose s_d as destination
9:             $UAV_c(X) \leftarrow s_d(X),\ UAV_c(Y) \leftarrow s_d(Y)$
10:            $\triangle E_{\mathrm{UAV}} \leftarrow \triangle E_{\mathrm{UAV}} - dist_d/v \times e_f$
11:            UAV charges the sensor
12:         **else**
13:             **if** $\exists s_{d'} \in V_c,\ dist_{d'} < dist_{\mathrm{UAV}}$ **then**
14:                 choose $s_{d'}$ as destination
15:                 $UAV_c(X) \leftarrow s_{d'}(X),\ UAV_c(Y) \leftarrow s_{d'}(Y)$
16:                 $\triangle E_{\mathrm{UAV}} \leftarrow \triangle E_{\mathrm{UAV}} - dist_{d'}/v \times e_f$
17:                 UAV charges the sensor
18:             **else**
19:                 UAV flies back to the v_{bs}
20:             **end if**
21:         **end if**
22:     **else**
23:         UAV destination $\leftarrow v_{\mathrm{bs}}$
24:     **end if**
25:     **if** $w_i \geq e_{\mathrm{thresh}}$ **then**
26:         $l_u \leftarrow s_i + i^{\mathrm{th}}$ node in l_w
27:         UAV charges all the sensor nodes in l_u, $e_j = \lfloor \frac{B_i - E_i}{2} \rfloor$
28:         **if** $l_u \leftarrow \emptyset$ **then**
29:             candidate nodes to be charged $\leftarrow l_w$
30:             UAV start to charge sensors in l_w
31:         **else**
32:             UAV flies back to v_{bs}
33:         **end if**
34:     **end if**
35: **end for**
36: **return** $TOUR$

To evaluate the performance of our proposed complete coverage energy knowledge partial charging scheme (Co-EPaCS), we compare Co-EPaCS with three existing algorithms, namely, TSP [5], NJNP [6] and PERS [22]. In algorithm Traveling Salesman Problem (TSP), an approximation of the shortest closed tour is calculated without considering the to-be-charged sensors energy expiration time. For Nearest Job Next with Preemption (NJNP), it acts greedily by prioritizing the requesting nodes located at the nearest position from the mobile charger. The mobile charger is forced to preempt its motion towards the next scheduled node if a new request from a closer node is received meanwhile. For Priority-based Energy Replenishment Scheme (PERS), sensors are sorted by the time they exhaust their energy in a round and the UAV charger will visit the sorted sensors one by one. Full charging model is adopted for all these three algorithms.

4.2   Results and Discussions

Firstly, we compared the ratio of total coverage area and energy consumption of all nodes for the four algorithms against the simulation of time in days, as shown in Fig. 2. The results in Fig. 2(a) show that our proposed Co-EPaCS can still cover 87.24% of the target region after simulating 100 days, whereas PERS covers 73.71%, TSP covers 65.02% and NJNP only covers 30.37%.

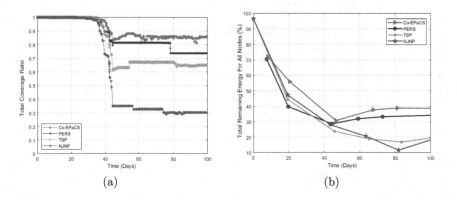

(a)   (b)

Fig. 2. (a) Total coverage ratio vs time. (b) Energy consumption of all nodes vs time.

Figure 2(b) illustrates the total remaining energy percentage of all nodes after running a simulation of 100 days. The remaining percentage energy of all nodes for the Co-EPaCS algorithm is 38.72%, PERS is 34.36%, TSP is 20.02%, and NJNP is 18.17%. It can be seen that for NJNP and TSP algorithms their total initial energy of all nodes at the beginning of the simulation is about 96% then it significantly decreases at the end of the simulation. For Co-EPaCS and PERS, their total remaining energy at the beginning of the simulation is about 70% then it decreases at the end of the simulation, however, not significantly compared to TSP and NJNP algorithms. The rationale behind this, TSP and NJNP algorithms sends request message to the UAV when their energy level is low. The UAV receives the message it immediately flies out to the field to start the charging process. As a result, the UAV will consume more energy by moving inefficiently and redundantly. In contrast to TSP and NJNP, our proposed Co-EPaCS and PERS both use an energy threshold e_{thresh} to determine when the UAV should start the charging task, avoiding redundant movement of the UAV. Despite this, our Co-EPaCS algorithm still outperforms PERS because the UAV partially charges the sensors, whereas PERS, TSP and NJNP all adopts the full charging strategy.

Secondly, we investigate the performance of the four algorithms on the impact of energy charging strategy, by decreasing the energy charging unit Ω from $\triangle_i$ to $\frac{\triangle_i}{5}$. As shown in Fig. 3, full charging strategy is adopted when $\Omega = \triangle_i$, while partial charging strategy is adopted when Ω is $\frac{\triangle_i}{2}$, $\frac{\triangle_i}{3}$, $\frac{\triangle_i}{4}$ or $\frac{\triangle_i}{5}$. Figure 3(a) shows that our CO-EPaCS algorithm outperforms PERS, TSP and NJNP in terms of shortening the sensors energy expiration time in full charging strategy and partial charging strategy. The average failure time per sensor of Co-EPaCS is stable from 5.04 days to 5.20 days, PERS is from 10.06 days to 10.96 days, TSP is from 17.35 days to 13.80 days and NJNP is from 17.31 days to 18.17 days.

On the other hand, Fig. 3(b) implies the network lifetime, which is defined as the duration from the start of the simulation till the time the first coverage hole occurs. The network lifetime for Co-EPaCS keeps increasing from 19.2% to 28.25% when Ω decreases. The network lifetime for PERS increases when the value of Ω decreases from $\triangle_i$ to $\frac{\triangle_i}{2}$, then it drops down to 8.4% when $\Omega = \frac{\triangle_i}{3}$ and when Ω decreases from $\frac{\triangle_i}{3}$ to $\frac{\triangle_i}{5}$ it significantly increases to 25.25%. The Network lifetime for TSP is stable all throughout from 8.25 days to 8.4 days. The Network lifetime for NJNP is also stable from 0.33 days to 0.25 days, before it significantly increases to 15.66 days when the value of Ω is from $\frac{\triangle_i}{3}$ to $\frac{\triangle_i}{5}$. In summary, we can see from Fig. 3 the performances of our proposed Co-EPaCS algorithm achieves the finest trade-off between minimizing the failure time per sensor and prolonging the network lifetime. It can be noted that both Co-EPaCS and PERS provide greater results, since they both consider residual energy and coverage of sensors whereas TSP and NJNP only take into account the residual energy of the sensors.

Thirdly, we investigate the impact of varying the UAV energy capacity by increasing $E_{UAV} = 10000\,J$ to $E_{UAV} = 350000\,J$. We compare the breach rate for the four algorithms against the UAV energy capacity, respectively.

In Fig. 4(a), it is not unexpected that the breach rate decreases as the E_{UAV} increases. Co-EPaCS outperforms PERS, TSP and NJNP by achieving the smallest and stable breach rate from 45% to 40%, PERS is from 47% to 42%, TSP is from 57% to 48% and NJNP is from 58% to 44%. We can see Co-EPaCS still outperforms other three algorithms. The reason for this is because PERS, TSP and NJNP all adopt the full charging model which increases the rate of coverage breach whereas our novel partial charging model can minimize the breach rate and provide a better result.

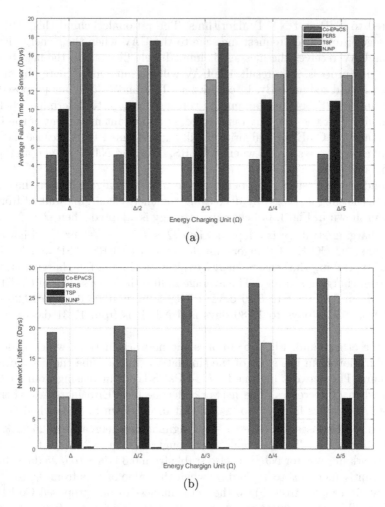

Fig. 3. (a) Average failure time per sensor vs time. (b) Network lifetime vs energy charging unit.

At last, we compared the changes of the four algorithms' cumulative distribution functions (CDFs) with the increase of burst value. A burst breach slot is defined as a coverage breach slot with two or more consecutive breach slots. The number of breach slots in each burst breach is defined here as burst value. As we can see in Fig. 4(b), the convergence speed for the proposed Co-EPaCS is faster than PERS, TSP and NJNP. Co-EPaCS outperforms the other three in terms of both the number of breach slot and burst breach. For example, when burst value is equal to 5, the cumulative probability for Co-EPaCS is 98.34%, for PERS is 91.60%, for TSP is 78.51% and for NJNP is 61.59%. This is because Co-EPaCS considers both the remaining energy and coverage degree of sensors.

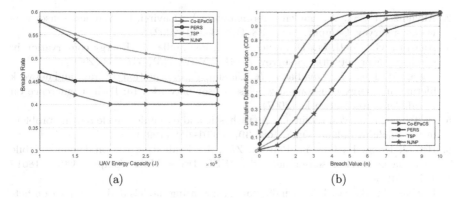

Fig. 4. (a) Breach rate vs energy capacity. (b) Cumulative distribution functions vs burst value.

Only the sensors who reaches e_{thresh} can be recharged in Co-EPaCS. In addition, the partial charging model can makes more sensors be recharged.

5   Conclusion

For past studies, the strategy widely used to recharge sensors is considering only the remaining energy of the sensors. However, in order to prevent the occurrence of coverage hole, it is insufficient taking into account only one factor. In this paper we consider both the remaining energy and coverage degree of sensors in terms of cover sets, propose Co-EPaCS, a complete coverage energy knowledge partial charging scheme that replenishes the energy of sensors in an efficient way to maintain the coverage of network and prolong the network lifetime. To validate the effectiveness of the proposed method, the total coverage ratio, energy consumption, network lifetime and Breach rate by Co-EPaCS are compared with PERS, TSP and NJNP in a wild scenario. Experimental results demonstrate that Co-EPaCS performs better than the compared approaches. In our future work, multiple UAV chargers will be considered. How to arrange multiple UAVs working together and recharging hundreds of sensor nodes effectively will be a challenge.

Acknowledgments. This work was supported in part by the National Natural Science Foundation of China (Nos. 61771209) and the Huazhong University of Science and Technology Special Funds for Development of Humanities and Social Sciences. The authors wish to thank the reviewers for their helpful comments.

References

1. Akhtar, F., Rehmani, M.H.: Energy replenishment using renewable and traditional energy resources for sustainable wireless sensor networks: a review. Renew. Sustain. Energy Rev. **45**, 769–784 (2015)

2. Akyildiz, I.F., Su, W., Sankarasubramaniam, Y., Cayirci, E.: Wireless sensor networks: a survey. Comput. Netw. **38**(4), 393–422 (2002)
3. Anastasi, G., Conti, M., Di Francesco, M., Passarella, A.: Energy conservation in wireless sensor networks: a survey. Ad Hoc Netw. **7**(3), 537–568 (2009)
4. Bagaa, M., Lasla, N., Ouadjaout, A., Challal, Y.: Information coverage and network lifetime in energy constrained wireless sensor networks. In: IEEE Conference on Local Computer Networks (2007)
5. Bertsimas, D.J., Van Ryzin, G.: A stochastic and dynamic vehicle routing problem in the Euclidean plane. Oper. Res. **39**(4), 601–615 (1991)
6. He, L., Kong, L., Gu, Y., Pan, J., Zhu, T.: Evaluating the on-demand mobile charging in wireless sensor networks. IEEE Trans. Mob. Comput. **14**(9), 1861–1875 (2014)
7. Hossain, A., Biswas, P.K., Chakrabarti, S.: Sensing models and its impact on network coverage in wireless sensor network. In: 2008 IEEE Region 10 and the Third international Conference on Industrial and Information Systems, pp. 1–5. IEEE (2008)
8. Huan, X., Wang, B., Mo, Y., Yang, L.T.: Rechargeable router placement based on efficiency and fairness in green wireless mesh networks. Comput. Netw. **78**, 83–94 (2015)
9. Johnson, J., Basha, E., Detweiler, C.: Charge selection algorithms for maximizing sensor network life with UAV-based limited wireless recharging. In: 2013 IEEE Eighth International Conference on Intelligent Sensors, Sensor Networks and Information Processing, pp. 159–164. IEEE (2013)
10. Kansal, A., Hsu, J., Zahedi, S., Srivastava, M.B.: Power management in energy harvesting sensor networks. ACM Trans. Embed. Comput. Syst. (TECS) **6**(4), 32 (2007)
11. Liang, W., Ren, X., Jia, X., Xu, X.: Monitoring quality maximization through fair rate allocation in harvesting sensor networks. IEEE Trans. Parallel Distrib. Syst. **24**(9), 1827–1840 (2013)
12. Mahfoudh, S.: Energy effciency in wireless ad hoc and sensor networks: routing, node activity scheduling and cross-layering. Bibliogr **12**(12), 4146–4151 (2012)
13. Ren, X., Liang, W., Xu, W.: Maximizing charging throughput in rechargeable sensor networks. In: 2014 23rd International Conference on Computer Communication and Networks (ICCCN), pp. 1–8. IEEE (2014)
14. Ren, X., Liang, W., Xu, W.: Quality-aware target coverage in energy harvesting sensor networks. IEEE Trans. Emerg. Top. Comput. **3**(1), 8–21 (2014)
15. Shi, Y., Xie, L., Hou, Y.T., Sherali, H.D.: On renewable sensor networks with wireless energy transfer. In: 2011 Proceedings IEEE INFOCOM, pp. 1350–1358. IEEE (2011)
16. Wang, B., Xu, H., Liu, W., Liang, H.: A novel node placement for long belt coverage in wireless networks. IEEE Trans. Comput. **62**(12), 2341–2353 (2012)
17. Wang, C., Li, J., Ye, F., Yang, Y.: Recharging schedules for wireless sensor networks with vehicle movement costs and capacity constraints. In: 2014 Eleventh Annual IEEE International Conference on Sensing, Communication, and Networking (SECON), pp. 468–476. IEEE (2014)
18. Wikipedia: Australianbushfires, January 2020. https://en.m.wikipedia.org/wiki/List_of_Australian_bushfire_seasons
19. Wikipedia: Bridgefailure, January 2020. https://en.m.wikipedia.org/wiki/List_of_bridge_failures

20. Xiong, Z., Bang, W., Wang, Z.: Priority-based greedy scheduling for confident information coverage in energy harvesting wireless sensor networks. In: International Conference on Mobile Ad-hoc and Sensor Networks (2016)
21. Xu, W., Liang, W., Jia, X., Xu, Z.: Maximizing sensor lifetime in a rechargeable sensor network via partial energy charging on sensors. In: 2016 13th Annual IEEE International Conference on Sensing, Communication, and Networking (SECON), pp. 1–9. IEEE (2016)
22. Yang, C.M., Shih, K.P., Chang, S.H.: A priority-based energy replenishment scheme for wireless rechargeable sensor networks. In: 2017 31st International Conference on Advanced Information Networking and Applications Workshops (WAINA), pp. 547–552. IEEE (2017)
23. Yick, J., Mukherjee, B., Ghosal, D.: Wireless sensor network survey. Comput. Netw. 52(12), 2292–2330 (2008)
24. Zhen, Z., Pang, H., Georgiadis, A., Cecati, C.: Wireless power transfer - an overview. IEEE Trans. Industr. Electron. 66(2), 1044–1058 (2019)

A Parallel Tasks Scheduling Algorithm with Markov Decision Process in Edge Computing

Jun Lu[1], Xing Guo[1(✉)], Xing-guang Zhao[1], and Hao Zhou[2]

[1] Anhui University, Hefei 230601, China
guox@ahu.edu.cn
[2] University of Science and Technology of China, Hefei 230026, China

Abstract. In edge computing, in order to obtain low latency and efficient service, users usually offload tasks from their devices to the nearby edge cloud for processing. How to schedule these tasks to the edge cloud efficiently and reliably is of particular interest to edge computing. In this paper, we design an online parallel tasks scheduling algorithm based on the theory of reinforcement learning, which not only saves the cost of edge server processing tasks, but also makes further optimization in ensuring the timeliness of task completion and shortening the response time. Finally, we conduct simulation experiments based on real data sets, compare our algorithm with existing algorithms in many aspects, and our algorithm is shown to be efficient and reliable.

Keywords: Task scheduling · Edge computing · Markov decision process · Reinforcement learning

1 Introduction

With the rapid development of the Internet of Things and the popularization of 5G wireless networks, the era of the Internet of Everything has arrived, and the number of edge devices on the network has increased rapidly, making the data generated by such devices reach the ZB level[1]. In the era of centralized big data processing with computing models as its core, its key technologies have been unable to efficiently process data generated by edge devices. For this reason, edge-based big data processing with massive data calculations generated by network edge devices with edge computing models as the core emerged at the historic moment[2,3], which combined with the existing centralized big data processing with cloud computing models as the core can solve the tricky problems encountered in big data processing in the era of the Internet of Everything, such as communication delay, energy cost [4–6]. Although edge computing breaks the

This work was supported in part by the Anhui University Natural Science Foundation-funded project under Grant KJ2019A0035, in part by the Nature Science Program of Anhui Province under Grant 1908085MF181.

new ground to solve the above problems, a new issue arises subsequently, that is, how to formulate an effective scheduling strategy for tasks offloading to edge servers, owing to the edge servers' own resources are limited compared with the remote cloud, the processing speed and total resources between edge servers are often not exactly even, what's more, competition between tasks would further aggravate the situation [7]. If within a certain period, there are many tasks unloading to edge nodes has not been handled properly, inevitably affecting the user experience. Therefore, how to formulate an effective scheduling strategy is becoming a key in edge computing [8].

The scheduling problem on edge servers is essentially an NP-hard problem to determine the placement order of N tasks on M servers. Due to the most prominent feature of edge computing is its low latency [9], using the traditional heuristic algorithm to solve the NP-hard scheduling problem on edge servers inevitably has the disadvantage of too long-running time, which means it cannot be used in large-scale scenarios. Online scheduling algorithm is the most promising solution to the scheduling problem of continuous arrival of such tasks. Reinforcement learning, an online learning technique that treats learning as a process of *exploration–evaluation*, is just a good way to solve this continuous decision problem. Our contributions can be summarized as follows.

1. In this paper, we design an online algorithm based on parallel-batch processing machines (P-BPM) transaction processing mode, called Online Parallel-batch Q-learning Algorithm (OnPQ-learning), to improve the concurrency of edge servers, Meanwhile, the tasks to be processed by our method do not need to be generated according to a specific mathematical distribution.
2. We take more evaluation indicator into account, including the time and energy consumption generated by edge servers in processing tasks, the amount of timeout tasks, and the average waiting processing time of tasks as the algorithm optimization goal. In addition, we make some personal insights on how to deal with the time and energy consumption of edge servers.

The remainder of the paper is organized as follows: in Sect. 2, we introduce some related work on task scheduling in edge computing. In Sect. 3, we would formalize the problems we posed. In Sect. 4, we would introduce algorithm overview, how to build the batch and use Q-learning to get the optimal strategy. Simulation results are shown in Sect. 5, followed by conclusions in Sect. 6.

2   Related Work

In this section, we first introduce the recent research on edge computing, and then introduce the application of reinforcement learning in scheduling problems. Finally, we discuss the shortcomings of these methods.

2.1   Research on Edge Computing

How to offload and schedule tasks is of particular interest to edge computing. Recently, considerable progress has been made in about this work.

Urgaonkar [10] transformed the workload scheduling problem into a Markov decision process and solved the problem through Lyapunov optimization strategy. Li et al. [11] proposed a task offloading strategy between edge devices in ad-hoc structure based on the idea of game theory. M Alicherry et al. [12] proposed an intelligent virtual machine layout to shorten the time of data transmission for scheduling strategies aiming at shortening the response time of tasks. As for the scheduling strategy aiming at reducing the operating energy consumption of the server, Zhang et al. [13] used LARAC algorithm to solve the energy saving cost of collaborative operation of the task on the mobile device and cloud in the mobile cloud environment. Zhu et al. [14] proposed a task-oriented energy saving algorithm EARH in the virtual cloud environment. For the scheduling strategy with balancing the number of tasks loaded on each server as the target, Wang et al. [15] used JLGA algorithm to not only shorten the completion time of each server's processing tasks, but also improve the resource utilization of each server. Based on the min-min algorithm, Chen et al. [16] proposed the LBIMM algorithm, which also optimized the completion time and resource utilization of the server. Tan et al. [17] proposed the first online approximate algorithm, called OnDisc to dispatching and scheduling tasks in edge-cloud systems.

2.2   Applications of Reinforcement Learning in Scheduling Problems

In research field of reinforcement learning, some scholars put forward their methods to solve scheduling problems. Peng et al. [18] proposed a fine-grained cloud computing system model and a new task scheduling scheme based on reinforcement learning and queuing theory to optimize task scheduling under resource constraints. Sharma et al. [19] believed that in the Internet of things (IoT) environment, guaranteeing quality of service (QoS) is the most important for real-time application of transmission latency sensitivity, and this paper proposes a scheduling scheme based on dynamic Markov chains to ensure QoS of delay-sensitive traffic in the Internet of things.

However, these methods also have some shortcomings in solving scheduling problems in edge computing. The most obvious disadvantage is that most of the processing of tasks adopts serial processing strategy, that is, the computing resources of an edge server can only process one single task simultaneously. Moreover, while selecting the optimization objective of the algorithm, it is often only considered optimizing a single time overhead or energy consumption, without taking into account the priority of task processing. Different from the above method, we make the tasks executed in parallel on the server to improve the concurrency, and take more evaluation indicator into account, including timeliness of task completion and the number of timeout task. Last but not least, the tasks to be processed by our method can be in arbitrary order and times.

3   Problem Definition

Definition of jobs: jobs are defined as $J = \{j_1, j_2, \ldots, j_n\}$, and each job j is represented by a quad (r_j, res_j, b_j, d_j), in which r_j is the release time of the job

j, res_j is the amount of computing resources needed for the job j, b_j is the data size of the job j, and d_j is the deadline of the job j. If the completion time of task j exceeds d_j, the task j would be regarded as timeout. There will be some transmission delay from one device to the edge server. We define $t_j = b_j/trans_v$ to indicate this delay and $trans_v$ to indicate the data transfer rate. The time that task j actually reaches the edge server is $r'_j = r_j + t_j$.

Definition of edge servers: edge servers are defined as $S = \{s_1, s_2, \ldots, s_n\}$, and each s is represented by a quad (p_s, c_s, v_s, s_s), where p_s represents the processing rate of the server s, c_s is the total amount of resources of the server s, v_s is the energy consumption factor per unit time when processing tasks, w_s is the energy consumption burden per unit time when the edge server s store tasks waiting for processing.

Definition of batchs: to take full advantage of concurrent processing on multi-core cpus, we propose a method of assigning multiple tasks to one batch for parallel processing. All tasks in the one batch will be processed at the same time Batch is defined as $B_{ks} = \{Rb_{ks}, Pb_{ks}, Sb_{ks}\}$, Rb_{ks}, Pb_{ks}, Sb_{ks} denote the generation time, processing time and total computation resource of all jobs in batch B_{ks} on the edge server s respectively, where $Rb_{ks} = \max\{r'_j | j \in B_{ks}\}$, $Pb_{ks} = \max\{p_j | j \in B_{ks}\}$, $Sb_{ks} = \sum_{j \in B_{ks}} res_j$. The start time and completion time of the batch B_{ks} on each server are recorded as $ST_{ks} = \max\{Rki, CT_{(k-1)i}\}$ and $CT_{ks} = ST_{ks} + PT_{ks}$ respectively, where $CT_{(k-1)i}$ refers to the previous one completion time before B_{ks} on the server s.

Energy Consume and Time Consume: the energy consume of a single job j on server s is $e_j = res_j * v_s$. The total energy consume for processing job set of the system is defined as follows:

$$E = \sum_{s=1}^{n} \sum_{j=1}^{n} e_j. \tag{1}$$

The total time consume is depend on the completion time of all jobs:

$$C_{\max} = \max\{CT_{ks}\}. \tag{2}$$

Definition of fail jobs: each task j has its own latest response time d_j, and if the task's completion time exceeds d_j, the processing of j is defined as timeout. We define a collection F to collect these failed tasks, defined as follows:

$$F = \{J_j | ct_j > r_s + d_j, j \in J\}. \tag{3}$$

Average waiting delay: the interval from generation to starting to execute of one task is defined as the waiting delay W_j, so the average waiting latency of the task is defined as:

$$\overline{W} = \sum_{j \in B_{ks}} (ST_{ks})/|J|. \tag{4}$$

There are three optimization objectives of our algorithm: reducing the energy consumption and time consumption caused by processing tasks of edge servers, the number of timeout tasks, and the average waiting delay.

$$Minimize \quad Z = C_{max} + E. \tag{5}$$

$$Minimize \quad |F|, F = \{J_j | cg_j > r_j + d_j, J_j \in J\}. \tag{6}$$

$$Minimize \quad \overline{W}. \tag{7}$$

4   Our Method

In this section, we start with the overall algorithm flow, then introduce how to set up batches and how to use Q-learning to get optimal strategy in detail.

4.1   Algorithm Overview

In order to design an efficient online task scheduling algorithm, we divide the time period of processing tasks into multiple decision cycles of equal length on average $T = \{1, 2, \ldots, t\}$. The task scheduling in each decision cycle, is essentially a sequential decision problem, and it satisfies the markov characteristic, so it can be modeled as the Markov decision process. For the MDP problem in each decision cycle t, we use a quad $M_t = (S(t), A(t), P_{sa}(t), R(s, a))$ to denote it, where $S(t) = 0, 1, 2, 3, \ldots, n$ represents the amount of unprocessed tasks in the current decision cycle, $A(t) = \{1, 2, 3, \ldots, m\}$ represents the number of edge servers selected to process tasks in different states. We define $R(s, a) = aT_{ks} + bE_{ks}$ as the reward when choosing action a in state s, where T_{ks} and E_{ks} represent time and energy consume of batch B_{ks} respectively, a and b are corresponding parameters. We will discuss the reward function in detail in Sect. 4.3. The key of MDP problem is to get an optimal strategy, and we usually use the value function to evaluate and update policies. Considering the actual situation, we define the strategy that can get the minimum value function as the best strategy and the optimal value function and optimal strategy are defined as follows:

$$V^*(s) = R(s) + \min_{a \in A} \lambda \sum_{s' \in S} P_{sa}(s')V^*(s'), \tag{8}$$

$$\pi^*(s_0) = \arg \min V^{\pi^*}(s_0). \tag{9}$$

Next, we will use Q-learning to get the optimal strategy in Sect. 4.3.

4.2   Establishment of Batch

As mentioned above, we divide the time period into multiple decision cycles with equal lengths. At the beginning point of decision cycle $T(t)$, as the limited computing resources of the edge server itself, it is often impossible to assign all unprocessed tasks to the edge server at once. Moreover, taking full advantage of concurrent processing on multi-core cpus is also essential. So it is necessary to set up an empty batch B_{ks} to collect the tasks assigned to the edge server s. In order to reduce the number of overtime tasks, we need to put the task with the highest priority into and initialize the empty batch. For the purpose of working out the priority of each task, we need define the latest start processing time $st_j^{\max}$ and the latest completion time $ct_j^{\max}$ for each task as $ct_j^{\max} = r_j + d_j$, $st_j^{max} = ct_j^{max} - res_j/p_s$, respectively. Then the definition of priority of tasks are as follows:

$$g_j = \frac{1}{st_j^{\max} - T(t)}, \tag{10}$$

where $T(t)$ is beginning point of each decision cycle. From the above definition, we can see that the nearer the latest starting point of a task is to the current time point, the higher the priority to be processed.

Besides, we establish a task candidate set CL to improve the search efficiency of tasks when putting in the appropriate remaining tasks. These candidate tasks need to satisfy two conditions: 1) the resource requirements of these tasks can not exceed the current remaining resources; 2) these tasks will not cause the existing tasks to process out of time. In order to distinguish whether the subsequent added tasks cause the processing time of previously added tasks to time out, we define the latest start processing time $ST_{ks}^{\max}$ of B_{ks} as follows:

$$ST_{ks}^{\max} = \min_{j \in B_{ks}} \{st_j^{\max}\}. \tag{11}$$

The task candidate set CL is defined as:

$$CL = \{j | res_j \leq c_s - Sb_{ks} \bigwedge r_j' \leq st_{ks}^{\max}\}. \tag{12}$$

After the task candidate set is established, the tasks are sorted in descending order according to the priority, and the tasks are selected and put into the batch according to the following mentioned Q-learning method under the precondition of $Sb_{ks} <= c_s$.

4.3   Q-learning Method

In Sect. 4.1, we convert the online task scheduling problem into an MDP problem. In fact, it is a very complex and time-consuming job to establish a complete MDP state transition process. So we need to use Q-learning method to solve the established MDP problem and get the optimal strategy. In Q-learning, for each Q value, the agent continuously selects corresponding behavior in different states with a certain strategy, and updates according to the newly arrived state and the obtained reward value until reaching the state of termination. The way to update the Q value is defined as follows:

$$Q(s,a) = Q(s,a) + \alpha[R(s,a) + \lambda \min_{a'} Q(s',a') - Q(s,a)]. \tag{13}$$

In Eq. (13), α represents the learning rate, and λ represents the discount factor.

Next we would introduce how to calculate the reward and adopt Polman strategy to select actions in the learning process. At last, we give the pseudo-code of the algorithm in Algorithm 1.

The Computation of Reward. In this paper, we consider the reward as an overhead incurred by the scheduler choosing an edge server to process the task set. Reward's computation includes two parts: time cost T and energy cost E of tasks during transmission, waiting and processing. Time cost for a single task is defined as follows:

$$T_j = b_j/trans_v + r_j - st_{ks} + res_j/p_s, \tag{14}$$

the computation of T_j consists of three parts: $b_j/trans_v$ represents the transmission time of the job j from the user equipment to the edge server, $r_j - st_j$ represents the waiting time from the production of the job j to the start of processing of the batch B_{ks} and res_j/p_s represents the time required for the job j to be processed on the edge server s.

The energy consumption of a single task is defined as follows:

$$E_j = b_j/trans_v \times trans_e + (r_j - st_j) \times w_s + res_j \times v_s, \tag{15}$$

the calculation of E_s consists of three parts: $b_j/trans_v \times trans_e$ denotes the transmission energy consumption from the task j generated by the client to the edge server, and $trans_e$ represents the energy consumption per unit time produced by the edge server to maintain communication with user devices, $(r_j - st_j) \times w_s$ represents the energy consumption of job j created by waiting for processing on edge server s, $res_j \times v_s$ is the energy consumed of job j by processing tasks on edge server s_s.

Based on the above analysis, we define the calculation method of time and energy consumption of the batch B_{ks} as follows:

$$T_{ks} = \sum_{j \in B_{ks}} T_j, \tag{16}$$

$$E_{ks} = \sum_{j \in B_{ks}} E_j. \tag{17}$$

At last, we define the reward function as follows:

$$R = aT_{ks} + bE_{ks}. \tag{18}$$

In order to calculate the energy and time consumption generated by batch in one equation, we need a way to unify the two different costs of energy consumption and time delay, so as to calculate the reward value. In some existing papers, however, most scholars do not use appropriate methods to deal with the relationship between time delay and energy consumption, but simply add two parts together as the total cost of edge servers processing tasks. This method is obviously inappropriate, since time delay and energy consumption are two different types of values, and simple addition is not in line with the actual situation, such as shown in [20,21]. In fact, if users offload their tasks to edge servers for processing, they will pay a corresponding fee according to the time spent on edge servers. On the other hand, users also need to pay for the energy consumption produced by edge server for processing their task, so the time and energy consumption produced by the edge server could be unified as the cost that the user needs to pay, which can be calculated as the result of reward value. As shown in Eq. (18), parameters a and b are used to calculate the unit cost of edge servers' occupancy time and energy consumption in processing respectively. Parameters a and b are usually related to the pricing strategy of edge servers operators.

Polman Strategy. During scheduling, the following situation may occur: in state s, $R(s, a_1) < R(s, a_2)$. While $R(s, a_1)$ is small, it's likely that the selected edge server handle fewer tasks, and $R(s, a_2)$ is large enough to allocate resources to more tasks. If you choose behavior based only on the values in the Q table, you are likely to fall into local optimization. In order to remedy this defect, we follow Polman strategy in our method to generate training samples:

$$\pi(s, a_i) = \frac{exp(\frac{Q(s,a_i)}{\tau})}{\sum_{j=1}^{|A|} exp(\frac{Q(s,a_j)}{\tau})}, \tag{19}$$

where $|A|$ is the size of actions, τ is the adjusting factor, the smaller τ is, the closer this strategy is to the greedy strategy, the greater the proportion of exploitation, the less exploration.

Algorithm 1 The OnPQ-learning Algorithm.

1: Initialize $T(t)$, Q table and other parameters, unscheduled job list $J = \{1, 2, 3, \ldots, n\}$.
2: **while** $T(t) \leq T_{max}$ **do**
3:    get start state S_t^s and end state S_t^e, count the numbers of jobs which have been released and calculate the g_j for them, and then initialize the batch B_{ks}.
4:    **for** *iteration* from 1 to Imax **do**
5:        For each action on the current state S_t^i, calculate $Q(s, a)$, choose a^* according to Polman strategy.
6:        Execution a^*, determine the next state S_{t+1}^i, update Q table.
7:        **if** $S_{t+1}^i \neq S_t^e$ **then**
8:            $S_t^i = S_{t+1}^i$ repeat (5).
9:        **end if**
10:    **end for**
11:    $T(t) = T(t + 1)$
12: **end while**

The Pseudo-code of the Algorithm. The pseudo-code is shown in Algorithm 1. With the continuous generation of tasks, at the time point of the beginning of each decision-making cycle, the number of the tasks that have been generated in the edge network are counted. At the same time, tasks come to the system during the decision cycle will be included in next decision cycle. The scheduling priority of the pending tasks is calculated according to its urgency (line 3). Subsequently, Q-learning method is used to find the scheduling strategy through multiple iterations for these unprocessed tasks (line 4–line 10). In each iteration, if all tasks in batchs are processed, the final state S_t^e is reached and meanwhile the iteration would be terminated. Select the appropriate action on the state reached at each stage, calculate the Q value, and update the Q table (line 5–line 6). After the training, the optimal scheduling strategy in the current decision-making period can be obtained according to the Q table.

5   Experiment

In this section, we will start with the experimental setup and the parameter settings, and then evaluate the performance of our algorithm in many aspects by conducting sufficient experiments in real dataset.

5.1   Experiment Settings

We implement our algorithm with Python 3.5. To make the experimental results more convincing, we use the Google cluster trace dataset as our experimental data sets. The three main indicators *release time*, *CPU request*, and *memory request* are selected to build one task sample. These tasks within a release time interval of 60 s are randomly selected to generate five experimental data sets of 100, 200, 300, 400, and 500. Four sets of edge servers were set up to simulate task processing. The parameters of each group of edge servers are (40, 100, 4, 1), (45, 100, 5, 1), (50, 100, 6, 1), (55, 100, 7, 1), $trans_v= 50$, $trans_e=1$. In addition, in order to better simulate the situation of edge cloud and remote cloud cooperation processing tasks, we additionally set up a server to simulate the remote cloud, the parameters are set to (100, 100, 20, 20), $trans_v= 20$, $trans_e= 2$. Other parameters involved in the experiments are shown in Table 1.

Table 1. Model parameter settings

Factors	Values
Polman strategy adjusting factor τ	0.4
Learning rate α	0.5
Discount factor γ	0.5
Decision cycle length $Timeslot$	2 s
Unit cost of occupancy time and energy consumption (a, b)	(0.8, 0.2)
Max decision cycle I_{max}	100
Max iteration T_{max}	60

The algorithm we choose to compare is OnDisc. The OnDisc is a preemptive task scheduling algorithm in the edge computing environment in where a new task is processed according to its own weighted waiting time WRT to select edge server for handling itself. In the meantime, the edge servers schedule the tasks to be processed according to the rules of Highest Residual Density First (HRDF).

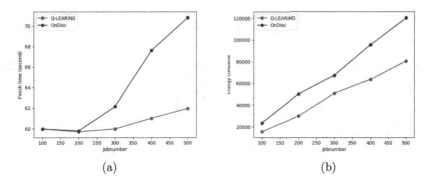

Fig. 1. The performance over time and energy cost.

5.2   Effectiveness Evaluation

Algorithm Performance Comparison. First, we will compare our algorithm with OnDisc algorithm on system performance cost, amount of timeout tasks and average waiting time in the environment without remote cloud participation.

System Overhead. Minimizing the running overhead of the entire edge server processing task is the primary optimization objective. We make statistics about the time and energy consumption of tasks completion, and show them in Fig. 1. In Fig. 1(a), it can be seen that OnPQ-learning algorithm completes tasks earlier than OnDisc algorithm. For OnDisc algorithm, although it reduces the WRT of the whole system, it adopts preemptive scheduling strategy according to HRDF rules while scheduling tasks, leading to inefficiency of edge servers in processing tasks and affecting the completion of tasks. Worse still, with the arrival of new tasks, switching tasks handled by edge servers and hanging up unfinished tasks will result in additional energy consumption overhead for edge servers, which can be seen from Fig. 1(b) that as the size of tasks increases, the energy consumption overhead for edge servers to store unfinished tasks will also increase.

Number of Timeout Tasks and Average Waiting Time. For the scheduling algorithm in the edge computing, ensuring the timely completion of the tasks and reducing the user waiting time for task completion are also two important evaluation criteria. Next, we will compare our algorithm with the OnDisc algorithm with the quantity of timeout tasks and the average task waiting delay. The comparison results are shown in Fig. 2. In Fig. 2(a), with the increase of tasks, the number of timeout tasks of both algorithms is increasing gradually. Compared with our algorithm, the amount of timeout tasks of OnDisc increases faster because: 1) The OnDisc algorithm adopts a preemptive scheduling strategy, and the efficiency of processing tasks is relatively low. When numerous tasks arrive, more tasks cannot be processed in time, which makes the magnitude of time-out tasks increase faster; 2) On the other hand, the HRDF scheduling mode

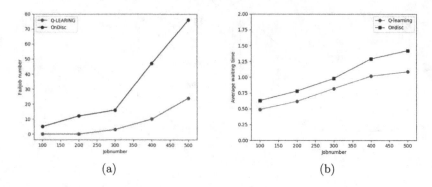

Fig. 2. The performance over quantity of overtime tasks and average waiting time.

adopted by OnDisc is mainly affected by the remaining processing time of tasks. Figure 2(b), can also attribute to two reasons mentioned before.

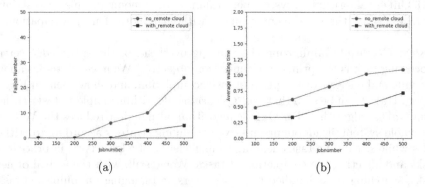

Fig. 3. The impact of using remote cloud over quantity of overtime tasks and average waiting time

The Influence of Remote Cloud on Experimental Results. In practical edge computing scenarios, it is not enough to deal with tasks only by limited edge cloud node resources. Usually, these tasks need to be handled in collaboration with remote cloud servers to meet the needs of computing resources for users tasks. In this section, we will mainly discuss the impact of the presence or absence of remote cloud on the edge cloud system, and the impact on the average waiting time of the task and the number of timeout tasks after adding the remote cloud.

The Impact of The Presence of Remote Cloud. The results of the two comparisons are shown in Fig. 3. From Fig. 3(a), we can see that there is no obvious difference between adding and not adding remote cloud processing tasks to the edge cloud system if the magnitude of tasks to be processed is small. The reason may be that the resources on the edge cloud are sufficient to handle the tasks in

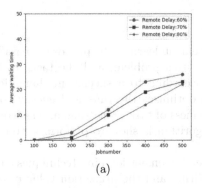 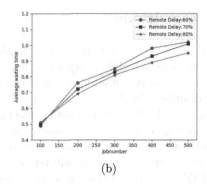

(a)   (b)

Fig. 4. The impact of latency to over quantity of overtime tasks and average waiting time.

instance of the total number of tasks is small. As the amount of tasks continues to increase, only using edge clouds to handle tasks could be no longer sufficient for task processing, compared to joining the remote cloud at this time, there are more overtime tasks without joining the remote cloud, owing to the computing resources on the edge cloud are less than those of the remote cloud, the same is true for processing speed. Similarly, as shown in Fig. 3(b), there is a longer average task waiting time if no remote cloud assisted edge cloud processing task, which is also caused by the edge server processing less resources and slower processing speed. Although the task transfer to the remote cloud will result in more transmission delay, which may make the task response time increase, it is still a good idea to undertake partial processing pressure by the remote cloud in order to ensure the user experience when edge cloud can't cope with more tasks.

The Impact of Communication Latency on Remote Cloud. Figure 4 shows the impact of communication delay variation between user and remote cloud computing center on the results of the two algorithms. We set up two remote cloud servers to assist the edge computing center to process tasks, and set the transmission speed between user and remote cloud to 80%, 70%, 60% of the user-edge cloud transmission speed respectively. By simulating the operation of our algorithm in the above environment, we observe the effect of the *user-remote cloud* transmission delay on the amount of timeout tasks and the average waiting time of these tasks. Based on the experimental results, we can find that as the transmission rate between users and remote clouds slows down, the amount of timeout tasks and average waiting time both increases. The reason for this phenomenon may be: some tasks must be transferred to the remote cloud for processing in order to ensure the timely completion of most tasks when the edge cloud receives too many tasks and exceeds its processing capacity, but in the process of decreasing transmission rate, more delay will be generated, which would not only result in more task latency but also more task timeouts.

6 Conclusion

In this paper, we use the idea of reinforcement learning to propose a parallel online tasks scheduling algorithm to solve this problem, and the tasks to be processed do not need to be generated according to a specific mathematical distribution. Furthermore, our algorithm optimizes the time and energy consumption of edge servers, ensures the timeliness of task processing, and shortens the waiting time of tasks. Finally, our algorithm is show to perform better in plenty of experiments in real data sets.

In the future work, we will try other reinforcement learning techniques such as DQN to improve the efficiency of algorithm and the utilization value of the algorithm in real scene.

References

1. Chen, Z., et al.: An empirical study of latency in an emerging class of edge computing applications for wearable cognitive assistance. In: The Second ACM/IEEE Symposium on Edge Computing, pp. 1–14, October 2017
2. Gouglidis, A., et al.: The extended cloud: review and analysis of mobile edge computing and fog from a security and resilience perspective. IEEE J. Sel. Areas Commun. **PP**(99), 1 (2016)
3. Ahmed, A., Ahmed, E.: A survey on mobile edge computing. In: International Conference on Intelligent Systems & Control (2016)
4. Guo, S., Xiao, B., Yang, Y., Yang, Y.: Energy-efficient dynamic offloading and resource scheduling in mobile cloud computing. In: IEEE Infocom-the IEEE International Conference on Computer Communications (2016)
5. Shi, W., Sun, H., Cao, J., Zhang, Q., Liu, W.: Edge computing-an emerging computing model for the internet of everything era. Jisuanji Yanjiu yu Fazhan/Comput. Res. Dev. **54**, 907–924 (2017)
6. Pan, J., McElhannon, J.: Future edge cloud and edge computing for internet of things applications. IEEE Internet of Things J. **5**(1), 439–449 (2018)
7. Yang, Z., Niyato, D., Ping, W.: Offloading in mobile cloudlet systems with intermittent connectivity. IEEE Trans. Mob. Comput. **14**(12), 2516–2529 (2015)
8. Mach, P., Becvar, Z.: Mobile edge computing: a survey on architecture and computation offloading. IEEE Commun. Surv. Tutor. **19**(3), 1628–1656 (2017)
9. Dolui, K., Datta, S.K.: Comparison of edge computing implementations: fog computing, cloudlet and mobile edge computing. In: Global Internet of Things (2017, Summit)
10. Urgaonkar, R., Wang, S., He, T., Zafer, M., Chan, K., Leung, K.K.: Dynamic service migration and workload scheduling in edge-clouds. Perform. Eval. **91**(C), 205–228 (2015)
11. Li, T., Wu, M., Min, Z., Liao, W.: An overhead-optimizing task scheduling strategy for ad-hoc based mobile edge computing. IEEE Access **5**, 5609–5622 (2017)
12. Alicherry, M., Lakshman, T.V.: Optimizing data access latencies in cloud systems by intelligent virtual machine placement. In: IEEE Infocom (2013)
13. Zhang, W., Wen, Y., Wu, D.O.: Energy-efficient scheduling policy for collaborative execution in mobile cloud computing. In: Infocom, IEEE (2013)

14. Zhu, X., Yang, L.T., Chen, H., Ji, W., Liu, X.: Real-time tasks oriented energy-aware scheduling in virtualized clouds. IEEE Trans. Cloud Comput. **2**(2), 168–180 (2014)
15. Wang, T., Liu, Z., Yi, C., Xu, Y., Dai, X.: Load balancing task scheduling based on genetic algorithm in cloud computing. In: Control Conference (2016)
16. Chen, H., Wang, F., Na, H., Akanmu, G.: User-priority guided min-min scheduling algorithm for load balancing in cloud computing. In: Parallel Computing Technologies (2013)
17. Tan, H., Han, Z., Li, X.Y., Lau, F.C.M.: Online job dispatching and scheduling in edge-clouds. In: IEEE Infocom -IEEE Conference on Computer Communications (2017)
18. Peng, Z., Cui, D., Zuo, J., Li, Q., Xu, B., Lin, W.: Random task scheduling scheme based on reinforcement learning in cloud computing. Cluster Comput. **18**(4), 1595–1607 (2015). https://doi.org/10.1007/s10586-015-0484-2
19. Kumar, N., Sharma, R.: QoS-alert Markov chain based scheduling scheme in internet of things. In: IEEE Globecom Workshops (2015)
20. Van Le, D., Tham, C.-K.: A deep reinforcement learning based offloading scheme in ad-hoc mobile clouds. In: IEEE INFOCOM 2018-IEEE Conference on Computer Communications Workshops (INFOCOM WKSHPS), pp. 760–765. IEEE (2018)
21. Le, D., Tham, C.K.: Quality of service aware computation offloading in an ad-hoc mobile cloud. IEEE Trans. Veh. Technol. **67**, 8890–8904 (2018)

Positioning

Localization Research Based on Low Cost Sensor

Jian Zuo[1], Chenghao Zhang[1], Kuang-I Shu[1,2], and Heng Zhang[1(✉)]

[1] College of Computer and Information Science, Southwest University, Chongqing,
China
dahaizhangheng@163.com
[2] E/E Architecture Department, Beijing New Energy Vehicle Technology Innovation
Center Co., Ltd., Beijing, China

Abstract. With the increasing demand for indoor navigation applications, indoor navigation has become a research hotspot in many technical fields. High-precision sensors are expensive, and they are often used in industrial and aerospace applications. Low-cost sensors can cause severe drift and noise. This paper uses a simple, low-cost Inertial measurement unit (IMU) and effectively evaluates the precise position of pedestrians. This paper designs a pedestrian position estimation based on low-cost inertial sensors. To solve the problem of inertial sensing noise and accumulated errors during the movement, based on the EKF algorithm, a multi-condition threshold detection method is proposed, and then a zero-speed update, an angular speed update, and a yaw angle update are designed. In the measurement state, the proposed measurement error vector effectively eliminates the cumulative error during walking. Finally, using this algorithm to perform straight and rectangular walking routes, corresponding experiments were performed on the effectiveness of the method used. The proposed method for estimating the inertial navigation of pedestrians has an error within 3.8%. This basic research is of great significance in rehabilitation training and somatosensory play.

Keywords: IMU · Multi-condition threshold detection · ZUPT · EKF

1 Introduction

In the past decades, people's demand for location-based services (LBS) is growing exponentially. Sensor hardware such as accelerometers, magnetometers, gyroscopes, barometers, Bluetooth, WiFi, and GPS makes precise positioning possible. Global Navigation Satellite System (GNSS) has been widely applied to electronic products, especially smartphones. The demand for LBS services in robotics, logistics, healthcare, travel, and entertainment is expected to grow in the coming years [7]. Owing to the developments of technology, the GPS receiver can be tracked outdoors within a 5-m margin of error [12]. Although GPS positioning is very successful out of doors, it is difficult to decode GPS indoors

© Springer Nature Switzerland AG 2020
Z. Yu et al. (Eds.): GPC 2020, LNCS 12398, pp. 379–390, 2020.
https://doi.org/10.1007/978-3-030-64243-3_28

due to the additional 10–30 dB signal loss caused by buildings and walls [13]. At present, there are several kinds of indoor location technologies, including fingerprint-based WLAN (WiFi) and magnetic fingerprint location, which are based on a hypothesis that each location has a specific signal feature. In the first stage, the signal features are extracted and stored and the radio map is created. In the second stage, the fingerprint is compared to the database for locating [3,18,19]. WiFi technology can cover the entire indoor location area to an increased extent with less equipment, and the equipment cost is low, the signal transmission is fast and easy to deploy, but a) data collection is labor-intensive and time-consuming. The surveyor needs to collect enough signal samples at each reference point to establish the fingerprint database. b) Database mainte-nance is difficult because signal patterns change over time and are susceptible to environmental changes. Impulse radio ultra-wideband (IR-UWB) is also an indoor location solution. Although the location solution based on UWB can achieve higher tracking accuracy (<1 m), it is usually used in industrial appli-cations, because the transmitter consumes a large amount of electricity. If there is no additional modify smartphone hardware, it is impossible to implement it on a smartphone. As a result, UWB based solutions are not suitable for pri-vate users. For the visualization based solution, the integrated camera of the smartphone is used to create images and compare them with the database [4]. An ultrasonic positioning system is a relatively simple indoor positioning solu-tion. Ultrasound is greatly affected by the multipath effect and no line of sight propagation, and ultrasonic frequency is affected by the Doppler effect and tem-perature. At the same time, a large number of basic hardware facilities are also required, with high cost [9]. Radiofrequency identification (RFID) is a low-cost indoor positioning solution. Also known as an electronic label, it can be used for fast read-write and long-term tracking management by using non-contact pattern recognition technology. However, its positioning accuracy is not high, the system stability is poor, and it is easy to miss [6,11]. At present, the inertial measurement unit has been widely used in robot positioning, human motion cap-ture and other fields in recent years. However, due to the drift of the sensor itself and the interference of the external complex environment to the magnetometer, the IMU can not provide stable and accurate positioning service for a long time. Therefore, using inertial sensors to provide long-term and accurate indoor and outdoor positioning has become a very challenging topic [15]. In the existing research, pedestrian track estimation (PDR) has stability and reliability. The dead reckoning device works by starting from the known position of the tracking device and then measuring the change of inertia on the device, which is achieved using an inertial measurement device (IMU) [6]. According to the data obtained by the sensor, the number of steps, step length, and direction of walkers were measured and counted in the periodic motion, and the walking trajectory and displacement of walkers were calculated [2]. Because PDR is autonomous and free from external interference, it can be operated in various complex situations. In recent years, many scholars focus on autonomous indoor navigation systems. Because of its low cost, small size, strong autonomy, and good environmental adaptability, MEMS inertial equipment have become the best choice for indoor positioning [1], especially for the unknown environment.

PDR is based on the characteristics of the pedestrian's periodic gait motion, using the accelerometer to measure the walking steps and estimate the step length, and combining the direction of the gyroscope to calculate the position, walking distance, speed, direction and other information, so the algorithm includes the step frequency detection, step length estimation, course estimation and position estimation. The Micro-electromechanical Systems MEMS consists of a triaxial accelerometer, a triaxial gyroscope, and a triaxial magnetometer that can calculate position by measuring step size and heading. However, only the PDR algorithm has a large error, and the sensor will cumulate error with the increase of time. Due to the inertia of motion, the sensor can not immediately return to zero when the foot is stationary. If PDR is used for drifting data, large errors will be generated and accumulated. A common algorithm to minimize positioning error is zero-speed update algorithm (ZUPT), which can effectively improve the accuracy of inertial navigation system by means of ZUPT's detection of the foot state and zeroing the foot speed in the static state. In addition, we also used the Extended Kalman Filter (EKF), which adopts the sequential steps as prediction - measurement - correction. According to the obtained system measurement value, the result with the greatest possibility is estimated from the system with errors, effectively reducing the error growth of the sensor itself [8, 10, 14, 17].

2   System Overview

In indoor positioning systems, pedestrian navigation is widely used. In many scholars' studies, inertial nodes are often placed on the feet [5, 16] to measure the position and direction of people walking. This article uses a low-cost MPU9250 inertial sensor bound to the instep. The direction of the sensor is the left side of the human body on the x axis, the y axis points behind the human body, and the z axis points above the human body, as shown in the Fig. 1. The sensors mainly include accelerometers, gyroscopes and magnetometers. The stability of acceleration and angular velocity is $0.01\,g$ and $0.05°/s$, respectively, and the ranges are $16\,g$ and $2000°/s$. The output frequency of the data $100\,Hz$. The MPU9250 is connected to the pc via wifi, and can output acceleration, angular velocity, and magnetometer raw data. In the next chapter we describe the design of the entire human position algorithm.

3   Agorithm Design

3.1   Flow Chart

In indoor navigation, the most basic way to calculate displacement is to directly perform double integration through acceleration. However, this process often

Fig. 1. Sensor attached to the instep

brings large cumulative errors, and effective error correction seems more necessary. The sensor is installed on the instep of the foot. According to the walking
characteristics, there is a zero-speed time interval during walking. In theory, the
speed of this interval should be zero, and the speed can be corrected. The idea of
a zero-velocity update proposes a method based on inertial navigation to calculate pedestrian position information. The algorithm flow is as follows. As shown
in the Fig. 2.

1) Perform mean filtering on the original signal acceleration and angular velocity.
2) Use a strapdown inertial navigation algorithm to solve speed and position.
3) Detect when pedestrians are in their stance phase.
4) When the speed is zero, the angular velocity and the speed error are used as
   the input of EKF.
5) Detect whether the pedestrian is walking straight. If it is walking straight,
   the yaw angle will not change. The yaw angle error will also be used as the
   input of the EKF. The final EKF output will obtain the speed and position
   information.

3.2   Walking State Detection

In the inertial navigation algorithm, due to the periodic movement of the human
gait, the cumulative error will become larger and larger. Considering the characteristics of the periodic movement of the human walking gait, it can be divided
into a stance phase and a swing phase as shown in Fig. 3. In the stationary state,
the heel touches the ground first, and the foot part touches the ground, and then
the foot completely touches the ground. At this stage, we think that the foot is
stationary, that is, the speed is zero, then the heel is off the ground, and the toe

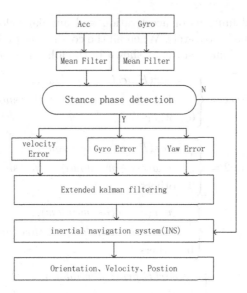

Fig. 2. Algorithm flowchart

is off the ground. Human gait periodic process. In order to accurately detect the movement state of pedestrians, a state detection algorithm must be proposed. In this paper, a multi-condition threshold is used to detect the stationary state. To detect the stationary state, the average acceleration and angular velocity data from the footstep sensor are first filtered. When the stationary state is used, the acceleration and angular velocity are both stable. When in the stationary state, the acceleration and angular velocity values change. Are relatively large, as shown in Fig. 4 and Fig. 5. According to the way of wearing in the experiment, when the human body walks periodically, the acceleration changes significantly with respect to the x-axis and the y-axis, and the z-axis does not change much during the walking of the human body. Similarly, the angular velocity is about the changes in the x-axis and y-axis obvious. The way to use energy, product and sum for acceleration signals is defined as the following formulas:

$$E_{acc} = \sqrt{(a_x)^2 + (a_y)^2}$$
$$P_{acc} = (a_x) * (a_y) \tag{1}$$
$$S_{acc} = (a_x) + (a_y)$$

Energy represents the square root of the sum of the square of the x-axis acceleration and the square of the y-axis acceleration. The product is the multiplication of the x-axis acceleration and the y-axis acceleration. The sum is the sum of the x-axis acceleration and the y-axis acceleration. The angle difference is defined by the following formula

$$E_{gro} = \sqrt{(w_x)^2 + (w_y)^2} \tag{2}$$

According to the definitions of acceleration and angular velocity, the window variances are obtained separately. When all the conditions are met, it is moving, otherwise, it is a stationary state, as shown in the following formula.

$$condition1 = \begin{cases} 1 & \begin{aligned}&var(E\_acc(i-window),...,\\&E\_acc(i+window)) < threshold\_E\end{aligned} \\ 0 & others \end{cases} \tag{3}$$

$$condition2 = \begin{cases} 1 & \begin{aligned}&var(P\_acc(i-window),...,\\&P\_acc(i+window)) < threshold\_P\end{aligned} \\ 0 & others \end{cases} \tag{4}$$

$$condition3 = \begin{cases} 1 & \begin{aligned}&var(S\_acc(i-window),...,\\&S\_acc(i+window)) < threshold\_S\end{aligned} \\ 0 & others \end{cases} \tag{5}$$

$$condition4 = \begin{cases} 1 & \begin{aligned}&var(E\_gro(i-window),...,\\&E\_gro(i+window)) < threshold\_Ew\end{aligned} \\ 0 & others \end{cases} \tag{6}$$

$$condition5 = \begin{cases} 1 & w(i) < threshold\_A \\ 0 & others \end{cases} \tag{7}$$

$$isStance = \begin{cases} 1 & \begin{aligned}&condition1\&\&condition2\&\&condition3\\&\&\&condition4\&\&condition5\end{aligned} \\ 0 & others \end{cases} \tag{8}$$

When all the conditions are met, it is marked as 1 and it is the starting phase, otherwise, it is the swing phase. In this article, the parameters set $threshold\_E = 1$, $threshold\_P = 15, threshold\_S = 1, threshold\_Ew = 1000, window = 12$.

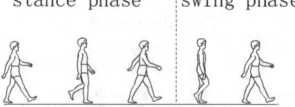

Fig. 3. Walking gait cycle

The following Fig. 6 shows the state detection effect diagram when a pedestrian is walking.

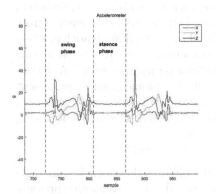

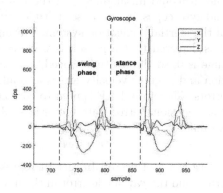

Fig. 4. Raw acceleration data

Fig. 5. Raw gyroscope data

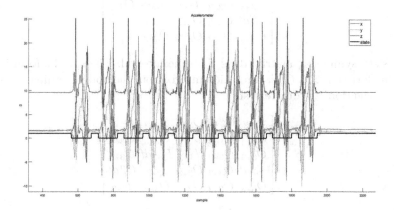

Fig. 6. Stance phase detection

3.3 Extended Kalman Filter Algorithm

This paper uses an inertial navigation system to calculate the speed, displacement, and direction of inertial sensors on the feet. Due to the problems of bias and drift and misalignment of the installation position, such as accelerometers and gyroscopes, it will cause attitude errors, speed errors and displacement errors of the inertial navigation system. Through the above detection algorithm, when it is detected that a person is walking in a stationary state, the speed at this time is 0, so the attitude, speed, and position can be used as errors. Acceleration and angular velocity errors also affect attitude, velocity, and displacement errors. Therefore, EKF is used to correct the corresponding errors. Therefore, a 15-dimensional error state vector is established, which is defined as the following formula:

$$\delta x = \{\delta \Psi \quad \delta w \quad \delta p \quad \delta v \quad \delta a\} \tag{9}$$

$\delta \Psi$ is a $3 * 1$ vector. In turn, it represents the pitch angle error, the roll angle error, and the yaw angle error in the navigation coordinate system. δp represents the position error in the navigation coordinate system. δv represents the velocity error in the navigation coordinate system. δa represents the accelerometer bias. This vector is used as the state vector of the EKF. This article designs EKF as follows:

$$\delta x_k = F \delta x_{k-1} + w_{k-1} \tag{10}$$

Where term δx_k is error state, δx_{k-1} is the last filter error state. w_{k-1} is the process noise. The transition matrix F is defined as follows:

$$F = \begin{bmatrix} I_{3*3} & C_b^n dt & O_{3*3} & O_{3*3} & O_{3*3} \\ O_{3*3} & I_{3*3} & O_{3*3} & O_{3*3} & O_{3*3} \\ O_{3*3} & O_{3*3} & I_{3*3} & I_{3*3} dt & O_{3*3} \\ -Sdt & O_{3*3} & O_{3*3} & I_{3*3} & C_b^n dt \\ O_{3*3} & O_{3*3} & O_{3*3} & O_{3*3} & I_{3*3} \end{bmatrix} \tag{11}$$

S is a skew symmetric matrix. dt is the time interval. The specific form is the following formula (13). C_b^n is a rotation matrix from the body coordinate system to the navigation coordinate system

$$S = \begin{bmatrix} I_{3*3} & C_b^n dt & O_{3*3} & O_{3*3} & O_{3*3} \\ O_{3*3} & I_{3*3} & O_{3*3} & O_{3*3} & O_{3*3} \\ O_{3*3} & O_{3*3} & I_{3*3} & I_{3*3} dt & O_{3*3} \\ -Sdt & O_{3*3} & O_{3*3} & I_{3*3} & C_b^n dt \\ O_{3*3} & O_{3*3} & O_{3*3} & O_{3*3} & I_{3*3} \end{bmatrix} \tag{12}$$

$$S = \begin{bmatrix} 0 & -a_z & a_y \\ a_z & 0 & -a_x \\ -a_y & a_y & 0 \end{bmatrix} \tag{13}$$

According to the zero speed more speed algorithm, when the pedestrian is stance phase, the velocity and angular velocity are theoretically 0, and the actual state is not 0, and an EKF filtering update is performed on this. Based on the idea that the yaw angle is constant during the process of straight walking, this paper adds the yaw angle to estimate the yaw angle error in the case of straight travel while adding the yaw angle to the straight line. This paper proposes that the measurement vector of EKF is defined as (14). The transition matrix of the EKF observation equation is defined as (15).

$$M = \begin{bmatrix} yaw_{error} & gyro_{error} & v_{error} \end{bmatrix} \tag{14}$$

$$H = \begin{bmatrix} [001] & O_{1*3} & O_{1*3} & O_{1*3} & O_{1*3} \\ O_{1*3} & I_{1*3} & O_{1*3} & O_{1*3} & O_{1*3} \\ O_{1*3} & O_{1*3} & O_{1*3} & I_{1*3} & O_{1*3} \end{bmatrix} \tag{15}$$

yaw_{error} is an update of the yaw angle. When a pedestrian walks straight, it can be observed that the yaw angle has not changed. We define the following formula 16 to detect the error of yaw angle when walking straight.

$$yaw_{error} = \begin{cases} 0 & yaw_t - yaw_{t-1} \\ & < threshold_{yaw} \\ yaw_t - \frac{yaw_{t-1} + yaw_{t-2} + yaw_{t-3}}{3} & others \end{cases} \tag{16}$$

where $threshold_{yaw}$ is set to 3 and yaw_{t-1} is yaw at k time.

The filter error state is available after the measurement is obtained at time k. The EKF update equation is as follows:

$$\delta x_{k|k} = \delta x_{k|k-1} + K * (M - H * \delta x_{k|k-1}) \tag{17}$$

K is Kalman gain and M is error measurement, as in formula 14. $\delta x_{k|k-1}$ is the predicted error state. Kalman gain is calculated as Eq. 18

$$K = \frac{(P * (H)')}{((H) * P * (H)' + R)} \tag{18}$$

P is the estimation error covarance matrix, which is a $15 * 15$ matrix R is the covariance matrix of the measurement state.

In the condition of multi-condition detection, when the footstep is in the stance phase, the EKF algorithm estimates the speed, angular velocity, and yaw angle as the measurement state estimation of the EKF to achieve the accurate estimation of the final displacement.

4   Experimental Results and Analysis

This experiment uses MPU9250 equipment, which is bound to the instep and worn as shown in Fig. 1. In order to verify the effectiveness of the algorithm, a straight path and a rectangular path are walked. In the course of straight walking, we separately verify the contrast effects of the ZUPT algorithm and yaw error correction. In the course of rectangular walking, this experiment verifies the effectiveness and accuracy of the algorithm through closed routes.

Experiment 1 The walking path of this experiment is a straight path. The actual distance is 21 * 0.6 m = 12.6 m. Figure 7 is an inertial navigation algorithm, without using any algorithm to correct the roadmap. It can be seen that the double integration using acceleration directly will result in serious route deviation. Figure 8 shows the effect of the route after the ZUPT algorithm which obviously corrects the actual path, and Fig. 9 shows the result of the yaw angle correction which has correction effect on the yaw angle deviation of straight line walking. From the experimental results, the uncorrected inertial navigation is divergent, which is far from the actual situation. After the ZUPT algorithm observes that the path matches the actual path, but there is a certain yaw angle difference, and finally the yaw correction method can be used to correct the final result.

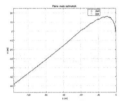   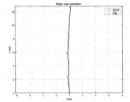

Fig. 7. Course without any correction   **Fig. 8.** Course with zupt correction   **Fig. 9.** Course with zupt and yaw correction

In experiment two, this experiment took a rectangular path. The actual walking rectangle is 30 * 0.6 m = 18 m in length and 18 * 0.6 m = 10.8 m in width. According to the proposed algorithm, the experimental simulation is performed, as shown in Fig. 10. This path is a closed matrix. The difference between the start position and the end position is used to calculate the error. The true error in this experiment is 3.8%.

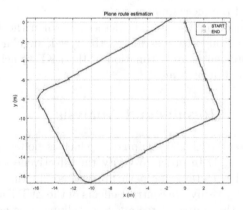

Fig. 10. Rectangular route

5 Conclusion

Positioning based on inertial sensing has become a hotspot in current research. In pedestrian navigation, high-precision sensor devices are often not suitable. This paper uses low-cost sensors based on the ZUPT method, adds angular velocity error measurement and yaw angle measurement, and finally uses Kalman filtering to estimate the position. The effectiveness of ZUPT and yaw angle correction is effectively verified through experiments. The rectangle calculates the accuracy of the algorithm with a final error of 3.8%. In this paper, high-precision pedestrian path navigation is finally achieved through low-cost sensors.

In the future. We will continue to study pedestrian gait patterns and will study multi-node fusion technology to more accurately explore pedestrian navigation issues. Subsequent in-depth research is urgently needed for the development of its related fields.

References

1. Cai, C.l., Liu, Y., Liu, Y.W.: Status quo and trend of inertial integrated navigation system based on mems. J. Chin. Inertial Technol. **5**, 562–567 (2009)
2. Diaz, E.M., Gonzalez, A.L.M., de Ponte Müller, F.: Standalone inertial pocket navigation system. In: 2014 IEEE/ION Position, Location and Navigation Symposium-PLANS 2014, pp. 241–251. IEEE (2014)
3. Du, Y., Arslan, T.: Magnetic field indoor positioning system based on automatic spatial-segmentation strategy. In: 2017 International Conference on Indoor Positioning and Indoor Navigation (IPIN), pp. 1–8. IEEE (2017)
4. Ebner, M., Zell, A.: Centering behavior with a mobile robot using monocular foveated vision. Robot. Auton. Syst. **32**(4), 207–218 (2000)
5. Foxlin, E.: Pedestrian tracking with shoe-mounted inertial sensors. IEEE Comput. Graphics Appl. **25**(6), 38–46 (2005)
6. House, S., Connell, S., Milligan, I., Austin, D., Hayes, T.L., Chiang, P.: Indoor localization using pedestrian dead reckoning updated with RFID-based fiducials. In: 2011 Annual International Conference of the IEEE Engineering in Medicine and Biology Society, pp. 7598–7601. IEEE (2011)
7. Husen, M.N., Lee, S.: Indoor location sensing with invariant WI-FI received signal strength fingerprinting. Sensors **16**(11), 1898 (2016)
8. Jiménez, A.R., Seco, F., Prieto, J.C., Guevara, J.: Indoor pedestrian navigation using an INS/EKF framework for yaw drift reduction and a foot-mounted IMU. In: 2010 7th Workshop on Positioning, Navigation and Communication, pp. 135–143. IEEE (2010)
9. Kim, Y.H., Song, U.K., Kim, B.K.: Development of an accurate low-cost ultrasonic localization system for autonomous mobile robots in indoor environments. J. Meas. Sci. Instrum. **1**, 16 (2010)
10. Ligorio, G., Sabatini, A.M.: A novel Kalman filter for human motion tracking with an inertial-based dynamic inclinometer. IEEE Trans. Biomed. Eng. **62**(8), 2033–2043 (2015)
11. Ni, L.M., Liu, Y., Lau, Y.C., Patil, A.P.: LANDMARC: indoor location sensing using active RFID. In: Proceedings of the First IEEE International Conference on Pervasive Computing and Communications (PerCom 2003), pp. 407–415. IEEE (2003)

12. Özsoy, K., Bozkurt, A., Tekin, İ.: 2D indoor positioning system using GPS signals. In: 2010 International Conference on Indoor Positioning and Indoor Navigation, pp. 1–6. IEEE (2010)

13. Peterson, B., Bruckner, D., Heye, S.: Measuring GPS signals indoors. In: 9th world congress of the International Association of Institutes of Navigation, Amsterdam, 18–21 November 1997 (1997)

14. Song, J.W., Park, C.G.: Enhanced pedestrian navigation based on course angle error estimation using cascaded Kalman filters. Sensors 18(4), 1281 (2018)

15. Tsai, F., Chiou, Y.S., Chang, H.: A positioning scheme combining location tracking with vision assisting for wireless sensor networks. J. Appl. Res. Technol. 11(2), 292–300 (2013)

16. Yun, X., Bachmann, E.R., Moore, H., Calusdian, J.: Self-contained position tracking of human movement using small inertial/magnetic sensor modules. In: Proceedings 2007 IEEE International Conference on Robotics and Automation, pp. 2526–2533. IEEE (2007)

17. Zhang, W., Li, X., Wei, D., Ji, X., Yuan, H.: A foot-mounted PDR system based on IMU/EKF+ HMM+ ZUPT+ ZARU+ HDR+ compass algorithm. In: 2017 International conference on indoor positioning and indoor navigation (IPIN), pp. 1–5. IEEE (2017)

18. Zhuang, Y., Shen, Z., Syed, Z., Georgy, J., Syed, H., El-Sheimy, N.: Autonomous WLAN heading and position for smartphones. In: 2014 IEEE/ION Position, Location and Navigation Symposium-PLANS 2014, pp. 1113–1121. IEEE (2014)

19. Zhuang, Y., Syed, Z., Georgy, J., El-Sheimy, N.: Autonomous smartphone-based WIFI positioning system by using access points localization and crowdsourcing. Pervasive Mob. Comput. 18, 118–136 (2015)

Relative Floor Estimation for Indoor Co-navigation: A Machine Learning Approach

Chanxin Zhou[✉], Ao Luo, and Bang Wang

School of Electronic Information and Communications,
Huazhong University of Science and Technology (HUST), Wuhan 430074, China
{chanxinzhou,latalio,wangbang}@hust.edu.cn

Abstract. Relative floor estimation plays an important role in infrastructure-free indoor co-navigation applications. Instead of locating exact floors for two users, we study the problem of estimating their floor relation from a machine learning approach to facilitate co-navigation. In this paper, we regard the floor relation estimation as a classification problem where a relation classifier is pre-trained to output the floor relation for two new samples. We extract various signals from smartphone internal sensors and then engineer relative features for training a relation classifier. We experiment those typical classification models with field measurements from two buildings and analyze the impacting factors on classification accuracy. Results show that the random forest model single out from other classifiers and can achieve 88.35% classification accuracy for training and testing in the same building and 61.67% for training and testing in different buildings.

Keywords: Relative floor estimation · Relative feature · Classification models · Random forest

1 Introduction

The growing demand for *location-based services* (LBS) has facilitated the rapid development of indoor and outdoor localization technologies. In the outdoor environment, *global positioning system* (GPS) works well in most daily situations. However, the performance of GPS could greatly degrade in indoor environments due to wall blocking and multi-path effects. Fortunately, positioning methods based on *mobile network* (MN) [1] or *wireless local area networks* (WLAN) [2,3] compensate for the limitations of GPS to some extent in indoor environments. Recently, many positioning and navigation schemes based on WLAN have been proposed [4,5]. However, most of them require pre-trained databases or detailed indoor layout, which is either expensive or cumbersome.

Recently, Li et al. [6] have designed and implemented an interesting co-navigation APP, called Let's Meet, to guide two indoor users to find each other

© Springer Nature Switzerland AG 2020
Z. Yu et al. (Eds.): GPC 2020, LNCS 12398, pp. 391–402, 2020.
https://doi.org/10.1007/978-3-030-64243-3_29

without estimating their exact locations. Although the co-navigation application is infrastructure-fee and localization-free, it cannot well address the relative floor problem. That is, the co-navigation should first prompt whether two users are on the same floor level; And if not, it should prompt at least which user is at a higher floor. We notice that such relative floor estimation is a key component for such co-navigation applications.

We further illustrate a scenario of using relative floor estimation in the initialization of a co-navigation process, as shown in Fig. 1. Alice and Bob want to find each other via the guidance of the co-navigation APP. At the start, both have no knowledge about their locations and layout information of this building. Obviously, the first step should be guiding two users to the same floor, if they are not; And then navigate them to each other on that floor using the methods like that proposed in Let's Meet. However, it is not an easy task to locate the absolute layer of a user without infrastructure based information, like fingerprint databases and indoor layouts. Yet barely based on GPS is with too large errors. As presented in Fig. 1, the vertical localization error of GPS may up to several layers of the building.

In the last decade, some solutions have been proposed for floor localization, yet all requiring indoor layouts, fingerprint databases or sensor calibrations, which are usually unavailable or time-consuming in practice. These methods can be generally divided into three categories: wireless signal-based methods [7,9,12], sensor signal-based methods [13,14] and fusion model-based methods [8,11]. The wireless signal approaches exploit the radio signal fingerprint to localize the user floor; The sensor approaches mainly use barometers to estimate location height and then the floor level from building information; While fusion models try to fuse different signal sources to improve the accuracy of floor estimation.

For wireless signal based methods, SkyLoc [12] first applied the global system for mobile (GSM) network to the floor localization by fingerprinting and achieve 73% accuracy within one floor error. However, such a method requires an offline burdensome fingerprint map construction process. Lohan [9] proposed to fit the signals propagation model for the indoor localization of multi-floor buildings; While [7] uses the RSS of AP to decide the floor of users, but the AP deployment information should be known as a prior for both [9] and [7], which are not always available in practice. As for sensor signal based methods, the accelerometer and barometer in smartphone have been exploited in [14] and [13] to detect the user's behavior of upstairs or downstairs, respectively. However, such sensor based methods require the calibration operation before localization, and some smartphone may not support specific sensors like barometer. Based on the above schemes, researcher in [11] and [8] proposed that fusing different source data to improve the estimation performance, yet burdensome calibration work or expensive hardware costs are still needed.

Per above discussions, we argue that relative floor estimation is important to infrastructure-free co-navigation, yet none of existing methods can meet the requirements. In this paper, we address the relative floor estimation from a machine learning approach and convert the task into a classification problem, where the objective is to estimate whether two users are on the same floor; And if not, which user is in the higher floor, so as to further facilitate their co-navigation. To train a relation classifier, we first propose to extract commonly available signals from GPS, mobile networks and wireless local access networks (WiFi); and then propose to engineer relative features from these signals. Furthermore, we experiment different classification models from field measurements in two different buildings and analyze the impacting factors on classification accuracy. Results show that the random forest model performs the best among other classifiers and can achieve 88.35% classification accuracy for training and testing in the same building and 61.69% for training and testing in different buildings.

The rest of this paper is organized as follows. Section 2 gives a detailed description and analysis of the research problem. The relative floor estimation is presented in Sect. 3 and experimented in Sect. 4. Section 5 concludes the paper and outlines future works.

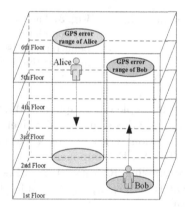

Fig. 1. An example of indoor navigation scenario without offline fingerprinting map or additional equipment in the building. Alice and Bob cannot know the floor and location of the other one but want to meet each other.

2 Problem Description

We study how to get the relative floor relationship between two users in a multistory building, where pre-trained databases and extra beacon deployments are unavailable. In this section, we first clarify what information can be used, then a detailed analysis of the problem is presented. Since most people carry their mobile phones in a daily indoor scenario, we choose GSM, Wi-Fi and GPS signals, the most common and available signals in the mobile device, as our raw data.

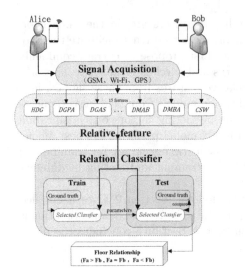

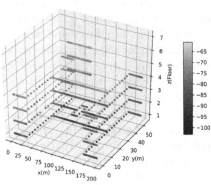

Fig. 2. The proposed system diagram

Fig. 3. The RSS distribution of GSM in the corridor area of NY building. Each point represents a sample, and the color indicates the RSS.

We denote each raw signal sample i as a tuple $\{C_i, W_i, G_i\}$ whose components represent GSM Cell, Wi-Fi and GPS signals, respectively. More specifically, the C_i contains scanned base station series B_i and corresponding *received signal strength* (RSS) series R_i; The Wi-Fi component W_i consists of scanned access point series A_i and corresponding RSS series S_i, while the GPS component is expressed as a 4-element tuple $(x_i, y_i, \alpha_i, n_i)$. Table 1 presents the detailed description for the raw data.

Recall the co-navigation scenario in Sect. 1. The target of the first step is to guide two users to the same floor. Let's denote the layers of user Alice and user Bob as f_a and f_b, respectively. It is obvious that there is no need to determine the value of f_a and f_b, as long as the relative relationship is known (for example, $f_a > f_b$), the following action will be clear (Alice going downstairs or Bob climbing upstairs). In general, there are three possible relative floor relations between two users in a building, that is, Alice is above Bob, Alice is below Bob and Alice and Bob are on the same floor, which could be regarded as a classification problem with 3 classes: $f_a > f_b$, $f_a = f_b$ and $f_a < f_b$.

Although these raw data can be directly inputted into a classification model, it is unwise to do so, as raw data are dependent on the particular building and location. A relation classifier trained via such data with absolute values could not be well adapted to other buildings. Furthermore, the dimensions of the input vectors are also different in different buildings. To deal with such issues, we propose to engineer some relative features for training classification models. Figure 2 presents the proposed system diagram.

Table 1. Detailed description of the acquired signal information.

Element	Description
$B_i = (b_i^1, b_i^2, ..., b_i^{M_i})$	GSM BS series. b_i^m denote identity of the m-th BS of sample i
$R_i = (r_i^1, r_i^2, ..., r_i^{M_i})$	GSM RSS series. r_i^m denote RSS from BS b_i^m
$A_i = (a_i^1, a_i^2, ..., a_i^{N_i})$	Wi-Fi AP series. a_i^n denote identity of the n-th AP of sample i
$S_i = (s_i^1, s_i^2, ..., s_i^{N_i})$	Wi-Fi RSS series. s_i^n denote RSS from AP a_i^n
x_i, y_i	Longitude and latitude obtained by GPS of sample i
α_i	GPS positioning accuracy of sample i
n_i	Number of available satellites of sample i

3 Relative Floor Classification

3.1 Relative Feature

As discussed in Sect. 2, using raw data as features cannot train a classifier adaptable to different buildings. On the other hand, we argue that relative features extracted from raw data with absolute values can not only reveal relative floor information but also help training adaptive classifiers. We next take GSM signal as an example to illustrate the effectiveness of the relative features. The factors affecting the user RSS mainly include the two-dimensional position l, the floor height f and the number of walls w that block the signal:

$$R = F(l, f, w). \tag{1}$$

Assume that the RSSs of Alice and Bob are $R_a = F(l_a, f_a, w_a)$ and $R_b = F(l_b, f_b, w_b)$, respectively. If $|l_a - l_b| < \delta$, Eq. 1 can be further derived as Eq. 2 for $w_a \simeq w_b$ when users are close to each other.

$$R_a - R_b = F_1(f_a - f_b) \tag{2}$$

As illustrated in Fig. 3, the wall structures of different floors are similar in many buildings. So when users are close to each other in the horizontal direction, the RSS difference is mainly related to the difference in floor height. In other words, we can exploit the relative GSM RSS between Alice and Bob to predict their floor relation.

In this paper, some relative features are only related to the difference between the signals of two users but not their absolute values. Specifically, we studied different signal distributions in a typical building and design in a total of 15 relative features. For ease of expression, we use a and b to denote two different raw samples in the remainder of this subsection.

The Horizontal Distance by GPS: Denote $l_i = (x_i, y_i)$ the GPS positioning result of sample i, then the horizontal distance by GPS between a and b is

$$HDG = ||l_a - l_b||_2 \tag{3}$$

The Difference of GPS Positioning Accuracy: Denote α_i the positioning accuracy of sample i, and the difference of GPS positioning accuracy between a and b can be represented as

$$DGPA = \frac{\alpha_a - \alpha_b}{\alpha_a + \alpha_b} \tag{4}$$

The Difference of GPS Available Satellites: Denote n_i the number of available satellites for sample i, and the difference of GPS available satelites between a and b is

$$DGAS = \frac{n_a - n_b}{n_a + n_b} \tag{5}$$

The Difference of Cell Average RSS: Denote R_i the GSM RSS series and M_i is the non-zero numbers of R_i. The difference of Cell (GSM) average RSS between a and b can be showed by

$$DCAR = \frac{\sum R_a}{M_a} - \frac{\sum R_b}{M_b} \tag{6}$$

The oOverlap Ratio of BS Series: Denote B_i the GSM BS series. We define the overlap ratio of B_a and B_b as

$$ORSB = \frac{len(B_a \cap B_b)}{len(B_a \cup B_b)} \tag{7}$$

The Union Distance of Cell RSS Series: Let $R_a = \{r_a^k\}_{k=1}^{M_a}$ and $R_b = \{r_b^k\}_{k=1}^{M_b}$ denote the RSS series of a and b, respectively. Note that r_i^k is the RSS value of BS k in sample i. Let B_a and B_b denote the BS series of a and b, respectively. We compute $B_u = B_a \cup B_b$ as their union set. The union distance of GSM RSS series is

$$UDCR = \sqrt{\sum_{k \in B_u} \left(r_a^k - r_b^k\right)^2} \tag{8}$$

The Intersection Distance of Cell RSS Series: Be similar to $UDCR$, we compute $B_i = B_a \cap B_b$ as their intersection set. The intersection distance of Cell (GSM) RSS series is computed by

$$IDCR = \sqrt{\sum_{k \in B_i} \left(r_a^k - r_b^k\right)^2} \tag{9}$$

The Vector Cosine Similarity of Cell: After extending R_a and R_b to their union format R'_a and R'_b, the vector cosine similarity of them can be calculated as

$$CSC = \frac{R'_a \cdot R'_b}{\|R'_a\| \times \|R'_b\|} \tag{10}$$

The Difference of Wi-Fi Average RSS: Let S_i denote the Wi-Fi RSS series of sample i and N_i represent the non-zero numbers of S_i. The difference of Wi-Fi average RSS can be represented by

$$DWAR = \frac{\sum S_a}{N_a} - \frac{\sum R_b}{N_b} \tag{11}$$

The Overlap Ratio of AP Series: Denote A_i the Wi-Fi AP series, and we define the overlap ratio of A_a and A_b as

$$ORA = \frac{len(A_a \cap A_b)}{len(A_a \cup A_b)} \tag{12}$$

The Union Distance of Wi-Fi RSS Series: Let $S_a = \{s_a^k\}_{k=1}^{N_a}$ and $S_b = \{s_b^k\}_{k=1}^{N_b}$ denote the Wi-Fi RSS series of a and b. s_i^k is the RSS value of AP k in sample i. Let A_a and A_b denote the AP series of a and b, respectively. We compute $A_u = A_a \cup A_b$ as their intersection set. The union distance of Wi-Fi RSS series is

$$UDWR = \sqrt{\sum_{k \in A_u} \left(s_a^k - s_b^k\right)^2} \tag{13}$$

The Intersection Distance of Wi-Fi RSS Series: Be similar to the union distance, the intersection distance of S_a and S_b can be showed by

$$IDWR = \sqrt{\sum_{k \in A_i} \left(s_a^k - s_b^k\right)^2} \tag{14}$$

where $A_i = A_a \cap A_b$ is computed as their intersection set.

The Difference from the Maximum Wi-Fi RSS of A to B: We define the difference between the maximum RSS of a and its corresponding AP RSS of b as

$$DMAB = s_a^j - s_b^j, \ j = \arg\min_i s_a^i \tag{15}$$

The Difference from the Maximum Wi-Fi RSS of B to A: We define the difference between the maximum RSS of b and its corresponding AP RSS of a as

$$DMBA = s_b^j - s_a^j, \ j = \arg\min_i s_b^i \tag{16}$$

The Vector Cosine Similarity of Wi-Fi: After extending S_a and S_b to their union format S'_a and S'_b, the vector cosine similarity of them can be calculated as

$$CSW = \frac{S'_a \cdot S'_b}{\|S'_a\| \times \|S'_b\|} \tag{17}$$

3.2   Relation Classifier

As mentioned earlier, the 15 relative features above will be used as the input of a classfication model. For the low input dimension, we mainly consider choosing the classification model from classical machine learning methods. Specifically, *k-nearest-neighbor* (KNN), *multi-layer perception* (MLP), *naive bayes* (NB), *support vector machine* (SVM), *decision tree* (DT), *random forest* (RF) [10] are studied and compared in this paper. The output of the classifier is the prediction of one of the relative floor relations, that is, $f_a > f_b$ (Alice above Bob), $f_a < f_b$ (Alice below Bob) or $f_a = f_b$ (Alice and Bob on the same floor). We define the classification accuracy as

$$Acc = \frac{\sum_{i=0}^{M} (T_i = P_i)}{M} \tag{18}$$

where T_i and P_i are the ground truth and the predicted result, respectively. M the number of the input samples.

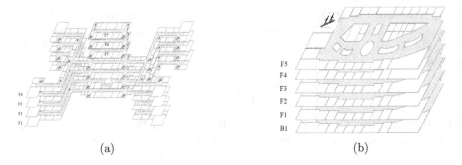

(a)   (b)

Fig. 4. (a) The layout of field NY. (b) The layout of field SJC.

4   Experiments

4.1   Experiment Settings

We conducted field measurements in a seven-story office building (called NY) and a five-story business building (called GW). Figure 4(a) and Fig. 4(b) present the layout of NY and GW, respectively. Students hold Mi6 and Mi8 Lite smartphones to collect raw data as listed in Table 1 on each floor. Specifically, each device collected 549 samples with a step of 3 m distance interval along the corridors in NY and 288 samples in total in GW with random intervals.

Each pair of two samples from different devices will be combined to generate the input sample tuples in a building. For example, let x_1^i and x_2^j denote the sample collected in NY by Mi6 and Mi8 Lite, respectively. Then we generate 301401 input sample tuples in the form of (x_1^i, x_2^j) $i, j = 1, ..., 549$ in NY building. Similarly, 81796 input sample tuples can be obtained in GW. Based on these tuples, three data sets are constructed for our experiments:

- DS1: All the tuples are from NY building, among which 80% of the tuples in NY building are chosen as training data and the rest 20% served as testing data ;
- DS2: All the tuples are from GW building, among which 80% of the tuples in GW building are chosen as training data and the rest 20% served as testing data;
- DS3: Tuples are from different buildings in this data set. Specifically, all the tuples from NY building are chosen as training data; While all the tuples from GW serve as the testing data.

4.2 Comparison of Different Classifiers

We first compare the classification performance of different classification models. In our experiments, all the classification models are implemented using the scikit-learn library in python. Specifically, we set the closest neighbor factor K to 3 in the KNN classifier, the number of trees N to 100 in the random forest classifier (RF) and set the hidden layer to 4 in multilayer perceptron (MLP) neural model, each with 50 nodes. The rest parameters are all default values.

Table 2 presents the prediction accuracy of different classifiers with different data sets. It can be observed that KNN achieved the best accuracy of 88.46% on DS1, but has worse performance than MLP, SVM and RF on DS3. Notice that the training and testing samples in DS3 come from different buildings and some features extracted in one building may be invalid in another building. Unfortunately, KNN exploits these features indiscriminately, which leads to worse accuracy on DS3 compared with other models. From the perspective of mean accuracy among different data sets, RF has the best performance among all the other classifiers, which may be due to its capability of detecting the importance and interrelatedness of different features.

Considering their mean performance among different data sets, only the top-3 models, KNN, MLP and RF, were further researched in the subsequent experiments. Besides, as sample tuples in DS3 are selected from different buildings, which can better evaluate the function of our extracted features and the generalization ability of a trained classifier, we conduct further experiments only based on DS3.

Table 2. Accuracy of different classifier.

	KNN	MLP	NB	SVM	DT	RF
DS1	88.46%	84.22%	61.14%	73.92%	79.59%	88.35%
DS2	74.46%	65.36%	56.66%	61.30%	66.05%	77.54%
DS3	46.88%	55.89%	54.96%	57.13%	45.56%	56.74%
Mean	69.93%	68.49%	57.58%	64.12%	67.73%	**74.21%**

Table 3. Accuracy with the limited data by GPS horizontal distance.

	20 m	30 m	40 m	50 m	60 m	70 m	80 m	90 m	100 m	Without limit
KNN	56.38%	56.70%	54.15%	52.82%	51.78%	50.49%	49.57%	49.22%	48.59%	46.88%
MLP	62.67%	62.41%	64.34%	63.35%	62.57%	61.94%	60.75%	61.88%	60.56%	55.89%
RF	63.84%	64.35%	63.63%	61.67%	62.43%	61.97%	60.44%	61.23%	60.49%	56.74%

4.3   The Impact of Horizontal Distance by GPS

We next investigate the impacts of the horizontal distance between Alice and Bob obtained by GPS. As discussed in Sect. 3, the RSS difference can reflect the difference on their floor relation on the condition that $|l_a - l_b| < \delta$. In this subsection, we study how the value of δ affects the accuracy of classification. Specifically, we set the value of δ from 20 m to 100 m and select the tuples whose observed horizontal distance by GPS is within δ for experiments. As presented in Table 3, the trends of different models are similar: the greater the value of δ, the lower the classification accuracy. A smaller value of δ means a smaller distance between two users. Therefore, RSS difference is mainly affected by the floor height when users are close to each other. From this insight, we set δ to 50 m in our subsequent experiments and do not make decisions for the tuples whose relative horizontal distances calculated from GPS are greater than 50 m. This actually enforces a simple rule of reject-to-classification, which, however, is only acceptable to some extent in practical co-navigation applications.

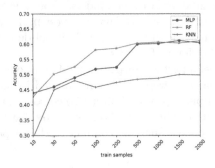

Fig. 5. Relation prediction accuracy of different classifiers against the number of train samples.

4.4   The Impact of Training Samples

We also investigate the impact of the number of training samples on different classification models. As reported by Fig. 5, the accuracy of the three classification models (i.e. RF, MLP and KNN) increases and gradually stabilizes as the number of training samples increases. Besides, the KNN algorithm requires the fewest samples to achieve stable accuracy, but its stable accuracy is also the worst; Although MLP can reach the same accuracy as that of RF, it requires more training samples. As for RF, it can make the decision about the depth and width when generating the random forest, which makes it more adaptable to the size of available samples. The result again validates the superiority of the RF model in terms of accuracy and adaptability.

Table 4. The impact of different signal sources.

	GSM	Wi-Fi	GPS	GSM & WIFI	GPS & GSM	GPS & WIFI	All
KNN	51.81%	45.23%	48.73%	53.13%	44.71%	48.03%	52.82%
MLP	58.81%	42.26%	42.20%	62.28%	58.72%	42.60%	63.35%
RF	57.53%	45.99%	52.00%	61.59%	57.50%	55.84%	61.67%

4.5 The Impact of Different Signal Sources

We finally study the impact of different signal sources. Different source data combinations are tested in our experiments. As reported by Table 4, models trained by using all the data sources achieve the best accuracy for the three classifiers, compared with other signal combination situations. Furthermore, we can also observe that models trained by using GSM and WiFi signals have similar accuracy to that using all the data sources, which may due to the weak influence of GPS in indoor environments.

5 Conclusion

In this paper, we have studied the relative floor estimation from a machine approach for co-navigation applications. We have proposed to engineer relative features for training relation classifiers. Field experiments have been conducted to examine the performance of different classifiers and the impact factors for classification accuracy. Results indicate that the random forest classifier can achieve the best performance among all the tested classifiers, and its relation classification accuracy can achieve 88.35% when all the samples are selected from the same building. In our further work, we shall exploit other available signal sources for relation classification and further examine the adaptivity of more classifiers.

Acknowledgments. This work was supported in part by the National Natural Science Foundation of China under Grant 61771209.

References

1. Shokry, A., Elhamshary, M., Youssef, M.: The tale of two localization technologies: enabling accurate low-overhead WIFI-based localization for low-end phones. In: Proceedings of the 25th ACM SIGSPATIAL International Conference on Advances in Geographic Information Systems, p. 42. ACM (2017)
2. Ye, Y., Wang, B.: RMapCS: radio map construction from crowdsourced samples for indoor localization. IEEE Access **6**, 24224–24238 (2018)
3. Lin, J., Wang, B., Yang, G., Zhou, M.: Indoor localization based on weighted surfacing from crowdsourced samples. MDPI Sens. **18**(9), 1–16 (2018)
4. Wang, B., Chen, Q., Yang, L., Chao, H.: Indoor smartphone localization via fingerprint crowdsourcing: challenges and approaches. IEEE Wirel. Commun. **23**(3), 82–89 (2016)
5. Li, W., Wang, B., Yang, L., Zhou, M.: RMapTAFA: radio map construction based on trajectory adjustment and fingerprint amendment. IEEE Access **7**, 14488–14500 (2019)
6. Li, W., Chen, Y., Zhou, C., Wang, B.: Let's meet: a smartphone co-navigation system based on relative direction and proximity change for indoor environments. In: 2019 IEEE 21st International Conference on High Performance Computing and Communications; IEEE 17th International Conference on Smart City; IEEE 5th International Conference on Data Science and Systems (HPCC/SmartCity/DSS), pp. 2535–2542. IEEE (2019)
7. Elbakly, R., Aly, H., Youssef, M.: Truestory: accurate and robust RF-based floor estimation for challenging indoor environments. IEEE Sens. J. **18**(24), 10115–10124 (2018)
8. Li, Y., Gao, Z., He, Z., Zhang, P., Chen, R., El-Sheimy, N.: Multi-sensor multi-floor 3D localization with robust floor detection. IEEE Access **6**, 76689–76699 (2018)
9. Lohan, E.S., Talvitie, J., e Silva, P.F., Nurminen, H., Ali-Löytty, S., Piché, R.: Received signal strength models for WLAN and BLE-based indoor positioning in multi-floor buildings. In: 2015 International Conference on Location and GNSS (ICL-GNSS), pp. 1–6. IEEE (2015)
10. Michie, D., Spiegelhalter, D.J., Taylor, C., et al.: Machine learning. Neural Stat. Classif. **13**, (1994)
11. Shen, X., Chen, Y., Zhang, J., Wang, L., Dai, G., He, T.: Barfi: barometer-aided wi-fi floor localization using crowdsourcing. In: 2015 IEEE 12th International Conference on Mobile Ad Hoc and Sensor Systems, pp. 416–424. IEEE (2015)
12. Varshavsky, A., LaMarca, A., Hightower, J., De Lara, E.: The skyloc floor localization system. In: Fifth Annual IEEE International Conference on Pervasive Computing and Communications (PerCom 2007), pp. 125–134. IEEE (2007)
13. Ye, H., Gu, T., Tao, X., Lu, J.: Scalable floor localization using barometer on smartphone. Wirel. Commun. Mob. Comput. **16**(16), 2557–2571 (2016)
14. Ye, H., Gu, T., Zhu, X., Xu, J., Tao, X., Lu, J., Jin, N.: Ftrack: infrastructure-free floor localization via mobile phone sensing. In: 2012 IEEE International Conference on Pervasive Computing and Communications, pp. 2–10. IEEE (2012)

Applications of Computer Vision

Defect Detection of Production Surface Based on CNN

Yi Sun[1] , Yuexiao Cai[1], Yang Li[2], and Yunlong Zhao[1(✉)]

[1] College of Computer Science and Technology, Nanjing University of Aeronautics and Astronautics, Nanjing 210016, China
{yi_sun,yuexiaocai,zhaoyunlong}@nuaa.edu.cn
[2] Harbin Engineering University, Harbin 150001, China
reeki@hrbeu.edu.cn

Abstract. With the continuous development of artificial intelligence, great progress has been made in the field of object detection. Defect detection is a branch of the field of object detection, as long as the purpose is to locate and classify defects on the surface of objects to help people further analyze product quality. In large-scale manufacturing, the demand for product surface defect detection has always been strong, and companies hope to reduce costs, while improving detection accuracy. This paper mainly proposes a method that is biased towards the detection of surface defects on smooth products, solving the problems including difficulty on detecting small scratches and imbalance between positive and negative samples. Finally, we achieve good results through the detector.

Keywords: Object detection · Defect detection · Deep learning

1 Introduction

In recent years, the development of object detection has reached a new height. Earlier, Ross Girshick et al. Proposed R-CNN [1], the first application of convolutional neural networks to object detection, which has further promoted the development of object detection. Subsequently, Ross Girshick proposed Fast R-CNN [2], which improved the speed of network training. Later, Kaiming He, Ross Girshick et al. Proposed Faster R-CNN [3] to improve Fast R-CNN, and used RPN (Region Proposal Networks) network to generate candidate frames, replacing the search selective process in Fast R-CNN. Since then, more and more CNN-based object detection models have appeared one after another.

However, although these network models have performed quite well on datasets such as COCO and Pascal VOC, they are still not ideal when detecting defects on the surface of industrial products (such as refrigerators). The reason is mainly different from common objects in life. Defects on the product surface have different shapes, large differences in size, large differences in materials, and sometimes difficult to distinguish. Among them, on some specific metal defect detection dataset, Yu He and K. Song proposed a multi-level feature fusion network (MFN) [4], which combines multiple hierarchical features

Z. Yu et al. (Eds.): GPC 2020, LNCS 12398, pp. 405–412, 2020.
https://doi.org/10.1007/978-3-030-64243-3_30

into one feature, which can contain more Details of defect location. Tao, X., Dapeng Zhang et al. Designed a novel cascaded autoencoder (CASAE) architecture [5] for segmenting and locating defects. The cascade network converts the input defect image into a pixel-level prediction mask based on semantic segmentation. The defect regions of the segmentation result are divided into specific categories by a compact convolutional neural network (CNN). Heying Wang et al. Proposed a strip surface defect detection algorithm based on a simple guide template [20]. Hongwen Dong et al. Proposed a pyramid feature fusion and global context attention network [6] for surface defect detection of pixel defects. This paper mainly proposes a method that is biased towards the detection of surface defects on smooth products, solving the problems including difficulty on detecting small scratches and imbalance between positive and negative samples. The data set used in this paper is from data collected by a large domestic manufacturing enterprise.

2 Related Work

At present, the methods applied to product surface defect detection can be divided into traditional methods and defect detection methods.

Traditional Methods. Win et al. [7] proposed two new thresholding methods for automated defect detection system for titanium-coated aluminum surfaces. Quintana et al. [8] proposed a computer vision system whose aim is to detect and classify cracks on road surfaces. Then, Bai et al. [9] proposed a new method that a collection of multiple test images are used as the input image for processing simultaneously in our method with two steps.

Deep Learning Methods. Multi-Scale Pyramidal Pooling Network is applied on detection classification [10]. Chen et al. [11] proposed a NB-CNN which is based on a convolutional neural network (CNN) and a Naïve Bayes data fusion scheme to analyze individual video frames for crack detection. A generic approach that requires small training data for ASIis proposed by Ren et al. [12]. This approach involves two tasks: 1) image classification and 2) defect segmentation. In contrast to these methods, which do not address the needs of large manufacturing companies, we propose a model that favors smooth surface defect detection to help quickly detect and locate defect locations.

3 Implement Details

3.1 Dataset

We use a product surface defect dataset provided by a large domestic manufacturing company. This dataset contains 1500 training pictures, of which 752 are pictures with defects and 748 are pictures without defects. For defective pictures, the location of the defect is indicated by a bounding box. For pictures without defects, this information is not available, as shown in Fig. 1.

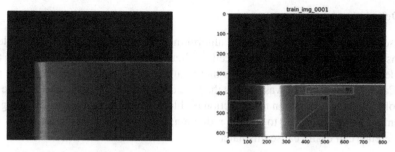

Fig. 1. Normal data (left) has nothing on it and defect data (right) has bounding boxes and label NG.

3.2 Data Augmentation

In view of the fact that our training data set contains fewer pictures, which may cause under-fitting or over-fitting during the training process, we take a data augmentation method to further expand our dataset. In our dataset, there are pictures with defects and pictures without defects. In order to be able to flexibly use these pictures without defects, we use mix-up [13] to randomly select normal pictures and pictures with defects, then combine them to generate new pictures. The effect is shown in Fig. 2.

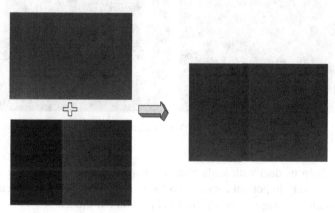

Fig. 2. Defect image (top-left) and normal image (bottom-left) are mixed into new image (right).

Other methods, such as translation, rotation, and flip are also commonly used, but according to the characteristics of our data defects, these do not change significantly after translation and flip.

3.3 Backbone

In the choice of the backbone model, we considered ResNet50, ResNet101 [14], and ResNext101 [15], and finally chose ResNet50 as the backbone. See the experimental section of Sect. 4 for specific effect comparison.

3.4 Detector

At present, in general object detection algorithms, one-stage detectors are suitable for systems that require high detection speed, such as some real-time systems, while two-stage detectors are suitable for systems that require high detection accuracy, so a two-stage Cascade R-CNN [16] was used as the base detector. This model can solve the IoU threshold selection problem in the detection problem, and better solve the following two problems: 1) overfitting due to sample reduction, 2) using different thresholds in train and inference can easily cause mismatch.

3.5 Extra Module

From experience, we all know that ordinary convolution kernels are square, which is not conducive to detecting irregular objects, such as defects in our data set, so we consider adding a Deformable Convolution Network [17] to the detection. As shown in Fig. 3, for defect features, DCN can focus the convolution process on defects as much as possible. The blue points in Fig. 3 on the left indicate the range of the receptive field after the shift. It can be seen that the receptive field can fit the defect shape well, so various scales of scratches can be detected.

Fig. 3. DCN (left) and traditional Conv.

DCN can help us deal with scale changes, but in the data picture, the context of the defect is also very important for the detector. Considering feature fusion to enhance feature presentation, we apply the idea of FPN [18] on our model.

3.6 Transfer Learning

Since our training data is small, there are a total of 1500 defective images and normal images. To prevent overfitting in training, we use the Fine-tuning method in transfer learning. Here we use a fabric surface defect dataset. The defect features in this dataset are similar to the defect features in our dataset, and there are 8000 pictures in this dataset, which is good for training a good detector. Example of pictures is as in Fig. 4 shown.

Fig. 4. Fabric defect sample.

4 Experiment

4.1 Experiment Setup

In our experiments, we reduced the original picture to half (1333, 800), the batch size was set to 4, and 2 pictures were placed on each GPU (GTX1080Ti). Use the model pre-trained on fabric surface defect dataset to initialize the entire network parameters, set the epoch to 120, use SGD as the optimizer, momentum is 0.9, weight decay is 0.0001, and the learning rate is 1e-3 for first 30 epochs, then we decrease it by a factor of 10 at 80 epochs and 100 epochs respectively. In order to solve the problem of imbalance of positive and negative samples at the RPN layer, we use Focal Loss [19] as the classification loss function of the RPN.

4.2 Multi-scale Anchors

In the experiment, we found that the size of the defects on the data picture varies greatly, and the bounding box changes accordingly. In order to adapt to multi-scale changes, we use K-Means clustering to obtain the appropriate size. we finally use a cluster number of 5 (as the Fig. 5 shows). Therefore, when RPN generates Anchor, five different aspect ratios are taken, which are 0.4, 0.5, 1, 2. 2.5.

4.3 Comparison

First, we use ResNet50, ResNet101, and ResNext101 as the backbones to train Faster R-CNN and Cascade R-CNN, respectively. Then we add DCN and FPN to the above model in turn, and the results are shown in Table 1. As can be seen from the table, compared to deeper networks such as ResNet101 and ResNeXt101, the results of ResNet50 are more impressive, which shows that without pre-training, the deepening of the network cannot bring better detection to our dataset.

Secondly, we choose YOLO and SSD as the comparison model for this experiment and further explore the differences between the two types of models. The results are shown in Table 2. From the perspective of accuracy, the structure of ResNet50 + Cascade R-CNN is obviously better than SSD300 (more than 7.5%) and YOLO (more than 4.1%), which fully shows that choosing a two-stage model is more conducive to improving detection accuracy. In terms of speed, the speed of ResNet50 + Cascade R-CNN

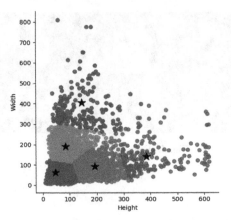

Fig. 5. K-Means result.

Table 1. Model results. The * means this model is pre-trained on fabric dataset.

Model	Accuracy	AUC
ResNet50 + FPN + Faster R-CNN	94.6%	0.8936
ResNet101 + FPN + Faster R-CNN	95.4%	0.9084
ResNeXt101 + FPN + Faster R-CNN	95%	0.9007
ResNet50 + FPN + Cascade R-CNN	97.6%	0.9534
ResNet101 + FPN + Cascade R-CNN	97.2%	0.945
ResNeXt101 + FPN + Cascade R-CNN	96.8%	0.9366
ReNet50 + DCN + FPN + Cascade R-CNN	97.4%	0.9492
ResNet101 + DCN + FPN + Cascade R-CNN	97.2%	0.9447
ResNet50 + DCN + FPN + Cascade R-CNN*	98%	0.9605

Table 2. Comparison between two-stage and one-stage detectors.

Model	Accuracy	FPS
SSD300	78.9%	44
YOLO	82.3%	21
ResNet50 + Cascade R-CNN	86.4%	16

is obviously the lowest. Compared with that, SSD300 has obvious speed advantage. Considering the accuracy and speed, and the task of the current research is to accurately identify defects, we still choose the two-stage detector.

4.4 Analysis

In this experiment, our data is a binary classification problem, so the main consideration is to use the accuracy and the AUC area under the ROC curve as the main measurement criteria.

As can be seen from Table 1, the effect of Cascade R-CNN is significantly better than Faster R-CNN, which relies on the cascade structure of Cascade R-CNN, which provides the accuracy of the detector's prediction of the bounding box position. It can be seen from Cascade R-CNN that the more complicated the backbone is, the better the performance of the detector does not mean. The model in the last row of the table uses the model trained on the fabric defect detection data set as a pre-trained model, and then tests on our dataset. It can be seen from the results that it is optimal. We think this is because of two distributions of the datasets are close, and the size and shape of the defects are similar, which is conducive to our detection of defects.

5 Conclusion

Aiming at the specific defect detection data set provided by the enterprise, this paper proposes a scheme that is biased towards the smooth surface defect detection of the product. First, we enhanced the data set with specific data, and expanded the diversity of the data set. Second, we modified the size of the default box, and used DCN and FPN in the detection process to solve the problem of scales. Finally, we further enhanced the generalization ability of the model by pre-training on another public dataset. It turns out that our model is suitable for the target dataset and can achieve good detection results.

Acknowledgements. This research was supported by Defense Industrial Technology Development Program under Grant No. JCKY2016605B006, Six talent peaks project in Jiangsu Province under Grant No. XYDXXJS-031.

References

1. Girshick, R., Donahue, J., Darrell, T., Malik, J.: Rich feature hierarchies for accurate object detection and semantic segmentation. In: 2014 IEEE Conference on Computer Vision and Pattern Recognition, CVPR 2014, pp. 580–587. IEEE, Columbus (2014)
2. Girshick, R.: Fast R-CNN. In: 2015 IEEE International Conference on Computer Vision, ICCV 2015, pp. 1440–1448. IEEE, Santiago (2015)
3. Ren, S., He, K., Girshick, R., Sun, J.: Faster R-CNN: towards real-time object detection with region proposal networks. In: The Twenty-ninth Conference on Neural Information Processing Systems, NIPS 2015, Canada (2015)
4. He, Y., Song, K., Meng, Q., Yan, Y.: An end-to-end steel surface defect detection approach via fusing multiple hierarchical features. IEEE Trans. Instrum. Meas. (Early Access) **69**(4), 1493–1504 (2019)
5. Tao, X., Zhang, D., Ma, W., Liu, X., Xu, D.: Automatic metallic surface defect detection and recognition with convolutional neural networks. Appl. Sci. **8**(9), 1575 (2018)
6. Dong, H., Song, K., He, Y., Xu, J., Yan, Y., Meng, Q.: PGA-Net: pyramid feature fusion and global context attention network for automated surface defect detection. IEEE Trans. Ind. Inf. (Early Access), 1–1 (2019)

7. Win, M., Bushroa, A.R., Hassan, M.A., Hilman, N.M., Ide-Ektessabi, A.: A contrast adjustment thresholding method for surface defect detection based on mesoscopy. IEEE Trans. Ind. Inf. **11**(3), 642–649 (2015)

8. Quintana, M., Torres, J., Menendez, J.: A simplified computer vision system for road surface inspection and maintenance. IEEE Trans. Intell. Transp. Syst. **17**(3), 608–619 (2016)

9. Bai, X., Fang, Y., Lin, W., Wang, L., Ju, B.-F.: Saliency-based defect detection in industrial images by using phase spectrum. IEEE Trans. Ind. Inform. **10**(4), 2135–2145 (2014)

10. Masci, J., Meier, U., Fricout, G., Schmidhuber, J.: Multi-scale pyramidal pooling network for generic steel defect classification. In: The 2013 International Joint Conference on Neural Networks, IJCNN 2013, pp. 1–8. IEEE, Dallas (2013)

11. Chen, Fu-chen, Jahanshahi, M.R.: NB-CNN: deep learning-based crack detection using convolutional neural network and naïve bayes data. IEEE Trans. Ind. Electron. **65**(5), 4392–4400 (2018)

12. Ren, R., Hung, T., Tan, K.C.: A generic deep-learning-based approach for automated surface inspection. IEEE Trans. Cybern. **48**(3), 929–940 (2018)

13. Zhang, Z., He, T., Zhang, H., Zhang, Z., Xie, J., Li, M.: Bag of freebies for training object detection neural networks. arXiv: 1902.04103v3 (2019)

14. He, K., Zhang, X., Ren, S., Sun, J.: Deep residual learning for image recognition. arXiv preprint arXiv:1512.03385 (2015)

15. Xie, S., Girshick, R., Dollar, P., Tu, Z., He, K.: Aggregated residual transformations for deep neural networks. In: 2017 IEEE Conference on Computer Vision and Pattern Recognition, CVPR 2017, pp. 5987–5995. IEEE, Honolulu (2017)

16. Cai, Z., Vasconcelos, N.: Cascade R-CNN: delving into high quality object detection. In: 2018 IEEE/CVF Conference on Computer Vision and Pattern Recognition, CVPR 2018, pp. 6154–6162. IEEE, Salt Lake City (2018)

17. Dai, J., et al.: Deformable convolutional networks. In: 2017 IEEE International Conference on Computer Vision, ICCV 2017, pp. 764–773. IEEE, Venice (2017)

18. Lin, T.-Y., Dollar, P., Girshick, R., He, K., Hariharan, B., Belongie, S.: Feature pyramid networks for object detection. In: 2017 IEEE Conference on Computer Vision and Pattern Recognition, CVPR 2017, pp. 936–944. IEEE, Honolulu (2017)

19. Lin, T.-Y., Goyal, P., et al.: Focal loss for dense object detection. In: 2017 IEEE International Conference on Computer Vision, ICCV 2017, pp. 2999–3007. IEEE, Venice (2017)

20. Wang, H., Zhang, J., Tian, Y., Chen, H., Sun, H., Liu, K.: A simple guidance template-based defect detection method for strip steel surfaces. IEEE Trans. Ind. Inform. **15**(5), 2798–2809 (2019)

An Image-Based Method for 3D Human Shapes Retrieval

Pengjie Li[✉] and Yanfei Shen

School of Sports Engineering, Beijing Sports University, Beijing 100000, China
lipj@bsu.edu.cn

Abstract. Automatically retrieving 3D human shapes from a single 2D image is a challenging problem. The 2D nature of one image makes it difficult to infer depth, pose and style. We propose a novel method for 3D human shape retrieval based on a single image. We present a single-network approach for keypoints detection, which entails simultaneous localization of internal region keypoints and the outer contour keypoints. The network is trained by using multi-task learning, which can handle scale differences between body/foot and face/hand keypoints through an improved architecture. Based on the keypoints, we can estimate the 3D pose, which is used for 3D pose retrieval. From the outer contour keypoints, the 2D closed boundary curve can be automatically generated. We formulate the 2D curve to 3D human shapes similarity calculation as an energy minimization problem for more sophisticated retrieval. Experimental results show that our method can achieve satisfactory retrieval performance on the two benchmark datasets.

Keywords: 3D human shapes retrieval · Internal region keypoints · Closed boundary curve · Single-Network

1 Introduction

Retrieving 3D shapes based on 2D images is extremely useful for 3D scene understanding, augmented reality and tasks like shape grasping or shape tracking. Recently, the emergence of large databases of 3D shapes such as ShapeNet [1, 2] initiated substantial interest in this topic and motivated research for matching 2D images of shapes against 3D shapes. However, there is no straight forward approach to compare 2D images and 3D shapes, since they have considerably different representations and characteristics. Retrieving 3D non-rigid shapes from a single 2D image has varied applications in areas such as Numerous works on content-based shape retrieval [3–5]. Typically, the query 3D shape and the shapes in datasets are represented as descriptor vectors aggregating some local geometric features. And retrieval is done efficiently by comparing such vectors [6]. However, the need for the query to be a 3D shape significantly limits the practical usefulness of such search engines: non-expert human users are typically not very skilled with 3D modeling, and thus providing a good query example can be challenging. As an alternative to 3D-to-3D shape retrieval, sever-al recent works proposed 2D-to-3D or sketch-based shape retrieval, where the query is a 2D image representing the projection

© Springer Nature Switzerland AG 2020
Z. Yu et al. (Eds.): GPC 2020, LNCS 12398, pp. 413–420, 2020.
https://doi.org/10.1007/978-3-030-64243-3_31

or the silhouette of a 3D shape as seen from some viewpoint [7–11]. This setting is more natural to human users who in most cases are capable of sketching a 2D drawing of the query shape; however, the underlying problem of multi-modal similarity between a 3D shape and its 2D representation is a very challenging one, especially if one desires to deal with non-rigid shapes such as 3D human shapes.

In this paper, we propose a novel method for 3D human shape retrieval based on a single image. Our method is based on the two-phase 2D-to-3D retrieval procedure. One phase is for 3D pose retrieval, which is based on the process of 3D pose estimation. The other phase is to use the 2D boundary curve to retrieval 3D human shape. The two-phase typically produces a good retrieval procedure. In order to estimate the 3D human pose, we need to predict the spatial coordinates of human keypoints in a given image. There are two main challenges for keypoints detection, one is that the inherent scale difference between body/foot and face/hand key points, the other is that we have to extract boundary keypoints for retrieval 3D shapes accurately. To solve these problems, we proposed the SinglePoseNet to complete the task of the extraction of keypoints and person detection. The keypoints include the internal keypoints in the image region and the outer contour keypoints. The internal keypoints can make the location of outer contour keypoints more accurately. Meanwhile, the accuracy of whole keypoints location can be improved by using the topological relation between the inner nodes and the outer nodes. Taking advantage of the outer contour key-points, the closed boundary curve can be automatically generated rather than the manual drawing of edges [9]. We formulate the 2D-to-3D similarity calculation as an energy minimization problem and its discretization and optimization. The input of our algorithm is a 2D image and the output is the most similar 3D shapes. The rest of this paper is organized as follows. In Sect. 2, we described our approach. In Sect. 3, we showed experimental results. Finally, in Sect. 4, we concluded the paper.

2   Method

This paper proposes a novel method for 3D human shape retrieval based on an image. The system takes, as input, a color image of size (Fig. 1a) and produces the location of the human, then generates 2D locations of anatomical key-points for the person in the image (Fig. 1c) and the boundary of a 2D human region. Figure 1 illustrates the input image, human detection, human keypoints and the boundary curve. The extracted keypoints not only contain information from the face, torso, arms, hands, legs, and feet but also contain information from the boundary of a 2D region. Based on the prior knowledge of human topological structure, we make the boundary of a 2D region to be a closed planar curve. we present an automatic algorithm for recovering 3D body pose from 2D landmarks in a single image. Based on the 2D location of keypoints on an image, we estimate the 3D human pose. To achieve this, we develop a statistical model of human pose variability that can describe a wide variety of actions while enforcing anthropometric regularity. In this paper, the process of 3D pose estimation is at the service of 3D pose retrieval, which is the first phase retrieval. Then we use the 2D boundary curve to retrieval 3D human shape, which is the second phase retrieval. The two-phase typically produces a good 2D-to-3D retrieval procedure.

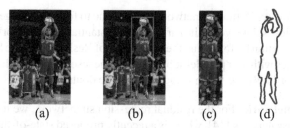

Fig. 1. (a) An input image. (b) human detection. (c) human keypoints detection. (d) the boundary curve.

2.1 The Spatial Coordinates of Human in the Image

In this paper, we focus on 3D human retrieval based on one person detected in the 2D image. In order to estimate the human pose, firstly we need to predict the spatial coordinates of human keypoints in a given image. The extracted keypoints contain information from the face, torso, arms, hands, legs, and feet. Integration of various CNN (Convolutional Neural Networks) architectures are designed for both detection and regression. Motivated by recent developments in pose estimation [12], we modified the backbone of MultiPoseNet to make it more suitable for single pose. In contrast to MultiPoseNet we call it SinglePoseNet. Based on the human keypoints, we first extract the human's closed boundary curve using a method [13]. The human's closed boundary curve is shown in Fig. 1 (d). Figure 2 shows the architecture of the keypoint subnet.

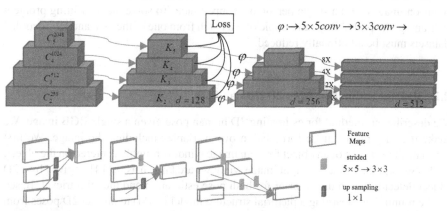

Fig. 2. The architecture of the keypoint subnet. It takes hierarchical CNN features as input and outputs keypoint.

Part Detection Subnetwork. To solve the inherent scale difference between body/foot and face/hand key points, we use the multi-resolution subnetworks. The subnetworks are built by connecting high-to low resolution stages, where each stage is composed of a sequence of convolutions. And there is a down-sample layer across adjacent subnetworks to halve the resolution. We start from a high-resolution subnetwork as the first stage.

We add high-to-low resolution subnetworks one by one to form new stages, and connect the multi-resolution subnetworks in parallel. We instantiate the network for keypoint heatmap [14] estimation by following the design rule of ResNet [12]. The SinglePoseNet contains four stages with four parallel subnetworks. The resolution is gradually decreased to a half and accordingly the width is increased to the double.

Regression Subnetwork. For the residual regression subnetwork, we used a (slightly) modified hourglass network [14], which is a recently proposed state-of-the- art architecture for bottom-up, top-down inference. The network is shown in Fig. 2. The network builds on top of the concepts described in [12], improving a few fundamental aspects. The first one is that extends within residual learning. The second one is that instead of passing the lower level futures through a convolution layer with the same number of channels as the final scoring layer, the network passes the features through a set of 3 convolutional blocks that allow the network to reanalyse and learn how to combine features extracted at different resolutions. See [12] for more details. Our modification was in the introduction of deconvolution layers for recovering the lost spatial resolution (as opposed to nearest neighbour upsampling).

Training. We train the CNN model based on two data sets [14]: the COCO 2016 keypoints challenge dataset and the MPII human multi-person dataset. In terms of human detection processing, we extend the human detection box to a fixed aspect ratio, and then crop the box from the image. The cropped bounding box is resized to a fixed size (256 × 256), which becomes the input image of the CNN. The human datasets mainly contain images with multiple people and low face and hand resolution. And the face datasets focus on images with a single person or cropped face. To solve the overfitting problem in training, the probability ratio of picking a batch from one of the face and lab-recorded datasets must be additionally reduced.

2.2 3D Pose Estimation from 2D Human Pose

We describe our method for estimating 3D human pose given a single RGB image. We make use of a probabilistic formulation over variables including the image. We first estimate the 3D pose of an object from an image window roughly centered on the object. In this work, we assume the input image windows are known as in [14] or given by a 2D object detector. It is a useful prior for both pose estimation and model retrieval. Based on the training, we learning a pictorial structure model (PSM) to predict 2D poses from images. We estimate the pose by minimizing the projection error under the constraint that the solution is close to the retrieved poses. In order to predict the 3D pose from an image, we first have to establish relations between 2D poses and 3D poses. This is achieved by using an estimated 2D pose as query for 3D pose retrieval.

In order to obtain the 3D pose, we have to estimate the unknown projection from the normalized pose space to the image and infer which joint set explains the image data best. To this end, we minimize the energy:

$$E(X, M, s) = \omega_p E_p(X, M, s) + \omega_r E_r(X, s) + \omega_a E_a(X, s) \tag{1}$$

There are three weighted terms on the right side of the equation. The first term measures the projection error of the 3D pose X and the projection M. The second term penalizes already deviations from the retrieved poses and therefore enforces implicitly anthropometric constraints. The third term is to add an additional term that enforces anthropometric constraints on the limbs. The approach can be iterated by using the refined 2D pose as query for 3D pose retrieval.

2.3 Similarity Computation for 3D Model Retrieval

Based on the keypoints and the topology prior information, we can generate closed boundary contour of the human efficiently and accurately. As an additional feature we use corresponding regions on the 2D query and the 3D shape. We are able to automatically extract compatible regions on the two shapes by consensus segmentation [15], a deformation-invariant region detection technique which directly operates with the Laplace-Beltrami eigenfunctions of a given shape. The region detection step on the two shapes is performed independently; we then obtain the 2D-to-3D region mapping by solving a simple linear assignment problem via the Hungarian algorithm [16]. The final feature maps are obtained by simple concatenation, namely Heat Kernel Signature (HKS). Figure 3 shows the illustrations of heat kernel signature (HKS). In this paper we advocate the adoption of spectral quantities to define compatible features between 2D and 3D shapes. Note that differently from existing methods for 2D-to-3D matching, we compute local features independently for each given pair of shapes.

In order to compare the feature maps on 2D curve and 3D shapes, we define the distance function as:

$$dist(f_{2D}(x), f_{3D}(y)) = \left\| f_{2D}^{HKS}(x) - f_{3D}^{HKS}(y) \right\|_1 \tag{2}$$

The similarity is the inverse of distance.

Fig. 3. Illustrations of heat kernel signature (HKS). There are four different human poses and the corresponding HKS features.

3   Experiments

Our image-based 3D human model retrieval algorithm is evaluated on two benchmark databases. The first dataset is the SHREC14 dataset and the second dataset is the FAUST dataset [7]. Comparison of our method against other methods: A 3D Model

Retrieval Method Using 2D Freehand Sketches [8], Efficient Globally Optimal 2D-to-3D Deformable Shape Matching [9], and Skeleton-based canonical forms for non-rigid 3D shape retrieval [10] on the two benchmarks in terms of precision-recall diagram.

To evaluate the retrieval performance of the proposed method on both the two datasets, the results are compared to the following three methods:

- A 3D Model Retrieval Method Using 2D Freehand Sketches [8], we abbreviate the method [8] as MRMUFS.
- Efficient Globally Optimal 2D-to-3D Deformable Shape Matching [9], we abbreviate the method [9] as EGODSM.
- Skeleton-based canonical forms for non-rigid 3D shape retrieval [10], we abbreviate the method [10] as SCFSR.

The retrieval performance was evaluated in terms of "precision" and "recall" (as shown in Fig. 4). We collect a dataset containing 100 images as the query input, and each image include a single human with different poses and background. Each image is input as the query for 3D retrieval. We draw precision-recall curve to visualize the retrieval performance of our proposed method and the state-of-the-art methods.

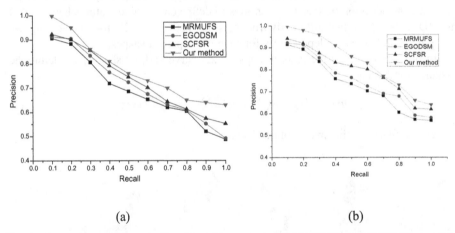

(a)   (b)

Fig. 4. Comparison of our method against other methods: MRMUFS [8], EGODSM [9], and the SCFSR method [10] on the two benchmarks in terms of precision-recall diagram. (a) Comparison for 3D human shapes retrieval on the SHREC14 dataset. (b) Comparison for 3D human shapes retrieval on the FAUST dataset.

From Fig. 4, we can see that our method gets better retrieval performance than other three methods on both the two shape benchmarks. Table 1 illustrate the partial retrieval results (two poses: "weightlifting" and "boxing") produced by using our method on the SHREC14 dataset.

All the four methods follow the retrieval task: Given a 2D image, return a list of 3D shapes, ordered by decreasing shape similarity to the query.

Table 1. Partial results using our method on SHREC14 dataset

Query	Best match	2nd match	3rd match	4th match

Table 2 illustrate the partial retrieval results produced by using our method on the FAUST dataset. Experiments are implemented for this benchmark on two poses: "akimbo" and "tiptoe".

Table 2. Partial results using our method on the FAUST dataset

Query	Best match	2nd match	3rd match	4th match

In Table 1 and 2, the query shapes are depicted in the first column. The first four retrieval 3D shapes are listed in the subsequent columns in accordance with the similarity. From the retrieval performance, we can see that our method is effective on both of the two benchmarks.

4 Conclusion

In this paper, we have presented an image-based 3D human shapes retrieval algorithm, which contained two phases: 3D pose retrieval and 3D shape retrieval. To retrieval the 3D pose, we estimated the 3D pose based on keypoints (internal region keypoints and the outer contour keypoints). To retrieval the 3D shape, we used the 2D closed boundary curve, which is automatically generated from the outer contour keypoints. We show that estimating the 2D human pose is a useful prior for 3D shape retrieval. For human pose estimation, we proposed the SinglePoseNet, which is a multi-task learning single-network. As a result, our method can achieve satisfactory retrieval performance on both the two benchmark datasets.

Acknowledgments. This work is supported by the National Natural Science Foundation of China under Grant No. 11901037.

References

1. Chang, A.: Shapenet: An Information-Rich 3D Model Repository. Technical report, Stanford University-Princeton University-Toyota Technological Institute at Chicago (2015)
2. Dyke, R., Stride, C., Lai, Y., Rosin, P.: SHREC-19: shape correspondence with isometric and non-isometric deformations. In: Eurographics Workshop on 3D Object Retrieval. Genova, Italy, 5–6 May (2019)
3. Ameesh, M., Kostas, D.: Spherical correlation of visual representations for 3D model retrieval. Int. J. Comput. Vis. **89**, 193–210 (2010)
4. Chao, M., Yulan, G., Jungang, Y., Wei, A.: Learning multi-view representation with LSTM for 3-D shape recognition and retrieval. IEEE Trans. Multimed. 21(5), 1169–1182 (2019)
5. Xun, Y., Yongsheng, G., Jun, Z.: Sparse 3D directional vertices vs continuous 3D curves: Efficient 3D surface matching and its application for single model face recognition. Pattern Recogn. **65**, 296–306 (2017)
6. Groueix, T., Fisher, M., Kim, V.G., Russell B.C., Aubry, M.: 3D-CODED: 3D correspondences by deep deformation. In: The European Conference on Computer Vision (ECCV) (2018)
7. Juefei, Y., et al.: SHREC' 18 Track: 2D scene sketch-based 3D scene retrieval. In: Eurographics Workshop on 3D Object Retrieval. Delft, The Netherlands (2018)
8. Jiantao, P., Karthik, R.: A 3D model retrieval method using 2D freehand sketches. In: International Conference on Computational Science. pp. 343–346, (2005)
9. Zorah, L., et al.: Efficient globally optimal 2D-to-3D deformable shape matching. In: IEEE Conference on Computer Vision and Pattern Recognition (CVPR) (2016)
10. Pickup, D., Sun, X., Rosin, P., Martin, R.: Skeleton-based canonical forms for non-rigid 3D shape retrieval. Comput. Visual Media 2(3), 231–243 (2016). https://doi.org/10.1007/s41095-016-0045-5
11. Jin, X., Guoxian, D., Fan, Z., Ling, S., Yi, F.: Deep nonlinear metric learning for 3-D shape retrieval. IEEE Trans. Cybernet. **48** (1), 412–422, (2018)
12. Kocabas, M., Salih, K., Emre, A.: MultiPoseNet: fast multi-person pose estimation using pose residual network. In: European Conference on Computer Vision (ECCV) (2018)
13. Alexander, G., Peter, M.R., Vincent, L.: 3D pose estimation and 3D model retrieval for objects in the wild. In: IEEE Conference on Computer Vision and Pattern Recognition (CVPR). pp. 99–110 (2018)
14. Nhat Vu, B.S.: Manjunath.: shape prior segmentation of multiple objects with graph cuts. In: IEEE Conference on Computer Vision and Pattern Recognition (CVPR), (2008)
15. Pengjie, L., Huadong, M., Anlong, M.: Non-rigid 3D model retrieval using multi-scale local features. In: ACM Multimedia. pp. 1425–1428 (2011)
16. Mehta, D., et al.: Vnect: Real-time 3d human pose estimation with a single rgb camera. ACM Trans. Graph. (TOG). **36**(4), 1–14 (2017)

MobiVision: A Novel Energy-Efficient Mobile Deep Learning Framework for Computer Vision

Xiaoming Dai[1], Xinyi Liu[1], Guoqing Liu[1], Qing Yang[1],
and Tianzhang Xing[1,2]

[1] School of Information Science and Technology, Northwest University, Xi'an, China
xtz@nwu.edu.cn
[2] Shaanxi International Joint Research Centre for the Internet of Things, Northwest University, Xi'an, China

Abstract. The development of mobile devices, such as smartphones, drones and augmented-reality headsets, have greatly promoted processing the convolutional neural network (CNN) model on them. One popular research topic is designing CNN models for image classification task on mobile terminals because these equipments would produce many videos or images data everyday generally. However, these pre-trained models usually possess complex structure and plenty of parameters so that they are difficult to be implemented on resource-limited mobile terminals for their serious time delay and energy consumption. A common solution is compressing neural networks to make them adapt to limited computation and memory resource in mobile devices, but it is not the best idea for pruned models always sacrificing accuracy. In this paper, We propose MobiVision, a novel neural network framework that conclude two main stages, which is defined as partitioning solution space and judging class for an image input. The former, utilizing deep learning-based clustering method, focuses on distinguishing which small solution space an image belongs to, while the latter calls a light-weight neural network associated to that solution space to recognize certain class of input. Series of experiments have proved that MobiVision achieves better performance than most of existing models serving for mobile devices because energy MobiVision consumed is little as well as accuracy of the model is equivalent to others meanwhile.

Keywords: Mobile devices · Convolutional neural network · Solution space · Image classification

1 Introduction

Mobile devices with high definition video cameras such as smart phones, drones, wearable cameras and autonomous vehicles have greatly revolutionized our living style. By processing streaming video data, mobile computing can provide

© Springer Nature Switzerland AG 2020
Z. Yu et al. (Eds.): GPC 2020, LNCS 12398, pp. 421–436, 2020.
https://doi.org/10.1007/978-3-030-64243-3_32

various service for users. For example, drones can monitor the traffic volumes, identify road signs in a certain area to enable mobile traffic surveillance. Compared with stable cameras, drones can provide more efficient performance. For another scene, an autonomous vehicle can recognize the objects, pedestrian, other vehicles and traffic lights by analyzing the streaming videos transmitted from in-vehicle cameras then response according to video processing result. Moreover, a user can interact with real world by wearing augmented-reality headsets. All these intelligent service all are supported by continuous video information analysis and computation generally. In the past few years, deep learning-based methods have shown impressively high accuracies in variety of computer vision tasks. It benefits from that convolutional neural networks (CNN) can extract high-level representation of images or frames of streaming video data.

Because of the high performance convolutional neural networks performing, a popular topic is to implement deep learning models on mobile terminals. Nowadays, The emergence of AI chipset, such as Apple A11 bionic neural engine, Intel Movidius VPU and Qualcomm XR1 VR chip efficiently enables the on-device deep learning on mobile vision systems. Contrast to the cloud, there are natural advantages in processing deep learning on mobile devices. One is that this work flow does not involve uploading data to cloud so it can still perform well even though without support of internet. Indeed, it will result in privacy risk once data uploading to cloud that mobile videos would record daily lives of users generally.

Though deep learning models have improved performance in a great deal, most of deep learning models are challenging to be implemented on mobile devices for limited computation and memory resource on terminals. Indeed, convolutional layer in CNN, a computing intensive layer in deep learning model, involves convolution computation which could consume much of computation and energy resource, giving a serious challenge in on-device deep learning. For example, AlexNet [17], VGG [22], GoogleNet [24] and ResNet [11] all are excellent works in ILSVRC. As the champion of ILSVRC, top5 error rate of AlexNet is 16.4%, but it possess 60 million parameters. If we store these parameters with float32, it will consume 228 MB memory in mobiles. Meanwhile, FLOPs of convolutional layers in AlexNet is 663M, about 92% of whole model FlOPs. It is obviously that AlexNet is not fit to resource-limited mobile devices. VGG, also a classic classification model, achieves 7.3% top5 error rate, which has a larger improvement on accuracy. However, VGG, a neural network model with 19 layers, possesses three times more parameters than AlexNet. It imposes a more serious challenge to implement the model on mobiles whether it is considered from the amount of computation or memory overhead. Though GoogleNet and ResNet are superior works too, they are inevitable to face the problem.

To solve this problem, a popular technique used by researchers is compressing pre-trained deep learning models to reduce their resource demand. Deep compression [10] proposed a compression method which utilizes model pruning, weight sharing and Huffman encoding to reduce model into a light weight model so that the pre-trained model can be performed on some mobile equipments.

AutoML [12], investigated an auto neural network compression method utilizing AI to prune model. These prune strategies can efficiently prune neural network models in a great deal but take a modest loss of accuracy meanwhile so that sometimes these pruned models can not achieve the demand of accuracy.

To analyze as many as images, a naive solution is expanding the data set. However, objects in real world is numberless, resulting in a serious problem neural network design. Different from existing models, we divide classification task into two stages. The first stage is defined as coarse-grained clustering process, and the most important function of this stage is to reduce the solution space (number of classes included in a data set that neural network model need to recognize). After this we can cluster the data into several small data sets irrelevant with each other but the images in same cluster have stronger similarity than those in different clusters. The second stage is classification process. In this stage, we design several customized lightweight classifiers separately recognize the specific class of an image.

To accomplish this work, we will face two main challenges. One is that we need to obtain a coarse-grained cluster pattern which could be straightly utilized to partition solution space of data set. Existing clustering models all aim to cluster images making them closed to their label as much as possible because their targets is to train a model inferring certain class-level image information. We solve this problem by proposing a coarse-grained clustering method which could roughly cluster the feature of images to distribute images into different clusters. The other is that we demand a criterion to consider if a model could be implemented on mobiles because computation cost and energy consumption is limited in mobile device. We solve the second challenge by proposing an energy prediction model, which could predict the energy a model will consume.

The main advantages of MobiVision and contributions of our work are as follows.

1. Note that our work is the first one to accomplish classification task by utilizing clustering and classification simultaneously. We use several light-weight neural networks replacing a single 'bulky' model to make it consume less mobile resource during every inference.

2. We propose an energy prediction method, which considers the relation of energy and amount of computation to obtain a conversion factor. We can predict the energy model will consume according to this factor and complexity of the model.

3. By partitioning solution space, our model could utilize light-weight neural networks in both two stages, achieving equivalent accuracy and taking less energy and time to infer.

2   Related Work

In this section, we introduce related works from two aspect, data clustering and classification.

Data Clustering. There are much of works related to data clustering. Most of existing clustering methods [9,25,26] are utilizing or improving traditional machine learning techniques to cluster data. Such as the K-means [20,25], and agglomerative clustering [8], find the correlation between images according the distance measurement of them. Density-based clustering methods [6] accomplish target by designing an appropriate density function. These machine learning clustering methods show poor accuracy on various data sets such as CIFAR-100 [16], ILSVRC2012 1K [7] because they are relying on feature extraction algorithm SIFT [19], SURF [1] resulting in the representation of images could not be improved. Recently, a popular topic is focusing deep learning-based cluster method such as [2,4,5], which utilize deep neural network to gradually extract more efficient feature representation. Deep Clustering [4] achieves preferable accuracy by utilizing K-means to cluster feature of data and then using cluster labels as pseudo labels to train Convnet. DAC [5] clusters data by transforming the image clustering task into a binary pairwise-classification problem to analyze whether pair of images belong to the same cluster. These deep learning-based cluster method improve cluster accuracy partly because of gradually improved feature, but the performance is still unsatisfied. Though these cluster methods are not superior, they provide valuable design method for our coarse-grained clustering. Our aim in clustering step is to partition solution space of target data set. To this end, we cluster data into several small data sets to make classifiers focusing on each cluster lightweight.

Data Classification. Image classification is a popular topic in computer vision and there are much of outstanding works [11,17,22,24]. These leading works provide many superb ideas for later researches such as [3]. However, a nonnegligible problem is that these models are much bulky making them difficult to be implemented on variety of mobiles. Thus, much of efforts [10,15,18,23] are devoted to compress a vanilla models into a appropriate one. [15] proposed a compression method that using linear combination of f * 1 and 1 * f filters substitute for f * f filter to accomplish low rank approximation. [18] processes filter-level pruning based on statistics of filter itself. These frameworks certainly reduce the size of models and even make them run on mobiles, but most of them pruning a model by sacrificing its accuracy. In contrast to these works, some neural network design methods [13,14,21,27] straightly design lightweight models rather compressing pre-trained models. SqueezeNet [14] proposes fire module which contains squeeze layer and expand layer to decrease the parameters of model. MobileNetV1 [13] applying depth-wise separable convolution to reduce quantity of parameters and speed up computing. ShuffleNet [27] utilize two operation, group convolution and channel shuffle, to reduce parameters. It is undeniable that these prevalent methods provide many superb ideas for Convnet. Nevertheless, as we mentioned in Sect. 3.1, these models are focusing on certain data set. As a result, while we gradually add samples into data set expanding solution space, Convnet must be more challenging to redesign and hard to be implemented on mobiles. Therefore, we provide MobiVision, an energy-efficient deep learning framework considering solution space and energy consumption, to make Convnet-based models performed on resource-aware mobile devices.

3   Method

In this section, we will introduce the details of our model. First of all, we clarify the necessity of coarse-grained clustering in our work. Indeed, we detail our cluster method. In the final, we propose a customized neural network framework to classify the data of each cluster produced by partitioning solution space.

3.1   Solution Space

We define solution space as the certain number of classes need to recognize of a whole data set, e.g. solution space being 1,000 for a data set with 1,000 classes of pictures. Naturally, when volume of sample data get increasing, solution space of a data set gets larger as well. Obviously, there are many outstanding works on images or video frames classification because they can analyze images with good accuracy. However, these neural network-based models usually bring plenty of parameters and extremely complex structure so that they are not fit to mobiles. Though compressed model can reduce consumption of model on computation and memory, it is still an nonnegligible problem for resource-limited mobile devices. Moreover, compressed model can not achieve same performance as original model generally because compression methods may prune some import filters which could generate good feature. Considering solution space, if we need to recognize an image input whose class does not exist in a specific data set, then we must redesign the model to retain the performance. Nevertheless, objects in real world is incalculable so single data set can not represent real world data and data distribution. That is to say, when we continuously add new images into original data set making solution space gets more bigger, traditional single neural network design methods could make models more complex and cumbersome, even difficult to design. For this situation, we propose a novel classification model which divides classification task into a two-step process, which are defined as large-scale solution space partitioning and customized neural network framework design.

3.2   Large-Scale Solution Space Partitioning

We insist that large-scale data sets make solution space increasing naturally, resulting in single models bulky very much so that models bring serious consumption for mobiles. Therefore, in our first step, we will partition a large whole data set into several small data sets to decrease solution space scale, making following neural network design for classification easier. These small data sets are distinguished from each other but an sample has strong relevance with other data in a same data set. Because of solution space decreasing, the classification models following this step can be more lightweight. This process is shown as

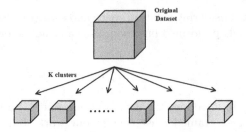

Fig. 1. Partition solution space.

Fig. 1. To partition data sets, a naive method is distributing images in a whole data set into K (K < N, N is the number of classes in a data set) small data sets randomly. This method is simple and can be processed quickly but the output generated from this process is unbeneficial to learn for neural networks because the data distribution are disorderly. Ideally, we would like to make small data sets have weak relevance even irrelevant with each other but data in each small data sets have strong relevance. Based on this idea, cluster is a reasonable way to achieve this target because cluster analysis techniques are usually utilized to find latent relation of data and distribute data into different clusters. Nevertheless, traditional machine learning techniques are not adapted to present requirements because of their low accuracy. Even though feature engineering makes this situation improved in a certain exact, compared with deep learning-based method, traditional machine learning methods still perform worse than the former. An important reason is that CNNs can gradually extract more effective features in training process to improve performance, but feature generated from feature engineering is fixed which could not be further improved. Thus, we take advantage of CNN-based model partitioning data sets to decrease solution space and we define this cluster model as coarse-grained clustering model for it just aim to find latent relationship of data. The architecture of our coarse-grained clustering model is shown as Table 1. As we all known, the computation and memory resource in mobiles are sensitive to CNNs because convolution operations are computational intensively so it will consume much of limited running resource and this situation results in that CNN models are more challenging to be implemented on mobile equipments. However, our proposed clustering model aims to find latent relevance of data and then partition a complete data set into several descendant data sets. Therefore, we just need to achieve the target that utilize clustering technique to find a rough clustering pattern. This starting point makes clustering problem get simple and clustering model lightweight for the reason that the number of clusters we need to recognize are less contrast to traditional CNNs based clustering models which aim to cluster data into concrete clusters. Although clustering problem gets simple, we take some techniques to improve model performance and make model easy to be implemented on mobiles meanwhile. In the following of this section, we will detail our CNN-based coarse-grained clustering method.

Table 1. The network architecture of coarse-grained clustering.

Layer	Size in	Size out	Kernel
conv1	$32 \times 32 \times 3$	$32 \times 32 \times 16$	$3 \times 3, 1$
conv2	$32 \times 32 \times 16$	$32 \times 32 \times 32$	$3 \times 3, 1$
conv3	$32 \times 32 \times 32$	$32 \times 32 \times 64$	$3 \times 3, 1$
pool1	$32 \times 32 \times 64$	$16 \times 16 \times 64$	$2 \times 2, 1$
lrn1	$16 \times 16 \times 64$	$16 \times 16 \times 64$	
conv4	$16 \times 16 \times 64$	$16 \times 16 \times 128$	$3 \times 3, 1$
conv5	$16 \times 16 \times 128$	$16 \times 16 \times 256$	$3 \times 3, 1$
pool2	$16 \times 16 \times 256$	$8 \times 8 \times 256$	$2 \times 2, 1$
lrn2	$8 \times 8 \times 256$	$8 \times 8 \times 256$	
Drop	$8 \times 8 \times 256$	$8 \times 8 \times 256$	
fc1	$8 \times 8 \times 256$	1024	
fc2	1024	K	
Restrict	K	K	

Convolutional Layer. Convolutional layer is the computation intensive layer in Convnet because it involves plenty of convolution computation. Therefore, choosing appropriate filter for Convnet is pretty significant. During neural network design for coarse-grained clustering, we just utilize kernels with size of 3 * 3 for the reason that contrasted to 1 * 1 kernels, 3 * 3 kernels possess larger receptive field. Receptive field decides the learning ability of filters partly because filters with large receptive field could get more information from previous layer output. However, we do not use 5 * 5 or 7 * 7 filters in our neural network design because we expect to reduce parameters and achieve equivalent performance. It is worth mentioning that two sequential 3 * 3 filters can analyze 25 pixels' information of a feature map which is equivalent to one 5 * 5 filter and this makes neural network possess comparable even superior learning capacity than others implementing 5 * 5 filters. Indeed, two 3 * 3 filters just bring 18 parameters, which is one third less than 5 * 5 filters with 25 parameters.

Restrict Layer. In our method, we expect to mainly utilize output of neural network to accomplish coarse-grained clustering. For obtaining better representation of feature and avoiding trivial solution, e.g. ln0 existed in loss function, we restrict the output generated from Convnet making it retain in a certain interval which could be beneficial for training Convnet. Specifically, we implement restrict layer after the last layer of neural network model to restrict every elements into (0, 1). This process is formulated as:

$$L^{out} = exp^{L_i^{in} - max(L_i^{in})}, i = 1, 2, \cdots, K \qquad (1)$$

$$L_i^{out} = \frac{L_i^{out}}{\|L^{out}\|_2}, i = 1, 2, \cdots, K \qquad (2)$$

$$s.t. 0 < L_i^{out} < 1, i = 1, 2, \cdots, K \tag{3}$$

$$\sum_{i=1}^{k} L_i^{out} = 1 \tag{4}$$

Where L^{in}, L^{out} are the input and output of restrict layer respectively. They both have dimension of K, which is a hyperparameter representing the number of clusters after coarse-grained clustering. We restrict all the elements of the neural network output by utilizing Eq. (1) and Eq. (2) is used to limit the output into a unit vector. This process just performs linear transformation for output of neural network making it more learnt more efficiently. Indeed, restrict process give us an interesting property that if L^{out}, k-dimensional label feature, is the optimal representation of an image, we can cluster the image according to its maximum of feature vector. We detail this process in Sect. 3.2. After implementing restrict layer, we cluster the output generated from restrict layer and take the clustering labels as pseudo labels to train model in classification manner.

Clustering Step. Inspired by Deep Clustering [4], we insist that choosing what method to cluster feature output is unimportant because performance of various clustering methods are equivalent by and large and we just demand a cluster patter which could give us a criteria for clusters images belong to. Therefore, in this work, we choose K-means clustering method to accomplish this step. When we obtain the cluster label, we change the clustering labels to one-hot vectors making every image $x_i \in x_n$ in data set is correlative to a one-hot label y_i in $\{0,1\}^k$ so that we can make the output of restrict and cluster labels possess identical dimension, where k is same as which in restrict layer representing the clustering numbers as well.

Ideally, if high-level representation generated from model can represent images very well, we will insist images with same response are both in a certain cluster. For instance, two k-dimensional feature, are probably in same cluster if the index of maximum are same. In reality, the images with same one-hot label are probably in the same cluster because we can not get superb feature by utilizing deep learning models to extract feature. After this process, we make the high-level feature and pseudo label have same dimension so that we can utilize both of them to compute loss.

Loss Function. In this part, we make distribution p(x), q(x) represent pseudo labels of sample images and output of neural network model respectively and x in both of them is feature information. We use Kullback-Leibler (KL) divergence to measure difference between feature representation and pseudo labels. Note that KL divergence is a measurement of asymmetric for two different distribution p(x) and q(x). The smaller the KL divergence, the higher the similarity of p(x) and q(x). According to Eq. (4), we find that the previous item on the right side is entropy of p(x), which is a constant during optimization. Thus, we just focus on the latter item, which is defined as cross entropy, propagating loss to update weights of neural network. Finally we compute loss by solving the following problem:

$$D_{KL}(p||q) = \sum_{i=1}^{n} p(x_i) log(\frac{p(x_i)}{q(x_i)}) \tag{5}$$

$$= \sum_{i=1}^{n} p(x_i) log p(x_i) - \sum_{i=1}^{n} p(x_i) log p(x_i) q(x_i) \tag{6}$$

$$= -H(p(x)) + [-\sum_{i=1}^{n} p(x_i) log p(x_i) q(x_i)] \tag{7}$$

Coarse-Grained Clustering Label Inference. For an image, it must belong to a certain cluster. Ideally, feature of the image could be a form of standard one-hot vector and the index of value 1 is the cluster the image belongs to. Based on this viewpoint, we analyze the output of neural network model to cluster images. After training, the Convnet-based cluster model would extract efficient feature from images so that analyzing output of neural network to classify the data is advisable and this process can be formulated as follows.

$$l_i := f(x_i; w) \tag{8}$$

$$c_i := argmax_h(l_{ih}) \tag{9}$$

Where l_i, a K-dimensional tensor, is the output of convolutional neural network of image i; f(*) is the mapping function and w is the weights of the model; c_i is the cluster label of image i, which is generated by the max value of tensor. Ideally, l_i, feature of an image, is a one-hot vector where 1 represents that image belongs to this cluster and 0 represents the image does not belong to this cluster. However, in reality, it is hard to get the global optima by training model. Thus, we take the largest response of high-level representation generated by convolutional neural network.

3.3 Customized Neural Network Framework Designing

In this section, we detail the design of customized neural network framework. Note that we will design K classifiers to classify the K data sets generated by coarse-grained clustering process respectively. We will obtain a meaningful analysis from cluster step which is the size of clusters must be different. Designing a same neural network for different clusters is naive because it is unnecessary to recognize a cluster of data using complex network structure. Thus, we proposed a customized neural network design strategy to make the model could efficiently perform on target device. In the following, we introduce the energy prediction model and other details in neural network design.

Energy Prediction Model. The most important problem for implementing deep learning models on mobiles is that energy consumption and computation. Energy produced by model performing inference once a time determines how long mobiles work. For a deep learning model, the energy consumption mainly generated from two aspects: one is the CPU resource it occupies and the other is data exchange between RAM and ROM. These two aspects are both be affected by the computation which produced by model processing images. More specifically, for CPU, size of computation straightly determines the required CPU resources. For data exchange, when size of memory is fixed, computation affects the rate of data exchange to a great extent. More specifically, For forward propagation, CPU performing inference will produce a certain amount of computation and energy consumption. For example, computation of using 3 * 3 filters to analyze images which have 32 * 32 pixels is different from the 128 * 128 pixels. Computation of the latter is 147,456, 16 times more than the former and this situation must lead to more energy consumption. In summary, the computation is positively correlated to energy consumption.

To make sure that our model could be performed on mobile devices efficiently, we propose an energy prediction model that could predict energy consumption according to computation generated from neural network process images. The method to predict energy consumption can be formulated as follows.

$$O = 2 * C_{in} * h_{j-1} * w_{j-1} * K^2 * C_{out} \tag{10}$$

$$O = \alpha * R_i \tag{11}$$

Where O represents the computation of neural network; C_{in}, C_{out} are the input channels and output channels of a j_{th} convolutional layer respectively; h_{j-1}, w_{j-1} are the size of input feature map; K is the size of kernel; R_i represents the energy consumption related to a certain computation; α is the conversion factor of computation and energy consumption and there are K α which associates to each of classifiers. Note that we just measure the energy consumption produced by convolution because we point the model inferring takes more than 90% of computation in Sect. 1.

To calculate the precise value of α, we design sufficiently small convolutional neural network models. In these small models, we just change the channels but keep size of kernels fixed (3 * 3). Specifically, We can calculate the computation of model by utilizing Eq. (10), then calculate the α according to the energy consumption and computation.

Other Details. Due to the solution space decreasing, we can utilize light weight-neural network to recognize images. Therefore, in the classifiers design, We broadly adopt the same neural network design strategy as the clustering method. To be exact, we just use 3 * 3 filters in convolutional layer to analyze information of images. We put in lrn (Local Response Normalization) after the final convolutional layer to make the feature distribution becoming stable. Note that we add the softmax layer following the final fully connected layer and loss function we utilized is the cross entropy. We take mini-batch gradient descent optimization function, which could solve the problem of loss unstable in stochastic gradient descent.

4 Model Performance

In this section, we apply the proposed MobiVision model to classify images and evaluate the performance on three popular data sets.

4.1 DataSets and Data Preprocessing

We perform our proposed model on three popular data sets, including CIFAR-10, CIFAR-100, ILSVRC2012 1K.

Data Sets. The two CIFAR data sets contain 50,000 training and 10,000 test RGB images of 32×32 pixels. CIFAR-10 comprises 10 classes, while CIFAR-100 includes 100 fine grained, which is further distributed to 20 coarse grained classes. ILSVRC2012 1k dataset possesses 1,000 classes, with a total of 1.2 million training data and 50,000 validation images of 96×96 pixels (we resize the images of ILSVRC2012 for processing conveniently). For we divide the images into several different clusters, the images of each clusters used to train correlative neural network get lessening. Therefore, we apply some data-augmentation techniques to expand datasets: images are zero-padded with 4 pixels, and then we randomly crop them to generate images with size of 32×32; We artificially create some noises into images; Z-score normalization are utilized to increasing the quality of raw data, in this step pixel data of an image are subtracted by channel means and then divided by standard deviations. This process is formulated as Eq. (12). These popular data-augmentation techniques are expanding the original datasets and strengthen the generation capability of neural networks.

$$x^* = \frac{x_i - min(x)}{std(x)}, 0 \leqslant i < n \tag{12}$$

Coarse-Grained Label. In the first stage of our model, we cluster images into several clusters. Though we do not need to utilize labels to train our model, we obviously demand labels to experiment performance of the model presumably. Thus, we apply a simple method to annotate the coarse-grained labels for images. Note that CIFAR-100 dataset naturally contains coarse-grained labels for every image to represent the superclass of an it, e.g. clocks, televisions, keyboards all are household appliances, so we do nothing for CIFAR-100 in this process. Before we train our proposed model MobiVision, firstly we collect coarse-grained labels to original datasets by analyzing the latent relationship of images artificially from 100 volunteers, and then we add the coarse-grained list for the dataset.

4.2 Coarse-Grained Clustering

In a preliminary of cluster performance assessment, we introduce the NMI to measure the information shared between two different assignment X, Y. NMI is formulated as Eq. (13). Note that we just utilize this way to analyze the update of the models in adjacent epochs.

$$NMI(X;Y) = \frac{I(X;Y)}{\sqrt{H(X)H(Y)}} \tag{13}$$

Where I(*) denotes the mutual information of X and Y; H(*) represents the entropy. Specifically, if value of NMI $\in [0,1]$ gets smaller, the correlation of two assignments are more independent.

Association Between Clusters and Coarse-Grained Labels. After neural network training, we show the dynamic association between clusters and artificial or natural coarse-grained labels by reporting the evolution of NMI. The target of this measurement is to measure the performance of the model to predict coarse-grained cluster level information of images. Naturally, when we process training a neural network model, the model will gradually update weight making inference more effectively. In Fig. 2, we show the trend of clusters and coarse-grained labels during training on CIFAR-10, CIFAR-100 and ILSVRC2012 1K datasets respectively. We can find that all the three curves sustain rising, i.e. the dependence between the coarse-grained clusters and labels continuously increasing, which denotes that our model could gradually produce effective feature information to improve the clustering performance.

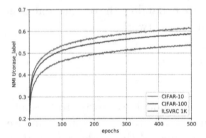

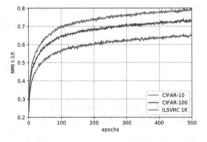

Fig. 2. Coarse-grained clustering inference quality on three datasets.

Fig. 3. Coarse-grained cluster stability on three datasets.

Association Between Clusters in Adjacent Training Epochs. In this part, we briefly analyze the stability of cluster model in training step. During training, the model distribute the images into different clusters according to the images feature information. However, we do not know the change situation of images assignment so that we can not assert the clusters getting stable. Therefore, we analyze the clusters distribution in adjacent epochs (t − 1 and t). In Fig. 3, we report the NMI of adjacent training epochs to represent internal change of our model. The figure shows that NMI continuously increasing, i.e. the number of reassigned images become less during training, and this measurement represents our model could effectively cluster images making images distribution stable.

Table 2. The clustering performance of various clustering methods on three datasets. Note that MobiVision* is the extended model making our model could fairly compare with other clustering methods, while MobiVision is the coarse-grained clustering.

Dataset method	CIFAR-10		CIFAR-100		ILSVRC	
	NMI	ACC	NMI	ACC	NMI	ACC
K-means	0.081	0.229	0.084	0.028	–	–
SC	0.103	0.247	0.090	0.136	–	–
DAC	0.396	0.522	0.185	0.238	–	–
DC	–	–	–	–	0.481	0.546
MobiVision*	0.298	0.397	0.138	0.184	0.107	0.146
MobiVision	0.621	0.763	0.583	0.628	0.549	0.597

Coarse-Grained Clusters Performance. To our knowledge, our work is the first one exploring coarse-grained cluster to partition solution space for original dataset so we do not compare cluster performance with other works which aim to predict certain classes level information. Thus, to compare our model with other existing work, we extend our model making it predict the certain class level information of images. For the reason that we do not utilize clustering method to predict the certain classes of images, performance of our model could not be highly efficient with other methods. We show the model performance in two aspects, NMI and accuracy, in Table 2. Firstly, We find that performance of the deep leaning-based methods (e.g. DAC) are superior to traditional machine learning methods (e.g. K-means). We can assert that feature information is more important than cluster method because DAC does not utilize machine learning cluster methods in its model. Secondly, compared with other works, our extended model shows modest performance for the reason that we just design a simple deep learning-based method to partition solution space of datasets. Because of this, our proposed coarse-grained clustering method shows the best performance among these cluster methods.

4.3 Classifiers

In the evaluation of image classification, we expect to show the performance of MobiVision from two aspects accuracy and energy consumption. The former validates effectiveness of model inference, while the latter guarantees that the model will perform well on target equipments. In this part, we apply the energy prediction method mentioned in Sect. 3.3 utilizing Eq. (10) to obtain an approximate energy consumption. Then the result is used to assess whether the model could work on a mobile by analyzing the predicted energy and the energy storage. Note that energy conversion factor is obtained by many experiments and then take the mean of tested values. In Fig. 4, we show the performance of MobiVision and other popular models on three datasets (data are taken from other papers). These MobiVision achieves equivalent accuracy with other models serving for mobiles, which represents our model achieving better response

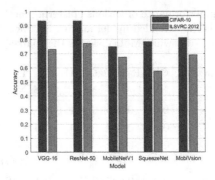

Fig. 4. Performance on two datasets: CIFAR-10 and ILSVRC 2012 1k.

to make the model satisfy requirement of users. However, our proposed model shows worse performance than models performing on desktop. This is caused by we design the model to serve on mobiles, so we do not utilize more complex neural network to accomplish design. After assessing the accuracy of *MobiVision*, we utilize the energy prediction model to calculate energy consumption and assess whether the model could effectively perform on mobiles. In Table 3, we show the energy consumption and some other characters for several model trained by ILSVRC 2012 1k. Because we do not reproduce these relevant works, we do not show energy of these works. However, amount of computation and weight parameters, which put tremendous pressure to memory and CPU or GPU so the computation and parameters could represent the energy consumption to a certain extent. Compared with other models, we can find that our model possesses more parameters than other existing popular models which is straightly to design lightweight neural networks. This is because we implement K (the same number as clusters) classifiers in our classification stage. Nevertheless, we just call a certain classifier in during classifying. As a result of this, computation of our model is less than other models. Meanwhile, our model processing inference once time just consumes 264 mA on drone. For much of existing

Table 3. Several models' characters on ILSVRC 2012 1k dataset. P is the number of parameters; C is the amount of computation, E is the energy consumption we predict.

Model	P(m)	C(m)	E(mA)
AlexNet	60	720	–
VGG-16	138.0	15300.0	–
MobileNetV1	4.2	56.9	–
GoogleNet	6.8	69.8	–
MobiVision	7.3	46.7	264

advanced mobile equipments, this value will produce little change. Therefore, our model is satisfied with majority of mobile devices nowadays.

5   Conclusion

We present MobiVision, a novel neural network to classify data by introducing two stages defined as partitioning solution space and classify data. The former, utilizing a coarse-grained cluster method, allows us distributing data into several clusters. The latter, a series of classifiers with the same number of clusters generated from last step, aims to precisely classify every cluster respectively. The advantage of this process is that we can relieve pressure of neural network model in both two steps, e.g. in cluster step we just need to find a roughly clustering pattern making neural network not bulky and in inference step we only call a lightweight model into memory, which may be a tiny fraction of size the occupied by a single model. The result of this process make our model consume much less energy which is beneficial for us to implement the model on various mobiles. In contrast to existing single neural network design methods, MobiVision is equivalently stable when solution space of a certain dataset changed because in the first stage partitioning solution space, our model will distribute the data into a one of the clusters, e.g. utilizing several datasets replacing original dataset to relieve the pressure of neural network produce by solution space increasing. Plenty of experiments show that our model performs well on datasets of CIFAR-10, CIFAR-100 and ILSVRC2012 1K, as well as consume less energy so that the model would efficiently be processed on mobiles.

Acknowledgements. This work was supported in part by China Postdoctoral Science Foundation (No. 201-7M613187), the Key Research and Development Project of Shaanxi Province (No. 2018SF-369), the International Cooperation Project of Shaanxi Province (No. 2020KW-004), and the Shaanxi Science and Technology Innovation Team Support Project under grant agreement (No. 2018TD-026).

References

1. Bay, H., Tuytelaars, T., Van Gool, L.: SURF: speeded up robust features. In: Leonardis, A., Bischof, H., Pinz, A. (eds.) ECCV 2006. LNCS, vol. 3951, pp. 404–417. Springer, Heidelberg (2006). https://doi.org/10.1007/11744023_32
2. Bengio, Y., Lamblin, P., Popovici, D., Larochelle, H.: Greedy layer-wise training of deep networks. In: Schölkopf, B., Platt, J.C., Hoffman, T. (eds.) Advances in Neural Information Processing Systems, vol. 19, pp. 153–160. MIT Press, Cambridge (2007)
3. Bhardwaj, S., Srinivasan, M., Khapra, M.M.: Efficient video classification using fewer frames. CoRR abs/1902.10640 (2019)
4. Caron, M., Bojanowski, P., Joulin, A., Douze, M.: Deep clustering for unsupervised learning of visual features (2018)
5. Chang, J., Wang, L., Meng, G., Xiang, S., Pan, C.: Deep adaptive image clustering. In: IEEE International Conference on Computer Vision (2017)

6. Chen, Y.: Density-based clustering for real-time stream data. In: ACM SIGKDD International Conference on Knowledge Discovery and Data Mining (2007)
7. Deng, J., Dong, W., Socher, R., Li, L.J., Li, F.F.: ImageNet: a large-scale hierarchical image database. In: IEEE Conference on Computer Vision and Pattern Recognition (2009)
8. Franti, P., Virmajoki, O., Hautamaki, V.: Fast agglomerative clustering using a k-nearest neighbor graph. IEEE Trans. Pattern Anal. Mach. Intell. **28**(11), 1875–1881 (2006)
9. Gowda, K.C., Krishna, G.: Agglomerative clustering using the concept of mutual nearest neighbourhood. IEEE Trans. Syst. Man Cybern. **10**(2), 105–112 (1978)
10. Han, S., Mao, H., Dally, W.J.: Deep compression: compressing deep neural networks with pruning, trained quantization and Huffman coding. Fiber **56**(4), 3–7 (2015)
11. He, K., Zhang, X., Ren, S., Sun, J.: Deep residual learning for image recognition. In: The IEEE Conference on Computer Vision and Pattern Recognition (CVPR), June 2016
12. He, Y., Lin, J., Liu, Z., Wang, H., Li, L.J., Han, S.: AMC: AutoML for model compression and acceleration on mobile devices (2018)
13. Howard, A.G., et al.: MobileNets: efficient convolutional neural networks for mobile vision applications (2017)
14. Iandola, F.N., Han, S., Moskewicz, M.W., Ashraf, K., Dally, W.J., Keutzer, K.: SqueezeNet: AlexNet-level accuracy with 50x fewer parameters and <0.5mb model size (2016)
15. Jaderberg, M., Vedaldi, A., Zisserman, A.: Speeding up convolutional neural networks with low rank expansions. Comput. Sci. **4**(4), XIII (2014)
16. Krizhevsky, A., Hinton, G.: Learning multiple layers of features from tiny images. Computer Science Department, University of Toronto, Technical report 1, January 2009
17. Krizhevsky, A., Sutskever, I., Hinton, G.: ImageNet classification with deep convolutional neural networks. In: International Conference on Neural Information Processing Systems (2012)
18. Li, H., Kadav, A., Durdanovic, I., Samet, H., Graf, H.P.: Pruning filters for efficient convnets (2016)
19. Lowe, D.G.: Distinctive image features from scale-invariant key points. Int. J. Comput. Vis. **60**(2), 91–110 (2004)
20. Norouzi, M., Fleet, D.J.: Cartesian k-means. In: 2013 IEEE Conference on Computer Vision and Pattern Recognition (2013)
21. Sandler, M., Howard, A., Zhu, M., Zhmoginov, A., Chen, L.C.: MobileNetv2: inverted residuals and linear bottlenecks (2018)
22. Simonyan, K., Zisserman, A.: Very deep convolutional networks for large-scale image recognition. Comput. Sci. (2014)
23. Sindhwani, V., Sainath, T.N., Kumar, S.: Structured transforms for small-footprint deep learning (2015)
24. Szegedy, C., et al.: Going deeper with convolutions (2014)
25. Wang, J., Wang, J., Song, J., Xu, X.S., Shen, H.T., Li, S.: Optimized cartesian k-means. IEEE Trans. Knowl. Data Eng. **27**(1), 180–192 (2015)
26. Yang, Y., Xu, D., Nie, F., Yan, S., Zhuang, Y.T.: Image clustering using local discriminant models and global integration. IEEE Trans. Image Process. **19**(10), 2761–2773 (2010)
27. Zhang, X., Zhou, X., Lin, M., Sun, J.: ShuffleNet: an extremely efficient convolutional neural network for mobile devices (2017)

CrowdSensing

Mobile Crowd-Sensing System Based on Participant Selection

Chunyu Tu[1,2], Lei Han[1,2], Leye Wang[4], and Zhiyong Yu[1,2,3](✉)

[1] College of Mathematics and Computer Science, Fuzhou University, Fuzhou, China
yuzhiyong@fzu.edu.cn
[2] Fujian Provincial Key Laboratory of Network Computing and Intelligent Information
Processing, Fuzhou University, Fuzhou, China
[3] Key Laboratory of Spatial Data Mining and Information Sharing, Ministry of Education,
Fuzhou, China
[4] Key Lab of High Confidence Software Technologies, Peking University, Beijing, China

Abstract. Mobile Crowdsensing (MCS) is often accompanied by various adverse objectives when performing data collection, which makes it difficult to collect accurate data of the entire target area with low cost. Therefore, how to collect a small part of the data to accurately infer the other data of the entire target area is a crucial issue. People's daily trajectories usually follow a certain pattern, for example, students go to school, company employees go to work. This pattern allows us to find participants who often pass through fixed areas within a certain time span, leading their collected partial data are near optimal for the entire data collection task. This paper models the problem and develops multiple methods to improve the participant selection and the data recovery. Particularly, we use a random method, reinforcement learning, and greedy algorithm to handle this problem and compare the differences among these methods by experiments.

Keywords: Crowdsensing · Participant selection · Reinforcement learning

1 Introduction

Once we collected city-scale data, such as vehicle flow data, air quality data and climate data, the method used was often to install dedicated sensors in fixed locations to collection data around the clock. However, this method has a lot of limitations. Various external factors will affect the accuracy of the data we collect, and even sometimes the sensor may be severely damaged and malfunction. Many times, the sensors we deploy cannot collect complete and accurate real data as we expect. Therefore, how to collect accurate and high-quality small parts of data to infer the data in the entire target area is a crucial issue.

With the continuous development of smart phones and mobile portable devices, more and more mobile devices are equipped with a variety of small sensors, which can easily detect temperature, air pressure, air quality and other data around users. These small sensors allows us to rely on MCS for data collection. Although MCS intelligence

© Springer Nature Switzerland AG 2020
Z. Yu et al. (Eds.): GPC 2020, LNCS 12398, pp. 439–450, 2020.
https://doi.org/10.1007/978-3-030-64243-3_33

has greatly facilitated our work, in the process of using MCS to assign tasks for data collection, we will inevitably encounter various problems. The most important issue is the low enthusiasm of the participants. It is difficult for us to find participants who are willing to take the initiative to complete the task for us. If we too deliberately ask the participants of the task to do something troublesome, then our task of finding the participants of the MCS task will be more difficult.

Considering the above issues, the data collection task we set up looks at the problem from the perspective of the participants, and selects the task participants we need from the appropriate candidates. In daily life, people's daily trajectories usually follow a certain pattern. Most people follow the same trajectory at the same time almost every day. For example, students go to school and company employees always have a fixed time and route to and from work. This pattern allows us to find participants who often pass through fixed areas within a certain time span, leading their collected partial data are near optimal for the entire data collection task. Participants can easily complete our data collection tasks with mobile devices with small sensors.

Specifically, our participant selection task is a MCS task based on the daily trajectory of person. When we need to monitor air quality data in a target city area, we will set a certain number of monitoring locations in different areas of the target city. And the locations of these monitoring sites are fixed throughout the mission. We need to collect data from some monitoring locations at each hour, so that the accuracy of the error obtained from the data of all locations is as small as possible. To this end, we need to combine the daily trajectory information of each candidate, select the participants of this task from them, and collect air quality data for us when they pass the monitoring location.

To construct the MCS task of this participant selection mechanism, we face the following problems. First, how do we infer the complete data from the collected data? The data we collect through the task is only a small part of the overall data, and our ultimate goal is to get a high approximation of the overall target area data. Another question is how to determine the participants in the next state of the task. Different participants will directly lead to huge differences in the data we collect, which will have a huge impact on our infer complete data. Therefore, among many task participants, selecting the most suitable participant for the next stage is a crucial issue. It is difficult to determine the participants of the next task without knowing the data collected by the participants selected in the next stage.

In this paper, we use Compressive Sensing to infer the air quality of unknown measurement locations. And this problem is modeled, random participants, reinforcement learning and greedy algorithms are used to select participants in this task. Finally, we compared the accuracy of data recovery after selecting participants under different methods.

2   Relative Work

Air quality has a profound impact on people's lives and health. Therefore, collecting and monitoring air quality has always been a matter of our close attention. Traditional methods of air quality collection are to install wireless sensors at fixed locations, and consist of wireless sensor networks and GPRS networks Air quality monitoring system realizes remote real-time data collection [1–4], but this is a coarse-grained and more expensive method. With the widespread application of MCS [6], we have more abundant data collection methods. Hasenfratz D et al. have designed a small portable air quality measurement system and calibrated the errors based on sensor readings from nearby monitoring stations to provide users with measurement recommendations [10]. Srinivas et al. Deployed sensors on public transport to monitor air quality in real time [5]. Wang et al. proposed a method of sparse MCS [7] which divided the target area into cells of equal size, and inferred the air quality data of the entire target area by collecting data from only a small number of cells [9]. Liu et al. added a reinforcement learning method on this basis to make the unit selection more accurate and effective [8]. In this paper, we study the participant selection strategy. How to select the appropriate number of participants to complete the air quality data collection task is our concern.

3 Problem Formulation

3.1 Definition

Before explaining our problem, we need to define the following:

Definition 1. Human trajectory: $T_{w,i,t}$ indicates that the wth participant passed the location i at time t and represented by a three-dimensional matrix. The first dimension of the matrix represents the participants' numbers, the second dimension corresponds to time and space, and the third dimension represents the time and space information of the participants for data collection.

Definition 2. Real Environment Data: E_{m*n} represents the real environmental data in the air quality collection tasks at m monitoring locations at n times. Among them, $E[i,j]$ represents the real air quality data at the j_{th} moment of the i_{th} monitoring location.

Definition 3. Selection Matrix: S_{m*n} simply represents the location and time information of the data we collected. For the trajectory $T_{w,i,t}$ of the task participant we selected, if he passed through location i at time t and collected data at location i, then set the i_{th} row and t column to 1 and the rest to 0.

Definition 4. Collecting Environmental Data: The matrix C_{m*n} is the result of multiplying the corresponding elements of the Selection Matrix and Real Environment Data, and represents the data collected by the task participants this time.

Definition 5. Reconstruction of Environmental Data: During the air quality collection task, we will use the air quality data collected on that day to infer the remaining uncollected data. We will use the matrix E_{m*n} to represent all collected data and estimated data. In MCS tasks, Compressive sensing is a commonly used data inference algorithm [11–13]. Therefore, in this paper we also use compressive sensing for this data inference work.

Definition 6. Participant Matrix: M_{W*1} is a w-dimensional vector. If participant w is selected to participate in the task, the n_{th} position is 1 and the rest are 0.

Definition 7. Task Evaluation Index: We use Mean Absolute Percentage *Error*(*MAPE*) as an evaluation indicator for the final task. Predicted is the value in the reconstructed environmental data matrix E', and observed is the corresponding value in the real environment data E. It is worth noting that we only take into account the uncollected data when calculating MAPE. For the data we have collected, the data in matrix C is not included in the calculation of MAPE.

$$MAPE = \sum_{t=1}^{n} \left| \frac{observed_t - predicted_t}{observed_t} \right| \times \frac{100}{n} \tag{1}$$

3.2 Assumptions

In this paper we need to make the following assumptions.

Assumption 1. Measurement Without Error: The data collected by all participants is not affected by instrument errors, and the measured data can be accurately returned. Some existing MCS work is addressing these issues, which is not the focus of this paper.

Assumption 2. Trajectory Certainty: In this paper, we consider that our candidate's trajectory is the same every day. Although the trajectory of human daily activities has a certain regularity, there are still some uncertainties. The work of this paper considers that the candidate's trajectory is the same every day. In fact, even if an individual candidate deviates from our preset after being selected as a task participant, the participant can still collect data from other monitoring locations and make predictions for us with enough task participants.

Assumption 3. Data Same Distribution: For the same area, the air quality data of this area has the same distribution law in different time periods. That is, we believe that the air quality data in January and the air quality data in February have the same distribution pattern.

3.3 Problem Formulation

Based on the premise of 3.1 and 3.2, we express the participant selection problem as follows: Given m monitoring locations and n time data inference tasks, ensure that the error of reconstructed data is minimized when the number of participants is less than or equal to q :

$$Min\ MAPE(E, E')$$

$$S.t.\ |\{k|M[k] = 1, 1 < k < w\}| \leq q \tag{2}$$

Where q is the upper limit of the predetermined number of participants, and w is the total number of candidates.

We will illustrate how our participants' selection tasks work specifically. First, we assume that the upper limit of the number of participants in the monitoring site is 1. It cause us just need select one participant at a time for data collection tasks. It is worth noting that each task we release is in units of days. If a participant is selected on that day, the participant will collect air quality data from that monitoring location when he passes the monitoring location we set on that day. We only record the air quality data of the monitoring location at the hour, and the air quality data of the site is recorded at the monitoring station that the participant passed at the hour. If the participant does not pass through the location at the hour, it is deemed that the participant has not collected data at that moment. Next, we will infer the air quality data of other monitoring locations based on the air quality data collected by our selected participants.

4 Method

In this section we describe in detail the methods we use in the participant selection problem. First, we use compressed sensing to make inferences about missing data. Then, the random selection method, greedy algorithm, and Q-learning for reinforcement learning were used to select participants, and various methods were compared.

4.1 Data Speculation

As we all know, compressed sensing [16] has a wide range of applications in recovering sparse spatiotemporal data. We have two parts that need to use compressive sensing for data inference:The first part is when calculating the reward in reinforcement learning and the setting and calculation of reward will be described in detail in the next section;The other part is that after the participants have collected the data, we need to use compressed sensing to infer complete air quality data. Below we will briefly introduce the principle of compressive sensing.

Any matrix can be decomposed into the form of Formula 3 by Singular Value Decomposition (SVD), We can create an r-rank approximation X by using only the r maximum singular values and discarding other values [17], like Formula 4.

$$\sum_{i=1}^{\min(n,t)} \sigma_i u_i v_i^T \tag{3}$$

$$\sum_{i=1}^{r} \sigma_i u_i v_i^T = X' \tag{4}$$

To find r, we can solve this problem:

$$\min \ rank \ (X') \quad s.t. \quad X' \circ S = C \tag{5}$$

Where $X' = LR^T$, So the problem can be transformed into:

$$min \ \|L\|_F^2 + \|R\|_F^2$$

$$s.t. \ X' \circ S = C \tag{6}$$

Furthermore, the formula can be reduced to

$$\min \ \lambda \left(\|L\|_F^2 + \|R\|_F^2 \right) + \left\| LR^T \circ S - C \right\|_F^2 \tag{7}$$

The final recovery matrix is the product of L and R.

4.2 Participant Selection

4.2.1 Reinforcement Learning

We use Q-learning algorithm [14] to solve the problem of participant selection. As we all know, the reinforcement learning model is mainly composed of $(S, A, T, R, \pi, \gamma)$ six parts. Where S is the set of states; A is the action set; T describes the transition probability of taking action at state St to the next state S_{t+1}; R represents the reward obtained immediately after taking action in a particular state and moving to the next state; π is a strategy that describes the possibility of taking an action in a particular state; γ is a time discount parameter. In order to apply reinforcement learning to our problem, we should first model the problem state, reward, and action:

1) **Action** is all possible choices we have when choosing participants. In the participant selection question, we set the action to the participant number we selected. Suppose that our candidates have a total of n and we select only one participant at a time for data collection, Then the action collection $A = \{1, 2, 3, \ldots\ldots, n\}$. Similarly, if we need to select two participants at a time for data collection tasks, Then the action collection $A' = \{(1,2), (1,3), \ldots\ldots, (1, n), (2,3), (2,4), \ldots\ldots, (n-1, n)\}$, There are C_n^2 element. It can be seen that when the number of participants we need is larger, the action space is larger. Whenever we need to make a decision to choose a participant, we choose one that we think is the best from the action set according to certain rules, and the selected action corresponds to the participant of the next air quality data collection task.

2) **State** indicates the situations of data collection. Data collection before this is a factor that we must consider when we are making a decision on the next participant choice. It's worth noting that we don't take all situation of data collection into consideration. If we only consider today's data collection, Then decide the action of the next day according to the collection of today, then the state can be simply expressed as $S = \{1,2,3, \ldots\ldots, n\}$. where n is the total number of candidate participants mentioned above. In the participant selection problem, since the trajectories of the participants are known and each participant passes a certain location at a certain time, it is fixed. Therefore, we can abstract the situation of data collection as the participant number and express it as states. In this paper, we consider the states to be multi-day. Suppose we determine to use K-day data collection to determine the participants for the next day, Then the state set S' is a set composed of A_n^k ordered sequences, and each element sequence has K participant numbers. The representation of the state set is similar to the action set, except that the elements in the state set are ordered and the elements in the action set are unordered.

3) **Reward** is used to indicate the quality of the action we choose. In reinforcement learning, we have several selectable actions in each state, each action will lead to different results and change the current state. Obviously, we definitely want to choose the action that can get the best results every time. This requires an indicator to evaluate our actions. In this paper, since our goal is to make the MAPE value

of the speculative data as small as possible, the reward is expressed by the MAPE value. Specifically, if we use the data collection of the previous k days to determine the participants of the next day, then we use $k + 1$ days of data to make an inference when calculating reward. The data collection in the first k days is the states, and the states of the participants who performed the data collection task on the $k + 1$ day is the action. The MAPE on the $k + 1$ day after the data recovery is completed is the reward. This completes the one-to-one correspondence of state, action, and reward.

When we described the action, we mentioned that whenever we need to make a decision to choose a participant, we need to choose an optimal action from the action set according to certain rules. How to choose the optimal action is the problem we need to pay attention to. We use the Q-learning algorithm to train a Q table with one-to-one correspondence of states and actions. Table 1 is a part of the Q target of the training completed in the experiment. As shown in the figure, the value in the Q table is the Q value, which is used to measure how much a certain action can be rewarded in a certain state.

Table 1. The form of Q-Table.

	Action 1	Action 2	Action 3	Action 4
State 1	24.20816507	23.94933957	23.79517444	23.01661363
State 2	52.01841281	42.21577166	44.01785144	39.07037176
State 3	66.94119158	56.87677433	57.37979283	43.80384588
State 4	23.80511464	22.99262492	23.54165504	22.30216311

The Q value in the Q table is updated according to Formula 8, and it represents the total expected return that can be obtained after taking this action in this state. In the formula, α is the learning rate and $max_{a'}Q(s', a')$ is the Q value of the optimal action in the next state. The Q table considers all states and the Q value of the corresponding action. In a specific state, we query the Q table to find the action with the highest Q value, and we consider this action to be the optimal action in this state. In the participant selection problem, the states is the situation of previous data collection and the action is the participant of the next day. After training the Q table [15], we can make the decision of the participant selection based on the Q table.

$$Q(s, a) = Q(s, a) + \alpha\left[r + \gamma max_{a'}Q(s', a') - Q(s, a)\right] \tag{8}$$

The specific Q-learning algorithm is shown in Algorithm 1. Through this algorithm we iteratively train the Q table until the table converges. Finally we make a decision through this Q table.

Algorithm 1. Q-learning algorithm

Input:α, γ

Initialize $Q(s,a)$ arbitrarily

Repeat (for each episode):

  Initialize s

  Repeat (for each step of episode):

    Choose a from s using policy derived from Q

    Take action a, observe r, s'

    $Q(s,a) \leftarrow Q(s,a) + \alpha[r + \gamma max_a Q(s',a') - Q(s,a)]$

    $s \leftarrow s'$

  Until s is terminal

4.2.2 Greedy Algorithm

Reinforcement learning's Q-learning algorithm takes into account the possibility of all states in the future and predicts the quality of the data recovery results for each state. However, when we consider each step, we will inevitably have errors. When the errors have accumulated to a certain degree, it is not a good thing to consider more steps instead. So we also use a greedy algorithm for the task of participant selection.

The greedy algorithm settings are mostly the same as Q-learning, except that the Q-learning algorithm trains the Q table until the Q table converges. However, the greedy algorithm does not train the Q table. In fact, the table of the greedy algorithm is the initial Q table, and the values in it are simply predictions of the MAPE of the next state. The difference between the greedy algorithm and the Q-learning algorithm is that the greedy algorithm only considers the next state when making decisions, and the Q-learning algorithm considers the situation of multiple states. In short, when we use the greedy algorithm, whenever we have to make a decision, we only consider the next best solution.

5 Experiment

To evaluate the effectiveness of the participants' choice of tasks, we used Beijing's July and August 2014 AQI data. Data from 4 locations were selected in the dataset for this experiment. In this experiment, we use July data for training and August data for testing.

5.1 Data Preprocessing

Due to the serious lack of AQI data in the data set, we chose to use linear interpolation to complete the data set. Linear interpolation uses a straight line passing through two known points to approximate the original function, so we can calculate the missing function value. Let (x_i, y_i), (x_{i+1}, y_{i+1}) be two adjacent points, and x is between the two points, then $y(x)$ can be calculated by the following formula. The speculation of data is not the focus we need to pay attention to. And both the completion of data preprocessing and the compressed sensing in the experiment are only a relative comparison, so we will not make too detailed instructions.

$$y(x) = y_i + \frac{y_{i+1} - y_i}{x_{i+1} - x_i}(x - x_i) \tag{9}$$

In the experiment, we used July data for training and August data for testing. We finally selected 4 adjacent locations from the multiple locations data in the dataset for this experiment. The final data form is shown in the Table 2, this is the E matrix in Definition 2.

Table 2. The form of Real Environment Data.

	1 o'clock	2 o'clock	3 o'clock	4 o'clock
location 1	63.0	64.0	62.0	60.0
location 2	61.0	60.0	55.0	52.0
location 3	61.0	62.0	56.0	53.0
location 4	60.0	64.0	63.0	54.0

After determining the air quality data for the monitoring location, we also need the trajectory data of the candidate participants. We simulated a fixed trajectory of 6 candidates and assumed that each participant could collect air quality data 8 times a day. The representation of the trajectory is a 6 * 2 * 8 three-dimensional matrix. The first dimension of the matrix corresponds to the number of 6 candidate participants; the second dimension of the matrix represents time and space; the third dimension of the matrix corresponds to the time and space information of the participants passing through the monitoring site. In other words, the matrix records the monitoring locations passed by each candidates and the time passed by the corresponding monitoring sites. For example, the second station that participant 1 passes through every day is station 3, and the time passing this station is 7 am, then our trajectory matrix is $[1, 1, 2] = 7$, $[1, 2, 2] = 3$.

5.2 State Setting Experiment

Our states is indicated by the data collection of the previous few days, but the specific number of days to collect the data will determine the participants of the next day. Therefore, in order to figure out how many days to predict the participants of the next day is valid, we did a data recovery experiment. In the experiment, we will use compressed sensing to recover the data of the whole month of the training set. Every day, we randomly select a participant for the data collection task, and then use the data collected by the participant to recover the complete data, and then calculate MAPE by comparing with the real data. First, we only use the data collected on the 31st to recover the data on the 31st, and then we add the data collected on the previous day of the day, the 30th, to recover the data on the 31st. Until the data of the 31st day is restored with the data of the entire month. Figure 1 shows the results of this experiment.

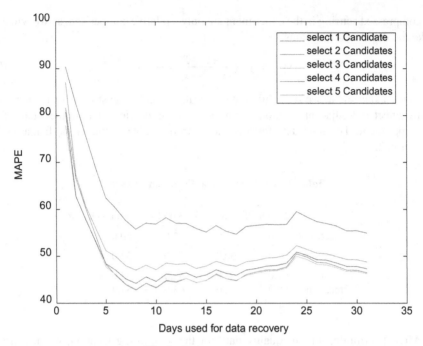

Fig. 1. Data recovery results

It can be seen that only one day for data recovery is the worst. And as the number of days used for data recovery increases, the effect of data recovery is also better. Although there are some slight improvements until last days, considering the capacity of the Q table and the calculation time, we decided to use the data collection of the first two days to determine the participants of the setting states.

5.3 Air Quality Data Experiment

Our experiments were performed based on 4 monitoring locations and 6 candidates. The methods used are random selection, greedy algorithm, and reinforcement learning. The random selection method is simply to randomly select n candidates from 6 candidates each time as participants in this task. Greedy algorithms and reinforcement learning methods have been introduced in detail in the previous section. We will elaborate on the states setting and reward setting in more detail. In the Q table, we set the states to the selection of participants in the previous two days, composed of ordered numbers. Further, we also take the date factor into the state, compared with the Q table without considering the date factor, after considering the date factor increased by 30 times. We set the reward to MAPE after compressed sensing recovery. It is worth noting that the smaller the MAPE, the better the choice, so in the experiment we need to choose the action with a small MAPE. The following table is the experimental result of this experiment. The experimental evaluation index was definition 7 MAPE.

Among them, Greedy (T) and Greedy are greedy algorithms. The difference is that when Greedy (T) sets the state, we treat different dates as different states. In the Greedy algorithm, we do not consider the date factor, and only consider the participants who collected the data before to determine the participants for the next day. In simple terms, we do not consider what day the date is when choosing participants. In the Greedy (T), we consider the date factor. For example, "Today is August 3, yesterday was the data collected by Participant No. 1" and "Today is August 4, and the data collected by Participant No. 1 yesterday" are two completely different states. Similarly, the difference between Q-learning (T) and Q-learning is the same.

From the Table 3, we can see that among the five methods, the best method is the Greedy algorithm, and the worst is Q-learning. The experimental results of Greedy (T) and Q-learning (T) are similar. For greedy algorithms, it is better to not consider dates than to consider dates. For reinforcement learning, considering the date is better than not considering the date. This shows that the factor of adding dates is effective when we consider multiple steps, but the greedy algorithm only considers one step so adding dates is not so effective. All the methods have little difference in selecting 4 and 5 people. This is because our candidate has only 6 people. Therefore, when the number of selected people is close to the number of candidates, the choice of actions is limited, which leads to a small gap.

Table 3. Air quality experiment results.

	Greedy(T)	Greedy	Qlearning(T)	Qlearning	Random
Select 1 Candidate	76.763	72.320	79.424	92.486	84.963
Select 2 Candidates	67.153	61.704	64.046	82.640	67.576
Select 3 Candidates	55.199	53.129	56.280	59.411	55.289
Select 4 Candidates	49.917	48.215	50.416	54.840	49.871
Select 5 Candidates	48.218	46.788	47.354	53.931	48.721

6 Conclusion

This paper assumes the participant selection problem and models this problem. Then we use a variety of different methods to conduct the participant selection problem and also compares the experimental results of each method.

In the future work, we would like to improve these methods based on our task process and reinforcement learning. Using more effective reinforcement learning models, considering various other factors in the state and some other factors will be taken into account by us. So that in the process of selecting participants, we can more accurately select participants suitable for our perception tasks.

Acknowledgements. This work is supported by the National Natural Science Foundation of China under grant No. 61772136.

References

1. Yingdong, L.: Research and Design of Ambient Air Quality Field Station Monitoring System. Wuhan University of Technology (2007)
2. Peiguo, H., Qiaoling, L.: Air quality monitoring system based on wireless sensor network. Ind. Instrum. Autom. **2009**(3), 109–112 (2012)
3. Kingsy Grace, R., Manju, S.: A comprehensive review of wireless sensor networks based air pollution monitoring systems. Wirel. Pers. Commun. **108**(4), 2499–2515 (2019). https://doi.org/10.1007/s11277-019-06535-3
4. Han, Q., Liu, P., Zhang, H., Cai, Z.A: A wireless sensor network for monitoring environmental quality in the manufacturing industry. IEEE Access. **7**, 78108–78119 (2019)
5. Devarakonda, S., Sevusu, P., Liu, H., Liu, R., Iftode, L., Nath, B.: Real-time air quality monitoring through mobile sensing in metropolitan areas. In: Proceedings of the 2nd ACM SIGKDD International Workshop on Urban Computing, pp. 1–8 (2013)
6. Ganti, R.K., Ye, F., Lei, H.: Mobile crowdsensing: current state and future challenges. IEEE Commun. Mag. **49**(11), 32–39 (2011)
7. Wang, L., Zhang, D., Wang, Y., Chen, C., Han, X., M'hamed, A.: Sparse mobile crowdsensing: challenges and opportunities. IEEE Commun. Mag. **54**(7), 161–167 (2016)
8. Liu, W., Wang, L., Wang, E., Yang, Y., Zeghlache, D., Zhang, D.: Reinforcement learning-based cell selection in sparse mobile crowdsensing. Comput. Netw. **161**, 102–114 (2019)
9. Wang, L., et al.: CCS-TA: quality-guaranteed online task allocation in compressive crowd-sensing. In: Proceedings of the 2015 ACM International Joint Conference on Pervasive and Ubiquitous Computing, pp. 683–694 (2015)
10. Hasenfratz, D., Saukh, O., Sturzenegger, S., et al.: Participatory air pollution monitoring using smartphones. Mob. Sens. **1**, 1–5 (2012)
11. Rana, R.K., Chou, C.T., Kanhere, S.S., Bulusu, N., Hu, W.: Ear-phone: an end-to-end participatory urban noise mapping system. In Proceedings of the 9th ACM/IEEE International Conference on Information Processing in Sensor Networks, pp. 105–116. ACM (2010)
12. Xu, L., Hao, X., Lane, N. D., Liu, X., Moscibroda, T.: Moscibroda: more with less: lowering user burden in mobile crowdsourcing through compressive sensing. In: Proceedings of the 2015 ACM International Joint Conference on Pervasive and Ubiquitous Computing, pp. 659–670. ACM (2015)
13. Zhu, Y., Li, Z., Zhu, H., Li, M., Zhang, Q.: A compressive sensing approach to urban traffiffiffic estimation with probe vehicles. IEEE Trans. Mob. Comput. **12**(11), 2289–2302 (2013)
14. Mnih, V., Kavukcuoglu, K., Silver, D., et al.: Playing Atari with deep reinforcement learning. arXiv preprint arXiv:1312.5602,99(2013)
15. Sutton, R.S., Barto, A.G.: Reinforcement Learning: An Introduction. MIT Press (1998)
16. Kong, L., Xia, M., Liu, X.Y., et al.: Data loss and reconstruction in sensor networks. In: Proceedings IEEE INFOCOM. IEEE, 1654–1662(2013)
17. Zhang, Y., Roughan, M., Willinger, W., et al.: Spatio-temporal compressive sensing and internet traffic matrices. In: Proceedings of the ACM SIGCOMM 2009 Conference on Data Communication, pp. 267–278 (2009)

Quality-Aware and Penalty-Sensitive Opportunistic Crowdsensing in Mobile Relay Networks

Ailun Song[1], Jingguang Zhou[1], Xiaofeng Gao[1]([✉]), Haotian Wang[2], Fan Wu[1], and Guihai Chen[1]

[1] Shanghai Key Laboratory of Scalable Computing and Systems,
Department of Computer Science and Engineering,
Shanghai Jiao Tong University,
Shanghai, China
salvatore@sjtu.edu.cn, jingguang.zhou5@gmail.com,
{gao-xf,fwu,gchen}@cs.sjtu.edu.cn
[2] Stony Brook University, New York City, USA
haotwang@cs.stonybrook.edu

Abstract. Mobile crowdsensing takes advantage of mobile devices to efficiently collect and process data in large scale sensing tasks. In this paper, our study focuses on opportunistic crowdsensing in mobile relay network constructed by user's D2D communication. Users participating in relaying a piece of data compose the corresponding detection sequence. We design a reward policy to encourage users to join the network. Moreover, we consider a scenario incorporating a crucial metric called total quality of information (TQoI), taking into account the different importance of the target locations. Obtaining data with high TQoI and limited cost in mobile relay networks is our primary goal. We investigate how to identify the data with high value and pay rewards to those users according to the corresponding detection sequences. We formulate the former problem as Relay-Encouraging Coverage Maximization (RECM) and prove its NP-hardness. Then, we design two algorithms to gain constant-factor approximation. One has low time complexity, while the other achieves a better bound. We also extend our scheme into penalty sensitive case where uncovered targets will bring various penalties. Extensive simulations are carried out to demonstrate the advantages of our approaches.

Keywords: Mobile crowdsensing · Opportunistic network · Incentive mechanism

1 Introduction

With the development of embedded sensors in mobile devices, opportunistic crowdsensing [9] has shown great potential in IoT system [16]. In a crowdsensing campaign [4], all end-users work during the same period of time, possibly at different places, cooperating for a specific task. It reflects great advantages [13]

Z. Yu et al. (Eds.): GPC 2020, LNCS 12398, pp. 451–465, 2020.
https://doi.org/10.1007/978-3-030-64243-3_34

over conventional sensing methods. The requester pays a reasonable price in return for massive data. These data can be possessed in mobile devices after they are collected, which further reduces the data load on the server side. The requester gets benefits and users get some rewards, which is a win-win result [1,2,15].

End-users are involved in opportunistic crowdsensing with their mobile devices sensing the environment automatically. Compared to participatory crowdsensing [5,6,19,21,25], opportunistic crowdsensing bid fewer rewards as users are not required to go to a specific area [2]. Thus, more users can be recruited to collect data. When users confront each other, data are shared and propagated via device-to-device communications. And users would upload data to the server while reaching a service point. So a mobile multi-hop relay network is constructed. It would enhance the performance of opportunistic crowdsensing as service point can access the data quickly through multi-hop transfers.

To accelerate the speed of data forwarding, incentive mechanisms [10,24] are proposed to reward user for both sensing and relaying. However, they only provided users with a fixed payment, which fails to arouse users' enthusiasm. In this paper, we attach value to each detection sequence, where the users who sense or relay this piece of data is tracked. For each user listed in the accepted detection sequences, our relay-encouraging policy will reward her for the contribution of sensing or relaying the data no matter if she went to the service points herself.

Furthermore, we consider how to maintain the sensing quality and manage the budget efficiently in mobile relay networks. We propose a crucial metric, total quality of information (TQoI) considering the different importance of target locations. Instead of simply treating targets without discrimination [10], we will give priority to those with high importance to get a larger TQoI. We formalize the problem of improving TQoI under limited budgets in mobile relay networks as a Relay Encouraging Coverage Maximization (RECM) problem and prove its NP-hardness. We first design our basic Relay-Encouraging Greedy algorithm (Basic-REG) with an approximation ratio of $\frac{1}{2}(1 - 1/e)$. Then we design our enhanced Relay-Encouraging Greedy algorithm (Enhanced-REG), improving the bound to $1 - 1/e$, which assures the quality.

To be more generalized, we consider that besides TQoI, requester will often be sensitive to some targets without which their follow-up data analysis will be badly hindered or ruined. Under the circumstance, those targets not included in the finally accepted data will cause some penalties to our crowdsensing campaign. We admit that these penalties exist due to limited budgets, but we prefer those algorithms that can help us decide which data to accept, simultaneously avoiding high penalties. We extend the Enhanced-REG to adapt with the generalized scenario where penalties exist. The introduction of penalties does not compromise the performance of our algorithm; instead, it would inherit the approximation ratio of $1 - 1/e$. Theoretical analysis and experiments are performed to validate the effectiveness of our algorithms.

Our main contribution includes:

1. We bring device-to-device communication into opportunistic crowdsensing, forming mobile relay networks. Then we design our relay-encouraging policy.
2. We introduce a new quality metric TQoI, formulate the Relay Encouraging Coverage Maximization (RECM) problem and prove its NP-hardness. Then, we design two approximation algorithms (Basic-REG, Enhanced-REG) to solve RECM, with quality guarantee and compatibility with limited budgets.
3. We are the first to consider and account for penalties in our algorithm design for crowdsensing. Penalty Sensitive case is solved by slightly modifying Enhanced-REG.
4. We present in-depth theoretical analysis on the approximation ratio and time complexity. We conduct several experiments to demonstrate the performance of our scheme.

The remainder of the paper is organized as follow. Section 2 introduces some related works in crowdsensing. Section 3 formulates the problem mathematically. Two approximated algorithms are proposed in Sect. 4 while the extension to penalty sensitive case is also discussed. Section 5 evaluates the performance of our scheme. We conclude this paper in Sect. 6.

2   Related Works

Crowdsensing can be participatory [22] or opportunistic [9,18]. The former requires end-users to go to a specific place at a specific time and then carry out their tasks while the latter allows end-users to maintain their daily trajectories and run the crowdsensing platform on the background of their mobile devices. Opportunistic crowdsensing could decrease the workload of core network. For example, Du et al. [3] proposed an grouping method of sharing and aggregating the sensing data to reduce the energy consumption of communication.

When crowdsensing emerged in 2011, researchers mainly focused on time-oriented tasks, such as [5,6,19–21,25]. However, they overlooked spatiality, another important factor in crowdsensing. The mechanisms proposed in these papers are often based on an assumption that end-users' trajectories and targets' spatial distribution will not affect the researchers' analysis and final results. However, these aspects should be taken into consideration in order to help to maximize profits. In subsequent years, some literature began to exploit spatiality. In [12,17], the distribution of targets are considered, but not consider the sensing quality. Zhang et al. [24] mentioned users' trajectories and analysed on sensing qualities. He et al. [7] explicitly considered users' trajectories but they assumed the budget was always abundant. And they only considered the single-user trajectories without interaction. Zhan et al. [23] proposed a routing protocol based on Nash bargaining theory which would maximize the sensing reward with time sensitivity. Jiang et al. [8] proposed a credit-based incentive mechanism for relay where the receiver should pay virtual currency to the forwarding service provider, where a trusted third party is needed. Karaliopoulos et al. [10] attempted the relay strategy in opportunistic network. However, the payment is fixed for each user, which discouraged users from exchanging data with others. And their goal is to cover all the targets with the same importance, which is inefficient under the budget constraint.

3 Problem Formulation

3.1 System Overview

We consider opportunistic crowdsensing tasks which require data for distributed objects $\mathcal{O} = \{o_1, o_2, \ldots, o_n\}$. Users $\mathcal{U} = \{u_1, u_2, \ldots, u_m\}$ who join the tasks will sense the data for the targets along their routes and keep records of the labels of the targets. In our scheme, we define the process through which users share data as "relay". Along the relay process, their mobile devices also keep records of each other. User's record list is noted as a Detection Sequence List (DSL). Each detection sequence represents a multi-hop notation for the data to flow into service points. Users upload their DSL's to the server when reaching the service points, while the crowdsourcer's server analyzes all DSL's, accepting a small portion of detection sequences with high total quality of information (TQoI) under a limited budget L. Here, we incorporate a crucial metric TQoI assessing the total value of crowdsensing task for one time. We then formulate the relay process policies in our scheme.

Definition 1 (DSL). *A Detection Sequence List (DSL) for a user is a set of all their detection sequences. A detection sequence contains labels of sensed objects and relevant users. A typical sequence would be $S_k = \{o_1^{(k)}, o_2^{(k)}, \ldots, o_i^{(k)} : u_1^{(k)}, u_2^{(k)}, \ldots, u_j^{(k)}\}$. The relevant users refer to those who have ever owned the data of these objects and have taken part in the relay process. Each detection sequence will satisfy the following conditions: 1) The last user $u_j^{(k)}$ owns the detection sequence S_k; 2) The objects are detected by the first user $u_j^{(1)}$; 3) The data are shared and relayed through the nodes $u_1^{(k)}, u_2^{(k)}, \ldots, u_j^{(k)}$; 4) The number of objects in the sequence depends on how many objects $u_j^{(1)}$ sensed; 5) Duplicate users or objects in a sequence are removed;*

Definition 2 (TQoI). *Given an object set $\mathcal{O}$, there is associative weight set $W = \{w_1, w_2, \ldots, w_n\}$ implicating the objects' importance. Total Quality of Information (TQoI) is defined as the weighted sum of those objects in selected detection sequences.*

Definition 3 (Sharing Policy). *When users meet each other, they share their data and DSL's as Fig. 1. They will append themselves to the detection sequences in the received DSL's. Specifically, if objects in two sequences S_i and S_j are the same and the user set in sequence S_i is a subset of user set in S_j, this user's mobile phone will delete S_j to avoid redundancy.*

Figure 1 gives an illustration of Detection Sequence List (DSL) and Sharing Policy. Before relay, the DSL of u_3 is composed of two detection sequences.

	Before Relay	After Relay
DSL of u_3	$\{o_1, o_3, o_4, o_{11} : u_3\}$ $\{o_5, o_3 : u_2, u_3\}$	$\{o_1, o_3, o_4, o_{11} : u_3\}$ Detection sequence gained by herself $\{o_5, o_3 : u_2, u_3\}$ $\{o_2, o_5, o_6 : u_5, u_3\}$ Detection sequence gained via relay $\{o_5, o_4 : u_1, u_5, u_3\}$
DSL of u_5	$\{o_2, o_5, o_6 : u_5\}$ $\{o_5, o_4 : u_1, u_5\}$	$\{o_2, o_5, o_6 : u_5\}$ $\{o_5, o_4 : u_1, u_5\}$ $\{o_1, o_3, o_4, o_{11} : u_3, u_5\}$ $\{o_5, o_3 : u_2, u_3, u_5\}$

Fig. 1. A example of detection sequence list and sharing policy

$\{o_1, o_3, o_4, o_{11} : u_3\}$ is a detection sequence gained individually, meaning it senses all of the objects in the sequence and she is the first user in the sequence. $\{o_5, o_3 : u_2, u_3\}$ is a detection sequence gained via relay because u_3 is not the first user and the sequence is shared with her by u_2 before. After u_3 meets u_5, they share data. u_3 copies u_5's data and detection sequences, then appends itself to the sequences and vice versa.

Finally, users arrive at service points where they can get access to the server through special transmission. They upload DSLs and their bids for one sequence to be selected. The bid set is denoted as $\mathcal{B} = \{b_1, b_2, \ldots, b_m\}$. We define $\mathcal{S} = \{s_1, s_2, \ldots, s_q\}$ to be the set of all detection sequences. Each time the server selects a sequence, it should pay once to all users appearing in the sequence. We propose our reward policy to encourage users to relay.

Definition 4 (Reward Policy). *Users are paid based on how many times they are involved in accepted detection sequences, i.e. the times that their contributions, such as sensing or sharing data, are admitted by the server. Let cnt_j denote the times u_j is involved in a selected sequence. If it is the cth time that she is involved, she will get $b_j^{(c)}$. The first time a user u_j is involved in a selected sequence, she will be paid the amount of reward $b_j^{(1)} = b_j$. To encourage users to relay, $b_j^{(c)}$ will be slightly more than $b_j^{(c-1)}$.*

3.2 Relay Encouraging Coverage Maximization (RECM)

The server needs to maximize QoI while its total cost cannot exceed budget L. We have indicating variables $\{x_1, x_2, \ldots, x_n\}$, in which $x_i = 1$ if the object o_i is covered and $x_i = 0$ otherwise. The server needs to select some detection sequences F and pay the users according to their appearance times in the sequences. If a sequence S_k is accepted by the server, we have a new indicating variable $z_k = 1$, otherwise $z_k = 0$. For each sequence S_k, indicating variables $\{y_1^{(k)}, y_2^{(k)}, \ldots, y_m^{(k)}\}$ denote whether associative users $\{u_1, u_2, \ldots, u_m\}$ are involved in the sequence. $y_j^{(k)} = 1$ if user u_j is involved and $y_j^{(k)} = 0$ otherwise.

Thus the problem can be formulated as Relay Encouraging Coverage Maximization (RECM):

$$\max \quad \sum_{o_i \in \mathcal{O}} w_i x_i$$

$$\text{s.t.} \quad \sum_{k=1}^{q} y_j^{(k)} = cnt_j, \qquad \forall j = 1, \ldots, m$$

$$\sum_{j=1}^{m} \sum_{c=1}^{cnt_j} b_j^{(c)} \leq L \tag{1}$$

$$\sum_{k:o_i \in S_k} z_k \geq x_i \qquad \forall i = 1, \ldots, n$$

$$\prod_{j:u_j \in S_k} y_j^{(k)} \geq z_k \qquad \forall k = 1, \ldots, q$$

$$x_i, y_j^{(k)}, z_k \in \{0,1\} \quad \forall i \in [1,n], j \in [1,m], k \in [1,q]$$

In our relay network, we say an object location is covered if it is included in our selected detection sequences. We aims to maximize QoI, which can be also regarded as the weighted sum of covered objects by F. The constraints include: 1) Appearances of u_j in all selected sequences is counted for cnt_j times. 2) Total expense cannot be greater than the budget L. The expense is the total reward given to all users according to their appearances. Each time the server will pay her a price $b_j^{(c)}$. 3) For each covered object, we have at least one accepted sequence from DSL's that covers the object. 4) If a sequence S_k is selected and accepted from DSL's, all users in this sequence should be rewarded.

Theorem 1. *The RECM problem is NP-hard.*

Proof. The budgeted maximum weighted coverage problem (BMWC) is NP-hard [11]: Given a collection $\mathcal{S}$ with associated costs defined over a domain of weighted elements, and a budget L, find a subset of $\mathcal{S}' \subseteq \mathcal{S}$ such that the total cost of sets in $\mathcal{S}'$ does not exceed L, and the total weight of elements covered by $\mathcal{S}'$ is maximized.

Now we have a reduction whose input is an instance of BMWC. Its output is a special instance of our problem (RECM). We let the weighted elements be our weighted object locations and let the collection of sets over a domain of weighted elements be the detection sequence set covering objects. The associated cost of each set can be regarded as the costs for all users in such a sequence. In this way, BMWC can be reduced into a special instance of RECM, that is, when each sequence is disjoint of users. To put in another way, each user only appears once and there cannot be a duplicate user in any two sequences. Since BMWC is NP-hard, RECM is apparently NP-hard. □

4   Mechanism Design

4.1   Basic-REG

Since Relay Encouraging Coverage maximization (RECM) is NP-hard, we design a basic version of Relay-Encouraging Greedy algorithm (basic-REG) to get a near-optimal solution. The entire process of basic-REG is illustrated in Algorithm 1. We define $W(F)$ as the total importance of the objects covered by sequences in F, and $B(F)$ as the total cost of the sequences in F. The total cost for one sequence is the sum of costs for all users in the sequence. Let W_i denote the total importance of the objects covered by S_i. Let W_i' denote the total weight of the objects that are covered by sequence S_i but not covered by any sequence in F. In the ith round, we repeatedly select a sequence maximizing the ratio of W_i' over the costs that have to paid to all users involved in the sequence (denoted by B_i). On the one hand, if the additional cost B_i does not cause the over-spending, we accept S_i and union the sequence S_i with our selected sequence set F. After that, the times cnt of users appearing on selected sequence should be updated. On the other hand, if the additional cost actually causes the over-spending, We do nothing. For both two cases, we have to remove sequence S_i from the sequence set $\mathcal{S}^0$. We repeat this process until the remaining sequence set becomes empty.

Algorithm 1: Basic-REG

---

1 $F \leftarrow \emptyset$; $\mathcal{S}^0 \leftarrow S$; $cnt \leftarrow \{0\} \times m$;
2 **repeat**
3   select $S_i \in \mathcal{S}^0$ which maximizes W_i'/B_i;
4   **if** $W_i' = 0$ **then** break
5   **if** $B(F) + B_i \leq L$ **then**
6          $F \leftarrow F \cup \{S_i\}$;
7   **for** $u_j \in S_i$ **do**
8              $b_j^{cnt_j+1} \leftarrow b_j^{cnt_j}$;
9              $cnt_j \leftarrow cnt_j + 1$;
10         $\mathcal{S}^0 \leftarrow S^0 \backslash \{S_i\}$;
11 **until** $\mathcal{S}^0 = \emptyset$;
12 Select a set S_t over S such that $B(S_t) \leq L$ and W_t is maximized;
13 **if** $W(F) \geq W_t$ **then return** F
14 **else return** S_t

Note that without extra processing, only the greedy selection (Line 1–11) will lead to infinitesimal approximation ratio for worst cases. To avoid it, in Line 12–14 we try to find the sequence S_t with the most importance W_t in S. Then comes the pivot. We compare the new W_t with $W(F)$. We choose the sequence set with larger QoI.

4.2   Approximation Analysis

In this part, we give an in-depth analysis on basic-REG algorithm and show its approximation ratio. We notice that sequences picked out may not belong to optimum sequences set F^*. Conversely, some sequences in F^* may not be selected. Repeat the pick-up process (Line 2) until the first sequence in F^* is not added to F for its addition would violate the budget L. Let r denote the number of executed loops and correspondingly let l denote the times that $B(F) + B_i \leq L$ (Line 5) is true. Without loss of generality, we renumber the sequences so that S_i is the ith sequence added to F. Then S_{l+1} is the first sequence which belongs to F^* but is not selected due to the budget limit.

Lemma 1. $\forall i \in (0, l+1]$, we have $\frac{L}{B_i}(W(F_i) - W(F_{i-1})) \geq W(F^*) - W(F_{i-1})$.

Proof. By set theory, we have $W(F^*) - W(F_{i-1}) \leq W(F^* \backslash F_{i-1})$. Then because of greedy selection, in the ith time we pick up the sequence S_i with a largest ratio W_i'/B_i. As the number of iterations increases, the cost for a unselected sequence will not decrease but increase or remain unchanged because users' count may increase. That is because the users in it accumulate more appearances on selected sequences and need to get higher reward. Furthermore, the weights of the objects for a unselected sequence will not increase but decrease or remain unchanged. Because objects in it may be covered by prior sequences. Hence $W_i'/(B_i - P_i')$ will decrease or remain unchanged.

Therefore when we get W_i'/B_i in the ith iteration, we multiple it with the budget L. The result will be greater than the remaining weight of the optimum after removing the first $i-1$ terms, i.e. $W(F^* \backslash F_{i-1})$. Thus we have $W(F^* \backslash F_{i-1}) \leq LW_i'/B_i$, where $W_i' = W(F_i) - W(F_{i-1})$. Combining two inequalities, the lemma is proved. □

Lemma 2. $\forall i \in (0, l+1]$, we have $W(F_i) \geq \left(1 - \prod_{k=1}^{i}(1 - \frac{B_k}{L})\right) W(F^*)$.

Proof. Mathematical Induction is utilized to prove the lemma. The base case $i = 1$ can be proved easily proved. For the inductive step, we suppose that the case for $i-1$ holds, i.e. $W(F_{i-1}) \geq \left(1 - \prod_{k=1}^{i-1}(1 - \frac{B_k}{L})\right) W(F^*)$. By reformulating Lemma 1, we have $W(F_i) \geq \frac{B_i}{L}W(F^*) + (1 - \frac{B_i}{L})W(F_{i-1})$. Combining two inequalities, we find that the case for i holds. So the statement holds for all $i \in (0, l+1]$. □

Lemma 3. We have $W(F_{l+1})/W(F^*) \geq 1 - 1/e$.

Proof. Since $\exp(-x) \geq 1 - x$, from Lemma 2, we have

$$W(F_{l+1})/W(F^*) \geq 1 - \exp\left(-\sum_{k=1}^{l+1}\frac{B_k}{L}\right).$$

And by Algorithm 1, S_{l+1} is the first sequence which belongs to F^* but not selected and we have $\sum_{k=1}^{l+1} B_k > L$. So the lemma is proved. □

Theorem 2. *The approximation ratio of the basic REG algorithm is $\frac{1}{2}(1-1/e)$ and its time complexity is $O(nq)$, where n is the number of objects and q is the number of sequences.*

Proof. By Lemma 3, we have $W(F_l) + W'_{l+1} \geq (1 - 1/e)W(F^*)$. Noticing that $W_i \geq W'_i$, so we have $W(F_l) + W_t \geq (1 - 1/e)W(F^*)$ where W_t is maximized. Algorithm 1 would choose $\max(W(F_l), W_t)$ which is larger than $\frac{1}{2}(1 - 1/e)W(F^*)$. So the approximation ratio is $\frac{1}{2}(1 - 1/e)$.

The subroutine at the repeat loop cost $O(q)$ time, where q is the number of detection sequences. Each loop we choose a sequence that at least covers one object, so we have $O(n)$ loops where n is the number of objects. So the time complexity is $O(nq)$. □

4.3   Enhanced-REG

The enhanced version of Relay Encouraging Coverage maximization (RECM) greedy algorithm is shown in Algorithm 2. It can achieve an approximation ratio of $1 - \frac{1}{e}$. We first give an intuitive explanation here and then provide detailed derivation.

We use a method called k enumeration technique. We assume the length of the optimum sequence set (F^*) is larger than 3, or we can easily find F^* by Brute Force. We order the sequences in F^* by selecting the sequence in F^* that covers uncovered elements with maximum total weight at each step. Let Y be the first k sequences in this order. The for each loop (Line 4) makes sure that we can always find the k-permutation Y with maximum weights by enumerating all k-permutations of n. When we get Y, we simultaneously update $B(F)$ and the corresponding counting times. the cost $B(F)$ should be less than or equal to the budget L. Then we use the greedy method on the remaining part, i.e. add the sequence with largest $\frac{W'_i}{B_i}$ one by one until the budget is exceeded. We denote Y' as the set of these sequences selected by greedy method. In this way, the output is composed of two parts $F = Y + Y'$ and we can calculate the ultimate approximation ratio using local ratio method.

Last but not least, we should not neglect the sequence set whose cardinality is smaller than k. This output H_1 will cover objects in less than k sequences with maximum weights. We should note that the high ratio of weight over cost does not mean it can be picked up because of the limited budget. Sometimes you will see the weights itself may play a crucial role in problem solving. Thus on Line 1 we first select the sequence set F in which the cardinality is smaller than k and the QoI are biggest. F will be used to be compared with H_2. Detailed analysis procedure is as follows. On the one hand, similar to the analysis in basic-REG before, due to the greedy process, we have $W(Y') + W'_{l+1} \geq (1-1/e)W(F^*\backslash Y)$. On the other hand, We sort sequences in F^* by finding the sequence that covers maximum weighted sum of uncovered elements at each step. Then Y represents the first k sequences and we have $W'_{l+1} \leq k^{-1}w(Y)$.

Theorem 3. *If $k \geq 3$, the approximation ratio of the enhanced-REG algorithm can achieve $1 - 1/e$. Its time complexity is $O(nq^{k+1})$, where n is the number of object locations and q is the number of sequences.*

Proof. By decomposing F into Y and Y', we have

$$
\begin{aligned}
W(F) &= W(Y) + W(Y') \\
&\geq W(Y) - W'_{l+1} + (1 - 1/e)W(F^* \backslash Y) \\
&\geq (1 - 1/k)W(Y) + (1 - 1/e)W(F^* \backslash Y) \\
&\geq (1 - 1/e)W(F^*) + (1/e - 1/k)W(Y).
\end{aligned}
$$

So while $k \geq 3$, $W(F) \geq (1 - 1/e)W(F^*)$.

From Theorem 2, the repeat loop cost $O(nq)$ time. And the foreach loop will execute $O(C_q^k) = O(q^k)$ times. Hence the total time complexity is $O(nq^{k+1})$. $\square$

Algorithm 2: Enhanced-REG

1 $H_1 \leftarrow \arg\max\{w(F)|F \subset S, |F| < k, B(F) \leq L\}; H_2 \leftarrow \emptyset$;
2 **for** $F \subset S, |F| = k, B(F) \leq L$ **do**
3     $S^0 \leftarrow S \backslash F$; $cnt \leftarrow \{0\} \times m$;
4   **repeat**
5   select $S_i \in S^0$ which maximizes W'_i / B_i;
6   **if** $W'_i = 0$ **then** break
7   **if** $B(F) + B_i \leq L$ **then**
8           $F \leftarrow F \cup \{S_i\}$;
9   **for** $u_j \in S_i$ **do**
10             $b_j^{cnt_j+1} \leftarrow b_j^{cnt_j}$;
11             $cnt_j \leftarrow cnt_j + 1$;
12          $S^0 \leftarrow S^0 \backslash \{S_i\}$;
13   **until** $S^0 = \emptyset$;
14   **if** $W(F) > W(H_2)$ **then** $H_2 \leftarrow F$
15 **if** $W(H_1) > W(H_2)$ **then return** H_1
16 **else return** H_2

4.4 Penalty Sensitive Scenario

Under the budget constraint, the server is much likely to fail to choose detection sequences covering all objects. On most occasions, those uncovered objects will cause a penalty $P = \{p_1, p_2, \ldots, p_n\}$ to the server. Consequently, we need to withdraw some money from the budget to cover the penalty. This scenario can be adapted into our previous model with a few modifications. We note the method as PA-REG. Intuitively, the sum of payment to users and penalty for uncovered objects should not exceed the budget. So the budget constraint in Problem (1) would be changed into

$$
\sum_{j=1}^{m} \sum_{c=1}^{cnt_j} b_j^c + \sum_{i:x_i=0} p_i \leq L.
$$

The modified variables in penalty sensitive scenario are compared with the original version in Table 1. We introduce notation $P(F)$ to represent the total penalty of the uncovered objects of F, and P'_i to represent the total penalty of the objects involved in sequence S_i but not involved in any sequence in F. For each DSL S_i adding into F, its cost would become $B_i - P'_i$ by subtracting all penalties of related objects in S_i to declare the coverage. It is worth noting that we consider only the items not involved in the current sequences of F each time. The upper bound of total cost would be $L - \sum_{i=1}^{n} p_i$ to accommodate with the budget constraint. It is an instance of Enhanced-REG. Thus, the approximation ratio of $1 - 1/e$ is inherited.

Table 1. Modification in penalty sensitive scenario

Enhanced-REG	L	B_i	$B(F)$
PA-REG	$L - \sum_{i=1}^{n} p_i$	$B_i - P'_i$	$B(F) - P(F)$

5 Performance Evaluation

To evaluate the performance of our schemes, we simulate the random walk scenario and implement our algorithms. Moreover, we implement the algorithm in [24] as comparison, denoted by MCQBC. We also implement randomized algorithm with different numbers of attempts.

5.1 Simulation Setup

We first simulate a scenario that 20 people walk randomly on a field with the size of 10×10. The users are initially at random position in this field. We randomly place 50 objects on this field. The importance of each object is randomly distributed on the interval $[4, 7]$. Then users walks 0.1 unit at each step. Each user has four directions: up, down, left, right. We set the probability of turning to other directions to be 0.2, which enable a user to go across a long distance rather than wandering in its neighborhood. Figure 2 demonstrates the users' trajectories in a random walk example. The sensing radius is set as 0.3 unit while the communication radius is set as 0.1 unit. The sensing and relaying process would be automatically triggered within the corresponding radius. The limited time is 500 steps of time. If a user does not reach terminal points uploading her data, then the server will not get the data. Fortunately, relay strategy helps the server to gain more detection sequences and data. A user's bid for one sequence containing her label is distributed randomly in $[1,6]$. The server has a budget L, and then decides how to choose sequences. If a user appears on more than one

selected sequence, for each selected sequence the server will pay her the associative bid b_j and extra reward $0.1(cnt_j - 1)$, depending on the counts of their
appearance on selected sequences. For each selected sequence, the server will pay
all users appearing in it according to the rules above.

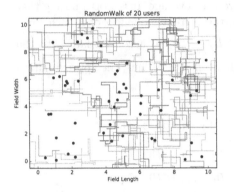

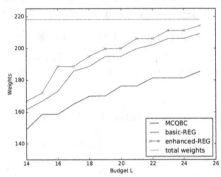

Fig. 2. Random Walk of 20 users   **Fig. 3.** Weight under different budget

5.2   Evaluation of RECM

In Fig. 3, we vary the budget L and see the QoI outputed by our two algorithms
and MCQBC algorithm. Enhanced-REG and Basic-REG perform better than
MCQBC. To better assess the algorithms, we introduce randomized algorithm
(RA) [14] as a criteria. It would randomly pick up a sequence continually until
the budget is exceeded. Running RA once can hardly get high QoI. Then we run
RA for multiple times and output the biggest weighted sum among them. We
find out that Basic-REG performs as well as 1024 attempts of RA and Enhanced-
REG performs better while MCQBC's performance is worse than 128 attempts
of RA.

We evaluate the impact of different object number, which is shown in Fig. 4.
We can see as the object number increases, the server will get a better QoI using
both Basic-REG and Enhanced-REG. Next we consider the dropout rate in real
scenario. Dropout rate means the percentage of people who have not arrived at
terminal points in a limited time. In opportunistic crowdsensing people will not
detect objects intentionally and they cannot guarantee they can upload their
DSLs and data at the terminal points timely. Although they cannot reach the
terminal points, they may have detected objects and relayed the data to other
users. Thus more objects can be accessible to the server and users will still get
reward it they have the contribution of relay. We fix the budget and vary the
dropout rate from 0.1 to 0.85. The result in Fig. 5. shows that when dropout
rate is high, MCQBC algorithm apparently has a bad performance and the gap
between MCQBC and Enhanced-REG is big. When the dropout rate is low

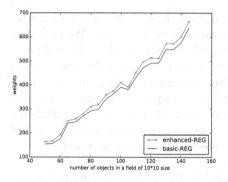

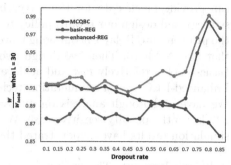

Fig. 4. Weight under different #objects   **Fig. 5.** %Weight with different %Dropout

Basic-REG may not get larger weights than MCQBC, but Enhanced-REG is always better than MCQBC.

5.3   Evaluation of Penalty Sensitive Scenario

We set the penalty for each object randomly on the interval $[0.1, 1]$. When budget L is 30, we compare the performance of Enhanced-REG and PA-REG in Fig. 6 and 7. They both have their own advantages. Enhanced-REG performs well on output weights while PA-REG can reduce the penalty. It shows that PA-REG is a better way to balance the penalty and quality under a limited budget. Thus the two algorithms are suitable for different situations.

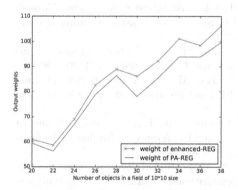

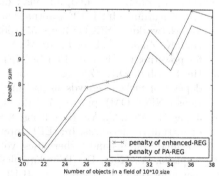

Fig. 6. Weight under different #objects   **Fig. 7.** Penalty under different #objects

6   Conclusion

In this paper, we focus on improving the quality of information (QoI) under budget constraint. In opportunistic crowdsensing, sharing data between users can provide much data for the server in a limited time. We adopt this relay strategy and design our reward policy to encourage users to relay. We formulate the problem into Relay Encouraging Coverage Maximization (RECM) and prove that it is NP-hard. Then, we design two approximation algorithms to solve it. Basic-REG is relatively fast and achieve an approximation ratio of $\frac{1}{2}(1 - 1/e)$. Enhanced-REG uses k-enumeration technique to improve the ratio to $1 - 1/e$. We have a thorough analysis on our algorithms. Then we extend Enhanced-REG into the penalty sensitive case. We conduct extensive simulations and the simulation results have demonstrated the effectiveness of our approaches.

Acknowledgement. This work was supported by the National Key R&D Program of China [2019YFB2102200], and the National Natural Science Foundation of China [61872238, 61972254].

References

1. Cardone, G., et al.: Fostering participation in smart cities: a geo-social crowdsensing platform. IEEE Commun. Mag. **51**(6), 112–119 (2013)
2. Chon, Y., Lane, N.D., Li, F., Cha, H., Zhao, F.: Automatically characterizing places with opportunistic crowdsensing using smartphones. In: ACM Conference on Ubiquitous Computing, pp. 481–490 (2012)
3. Du, Y., Sailhan, F., Issarny, V.: Let opportunistic crowd sensors work together for resource-efficient, quality-aware observations. In: IEEE International Conference on Pervasive Computing and Communications (2020)
4. Guo, B., et al.: Mobile crowd sensing and computing: the review of an emerging human-powered sensing paradigm. ACM Comput. Surv. (CSUR) **48**(1), 1–31 (2015)
5. Han, K., Zhang, C., Luo, J.: Bliss: budget limited robust crowdsensing through online learning. In: IEEE International Conference on Sensing, Communication, and Networking (SECON), pp. 555–563 (2014)
6. Han, K., Zhang, C., Luo, J., Hu, M., Veeravalli, B.: Truthful scheduling mechanisms for powering mobile crowdsensing. IEEE Trans. Comput. **65**(1), 294–307 (2015)
7. He, S., Shin, D.H., Zhang, J., Chen, J.: Toward optimal allocation of location dependent tasks in crowdsensing. In: IEEE Conference on Computer Communications (INFOCOM), pp. 745–753 (2014)
8. Jiang, Q., Men, C., Yu, H., Cheng, X.: A secure credit-based incentive scheme for opportunistic networks. In: IEEE International Conference on Intelligent Human-Machine Systems and Cybernetics, vol. 1, pp. 87–91 (2015)
9. Kapadia, A., Kotz, D., Triandopoulos, N.: Opportunistic sensing: security challenges for the new paradigm. In: IEEE International Communication Systems and Networks and Workshops, pp. 1–10 (2009)
10. Karaliopoulos, M., Telelis, O., Koutsopoulos, I.: User recruitment for mobile crowdsensing over opportunistic networks. In: IEEE Conference on Computer Communications (INFOCOM), pp. 2254–2262 (2015)
11. Khuller, S., Moss, A., Naor, J.S.: The budgeted maximum coverage problem. Inf. Process. Lett. **70**(1), 39–45 (1999)
12. Liu, X., Ota, K., Liu, A., Chen, Z.: An incentive game based evolutionary model for crowd sensing networks. Peer-to-Peer Netw. Appl. **9**(4), 692–711 (2015). https://doi.org/10.1007/s12083-015-0342-2

13. Ma, H., Zhao, D., Yuan, P.: Opportunities in mobile crowd sensing. IEEE Commun. Mag. **52**(8), 29–35 (2014)
14. Motwani, R., Raghavan, P.: Randomized Algorithms. Cambridge University Press, Cambridge (1995)
15. Pan, B., Zheng, Y., Wilkie, D., Shahabi, C.: Crowd sensing of traffic anomalies based on human mobility and social media. In: ACM SIGSPATIAL International Conference on Advances in Geographic Information Systems, pp. 344–353 (2013)
16. Petrov, V., et al.: Vehicle-based relay assistance for opportunistic crowdsensing over narrowband IoT (NB-IoT). IEEE Internet of Things J. **5**(5), 3710–3723 (2017)
17. Wang, L., Zhang, D., Xiong, H., Gibson, J.P., Chen, C., Xie, B.: EcoSense: Minimize participants' total 3G data cost in mobile crowdsensing using opportunistic relays. IEEE Trans. Syst. Man Cybern. Syst. **47**(6), 965–978 (2016)
18. Wang, L., Yu, Z., Yang, D., Ku, T., Guo, B., Ma, H.: Collaborative mobile crowdsensing in opportunistic d2d networks: a graph-based approach. ACM Trans. Sensor Networks (TOSN) **15**(3), 1–30 (2019)
19. Xu, J., Xiang, J., Yang, D.: Incentive mechanisms for time window dependent tasks in mobile crowdsensing. IEEE Trans. Wireless Commun. **14**(11), 6353–6364 (2015)
20. Yan, H., Zhao, M.: Time-based quality-aware incentive mechanism for mobile crowd sensing. In: International Conference on Green, Pervasive, and Cloud Computing (GPC), pp. 138–151 (2018)
21. Yang, D., Xue, G., Fang, X., Tang, J.: Crowdsourcing to smartphones: incentive mechanism design for mobile phone sensing. In: International Conference on Mobile Computing and Networking, pp. 173–184 (2012)
22. Yucel, F., Bulut, E.: Location-dependent task assignment for opportunistic mobile crowdsensing. In: IEEE Consumer Communications & Networking Conference (CCNC), pp. 1–6 (2020)
23. Zhan, Y., Xia, Y., Zhang, J., Wang, Y.: Incentive mechanism design in mobile opportunistic data collection with time sensitivity. IEEE Internet of Things J. **5**(1), 246–256 (2017)
24. Zhang, M., et al.: Quality-aware sensing coverage in budget-constrained mobile crowdsensing networks. IEEE Trans. Veh. Technol. **65**(9), 7698–7707 (2015)
25. Zhao, D., Li, X.Y., Ma, H.: Budget-feasible online incentive mechanisms for crowdsourcing tasks truthfully. IEEE/ACM Trans. Netw. **24**(2), 647–661 (2014)

Cloud and Related Technologies

Failure Prediction with Hierarchical Approach in Private Cloud

Yaru Bao[1](✉), Feilong Tang[1], and Lijun Cao[2]

[1] Department of Computer Science and Engineering, Shanghai Jiao Tong University,
Shanghai, China
794998378@qq.com, tang-fl@cs.sjtu.edu.cn
[2] Suzhou Kedacom Technology CO., LTD., Suzhou, China
caolijun@kedacom.com

Abstract. Cloud computing is widely adopted in real-world data centers. Most companies choose to build a private cloud service with the consideration of privacy. In these circumstances, they provide the service through Infrastructure as a Service (**IaaS**). However, with the scale of the data center, the possibility of cloud failure is increasing and become urgent in cloud computing. Current methods mainly use the proactive approach that monitors the failure and process it afterward. These methods are inefficient, and may always cause the service to break down. In this paper, we propose a new approach **HFP** (Hierarchical Failure Prediction) that can effectively monitor and predict the failure in advance. We firstly design and implement a new monitor structure that can effectively collect data. Then, a failure prediction method is proposed to predict the failure in advance. We implement this system with OpenStack, the synthetic result on the collected dataset shows that our method can achieve 98.3% accuracy in the prediction of cloud failure.

Keywords: Cloud computing · Failure prediction · Machine learning

1 Introduction

Cloud computing is a shared computing method which relies on Internet technology, allocating software and hardware resources dynamically and stably for users according to their demands [5,22,27]. In recent years, cloud computing is in a state of rapid development and has been praised as the future of enterprise technology. By taking cloud facilities as the foundation, further building the system on the cloud platform and making dynamic use of available resources, the operation cost of enterprises can be greatly reduced [18,23]. Among different cloud computing paradigm, private cloud has become a hot field in cloud computing technology due to its features of data security, convenient update and maintenance, low cost, convenient deployment, and strong customization, etc., which have been widely applied in enterprise practice [5,17].

Although the cloud computing industry is maturing, it will face many challenges in its development. The occurrence of cloud failures is not so frequent,

© Springer Nature Switzerland AG 2020
Z. Yu et al. (Eds.): GPC 2020, LNCS 12398, pp. 469–480, 2020.
https://doi.org/10.1007/978-3-030-64243-3_35

but enterprises are very vulnerable to the risk of downtime, which will seriously affect the reliability and availability of cloud computing platforms and even cause untold losses to enterprises and users. In order to ensure the high availability and continuity of daily services of the cloud platform, it is necessary to ensure the timely recovery of discontinuities or faults during the application of cloud services. In 2010, several virtual machines of Amazon went down and all the running instances on them failed, which indirectly led to heavy losses for companies using corresponding instances. The key reason lies in the lack of real-time monitoring of the cloud platform, or even the accurate detection of upcoming failures. Since the cloud infrastructure is large in scale, it is not enough to rely solely on the cloud system administrator to manage a large number of devices and prevent system failures. Therefore, the infrastructure that can automatically monitor and even predict failures to ensure the stable operation of the cloud platform cannot be ignored in the cloud platform management.

Private cloud systems often employ fault solutions for passively managing failures, monitoring physical machines and setting alarm thresholds for each observed resource, where there is usually no time to trigger an alarm and potential loss is hard to avoid. We propose a cloud failure prediction algorithm to implement virtual machine failure prediction in the cloud environment, that is, to monitor each virtual machine in the cloud platform, analyzing its historical data and failure scenarios, and then predict its state of next moment, detect the possibility of the fault before it occurs and causes serious consequences. To improve stability and intelligent level of the system, we analyze potential hot spots and ensure reliable operations, which will help cloud platform to take the initiative to adjust resource usage, and make corresponding treatment in time, the experimental results show that the forecasting method we used to forecast can achieve the accuracy close to 98.3% of failure.

To summarize, we make the following contributions,

- We propose a new approach to deal with cloud failure problem, that uses prediction to actively deal with failure.
- We design and implement a new monitoring and prediction system based on OpenStack.
- We propose a new prediction algorithm that can deal with cloud failures fast and accurately.
- We conduct extensive experiments, the results show that our approach can improve the stability of the cloud data center.

2   Related Work

The research in the field of fault prediction for the virtual machine is quite rare. At present, many researchers focused on just how to detect a virtual machine failure [2, 6, 7], but does not take into account how to predict these failures purposefully and warn the users accurately [1, 4, 13, 24]. There are many different approaches can be used to predict the failure. The regression prediction method is often used to predict the virtual machine fault [20]. The method of regression analysis and prediction is to analyze the correlation between independent variables and dependent variables, then establish the corresponding regression prediction equation. Based on the obtained regression equation, the values of all independent variables are substituted into the regression equation to obtain the values of dependent variables, so as to achieve the purpose of predicting some future data [14,21].

Some works use bayesian method [8,11]. E.g., Guan proposed a mechanism which combines Bayesian algorithm and Decision Tree algorithm to dynamically predict faults in cloud computing systems [11]. Bayesian model is used as a way of unsupervised learning and it processes the unlabelled data set. Tan developed a predictive fail-prevention system to prevent virtual machine failures automatically [11]. The system is mainly composed of four modules includes the virtual machine monitoring module, the fault prediction module, the fault reasoning module and the fault prevention module [10,12,15].

Wu T. proposes a virtual machine anomaly detection strategy based on detection domain division [25]. Virtual machines in the cloud platform are divided into detection domains based on similarity, and k-medoids clustering method is adopted to classify virtual machines based on the similarity of running environment, which can avoid the influence of noise data and achieve better clustering effect. Zhang proposed a dynamic adaptive monitoring network building mechanism based on local neighbor optimization division [19].

The scale of cloud platform is expanding continuously, and the number of applications deployed on it is increasing day by day. Users' requests for service of cloud platform resources are highly dynamic and instantaneous, which puts forward higher requirements for cloud computing system to be able to reflect the actual running state of a large number of virtual machines dynamically in real time. Monitoring intervals need to be more granular and virtual machine data needs to capture anticipate failures that may occur at a future time accurately and make adjustments in time to provide higher quality service. Besides, there are some researches focus on disk failure prediction [3,9,16,26], which is different from the topic we discuss in this paper.

3   System Architecture

In this section, we introduce the system architecture as shown in Fig. 1. It contains the following modules.

3.1   Data Collection Module

The data acquisition module is mainly responsible for data acquisition, providing data support for subsequent fault warning. The cloud platform transmits the performance indicator data of each virtual machine to the data center every 5 min. The data center classifies the collected data and sends the collected performance indicator data to the upper data processing module. The services of

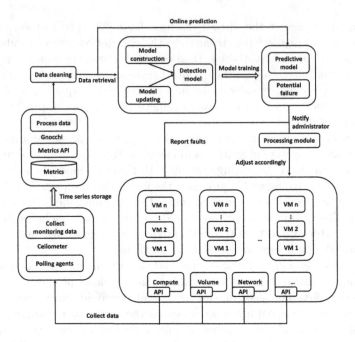

Fig. 1. System architecture.

Compute (nova compute), Volume (swift), Network (neutron), Image (glance), Object storage (cinder) and other modules will actively send some data to the Notification Bus. The Notification Agent will obtain the data through the Notification Listener and transfer it to the Sample Pipeline for the next processing.

3.2 Data Storage Module

The data storage module, Gnocchi handles the data, splitting it into two parts, one through storage driver and one through index driver. When retrieving data, the resource is found through index, and then the corresponding metric is found, and then the measure of metric is obtained, which greatly reduces the complexity of information. Gnocchi takes a unique approach to time series storage: instead of storing raw data points, it aggregates them for pre-defined policies before storing them, saving only the processed data. So Gnocchi is very fast at reading this data, because it only needs to read the pre-aggregated results.

3.3 VM Fault Monitoring Module

We use a monitor-based predictive mechanism, where the monitoring component periodically collects and checks key system values to prevent resource exhaustion from interrupting work. With the help of this, we can find the abnormal system measures in advance to summarize the situation for the fault management module, so as to respond to the possible faults actively. When the abnormal state is predicted or detected, the alarm information is reported to the fault diagnosis module for further analysis. The virtual machine fault detection module mainly treats the virtual machine fault warning. The performance data of the virtual machine to be tested are mainly processed in the lower layer, and the fault warning model is built through machine learning. Finally, the built warning model is used to predict the state of the detected virtual machine at the next moment.

3.4   Processing Behavior Management

The virtual machine fault diagnosis module mainly uses the results of the virtual machine fault detection module to predict and judge whether the running virtual machine has the possibility of failure. If a fault is likely to occur, it will send an email to the administrator immediately and inform the virtual machine ID, so that the administrator can take corresponding measures according to the node information obtained by the module, and help the user to make decisions such as whether the fault is acceptable or whether it must be repaired immediately.

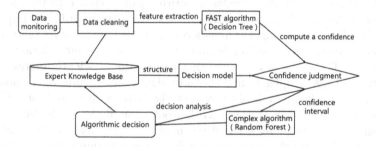

Fig. 2. The Procedure of the HFD algorithm.

4   Proposed Method

In this section, we introduce the method we proposed to predict cloud failure. Recall that our goal is to improve the availability of cloud platform services through failure prediction, that is, to start processing when nodes in the cloud service system have a tendency to fail. Machine learning technology is used to learn the characteristics of historical fault data, and a fault prediction model is established to predict the failure of nodes in the future. By predicting the failure nodes, the cloud service system can adjust the running virtual machines and assign tasks to healthier nodes, which can greatly reduce the number of failures and the virtual machine downtime caused by the continuous failure of nodes. In addition, if the node is predicted to fail, the cloud service system can perform active migration from the failed virtual machine node to the node in good working condition without disconnecting the service.

The prediction algorithm is designed to meet the requirements of the prediction accuracy and the time. The overall structure is shown in Fig. 2. It contains the following components.

4.1   Data Cleaning

We firstly clean the data to Gaussian distribution with zero mean and unit variance. Since many algorithms might behave badly if the individual features do not more or less look like standard normally distributed data. The standardization is done by,

$$z = \frac{x - \mu}{\sigma} \tag{1}$$

where μ is the mean of the data in a time period, and σ is the standard deviation.

4.2   Fast Filtering

In real-world settings, the prediction algorithm must be fast to complete most requests, in this step we propose to use fast algorithms to determine the possibility of the server is in danger. The fast algorithm can be chosen by the preference of system operators. Here, we use the decision tree algorithm in our implementation. The decision tree algorithm uses certain rules to analyze and sort out the data, generates the decision tree by induction, and carries out relevant classification work. The decision tree algorithm can conduct in-depth analysis on all the features of the samples to find the most significant features of the predicted results. Through the analysis of the results, the features that can best determine the predicted results will be taken as the root node of the whole decision tree, and then continue to analyze the determinacy of other features to establish a decision tree. We use the information gain as the splitting criterion, it can be calculate as,

$$\text{Gain}(S, A) = \text{Entropy } (S) - \sum_{v \in \text{ Values } (A)} \frac{|S_v|}{|S|} \cdot \text{Entropy } (S_v) \tag{2}$$

where the entropy is calculated as,

$$\text{Entropy} = \sum_{i=0}^{n} p(x_i) l(x_i) = - \sum_{i=0}^{n} p(x_i) \log_2 p(x_i) \tag{3}$$

4.3   Confidence Judgment

After the filtering of the algorithm, we use an experience-driven threshold-based approach to determine the need for more analysis. The threshold can be calculated based on the frequency of the appearance of the failure event. It can be calculated as,

$$t = \alpha \log \sum_{t=0}^{t=slot} err_t \tag{4}$$

where err_t is the number of failure event in time t, and α is the weight parameter.

Algorithm 1. HFP Algorithm

1: **while** system running **do**
2:      Collect and storing data as described in Section 3.
3:      Clean data using equation 1.
4:      Update statistics in knowledge base.
5:      Extract features and perform fast filtering as described in Section 4.2.
6:      **if** confidence above threshold **then**
7:          Release judgment.
8:      **else**
9:          Perform complex decision as described in Section 4.4
10:         Release judgment.
11:     **end if**
12: **end while**

4.4 Complex Model

In the previous steps find that is a high risk of failure, it will call a complex model that trained with more data. Similarly, the choice of this model is also user-specific. Here we choose the random forest algorithm in our implementation. The random forest algorithm is an ensemble algorithm that combines the decision of multiple decision trees by,

$$H(x) = \frac{1}{T} \sum_{i=1}^{T} h_i(x) \tag{5}$$

The algorithm works as follows: for each tree in the forest, we select a bootstrap sample from S where $S^{(i)}$ denotes the ith bootstrap. We then learn a decision-tree using a modified decision-tree learning algorithm. The algorithm is modified as follows: at each node of the tree, instead of examining all possible feature-splits, we randomly select some subset of the features $f \subseteq F$. where F is the set of features. The node then splits on the best feature in f rather than F. In practice f is much, much smaller than F. Deciding on which feature to split is oftentimes the most computationally expensive aspect of decision tree learning. By narrowing the set of features, we drastically speed up the learning of the tree.

4.5 The HFP Algorithm

Based on the previous components, we derive the following **HFP** algorithm. The procedure of the algorithm is describe in Fig. 2. The pseudo code is show in algorithm 1, it works as following,

- Store and clean the data for training the model. (line 2–4)
- Extract features and train a fast model. (line 5)
- Judge if the prediction is confident enough. (line 6)
- Release the judgment to the system and perform alerts if needed. (line 7)
- If confidence not enough it will perform the complex model and release the judgment. (line 9–10)

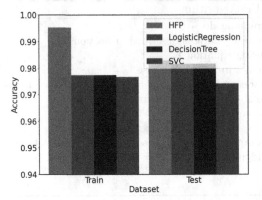

Fig. 3. Accuracy of different algorithms.

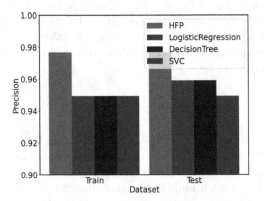

Fig. 4. Precision of different algorithms.

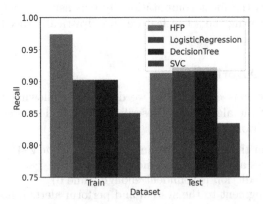

Fig. 5. Recall of different algorithms.

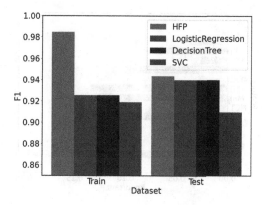

Fig. 6. F1 of different algorithms.

5 Result Analysis

5.1 Experiments Setup

The FTA (Failure Trace Archive) is a centralized, public data archive, which is collected, managed and maintained by Western Sydney University, Australia. The purpose of this data archive is to provide a standard dataset for the design, validation, and comparison of fault-tolerant models and algorithms. The EGEE data set in the FTA file contains the status information of each node of a grid system within a month, and each status information contains 15 performance indicators flags, and fault markers. The EGEE data set can be used to mine the unknown patterns hidden in multiple performance indicators that cause grid system failure. In this paper, we use the data of virtual machines monitored on the cloud platform in real time and EGEE data set in FTA archive for experimental analysis. And finally we selected 5871 virtual machine parameter samples. In a ratio of 3:1, 4403 groups were randomly selected as training samples and the remaining 1468 groups were taken as test samples.

We compare the algorithm with Logistic Regression, Decision Tree and Support Vector Classifier. In order to compare the prediction performance, we use four metrics, namely, *accuracy*, *precision*, *recall* and *F1 score*.

5.2 Performance Analysis

We plot the performance in Figs. 3, 4, 5 and 6. As we can see in Fig. 3, the HFP algorithm achieves the highest accuracy in the training set and the testing set, it also achieves the highest accuracy in the testing set. The other algorithms are worse, and it seems the SVC it not suitable for this problem.

And as we can see in Fig. 4, Fig. 5 and Fig. 6, HFP we proposed achieves better performance, and it seems the simper algorithm logistic regression and decision tree can achieve better recall but they are much worse in precision which results in that the algorithms is much worse in F1 score.

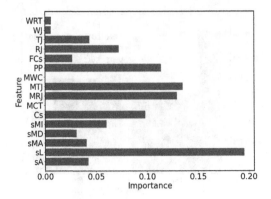

Fig. 7. Feature importance analysis.

5.3 Feature Analysis

After running the experiments, we also analyze the importance of different features as shown in Fig. 7. As we can, see different features have different importance. The features including lossless forwarding rate (sL), the maximum number of total jobs (MTJ), the maximum number of concurrent running jobs (MRJ) are the most important in our problem. We think this is reasonable and in line with our assumptions. To be specific,

- The higher lossless forwarding rate is, the better the performance is because it indicates network of the virtual machine is in normal operation and maintains little loss.
- The maximum number of total jobs and the maximum number of concurrent running jobs on the non-fault node are relatively more than that on the failure node because normal nodes have a higher system throughput and failure significantly leads to the decrease of performance on the cloud platform.

6   Conclusions

In many cases, the abnormal situation of some key indicators will lead to performance problems of the virtual machine, which will cause downtime and greatly reduce the use efficiency of the cloud platform. In this paper, we take virtual machines in the cloud platform as an object of fault prediction. We design and implement HFP in the Openstack platform. Meanwhile, the open data set of fault research is used to conduct extensive experiments and analysis on the algorithms which involved in feature extraction, feature selection and fault prediction. Through the analysis of the monitoring data, we can estimate the states of the virtual machine in the next moment and predict whether there is a possibility of failure, which can improve the stability and availability of the cloud platform.

Acknowledgments. This work was supported in part by the National Key Research and Development Program of China (No. 2019YFB2102204).

References

1. Aceto, G., Botta, A., de Donato, W., Pescapè, A.: Cloud monitoring: a survey. Comput. Netw. **57**, 2093–2115 (2013)
2. Bambharolia, P., Bhavsar, P., Prasad, V.: Failure prediction and detection in cloud datacenters (2017)
3. Bessani, A.N., Correia, M., Quaresma, B., André, F., Sousa, P.: DepSky: dependable and secure storage in a cloud-of-clouds. TOS **9**, 12:1–12:33 (2013)
4. Botta, A., de Donato, W., Persico, V., Pescapè, A.: Integration of cloud computing and internet of things: a survey. Future Gener. Comput. Syst. **56**, 684–700 (2016)
5. Chen, H., Tang, F., Kong, L., Xu, W., Zhang, X., Yang, Y.: Optimal resource allocation through joint VM selection and placement in private clouds. In: NPC (2019)
6. Chen, X.: Failure analysis and prediction in compute clouds (2014)
7. Chen, X., Jiao, L., Li, W., Fu, X.: Efficient multi-user computation offloading for mobile-edge cloud computing. IEEE/ACM Trans. Netw. **24**, 2795–2808 (2015)
8. Di, S., Kondo, D., Cirne, W.: Host load prediction in a google compute cloud with a Bayesian model. In: 2012 International Conference for High Performance Computing, Networking, Storage and Analysis, pp. 1–11 (2012)
9. Ganguly, S., Consul, A., Khan, A., Bussone, B., Richards, J., Miguel, A.: A practical approach to hard disk failure prediction in cloud platforms: Big data model for failure management in datacenters. In: 2016 IEEE Second International Conference on Big Data Computing Service and Applications (BigDataService), pp. 105–116 (2016)
10. Garraghan, P., Moreno, I.S., Townend, P., Xu, J.: An analysis of failure-related energy waste in a large-scale cloud environment. IEEE Trans. Emerg. Top. Comput. **2**, 166–180 (2014)
11. Guan, Q., Zhang, Z., Fu, S.: Proactive failure management by integrated unsupervised and semi-supervised learning for dependable cloud systems. In: 2011 Sixth International Conference on Availability, Reliability and Security, pp. 83–90 (2011)
12. Guan, Q., Zhang, Z., Fu, S.: Ensemble of Bayesian predictors and decision trees for proactive failure management in cloud computing systems. JCM **7**, 52–61 (2012)
13. Huang, P., et al.: Gray failure: The achilles' heel of cloud-scale systems. In: HotOS 2017 (2017)
14. Islam, S., Keung, J.W., Lee, K., Liu, A.: Empirical prediction models for adaptive resource provisioning in the cloud. Future Gener. Comput. Syst. **28**, 155–162 (2012)
15. Javadi, B., Abawajy, J.H., Buyya, R.: Failure-aware resource provisioning for hybrid cloud infrastructure. J. Parallel Distrib. Comput. **72**, 1318–1331 (2012)
16. Li, J., et al.: Hard drive failure prediction using classification and regression trees. In: 2014 44th Annual IEEE/IFIP International Conference on Dependable Systems and Networks, pp. 383–394 (2014)
17. Liu, J., Tang, F., Chen, L., Qiao, L., Yang, Y., Xu, W.: Converging human knowledge for opinion mining. In: IMIS (2017)
18. Qiao, L., Tang, F., Liu, J.: Feedback based high-quality task assignment in collaborative crowdsourcing. In: 2018 IEEE 32nd International Conference on Advanced Information Networking and Applications (AINA), pp. 1139–1146 (2018)

19. Qin, D., Chen, S., Zhang, H.: Virtual machine anomaly detection based on partitioning detection domain. In: IEEE International Conference on Software Engineering and Service Science, pp. 434–437 (2017)
20. Reiss, C., Tumanov, A., Ganger, G.R., Katz, R.H., Kozuch, M.A.: Heterogeneity and dynamicity of clouds at scale: google trace analysis. In: SoCC 2012 (2012)
21. Taleb, T., Ksentini, A.: Follow me cloud: interworking federated clouds and distributed mobile networks. IEEE Netw. **27**, 12–19 (2013)
22. Tang, F., Yang, L.T., Tang, C., Li, J., Guo, M.: A dynamical and load-balanced flow scheduling approach for big data centers in clouds. IEEE Trans. Cloud Comput. **6**, 915–928 (2018)
23. Tang, F., Zhang, H.: Spatial task assignment based on information gain in crowdsourcing. IEEE Trans. Netw. Sci. Eng. **7**, 139–152 (2020)
24. Whaiduzzaman, M., Sookhak, M., Gani, A., Buyya, R.: A survey on vehicular cloud computing. J. Netw. Comput. Appl. **40**, 325–344 (2014)
25. Wu, T.: A virtual machine anomaly detection algorithm based on detection domain partition. In: 2011 Sixth International Conference on Availability, Reliability and Security, pp. 83–90 (2016)
26. Xu, C., Wang, G., Liu, X., Guo, D., Liu, T.Y.: Health status assessment and failure prediction for hard drives with recurrent neural networks. IEEE Trans. Comput. **65**, 3502–3508 (2016)
27. Zhang, H., Tang, F., Barolli, L.: Efficient flow detection and scheduling for SDN-based big data centers. J. Ambient Intell. Humaniz. Comput. **10**, 1915–1926 (2019)

Research on Job Scheduling Algorithms Based on Cloud Computing

Gang Qiu[1,2], Yang Gao[1], and Yajun Zhang[2,3]($\boxtimes$)

[1] Changji College, Changji 831100, China
coral1001@163.com
[2] Shandong University, Jinan 250100, China
Yajunzhang369@163.com
[3] Xinjiang University, Urumqi 830046, China

Abstract. With the rapid development of digital technology, from the application of traditional databases and scientific computing to the emerging cloud computing services, the analysis and processing of massive data has become the focus of society. Providing low-cost, scalable, and configurable shared cloud services to users on cloud service platforms is a new hotspot for the development of major cloud service providers. Job scheduling plays an important role in improving the overall system performance of cloud service capabilities. Simple job scheduling strategies (such as Fair and FIFO scheduling) do not consider job size and may degrade performance when jobs of different sizes arrive. This paper proposes the MQWAG (Multi-queue Load-Sensitive Greedy Scheduling Algorithm) job scheduling algorithm to reorder multi-queue jobs so that short jobs are executed preferentially in multiple queues. In our experiments, our algorithm shortened the average job completion time by about 26% compared with other algorithms.

Keywords: Cloud computing · Job scheduling · Reordering

1 Introduction

With the vigorous development of information technology, from the traditional database and the application of scientific computing, the analysis, and processing of massive data has become the focus of society. Providing low-cost, scalable, and configurable shared cloud services on the cloud service platform is a new hotspot for major cloud service providers. Companies such as world-renowned IT companies such as Microsoft and Google have joined in the development of cloud computing, and have developed a number of cloud service products, such as Microsoft's OneDrive and Google's Google App Engine. China has also conducted a lot of explorations and attempts in many fields such as the academic field and technology application field of cloud computing and has achieved remarkable results. For example, the distributed data warehouse based on the MapReduce (MR) computing framework developed by Tencent; the real-time data processing platform developed by JD.com can efficiently deal with real-time access, real-time analysis, real-time transmission, real-time calculation and real-time query of large amounts of data.

© Springer Nature Switzerland AG 2020
Z. Yu et al. (Eds.): GPC 2020, LNCS 12398, pp. 481–495, 2020.
https://doi.org/10.1007/978-3-030-64243-3_36

2 Related Work

Generally, cloud service providers focus on resource utilization and service revenue of big data platforms, while users care about job completion time and rental costs. However, the jobs submitted by users are usually multi-type, such as compute-intensive, data-intensive, and I/O-intensive. Especially when running data-intensive jobs, it will generate a huge workload on the cluster computing system, such as web search, Consumer behavior, and consumer intelligence and business intelligence services. In such an application environment, when a cloud service provider submits jobs to multiple users, the cloud service provider considers multiple SLA (Service-Level Agreement) constraints based on different users, the size, characteristics, and benefits of the submitted job aspect.

Job scheduling in cloud service platforms is critical to platform performance optimization. Optimizing job scheduling algorithms is very important for cloud service platforms. At present, many scholars have done extensive research on task scheduling under the constraints of resource availability. References [1, 4, 5] flexibly schedule users' jobs based on the available resources of the platform to optimize the performance indicators of various platforms and provide guidance for the research of resource scheduling in this paper. Reference [2] aimed at the different real-time requirements of jobs and divided the jobs into high and low dual priorities. The two-level preemption strategy ensures that high-priority jobs can be completed quickly without sacrificing the completion time of low-priority jobs. The job scheduling method can improve the utilization of resources, which has great inspiration for this article. Reference [3] proposed a new cloud job scheduling mechanism. For each tenant, the deadline for the job is specified. The scheduling mechanism is based on the principle of maximizing global revenue. It allocates network bandwidth resources for each user job. In addition, the tuning mechanism also focuses on the review. Optimize the execution time of each job to reduce the overall job execution time. Reference [6] proposed a job-aware priority scheduling algorithm by real-time monitoring of the application layer. This algorithm not only achieves network load balancing but also reduces the delay between jobs of the same priority, improves job execution efficiency and reduces jobs Complete time.

Many experts and scholars have conducted in-depth research on the optimization of job scheduling algorithms in cloud service platforms, thereby improving the efficiency of job execution and resource utilization in cloud service platforms. in [7–9], in order to improve job execution efficiency and reduce data transmission time, data placement strategies and job scheduling algorithms based on minimum data transmission time are proposed. The issue of platform job execution time is not considered. Although the three methods proposed in [10–12] optimize the performance of the platform, they do not take into account the issue of job execution time. The Reference [13–17] mainly optimized the performance of the platform through reasonable job scheduling, but they did not consider both the short job runtime and cost issues at the same time.

In summary, the current popular cloud computing job scheduling mechanism has many deficiencies and faces great challenges when facing the above problems:

(1). Lack of standardized measurement models for assignments. There is no quantitative description of the job based on the characteristics of the job itself and the SLA constraints of the job;

(2). Most of the existing scheduling strategies take into account the problem of multiple job scheduling in the same queue, and there is no research on the job scheduling mechanism of multiple jobs in multiple queues.

In order to deal with the multi-tenant service problem based on the Hadoop cluster and allow the platform provider to obtain the maximum cost model, under the SLA constraint, This paper proposes MQWAGS (Multi-Queue Load-Aware Greedy Scheduling) job scheduling algorithm. The main contributions of this paper are as follows:

(1) A model for obtaining the maximum benefit execution cost is proposed. The model considers various parameters that affect the completion time of Hadoop jobs, such as the running time of map tasks and reduce tasks, and the size of map and reduce input data.

(2) Provide users with MQWAGS multi-queue load-sensing greedy scheduling strategy based on SLA constraints. This scheduling strategy takes the user's deadline as part of the input and determines the schedule ability of the job based on the job execution cost model. It depends on the type of job in. Ability to complete user-submitted jobs under specified SLA constraints. The above two methods aim to improve the average response time of the job and the average completion time of the job, and on this basis, improve the utilization of resources.

The organizational structure of this paper is as follows: Sect. 2 introduces related research; Sect. 3 describes the model for estimating job execution costs; Sect. 4 introduces the multi-queue job scheduling model and algorithm implementation; Sect. 5 is the experimental part; Sect. 6 gives a brief summary.

3 Evaluation Model

The size of the job is an important indicator that affects the performance of the job scheduling algorithm, and in most cases, this information is known or accurately estimated in advance. In our system, the job scheduling strategy evaluates multiple job costs at the time of job arrival and departure, and after the job cost assessment, the job is reasonably scheduled using MQWAGS job scheduling strategy.

3.1 Problem Definition

Based on the characteristics of the job (the computational complexity of the job, the size of the job data size, etc.), according to the configuration of the Hadoop platform cluster, we establish a job execution cost assessment model to estimate the minimum job execution time and the cost of completing the job.

We assume that there are N nodes in the cluster under the Hadoop 2.0 platform, each node has m containers, given a MapReduce job J, and the data of size σ must be completed within the deadline D under the user SLA constraint. The query q is executed in the MapReduce framework, and q has corresponding map tasks and reduce tasks for job J. After submitting the job, the scheduler first determines whether the user can complete the job within the established SLA constraint period. We do not determine the schedulability based on all the jobs running in the system. We assume that all tasks can get system resources, and do not consider the problem of repeated scheduling of tasks. After it is determined that the operation is completed within the prescribed SLA constraint period, we can enter the scheduling link. In order to ensure the deadline of the task, we have developed some strategies including:

All map and reduce tasks are allocated: if the number of tasks is less than the number of containers, all tasks are allocated. Otherwise, assign tasks to the available containers in the cluster. Although this will cause the jobs submitted later to not have enough containers to run, the system has reached a saturation state at this time, and the tasks can only wait afterwards.

3.2 Deadline Estimation Model

We design the initial estimation model based on a series of assumptions:

1) Suppose our cluster is in a homogeneous environment. Therefore, the unit cost of each node processing tasks is equal; (2) all jobs start to reduce tasks after the map task is completed; (3) input data is available under HDFS.

In order to find the expressions for the minimum number of map tasks n_m^{min} and the minimum number of reduce tasks n_r^{min}, we introduce a series of symbols as follows:

① J is a collection of all jobs running on the cloud service platform.

$$J = (j_1, j_2, j_3 \cdots j_n)$$

$$T = (m_{j_1}^1, m_{j_1}^2 \cdots m_{j_1}^i, r_{j_1}^1, r_{j_1}^2 \cdots r_{j_1}^k, m_{j_2}^1, m_{j_2}^2 \cdots m_{j_2}^i, r_{j_2}^1, r_{j_2}^2 \cdots r_{j_2}^k, m_{j_n}^1, m_{j_n}^2 \cdots m_{j_n}^i, r_{j_n}^1, r_{j_n}^2 \cdots r_{j_n}^k)$$

② T is a collection of all tasks running on the cloud service platform.

Among them, $m_{j_i}^i$ and $r_{j_1}^k$ represent the i-th map task in the j-th job and the k-th reduce task in the j-th job, respectively. Where $1 \leq i \leq u$, $1 \leq j \leq v$, (u is the total number of map tasks for job J, and v is the total number of reduce tasks).

③ q means run the query. We use a three-tuple $q = (R, \sigma, D)$ representation, where R is the arrival time (job submission time), σ is the input job size, and D is the relative deadline time under the SLA constraint.

④ f is the filtering ratio. The output of the map process is used as input to the reduce process. Generally, the number of map tasks is greater than the number of reduce tasks, and the filtering ratio is $0 \leq f \leq 1$.

⑤ C is the total number of containers that can be allocated to job J in the Hadoop cluster.

⑥ f_σ is reduce input (map output), $f_\sigma = f \times map$ output.

⑦Data processing cost DC. DC_m is the processing cost of map task unit data. DC_r is the cost of data processing for reduce task units.

⑧The data transmission cost DCT_d represents the communication cost for transmitting unit data from the map task to the reduce task.

⑨ $f_{j_n}^m$ is the start time of the first map task of job j_n.

⑩ $f_{j_n}^i$ is the start time of the first map task of job j_n.

⑪Job arrival time R and deadline D.

In order to estimate the duration of the job, we need to consider factors such as map completion time, reduce task completion time and R phase data transmission time, and the total cost of job processing.

The job execution time expression is:

$$JFT = \frac{DC}{C} + f\sigma \times DTC_d \tag{1}$$

Total cost of job processing:

$$DC = \sigma \times DC_m + f_\sigma \times DC_r \tag{2}$$

Completion time of the job:

$$FT(JFT_i) = f_{j_n}^m + JFT_i \tag{3}$$

where, $f_{j_n}^m + JFT \leq R + D$

Therefore, the maximum value of the starting execution time of the reduce task of job J_n:

$$f_{r_{j_n}^k}^{max} = R + D - \frac{f_\sigma \times DC_r}{C} - f_\sigma \times DTC_d \tag{4}$$

where $f_{j_n}^m + \frac{f_\sigma \times DC_m}{C} \leq f_{r_{j_n}^k}^{max}$, so

$$n_m^{min} = \left\lceil \frac{\sigma \times DC_m}{f_{r_{j_n}^k}^{max} - f_{j_n}^m} \right\rceil \tag{5}$$

Similar to it:

$$n_r^{min} = \left\lceil \frac{f_\sigma \times DC_m}{R + D - f_\sigma \times DTC_d - f_{j_n}^m} \right\rceil \tag{6}$$

$$n_j^{min} = n_m^{min} + n_r^{min} \tag{7}$$

Our job scheduling strategy introduced in the following sections is based on this criterion to constrain scheduling.

4 (MQWAGS) Job Scheduling Algorithm

In this chapter, the design goals of the deadline estimation model are proposed in Sect. 4.1. Section 4.2 uses examples to illustrate the differences between MQWAGS job scheduling and traditional FIFO, Capacity, and Fair job scheduling. Section 4.3 describes the specific implementation of job scheduling.

4.1 Deadline Estimation Model Design Goals

In Hadoop, users can design job schedulers according to their actual application requirements. We use the minimum task scheduling algorithm to implement constrained
scheduling.

Deadline estimation models are able to complete job within a given deadline. Our
estimation model calculates the minimum number of map tasks and the minimum number
of reduce tasks for the user, and determines whether the job can be completed within the
deadline of the user's SLA constraint by detecting the number of remaining containers
in the system. Otherwise, the user can choose to resubmit and modify the deadline for
the job. When the job is submitted, we perform a schedulable test. First calculate the
minimum map task. If the system cannot meet the minimum map task for submitting a
job, the job will be rejected, and the job needs to be submitted again after the system is
idle. Then, we calculate f_r^{max} (the maximum start time of the reduce task) based on the
reduce task specified by the job.

Calculate the final completion time of the job according to $f_{j_n}^m + JFT$, and infer to
$f_{(j_n)}^m + JFT \leq R + D$ from the above formula.

②Maximize the number of jobs that can run in the cluster while satisfying the completion of all jobs. Because in the cloud service cluster system, our user types are diverse.
Therefore, according to the user's deadline estimation model and job scheduling strategy MQWAGS, the job execution efficiency can be further optimized, so that the cloud
computing cluster can maximize the benefits while meeting the user's SLA constraints.

4.2 Examples of Job Scheduling Strategies

In a cloud computing cluster, it is important to run an excellent job scheduling strategy
due to the different job types and job sizes. In order to explain the differences in various
job scheduling strategies. We use a simple example to illustrate. Table 1 describes the
arrival order of the three jobs A, B, and C; Fig. 1 provides the scheduling results of
various scheduling technologies involved in this paper. In this example, three jobs A, B,
and C arrive in sequence, each job is different in size, and the final completion time of
the job is also different. Assume that the three jobs run in three different queues.

Table 1. The job collection, arrival order and task assignment

Job ID	Task arrival order	Number of tasks in queue 1	Number of tasks in queue 2	Number of tasks in queue 3	Total tasks
Job_A	1	6	5	3	14
Job_B	2	3	7	3	13
Job_C	3	5	4	6	15

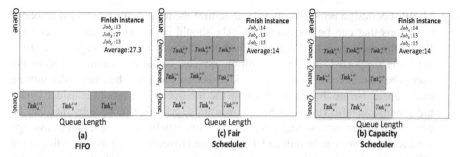

Fig. 1. Job submission order, completion time, and average job completion time in different scheduling algorithms

Let's calculate the average job completion time of n jobs, where n = $\{1, 2, 3 \cdots n\}$, then the average completion time of n jobs can be expressed as:

$$\frac{1}{n} \times \sum_{i=1}^{n} JFT \tag{8}$$

We can reduce the average job completion time by reducing the job completion time.

In order to illustrate the completion time of jobs A, B, and C in different scheduling strategies in the three queues, we assume that the number of tasks assigned to the three queues is different. The completion time of a job depends on the time when the last task of the job is completed $T_{i,d}$ (i represents the job number, and d represents the task number), the completion time of the subtask is a monotonic indicator for measuring the completion time of the job and the completion time $T_{i,d} \leq R + D$ of the subtask. Task scheduling sequence and execution time are shown in Fig. 1.

Figure 1 (a) uses the FIFO job scheduling algorithm. The completion time of the three jobs is A → B→C, and the average job completion time is 27.3; Fig. 1 (b) uses the Capacity Scheduler job scheduling algorithm. The completion order of the three jobs is B → A→C, and the average job completion time is 14. Figure 1 (c) uses Fair Scheduler job scheduling algorithm. The completion order of the three jobs is B → A→C, and the average job completion time is 14.

4.3 Multi-queue Load-Aware Greedy Scheduling (MQWAGS)

The completion time of a job is composed of waiting time and service time. Traditional FIFO scheduling strategy jobs can only be executed sequentially. Capacity Scheduler users can only submit tasks to their own queues, and cannot modify or access tasks in other queues. The Fair Scheduler divides the entire Yarn's available resources into multiple resource pools. Each resource pool can be configured with the minimum and maximum available resources. When there are no tasks in the queue, the minimum resources can be snatched by other queues; when new tasks come in At this time, if the cluster has resources, it will obtain resources, if not, it will grab resources from other low-priority queues and execute tasks. Preemption will reduce the execution efficiency of the cluster, because terminated containers need to be re-executed.

(1) MQWAGS design principle: In order to reduce the total waiting time and response time, jobs that can be completed quickly should be arranged before other jobs. But in the multi-task-multi-queue scheduler, the principle of short job priority is generally supported. In fact, in multiple queues, because sometimes a short job cannot be guaranteed to complete quickly, because there may be other tasks running in the queue before the short job enters the job queue, we should consider Under the premise of affecting user SLA constraints, prioritize those jobs that can be completed in advance, so that job execution time can be shortened, that is, average job execution time can be reduced. Here we need to reorder the jobs according to the different finish times in different queues. Get the optimal job scheduling sequence. We use an example to illustrate MQWAGS. As shown in Fig. 2, there are two scheduling strategies, Capacity and MQWAGS, in which three jobs are A, B, and C. A task has 13 tasks, B task has 14 tasks, and C task has 15 subtasks; they are respectively distributed in three different queues. But we find that the B task has the fewest tasks, so we can prioritize the tasks of the B task, and then execute the A and C tasks. Next we introduce MQWAGS job scheduling algorithm.

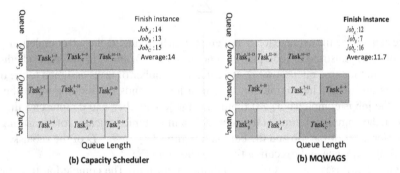

Fig. 2. Capaciyt and MQWAGS job average completion time comparison

(2) MQWAGS job scheduling algorithm. In the MQWAGS job scheduling algorithm, we first propose reordering. Our reordering is based on the task already in a certain queue and shortens the overall job in the cluster without delaying the user's SLA constraint final completion time, Based on average completion time.

  The reordering mechanism is as follows. In a given job scheduling algorithm and job queue, in each iteration we identify the queue with the most tasks and reorder them. Find the target task with the largest number of tasks in the queue under the same job, and place this job task in queue L, and then operate in a loop to calculate a new queue L in reverse order by reordering.

  In general, we use Capacity scheduler and Fair Scheduler multi-queue job scheduling algorithms to perform job scheduling under the cloud service platform. The MQWAGS multi-queue job scheduling algorithm proposed in this paper uses reordering to perform queue internal scheduling. Next we will prove the superiority of using the reordering algorithm. In addition, our reordering scheduling algorithm can be used in arbitrary multi-queue job scheduling.

Algorithm 1. reordering algorithm

---

① procedure reordering ($T_{j,q}, \forall j \in J$)

② J ← j

③ L← 0/ // an ordered list

④ **while** J≠φ **do**

⑤ target-Queue← $\max_q$, ($q \in Queue$)

⑥ target-Task←max ($T_{j,q}$), ($j \in J$)

⑦ L.list(target-Task)

⑧ Q←Q-q, ($q \in Queue$)

⑨ J←J-j, ($j \in J$)

⑩ **end while**

In the reordering algorithm, we use the job completion time to approximate the job end time. The job completion time is exactly the job completion time: (1) uniform task service time, that is, all tasks have the same continuous service time; (2) the same Efficiency services. All servers in the cluster system run tasks with the same efficiency.

(3) Each node has the same number of containers.Based on the appeal assumption, reordering does not lead to a reduction in completion time. The specific proof is as follows:

Theorem: Reordering provides non-decreasing performance improvement for our proposed MQWAGS job scheduling algorithm.

Let the position of f_j be the completion time of job J in queue q; that is, $f_j = \{ i_{j,q} | (q \in Q) \}$. Let O be the job scheduling algorithm and the result of the entire job completion time; C $F_O = \frac{1}{t} \sum_{j \in J} f_j$ C (t represents the total number of tasks of job j)

Let R represent the reordering algorithm, $F_{O,R}$ indicates that algorithm O and algorithm R are executed in sequence. Need to prove $F_{O,R} \leq F_O$.

Proof: We use mathematical induction to prove. When n = 1, the theorem obviously holds. Assuming n = k, the theorem holds. We define F (k) as k at the last completion time for job J in all queues. So, $F_{O,R}(k) \leq F_O(k)$, when n = k + 1, suppose we prefer to select processing job a, which is the one with the most tasks selected from all the queues. After processing, the completion time f'_a is the same as f_a, and $F_{O,R}(k) \leq F_O(k)$, So

$$F_{O,R}(k+1) = \frac{k \times F_{O,R}(k) + f'_a}{k+1} \leq \frac{k \times F_{O,R}(k) + f_a}{k+1} = F_o(k+1) \qquad (9)$$

Algorithm 2. MQWAGS algorithm

---

① procedure MQWAGS $(J, T_{j,q}, \forall j \in J, \forall q \in Q)$

② L←φ // an ordered list

③ q_i ←0, $\forall q_i \in Q$

④ J// Collection of assignments

⑤ while $Q \neq \phi$ do

⑥targetJob←find_Mintask(J)// Find the job with the
                      fewest tasks from set J

⑦while |L|≠|J| do

⑧ targetTask←$T_{t \arg etJob,q}$, $\forall j \in J$ // Find the task of the
                      target job

⑨L.list(targetTask)// Put the task of the target job
                   into the linked list

⑩ $q_i \leftarrow q_i + |T_{t \arg etTask,q_i}|$ // Put tasks in the queue

⑪end while

⑫end while

⑬return N

The proof of the above theorem shows that the reordering algorithm has improved the job scheduling, or that there is no harm. It is assumed that the completion time of the job can be estimated, and the reordering improves the average job completion time, and the result also reduces the average job response time of the job.

MQWAGS job scheduling strategy is an improvement on Capacity job scheduling strategy. Capacity job scheduling can configure a certain amount of resources for each queue, and each queue uses FIFO scheduling strategy, and our MQWAGS uses a greedy algorithm inside the queue. Our main idea is to calculate the job with the least number of tasks, and The job with the least number of tasks within each queue is shown in Fig. 2 (b). We prioritize the task of job B in all queues. In our algorithm, the order of job completion is B → A → C. The average job completion time is about 11.7.

5 Experiment

In this section, we will introduce the experimental and simulation results of MQWAGS job scheduling. Our lab is based on a big data platform based on the MapReduce computing framework.

5.1 Experimental and Simulation Setup

Experimental platform: Our experimental test platform consists of 21 workstations, including a master node and 20 slave nodes with the same configuration information. The configuration information of each node is Intel Xeon CPU E7-4809 v4 @ 2.10 GHz 10cores, memory 8 GB, hard disk 1 TB, Red Hat Enterprise Linux 6.2 System, and Hadoop version 2.8.4. We use the number of Containers to represent the number of computing resources. Each Container has a size of 1 core and 2G memory. In this way, there are 4 Containers on each node and there are 80 Containers in the entire platform. In HDFS, the block size is 128 M and the replication factor is set to 2.

Workload and Input: Our workload contains 200 jobs, and each job input is randomly selected from WordCount, TeraSort, SelfJoin, SequenceCount, Classification, HistogramMovies, HistogramRatings. Job arrivals follow a Poisson distribution. We will use different time intervals in the job input.

WordCount is a dataset consisting of Random Words generated by RandomTextWriter provided by Hadoop. TeraSort sorts the dataset in a logical order. For SelfJoin, we use synthetic data. For Classification, HistogramMovies, HistogramRatings, we use the movie dataset. Divide the workload into 3 BINS based on the size of the input. Related workloads used in the experiments in Table 2.

Table 2. Workload in the experiment

Bin	Job name	Data size	Map quantity	Reduce quantity	Job quantity
1	TeraSort	2 GB	200	20	4
1	SelfJoin	2 GB	204	20	20
2	WordCount	200 GB	1442	160	20
3	Classification	20 GB	204	40	15
3	HistograMovies	20 GB	204	40	10
3	HistograRatings	20 GB	204	40	6

5.2 Experimental Results and Analysis and Simulation Setup

Our evaluation index is based on the average job response time, average job completion time, and platform resource utilization. The target calculation formula is as follows:

Platform resource utilization = number of resources used for job execution/ total number of platform resources.

Average job completion time = execution time of all jobs/ number of jobs.

Average job response time = entry time of all jobs + job waiting time/ number of jobs.

(1) Average job response time: In Fig. 3 (a), the average interval between job arrivals is set to 80 s. We divide the input workload size into 3 BINs according to the different job input scales. From Fig. 3 (a), we can see that the performance of different scheduling algorithms in the same BIN is different. In Fig. 3 (a), except for Bin3's FIFO, our scheduling algorithm performs better than Capacity, Fair, and FIFO. In all BINs, our scheduling algorithm reduced the average response time of jobs by nearly 40% and the average response time of FIFO jobs by nearly 46%. Our experimental results show that, first, we can see it in Bin 1-3. Our solution can effectively find and give higher priority to short jobs. Secondly, only some FIFO jobs perform better than ours. This is because most of the video files are long jobs and their jobs are executed by The sequence is related to the time of joining the team. As far as we are concerned, our job scheduling algorithm will give priority to newly arrived short jobs and execute long jobs only after the short jobs have been executed. Therefore, in our scheduling policy, long jobs will free up resources for smaller jobs and wait longer to get more resources. Third, the average job response time of the FIFO job scheduling algorithm is similar across all BINs, because it is performed sequentially, regardless of the amount. Finally, the performance of Capacity and Fair job scheduling is basically close. They excel in short assignments, but at the same time are facing resource sharing for a lot of assignments.

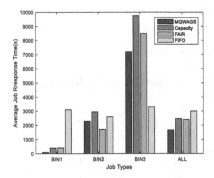 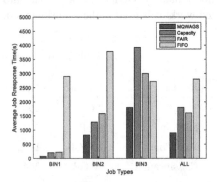

(a) Performance of workload with an average arrival interval of 80 seconds

(b) Performance of workload with an job average job arrival interval of 40 seconds

Fig. 3. (. a) Performance of workload with an average (b) Performance of workload with an job arrival interval of 80 s average job arrival interval of 40 s

(2) Performance comparison under different workloads: Different workloads are the key factors for measuring job scheduling performance. Therefore, we changed the average arrival time interval of the workload from 80 s in Fig. 3 (a) to 50 s in Fig. 3 (b). In Fig. 3 (b), our job scheduling is more prominent than the previous 80 s. In our solution, when the job arrival time is set to 80 s, about 90% of the jobs have

an average job response time of less than 2000 s, while the response values of the Capacity and Fair job schedulers are only about 70%. In Fig. 32 (b), our scheduling algorithm reduces the average response time of the job by nearly 43% and reduces the average response time of the FIFO job by nearly 62%.

(3) Platform resource utilization: In Fig. 4 we show the impact of different data volumes and different data types on resource utilization. From Fig. 4 we can see that with the continuous increase in data volume, our job scheduling The algorithm continues to improve in resource utilization, while the resource utilization of the Capacity and Fair job scheduling algorithms remains basically unchanged. Because Fair job scheduling algorithm users have independent resource pools, and resource pools have restrictions, as the amount of data continues As resources increase, resource utilization decreases. When the amount of data increased from 2G to 20G, our job scheduling algorithm increased by38%. When the amount of data increased from 20G to 200G, our job scheduling algorithm increased by 14%. Looking at the overall resource utilization of the FIFO job scheduling algorithm The rate is lower.

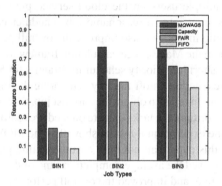

Fig. 4. Impact of data on resource utilization

(4) Workloads with different distributions: We compared the performance of workload algorithms under heavy-tailed and light-tailed distributions. In Fig. 5 (a), we can see that for heavy-tailed distribution, our algorithm performs best, followed by Capacity and Fair scheduling. Compared with other algorithms, the average job completion time is reduced by about 26%. FIFO is much worse than the other three algorithms, mainly because small jobs can be severely delayed by large jobs. Since our algorithm puts the tasks in short jobs into the head of each queue, the superiority of the algorithm becomes better as the number of jobs increases. In the case of even distribution, the performance of FIFO and MQWAGS is basically the same, while Fair and Capacity are both half their average response time. Because in this case, Fair scheduling and Capacity will share the processor.

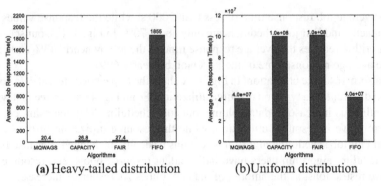

(a) Heavy-tailed distribution   (b) Uniform distribution

Fig. 5. (a) Heavy-tailed distribution (b) Uniform distribution

6   Conclusions

Provide services for multiple users on the cloud service platform at the same time. When multiple users submit jobs, a reasonable job scheduler can not only meet the user's performance requirements, but also improve the overall performance of the platform. Therefore, based on the MapReduce calculation framework, this paper proposes a reordering multi-queue short job priority scheduling strategy for SLA-constrained jobs. The algorithm calculates the job cutoff time by estimating the model based on the job cutoff time as a constraint. In order to obtain the shortest job, then according to the multi-queue job scheduling algorithm, the tasks that are queued are reordered, and the short job tasks are prioritized. The experimental results show that the MQWAGS job scheduling algorithm proposed in this paper can not only ensure that the job is completed before the deadline, It also increased the average completion time of the job by 26%, increased the platform's resource rate, and improved the overall performance of the platform.

Acknowledgments. The work is partially supported by The 2019 Xinjiang Uygur Autonomous Region Higher Education Scientific Research Project (XJEDU2019Y057,XJEDU2019Y049).

References

1. Mao, M.: Auto-scaling to minimize cost and meet application deadlines in cloud workflows. In: High PERFORMANCE Computing, Networking, Storage and Analysis. pp. 1–12, IEEE (2011)
2. Cho, B., Rahman, M., Chajed, T., et al.: Natjam:design and evaluation of eviction policies for supporting priorities and deadlines in mapreduce clusters. In: Symposium on Cloud Computing. pp. 1–17 (2013)
3. Shen, H.Y., Yu, L., Chen, L.H., Li, Z.Z.: Goodbye to fixed bandwidth reservation: Job scheduling with elastic bandwidth reservation in clouds. In: 8th IEEE International Conference on Cloud Computing Technology and Science. pp. 1–8 Luxembourg, Luxembourg, December 12-15 (2016)
4. Ghosh, T.K., Das, S., Barman, S., Goswami, R.: Job scheduling in computational grid based on an improved cuckoo search method. Int. J. Comput. Appl. Technol. **55**(2), 138–146 (2017)

5. Gasior, J., Seredynski, F.: Metaheuristic approaches to multiobjective job scheduling in cloud computing systems. In: 8th IEEE International Conference on Cloud Computing Technology and Science. pp. 222–229, Luxembourg, Luxembourg, December 12-15 (2016)
6. Liu, W., Wang, Z.G., Shen, Y.M.: Job-aware network scheduling for Hadoop cluster. KSII Trans. Internet Inf. Syst. **11**(1), 237–252 (2017)
7. Clinkenbeard, T., Nica, A.: Job scheduling with minimizing data communication costs. In: ACM SIGMOD International Conference on Management of Data. pp. 2071–2072, ACM (2015)
8. Wang, Q., Li, X., Wang, J.: A data placement and task scheduling algorithm in cloud computing. J. Comput Res. Develop. **51**(11), 2416–2426 (2014)
9. Sun, M., Zhuang, H., Li, C., et al.: Scheduling algorithm based on prefetching in MapReduce clusters. Appl. Soft Comput. **38**, 1109–1118 (2016)
10. Zhen, X., Xiang, M., Zhang, D.: An adaptive tasks scheduling method based on the ablility of node in hadoop cluster. J. Comput. Res. Develop. **51**(3), 618–626 (2014)
11. Li, Z., Chen, M., Yang, B.: Multi-objective memetic algorithm for task scheduling on heterogeneous cloud. Chinese J. Comput. **39**(2), 377–390 (2016)
12. Lee, M.C., Lin, J.C., Yahyapour, R.: Hybrid job-driven scheduling for virtual mapreduce clusters. IEEE Trans. Parallel Dist. Syst. **27**(6), 1687–1699 (2016)
13. Kumar, K.A., Konishetty, V.K., Voruganti, K., et al.: CASH: context aware scheduler for Hadoop. In: International Conference on Advances in Computing, Communications and Informatics. pp. 52–61 (2012)
14. Wang, X., Shen, D., Bai, M., Nie, T., Kou, Y., Yu, G.: SAMES: deadline-constraint scheduling in MapReduce. Front. Comput. Sci. **9**(1), 128–141 (2015). https://doi.org/10.1007/s11704-014-4138-y
15. Wang, Y., Shi, W.: Budget-driven scheduling algorithms for batches of MapReduce jobs in heterogeneous clouds. IEEE Trans. Cloud Comput. **2**(3), 306–319 (2014)
16. Song, Y., Sun, Y., Shi, W.: A two-tiered on-demand resource allocation mechanism for VM-based data centers. IEEE Trans. Serv. Comput. **6**(1), 116–129 (2013)
17. Rasooli, A., Down, D.G.: An adaptive scheduling algorithm for dynamic heterogeneous Hadoop systems. In: Conference of the Center for Advanced Studies on Collaborative Research. IBM Corp. (2011)

Recovering Cloud Services Using Hybrid Clouds Under Power Outage

Yu Xia[1,2(✉)], Xueyong Xu[2], Wanyuan Wang[1], Xiujun He[1], Weiwei Wu[1], and Xiaolin Fang[1]

[1] School of Computer Science and Engineering, Southeast University, Nanjing, China
`xiayu528@126.com`, `weiweiwu@seu.edu.cn`
[2] North Information Control Research Academy Group Co., Ltd, Nanjing, China

Abstract. The rapid development of the Internet and cloud computing are giving people high quality online services, which are usually deployed in cloud data centers. While the clouds are not always failure-free, in case of a power failure in a cloud data center, it is important to reduce the cost of disaster recovery meanwhile ensuring cloud service performance. To solve the service recovery problem of cloud data center under a power outage, in this paper, we propose an online solution based on hybrid cloud framework, which resolves the service workload management optimization between private cloud and public one. By using Lyapunov optimization technology, the long-term online optimization problem can be transformed into a general one. Besides, we present a power-aware online control algorithm (POCA) which achieves a trade-off between power consumption and cost, and the simulation results show that the proposed POCA algorithm can give a better and efficient performance.

Keywords: Cloud computing · Power outage · Cloud recovery · Lyapunov optimization

1 Introduction

With rapid development of the Internet and cloud computing, people can acquire various and high quality services conveniently through visiting websites and client applications provided by Internet enterprises. For instance, e-commerce websites, which provide cheaper commodities and instant shopping every day, are facing a mass of user requests due to an increasing number of consumers. To satisfy the ever-growing user demands, many large websites usually choose establishing their own private cloud. However, in reality the cloud may unavoidably suffer outage issues for technical or nontechnical reasons, which will result in a continually disturbance on business continuity and service availability. One of the most common but serious issues is power outage [1,2]. To cope with the accident disaster, almost all data centers should possess emergency power, which contains limited energy storing and is generally not enough before the disaster recovers. One existing research direction is to process user requests as many as

© Springer Nature Switzerland AG 2020
Z. Yu et al. (Eds.): GPC 2020, LNCS 12398, pp. 496–503, 2020.
https://doi.org/10.1007/978-3-030-64243-3_37

possible by making full use of the limited energy, and in this situation, part of user requests couldn't be effective processed inevitably, which could result in the dissatisfaction of users. A better and user-friendly solution should be one that makes users feel as if power outage doesn't occur ever during visiting the websites. In this paper, we propose a viable solution by introducing the hybrid clouds framework, which can solve power outage issues by outsourcing the excessive user requests from private cloud to the public one.

As we know, the public cloud is able to dynamically provision scalable computing resources according to the workload from the cloud consumer. In the scene of e-commence service, for instance, communication will running among the private and public cloud, over a non-trusted and latency-inconsistent network. While a dedicated tunnel, such as, AWS Direct Connect which provide private connectivity over the Internet [3], can easily scale the connection in time to meet different transmission rate needs and pay corresponding fee at the same time, and it is also essential for outsourcing users' requests into the public cloud.

Based on such recognition, we specifically study the dynamically distribution problem of real time workloads, to optimize the whole cost spent on the public cloud and the tunnel, constrained by the QoS guarantee of workloads and the limited energy in the private cloud. First, we use the $M/M/1$ queuing model in Queuing Theory to estimate the delay of workloads, and propose a widely acknowledged energy consumption model to trace real time energy consumption. To solve the proposed optimization problem, we present a power-aware online control algorithm(POCA) using Lyapunov optimization technique, which implements a trade-off between the power expenditure and the outsourcing cost. The simulation result shows that $POCA$ implements better performance than greedy private cloud priority scheduling strategy.

The remainder of the paper is organized as follows. In Sect. 2 we make an introduction on the system model and formulate the cloud service recovery problem. In Sect. 3 develops a power-aware online algorithm using Lyapunov optimization technique with unknown future workloads. Numerical experiment details as well as simulation results are represented in Sect. 4. In the end, we conclude the paper in Sect. 5.

2   Model and Problem Formulation

We establish the system model by analyzing the real flow of requests. In most popular way, requests from users arrive at web servers and are transferring to the private cloud data center to be processed. By introducing the public cloud, partial requests are redirected to the public cloud data center which provides the same processing service.

Suppose the power supply outside the private cloud data center is interrupted at time 0 due to a disaster and is expected to restored at time T. In order to keep the service continuity, the private cloud data center has to process some requests within limited energy and redirects additional requests to the public cloud data center via a dedicated tunnel for the sake of security until time T.

To address the limited energy in the private cloud, we discuss the power consumption model. It has been widely acknowledged that, the amount of power consumed by a server running at speed μ can be denoted as follow [4]:

$$E = \alpha_0 \mu^v + \beta_0 \tag{1}$$

where α_0 is a positive factor, β_0 is the power consumption in idle state, and the exponent parameter v is empirically determined as $v \geq 1$. In this paper, we utilize the previous power consumption of model with a reasonable value $v = 1$.

In order to provide reliable service quality, we have to estimate the average delay of serving requests, i.e., the average response time which include waiting delay and service time in a formal way. We take the $M/M/1$ queuing model to establish related functions according to queuing theory [5]. To make it work effectively, we assume that the requests arrive at the website as a Poisson process. The time interval between two requests that are served is assumed to be exponentially distributed. Then the average response time d can be computed using Little's law [6] as

$$d = \frac{1}{\mu - \lambda}, \quad \lambda < \mu. \tag{2}$$

where parameter λ is the average arrival rate according to a Poisson process and parameter μ is the average service rate. The model is considered stable only if $\lambda < \mu$.

Based on the model and assumption mentioned in the previous work, we can take up formulating the cloud recovery problem.

The average response time of requests is the essential factor which we have to consider in our problem. We typically require that the average response time is enforced at an acceptable limit. In this paper, we enforce the following constraint

$$D(t) \leq d, \quad \forall 1 \leq t < T. \tag{3}$$

where $D(t)$ is the average response time of requests at time slot t. The constant limit d reflects the maximum time delay which users can tolerate.

Due to the limited energy under power outage scenario in the private cloud, we have to formulate the power usage constraint. In this paper, we impose a long-term time-averaged power provision budget e for the private cloud during power outage period. For each time slot t, the power consumption includes the processing consumption and the transferred consumption. Based on the power consumption model (1) in the previous work, the processing consumption can be written as $N^V(t)(\alpha_0 \frac{x(t)}{N^V(t)} + \beta_0)$. The transferring consumption is $e_t \lambda^R(t)$, where e_t is the energy consumption of unit request using to transfer to the public cloud. Therefore, the constraint on the time-averaged power usage in the private cloud can be enforced as follows

$$\lim_{T \to \infty} \frac{1}{T} \sum_{t=0}^{T-1} \left\{ N^V(t) \left(\alpha_0 \frac{x(t)}{N^V(t)} + \beta_0 \right) + e_t \lambda^R(t) \right\} \leq e. \tag{4}$$

From the perspective of expenditure, we hope that the cost spent on the public cloud is as less as possible. In our practical model, the cost include the cost of renting the tunnel and EC2 instances. The cost of renting the tunnel during the tth time slot, i.e., the fee of renting the l-level tunnel which has defined before, can be displayed as follows

$$F(t) = \sum_{l=0}^{L} f_l x_l(t). \tag{5}$$

And the cost of renting EC2 instances during the tth time slot can be denoted as

$$C(t) = AN^U(t). \tag{6}$$

where A is the price of renting one running EC2 instance.

To evaluate the negative impact of dropout, we add an extra penalty item to the objective function. The penalty item is define as follow

$$J(t) = Q\lambda^D(t) \tag{7}$$

where $\lambda^D(t)$ is the number of dropout requests at time slot t, Q represents the penalty of unit dropout request.

Our objective is to minimize the total cost spent on the public cloud, combined with the penalty cost due to dropout. The optimization problem can be formulated as follows

$$min \quad \lim_{T \to \infty} \frac{1}{T} \sum_{t=0}^{T-1} F(t) + C(t) + J(t) \tag{8}$$

$$s.t. \quad constraints \ (4)$$

3   Online Algorithm

To address the challenge of the optimization problem (8), one solution is to provide an online algorithm for choosing control actions over time in reaction to the existing network state. We use Lyapunov optimization techniques [7] to design power-aware online control algorithm, called POCA.

3.1   Problem Transformation Using Lyapunov Optimization

Firstly, we transform the constraint (4) into a queue stability problem by introducing a virtual queue $Q(t)$. Initially, we define $Q(0) = 0$ and update the queue per each time slot as follows

$$Q(t+1) = max\{Q(t) + a(t) - e, 0\}. \tag{9}$$

where $a(t) = N^V(t)\left(\alpha_0 \frac{x(t)}{N^V(t)} + \beta_0\right) + e_t\lambda^R(t)$ is the power usage during the tth time slot. But a large value of $Q(T)$ in the end is not plausible. One intuition is that we can reduce $a(t)$ if the value of $Q(t)$ is large. Therefore, the problem (8) can be transformed as follows

$$\min \ Q(t)(a(t) - e) + V(F(t) + C(t) + J(t)) \tag{10}$$

where V is a non-negative control parameter chosen.

3.2   Power-Aware Online Algorithm

We observe some variables which exist in the (10) and attempt to figure out the relationship among these variables and their effect on the objective function. To minimize the objective function, we hope that those decision variables should be as small as possible. We use the decision variable $\alpha(t) = \lambda^V(t)/\lambda(t)$ and $\beta(t) = \lambda^R(t)/\lambda(t)$ to represent the proportion of requests distributed to the private cloud and to dropout, respectively. And we have

$$0 \leq \alpha(t), \beta(t) \leq 1 \tag{11}$$

Therefore, the optimization problem (10) can be expanded as follows

minimize

$$\begin{aligned}
z(t) = & \ Q(t)(\alpha_0 x(t) + \beta_0 N^V(t) + e_t(1 - \alpha(t) - \beta(t))\lambda(t) - e) \\
& + V\left(\sum_{l=0}^{L} f_l x_l(t) + A N^U(t) + Q\beta(t)\lambda(t)\right)
\end{aligned} \tag{12}$$

s.t.

$$\frac{1}{x(t) - \alpha(t)\lambda(t)} \leq d, \tag{13}$$

$$\frac{1}{\mu^R(t) - (1 - \alpha(t) - \beta(t))\lambda(t)} + \frac{1}{\mu^U N^U(t) - \lambda^U(t)} \leq d,$$
$$\text{constraints (11).} \tag{14}$$

The optimal solution demands that the equality holds in the delay constraints (13) and (14). Note that the variable $N^V(t)$ is only related to the variable $x(t)$. Therefore, for a given $x(t)$ satisfying the constraints, we hope that $N^V(t)$ is as small as possible. Then we can represent the variable $x(t)$ as $x(t) = \mu^V N^V(t)$, where μ^V is the maximal service rate of each server in the private cloud. Based on the analysis above, we propose our online algorithm.

Firstly, we enumerate the variable $\mu^R(t)$ with L kinds of tunnel bandwidth levels. Secondly, both the variable $x(t)$ and $N^U(t)$ can be represented by the variable $\alpha(t)$ with the delay constraints (13) and (14), respectively. Finally, the objective function can be represented by the variable $\alpha(t)$ and the variable $\beta(t)$. We first consider $\beta(t)$ is a given constant. In this case, we can take the derivative of the variable $\alpha(t)$ and find a feasible value of $\alpha(t)$ to make the objective

function globally minimum. Based on this, we further take $\beta(t)$ into consideration. Consider the complexity, our solution simply enumerates the variable $\beta(t)$
with the precision δ. Therefore, our algorithm can be displayed below. Our algorithm has an $O(L/\delta)$ time complexity, where $1/\delta$ is the enumeration times of
the variable $\beta(t)$ with the precision δ.

Algorithm 1. Power-aware Online Algorithm

1: initiate $z_{opt}(t) = \infty, \alpha_{opt}(t) = 0, l_{opt}(t) = 0, \beta_{opt}(t) = 0$
2: **for** each $\beta(t)$ with precision δ **do**
3:     calculate $z_{min}(t), \alpha_{min}(t), l_{min}(t)$ by algorithm 1
4:     **if** $z_{min}(t) < z_{opt}(t)$ **then**
5:         $z_{opt}(t) \leftarrow z_{min}(t)$
6:         $\alpha_{opt}(t) \leftarrow \alpha_{min}(t)$
7:         $l_{opt}(t) \leftarrow l_{min}(t)$
8:         $\beta_{opt}(t) \leftarrow \beta(t)$
9:     **end if**
10: **end for**

---

4 Performance Evaluation

In this section, we conduct trace-driven simulations to evaluate the performance
of our power-aware online control algorithm (POCA). We conduct the experiments based on real data sets from Google to enhance the reliability of our
proposed algorithm.

In order to validate the performance, we compare POCA with a greedy private cloud first (PCF) scheduling policy which dispatches requests to the private
cloud first and consequently make full use of the limited energy.

Furthermore, we propose a α-PCF scheduler for comparison, where α represents the proportion of arrival requests distributed to the private cloud while
the rest is distributed to the public cloud at each time slot.

In the simulation, we set some benchmark parameters as follows. We get each
time slot workloads at intervals of $100(s)$ and the corresponding values ranging
from 100 to 50000. And we set $T = 5000$. And we assume that the maximum
time delay which users can tolerate is $d = 0.05(s)$. The parameters of the power
consumption function are set with $\alpha_0 = 0.25, \beta_0 = 100.0$, and $v = 1$. We set the
time-averaged power budget $e = 800.0$ and the transferring energy consumption
of unit request $e_t = 0.05$. With respect to dropout, we set the dropout cost of
the unit request as $Q = 20.0$. We initiate the dropout precision $\delta = 0.01$.

We have transformed the original Google data sets into the time slot workloads above and set corresponding benchmark parameters. The experimental
results of real data sets validate the performance of the proposed algorithm.

As a consequence, we simply display the corresponding experimental results
without redundancy.

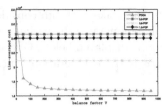

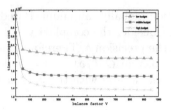

Fig. 1. Time-averaged service cost under different scheduling policies using real trace.

Fig. 2. Time-averaged service cost under different time-averaged energy budget e using real trace.

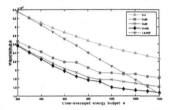

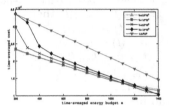

Fig. 3. Time-averaged service cost under different balance factor. ($V = 1/2/50/100$)

Fig. 4. Time-averaged service cost under different balance factor. ($V = 0.5/1/5/10 * 10^4$)

Figure 1 shows the time-averaged service cost change by different scheduling policies when the balance factor V varies form 1 to 1000, with a step size of 50. Figure 2, 3 and 4 show results of the impact of the balance factor V and the energy budget e on the service cost in our problem. Figure 2 describes the time-averaged service cost as V increases under three degrees of time-averaged energy budget e (low, middle, and high). Figure 3 and 4 show the time-averaged service cost consumed under obvious different values of balance factor V when the energy budget e increases in the range of $[200, 1400]$, with a step size of 100. It is apparent from Fig. 3 that the overall time-averaged service cost decreases as the balance factor V increases when V takes small values, while Fig. 4 illustrates opposite trend when V is large enough. All these results validate the efficiancy of our propose algorithm.

5   Conclusion

In order to deal with the situation of limited power supply under power outages in enterprise cloud data centers, we propose a hybrid cloud model to ensure the continuous operation of services by outsourcing some users' requests to the public cloud. We study the specific energy consumption model and queuing model to explicitly model the cloud service recovery problem. In order to deal with the challenge of task scheduling and resource allocation in online scenario, we design a power-aware online control algorithm, which transforms the long-term online optimization problem into a general optimization problem at each time slot by using Lyapunov optimization technology. We introduce a balance factor V to balance the tradeoff between energy consumption and outsourcing cost, and it achieves a trade-off between power consumption and outsourcing cost. Simulation results show that $POCA$ has efficient performance for the cloud recovery problem.

Acknowledgement. The work is supported in part by the national key research and development program of China under grant No. 2019YFB2102200, National Natural Science Foundation of China under Grant No. 61672154, 61672370, 61972086.

References

1. QPS Team: Average Cost of Data Center Outages: $627,418 PER INCIDENT. Quality Power Solutions Ltd, Location (2015)
2. Aliyun Data Center in HK Suffers 14-Hour Disruption. http://english.caixin.com/2015-06-24/100822037.html. Accessed June 2015
3. AWS Direct Connect Pricing. https://aws.amazon.com/directconnect/pricing
4. Zhou, Z., et al.: Carbon-aware load balancing for geo-distributed cloud services. In: 2014 IEEE 21st International Symposium on Modeling, Analysis & Simulation of Computer and Telecommunication Systems (MASCOTS), Location, pp. 232–241. IEEE (2013)
5. Kleinrock, L.: Queueing Systems, Volume 2: Computer Applications. Wiley, New York (1976)
6. Little, J.D.C., Graves, S.C.: Little's law. In: Chhajed, D., Lowe, T.J. (eds.) Building Intuition, pp. 81–100. Springer, Boston (2008). https://doi.org/10.1007/978-0-387-73699-0_5
7. Neely, M.J.: Stochastic network optimization with application to communication and queueing systems. Synth. Lect. Commun. Netw. **31**, 1–211 (2010)

BED: A Block-Level Deduplication-Based Container Deployment Framework

Shiqiang Zhang, Song Wu, Hao Fan$^{(\boxtimes)}$, Deqing Zou, and Hai Jin

National Engineering Research Center for Big Data Technology and System,
Services Computing Technology and System Lab,
Cluster and Grid Computing Lab,
School of Computer Science and Technology,
Huazhong University of Scinece and Technology, Wuhan 430074, China
{zhangshiqiang,wusong,fanh,deqingzou,hjin}@hust.edu.cn

Abstract. Container technology has gained great popularity in cloud environment since containers provide near-native performance and are lighter and less expensive than traditional virtual machines. However, starting up a non-local container, whose image is unavailable locally, is time-consuming. The reason is that pulling an image from a remote registry requires a long time. In this paper, we experimentally find that a lot of redundant data exists among image layers when we pull images from the registry. This redundant data causes additional pull time and makes the startup of a non-local container slower. To minimize the amount of pulled data while providing intact images, we propose a container deployment framework, BED, based on block-level deduplication. To be specific, BED stores an image layer as numerous data blocks and a fingerprint list which is generated based on these data blocks. When BED needs to pull an image, it pulls the fingerprint lists of the image, deduplicates these fingerprint lists, and pulls the data blocks non-existing locally from the registry. Based on the local and pulled blocks, BED reconstructs the image layers for a container. Experiments show that compared with original Docker, BED reduces the time of pulling images by 35% on average and saves about 48% data transmission in the network.

Keywords: Container · Block-level deduplication · Pull time · Network traffic

1 Introduction

In recent years, cloud computing has been developing rapidly. Container technology [1,10], an operating system-level virtualization, is more and more popular due to its lightweight and convenience compared with traditional virtualization [13,20]. Instead of providing a full kernel for each *virtual machine* (VM) like traditional virtualization, container technology leverages *Cgroups* [5] and *Name-spaces* [6] to provide isolated execution environments for processes on a shared host kernel [13,14]. However, running a non-local container whose image

© Springer Nature Switzerland AG 2020
Z. Yu et al. (Eds.): GPC 2020, LNCS 12398, pp. 504–518, 2020.
https://doi.org/10.1007/978-3-030-64243-3_38

is unavailable locally takes a long time sometimes, because an image which consists of application binary, shared libraries, and Linux distribution is usually large and must be transmitted to the host from registry before starting up the container. Taking widely used Docker [2] and Kubernetes [4] for example, pulling an image takes up 76% of the entire time in deploying a non-local container on average [13]. Moreover, huge network traffic is required, because the sizes of images to be transmitted are getting bigger and bigger [9, 25].

To speed up the process of pulling container images as well as save network traffic, images with small sizes are required. There are two primary ways to reduce the sizes of images. First, reducing useless data by building a simplified image that only contains data required by starting up a container [13, 25], instead of a complete image. This method can significantly improve the startup time of a container. However, a container may show a long response time when it needs data that is not in the simplified image. Second, reducing redundant data by file-level sharing among different native container images. File-level sharing [15] can prevent the remote host from pulling redundant files that widely exist among different image layers, while guaranteeing an intact image. However, file-level sharing cannot reduce redundant data thoroughly. Furthermore, special files within layers, such as special block devices and hard links, are difficult to share and file-level sharing may cause security and privacy issues [16, 22].

For the purpose of a minimal and intact image, we propose to conduct block-level deduplication [17] during pulling an image. This enables us to only pull the data blocks that cannot be found locally and provides an intact image by combining the local and pulled data blocks. We are faced with three challenges to achieve the above goal. First, block-level deduplication cannot be applied to the existing container management framework, because an image is transmitted in the form of compressed packages and block-level deduplication shows few effects on them even if there are a lot of redundant data after uncompressing the packages. Second, even if we realize block-level deduplication, reconstructing intact images is hard based on pulled data blocks. Because the container manager provides an image by organizing image layers, it cannot recognize data blocks. Third, block-level deduplication brings additional overhead due to decompressing blocks and reconstructing images.

Accordingly, we propose a container deployment framework, BED, based on block-level deduplication. BED conducts block-level deduplication in two places. In the registry, BED divides an image layer into blocks and generates a *fingerprint list* which contains the fingerprints [23] of all data blocks within the image layer. These blocks are deduplicated and compressed to reduce data size. In the pull phase, when local BED needs to pull an image layer, it deduplicates the data blocks to be pulled based on the corresponding fingerprint list. Then BED generates a *deduplicated fingerprint list* recording fingerprints that cannot be found locally. BED only pulls blocks recorded by the *deduplicated fingerprint list* from the registry. On the native host, BED reconstructs an intact image using pulled blocks, local blocks, and the corresponding *fingerprint lists*. Data block decompression phase, pull phase, and layer reconstruction phase are overlapped to cover up additional overhead. In summary, the main contributions are as follows:

1. We experimentally find that compared with original image, those intact images constructed by block-level deduplication and block compression have smaller size.
2. We propose BED, which can couple block-level deduplication with container deployment process and reconstruct image layers based on deduplicated data blocks, to accelerate container deployment and reduce network traffic at the same time.
3. We testify BED on a Docker platform. Experiments show that compared with original Docker, BED can accelerate the time of pulling images by 35% and reduce network traffic by 48% when deploying non-local containers. Notably, BED can be implemented on any container-based platform that supports OCI [8].

The rest paper is organized as follows. Section 2 introduces the background, benefits, and challenges of applying block-level deduplication in container deployment. Section 3 introduces the design of the block-level deduplication-based container deployment framework. Section 4 introduces the experimental environments and proves the benefits of BED. Section 5 discusses the related works. And conclusions are in Sect. 6.

2   Background and Motivation

2.1   Deploying a Non-local Container

To deploy a non-local container, the local host needs to pull the corresponding container image to the local host and starts the container based on the image. Pulling an image from the registry is a time-consuming process. So, reducing the size of an image during the pull phase is critical for a container manager (i.e., Kubernetes and Docker) to accelerate the deployment of non-local containers. Currently, the container manager usually adopts two methods to reduce the size of an image during the pull phase. First, layer-level sharing. An image of a container is composed of several image layers, and each image layer contains many files of the image. Images can share their base image layers. When a client deploys a non-local container by *docker run* or *docker pull*, the container manager uses the same image layers on the local host at first. If there is a non-local image layer, the container manager begins to pull image layers from the registry. Second, data compression. Image layers are compressed into packages by the registry before they are sent to the local host.

2.2   Large Image Size Caused by Data Redundancy

Sharing and compressing image layers can reduce data size during the pull phase. However, the size of compressed packages of image layers is still large during the

Table 1. 20 types of frequently downloaded images

Categories	Images
Linux Distro	**alpine, debian, centos, fedora**
Database	**neo4j, mysql, cassandra, couchdb**
Language	**python, php, java, openjdk**
Web Component	**django, kibana, tomcat, rails**
Application Platform	**wordpress, owncloud, xwiki, nextcloud**

pull phase because of redundant data among image layers. On the one hand, coarse-grained layer-level sharing provided by the container manager cannot share identical files and blocks of different layers. On the other hand, compressing an image layer cannot reduce data redundancy among image layers.

2.3 Deduplication for Container Image

Deduplication [28] is a possible way to reduce redundant data. Deduplication can be classified into file-level deduplication and block-level deduplication based on data granularity. File-level deduplication identifies duplicate files based on the content hash of the entire file. Block-level deduplication achieves better deduplication ratio by dividing the file into more fine-grained blocks and judging whether the blocks are redundant. Block-level deduplication has two chunking approaches. One is *Fixed-Size Chunking* (FSC) and another is variable-Size Chunking, referred to as *Content-Defined Chunking* (CDC) [21,27]. CDC solves the boundary-shift problem, which is better than FSC.

To observe total data redundancy of normal images (i.e., images on the native host) and compressed images (i.e., *Gzip* compressed packages during pull phase), we select 20 types of images in the Docker Hub based on download times (i.e., the image has been downloaded more than 10M times) and category (i.e., *Linux Distro, Database*, and so on). For every type of image, the latest five versions are used. Table 1 shows the detail information of these images and Table 2 shows the size of images after using different methods to reduce redundant data. $D+C$ means deduplicating images first, and then compressing these deduplicated images. $C+D$ means compressing images first, and then deduplicating these compressed images. The total size of all normal images (i.e., *Raw*) is 35.79GB and the total size of all compressed images (i.e., *Gzip*) is 13.83 GB. Both file-level deduplication for compressed images (i.e., *File(C+D)*) and block-level deduplication for compressed images (i.e., *Block(C+D)*) show few effects even if there are a lot of redundant data among the corresponding uncompressed image layers, because the data structure has changed after compression [24]. While, by deduplicating and compressing normal images in block-level (i.e., *Block(D+C)*) and file-level (i.e., *File(D+C)*), data sizes are 7.46 GB and 8.51 GB, respectively. Deduplicating and compressing data in block-level (i.e., *Block(D+C)*) shows minimal data size.

Table 2. Images size under different methods

Dateset	Method	Size(GB, including metadata)
Normal images	Raw	**35.79**
	File(D)	**15.76**
	File(D+C)	**8.51**
	Block(D)	**14.06**
	Block(D+C)	**7.46**
Compressed images	Gzip	**13.83**
	Block(C+D)	**13.23**
	File(C+D)	**13.83**

However, effective block-level deduplication is inapplicable for the existing container management framework. First, an image is transmitted in the form of compressed packages. Block-level deduplication shows few effects on compressed packages of image layers as mentioned above. Second, even if we can divide the packages into data blocks and transmit the unique blocks to the native host, the container manager cannot provide an intact image based on these blocks, because the container manages the image in the granularity of files. Third, decompressing blocks and reconstructing image layers with blocks introduce additional overhead.

3   System Design

According to the previous discussion, we conclude that deduplication can speed up container deployment by reducing data size during the pull phase. However, existing architecture does not support block-level deduplication. In this section, we introduce BED, a container deployment framework based on block-level deduplication.

3.1   Overview

In face of the challenges we mentioned before, BED needs to achieve the following goals:

1. Enabling effective block-level deduplication during pulling image layers. Block-level deduplication does not work well on compressed image layers. BED needs to divide the images into blocks and perform deduplication and compression based on blocks to effectively reduce data size as mentioned in Sect. 2.3.
2. Providing a complete image layer based on data blocks. Current container manager cannot work with blocks. BED needs to organize data blocks to reconstruct the complete image layer according to the orders of these blocks in the original image layer.

3. Decompression and reconstruction bring additional overhead to pull phase, so BED needs to cover up this overhead in the time of downloading images.

Figure 1 shows the architecture of the BED. BED is implemented as a separate component and does not impose any modifications to the container architecture. So BED can be used easily in native host and registry (i.e., private registry and public registry). In order to support block-level deduplication, BED first stores image layers as numerous data blocks in the registry and local host, and then deduplicates blocks in the registry and during pulling image layers. In the registry, BED divides an image layer into blocks and deduplicates these blocks. These blocks are compressed and stored in *Block Store*. At the same time, a *fingerprint list* of the image layer, which contains fingerprints of all blocks within the image layer, is generated and stored in *Metadata Sotre*.

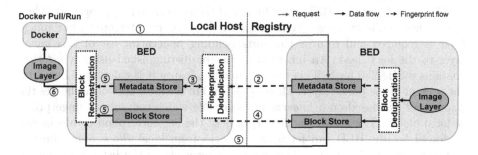

Fig. 1. Architecture of BED

When a local host pulls an image, BED in the registry ① intercepts what image layers are required and ② sends *fingerprint lists* of these image layers from *Metadata Store* to the local host. ③ Then, BED in the local host will store these *fingerprint lists* into *Metadata Store* for image reconstruction as well as deduplicate the *fingerprint lists* based on the local fingerprints stored in *Metadata Store* and then get unique fingerprints. Based on these fingerprints, ④ BED only requests blocks that the local host does not have from *Block Store* in the registry. Finally, ⑤ BED receives and decompresses the pulled blocks. Meanwhile, BED reconstructs the image layers based on pulled blocks, local blocks, and corresponding *fingerprint lists*. Besides, BED overlaps decompression phase, pull phase, and reconstruction phase to cover up overhead caused by decompression and reconstruction.

3.2   Enabling Block-Level Deduplication During Pulling an Image

Block-level deduplication does not work well on compressed layers under the existing architecture, even if images show high redundancy. BED conducts block-level deduplication on image layers and compresses the deduplicated blocks in the registry. During the pull phase, BED only pulls blocks that the local host does not have according to a *deduplicated fingerprint list* which only has the fingerprints of blocks the local does not have.

As we mentioned in Sect. 2.3, we can get minimum data size during image pull by deduplicating and compressing the image layers in block-level [11,18]. However, compressed image layers in the registry cannot be deduplicated effectively as shown in Table 2. Accordingly, we modify the data format in the registry. A normal image layer is divided into blocks with corresponding 128-bit MD5 fingerprints. A *fingerprint list*, which contains the fingerprints of all blocks within an image layer, is generated by putting all fingerprints in a *Python list* orderly at the same time. The blocks are deduplicated and compressed to reduce data size. *Fingerprint lists* and all fingerprints of image layers are stored in the *Metadata Store*. Meanwhile compressed blocks are stored in the *Block Store*. Notably, fingerprints in a *fingerprint list* are ordered based on the orders of blocks within the corresponding image layer.

Figure 2 shows how BED pulls blocks of the corresponding image. ① When a local host pulls an image layer, BED in the registry intercepts what image layer is required and returns the corresponding *fingerprint list* of this image layer to the local host. An image layer can be distinguished using a *url* that contains a SHA256 hash. This hash is unique because it is calculated based on the content of the pulled layer. Then, ②③ BED in the local host deduplicates the *fingerprint list* based on a *fingerprint hash table* which contains all fingerprints of local blocks. The redundant fingerprints of the list correspond to blocks can be found locally. BED can fetch these blocks from local *Block Store* directly in the reconstruction phase. The unique fingerprints of the list correspond to blocks that do not exist locally. So BED collects the unique fingerprints into a *deduplicated fingerprint list*. ④ Based on the *deduplicated fingerprint list*, BED requests the unique blocks from *Block Store* in the registry. The requested image is transmitted in discrete compressed data blocks and the content of image is opaque. So BED has good security. After pulling, all pulled blocks are stored in the local *Block Store* and their corresponding *fingerprints* are stored in the *fingerprint hash table* in local *Metadata Store*.

3.3 Reconstructing Image Layer with Blocks

The container manager cannot handle the blocks pulled from the registry, because it manages images in the granularity of files. BED reconstructs an image layer with pulled and local blocks using a *fingerprint list* which consists of all fingerprints of an image layer.

Figure 2 shows how BED reconstructs an image layer based on unique blocks. To reconstruct an image layer, BED needs to get corresponding *fingerprint list* and blocks. The orders of fingerprints in the list are the same as the orders of the corresponding blocks within the image layer. In order to bind a *fingerprint list* to its corresponding image layer, BED maps the *fingerprint list* to the SHA256 of its corresponding image layer.

After pulling the *fingerprint list* and ⑤ blocks of an image layer, BED uses this *fingerprint list* to read local blocks from the *Block Store*. Pulled blocks

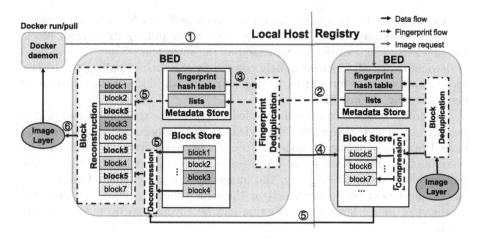

Fig. 2. Pulling blocks and reconstructing image layer

and local blocks are decompressed and arranged according to their orders in *fingerprint list* to reconstruct an image layer. Although a block may be used many times in some layers (for example, *block5* in Fig. 2), BED does not pull this block or read it from the local repeatedly, because pulling or reading a block is time-consuming. BED solves this problem by traversing the *fingerprint list*, recording all the positions of each block in the entire layer, and then fetching the corresponding blocks only once and placing them where they should be.

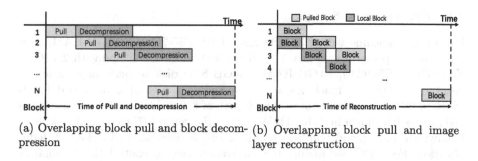

(a) Overlapping block pull and block decompression

(b) Overlapping block pull and image layer reconstruction

Fig. 3. Overlapping decompression, pull, and reconstruction

3.4 Overlapping Decompression, Pull, and Reconstruction

Block-level deduplication divides the intact layer into compressed blocks. Unlike pulling an intact layer, blocks decompression and layer reconstruction bring additional overhead compared to original Docker framework.

To cover up decompression overhead, block pull and block decompression phases are overlapped, as shown in Fig. 3(a). While pulling the current block, the previous block can be decompressed at the same time. Then the overhead of decompressing all blocks is mostly covered by the time of pulling the blocks. Ideally, the overhead introduced by decompressing all blocks equals the time of decompressing the last block.

The intact image is composed of pulled blocks and local blocks. If we begin to reconstruct an image layer after all needed blocks have been pulled, the overhead caused by reconstruction is obvious. To cover up reconstruction overhead, pull phase and reconstruction phase are overlapped, as shown in Fig. 3(b). While pulling blocks from the registry, the image layer is reconstructed using local blocks and blocks pulled previously at the same time. Therefore, a part of the overhead of image layer reconstruction can be covered up by pulling remote blocks.

4   Evaluation

We integrate BED into Docker and compare performance in pulling images against the original Docker framework. We measured the time of pull, data size, and network traffic. In what follows, firstly, we introduce our experimental setups. Secondly, we evaluate the total time, data size, and network traffic of pulling 100 images. Thirdly, we evaluate the time of each type of images when we pull 20 types of images (100 images in total) on one host. Fourthly, we testify the benefit brought by overlapping decompression, pull, and reconstruction.

4.1   Experimental Setups

We use one machine with 2.30 GHz Xeon CPU (E5-2650), 128 GB RAM, 2TB HDD disk to perform as a private registry and another machine with 2.10 GHz Xeon CPU (E5-2620), 64 GB RAM, 500GB SSD disk to perform as a native client host. The two machines are connected at a measured download bandwidth of 930.23 Mbps and upload bandwidth of 820.08 Mbps. The registry stores 100 images (as shown in Table 1). We use *traffic control* [7] to control download bandwidth and upload bandwidth. Block size is essential to block-level deduplication. For CDC, we mainly use an average size to control the granularity of deduplication. The minimum size is set to half of the average size, and the maximum size is twice the average size. Smaller block can bring a higher deduplication rate, but it is harmful to image reconstruction. So we implement BED with different block sizes. The average size ranges from 4KB to 64KB. This is because we consider that 4KB is the smallest unit that a filesystem can handle. And many image layers are about 1MB in size, and 64KB is enough for deduplication.

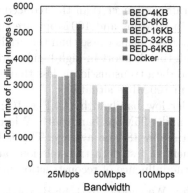
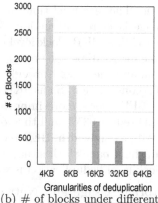

(a) Total time of pulling images under different bandwidths

(b) # of blocks under different granularities of deduplication

Fig. 4. Experimental result about pull time and number of blocks

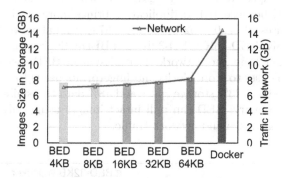

Fig. 5. Data size in storage and network traffic when pulling images

4.2   Overall Performance When Pulling Images in Batch

We evaluate data size, network traffic, and total time against original Docker when pulling 100 images sequentially. These images are top 20 of 5 different kinds of images (ie, Linux distro, language, database, and so on). Results are shown in Fig. 4 and Fig. 5.

Total Time of Pulling Images. As shown in Fig. 4(a), when bandwidth is 25 Mbps, deduplication in all granularities works better than the original Docker. BED shows 30%, 36%, 38%, 37%, and 34% improvement in pull time for 4KB, 8KB, 16KB, 32KB, and 64KB block-level deduplication, respectively. Pull time decreases when the average size of deduplication increases from 4KB to 16KB. The reason is that the number of transmitted blocks decreases and BED needs less time to reconstruct the image layer as shown in Fig. 4(b). The pull time of 32KB and 64KB block-level deduplication goes up. The reason is that BED needs to pull more data under larger block sizes due to the lower deduplication ratio. The increased time in network traffic is longer than the reduced time in image layer reconstruction. Situations in 50 Mbps and 100 Mbps are the same as 25 Mbps. 4KB block-level deduplication performs worse than the original pull time for 50 Mbps. The reason is that pull time is short in high bandwidth situation, and the benefit brought by reduced data transmission is less than the cost of reconstruction. So as 4KB and 8KB in 100 Mbps situations.

BED shows more improvement under low bandwidth. As Fig. 4(a) shows, BED reduces 35% pull time on average under 25Mbps bandwidth. While, under 50Mbps bandwidth, BED reduces pull time by 18% on average. This is because in a high bandwidth situation, the benefit of less data transmission caused by block-level deduplication is weak, and the influence of reconstruction increases.

Storage Usage and Network Traffic. We choose 4KB, 8KB, 16KB, 32KB, and 64KB block-level deduplication and 50Mbps bandwidth to evaluate storage usage and network traffic. As shown in Fig. 5, BED uses 56%, 55%, 56%, 57%, and 60% original storage space under BED-4K, BED-8K, BED-16K, BED-32K, and BED-64K, respectively. Storage usage of BED-4K is larger than storage usage in BED-8K because 4KB deduplication brings more blocks and more fingerprints. BED uses 49%, 50%, 52%, 54%, and 57% original network traffic under BED-4K, BED-8K, BED-16K, BED-32K, and BED-64K, respectively. The storage space is larger than the network transmission in BED, because key-value storage that BED uses to store blocks and fingerprints needs to store extra data for itself. BED reduces 43% storage space and 48% data transmission in network on average. In summary, BED can pull intact images using only about half of the original storage space and network traffic.

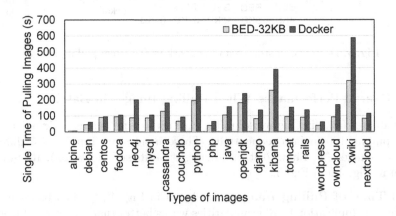

Fig. 6. Pull time of each type of images

4.3 Pull Time of Each Type of Images

Based on the conclusion of Sect. 4.2, the experimental results show similar trends. For the convenience of analysis in a common situation, we choose 32KB block-level deduplication with 50Mbps bandwidth to evaluate the pull time of each

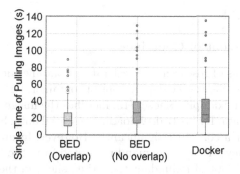

Fig. 7. Pull time when execution phases are overlapped

type of images against the original Docker. We pull 20 types of images (each type contains five latest versions) in a row. As shown in Fig. 6, the y-axis represents the time of pulling all five images of a type. We can see that the pull time of the first four types in BED are similar to Docker, because few blocks can be deduplicated on local host, and BED needs to pull most of the data blocks from the registry. As the number of local images increases, there are more and more blocks can be found locally in general. So deploying a non-local container in BED becomes faster and faster because of pulling image efficiently. BED shows 31% average improvement in pull time. We can also observe that BED shows 56% maximum improvement when pulling one type of images. In summary, only when pulling a few images, BED can show its power to accelerate the pulling of the images. The more images are pulled, the faster BED shows. Accordingly, we can store some commonly used images locally at first, and BED will work more efficiently.

4.4   Benefit of Overlapping

We still choose 32KB block-level deduplication with 50Mbps bandwidth to evaluate the benefit caused by overlapping decompression, pull, and reconstruction when pulling 100 images in a row. As shown in Fig. 7, the y-axis represents the pull time of each image. We can see that using overlap can significantly reduce the time of pulling images. On the one hand, overlapping pull and decompression can fully use the bandwidth, because BED does not need to wait until all blocks are pulled. On the other hand, overlapping pull and reconstruction enables BED to begin to reconstruct an image layer before getting all blocks of the layer. BED with overlap shows 18% average improvement against BED without overlap and 29% average improvement against Docker. However, BED without overlap shows 3% average decrease against Docker. With overlap, BED performs better than Docker after pulling a few images. But without overlap, BED performs better than Docker until pulling enough images. In summary, we cover up the overhead caused by blocks decompression and image layer reconstruction by overlapping the execution of different phases.

5   Related Work

5.1   Fast Deployment of Container

There are many types of research on accelerating container deployment. Reducing image size can accelerate the deployment of container. One of the ways is the simplified image. For example, Slacker [13] modifies the image format and marks the essential set of data. By lazily downloading essential data, Slacker reduces the deployment time for a container significantly. However, future data access may become slower as they will be on-demand requested from the Internet. Cntr [25] finds that there are a lot of redundant tools (i.e., shell) in the container image. Accordingly, Cntr proposes to share these tools among containers. Cntr builds a slim image that contains an application and a shared fat image that contains all tools. The slim image cannot provide all services, so sometimes the performance of Cntr is limited by the fat image. Another way to reduce image size is file-level sharing. For example, Fastbuild [15] builds a file cache on a native host. When generating a container, Fastbuild searches necessary files in the native cache first. In this way, Fastbuild significantly reduces redundant data among native image layers. However, the file-level share is not enough for container image, because there are still many redundant data blocks among layers.

Besides, some methods are used to speed up pulling images by optimizing the registry. First, Anwar [9] believes that more and more images are stored in the registry, and pulling images from the registry becomes a performance bottleneck. It optimizes the pull time by prefetching the base images that may be pulled into memory. BED uses block-level deduplication in the registry to reduce the size of the images, so more images can be put into memory. Therefore, BED is orthogonal to the work of Anwar. Second, FID [26] and Dragonfly [3] think that the registry will decrease the performance of pulling images as the number of pull requests increases. They use P2P to share images among different clients and make use of bandwidth among users. However, they cannot reduce data sizes of images while transmitting. However, BED can not only reduce the size of images but also cooperate with FID and Dragonfly.

5.2   Deduplication in Virtualized Environments

Data deduplication on virtual machines is widely studied. Nitro [12] proposes to combine a network-aware p2p with deduplication to reduce the redundant data in VMs as well as accelerate the transmission of VM images. HPDV [17] uses parallel CDC deduplication for different VMs. Based on data locality, HPDV only holds a very small fingerprint table in RAM to save RAM space and accelerate blocks finding. Furthermore, HPDV dynamically controls the parallelism of deduplication to prevent sensitive front-end from the interferences caused by heavy deduplication. Dmdedup [19] finds that deduplicating unique data, such as metadata, is unnecessary, because it may hurt the performance of block-level deduplication. So Dmdedup adds a hinting interface to the operating system. Users can send hints to the lower system using this interface for avoiding unnecessary deduplication.

6 Conclusion

Data size during the pull phase is critical to the deployment time of a non-local container. In this paper, we experimentally find that a lot of redundant data exists among image layers even if compressed packages of the layers show few data redundancy. Accordingly, we couple block-level deduplication with container deployment procedure by proposing BED. BED divides image layers into compressed data blocks and only pulls data blocks that cannot be found locally. Based on these blocks, BED reconstructs image layers for a container. Experiments show that compared with original Docker, BED reduces the time of pulling images by 35% on average. BED also saves about 48% data transmission in the network.

Acknowledgment. We thank Shadi Ibrahim for his valuable advice. This work is supported by National Key Research and Development Program under grant 2016YFB1000501, National Science Foundation of China under grants No.61872155 and 61732010.

References

1. Container. https://www.docker.com/resources/what-container
2. Docker. https://www.docker.com/
3. Dragonfly. https://d7y.io/en-us/
4. Kubernetes. https://kubernetes.io/
5. Linux Cgroups. https://www.kernel.org/doc/Documentation/cgroup-v1/
6. Linux Namespaces. https://www.kernel.org/doc/Documentation/namespaces/
7. Linux Traffic Control. https://www.lartc.org/
8. Open Container Initiative. https://www.opencontainers.org/
9. Anwar, A., et al.: Improving docker registry design based on production workload analysis. In: Proceedings of FAST, pp. 265–278. USENIX (2018)
10. Bernstein, D.: Containers and cloud: from LXC to docker to kubernetes. IEEE Cloud Comput. 1(3), 81–84 (2014)
11. Constantinescu, C., Glider, J.S., Chambliss, D.D.: Mixing deduplication and compression on active data sets. In: Proceedings of DCC, pp. 393–402. IEEE (2011)
12. Darrous, J., Ibrahim, S., Zhou, A.C., Pérez, C.: Nitro: network-aware virtual machine image management in geo-distributed clouds. In: Proceedings of CCGRID, pp. 553–562. IEEE (2018)
13. Harter, T., Salmon, B., Liu, R., Arpaci-Dusseau, A.C., Arpaci-Dusseau, R.H.: Slacker: fast distribution with lazy docker containers. In: Proceedings of FAST, pp. 181–195. USENIX (2016)
14. Herbein, S., et al.: Resource management for running HPC applications in container clouds. In: Kunkel, J.M., Balaji, P., Dongarra, J. (eds.) ISC High Performance 2016. LNCS, vol. 9697, pp. 261–278. Springer, Cham (2016). https://doi.org/10.1007/978-3-319-41321-1_14
15. Huang, Z., Wu, S., Jiang, S., Jin, H.: FastBuild: accelerating docker image building for efficient development and deployment of container. In: Proceedings of MSST, pp. 28–37. IEEE (2019)
16. Keelveedhi, S., Bellare, M., Ristenpart, T.: DupLESS: server-aided encryption for deduplicated storage. In: Proceedings of the 22th USENIX Security Symposium, pp. 179–194. USENIX (2013)

17. Lin, C., Cao, Q., Huang, J., Yao, J., Li, X., Xie, C.: HPDV: a highly parallel deduplication cluster for virtual machine images. In: Proceedings of CCGRID, pp. 472–481. IEEE (2018)
18. Lin, X., Hibler, M., Eide, E., Ricci, R.: Using deduplicating storage for efficient disk image deployment. EAI Endorsed Trans. Scalable Inf. Syst. **2**(6), e1 (2015)
19. Mandal, S., et al.: Using hints to improve inline block-layer deduplication. In: Proceedings of FAST, pp. 315–322. USENIX (2016)
20. Merkel, D.: Docker: lightweight Linux containers for consistent development and deployment. Linux J. **2014**(239), 2–6 (2014)
21. Muthitacharoen, A., Chen, B., Mazières, D.: A low-bandwidth network file system. In: Proceedings of SOSP, pp. 174–187. ACM (2001)
22. Puzio, P., Molva, R., Önen, M., Loureiro, S.: ClouDedup: secure deduplication with encrypted data for cloud storage. In: Proceedings of CloudCom, pp. 363–370. IEEE (2013)
23. Quinlan, S., Dorward, S.: Venti: a new approach to archival storage. In: Proceedings of FAST, pp. 89–101. USENIX (2002)
24. Süß, T., Kaya, T., Mäsker, M., Brinkmann, A.: Deduplication analyses of multimedia system images. In: Proceedings of HotEdge. USENIX (2018)
25. Thalheim, J., Bhatotia, P., Fonseca, P., Kasikci, B.: CNTR: lightweight OS containers. In: Proceedings of ATC, pp. 199–212. USENIX (2018)
26. Wang, K., Yang, Y., Li, Y., Luo, H., Ma, L.: FID: a faster image distribution system for docker platform. In: Proceedings of FAS*W@SASO/ICCAC, pp. 191–198. IEEE (2017)
27. Xia, W., et al.: FastCDC: a fast and efficient content-defined chunking approach for data deduplication. In: Proceedings of ATC, pp. 101–114. USENIX (2016)
28. Zhu, B., Li, K., Patterson, R.H.: Avoiding the disk bottleneck in the data domain deduplication file system. In: Proceedings of FAST, pp. 269–282. USENIX (2008)

Author Index

Printed in the United States
By Bookmasters